A HANDBOOK FOR DATA ANALYSIS IN THE BEHAVIORAL SCIENCES: Methodological Issues

Edited by

Gideon Keren
Free University of Amsterdam

Charles Lewis
Educational Testing Service

LEA LAWRENCE ERLBAUM ASSOCIATES, PUBLISHERS
1993   Hillsdale, New Jersey   Hove & London

Lawrence Erlbaum Associates, Inc., Publishers
365 Broadway
Hillsdale, New Jersey 07642

Library of Congress Cataloging-in-Publication Data

A Handbook for data analysis in the behavioral sciences :
  methodological issues / edited by Gideon Keren, Charles Lewis.
       p.   cm.
    Includes bibliographical references and index.
    ISBN 0-8058-1036-6. — ISBN 0-8058-1037-4 (pbk.)
    1. Psychology—Statistical methods.   2. Social sciences—
Statistical methods.   3. Psychology—Research—Methodology.
4. Social sciences—Research—Methodology.   I. Keren, Gideon.
II. Lewis, Charles, 1943–   .
BF39.H26435   1992
150'.72—dc20   92-23007
                                                              CIP

Books published by Lawrence Erlbaum Associates are printed
on acid-free paper, and their bindings are chosen for strength
and durability.

Printed in the United States of America
10   9   8   7   6   5   4   3   2   1

Contents

Preface

Science is supposed to be an ever *changing* enterprise. Yet "change is not made without inconvenience, even from worse to better" (quoted by Johnson in the preface to the *English Dictionary*). This inherent resistance to change may account (at least partly) for the recent claim made by Aiken, West, Sechrest, and Reno (1990) that statistical and methodological training of psychologists has barely advanced during the past 20 years. Their conclusions are based, among other things, on a survey conducted in close to 200 psychology departments in North America, and are further supported by examining the leading psychological journals from which it is apparent that the methodology and methods of data analysis have hardly changed. For instance, the conventional null hypothesis testing remains by far the most common and preferred method for analyzing empirical data. The continuous and growing number of articles that appeared in methodological- and statistical-oriented journals such as the *Psychological Bulletin* point out the pitfalls of null hypotheses testing (see chapter 6 of the *Methodological Issues* volume) and offer some remedies or alternative methods of data analysis, but apparently had little impact (see chapter 11 of the *Methodological Issues* volume for a more elaborated discussion).

The lack of change is further accompanied by some misunderstandings of the use of statistical tools. Apparently, people are poor intuitive statisticians, (chapters 12 and 13 of the *Methodological Issues* volume), and even social scientists have been shown to possess some fundamental misunderstanding regarding statistical theory. Unfortunately, statistical methodology is often conceived by social scientists in a technical manner, and its utilization resembles a drunken man's use of lamp posts: for support rather than for illumination. There are several causes that have led to this state of affairs and a few of these are mentioned here.

As pointed out earlier, most graduate programs offer a rather narrow number of courses. Psychology departments usually require a single course that is mainly centered on hypothesis testing and analysis of variance. Other courses, which are usually considered as advanced, are not required and consequently have a low attendance.

Most of the methodology and statistical textbooks (particularly those for the social sciences) do not improve the situation. They are typically written in the technical style of a cookbook, and provide straightforward algorithms usually avoiding the controversial issues, confusions, and complexity that characterize our knowledge. In particular, they do not sufficiently introduce the uncertainties involved in the use and application of statistical tools. Consequently, many readers are led to believe that once they know and understand well the algorithm or procedure of a certain method, the major goal has been achieved. Statistical procedures are thus frequently performed mechanically by a "blind" process (Wertheimer, 1959), rather than in a genuine constructive mode. In fact, the use of statistical methodology often requires careful considerations (e.g., what is the appropriate tool for a given question, what are the underlying assumptions of a particular methodology) and several subjective decisions—even if one is not a Bayesian! It is especially the latter aspect that is often ignored or misunderstood: Any statistical tool may aid researchers in their scientific inquiry, but it cannot substitute for the subjective judgments and personal interpretations that have to be made by the researcher.

Another source of difficulty lies in the fact that many of the methodological and statistical developments appear in specialized journals, frequently in journals with little relation to the substantive area of the researcher (e.g., pure statistical journals). Moreover, such articles are frequently written in a highly technical language and include mathematical sophistication that social scientists often find difficult to follow. Finally, methodological and statistical methods constitute such a broad area that it is difficult to systematically follow the progress on so many different fronts.

The present two-volume book is an attempt to provide some partial remedy to the aforementioned problems. The first volume is devoted to methodological issues and related topics such as mathematical modeling, measurement, and scaling. The second volume focuses on statistical issues: In addition to covering traditional topics of classical statistics (e.g., hypothesis testing, analysis of variance, multiple regression) it also offers an extensive treatment of the Bayesian approach as well as some recent developments like Exploratory Data Analysis (EDA). Indeed, our choice of topics (for both volumes) was guided by including traditional issues as well as more novel and recent developments that we believe to be of growing importance for the social sciences. All the chapters were written under the assumption that potential readers have a limited acquaintance with the basics of statistical methodology and possess only elementary mathematical skills. Indeed, all authors were asked to follow three major guidelines: (a) Present the material in a simple and clear style (including intuitive explanations), avoiding complex mathematical formulations unless necessary; (b) emphasize applications by using as many examples as possible, explaining the rationale underlying each analysis and briefly summarizing potential difficulties associated with the application of a specific tool; and (c) provide as many references as possible so that the interested reader can refer to other sources for elaboration. It is our hope that, to the extent that we were able to follow these guidelines, these two volumes will enable the reader to overcome some of the aforementioned difficulties. In particular, our aim is to provide an updated survey on different aspects of empirical research and data analysis, facilitate the understanding of the internal logic underlying different methods, and provide novel and broader perspectives beyond what is usually covered in traditional curricula.

This book constitutes a considerable and elaborated revision of *Statistical and Methodological Issues in Psychology and Social Sciences Research* published in 1982. Some chapters from the previous book have been substantially revised (these are marked in the table of contents by an asterisk). A few chapters are based on journal articles that have been specifically revised to accommodate the book.[1] Most of the chapters, however, are original contributions to this edition.

The present edition departs from the previous book in several fundamental respects. According to the basic assumption of these volumes, philosophy of science, research methodology, and statistics are deeply interrelated in most applications. Consequently, we make an attempt to cover these different facets rather than to focus solely on statistical methodology. We also include several chapters dealing with descriptive data. A growing body of empirical psychological research indicates that people are not always good "intuitive statisticians." This research suggests that reasoning is sometimes guided by unwarranted heuristics and hampered by (logically) unjustified biases. Any scientific activity results from operations carried by the human's cognitive system, so it seems to us that the study of this cognitive system and its limitations are an integral part of the scientific endeavor. It is also our belief that realization of one's own weaknesses is a necessary condition for change.

Our emphasis on the cognitive facet has another aspect, namely the tendency of practitioners to view and apply methodological and statistical methods in a mechanical and technical manner. We believe that analysis and explanation of empirical data requires creativity as well as judgments (as is reflected explicitly in many chapters in this book). Data as well as results of statistical analysis can be interpreted in different ways. In fact, the initial decision of which particular method or statistical technique is most appropriate requires careful and meticulous considerations. We deliberately chose a broad spectrum of methods, some of which are known to be conflicting (e.g., Bayesian vs. classical statistics). We are

---

[1] Only chapters 12 and 16 of the *Methodological Issues* volume have been reprinted without any modifications.

also aware that the views expressed by different authors may occasionally be incompatible. The decision of which method to use, how, and when, is, in our opinion, part of the researcher's task. We believe there is not always one right approach or method, and the final choice depends on the particular question the researcher wants to address, the nature of the data, and the larger context in which it was collected. The choice of which method is the appropriate one under given circumstances is part of what constitutes the art of the scientific inquiry.

GIDEON KEREN
CHARLES LEWIS

REFERENCES

Aiken, L. S., West, S. G., Sechrest, L., & Reno, R. R. (1990). Graduate training in statistics, methodology, and measurement in psychology. *American Pscyhologist, 45,* 721–734.
Keren, G. (1982). *Statistical and methodological issues in psychology and social sciences research.* Hillsdale, NJ: Lawrence Erlbaum Associates.
Wertheimer, M. (1959). *Productive thinking.* New York: Harper & Row.

MODELS AND
MEASUREMENT

The first section of this book is concerned with two essential topics: Mathematical models, and the measurement and scaling of psychological attributes.

Robin Hogarth from the University of Chicago has recently claimed that economics is a discipline of theory without data, whereas psychology is a discipline of data without theory. With minor modifications, we tend to endorse this statement. Our choice to start this book with a review of mathematical modeling, is meant to encourage researchers to modify their orientation and be more geared toward theory building. Stimulating the use of mathematical models is one possible step in this direction.

Strictly speaking, our (the editors) position is that every model (certainly in the behavioral sciences) is incorrect and at best can serve as a rough approximation. The importance of a model in our view is not just to provide an approximation that will be as close as possible to the "true" model, but also offer simultaneously a framework that enables researchers to ask meaningful questions and establish a consistent research program.

Representing psychological phenomena in the form of a mathematical model is not an easy task, which may account for the relative scarcity of such models. The first chapter, by Estes, provides a brief overview of models employed in various areas of psychology, their function, and how they should be tested. The following chapter, by Macmillan, introduces one of the more successful approaches to modeling in psychology, namely the Theory of Signal Detection (TSD). Although the roots of TSD are to be found in electrical engineering, it has been widely applied in different ways in the psychological literature.

Theories and models, especially when formulated in mathematical terms, require input. The meaning attached to any quantification of such input depends on the underlying measurement theory, which is presented in chapter 3, written by Norman Cliff. Measurement theory provides the justification, rationale, and underlying assumptions of the measurement operation. The concrete process by which multiple numbers are assigned to objects, attributes, or any other psychological properties is termed multidimensional scaling, and is reviewed in chapter 4 by Jones and Koehly.

Both chapters 3 and 4 are concerned with the quantification of psychological entities. Chapter 5 focuses on the quantification of a particular psychological entity namely uncertainty. Indeed, the theory of probability plays a major role in the present book. Although it is obviously impossible to summarize in one chapter the numerous books written on the topic, the chapter by Shafer provides an excellent overview of the different interpretations of the concept of probability, and offers a stimulating perspective for reconcilation among conflicting views.

1 Mathematical Models in Psychology

W. K. Estes
Harvard University

From the time when the earliest predecessors of experimental psychology began collecting quantitative observations of behavior, mathematical methods have been drawn on to aid in ordering and interpreting data. Measurements of the accuracy with which observers could detect simultaneous occurrences of events in astronomical observatories and determinations of sensory thresholds—that is, the intensities of stimuli just capable of evoking responses—in physiological experiments could be accomplished using only simple methods long familiar in physical science. However, these measurements were only the first steps toward a new discipline of psychophysics, or, more broadly, experimental psychology, with the new goal of generating quantitative representations of psychological attributes such as sensations, action tendencies, or values that could be inferred from observations. Moving toward this goal required a new theoretical apparatus that has come to be known as psychological measurement, or scaling, theory, and means of dealing with problems of reliability of measurements, met by the importation of statistical methods and theory developed in physical and biological sciences.

Finally, toward the middle of the first century of scientific psychology, mathematics began to be used as in older sciences, to aid the formulation of theoretical models capable of setting the stage for incisive tests of hypotheses and bringing significant relationships out of the welter of empirical facts and local theories. The term *model* is most commonly associated with this highest level of theoretical formulations but can well apply also to applications of formal methodology, often but not always mathematical, in measurement and statistics. New developments in the application of statistical models to psychological data constitute the main theme of this volume. This chapter focuses on theoretical models but also touches on some relationships between these and statistical models. I start with a bit of history, then discuss some salient aspects of the modeling enterprise.

By *model* I denote any theoretical formulation, whether mathematical, logical, or computer implemented, that allows exact computations. Embodying a scientific hypothesis or theory in a model enables us to know exactly what is assumed and to determine unambiguously the implications of the assumptions. Thus the emergence of useful theoretical models in any field is one of the prime indicants of theoretical progress. Though the term *model* first came into common use among psychologists only in the 1950s, efforts to formulate mathematical models as constituents of theory actually began much earlier and have played an important role in shaping the course of research.

A THUMBNAIL HISTORY OF MODELS IN PSYCHOLOGY

I group modeling efforts into three main classes: (a) the extraction of numerical laws and invariances from data, (b) the inference of structures underlying behavioral observations, and (c) the modeling of behavioral or cognitive systems.

Laws

Under this heading I include work done in the tradition of the natural sciences as explicated by Langley, Simon, Bradshaw, and Zytkow (1987). Among the earliest instances are some well-known invariances discovered in sensory psychophysiology in the 18th and 19th centuries. One example is Bloch's law, which states that the product of intensity and duration of a brief visual stimulus is a constant; a more famous example is Weber's law, dating from the early 19th century, which states that a just discriminable change in a stimulus is a constant fraction of its intensity. Weber's law was incorporated by Fechner (1907) into his expression of a logarithmic relation between psychological and physical stimulus magnitudes. Though still treated as gospel in some quarters, Fechner's law has been superseded for many experimental psychologists by the work of Stevens (1957, 1971), who distinguished classes of experimental situations in which the Weber–Fechner function is and is not approximated and showed that both could be accommodated by a power law.

The breakout of this strand of mathematical psychology from the narrow domain of sensory processes must be largely credited to L. L. Thurstone, the originator of psychological scaling theory. He showed that a model incorporating response variability could be used to transform data for judgments about stimuli that are definable only on qualitative dimensions (handwriting quality, employee performance, esthetic value) to scales calibrated in "just-noticeable differences," thus vastly facilitating the search for invariants or simple predictive relationships

(Thurstone, 1927). The line of development from Thurstone's pioneering work led, somewhat indirectly, to the currently extremely influential "choice model" of Luce (1959, 1963). Luce's model differed from Thurstone's in being based on a small number of axioms derived from intuitions about the psychological basis of choice behavior. The principal axiom expresses a property of choices sometimes known as *independence of irrelevant alternatives,* which implies that the relative probability of choosing two objects, or other choice alternatives, is independent of the size of the set of alternatives presented to the chooser (so that, e.g., the probability of a buyer's choosing grey over blue as an automobile color would be predicted to be the same whether only grey and blue or grey, blue, and red were the alternatives offered by a dealer). The axioms imply that the utility of any alternative to a chooser can be represented as a value on a ratio scale of measurement, with the important property that probability of choosing any given alternative from a set is given by the ratio of the scale value of the given alternative to the sum of scale values for all members of the set. The choice model has received some support from direct empirical tests (e.g., Atkinson, Bower, & Crothers, 1965), but more importantly, provides the basis for computation of choice probabilities in many current cognitive theories.

A development in this tradition that once seemed extremely promising was the importation of the mathematical theory of communication of Shannon (1948) into psychology under the rubric *information theory* (Attneave, 1959). A most attractive prospect was that expressing quantities of information stored in memory in informational units would reveal invariants (e.g., invariance of short-term memory span over types of materials) not apparent when the units are items such as digits, letters, or words. The promise was not realized, however, and applications of information theory are now seen mainly in the interpretation of some types of perceptual information processing (Garner, 1962).

The importance of descriptive quantitative laws is not limited to simple sensory and perceptual processing. A notable example in the domain of research on animal learning and behavior is the *matching law,* expressing a proportionality between rate of responding and rate of reinforcement (reward) in a variety of instrumental, or trial and error, learning situations (Herrnstein, 1974; Williams, 1988). The matching law has been extended to the human level as an ingredient in the interpretation of economic behaviors (Herrnstein, 1990).

Cognitive Structures

Another group of models with a long history in psychology is concerned not with the reduction and smoothing of data, but with the task of inferring mental structures that lie behind observed behaviors. The earliest entry in this tradition is factor analysis, a methodology for extracting estimates of the weights of factors, such as components of mental abilities, from intercorrelations of test scores. One of the first and most famous results was the extraction of a general intelligence, or g, factor from intelligence test data by Spearman (1904). The conception of an important general factor did not stand up well over the years, however, and multiple factor theories pioneered by Thurstone (1935) have come to dominate the field of ability and personality assessment. Mental factors based on correlational data have never become significant in psychological theorizing outside the testing area, however. Much more important is the approach of multidimensional scaling, a generalization and extension of Thurstone's scaling methods that maps judgmental data onto distances in psychological spaces. This mapping is theoretically significant because functional relations (as, e.g., stimulus generalization gradients, Shepard, 1958) expressed in terms of distances on psychological scales often prove to exhibit much greater generality than functions expressed in terms of physical stimulus dimensions. This tradition has given rise to some of the most elegant formal developments to be found in psychological research, most notably work on the foundations of psychological scales of measurement (Krantz, Luce, Suppes, & Tversky, 1971).

Models of Cognitive and Behavioral Systems

Models of cognitive function that include assumptions about both structure and process date from the early 19th century and are currently the focus of so much activity that they almost preempt the term *model* for most psychologists. The first important entry was Herbart's (1891) model of the interplay of ideas in competition for access to consciousness. The model was elaborated in considerable detail but, perhaps because of the lack of any link with behavior, it did not enter into any continuing stream of research. Some of its elements did, however, reappear in later theories, as, for example, the treatment of variability of response latencies in the work of Clark L. Hull and his associates (Gladstone, Yamaguchi, Hull, & Felsinger, 1947; Hull, 1951). The first cognitive model that could actually be interpreted experimentally was a probabilistic model for trial-and-error learning, the work of the ubiquitous Thurstone (1930). This model fell on infertile ground, but after a dozen subsequent years of rapidly accelerating research in animal learning, the situation was much more auspicious for Hull (1943) to produce an axiomatic mathematical theory of behavior and learning. Hull's system was largely programmatic, and although he did not live to supply more rigorous mathematical development, his vision was an important source of motivation for the emergence of mathematical learning theories in the 1950s (Bush & Mosteller, 1951, 1955; Estes, 1950). The continuing development of mathematical learning theory after about 1960 was eclipsed in the eyes of the psychological public by the impact of digital computers and the beginnings of artificial intelligence, which led to the flourishing of cognitive models based on computer and information-processing metaphors (e.g., Atkinson & Shiffrin, 1968; Feigenbaum, 1963; Hunt, 1962; Newell, Shaw, & Simon, 1958; Norman & Rumelhart, 1970).

CONTEMPORARY MODELS

The use of mathematical and computer models in behavioral and cognitive science has expanded during the last decade to the degree that even a book-length survey could scarcely do justice to all of the major developments. I limit the following sketch to areas in which nearly all theoretically oriented research is model driven and try only to give an idea of the range and kinds of highly visible and influential efforts.

Psychophysiology and Behavioral Neuroscience

Even within the area of elementary, *low-level,* sensory and perceptual processes, which looks to outsiders like a narrow and homogeneous specialty, research is directed and interpreted by a bewildering diversity of formal models. It appears that almost every basic problem can be approached from many different perspectives, each giving rise to a particular kind of modeling effort and with little sign of convergence on any common framework. In the psychophysiology of the retina, models based on lateral excitatory and inhibitory interactions of retinal elements (Graham & Ratliff, 1974) have been moved somewhat out of the limelight, but by no means supplanted, by models based on Fourier analyses of spatial frequency channels (Graham, 1981). At a slightly higher level, efforts to model the way the visual system extracts information from a scene are associated with the new field of *computer vision* and models intended to simulate early visual function by programs utilizing parallel computation by large numbers of processing units (Marr, 1982; Marr & Poggio, 1977) or cooperative/competitive interactions in networks of *mathematical neurons* (Sperling, 1980). In audition, networks seem to be a less natural medium of representation, and problems of discrimination on basic acoustic dimensions are approached by counting and timing models for the accumulation of information in random walk or race processes (Green & Luce, 1974) or by extensions of traditional psychophysical models that incorporate stochastic elements (Falmagne, 1974). There is also continuing concern with connections of psychophysical models to measurement theory (Krantz, 1974). Outside the sensory area, there has recently been a resurgence of interest in neural models for learning and memory. An important class of these models involves *neural networks,* that is, parallel processing in networks of abstract units whose properties resemble in some respects those of neurons (Hawkins & Bower, 1989).

Cognitive Psychology and Cognitive Science

Some investigators are pursuing the ambitious goal of constructing comprehensive theoretical architectures for a unified cognitive science (Anderson, 1983; Newell, 1990), but so far these are of only limited influence and most research is carried out within the frameworks of more limited models.

One of the most seminal developments in modern cognitive psychology has been the use of reaction time data in efforts to trace the time course of mental processes (reviewed by Luce, 1986). A technique originated by a 19th-century physiologist, Donders (1868/1969), which took the difference in reaction time between two tasks of different complexity as a measure of the duration of an added process, was refined and extended by Sternberg (1969) to constitute what is known as the *additive factors method*. Application to a recognition task originated by Sternberg (1966) suggested that, in making a decision about recognition of a recent event, an individual examines the contents of short-term memory by a process of sequential search in which the durations of cognitive operations such as stimulus encoding and comparison can be determined. The exciting prospect of getting directly at temporal properties of mental events was dimmed somewhat by research showing that people often tend to trade off speed and accuracy when making decisions, so that measures of response time cannot safely be assumed to reflect only the durations of underlying processes. The positive return for recognizing this complication was the flourishing of models with richer structures that could accommodate both speed and accuracy data (Ratcliff, 1978; Townsend & Ashby, 1983; Townsend & Schweikert, 1989).

Another fertile line of application of reaction-time methods has been the exploration of semantic and propositional network models. A profusion of research on semantic memory over nearly 2 decades has been guided by models in which it is assumed that words or concepts that an individual has learned can be represented by nodes in an associative network that takes the form of a directed graph (Collins & Loftus, 1975; Collins & Quillian, 1972). The nodes are connected by links, and the network has the property that perception of a word excites its node in the memory representation and then activation spreads over the connecting links to the nodes for other semantically related words or concepts. Early support for this type of model came from experimental phenomena such as the *semantic distance effect*, which refers to the observation that, under some conditions, reaction time to verify the statement of a relation between two words or concepts varies directly with the distance between the corresponding nodes in the memory net. The architecture of semantic networks has been extended to propositional network models for factual memory (Anderson, 1983; Anderson & Bower, 1973). Memory for events (episodic as distinguished from semantic memory in a currently popular classification) also lends itself to network models; some of the currently influential models assume localized storage of "images" of experienced events at the nodes of a network (Raaijmakers & Shiffrin, 1981) and others assume storage of representations in a composite, distributed memory system (Anderson, 1973; Murdock, 1982).

Research on learning has been similarly model driven. A great part of theoretically oriented research on conditioning and animal learning is now conducted in connection with a model developed by Rescorla and Wagner (1972), which combines the linear recursive learning function familiar from earlier learning theory (Bush & Mosteller, 1951; Estes, 1950; Hull, 1943) with a competitive learning principle. Gluck and Bower (1988) showed that this model can be interpreted as a special case of an adaptive network (Widrow & Hoff, 1960) and have extended it successfully to apply to some instances of human learning.

For some years, the learning of both rule-defined and fuzzy (probabilistically defined) categories by human subjects has been the scene of very active developments and testing of a variety of information-processing models. Among the earliest quantitative models to receive attention were feature-frequency and prototype models (Reed, 1972). In feature-frequency models, it is assumed that the learner accumulates information about the relative frequencies of exemplar-features in different categories and from these computes categorization probabilities for both previously experienced and new patterns. In prototype models, it is assumed that the learner forms a mental prototype of each category, comprising the average or modal feature values for exemplars of the category. Although these models appear quite different on the surface, it has been shown that, under a fairly general set of conditions, they are actually isomorphic (Estes, 1986). These models account quite well for categorization performance under some circumstances, but they fail when feature values are correlated within categories (Estes, 1986; Norman & Rumelhart, 1970; Nosofsky, 1986). This limitation is not true of exemplar-memory models, in which it is assumed that the learner stores whole exemplar patterns in memory and categorizes new exemplars on the basis of their similarity (computed by a multiplicative algorithm) to the stored patterns (Medin & Schaffer, 1978; Nosofsky, 1984). Very current work in this line involves comparisons between the exemplar-memory models and adaptive network models (Estes, Campbell, Hatsopoulos, & Hurwitz, 1989; Gluck & Bower, 1988).

ON THE FUNCTIONS OF MODELS

Why do we need models in behavioral science? Several reasons deserve attention.

Models are essential to set the stage for tests of hypotheses about theoretical concepts. In behavioral science, we are dealing with complex systems in which processes and mechanisms do not exist alone. When a biologist is concerned with properties of transmission along a nerve fiber of a crustacean, it is possible to remove a bit of tissue including the fiber, keep it alive in a preparation that stimulates its context in the body, and study the fiber in isolation. But when our concern is with mental processes of live human beings, nothing of the sort can be done. If we wish to test hypotheses about a particular process, we can proceed only by including the process along with other processes and structures in a model that can represent some form of mental activity or behavior. Then we may be able to discover whether our observations are better accounted for by a model including the process of interest or by an otherwise identical model in which it is lacking or is replaced by some alternative. A good example appears in a recent study by Murdock and Lamon (1988). In order to address the question of whether learning in standard recognition experiments has the property that the amount of relevant information stored from any learning experience depends on the amount already present in memory, they compared two versions of the *matched-filter model* of Anderson (1973) that differed only with respect to this property. Only the version incorporating the hypothesized dependence proved able to account for the effects of repetition on recognition, a result of interest because mention of such a property had been missing from the literature on recognition.

Another approach to hypothesis testing is based on estimation of model parameters. In a recent study (Estes & Brunn, 1987), a colleague and I were interested in the *word superiority effect*, that is, the observation that letters imbedded in briefly displayed printed words are better identified than the same letters imbedded in nonwords (strings of unrelated letters). At issue was the hypothesis that letters in a word context are better discriminated at a perceptual level versus the alternative hypothesis that the word advantage is due only to a bias for reporting letters that complete words. Our procedure was to formulate a model including a parameter representing discriminability and a parameter representing bias. By fitting the model to our experimental data, we obtained estimates of these parameters and could determine whether the values of either or both would differ between words and nonwords (the result proving to be both).

Models are also essential to the analysis of complex situations. In psychological research, we are always dealing with complex systems in which any observed behavior can be the resultant of many different, and often interacting, causal factors. Thus the outcomes of experiments can only be interpreted by comparing what is observed with what was expected on the basis of some simplified view of the situation, that is, a model. Put more elegantly,

> It seems that the human mind has first to construct forms, independently, before we can find them in things. Kepler's marvelous achievement [his law concerning the elliptical orbits of the planets] is a particularly fine example of the fact that knowledge cannot spring from experience alone but only from a comparison of the inventions of the intellect with the facts of observation. (quoted from Albert Einstein by Chandrasekhar, 1990, p. 285)

Unfortunately, a common malady among behavioral scientists is to complicate their models in an effort to make them all-encompassing for a particular domain, and therefore irrefutable, and to take an unbroken string of correct predictions as the prime indicator of success. The effort is self-defeating, for we learn only by comparing successes and failures. A useful model needs the property I have denoted as *sharpness* (Estes, 1975). That is, the model must capture aspects of a situation that are believed to be important in a simple enough form that unambiguous empirical implications can be derived and disparities between predictions and observations will be instructive.

An excellent example of a model meeting all criteria of usefulness was imported into psychology from signal detectability theory (Estes, 1975; Green & Swets, 1966; Tanner & Swets, 1954). In a common type of decision task, an individual is confronted from time to time with perceptual inputs, which only sometimes include a designated target or signal. For example, an aircraft controller viewing a radar screen occasionally sees small "blips" on the screen, which sometimes represent aircraft but sometimes only visual noise; or a radiologist studying a series of x-rays occasionally sees a faint shadow, which may represent a lesion but may represent only a random variation in texture. An important psychological problem is to understand how the observer's decisions are determined jointly by physical characteristics of the display and by the observer's expectations or biases. In the model drawn from signal detectability theory, it is assumed that corresponding to the set of possible sensory inputs in such a task are two sets of internal states, those generated by inputs that contain a target and those generated by inputs that do not. In general, these sets overlap, so the observer must have some criterion for deciding whether a given input contains a target, and the value of this criterion is assumed to be determined by experience with frequencies of target and noise inputs and by values and costs of correct and incorrect decisions. The model provides a standard way of estimating parameters that separately represent the observer's decision criterion and sensitivity to differences between target and noise distributions. The estimates can be used to test hypotheses about such matters as the effect of training on these aspects of the decision process. Although it is too simple to represent any one situation fully, the model has—in part for that very reason—come into nearly universal use as an aid to the analysis of decision making.

ON TESTING MODELS

General Issues

I start with a summary of some of my ideas, perhaps aptly termed *biases,* on the testing of theoretical models. First, although psychologists continually speak of testing models, they rarely do so in any strict sense. There are several prerequisites to the useful testing of a model. Almost everyone recognizes that the model must be well enough specified that investigators other than the originator of the model can agree on its empirical implications. And of course it must be possible also to agree on a test situation capable of yielding data that the model should be expected to account for. Less obvious is the fact that, because experiments yield only comparative judgments, a model cannot be effectively tested in isolation; a comparison with one or more alternative models (even if the alternative is only a "chance" base line) is essential to any rigorous interpretation. In practice, there are often many relevant test situations with no objective criterion for selecting the most appropriate and with the possibility, nay, likelihood, that different experiments will yield conflicting results. As a consequence, effective evaluation of a model comes from assessment of how well it stands up over multiple tests in comparison with competitors.

This last conclusion is not as widely understood among psychologists and cognitive scientists as would be desirable, perhaps because many come to this area with little prior background in natural sciences. A pointed illustration can be given in terms of the information-processing model of Atkinson and Shiffrin (1968), which accrued so much support in experimental applications over a period of several years that it came to be known as the *modal model* of human short-term memory. An apparent break in the string of successes occurred on the appearance of a study by Craik and Lockhart (1972) suggesting a limitation of the model, in that it had not provided for multiple levels of stimulus encoding. This result was immediately seized on by many investigators (not, to my knowledge, including Craik or Lockhart) as "disconfirming" Atkinson and Shiffrin's model and leaving the way open for some newcomer. But science does not work that way. It is reasonable to interpret this as meaning that the evidence for multiple levels of encoding suggests a desirable direction of extension or elaboration of the model. That step seems not to have been explicitly taken, with the result that Atkinson and Shiffrin's model has yet to be superseded as the most useful quantitative interpretation of a fairly wide range of research in short-term memory whereas the concept of multiple levels of coding has come to be incorporated as a matter of course in newer theories for various aspects of memory.

Why do investigators of cognition expend so much time and effort in testing models if the tests are rarely definitive? Primarily, I think, because the most valuable products of model testing are not the support or disconfirmation of particular models, but the generation of information bearing on theoretical assumptions. As soon as theory in any domain has reached any appreciable degree of richness or complexity, it becomes impossible to carry out direct tests of hypotheses about individual component structures and processes because a negative result may be attributable to other components than the one under test. The way to progress then, though not necessarily easy, is to compare two models that differ only with respect to the component of interest. An illustration can be given in terms of the study of human category learning discussed earlier (Estes et al., 1989). It was found that a simple adaptive network model introduced by Gluck and Bower (1988) provided a close account of the acquisition data. This result set the stage for a test of the hypothesis that this form of learning manifests a competitive property such that the amount learned on any acquisition trial about the relation between a given stimulus feature and a category depends (negatively) on the degree to which other features present in the stimulus already predict the category. This competitive property is characteristic of many neural network models but not of traditional information-processing models. The desired test was achieved by fitting the acquisition data with two network models that had identical structures and process assumptions except that only one incorporated the competitive property in the algorithm for adjusting the weights on feature-category associations during learning experiences. In several such tests, the competitive version proved superior, a result providing convincing support for the hypothesis at issue. It is not always possible to meet the requirement of strict comparability completely, but it is important to keep the goal in mind.

Procedures for Statistical Tests of Models

More extended discussions of test procedures are available in a number of sources, among them Sternberg (1963) and Wickens (1982). Here I only touch on some issues germane to the interrelations between theoretical and statistical models.

When a new model is formulated, a natural question is whether it yields a satisfactory account of relevant data. But how is one to decide what is satisfactory? Comparisons with existing models are relevant when possible, but sometimes there is no prior model. Consider, for example, the situation when Sternberg (1966) first reported short-term recognition data that appeared to be well described by predictions from a serial search model. The experimental paradigm was new and there were no relevant models in the literature, but it was nonetheless desirable to make some judgment about the adequacy of the search model. A very common procedure is simply to fit the model to the data, correlate theoretical with observed values, and report the obtained correlation coefficient, r, expressing satisfaction if the correlation is high. Aside from the lack of any generally accepted criterion for a high correlation, this procedure has the drawback that the absolute value of r strongly depends on the experimenter's choice of the spacing and range of values of the independent variable (in Sternberg's experiment the length of the list of items presented for study). Also, there is no way to make a satisfactory statement about the significance of the correspondence between theory and data. Testing the significance of the obtained r is no help, because a negative result may signify only lack of sensitivity and a significant result only justifies some confidence that the true correlation is nonzero and provides no help at selecting the given model over alternatives. Testing the significance of the differences between correlations obtained for alternative models is unlikely to be rewarding because standard errors associated with correlation coefficients are usually very large and thus significance is hard to demonstrate even when differences are substantial.

Another common procedure is to estimate the parameters of a model by a procedure such as minimizing chi-square and claim support for the model if the chi-square is short of significance at some prescribed level. This tactic shares the weaknesses of all statistical tests that depend on failure to reject a null hypothesis. Lack of significance may signify only that the data are too meager or too variable to provide a test with satisfactory power; significance may be obtained with nearly any model if the test is sufficiently powerful, and in any event provides no clue as to why or how the model tested is unsatisfactory.

What is needed is a statistical test procedure constructed so that a significant outcome lends support to the model tested and yields some information as to the aspect of the model that gives it an advantage over less satisfactory ones. To meet these requirements, it is necessary that a test involve a comparison of models. Optimally, the model tested should be nested in a family of models so that it differs from another member of the family only in the aspects of particular interest. A good example is provided in a study reported by Young (1971). The study was concerned with paired-associate learning, and special interest attached to the hypothesis that information stored in memory about newly studied associations is represented in multiple short-term memory stores with some unique properties. In one analysis, Young's procedure was to fit his data by minimizing chi-square to a Markovian model with seven free parameters and then to a reduced, five-parameter, model in which some distinctions among memory stores were eliminated, allowing two of the original seven parameters to be dropped. The unrestricted model yielded a description of the data that appears impressive to the eye and a chi-square short of significance at even the .25 level. More important, the difference between the chi-square values for the two versions was highly significant, and thus there was reason to claim positive support for the assumptions that differentiated the general and restricted models.

When data are appropriate for analysis of variance rather than chi-square methods, it is sometimes possible to devise similar test procedures based on comparisons of models. To illustrate, I use data from the study of Estes et al. (1989) cited previously. In that study, the task was learning to assign symptom patterns of hypothetical patients to disease categories. There were four symptoms, correlated to different degrees with the categories, and they occurred in all 16 possible patterns. We were interested in assessing the ability of the adaptive network model of Gluck and Bower (1988) to predict asymptotic response percentages, so the first step was to compute theoretical values for the asymptotic percentages of choices of a given category for each of the symptom patterns (these values being a priori predictions, not depending on fitted parameters). For one group, the resulting data are shown in Table 1.1, in part,

TABLE 1.1
Fit of Network Model to Categorization Data

Symptom Pattern	Data	Prediction
1	78	78
2	39	34
3	6	18
4	2	10
1,2	73	75
1,3	40	54
1,4	41	30
.	.	.
.	.	.
1,2,3,4	0	4

where the numerals under Symptom Pattern denote individual symptoms. The correlation between observed and predicted values was .93, and the r^2 of .87 indicates that a large part of the variance in the data was accounted for by the model. What we do not know at this point in the analysis is how much of the remaining variance is due to error and how much, if any, to systematic factors not represented in the model but possibly in a superior model.

To complete the analysis, we follow a procedure, discussed in detail by Estes et al. (1989) and Estes (1991), that begins with an analysis of variance (ANOVA) of the observed response percentages. The F for variation between patterns is highly significant, which is unsurprising and of no great interest in itself. The crucial step is to partition the sum of squares between patterns into a component attributable to the model and a residual attributable to (nonerror) sources other than this component. The partitioning is accomplished by defining a contrast over the mean response percentages for the 16 patterns. The contrast is a weighted sum of the means with the constraint that the weights sum to zero. In this case, the contrast weights are the predicted values, expressed as deviations from their mean. The sum of squares for the contrast yields an F significant at the .001 level, whereas the residual (obtained by subtracting the sum of squares for the contrast from the sum of squares between patterns) yields an F that does not approach significance even at the .05 level. Thus the network model survives this particular test satisfactorily in that we have some statistical justification for concluding that its predictions account for all of the systematic variance in the data. That is not to say, of course, that the data have selected this model as the only one for which the same claim could be made. If there should prove to be a competing model that survives the same test, we may be able to extend our procedure by applying a t test to the difference between the contrasts defined for the two models and ascertain whether there is statistical justification for choosing one over the other.

This last step is straightforward only if the models are parameter free, as in the example just described. Most often in the behavioral sciences, however, models include free parameters that must be evaluated from data when the model is being applied; and comparisons of models with free parameters are fraught with hazards. If two models being compared have different numbers of free parameters, then a statistical comparison is unfair in the sense that the model with more parameters has to account for fewer degrees of freedom in the data and may yield a better fit simply on that account. For the very special case of linear regression models, there is a standard way of adjusting a statistic such as a squared multiple correlation coeffient for different numbers of free parameters (Cohen & Cohen, 1975); the same is not true for nonlinear models. And, even if theoretical models can be put in linear form (sometimes accomplishable, for example, by transformations of variables), the parameters in two models being compared may not reflect the same aspects of the data, in which case no way of allowing for different numbers of parameters can be justified. We simply have to live with the fact that, for the most part, fully satisfactory statistical comparisons of models are limited to cases when the models are nested in the sense already defined in connection with minimum chi-square tests.

Theorists in the behavioral sciences may find it discouraging that statistical methods are not available to support all of the kinds of model comparisons they wish to make. The brighter side of the coin is that, at least for some problems, useful statistical methods are available. For the remainder, behavioral scientists are in the same boat as their fellows in the biological and physical sciences, but with the advantage of being able to draw on the experience of those sciences in comparing models by heuristic methods that emphasize multiple tests and converging evidence from independent sources. One can scarcely be reminded too often that models, both statistical and theoretical, are devices that augment but cannot substitute for the judgment of the investigator in reasoning about scientific problems.

ACKNOWLEDGMENT

Preparation of this chapter was supported by Grants BNS 86-09232 and BNS 90-09001 from the National Science Foundation.

REFERENCES

Anderson, J. A. (1973). A theory for the recognition of items from short memorized lists. *Psychological Review, 80*, 417–438.

Anderson, J. R. (1983). *The architecture of cognition.* Cambridge, MA: Harvard University Press.

Anderson, J. R., & Bower, G. H. (1973). *Human associative memory.* Washington, DC: Winston.

Atkinson, R. C., Bower, G. H., & Crothers, E. J. (1965). *An introduction to mathematical learning theory.* New York: Wiley.

Atkinson, R. C., & Shiffrin, R. M. (1968). Human memory: A proposed system and its control processes. In K. W. Spence & J. T. Spence (Ed.), *The psychology of learning and motivation: Advances in research and theory* (pp. 89–105). New York: Academic Press.

Attneave, F. (1959). *Applications of information theory to psychology: A summary of basic concepts, methods, and results.* New York: Holt, Rinehart & Winston.

Bush, R. R., & Mosteller, F. (1951). A mathematical model for simple learning. *Psychological Review, 58*, 313–323.

Bush, R. R., & Mosteller, F. (1955). *Stochastic models for learning.* New York: Wiley.

Chandrasekhar, S. (1990). Science and scientific attitudes. *Nature, 344* (22 March), 285–286.

Cohen, J., & Cohen, P. (1975). *Applied multiple correlation/regression analysis for the behavioral sciences.* Hillsdale, NJ: Lawrence Erlbaum Associates.

Collins, A. M., & Loftus, E. F. (1975). A spreading-activation theory of semantic processing. *Psychological Review, 82*, 407–428.

Collins, A. M., & Quillian, M. R. (1972). How to make a language user. In E. Tulving & W. Donaldson (Ed.), *Organization of memory* (pp. 310–351). New York: Academic Press.

Craik, F. I. M., & Lockhart, R. S. (1972). Levels of processing: A framework for memory research. *Journal of Verbal Learning and Verbal Behavior, 11*, 671–684.

Donders, F. C. (1969). Over de snelheid van psychische processen [on the speed of mental processes, translated by W. G. Koster]. *Acta Psychologica, 30,* 412–431. (Original work published 1868)

Estes, W. K. (1950). Toward a statistical theory of learning. *Psychological Review, 57,* 94–107.

Estes, W. K. (1975). Some targets for mathematical psychology. *Journal of Mathematical Psychology, 12,* 263–282.

Estes, W. K. (1986). Array models for category learning. *Cognitive Psychology, 18,* 500–549.

Estes, W. K. (1991). *Statistical models in behavioral research.* Hillsdale, NJ: Lawrence Erlbaum Associates.

Estes, W. K., & Brunn, J. L. (1987). Discriminability and bias in the word-superiority effect. *Perception and Psychophysics, 42,* 411–422.

Estes, W. K., Campbell, J. A., Hatsopoulos, N., & Hurwitz, J. B. (1989). Base-rate effects in category learning: A comparison of parallel network and memory storage-retrieval models. *Journal of Experimental Psychology: Learning, Memory, and Cognition, 15,* 556–571.

Falmagne, J. C. (1974). Foundations of Fechnerian psychophysics. In D. H. Krantz, R. C. Atkinson, R. D. Luce, & P. Suppes (Ed.), *Contemporary developments in mathematical psychology: Vol. 2. Measurement, Psychophysics, and Neural Information Processing* (pp. 121–159). San Francisco: W. H. Freeman.

Fechner, G. T. (1907). *Elemente der psychophysik* (3rd ed.). Leipzig: Breithopf & Hartel.

Feigenbaum, E. A. (1963). Simulation of verbal learning behavior. In E. A. Feigenbaum & J. Feldman (Eds.), *Computers and thought* (pp. 297–309). New York: McGraw-Hill.

Garner, W. R. (1962). *Uncertainty and structure as psychological concepts.* New York: Wiley.

Gladstone, A. I., Yamaguchi, H. G., Hull, C. L., & Felsinger, J. M. (1947). Some functional relationships of reaction potential (sEr) and related phenomena. *Journal of Experimental Psychology, 37,* 510–526.

Gluck, M. A., & Bower, G. H. (1988). From conditioning to category learning: An adaptive network model. *Journal of Experimental Psychology: General, 117,* 225–244.

Graham, N. (1981). The visual system does a crude Fourier analysis of patterns. In S. Grossberg (Ed.), *Mathematical psychology and psychophysiology* (pp. 1–16). Providence, RI: American Mathematical Society.

Graham, N., & Ratliff, F. (1974). Quantitative theories of the integrative action of the retina. In D. H. Krantz, R. C. Atkinson, R. D. Luce, & P. Suppes (Eds.), *Contemporary developments in mathematical psychology: Vol. 2. Measurement, psychophysics, and neural information processing* (pp. 306–371). San Francisco: W. H. Freeman.

Green, D. M., & Luce, R. D. (1974). Counting and timing mechanisms in auditory discrimination and reaction time. In D. A. Krantz, R. C. Atkinson, R. D. Luce, & P. Suppes (Eds.), *Contemporary developments in mathematical psychology. Volume II. Measurement, psychophysics, and neural information processing* (pp. 372–415). San Francisco: W. H. Freeman.

Green, D. M., & Swets, J. A. (1966). *Signal detection theory and psychophysics.* New York: Wiley.

Hawkins, R. D., & Bower, G. H. (1989). *Computational models of learning in simple neural systems.* New York: Academic Press.

Herbart, J. R. (1891). *Lehrbuch der Psychologie* [A Textbook of Psychology]. New York: Appleton.

Herrnstein, R. J. (1974). Formal properties of the matching law. *Journal of the Experimental Analysis of Behavior, 21,* 159–164.

Herrnstein, R. J. (1990). Behavior, reinforcement, and utility. *Psychological Science, 1,* 217–224.

Hull, C. L. (1943). *Principles of behavior.* New York: Appleton.

Hull, C. L. (1951). *Essentials of behavior.* New Haven: Yale University Press.

Hunt, E. B. (1962). *Concept learning: An information processing problem.* New York: Wiley.

Krantz, D. H. (1974). Measurement theory and qualitative laws in psychophysics. In D. H. Krantz, R. C. Atkinson, R. D. Luce, & P. Suppes (Eds.), *Contemporary developments in mathematical psychology: Vol. 2. Measurement, psychophysics, and neural information processing* (pp. 161–199). San Francisco: W. H. Freeman.

Krantz, D. H., Luce, R. D., Suppes, P., & Tversky, A. (1971). *Foundations of measurement* (Vol. 1). New York: Academic Press.

Langley, P., Simon, H. A., Bradshaw, G. L., & Zytkow, J. M. (1987). *Scientific discovery: Computational explorations of the creative process.* Cambridge, MA: MIT Press.

Luce, R. D. (1959). *Individual choice behavior.* New York: Wiley.

Luce, R. D. (1963). Detection and recognition. In R. D. Luce, R. R. Bush, & E. Galanter (Ed.), *Handbook of mathematical psychology* (Vol. 1, pp. 103–189). New York: Wiley.

Luce, R. D. (1986). *Response times: Their role in inferring elementary mental organization.* New York: Oxford University Press.

Marr, D. (1982). *Vision: A computational investigation into the human representation and processing of visual information.* San Francisco: W. H. Freeman.

Marr, D., & Poggio, T. (1977). Cooperative computation of stereo disparity. *Science, 194,* 283–287.

Medin, D. L., & Schaffer, M. M. (1978). Context theory of classification learning. *Psychological Review, 85,* 207–238.

Murdock, B. B. J. (1982). A theory for the storage and retrieval of item and associative information. *Psychological Review, 89,* 609–626.

Murdock, B. B., Jr., & Lamon, M. (1988). The replacement effect: Repeating some items while replacing others. *Memory & Cognition, 16,* 91–101.

Newell, A. (1990). *A unified theory of cognition.* Cambridge, MA: Harvard University Press.

Newell, A., Shaw, J. C., & Simon, H. A. (1958). Elements of a theory of human problem solving. *Psychological Review, 65,* 151–166.

Norman, D. A., & Rumelhart, D. E. (1970). A system for perception and memory. In D. A. Norman (Ed.), *Models of human memory* (pp. 21–64). New York: Academic Press.

Nosofsky, R. M. (1984). Choice, similarity, and the context theory of classification. *Journal of Experimental Psychology: Learning, Memory, and Cognition, 10,* 104–114.

Nosofsky, R. M. (1986). Attention, similarity, and the identification-categorization relationship. *Journal of Experimental Psychology: General, 115,* 39–57.

Raaijmakers, J. G. W., & Shiffrin, R. M. (1981). Search of associative memory. *Psychological Review, 88,* 93–134.

Ratcliff, R. (1978). A theory of memory retrieval. *Psychological Review, 85,* 59–108.

Reed, S. K. (1972). Pattern recognition and categorization. *Cognitive Psychology, 3,* 382–407.

Rescorla, R. A., & Wagner, A. R. (1972). A theory of Pavlovian conditioning: Variations in the effectiveness of reinforcement and non-reinforcement. In A. H. Black & W. F. Prokasy (Eds.), *Classical conditioning II: Current research and theory* (pp. 64–99). New York: Appleton-Century-Crofts.

Shannon, C. E. (1948). A mathematical theory of communication. *Bell System Technical Journal, 27,* 379–423, 623–656.

Shepard, R. N. (1958). Stimulus and response generalization: Deduction of the generalization gradient from a trace model. *Psychological Review, 65,* 242–256.

Spearman, C. (1904). "General intelligence" objectively determined and measured. *American Journal of Psychology, 15,* 201–293.

Sperling, G. (1980). Mathematical models of binocular vision. In S. Grossberg (Ed.), *Mathematical Psychology and Psychophysiology* (pp. 281–300). Providence, RI: American Mathematical Society.

Sternberg, S. (1963). Stochastic learning theory. In R. D. Luce, R. R. Bush, & E. Galanter (Eds.), *Handbook of mathematical psychology* (Vol. 2, pp. 1–120). New York: Wiley.

Sternberg, S. (1966). High-speed scanning in human memory. *Science, 153,* 652–654.

Sternberg, S. (1969). The discovery of processing stages: Extensions of Donders' method. In W. G. Koster (Ed.), *Attention and Performance II* (pp. 276–315). Amsterdam: North Holland.

Stevens, S. S. (1957). On the psychophysical law. *Psychological Review, 64*, 153–181.

Stevens, S. S. (1971). Issues in psychological measurement. *Psychological Review, 78*, 426–450.

Tanner, W. P., Jr., & Swets, J. A. (1954). A decision-making theory of visual detection. *Psychological Review, 61*, 401–409.

Thurstone, L. L. (1927). A law of comparative judgment. *Psychological Review, 34*, 273–286.

Thurstone, L. L. (1930). The learning function. *Journal of General Psychology, 3*, 469–493.

Thurstone, L. L. (1935). *The vectors of mind*. Chicago: University of Chicago Press.

Townsend, J. T., & Ashby, F. G. (1983). *The stochastic modeling of elementary psychological processes*. New York: Cambridge University Press.

Townsend, J. T., & Schweickert, R. S. (1989). Toward the trichotomy method of reaction times: Laying the foundation of stochastic mental networks. *Journal of Mathematical Psychology, 33*, 309–327.

Wickens, T. D. (1982). *Models for behavior*. San Francisco: W. H. Freeman.

Widrow, B., & Hoff, M. E. (1960). Adaptive switching circuits. *WESCON Convention Record*, Part IV, 96–104.

Williams, B. A. (1988). Reinforcement, choice, and response strength. In R. C. Atkinson, R. J. Herrnstein, G. Lindzey, & R. D. Luce (Eds.), *Stevens' handbook of experimental psychology: Vol. 2. Learning and cognition* (2nd ed., pp. 167–244). New York: Wiley.

Young, J. L. (1971). Reinforcement-test intervals in paired-associate learning. *Journal of Mathematical Psychology, 8*, 58–81.

2 Signal Detection Theory as Data Analysis Method and Psychological Decision Model

Neil A. Macmillan
Brooklyn College, City University of New York

Signal Detection Theory (SDT) can be applied, in principle, to any experiment in which error rates are the primary dependent variables. The theory derives its name from its original application in psychology to the detection of weak signals (Green & Swets, 1966), but has since spread widely through cognitive psychology and other behavioral fields. Swets (1988) presented an assessment of the application of detection theory to such diagnostic fields as medical imaging, materials testing, weather forecasting, information retrieval, polygraph lie detection, and aptitude testing.

Detection theory is both a set of methods for reducing confusion data (i.e., data from experiments in subjects display some confusion between stimuli by making errors) and a proposal about decision processes. The first section of this chapter provides an account of SDT from both points of view. My goal is to present enough information so that the reader can analyze simple experiments and understand the principles that permit extensions to more complex situations. Following this summary description, I briefly enumerate the most significant (largely practical) advantages of the SDT approach.

My second aim is to evaluate SDT as a decision model. In the final section I ask whether the explicit assumptions of the theory are correct, and what the implications are if they are incorrect.

What makes this enterprise worthwhile, and necessary, is the availability of alternative methods for analyzing error data. Many experimenters summarize confusion data in terms of proportion correct, a natural and apparently assumption-free statistic. Other summary statistics claiming to be nonparametric have been proposed as well. If SDT makes assumptions that other methods do not, why should not a neutral procedure be preferred?

The problem with this question is in its premise. Like many previous authors (e.g., Macmillan & Kaplan, 1985; Swets, 1986a), I argue that all data analysis methods make assumptions. Signal Detection Theory has invited attacks on its assumptions primarily, I believe, by making them explicit. A direct comparison of the assumptions of SDT and of alternative methods leads to the narrow conclusion that SDT's assumptions are at least as correct as those of other approaches. More broadly, I wish to point out that the advantages and assumptions of SDT—or any theory—are best evaluated against specific alternatives.[1]

ELEMENTS OF SDT

To maintain the distinction between data analysis and decision theory, the next two subsections introduce SDT in each of these ways. In describing SDT as a data analysis tool, no mention is made of its decision-theoretic assumptions, and explicit comparison is made to common alternative methods in which proportion correct and related statistics are used. I hope to demonstrate that elementary SDT procedures can be motivated heuristically, without recourse to "underlying processes." The second subsection demonstrates the close relation between these pragmatic arguments and inferences about psychological mechanism. Later subsections sketch the extension of SDT to more complex experiments.

SDT as Data Analysis

In the simplest experiment to which SDT can be applied, observers attempt to discriminate two stimulus classes S_2 and S_1. These might be Signals and Noise, as in the original detection application, but also might be Old and New words in a recognition memory experiment, Abnormal and Normal X rays in a diagnostic study, or Lies and Truths in a polygraph evaluation. Numerous examples of experiments from these and other fields can be found in Swets (1986b). To each stimulus, the observer responds either "yes" (an element of S_2 was presented) or "no" (it was S_1). Table 2.1 summarizes the situation.

There are four possible outcomes on one trial of such an experiment, so four numbers are needed to describe the result of many trials. However, the experimenter determines the total number of each type of stimulus presented, so the

---

[1]Space limitations have all but eliminated coverage of two important topics. One is Choice Theory (Luce, 1959, 1963), a way of analyzing choice experiments that is closely related to SDT. The other is the application of SDT to multidimensional stimulus sets, a recently flourishing field of study. (The two topics are related: Choice Theory can be applied more easily to multidimensional stimulus sets than can SDT.) Sample entry points to these areas are found in Ashby and Townsend (1986) and Nosofsky (1984, 1986).

TABLE 2.1
SDT Analysis of the Yes-No Experiment

Stimulus–Response Matrix:

	"yes"	"no"
S_2	x_1 = hit	x_2 = miss
S_1	y_1 = false alarm	y_2 = correct rejection

Summary statistics:

hit rate = $H = x_1/(x_1 + x_2)$
false-alarm rate = $F = y_1/(y_1 + y_2)$
sensitivity = $d' = z(H) - z(F)$
response bias = $c = -0.5[z(H) + z(F)]$

Example:

	"yes"	"no"
S_2	20	5
S_1	10	15

$H = .8, F = .4$
$z(H) = 0.842, z(F) = -0.253$
$d' = 1.095, c = -0.294$

performance of the subject can be completely described by two values. One choice of such a pair is the *hit rate (H)* and the *false-alarm rate (F)*:

$$H = P(\text{"yes"}|S_2)$$
$$F = P(\text{"yes"}|S_1). \tag{1}$$

Sensitivity.   Often, two statistics is one too many: The experimenter would like a single numerical summary of *accuracy* or *sensitivity*. Such a measure should depend directly on H and inversely on F, a *monotonicity* requirement. Many sensitivity measures satisfy a more stringent *symmetry* condition. These indexes can be written as a monotonic function of the difference between the transformed hit and false-alarm rates:

$$\text{sensitivity} = v[u(H) - u(F)], \tag{2}$$

where u and v are monotonic functions.

For the most widely used detection theory index of sensitivity, d', the function u is the z-transformation, which converts a proportion p to a standardized score, so that p is the area under a normal distribution below the point z; and v is the identity function. Thus

$$d' = z(H) - z(F). \tag{3}$$

Clearly there are many (hit, false-alarm) pairs that will lead to the same d'. For example, the pairs ($H = .8, F = .4$) and ($H = .6, F = .2$) each reflect a d' of 1.095. The manner in which H and F covary when accuracy is constant is called an *isosensitivity curve* or *receiver operating characteristic (ROC)*. Examples of ROCs implied by d' are shown in Fig. 2.1a. Chance performance ($d' = 0$) occurs when $H = F$. As sensitivity increases, the curves move toward the upper left corner, where $H = 1$ and $F = 0$. Figure 2.1a displays a prediction of the simple SDT model: If the tendency to say "yes" changes while sensitivity does not, H and F should vary along a curve from this family.

The isosensitivity curves of SDT take on a simpler geometric form when plotted on *transformed* coordinates. If instead of H and F the variables $z(H)$ and $z(F)$ are used, Equation 3 implies that the ROC will be a straight line with unit slope. Examples of such curves are shown in Fig. 2.1b. The value of d' is simply the intercept of the transformed curve.

This approach to analyzing the data in Table 2.1 may or may not be intuitively appealing, but it is likely to seem a complete departure from traditional methods based on proportion correct [$p(c)$]. In fact, however, d' and $p(c)$ are parallel constructs: For experiments in which S_1 and S_2 are equally likely, proportion correct [$p(c)$] is also consistent with Equation 2. In this case, $p(c)$ is the average of the hit and correct-rejection rates:

$$p(c) = 0.5(H + 1 - F) = 0.5 + (0.5H - 0.5F). \tag{4}$$

Thus the transformation u is multiplication by a constant, and v is addition of a constant.

Like Equation 3, Equation 4 implies a specific form for isosensitivity curves. As shown in Fig. 2.2, they are straight lines with unit slope on *linear* (not z) coordinates. The dependence of H on F implied by the use of $p(c)$ is quite different from that implied by d', so empirical ROC curves provide a simple test between the measures. Data from a wide variety of content areas (see Green & Swets, 1966, chaps. 4 and 5 for detection experiments; Swets, 1986b, and Swets & Pickett, 1982, for other applications) support a consistent result: Empirical ROCs are better described as straight lines in z coordinates than as straight lines in linear coordinates.

Response Bias.   Two observers operating at different points on the same ROC have the same sensitivity, but differ in *response bias,* the tendency to say "yes." It is often valuable to summarize this bias by a single number, for example to be able to compare the bias of two ROC points. A monotonicity condition analogous to that for sensitivity suggests that bias toward "yes" should increase

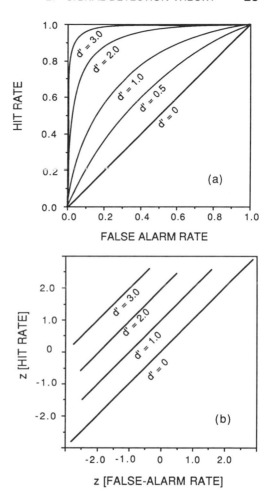

FIG. 2.1. (a) ROCs for SDT on linear coordinates. Curves connect locations with constant d'. (b) ROCs for SDT on z-coordinates.

when either H or F increases. A symmetry condition analogous to Equation 2 is (u and v again being monotonic functions)

$$\text{bias} = v[u(H) + u(F)]. \tag{5}$$

One detection theory index of response bias, c, satisfies Equation 5 and forms a natural pair with d':

$$c = -0.5[z(H) + z(F)]. \tag{6}$$

For the (H, F) pairs (.8, .4) and (.6, .2), $c = -0.294$ and 0.294 respectively.

Many (hit, false-alarm) pairs lead to the same value of c. For example, the pairs (.62, .62) and (.72, .5) have about the same value of $c = -0.294$ as the

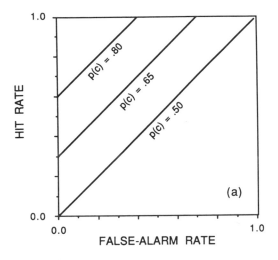

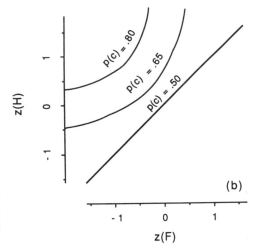

FIG. 2.2. ROCs consistent with
p(c) as a measure of sensitivity,
on (a) linear coordinates and (b)
z-coordinates.

pair (.8, .4). The manner in which H and F covary when response bias is constant
but sensitivity varies is called an *isobias curve*. Examples of isobias curves
implied by c are shown in Fig. 2.3. Unbiased performance ($c = 0$) occurs when
$H = 1 - F$, so that the observer is equally likely to be correct on S_1 and S_2 trials.
As bias increases in absolute value, the curves move toward the upper (for
negative c) or left (for positive c) boundaries of ROC space.

Many other measures of bias can be formulated within detection theory, but
most of these satisfy the monotonicity condition only in part of ROC space. A
theoretical interpretation of one candidate, the *likelihood ratio*, is given later;

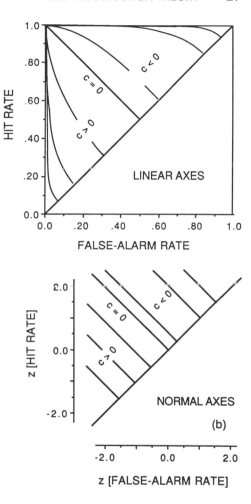

FIG. 2.3. Isobias curves (hit rate vs. false-alarm rate, d' varying) for constant values of the bias statistic c, on (a) linear and (b) z-axes.

Macmillan and Creelman (1990) presented a more detailed comparison of many bias indexes.

A plausible alternative measure of bias, sometimes used in conjunction with $p(c)$ as a sensitivity index, is the *yes rate* (Dusoir, 1975), the overall proportion of "yes" responses. When the presentation probabilities of S_1 and S_2 are equal,

$$yes\ rate = 0.5(H + F). \qquad (7)$$

The yes rate obviously satisfies Equation 5; it also predicts isobias curves that differ in shape from those generated by c. To decide between c and the yes rate (and other possible bias measures), it is natural to examine empirical isobias curves. The results of such experiments, unfortunately, have been inconclusive (see Dusoir, 1983; Macmillan & Creelman, 1990).

SDT as Decision Model

So far we have seen that sensitivity can be thought of as the difference between transformed hit and false alarm rates, and if the z-transformation is used the resulting relation between H and F provides a good description of ROC data. I now describe detection theory's picture of the discrimination process—its decision model—and show that it is consistent with these pragmatic conclusions.

The Decision Space. The SDT model imagines a *decision space* in which the effects of the stimuli are evaluated by the observer. Repeated presentations of stimuli from a given class (e.g., S_1) lead to an *underlying distribution* of values on an internal decision axis; stimuli from S_2 also generate a distribution. The two distributions have different means M_i, but are identical in variance and all other respects, as shown in Fig. 2.4. On one trial of a discrimination experiment, the information available to the subject is the value of a single observation on the decision axis. In general, this observation could have arisen from either S_1 or S_2.

The optimal procedure for selecting a response (that is, the one guaranteeing the best performance; see Green & Swets, 1966, chap. 1) is to establish a *criterion* (k in Fig. 2.4) and to respond "yes" for values above it, "no" for values below it. The conditional response rates H and F can be interpreted as areas under one or the other of the two distributions. If the location of the criterion is

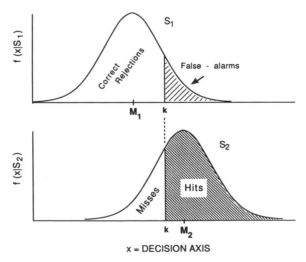

FIG. 2.4. Underlying distributions for S_1 and S_2 items. Top curve shows distribution due to S_1 items; values above the criterion k lead to false alarms, and those below to correct rejections. Lower curve shows distribution due to S_2 items; values above criterion lead to hits, those below to misses. The means of the distributions are M_1 and M_2.

very high, both H and F will be near 0. As it takes on smaller values, H and F will increase along an ROC curve until both are near 1.

The S_1 and S_2 distributions have the same shape, so each of the two yes rates H and F is the same function of the location of the criterion relative to the appropriate mean (i.e., of $M_i - k$). The form of the dependence, shown in Fig. 2.5, is the integral of one of the densities in Fig. 2.4. When the criterion is located at the mean of one distribution, the yes rate for that distribution equals 0.5. Positive $M_i - k$ differences lead to higher rates, negative differences to lower ones.

So far we have said nothing about the shape of the densities in Fig. 2.4; we now adopt the SDT assumption that they are Gaussian. In that case, Fig. 2.5 displays the normal distribution function, denoted Φ.

Sensitivity and Bias in the Decision Space. We can now connect the pragmatically motivated measures of sensitivity and bias, d' and c, with aspects of the decision space. Letting the variances of the distributions equal unity, the two yes rates can be written:

$$H = \Phi(M_2 - k),$$
$$F = \Phi(M_1 - k). \tag{8}$$

The function Φ is simply the inverse of the z-transformation, so

$$z(H) = M_2 - k,$$
$$z(F) = M_1 - k. \tag{9}$$

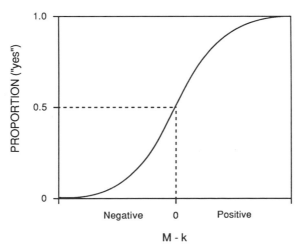

FIG. 2.5.   A cumulative distribution function (the integral of one of the densities in Fig. 2.4) giving the proportion of "yes" responses as a function of the difference between the distribution mean and the criterion.

Subtracting Equations 9 yields

$$d' = z(H) - z(F) = M_2 - M_1, \tag{10}$$

so sensitivity is represented as the difference between the means of the S_2 and S_1 distributions. The mean difference is a desirable interpretation of sensitivity because it does not depend on criterion location, but only on the relative locations of the distributions.

The criterion c is a function of the *sum* of Equations 9:

$$c = -0.5[z(H) + z(F)] = k - 0.5(M_2 + M_1). \tag{11}$$

Our response bias measure c is simply the location of the criterion relative to the halfway-point between the two means, the point of unbiased responding. To put it differently, if the equal-bias point on the decision axis is assigned the value of 0, c *is* the criterion location. This is of course a very natural interpretation of a statistic that purports to measure response bias.[2]

Likelihood Ratio.   One important aspect of the decision space that has been neglected so far is the *likelihood ratio,* the relative likelihood that an observation is due to S_2 rather than S_1. (For a discussion of the importance of the likelihood ratio in decision processes generally, see chapter 7 in the companion to this volume, subtitled *Statistical Issues.*) At each point along the decision axis, the likelihood ratio equals the height of the S_2 density divided by the height of the S_1 density. For equal-variance normal distributions, the likelihood ratio is monotonically related to the decision axis.

The value of likelihood ratio at the criterion, denoted β, is a possible measure of response bias. If the likelihood ratio is monotonic with the decision axis, one should expect β and c to be monotonically related, and they are (Macmillan & Creelman, 1990):

$$\log(\beta) = cd', \tag{12}$$

where "log" is the natural (base e) logarithm. For a constant d', therefore, β and c lead to identical conclusions in comparing different experimental conditions. When d' varies, however, the isobias curves traced by the two statistics are quite different; an experimenter wishing to compare bias in conditions for which sensitivity also differs will often reach different conclusions using β and c. Primarily because likelihood ratio does not satisfy the monotonicity condition for bias, several writers have argued that c is preferable (Banks, 1970; Ingham, 1970; Macmillan & Creelman, 1990).

The concept of likelihood ratio is nonetheless of great importance, because a

---

[2]In presenting SDT as data analysis, I drew explicit parallels between SDT indexes of sensitivity and bias and proportion-based measures like $p(c)$. There is also a parallel decision-space representation; it is described later, in the discussion of SDT's assumptions.

decision rule based on it is always optimal. For more complex experimental designs, in which the construct of a *decision axis* is too simple, decision rules based on likelihood ratio can always be stated. We encounter this application of the likelihood-ratio statistic in a later section.

Empirical ROCs and the Rating Experiment

To test the only prediction of SDT so far discussed, the shape of the ROC, requires measuring (H, F) pairs at several different biases while holding sensitivity constant. This can be accomplished through a number of manipulations.

1. Instructions can be varied, so that subjects are to respond "yes" only if they are quite sure that S_2 was presented in one block of trials, respond "yes" if there is any possibility S_2 was presented in another, and so forth.
2. The instructional variable can be implemented in the form of *payoffs*, financial incentives for each of the four possible trial outcomes in Table 2.1.
3. The probabilities with which the two stimuli are presented can be manipulated; a subject who is trying to maximize proportion correct (and who knows the presentation probabilities) will increase use of the response corresponding to the more popular stimulus.

All of these methods have been used (see Green & Swets, 1966, chap. 4), but none is now common. All have the disadvantage of tedium: A three-point ROC curve requires three times as many trials as a single ROC point. In addition, the probability manipulation is suspected to affect sensitivity as well as bias (Dusoir, 1975, Markowitz & Swets, 1967). And there is a more efficient method.

Suppose the subject is asked to provide a *confidence rating*, rather than a simple yes–no judgment, about whether S_2 was presented. This is sometimes done using verbal categories ("sure it was S_1," "perhaps S_1," "perhaps S_2," "sure it was S_2"), and sometimes with numerical categories ("1" = "sure it was S_1," "2" = "perhaps S_1," etc.). In the popular *double-response method*, the subject is asked for a yes–no response, then for a confidence judgment about the response. A continuum of confidence in S_2 can then be created by arranging the responses in the order "yes, highest confidence rating," "yes, second highest confidence rating," . . . , "yes, lowest confidence rating," "no, lowest confidence rating," . . . , "no, highest confidence rating."

Figure 2.6 provides an SDT interpretation of the rating experiment. An observer in a yes–no experiment, we have assumed, can vary the criterion location from one block of trials to the next. In a rating experiment, several of these alternative criteria are maintained simultaneously. If there are m possible response categories, $m - 1$ criteria are required. If responses are numbered from 1 (highest confidence in S_1) to m (highest confidence in S_2), then an observation between the $(j - 1)$st and jth criteria leads to response j.

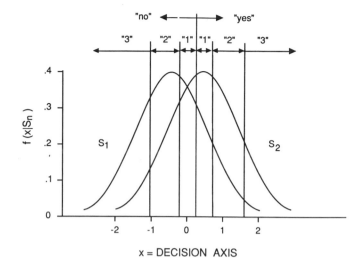

FIG. 2.6.   Decision space and response criteria for a rating experiment in which the subject first responds "yes" or "no", then gives a confidence judgment on a three-point scale.

Table 2.2 illustrates the method of collating the data for the double-response method. The highest value of the criterion is assumed to divide the "yes, highest confidence" responses from all the others, so one (H, F) pair is (in the notation of Table 2.2) $H = x_1/T_2$, $F = y_1/T_1$. To find the next point, we divide the two highest-confidence "yes" responses from all the others; the corresponding ROC point is $H = (x_1 + x_2)/T_2$, $F = (y_1 + y_2)/T_1$. The process continues to the lowest value of criterion, which divides the "no, highest confidence" responses from all the others.

Many empirical ROCs have been collected, mostly using the rating method. Maximum-likelihood methods are commonly used for fitting ROCs to data (Dorfman & Alf, 1969). As noted earlier, most ROCs are well-described by straight lines in the transformed space of Fig. 2.1b, as predicted by SDT. However, another prediction of the model fails: The slopes of empirical ROCs often do not equal 1. We now consider factors that might account for this discrepancy, and modifications to the model that accommodate the data.

Unequal-Variance Models

An ROC of nonunit slope on z-coordinates (Fig. 2.7) presents an immediate problem of interpretation. The sensitivity measure d' is the distance between an ROC and the major diagonal, but when the slope does not equal one this distance varies. For example, a large value (d'_1 in the figure) can be measured when $z(H) = 0$, a smaller one d'_2 when $z(F) = 0$. These points differ in criterion location, so

TABLE 2.2
Calculation of Hit and False-alarm Rates for a Rating
Experiment in which Subjects Make Both a Binary
("Yes-No") and Rating (1 to n)
Response on Each Trial

Stimulus–Response Matrix:

binary response:	"yes"		"no"	
rating:	$n \; n-1 \ldots 1$		$1 \ldots \ldots n$	
S_2	$x_1 \, x_2 \ldots x_n$		$x_{n+1} \ldots x_{2n}$	T_2
S_1	$y_1 \, y_2 \ldots y_n$		$y_{n+1} \ldots y_{2n}$	T_1

(Hit,false-alarm) pairs:

Highest value of c:	$H = x_1/T_2$
	$F = y_1/T_1$
Next highest value of c:	$H = (x_1 + x_2)/T_2$
	$F = (y_1 + y_2)/T_1$
....	
Lowest value of c:	$H = (x_1 + \ldots + x_{2n-1})/T_2$
	$F = (y_1 + \ldots + y_{2n-1})/T_1$

Example:

binary response:	"yes"		"no"		
rating (n = 2):	2	1	1	2	
S_2	40	20	10	5	75
S_1	20	15	10	30	75

(Hit,false-alarm) pairs:

(40/75, 20/75) = (.53, .27)
([40 + 20]/75, [20 + 15]/75) = (.80, .47)
([40 + 20 + 10]/75, [20 + 15 + 10]/75) = (.93, .60)

the apparent value of d' changes with the criterion. This is exactly the confounding that SDT is supposed to prevent.

Examination of Fig. 2.7 reveals that s, the slope of the ROC, is equal to

$$s = d'_2/d'_1, \tag{13}$$

and the equation of the ROC can be written

$$z(H) = d'_2 + sz(F). \tag{14}$$

In terms of underlying distributions, an ROC slope less than 1 means that moving one z-unit, or one standard deviation, on the F axis produces a change of

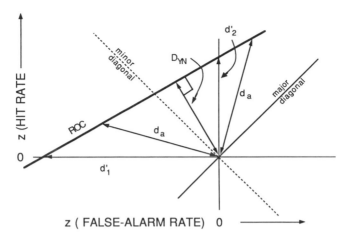

FIG. 2.7. Non-unit slope ROC, in z-coordinates. Several alternative indexes of sensitivity are shown: d'_1 (unit is the standard deviation of S_1), d'_2 (unit is the standard deviation of S_2), d_a (unit is the rms average of the two standard deviations). The distance d_a is $\sqrt{2}$ times as long as D_{YN}, the perpendicular distance from the origin to the ROC.

only s units on the H axis. That is, the standard deviations of the S_1 and S_2 distributions are in the ratio $s{:}1$ rather than $1{:}1$ as the simplest model requires. Pairs of distributions having this characteristic (with $s = 0.5$) are shown in Fig. 2.8.

The alternate measures of sensitivity d'_1 and d'_2 each rely on one of these two standard deviations; each corresponds to a different distance in the decision space. The index d'_1 is measured for a criterion set at the mean of the S_2 distribution, as in Fig. 2.8a. At that point, d'_1 equals $-z(F)$, and thus depends only on the standard deviation of the S_1 distribution. On the other hand, d'_2 is measured so that the criterion is at the mean of the S_1 distribution (Fig. 2.8b). Here d'_2 equals $z(H)$, and depends only on the standard deviation of the S_2 distribution.

The best single measure of sensitivity in this situation is neither d'_1 nor d'_2, but a compromise. In ROC space, it should be a distance between the ROC and the chance line that is shorter than d'_1 but longer than d'_2. In the decision space, it should measure the mean distance between distributions in units of some kind of average of the two standard deviations.

Figure 2.7 illustrates such a measure. Instead of selecting the horizontal or vertical distance from the origin to the ROC, consider the shortest distance between them. This statistic, termed D_{YN} by its inventors (Schulman & Mitchell, 1966), is always smaller than either d'_1 or d'_2. The appropriate generalization of d' to the unequal-variance case, d_a, is the length of the hypotenuse of the equilateral right triangle whose legs have length D_{YN} (Simpson & Fitter, 1973). As shown in Fig. 2.7, d_a equals $\sqrt{2}D_{YN}$, is intermediate in size between d'_1 and

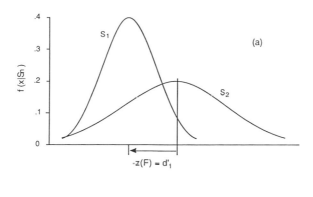

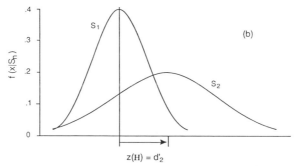

FIG. 2.8.   Decision space for non-unit slope ROC, standard deviation of S_2 double that of S_1: (a) criterion at mean of S_2, d' measured in units of the S_1 standard deviation; (b) criterion at mean of S_1, d' measured in units of the S_2 standard deviation.

d'_2, and is equivalent to d' when the ROC slope is 1. In terms of the decision space, d_a is equivalent to the difference between the means in units of the root mean square standard deviation:

$$d_a = d'_2/[0.5(1 + s^2)]^{1/2} = [2/(1 + s^2)]^{1/2}d'_2. \tag{15}$$

Sometimes a measure of performance expressed as a proportion is preferred to one expressed as a distance. The index A_z, which is simply the Φ-transform of D_{YN}, is appropriate in such circumstances (Swets & Pickett, 1982):

$$A_z = \Phi(D_{YN}) = \Phi(d_a/\sqrt{2}). \tag{16}$$

This statistic equals the area under the ROC curve, assuming that SDT is correct; we discuss area under the ROC in more detail later.

Discrimination Paradigms with Sequences of Stimuli

The goal of the yes–no experiment—to measure the ability of an observer to distinguish between two stimuli or stimulus classes—can also be reached by presenting a sequence of stimuli on each trial. For example, observers may be asked whether two stimuli are the same or different, or which of three stimuli differs from the other two. These more complex paradigms may be preferred because they reduce bias, improve precision, or are easy to explain to subjects.

Detection theory analysis allows the experimenter to estimate the same sensitivity statistic from all paradigms. This does not mean that all discrimination tasks are equally difficult for the observer; they are not. Rather, by analyzing the decision space for a paradigm and determining the optimal response strategy, SDT predicts that a constant d' leads to different proportions of correct responding for different paradigms. The prediction of performance across paradigms provides a second test of SDT (prediction of ROC shape being the first).

Two-Alternative Forced-Choice.   The design that has received the most attention is two-alternative forced-choice (2AFC), in which both stimuli are presented on each trial and the observer must determine the (spatial or temporal) order of their occurrence. For example, in a detection experiment, Signal and Noise are presented in either order, in temporal or spatial sequence; in recognition memory, an Old and a New item are presented, probably simultaneously. The possible stimulus sequences can be denoted $\langle S_1 S_2 \rangle$ and $\langle S_2 S_1 \rangle$. If the observer is asked to choose the interval in which S_2 was presented, the hit rate is $P(\text{``2''} \mid \langle S_1 S_2 \rangle)$, the false-alarm rate $P(\text{``2''} \mid \langle S_2 S_1 \rangle)$.

Having two intervals allows the subject to make two observations; if these are assumed to be independent, the decision space is as shown in Fig. 2.9. The coordinates of the space, A and B, are the strengths of the observations in the two intervals, so the two possible sequences generate unit-variance bivariate distribu-

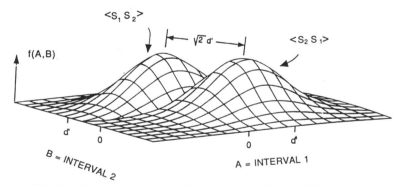

FIG. 2.9.   A three-dimensional interpretation of the 2AFC task. On the *A* axis are values obtained in the first interval, and on the *B* axis values from the second interval. The heights of two distributions give the likelihoods of (*A,B*) points for each possible stimulus sequence.

tions with means at either $(0, d')$ or $(d', 0)$. The distance between the means is readily seen to be $\sqrt{2}d'$; to estimate d', one should therefore calculate

$$d' = (1/\sqrt{2}) \, [z(H) - z(F)]. \qquad (17)$$

The response criterion must divide the decision space into two regions at a fixed value of likelihood ratio, the relative likelihood that an observation arose from $\langle S_1 S_2 \rangle$ and $\langle S_2 S_1 \rangle$. Curves along which likelihood ratio is constant are straight lines with unit slope, of the form $A - B = k$. Thus it is only the difference between the two observations that matters, and the decision space can be represented in one dimension instead of two.

Figure 2.10 shows such a representation. The difference distribution of $A - B$ has a mean of d' when $\langle S_2 S_1 \rangle$ occurs, $-d'$ for $\langle S_1 S_2 \rangle$. The variance of the difference is 2, so the difference between the two means, in standard deviation units, is indeed $\sqrt{2}d'$.

Implications of 2AFC Analysis for the One-interval Experiment   The 2AFC paradigm is popular for the practical reason that it tends to induce a symmetric response criterion. It is also of theoretical interest, because it suggests two measures of sensitivity for the one-interval (yes–no or rating) design, one under the usual SDT assumption of normal distributions, and the other without such assumptions.

Consider the nonparametric measure first. We saw earlier that the area under the ROC curve is a natural measure of accuracy in the one-interval experiment. Green and Swets (1966, chap. 2) showed that this area is equal to the proportion correct obtained by an unbiased observer in 2AFC. This *area theorem*, which does not depend on any assumptions about the form of the underlying distributions, provides a rationale for the area under the ROC as a nonparametric measure of performance.

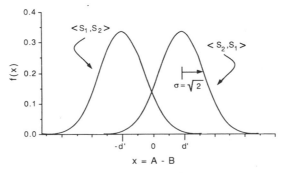

FIG. 2.10.   A one-dimensional interpretation of the 2AFC task (view from the front corner in Fig. 2.9). The decision axis is the difference between observations in the two intervals.

The parametric measure supported by the relation between the one- and two-interval experiments is d_a (Equation 15). To see this, let us extend the one-dimensional analysis of 2AFC illustrated in Fig. 2.10 to the case of unequal variances. For an ROC of slope s, we may arbitrarily set the variance of the S_2 distribution to 1, and the variance of the S_1 distribution to s^2. The decision space in the one-interval task is therefore as in Fig. 2.11a.

If the subtraction decision rule is used in 2AFC, the two underlying distributions will each have variance $1 + s^2$, and their means will differ by $2d'_2$ (Fig. 2.11b). The mean difference divided by the common standard deviation can be estimated by subtracting the z-transformed hit and false-alarm rates:

$$z(H) - z(F) = 2d'_2/(1 + s^2)^{1/2} = \sqrt{2}d_a. \qquad (18)$$

We have already seen (Equation 17) that in the equal-variance case ($s = 1$) d' can be estimated from 2AFC by dividing $z(H) - z(F)$ by $\sqrt{2}$. It now appears that

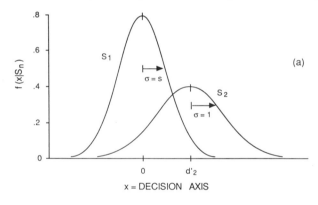

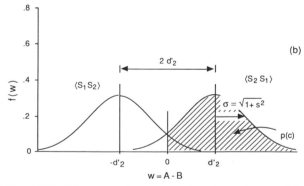

FIG. 2.11.   (a) Decision space for yes-no when the variances of S_1 and S_2 are unequal. (b) Decision space (in the style of Fig. 2.10) for 2AFC, according to SDT, when the variances of S_1 and S_2 are unequal and the observer uses an unbiased cut-point decision rule. The area under the $\langle S_2, S_1 \rangle$ distribution to the right of the criterion (and the area under the $\langle S_1, S_2 \rangle$ distribution to its left) equals $p(c)$, which by the area theorem equals the area under the unequal-variance yes-no ROC.

when the unit-slope assumption is unwarranted, this method is still appropriate, and yields an estimate of d_a.

Finally, the two desirable measures d_a and area under the ROC can be related to each other (Simpson & Fitter, 1973). Proportion correct by an unbiased observer in the unequal-variance case (Fig. 2.11b) equals

$$p(c)_{2AFC} = P(A - B > 0)$$
$$= \Phi[d'_2/(1 + s^2)^{1/2}]$$
$$= \Phi(d_a/\sqrt{2}) = A_z. \quad (19)$$

According to the area theorem, unbiased $p(c)_{2AFC}$ equals the area under the yes–no ROC, denoted A_z in the SDT case (Equation 16). The equivalence of d_a to the area under the yes–no ROC is a strong argument for preferring it to other possible distance measures of sensitivity in the one-interval experiment.

Note that the area measure A_z, like the equivalent distance measure d_a, requires the Gaussian assumption of SDT. Other area measures are considered later.

Other Paradigms.   Any multi-interval paradigm can be analyzed in SDT terms, using a generalization of our approach to 2AFC. The method can be illustrated by sketching an analysis of the same-different experiment. The four possible stimulus sequences in this design—$\langle S_1S_1 \rangle$, $\langle S_2S_2 \rangle$, $\langle S_1S_2 \rangle$, and $\langle S_2S_1 \rangle$—are arranged in the two-dimensional decision space as shown in Fig. 2.12. The axes of the space correspond to activity in the two intervals, as in Fig. 2.9, but the view is from above rather than in perspective. The centers of the circles represent the means of the distributions, and the circles themselves connect points of equal likelihood.

The unbiased observer should respond "different" in the upper-left and lower-right corners of the space, "same" otherwise. The criterion lines dividing the two responses are parallel to the horizontal and vertical axes; along these lines, the likelihood ratio (in this paradigm, the ratio of the average height of the $\langle S_1S_2 \rangle$ and $\langle S_2S_1 \rangle$ densities to the average height of the $\langle S_1S_1 \rangle$ and $\langle S_2S_2 \rangle$ densities) equals 1. For biased subjects, the critical likelihood ratio is something other than 1, and the hit and false-alarm rates are volumes under the appropriate distributions bounded by curved criteria. (See Noreen, 1981, and Macmillan and Creelman, 1991, for more detail.)

This paradigm is clearly more complex analytically than yes–no or 2AFC, but the meaning of d' is unchanged: It is always the normalized distance between two distributions due to stimulus sequences that are identical except for a single replacement of S_1 by S_2. What does change is the relation between response proportions and d'. Figure 2.13 shows how unbiased $p(c)$ depends on d' for a variety of popular discrimination paradigms. The discrepancies between predicted performance in the different paradigms are large, and depend on overall accuracy. In some cases, even the ordering of the conditions changes with performance level.

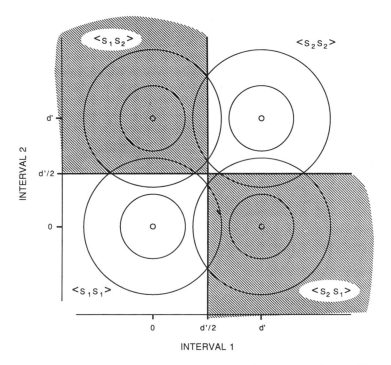

FIG. 2.12. Decision space for the same-different experiment. The effects of the two observations are combined independently. The unbiased decision rule is to respond "different" in the shaded area.

ADVANTAGES OF SDT

With some understanding of the practical and theoretical elements of SDT, we now ask why one should want to use it. This question immediately raises another: What strategies are available to nonusers? Alternatives to SDT have traditionally been divided into three camps: *parametric* models, which assume a form other than Gaussian for the underlying distributions; *nonparametric* models, which make no mention of distributions; and *threshold* models, which postulate discrete internal states. Prototypical sensitivity indexes in these categories are η, a Choice Theory statistic usually interpreted as *similarity* (Luce, 1963); A', an estimate of the area under the ROC (Pollack & Norman, 1964); and the proportion correct, $p(c)$. Further analysis of these and other measures follows in a later section; I mention them here to suggest the field in which d' and other SDT measures are competing.

Advocates of SDT have offered three pragmatic arguments for its use: The theory distinguishes between sensitivity and response bias; its sensitivity index is a distance measure; and performance in one paradigm can be predicted from

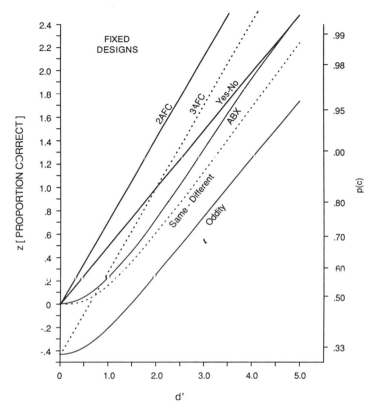

FIG. 2.13.   Proportion correct as a function of d' for six different experimental paradigms. Paradigms are "fixed" in the sense that the
same two stimuli occur throughout a block of trials. Unbiased responding is assumed for all paradigms.

performance in others. A fourth advantage arises from the theory's status as a
decision model: It provides a context for studying complex decision processes.

Separation of Sensitivity and Response Bias

In providing recipes for distinct indexes of sensitivity and of bias, SDT makes
two claims: (a) Changes in response bias do not affect sensitivity, and (b) changes
in sensitivity do not affect bias.

The first claim—in effect, that SDT can predict the shape of ROCs—has
received both more study and more support. Early experiments (summarized in
Green & Swets, 1966, chap. 4) showed that shifts in response bias did not greatly
change estimated d'. Specifically, SDT was more successful than the then-
current threshold theories ("corrections for guessing") in this respect. The bias-
free measure d' can be estimated from a single (hit, false-alarm) pair if the ROC

has unit slope; and the measures d_a and A_z from the complete ROC if the slope is not unity, as described earlier.

The second claim—that SDT can predict the shape of isobias curves—has not been well supported. There are multiple interpretations of *constant bias* within the SDT framework—we have discussed both the criterion location c and the likelihood ratio β—and subjects do not appear to agree on which meaning is intended when an experimenter instructs them to maintain a constant response strategy in the face of varying sensitivity (Dusoir, 1975; Macmillan & Creelman, 1990). Other approaches are no more successful: Our understanding of response bias is simply not as deep as that of accuracy.

Distance Measures of Accuracy

Most sensitivity indexes estimate a proportion: proportion correct, maximum possible proportion correct, proportion of the maximum area under the ROC, and so forth. The detection theory index d' [and also a transformation of the Choice Theory statistic, $-\log(\eta)$] is a *distance measure*. That is, it is positive $(d' > 0)$, symmetric $[d'(x,y) = d'(y,x)]$, and satisfies the triangle inequality:

$$d'(x,z) < d'(x,y) + d'(y,z). \tag{20}$$

For purposes of comparing two qualitatively different conditions—face recognition at two delays, for example—proportion and distance measures are equally valuable. Distance measures have an advantage, however, when quantitatively different conditions are being compared. Suppose $p(c) = .77$ for stimuli differing by one unit and $p(c) = .93$ for stimuli two units apart. For which pair is sensitivity greater? There is no way to tell. But a report that d' equals 1.5 and 3.0 in these two conditions (as it does if the above values of $p(c)$ result from unbiased responding) makes it clear that sensitivity per stimulus unit is the same in the two conditions.

The need to make comparisons of this sort arises in two contexts. First, an experimenter may wish to investigate a continuum along which sensitivity varies substantially. If a constant physical difference is used, some estimates of performance are likely to produce chance or perfect outcomes. The use of a distance measure allows the physical discrepancy to be varied. Second, experimenters conducting similar experiments often choose different stimulus values. Comparing results obtained in different laboratories is easily done using a distance measure. Examples of both applications can be found in the speech sound resolution experiments of Macmillan, Goldberg, and Braida (1988).

Most experiments study more than a single pair of stimuli, and distance measures can also be used to summarize multiple measurements. When the resolution of stimuli along a dimension is being investigated, a useful statistic is *total sensitivity,* the sum of sensitivities across the range. Durlach, Braida, and their colleagues (Braida & Durlach, 1988; Durlach & Braida, 1969) used total d' to compare a variety of discrimination and identification paradigms.

Relations Among Experimental Paradigms

In SDT the same d' statistic can be estimated from many experimental paradigms, and this ability to translate between different discrimination paradigms is a strength of the detection theory approach. Other indexes, such as $p(c)$, can also be estimated from many designs, but there is no reason to expect the value obtained to be fixed. In fact, SDT predicts that $p(c)$ will vary substantially across paradigms when d' is fixed (see Fig. 2.13, and also Macmillan & Creelman, 1991, chap. 7).

In general, the success of SDT's predictions has been quite good, although the data base is sparse and there are some systematic deviations (discussed later). Even when the theory fails, however, the ability to calculate theoretically equivalent performance is helpful in explorating task-dependent limitations within the observer.

It is also possible to estimate d' from classification and identification designs, in which the subject attempts to sort stimuli into categories. In the one-dimensional case, the relation between discrimination and identification d' values has been extensively studied by Braida and Durlach (1988). For multidimensional stimulus sets, Choice Theory measures are more commonly used (e.g., Nosofsky, 1984, 1986).

Studying Decision Processes

The decision process is an explicit part of SDT. Most often, the purpose of using the theory is to factor out this process, but it is also possible to study the decision rule itself. Applications of this sort typically involve complex stimulus situations in which a variety of decision processes is possible. We discuss such experiments in the next section.

ASSUMPTIONS OF SDT

Let us now examine some of the assumptions made by SDT, or by users in some applications. Four categories of such assumptions can be distinguished: the form of the underlying distributions; the nature of the decision rule; the optimality of processing; and the homogeneity of stimuli and observers.

As all of these categories contain more than one element, it may seem that SDT is heavily theory-dependent. Two observations mitigate this concern. First, when the assumptions of SDT are compared with those of alternative approaches, no discrepancy in theory-dependence is evident. In particular, most approaches dubbed nonparametric by their users are just as model-laden as SDT. Assumptions about underlying distributions illustrate this parallelism particularly well.

Second, some assumptions are necessary only to describe ideal performance.

In early SDT work, for example, the performance of an "ideal observer" in sensory discrimination was predicted from stimulus characteristics (Green & Swets, 1966, chap. 6). Actual performance was compared with this ideal to determine the "efficiency" of the observer. Efficiencies less than unity do not reveal a failure of SDT assumptions, but provide an indication of the subject's processing capacity. Several of the assumptions we consider invoke optimality in this familiar way (see Sperling & Dosher, 1986, for a thorough-going example of this approach).

Form of Underlying Distributions

Distribution Shape.   Using d' to measure discriminability requires the assumption that the S_1 and S_2 distributions are normal with equal variance. To evaluate d' in this respect, let us compare it with another parametric measure (Choice Theory's η), a nonparametric measure (A'), and a threshold measure $[p(c)]$.

The distinctions between these measures are not well-captured by the parametric-nonparametric-threshold trichotomy. A deeper understanding of their similarities and differences can be reached by trying to infer the transformation u (Equation 2) and a pair of underlying distributions for each measure, as was done for d'. That this analysis can be performed at all implies that no sensitivity measure for two-response experiments is truly nonparametric (Macmillan & Kaplan, 1985; Swets, 1986a). Perhaps because SDT is frequently introduced in terms of underlying distributions (e.g., Green & Swets, 1966, chap. 1), whereas other approaches are not, comparisons of discrimination theories or indexes sometimes discuss the distributional assumptions of SDT and ignore those of other measures (e.g., Massaro & Friedman, 1990; Nelson, 1984). There is no rationale for according SDT such special treatment.

Applying this strategy to the measures described previously leads to the following conclusions:

For the one-interval experiment, Choice Theory is equivalent to SDT, but with logistic rather than Gaussian distributions (Luce, 1959; McNicol, 1972; Noreen, 1977). The u transformation of the yes rate implied by this model is from a proportion p to $\log[p/(1 - p)]$, or *log odds*. As logistic and Gaussian distributions are very similar in shape, a choice between them depends on factors other than the shape of the ROC.

Proportion correct is the sensitivity statistic of double threshold theory, in which there are three internal states: One activated only by S_1, one only by S_2, and one by either stimulus class (Egan, 1958; Snodgrass & Corwin, 1988). The decision space can be represented as two overlapping, congruent *rectangular* distributions (Macmillan & Creelman, 1990, 1991). As we saw earlier, the implied u transformation is linear, and the predicted ROC is a straight line on linear coordinates.

That the area under the *complete* ROC is a desirable nonparametric measure of accuracy is a corollary of the area theorem. The index A', however, is estimated from a single ROC point. No one has presented pairs of underlying distributions corresponding to A'. However, it is known (Macmillan & Kaplan, 1985; Pollack & Norman, 1964) that the ROC implied by this measure resembles that of SDT at low sensitivity, that of double threshold theory at high sensitivity.

Each of these measures, therefore, can be characterized in terms of its implied ROC; for two of them transformations and underlying distributions can be identified. The primary empirical test of these competing assumptions is the shape of the ROC. If the underlying distributions are normal (or logistic), the ROC is linear (or nearly so) on z-coordinates; if the distributions are rectangular (as required by threshold theories), the ROC is linear on probability coordinates. The substantial majority of ROCs in the literature, we have noted, are consistent with SDT assumptions. In the absence of other information, therefore, d' should be preferred to $p(c)$. Because A' resembles d' at low levels and $p(c)$ at high levels, it is also inferior to d'. Of course, the shape of the underlying distributions depends on the stimuli, and a new stimulus domain could in principle lead to distributions of any form. The collection of ROCs is therefore especially important for unfamiliar stimulus sets.

Bias indexes can be analyzed similarly. Macmillan and Creelman (1990) classified eight proposed bias measures according to the implied underlying distributions (Gaussian, logistic, or rectangular), and the decision-space construct (criterion, criterion relative to sensitivity, or likelihood ratio). The three nonparametric measures considered were all consistent with one or another distributional assumption. Most surprisingly, B'' (Hodos, 1970), a measure motivated solely from the geometry of ROC space, was shown to be equivalent to likelihood ratio in the logistic model.

Relative Magnitude of Variances.   A common use of SDT is to calculate d' (and perhaps a bias statistic) from a 2×2 stimulus-response matrix like that in Table 2.1. To interpret such a d' as bias-free requires that the (unknown) empirical ROC have unit slope, so that all points on the curve provide the same estimate of sensitivity. This is true only if the variances of the S_1 and S_2 distributions are equal.

In a survey of many content areas, Swets (1986b; Swets & Pickett, 1982) concluded that the slopes of empirical ROCs range from about 0.5 to 2.0. Desirable sensitivity measures for such curves, described earlier, require that an ROC be collected. The assumption of equal variances, though often wrong, can be avoided by soliciting a rating rather than (or, as in the example of Table 2.2, in addition to) a yes–no response.

Collection of ROCs would be unnecessary, even if slopes did not equal 1, if slopes were known. Several models predict that slope should be systematically related to sensitivity. Green and Swets (1966, chap. 4) proposed that the slope

$s = 4/(4 + d'_l)$, so that ROCs reflecting low sensitivity have slopes near 1, and those measuring good performance have increasingly shallow slopes. Other families of ROCs that show a negative correlation between sensitivity and slope are those that take the underlying distributions to be chi-square, Poisson, or exponential. Egan (1975) provided a thorough description of each of these ROC families.

The key question is whether the intercept and slope of ROCs (equivalently, the relative means and variances of the underlying distributions) are actually related in a monotonic fashion. Early enthusiasm for this idea was based on psychoacoustic stimulus models, but models of this sort have met with only limited success in hearing and vision, and are in any case unhelpful in applying detection theory to cognitive and applied fields. Swets's (1986b) survey uncovered no systematic relation between accuracy and slope.

In most applications, therefore, ROC slope is unpredictable, and the user of SDT who does not collect ratings is at risk. For purposes of comparing two points in ROC space, the risk is least if bias is held constant, but we have seen that there is no agreement about the meaning of constant bias. Whenever possible, therefore, discrimination experiments should include a rating response; when they do, there is no need to make any assumption about the relative magnitude of the two underlying variances.

Decision Rule

Detection theory proposes that subjects use a decision rule based on likelihood ratio. To discover whether this is true, and to characterize the actual decision rule if it is not, requires an extension of the basic discrimination experiment. Two general strategies have been employed: First, the hypothesized internal observations can be made external. The discrimination task is thereby transformed into classification, and the mapping of observation to response is uncovered. Second, different tasks (or different aspects of the same complex task) can be compared. Changes in the decision rule are then inferred from the relation between tasks.

We first consider one-interval experiments with one-dimensional stimuli, then relax both constraints. In multi-interval or multidimensional experiments, the number of sensible alternative decision rules from which a subject might choose increases greatly (see Graham, 1989), and it is possible to distinguish many types of possible interactions among the intervals or dimensions (Ashby & Townsend, 1986).

One-interval Experiment, One-dimensional Stimuli.   Artificial distribution experiments have used both numeric and nonnumeric stimuli (e.g., dot location, shade of gray). A number of early studies (e.g., Lee, 1963; Kubovy, Rapoport, & Tversky, 1971) supported the SDT claim that subjects' responses in the equal-variance case are determined by fixed criteria.

The criterion rule and the likelihood-ratio rule are equivalent in the equal-variance case, but not in general. If variances are unequal, the distributions intersect twice (Luce, 1963); the decision axis thus contains two locations at which the likelihood ratio equals one, and cannot be monotonic with it. Ashby and Perrin (1988) studied the extreme case of two distributions differing *only* in variance. The optimal (likelihood ratio) strategy was closely approached by all subjects.

The strategy of examining the relation between results in different experiments, as predicted by the optimal rule and a specific nonoptimal one, was followed in a study of line orientation discrimination by Vogels and Orban (1986a). Using a one-interval task in which five stimuli were sorted into two categories, they compared the fixed-criterion strategy with an alternative "paired comparison" rule in which the subject compares each observation with a previous one. By varying the spacing between the stimuli, they were able to reject the paired-comparison model in favor of the fixed-criterion SDT hypothesis.

One-interval Experiment, Multidimensional Stimuli   In multidimensional experiments, the subject may combine decisions for each dimension independently, or may construct a single decision variable by adding or subtracting inputs for the dimensions. The optimal decision rule may be one or the other of these, or something else entirely.

Ashby and Gott (1988) generated stimuli composed of a horizontal and vertical line segment joined at a corner. Two classes of stimuli were derived having means at prototype values, and prescribed variances and horizontal-vertical correlation. In separate experiments, a differencing rule or an independent-decision rule was optimal. Observers were excellent at following the differencing rule when it was appropriate, but tended also to use it when an independent-decision rule would have been better.

Complex Designs.   Designs other than one-interval provide an important special case of the general multidimensional problem. We can view each interval in a multi-interval experiment as a perceptual dimension, as in Figs. 2.9 and 2.12 (see Macmillan & Creelman, 1991, chaps. 5–7). Some complexities that are significant in the general multidimensional case can be neglected in this application; for example, as long as observation intervals are adequately separated in time and space, perceptual independence of the effects of the two observations seems a natural assumption.

Johnson (1980) showed how the relation between performance in different two-interval tasks depends on the decision rules, correlations among effects due to the stimulus intervals, and memory noise. Vogels and Orban (1986b) applied Johnson's scheme in a study of the oblique effect (discrimination of orientation is worse for oblique lines than near the horizontal and vertical axes). Comparing three different two-interval tasks, they found a differencing strategy was used in all, although it was optimal in only one. The strategy did not change with angle, however, and was therefore not a candidate to explain the oblique effect.

In designs with more than two stimulus classes, decision rules can be determined by examining the several different hit and false-alarm rates. Shaw (1982) showed how independent-decision and integration rules could be distinguished in some experiments of this type. For example, observers discriminating a signal that can be either auditory, visual, or both from background noise were shown by her method to use the (near-optimal) independent-decision rule rather than integration (Mulligan & Shaw, 1980).

In summary, observers in simple discrimination tasks appear to use the optimal SDT rule. In more complex tasks, they are capable of using any of several distinct decision rules, and frequently (but not always) use one that is near optimal. In these tasks it is often possible to diagnose the rule that is in use.

Processing Assumptions

There is no rigid boundary between the optimality of the decision rule (considered in the last section) and the optimality of processing (which we now assess), but it is useful to draw the fuzzy distinction between the subject's plan and how well it is carried out. An important question is whether limitations on the observer's memory impede performance; we first look at memory for criterion location, then at memory more generally. Another issue concerns the possibility that discrimination is a multistage process. In each case, the primary issues are how such complexity can be diagnosed, and how an analysis that ignores it would be wrong.

Stability of the Criterion.   What if the subject in a one-interval experiment uses a criterion decision rule, but the location of the criterion varies from trial to trial? Wickelgren (1968) described a generalization of SDT in which criterion location is a random variable, independent of the effects of S_1 and S_2, so that criterion variance and the variance of the underlying distributions add to limit performance. If this is an apt characterization, several conclusions reached earlier must be modified: (a) d' will be smaller than if criterion variability were zero. (b) If criterion variability is constant across tasks, relative performance levels across tasks will be more similar (i.e., d' ratios will be nearer to unity) than if variability were zero. (c) The slope of the ROC will no longer be an estimate of the ratio of the standard deviations of S_1 and S_2; if criterion variability is constant, this slope is nearer to unity than if variability were zero.

To estimate the magnitude of criterion variability (and thereby decide how concerned to be about the effects enumerated earlier) requires more than one experimental condition. One possible comparison is between a standard condition and one in which the stimulus is presented multiple times on each trial. On the assumption that multiple presentations affect only sensory variability, the amount of criterion variability can be assessed (Nosofsky, 1983).

Treisman and Williams (1984) have proposed the most detailed theory of criterion changes. Their two-process model postulates a long-term stabilization mechanism that tends towards unbiased responding and a tracking mechanism that reacts to short-term changes in the probability of the signal. The model successfully accounts for sequential effects in a number of auditory experiments, including the double-response rating task (Treisman & Faulkner, 1986).

Vogels and Orban (1986b) asked whether the oblique effect could be due to differential amounts of criterion variability at horizontal and oblique orientations. They first assumed this to be true, and in particular supposed that criterion variability occurred *only* in the oblique condition. They then calculated the distance between the extreme criteria in their four-response rating task; this turned out to be about 1.8 sensory standard deviations. (If the assumption of no variability in the horizontal condition is abandoned, this distance is even smaller.) But they estimate that unless this distance were about 4.0, criteria are likely to change places. This is implausible (if not impossible), so Vogels and Orban concluded that the oblique effect in their data is not due to differential criterion variability.

Memory Effects.   Criterion variability can be viewed as an example of the observer's more general problem of remembering the various components of the underlying space until a decision can be made. Two-interval tasks (temporal ones, at least) involve the additional requirement of remembering the effect of the first interval until the second occurs. Evidence that such memory is imperfect is obtained by varying the interstimulus interval (ISI). Kinchla and Smyzer (1967) and Wickelgren (1969) systematically varied ISI and found sensitivity to be a decreasing function of time. By using several different two-interval designs, Vogels and Organ (1986b) were able to show that deviations from a simple functional relation between the jnd (just noticeable difference) and ISI were due to a change in decision rule at long ISIs.

Berliner and Durlach (1973) and Berliner, Durlach, and Braida (1977) showed that the effect of ISI increased with the range of stimuli that could occur in a block of trials. They interpreted their data in terms of the resolution theory of Durlach and Braida (1969; Braida & Durlach, 1988), who postulated two types of memory noise, a *trace variance* that depends on ISI and a *context variance* that depends on stimulus range. The two types of memory combine in such a way that the smaller variance dominates; the total memory variance is added to the task-independent *sensory variance*. When the stimulus range is small, context variance is minimal; observers operate in the context mode, and ISI effects are therefore slight.

If ISI were to equal the inter-*trial* interval, the problem of remembering information from the first interval would be similar to the problem faced by subjects in one-interval experiments. Berliner and Durlach showed that performance in these two situations was in fact similar. This result is inconsistent with the memory-free prediction of a $\sqrt{2}$ ratio between yes–no and 2AFC (Equation 17). Although some early auditory and visual detection experiments supported this prediction (see Green & Swets, 1966, chap. 4 and Luce, 1963 for summaries), most subsequent research has suggested instead that yes–no suffers from a memory constraint. Jesteadt and Bilger (1974) found that 2AFC performance was a factor of 2, rather than $\sqrt{2}$, better than yes–no, both in their own frequency-discrimination experiments and others they surveyed. Creelman and Macmillan (1979) found the same result for discrimination of both auditory frequency and monaural phase.

In detection tasks, weak stimuli may be particularly unmemorable. Taylor, Forbes, and Creelman (1983) compared psychometric functions collected under both a fixed-level and an adaptive method. They found that memory for weak signals was worse in the fixed condition, and the decline could be accounted for by the strong sequential effects in that condition.

Memory effects of various kinds are clearly part of the discrimination process; what implications does this have for the user of detection theory? First, memory and decision effects can be distinguished from sensory ones by comparing tasks. The work of Johnson (1980) and Vogels and Orban (1986a, 1986b) illustrates how these components can be systematically teased apart. Second, the investigator who uses a single task to compare conditions risks finding an effect whose source is unknown. Detection theory is in the position of a messenger bearing the bad news that firm theoretical conclusions require more complex experiments. Other approaches to discrimination are less informative about these interactions, and also about how to diagnose them.

Multistage Discrimination.   The finding that both memory and sensory sources affect accuracy raises a more general issue about combining information. In many applications, two or more inputs are relevant, and the observer must combine them in an effective manner.

Suppose, for example, that a decision maker looks for possible stimuli, and when one seems to have occurred, passes the fact to a second decision maker. Action requires both stages to decide that a stimulus was present. Alarm systems represent one such situation: Automatic alarms pass information about a possible failure to pilots or factory managers who must in turn confirm and identify the malfunction. In a rather different application, some theoretical models of cognitive processing postulate that one (perhaps pre-attentive) detector leads another to evaluate a stimulus (e.g., Erdelyi, 1974).

Sorkin and Woods (1985) calculated the behavior of a combined automated-human system in which a human operator checks to see whether an alarm signals a real problem, and makes the ultimate decision about action. Their work was motivated by reports of alarms that were ignored by commercial pilots (e.g., Sorkin, 1988). Sorkin and Woods showed that a combination of two detectors, even with a serial decision system, can perform better than either can separately, but that such systems have an interesting limitation.

Suppose the criterion of the human observer depends on the false-alarm rate of the automated system, or that the human looks for trouble following only a portion of the alarms (for instance when not busy landing an aircraft), or that the human's sensitivity depends on the machine's false-alarm rate. ROC curves for the combined system in these cases do not range from one corner of the ROC space to the other. Rather, under not unreasonable assumptions, H is limited, even at quite high F rates. Thus nonindependence between relevant processes can substantially undermine overall performance.

Homogeneity of Stimuli and Observers

According to detection theory, the observer partitions a stable underlying distribution by use of a fixed criterion. This story of the decision process is most convincing if the experiment uses only one pair of stimuli, all data are collected in one session, and the analysis is applied to a single observer. In experiments with multiple stimuli, sessions, or observers—that is, all experiments of real interest—some kind of averaging must be done. The data analysis procedure most consistent with our assumptions is to calculate sensitivity and bias separately for each combination of stimulus, session, and observer, then average the resulting estimates.

This idealized approach is often not possible, because the number of trials contributing to a single estimate is small. In this case, some of the cells in the stimulus-response matrix are likely to contain zeroes, and SDT statistics cannot be computed unless ad hoc adjustments are made (see Macmillan & Kaplan, 1985). An extreme example is provided by *class discrimination*, in which a single stimulus occurs only once per observer. Less dramatically, a single session using a roving design often contains few trials per stimulus. And with some observers—infants, for example—a few trials is all one can hope for.

Class Discrimination.   In discrimination between individual simulus *tokens,* there is a one-to-one correspondence between possible stimulus events, stimulus classes, and the responses available to the observer. In studies of sensory discrimination, two specific stimuli are often used for a long run, and individual trials differ only in presentation order.

In *class discrimination* tasks, the stimuli comprise two large sets, such as Old and New words. On each trial one or more stimuli is sampled from these classes. Discrimination between specific tokens would be of no interest in this experiment. Many discrimination experiments in the study of memory and language are of the class variety. Wickelgren (1968) showed that under fairly general conditions the assumption of Gaussian distributions was plausible for class discrimination. Lockhart and Murdock (1970) pointed out that the class discrimination design can produce nonindependence between stimulus presentations, as when presentation of one item in a recognition memory task affects the availability of other, related items.

A more significant step away from the detection model is taken when stimuli cannot be classified reliably. This is often the situation in medical applications, in which no diagnosis procedure is perfect. Kraemer (1988) suggested a generalization of SDT that allows for this type of variability.

Group Data.   In dealing with groups of subjects, a frequently used strategy is to estimate sensitivity from data that have been combined across multiple stimuli, sessions, or observers. The resulting statistic is called *pooled* or *collapsed sensitivity.* This method can be compared to the ideal approach, in which parameter estimates from different subsets of the data are averaged to yield *mean sensitivity.* The questions to be asked fall into two classes. First, how much does pooled sensitivity differ from mean sensitivity? In statistical language, how much statistical bias does the method entail? The second question is one of *efficiency:* How variable are estimates of pooled sensitivity, compared to those of mean sensitivity?

To illustrate these statistical problems, let us consider subjects with the same sensitivity but different biases. (Other situations are discussed by Macmillan and Kaplan, 1985.) Two observers whose sensitivity is the same will produce hit and false-alarm rates that lie on the same ROC curve, but (in general) at different points. If their hit and false-alarm rates are averaged, the resulting point will be halfway along a line connecting the original points. These ROC curves are concave downward, so the average-performance point will be lower than the original points, and will yield a lower estimate of sensitivity, as shown in Fig. 2.14.

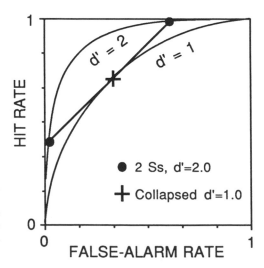

FIG. 2.14. In SDT, averaging two points on the same ROC curve yields a point on a curve with a lower value of d'. Adapted from Macmillan and Kaplan (1985) by permission of the publisher. Copyright 1985 by the American Psychological Association.

It is clear from Fig. 2.14 that the decrement in estimated sensitivity will be severe only if the two points are quite discrepant in bias. The exact size of the effect depends on the difference between the two criteria, and is large only when they are very different, perhaps 1.5 standard deviations apart. The average location of the two criteria on the ROC matters little (Macmillan & Kaplan, 1985).

Clearly it is desirable to average proportions from only those subjects whose criteria are similar. A possible procedure is to divide subjects into subgroups so that each member of a subgroup has similar bias. Collapsed d' can be computed for each subgroup, and the results averaged to estimate d' for the entire group.

The *efficiency* of collapsed d' is calculated by dividing its variance into the variance of *mean d'*, for a constant number of trials. Figure 2.15 illustrates the result of such a calculation, using a technique based on that of Gourevitch and Galanter (1967) (see Macmillan & Kaplan 1985 for details). The figure reveals that collapsed d' is always *less* variable than average d', and its variance decreases as the discrepancy between the subjects increases. There is also a tendency, other things being equal, for variance to decrease (relative to that of mean d') as the false-alarm rates of the subjects become more extreme.

These effects result from the fact that the variability of a z-score computed

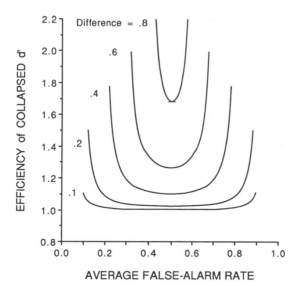

FIG. 2.15. The efficiency of collapsed d' (its variance divided into that of average d') for two subjects with the same hit rate ($H = .9$) and different false-alarm rates. The abscissa value is the average of the two values F, the parameter of the curve the difference between them. Collapsed d' is always more efficient, especially so if the two false-alarm rates are very different or if either of them is extremely large or small. Adapted from Macmillan and Kaplan (1985) by permission of the publisher. Copyright 1985 by the American Psychological Association.

from an observed proportion increases nonlinearly with the absolute value of z. When data from two or more subjects are collapsed, the z-score of the average has less variability than the average of the two z-scores. The one important exception to this rule occurs when hit or false-alarm rates equal 0 or 1: The variability of a z-score for those proportions is not finite.

Finally, ROC curves obtained by averaging data across subjects require special estimation techniques. This problem has been solved by Dorfman and Bernbaum (1986), who use a "jackknife" statistical procedure. Their article provides both a listing of their computer program and an explanation of the jackknife method.

CONCLUSIONS

The assumptions made by SDT fall roughly into two classes. In the first, smaller class are those that can be said to be "correct"; in the second, larger class are those that cannot be said to be either correct or incorrect in general. The correct assumptions appear to be the normality of underlying distributions (at least in those cases that have been studied) and the optimal nature of the decision rule in simple experiments. This is enough for experiments in which d' (or perhaps c) is used as an index to compare qualitatively different conditions.

The class of unresolved assertions holds the other assumptions: equality of variances, optimal decision rules in complex cases, stability of the criterion, perfect memory in multi-interval tasks, and independence of processing stages. (The homogeneity issues, being more pragmatic than theoretical, are neglected in this dichotomy.) All class-2 assumptions can be tested, and testing them requires either more complex tasks (ratings to test variance equality) or more tasks.

Some resolution of these questions is necessary for quantitative comparison of experimental conditions. The number of studies in which theoretically motivated comparisons between paradigms are made is small, but few would deny the value of this "converging operations" strategy. As the study of complex, multidimensional stimuli and paradigms progresses, the need for this strategy will increase.

The ability of SDT to identify and evaluate assumptions is a strength, but there is a temptation to view it as a weakness, a rationale for adopting other methods of data analysis. We have seen that SDT's alternatives—threshold and nonparametric methods—are not assumption-free, and the assumptions they do make are often unattractive. In being less explicit and less easily extendable than SDT, however, these approaches are what be called *assumption-innocent*. Although one cannot use, for example, $p(c)$ without threshold entailments, it is possible to use it without awareness of them. A goal of this chapter has been to undermine this innocence.

ACKNOWLEDGMENTS

A fuller discussion of detection theory, and of many of the specific issues discussed here, can be found in Macmillan and Creelman (1991). Figures 2.4, 2.5, 2.7–2.9, and 2.11–2.13 are reprinted or adapted from this book, with the permission of Cambridge University Press. I am grateful to Douglas Creelman for his (successful and unsuccessful) attempts to change my mind about some of these problems. Preparation of this chapter was supported by a PSC-CUNY award from the Research Foundation of CUNY.

REFERENCES

Ashby, F. G., & Gott, R. E. (1988). Decision rules in the perception and categorization of multidimensional stimuli. *Journal of Experimental Psychology: Learning, Memory, and Cognition, 14,* 33–53.

Ashby, F. G., & Perrin, N. A. (1988). Toward a unified theory of similarity and recognition. *Psychological Review, 95,* 124–150.

Ashby, F. G., & Townsend, J. T. (1986). Varieties of perceptual independence. *Psychological Review, 93,* 154–179.

Banks, W. P. (1970). Signal detection theory and human memory. *Psychological Bulletin, 74,* 81–99.

Berliner, J. E., & Durlach, N. I. (1973). Intensity perception. IV. Resolution in roving-level discrimination. *Journal of the Acoustical Society of America, 53,* 1270–1287.

Berliner, J. E., Durlach, N. E., & Braida, L. D. (1977). Intensity perception. VII. Further data on roving-level discrimination and the resolution and bias edge effects. *Journal of the Acoustical Society of America, 61,* 1577–1585.

Braida, L. D., & Durlach, N. I. (1988). Peripheral and central factors in intensity perception. In G. M. Edelman, W. E. Gall, & W. M. Cowan (Eds.), *Auditory function* (pp. 559–583). New York: Wiley.

Creelman, C. D., & Macmillan, N. A. (1979). Auditory phase and frequency discrimination: A comparison of nine procedures. *Journal of Experimental Psychology: Human Perception and Performance, 5,* 146–156.

Dorfman, D. D., & Alf, E. Jr. (1969). Maximum likelihood estimation of parameters of signal detection theory and determination of confidence intervals—rating-method data. *Journal of Mathematical Psychology, 6,* 487–496.

Dorfman, D. D., & Bernbaum, K. S. (1986). RSCORE-J: Pooled rating-method data: A computer program for analyzing pooled ROC curves. *Behavioral Research Methods, Instrumentation, & Computers, 18,* 452–462.

Durlach, N. I., & Braida, L. D. (1969). Intensity perception. I. Preliminary theory of intensity resolution. *Journal of the Acoustical Society of America, 46,* 372–383.

Dusoir, A. E. (1975). Treatments of bias in detection and recognition models: A review. *Perception & Psychophysics, 17,* 167–178.

Dusoir, T. (1983). Isobias curves in some detection tasks. *Perception & Psychophysics, 33,* 403–412.

Egan, J. P. (1958). *Recognition memory and the operating characteristic* (Tech. Note AFCRC-TN-58-51). Bloomington: Indiana University, Hearing and Communication Laboratory.

Egan, J. P. (1975). *Signal detection theory and ROC analysis.* New York: Academic Press.

Erdelyi, M. H. (1974). A new look at the New Look: Perceptual defense and vigilance. *Psychological Review, 81,* 1–25.

Gourevitch, G., & Galanter, E. (1967). A significance test for one-parameter isosensitivity functions. *Psychometrika, 32,* 25–33.

Graham, N. V. (1989). *Visual pattern analyzers.* New York: Oxford University Press.

Green, D. M., & Swets, J. A. (1966). *Signal Detection Theory and Psychophysics.* New York: Wiley.

Hodos, W. (1970). Nonparametric index of response bias for use in detection and recognition experiments. *Psychological Bulletin, 74,* 351–354.

Ingham, J. G. (1970). Individual differences in signal detection. *Acta Psychologica, 34,* 39–50.

Jesteadt, W., & Bilger, R. C. (1974). Intensity and frequency discrimination in one- and two-interval paradigms. *Journal of the Acoustical Society of America, 55,* 1266–1276.

Johnson, K. O. (1980). Sensory discrimination: Decision process. *Neurophysiology, 43,* 1771–1792.

Kinchla, R., & Smyzer, F. (1967). A diffusion model of perceptual memory. *Perception & Psychophysics, 2,* 219–229.

Kraemer, H. C. (1988). Assessment of 2×2 associations: Generalization of signal-detection methodology. *American Statistician, 42,* 37–49.

Kubovy, M., Rapoport, A., & Tversky, A. (1971). Deterministic vs. probabilistic strategies in detection. *Perception & Psychophysics, 9,* 427–429.

Lee, W. (1963). Choosing among confusably distributed stimuli with specific likelihood ratios. *Perceptual and Motor Skills, 16,* 445–467.

Lockhart, R. S., & Murdock, B. B., Jr. (1970). Memory and the theory of signal detection. *Psychological Bulletin, 74,* 100–109.

Luce, R. D. (1959). *Individual choice behavior.* New York: Wiley.

Luce, R. D. (1963). Detection and recognition. In R. D. Luce, R. R. Bush, & E. Galanter (Eds.), *Handbook of mathematical psychology* (Vol. 1, pp. 103–189). New York: Wiley.

Macmillan, N. A., & Creelman, C. D. (1990). Response bias: Characteristics of detection-theory, threshold-theory, and "nonparametric" indexes. *Psychological Bulletin, 107,* 401–413.

Macmillan, N. A., & Creelman, C. D. (1991). *Detection theory: A user's guide.* New York: Cambridge University Press.

Macmillan, N. A., Goldberg, R. F., & Braida, L. D. (1988). Resolution for speech sounds: Basic sensitivity and context memory on vowel and consonant continua. *Journal of the Acoustical Society of America, 84,* 1262–1280.

Macmillan, N. A., & Kaplan, H. L. (1985). Detection theory analysis of group data: Estimating sensitivity from average hit and false-alarm rates. *Psychological Bulletin, 98,* 185–199.

Markowitz, J., & Swets, J. A. (1967). Factors affecting the slope of empirical ROC curves: Comparison of binary and rating responses. *Perception & Psychophysics, 2,* 91–100.

Massaro, D. W., & Friedman, D. (1990). Models of integration given multiple sources of information. *Psychological Review, 97,* 225–252.

McNicol, D. (1972). *A primer of signal detection theory.* London: Allen & Unwin.

Mulligan, R. M., & Shaw, M. L. (1980). Multimodal signal detection: Independent decisions vs. integration. *Perception & Psychophysics, 28,* 471–478.

Nelson, T. O. (1984). A comparison of current measures of the accuracy of feeling-of-knowing predictions. *Psychological Bulletin, 95,* 109–133.

Noreen, D. L. (1977). *Relations among some models of choice.* Paper presented at Mathematical Psychology meetings, Los Angeles.

Noreen, D. L. (1981). Optimal decision rules for some common psychophysical paradigms. In S. Grossberg (Ed.), *Mathematical psychology and psychophysiology: Vol. 13. Seminars in applied mathematics* (pp. 237–280). Providence, RI: American Mathematical Society.

Nosofsky, R. M. (1983). Shifts of attention in the identification and discrimination of intensity. *Perception & Psychophysics, 33*, 103–112.

Nosofsky, R. M. (1984). Choice, similarity, and the context theory of classification. *Journal of Experimental Psychology: Learning, Memory, and Cognition, 10*, 299–309.

Nosofsky, R. M. (1986). Attention, similarity, and the identification-categorization relationship. *Journal of Experimental Psychology: General, 115*, 39–57.

Pollack, I., & Norman, D. A. (1964). A nonparametric analysis of recognition experiments. *Psychonomic Science, 1*, 125–126.

Schulman, A. I., & Mitchell, R. R. (1966). Operating characteristics from yes-no and forced choice procedures. *Journal of the Acoustical Society of America, 40*, 473–477.

Shaw, M. L. (1982). Attending to multiple sources of information: I. The integration of information in decision making. *Cognitive Psychology, 14*, 353–409.

Simpson, A. J., & Fitter, M. J. (1973). What is the best index of detectability? *Psychological Bulletin, 80*, 481–488.

Snodgrass, J. G., & Corwin, J. (1988). Pragmatics of measuring recognition memory: Applications to dementia and amnesia. *Journal of Experimental Psychology: General, 117*, 34–50.

Sorkin, R. D. (1988). Why are people turning off our alarms? *Journal of the Acoustical Society of America, 84*, 1107–1108.

Sorkin, R. D., & Woods, D. D. (1985). Systems with human monitors: A signal detection analysis. *Human-Computer Interaction, 1*, 49–75.

Sperling, G., & Dosher, B. (1986). Strategy and optimization in human information processing. In K. Boff, L. Kaufman, & J. Thomas (Eds.), *Handbook of perception and performance* (Vol. 1). New York: Wiley.

Swets, J. A. (1986a). Indices of discrimination or diagnostic accuracy: Their ROCs and implied models. *Psychological Bulletin, 99*, 100–117.

Swets, J. A. (1986b). Form of empirical ROCs in discrimination and diagnostic tasks. *Psychological Bulletin, 99*, 181–198.

Swets, J. A. (1988). Measuring the accuracy of diagnostic systems. *Science, 240*, 1285–1293.

Swets, J. A., & Pickett, R. M. (1982). *Evaluation of diagnostic systems: Methods from signal detection theory.* New York: Academic Press.

Taylor, M. M., Forbes, S. F., & Creelman, C. D. (1983). PEST reduces bias in forced choice psychophysics. *Journal of the Acoustical Society of America, 74*, 1367–1374.

Treisman, M., & Faulkner, A. (1986). The setting and maintenance of criteria representing levels of confidence. *Journal of Experimental Psychology: Human Perception and Performance, 10*, 119–139.

Treisman, M., & Williams, T. C. (1984). A theory of criterion setting with an application to sequential dependencies. *Psychological Review, 91*, 69–111.

Vogels, R., & Orban, G. A. (1986a). Decision factors affecting line orientation judgments in the method of single stimuli. *Perception & Psychophysics, 40*, 74–84.

Vogels, R., & Orban, G. A. (1986b). Decision processes in visual discrimination of line orientation. *Journal of Experimental Psychology: Human Perception and Performance, 12*, 115–132.

Wickelgren, W. A. (1968). Unidimensional strength theory and component analysis of noise in absolute and comparative judgments. *Journal of Mathematical Psychology, 5*, 102–122.

Wickelgren, W. A. (1969). Associative strength theory of recognition memory for pitch. *Journal of Mathematical Psychology, 6*, 13–61.

3 What Is and Isn't Measurement

Norman Cliff
University of Southern California

"MYTHS" ABOUT MEASUREMENT

Specialization is inevitable in scholarly work, but it carries with it penalties. Among these is a tendency toward divergence between the views of active workers in an area and those of nonspecialists. Such divergence can be particularly costly to both sides if a field is central or fundamental to other fields. The present chapter has been written in the belief that such a divergence has taken place in psychology with respect to measurement concepts, and the chapter's main purpose is to orient the nonspecialist in measurement toward what is felt to be a contemporary view of measurement matters.

It has been prepared from a particular perception of how a large segment of research psychologists view measurement, a perception based on reading and conversation with psychologists and through familiarity with the statistical and methodological texts that seem to be widely used and influential in forming the orientation of many psychologists. Such reading and conversation has led to the conclusion that measurement specialists have quite a different conception of measurement than does the more typical research psychologist. This perception, like any other, may be mistaken, and if so the present chapter is unnecessary, but the chapter is written in the belief that at least some part of psychology would benefit from a consideration of the issues discussed here.

The major point that measurement specialists would make about measurements is their intimate relation with the empirical-theoretical structure of a scientific field. Measurement does not take place separately from science but rather is part of the complex of interlocking observations and ideas. This is not put forth as a particularly new or unique view (see, e.g., Anderson, 1970, 1974; Cliff,

1971, 1972; Guttman, 1971; Luce, 1972; Zinnes, 1969), but rather as one from which there does seem to have been some divergence in recent decades. As Anderson (1974) says: "Measurement is thus an organic part of experimental analysis . . . Measurement and substantive theory are co-functional in their development [p. 291]." If such a conception is already clear to the reader, then the major point has already been made. However, it seems to be easy to gain the impression from some influential works, particularly those of S. S. Stevens (e.g., 1951, 1959), that measurements and their properties somehow have a status independent of a supporting network of relations. Even if it was not Stevens's intention to give this impression, it can certainly be gained from some of his writings, and this is even more true of secondary and tertiary sources.

As an expository device, several attitudes toward measurement are referred to here as "myths." This term is felt to be quite descriptive in several ways. For example, myths may not constitute the literal beliefs of individuals, or at most only the most naive, but they nevertheless have some currency in that even professed nonbelievers may sometimes give the impression of accepting their basis if not their literal truth. Also, they are rooted in generally accepted concepts even though they represent exaggerations or distortions of them. It is hoped that this somewhat informal approach is not counterproductive.

Myths About Physical Measurement

One myth about physical measurement is that "length is measured by laying rods end to end." If anyone thinks that is not a myth, we invite him to use that method and *only that method* for some practical purpose, as specified by responsible, reliable authorities (e.g., Campbell, 1920; Ellis, 1966; Krantz, Luce, Suppes, & Tversky, 1971; Michell, 1990), and we bet him that he cannot do so successfully. The statement is like most myths in that it carries a seed of truth, but one that can only be used if a system of culturally derived implicit assumptions is called into play; if this system is actually used with any success, close examination will reveal that many things are being done besides just laying rods end to end. Also, as with many myths, this one has an inner myth—that length, in the literal sense of how long an object is, is a basic variable in physics—and it has a companion myth—that the primary physical variables are measured on ratio scales.

Suppose that the bet is accepted, and we stipulate that the task is to lay a carpet to fit our living room. If the taker is successful (by ordinary socially defined standards of fit, i.e., no creases and no bare floor), we are to pay him double the regular cost. If he is unsuccessful, then *he* pays a professional to do the carpet laying.

We are very likely to win the bet. The reasons one cannot lay carpet using rods laid end to end are threefold. Most importantly, it is not sufficient to lay them end to end; they must be *parallel*. This requires a means of ensuring that they are parallel, not just end to end. In addition, there must be a means of dividing up rods into fractions. Otherwise the measurer must either be satisfied with crude measurement or use a large number of rods of different sizes. Furthermore, any errors that are made tend to cumulate as the number of rods increases, partly because they tend to be in the same direction, but also because of the elementary statistical principle that the sum of two random errors tends to have a larger variance than either.

Contrast these difficulties with the casual nonchalance of the professional carpet layer as he unreels his tape measure a few times and writes down the results. Contrast it also with our antagonist's own success if we were to allow him Euclid's straightedge and compass instead of forcing him to use his own rigid rods. Euclid's methods would reduce error because, for example, the procedures for dividing a line in half or doubling it are quite accurate, and furthermore they are subject to check and correction by such means as using the bisecting point as the center of a circle and checking to see that the line is a diameter.

In a three-dimensional world, concatenating lines is a complex process. Guttman (1971) makes much the same point concerning the complexities involved in concatenating weights. The kernel of truth in the myth of the concatenated rods is that it is a quite internally consistent method and it does agree, or rather, can be made to agree, with a variety of other methods of measuring length. It has a homely forthrightness to it, and putting rods end to end has a superficially concrete flavor, and it is a good physical exemplar of the process of concatenation. It works when no other, more elegant or exact, method is available, but only if no heavy demands are placed on it.

Length Versus Distance.   It was asserted at the outset that "length" is not a variable in physics. This assertion is the result of noting that the variable that is referred to as length in classical mechanics is actually *distance,* defined by two points in a Euclidean three-space. In the preceding discussion, then, it would have been more accurate to substitute the terms *distance* for *length.*

Consideration of distance as a Newtonian physical variable makes it clear that it refers back to differences in the coordinates of points in a Euclidean space. The space itself has no *origin* or zero point. So what is done is to make the physical variable a function of coordinate *differences* (distance).

Similarly, time, as a variable in Newtonian physics, is actually a time difference, $t - t_0$, where t_0 is the time we begin to observe. It is this difference that enters into the equations. Relativity theory unites distance and time into a four-dimensional system. Thus it is spatial *difference* and time *differences* that enter into the equations of physics. It is true that modern cosmology has been reasonably convincing in deriving a space–time zero point, the Big Bang, but for almost all purposes, it is differences in the space–time system that are important.

Physics and Psychology.   In concluding this section, I may suggest, but only suggest, with Guttman (1971), that the main myth is that the details of physical measurement have any relevance at all to measurement in other fields. For one thing, it is not at all certain that a nonphysicist has a clear understanding of what the nature of physical measurement is, or even what is being measured in a given instance. The example of Hooke's law used by Krantz et al. (1971, p. 484 *et seq.*) is again one in which length is not really the variable involved. Rather, there is a transfer of potential energy from the weight to the spring as the weight falls, and the amount that the spring stretches is proportional to the energy transferred. For a limited set of materials, the amount of energy transferred to the spring is proportional to its length and cross section, and the amount is constant for a given material. This is important for various engineering applications, provided the engineer can be sure of the material he is dealing with, and is interesting from the point of view of physical chemistry. What it tells us about the nature of psychological measurement is questionable, and this may be generally true of analogies to physical measurement.

What Is True About Physical Measurement?

The point of the example of carpet laying is that it is at best barely possible to measure length by the concatenating rods procedure, and perhaps not possible at all without including some external principle and process such as the concept of a straight line and a means of defining it. Measuring length is much more effectively and efficiently done if it is imbedded in a larger system, in this instance the science of geometry. It is true that we are currently used to referring to geometry as a branch of abstract mathematics, rather than empirical science, but it is also true that it is the latter. Certainly it was an empirical science before it became a mathematical toy. Humanity has been measuring land and buildings for 50 or more centuries, at least back to the time of the pyramids. Thus it seems likely that it started as an empirical science in the modern sense of providing a tightly woven empirical fabric that could be tied to an abstract theoretical framework. The fact that the theoretical structure has become an abstract system does not detract from the likelihood that it first permitted the accurate measurement of length through showing how a line could be found straight, how it could be extended to twice its length, and so on, even when only the most primitive apparatus was available. It still provides the basic means by which accurate measurement and construction are possible.

It seems plausible that measurement never exists in an isolated, abstract system such as one of the concatenating rods end to end; rather it relies on a much broader system whereby results from one method can be cross-checked with those from another, implying that a multiplicity of empirical relationships, rather than a single one, is available. Indeed, the most advanced methods of measuring length rely on physical principles rather than merely geometrical ones. It has been proposed (Hall, 1978) that the standard definition of the meter be defined in terms of the assumed constancy in the period and wavelength of a laser!

What is clear about physical measurement is its intimate entanglement with the science itself. Somehow, someone hits upon a way of taking observations that results in regular relations of a quantifiable sort. Someone else finds a way of making observations that are highly correlated with the first sort, but whose relations are even more precise. It is thus that empirical variables are defined operationally and theoretical variables are born. A new set of observations is made that agree with the others for the most part but differ in details, causing a revision of the theory and a concomitant redefinition of the original variables. As the science becomes more differentiated, empirical variables that have been found to behave well in one context are taken over into a new one where they are found to work equally well and provide new insights and explanations of old findings. Ways of defining variables are found that are cheaper, more efficient, more convenient. The process goes on and on, and which part of it should be isolated and called "measurement" is debatable. The important thing is that the empirical definition of variables is made in such a way as to simplify and make more precise their interrelations and the clarity of theoretical interpretations. Such empirically defined variables, supported by a theoretical structure, is the closest we can come to a definition of measurement.

Myths About Psychological Measurement

There Is None.   The biggest myth about psychological measurement is that it is a myth. That this is a myth can be demonstrated by a perusal of a sample of journal articles, albeit a selective perusal. The tenet here is that at least some of the results in those articles will show regular relations among empirically defined variables. Furthermore, some of these variables are not physical variables such as times and voltages—if they were it would reduce psychology directly to physics—but rather are more psychologically defined ones such as the frequency of a certain type of response or the nature of a stimulus word. Such regularities could not be observed if reasonably appropriate measurement—empirical definition of variables in a theoretical context—had not taken place.

Some unsystematic scanning of recent journals (in the fall of 1978) fairly quickly produced examples, of which two of the clearest are mentioned here. Curtis and Rule (1978) had subjects judge brightness of illumination when the intensity was varied independently for each eye. It is well established that brightness judgments are consistent with ordinal interpretation for the responses at the very least. They were able to show that the ordinal relations among responses as a function of the intensities presented to the individual eyes were consistent with a rather simple but nonobvious model. The fit was nontrivial in the sense that there were many fewer parameters than data points. Furthermore, the parameters of the model were quite similar for different individuals, although not identical. The various types of consistency are impossible to explain unless this is "measurement" of a fairly high-level kind. Swets (1986) provided a compilation of results applying signal detection theory to psychological examples that is likewise consistent enough to support the idea that measurement is possible in psychology.

Wainer, Fairbank, and Hough (1978) studied responses to a questionnaire concerning the seriousness of the impact of "life events." They found first that, at least for a subset of the events, the individuals' responses concerning their estimates of degree of impact were consistent with an underlying model, which has a single parameter for the individual and one on the same scale for the item. The item scales could be related across four separate subgroups of subjects, even though the response distributions were not the same. Furthermore, subjects' reports of the combined impact of two life events were related to the impact of the individual events according to still another model. These various consistencies among the observations, which here are the questionnaire responses of persons, again require the interpretation that measurement is going on here.

Type of Scale. A second myth is that the place of a scale in the nominal-ordinal-interval-ratio hierarchy is somehow a given; that is, the scale status of a variable does not depend on its empirical exhibition of the requisite properties for its class and its empirical failure to display the ones for the higher classes. One tends to get the impression from reading the original sources on this question of scale type (Stevens, 1951, 1959) that it was not necessary to make these empirical demonstrations. To some extent this may be a function of the examples he used in trying to convey a novel idea as simply as possible, but it is also possible that there was some degree of intrinsic confusion on this point in view of Stevens' apparent conclusions (Stevens, 1957, 1959; Stevens & Galanter, 1957) concerning the nature of the scales that result when subjects give "ratio" judgments. If they are told to judge on ratios, it appears that the resulting numerals are to be treated as directly corresponding to a ratio scale *in the absence of any confirmatory data*.

On the other hand, there may have been no confusion on this point. Stevens's table (1959, p. 25) is quite precise in this regard. It includes a column labeled "Basic Empirical Operations" for each of the scale types, indicating a recognition of the need to define scale properties empirically. These properties are "the determination of equality," "of greater or less," "of the equality of intervals or of differences," and "of the equality of ratios," for the nominal, ordinal, interval, and ratio scales, respectively. The formal, mathematical nature of these demonstrations has only been made clear relatively recently, receiving a rather complete treatment in the book by Krantz et al. (1971).

It may be useful to make a distinction between a *proposed* scale and a scale. A proposed scale is one that some investigator(s) put forward as having the requisite properties, and if it is indeed shown to have them, then it is recognized as a scale. Psychiatric classification is an example of a proposed scale, in this case a nominal one. That is, it is asserted (e.g., American Psychiatric Association, 1968) that there exists a set of categories—schizophrenia, manic-depression, paranoia, psychopathy, etc.—and that persons with substantially aberrant behavior can be placed in one of those categories. The question of whether this is actually a nominal scale needs to be examined.

In order to answer this question, we may accept Stevens's requirement of an *empirical* determination of equality but elaborate it slightly to require that there not only be equality of some sort for persons in the same category but difference between members of different categories. Now, any collection of persons or other things can be put into any arbitrary collection of categories. This is not sufficient to make the psychiatric classification a scale. We would require that the categorization be made on some set of criteria that are relevant to abnormal behavior, not something superficial such as fingerprint patterns. We would further require that it be done reliably; there must be more-or-less equivalent, more-or-less interchangeable methods for making the classification, which agree with each other. Agreement between human classifiers is a good start on this. If there is only one method of classification and no opportunity for comparison of different but supposedly equivalent means, what we have is a dogma, not a scale.

For this purpose, but not necessarily in other instances, it would also seem that some degree of temporal stability is required of the nominal scale of psychiatric classification. That is, we do not want to classify a person as a schizophrenic one day and a psychopath the next. Thus we would want a sort of test-retest reliability as well as interchangeable methods for the classification. If this is not found, then again we would tend to abandon the scale. This might be premature. If careful observations are made and records are kept, it might be that only certain shifts were found. For example, it might be that a person who was classified as a schizophrenic one day was always either schizophrenic or manic the next, and never any of the others, and similar restrictive relations were found for other categories. This would be much more interesting than mere consistency of classification. However, most of the available evidence (e.g., Aschenbach & Edelbrock, 1978) casts doubt on the nominal scale status of the traditional psychiatric classification scheme, but this is not to say that there is not some alternative in this area that would serve that purpose.

The determination of "greater or less" is also not a self-evident matter. Even Guilford (1954, p. 9) gives some examples that may be misleading if taken at face value. If there is such a thing as a dominance order for chickens, then this is *not* demonstrated by the fact that one chicken pecks another, as suggested there. Two further requirements are necessary. One is perhaps implicit: The second must not also peck the first, or at least must do so reliably less frequently. The other requires the presence of a third chicken. That is, if the first chicken pecks the second, and the second pecks a third, then it must be that the first also pecks the third. This is called *transitivity,* and it is a requirement of most relations which constitute an order, and so is the asymmetry that is implied when the second does not peck the first. The important point here is that there is no order, no ordinal scale, unless all these properties can be demonstrated. If someone says there is an ordinal scale, he must be prepared to demonstrate that in a nontrivial way these properties hold.[1] The observations of Scott (1973) cast doubt on the proposition that they do hold.

Note that the mere attachment of a number to a person, a stimulus, or a response is not enough to constitute an order in more than a trivial way. If one person gets a 90 on a test, and another gets a 40, does this order them? In itself it does not, any more than the fact that one lives on 90th Street and the other on 40th would. However, there is a likelihood that the score number has a richer definition than mere arbitrary assignment. For example, it may be an index of the probability that the individual will give the accepted answer for a certain domain of questions. Thus the scores order the persons with respect to this probability. The ordinal property of the scores may still be present if the scores are subjectively assigned, but again there must be some empirical verification of this. For example, we could require that there at least be a good degree of interjudge consensus: If one judge assigns a higher number to one paper than to a second, then the odds should be high that a second judge does also. These are quite minimal requirements, and there would be little point to assigning the numbers if they were not of more general import.

Why is a scale an ordinal scale and not an interval scale? This, too, is an empirical matter, not something that is decided by a commissar of scales on the basis of whether it feels right to him to call it one thing rather than another. Stevens's system says that an ordinal scale is one on which any monotonic transformation is allowable. "Allowable" must mean that the proposed transformation can be made without disturbing any empirical relationships. Again, there is a kind of convergent validation required. If judges rate stimuli and if when the ratings of one judge are plotted against those of another it is found that there is pretty good ordinal agreement but the relation is often curvilinear, it would seem arbitrary to call this more than an ordinal scale. All that is consistently verifiable is the order. An elegant and precise specification of the circumstances that provide a basis for converting an ordinal scale into an interval one was provided by Luce and Tukey (1964) and elaborated by Krantz (1964). Levine (1970) provides an interesting geometric interpretation. These will be considered more fully later.

---

[1]What we have described here is a dominance order, and there is another quite different type of order, a proximity order, that is symmetric rather than asymmetric and also nontransitive in a special way. See Roberts (1970, 1971) and Fishburn (1970) for a rather technical discussion of this type, and see Coombs (1964) for a somewhat less technical discussion. Cliff, Collins, Zatkin, Gallipeau, and McCormick (1988) provided a method for scaling this kind of data.

The simplest way to formulate the requirements for defining an interval scale is to focus on the necessity of equating and comparing differences at different points on a scale. (We return to this issue from a more technical point of view in the section on conjoint measurement.) It is difficult to provide supporting evidence of equality of differences for many psychological variables. For example, is there any way of equating the difference between IQs of 80 and 90 with that between 120 and 130, much less showing in a meaningful way that it is half as big as the difference between 120 and 140? Similar questions arise in an experimental context, particularly with the manipulation of stimulus conditions. It is the exception rather than the rule to find even suggestive evidence that, as *psychological* variables, there is any way in which nominally equal steps at different points on the scale are equal.

Response time is perhaps an exception because it often seems to behave in a regular enough way to support the conclusion that a response time difference from 400 to 800 milliseconds is equivalent to the difference between 1,200 and 1,600. We return to this later also. Even here, however, it may turn out that the appropriate version of this variable is processing rate rather than response time.

In the same way, in order to to say that a certain variable is a ratio scale it must be possible to show that it has ratio scale properties (i.e., that some empirical property of the scales relations will be destroyed if a constant is added to all the scale values). Again, it should not be taken as self-evident that this will happen. Stevens's magnitude estimation procedure (Stevens, 1957, 1959; Stevens & Galanter, 1957) was taken by him to furnish ratio scales. However, this is only legitimate if subjects' responses are taken literally. There is no overriding reason for doing so; if anything, the contrary is more reasonable (Poulton, 1968; Teghtsoonian, 1971; Treisman, 1964). In that case, the magnitude scales are only log-interval scales, not ratio scales, because the corresponding family of transformation may be applied without disturbing the empirical relations.

It may be worth noting that Krantz (1972; see also Krantz et al., 1971, Weitzenhoffer, n.d.) has shown that if a cross-modality matching procedure (Stevens, 1971, 1974) is used and the results are sufficiently consistent across several intercomparisons of modalities, then ratio scales are determined for all if they are determined for one. However, the point is that if the experimenter says to the subject, "Tell me ratios," and the subject says, "I am indeed telling you ratios," that is not grounds for the rest of psychology to believe that the responses are ratios, any more than if the experimenter says "See ghosts," and the subject replies, "I am indeed seeing ghosts," we are to assume that he is seeing ghosts. There has to be some sort of additional evidence, and, in the case of ratios, what is required is some empirical property of data that requires a ratio interpretation.

Just as a special set of relations can be used to convert ordinal scales to interval scale, empirical relations may be used to derive a "rational" zero point on an interval scale, thus converting it to ratio status. The suggestion that cosmology is trying to do this for the interval spacetime continuum may be recalled.

Cliff (1959, 1988) provided an interesting instance of this in psychology, using a set of consistent relations among interval scales to conclude that there must be an underlying zero point.

It seems, at least to the layman, that an important instance of the use of relations to make what had been an ordinal scale into an interval scale has occurred in geology. Stratigraphy, the way in which rocks of specific kinds occur in layers, provides the basis for an ordinal scale of geologic time. Deeper layers are, generally speaking, older than shallower ones. Careful correlation of different strata, including allowing for faults, uplifts, weathering, and even folding over, permitted a rather complete ordering of rock strata with respect to age. However, absolute ages could only be defined rather vaguely, if at all. The advent of physical procedures, particularly radioactive dating by determination of isotope ratios, has permitted the conversion of much of the geological time scale to an interval status through the assumption that the underlying nuclear processes have taken place at a constant rate.

The burden of this rather long argument is the suggestion that the scale status of a variable is not self-evident but rather must be earned and can be earned. If a scale is proposed as a certain type—physical variables in a psychological context are a salient example—there must be supporting data that shows that it has the properties of a scale of this type. Although it is not necessary to provide a full demonstration of these properties in every application of a particular variable, there must be a background of such demonstrations for it, support by sufficient checks in the present instance to show that nothing has gone haywire. Guttman (1971) and Anderson (1974) present rather similar views.

Ubiquity of Error. Another myth about psychological measurement— complementary to the nihilistic one that there is no measurement—is that in order for there to be measurement it must be made without error. Perhaps no one holds this view, but one can gain the impression from Coombs (1964) that scales only are definable when the data are perfectly consistent. Also, viewed in isolation the axiomatic measurement theory seems only to apply when the axioms are fully satisfied, and what to do when they are not is rather unclear.

The trouble with this is that it leaves us with no scales at all, or, worse, with only those that have not been examined very closely. There is an old country saying, "you can't have beef without bones nor a farm without stones," to which we would append, "nor a measurement without error." Every field of science has to take account of the fact that its observations are not the pure phenomena it is studying, but rather that they are alloyed with a greater or lesser variety of events which cause bias and randomness. Thus no system of relations which is at all extensive can be expected to be perfectly consistent, either with itself or with a model proposed to account for it.

In all measurement there is the necessity of distinguishing between the variable one directly observes or manipulates and its theoretical or verbal counterpart. This is recognized in some areas of research but may be ignored or glossed over in others. Surely one always wants to interpret a variable beyond the immediate, exact observed values when one has employed it. Then two kinds of questions of level of generality can be raised. One kind of generality has historically been known as *reliability*. It refers to degree of measurement error in the observations, reflected by the amount of variation there would be in the numbers over replications of the same operations. Depending on the context, replication can occur across many kinds of factors: repetitions of the same task, randomly different stimuli, forms of a test, times of observation, observers or raters or experimenters. Cronbach and his coworkers (e.g., Cronbach, Gleser, Nanda, & Rajaratnam, 1972; see also Shavelson, Webb, & Rowley, 1989) formulated an extended system for assessing reliability in an analysis of variance framework, calling it *generalizability theory* although here that term is used in a more general sense.

The second issue concerning level of generalizability is most often referred to as the *construct validity* of a variable, the extent to which it is demonstrable that different measures of the same variable are in agreement. The concept arose in the measurement of traits, but has wide generality. In an experimental context, it might refer to the degree to which different operational definitions of a variable behave in the same way or that an effect generalizes across theoretically equivalent but operationally different paradigms. In assessing construct validity, there are two aspects that require attention: convergent and discriminant validation (Campbell & Fiske, 1959). These refer, respectively, to the demonstration that different definitions of the same underlying variable agree and, equally important, that they be independent of observed variables that are supposed to reflect *different* underlying variables. Variables without demonstrated construct validity are of dubious scientific value.

The fundamental issue here is the necessity of recognizing the distinction between the manifest or observed values of variables and the latent or theoretical variables for which they are surrogates. This distinction seems to be more easily recognized in some research areas than others, but it is of universal generality. The researcher not only has to recognize the influence of unreliability or measurement error, that is, differences between more-or-less interchangeable observations, but also the possibility that the same conceptual variable may give different results when defined in different ways.

What does one do with such inconsistency? That depends on what the options are. Certainly the preferred approach is to reduce the inconsistency as much as possible. This can sometimes be done by refining the observational methods or inventing new ones. This may have the effect of reducing random variation, but also may show that inconsistencies were the result of biases in the way the data is gathered; methods that are adequate for initial explorations of an area may need to be replaced by more sophisticated ones. One gets the impression that this goes on in physics all the time.

Inconsistency may be removed by improvements in theory as well as in observational technique. Persistent apparent inconsistency may be removed by the creation of a new theory that accounts for the apparent aberrations. There is, of course, the danger of a pure post-hoc fixup of theory in this context, but adequate safeguards may be incorporated by the usual requirements of replicability and generality of effects. A more elaborate theoretical model should not be rejected just because it is more elaborate; Occam's razor may amputate rather than simply remove unwanted growths.

Thus, measurements may not be entirely consistent with a mathematical model or theory, whether the latter takes the form of a set of equations or a system of axioms. However, it is to be expected that the size of the errors, whether random or systematic, should be relatively small, accounting for only a small part of the variance. Ideally one would want his measurements to be consistent with a theory except for very small and apparently random deviations, where randomness can be defined by the sort of replication that leads, say, to an error term in analysis of variance. What does one do if the measurements show satisfactorily small but apparently systematic deviations from the model? Literal application of the hypothesis-testing procedures, which form the basis of the quantitative training of most psychologists, would give the impression that the model is to be rejected in this case. One can even gain the impression from writers such as Anderson and Shanteau (1977) and Birnbaum (1973, 1974), that it is preferable to have data where the proportion of error is large but where the model cannot be rejected.

The history of science shows that it is frequently the case that systematic departures from theory can occur for reasons which are essentially irrelevant to the phenomenon being studied. Astronomical observations which are distorted by apparent curvature introduced by the lens would be an example. Apparent inconsistencies may also lead to the discovery of new phenomena which are within the same theoretical rubric. There is the well-known example from astronomy, where persistent, systematic departures remained after all observational biases were accounted for. Rather than abandoning the theoretical-observational complex furnished by Newtonian mechanics and the technology of the time, a yet undiscovered planetary body was hypothesized. The existence of this body was eventually confirmed. Also, as Eisler and Montgomery note (1974), a model that is correct may correspond exactly to observations only in ideal limiting cases, otherwise there are consistent deviations.

Ideally, one would like to account for such deviations, but this may not be possible immediately. In the interim, it would seem sensible to retain a model which accounts for a large part of the data rather than rejecting it, at least until a persuasive replacement appears. Theories are supposedly overthrown by better theories, not by data. However, the current preoccupation with significance testing as a means of scientific inference may act against this notion. In any event, the present author states a preference for experiments where a model accounts for almost all, but significantly less than all, of the data over those where much of the variance is error.

Note that the preceding argues that we must expect error, but not that we must simply accept it. Rather, it is important to strive to eliminate it by improvements in either theory or technique. The other side of the myth that it does not exist is the myth that nothing can be done about it and the best that can be hoped for is a *modus vivendi* for coexistence. This is as fruitless as the denial of its existence.

Mental test theory, as exemplified by Lord and Novick (1968), may nearly represent an example of this latter attitude. Responses to test items display a high degree of inconsistency, and test theory may be looked on as an attempt to winnow something stable out of that inconsistency. The extent to which it has been possible to do so and derive useful information out of responses to test items is a tribute to the ingenuity of test theorists and item writers, but very little practical progress has been made since perhaps the 1930s, in spite of the enormous increase in the sophistication of models. The most recent developments in test theory follow the same general pattern, albeit using much more sophisticated models. Item response theory (Lord, 1980) is currently the dominant model there, but its applications are based on the same response systems as earlier ones. In terms of making different tests the improvements it offers seem to be more comparable than in increased precision or validity of measurement on any given test. Psychometricians are attempting to increase the psychological sophistication of the models they use (e.g., Mislevy, 1989; Embretson, in press) although so far the results are encouraging rather than definitive. Errors of measurement are rather like fleas; one cannot deny their existence, but it is better to try and find a way of getting rid of them—even if it involves moving—than it is to simply put up with them.

Statistics and Scales.   There is another myth, or collection of myths, about measurement that centers around the appropriateness of statistical analysis of different kinds of scales. These receive extensive discussion by Stevens (1959), and they form the basis for the still widely used reference on nonparametric statistics (Siegel, 1956; Siegel and Castellan, 1988), but there are a number of issues involved here which should not be treated in a simplistic fashion.

Statistics have two functions that are traditionally separated for expository purposes. One is *description,* summarizing what is going on in the data that is at hand. The other is *inference,* suggesting what may be concluded about a universe of more or less equivalent data that might have been gathered instead. Let us consider the problem of possible transformation from both of these points of view and see wherein lies its validity and its limitations.

Suppose we have some data in the form of numbers assigned to definable observations according to a specifiable rule. If the operations are repeated by ourselves or some colleagues somewhere, the observations are expected to be similar, and if the rules of number assignment that have been followed are followed again, then the data are expected to be similar; otherwise what we have is something outside the realm of science. Transforming the data is equivalent to changing the rules whereby the numbers are assigned. If such a change is made, would it make any difference to conclusions from the data, and would anyone make such a change? These are the questions which are of concern.

The question of which statistics are appropriate for which variables has facets that touch all the combinations of scale types, but there is not space here to deal with all of them. Instead, we will focus on the ordinal-interval distinction, because that is perhaps the most frequently encountered issue. The ordinary "parametric" statistics which involve the computation of means and variances are deemed appropriate only for interval scale variables (e.g., Stevens, 1959). The reason is that although the general linear transformation, $x' = bx + a$, has quite predictable effects on means, variances, and correlations and all the statistics and tests derived from them, the effect of an arbitrary monotonic transformation is unpredictable. If a linear transformation is made, then $\bar{x}' = b\bar{x} + a;\ s_{x'}^2 = b^2 s_x^2;$ and $r_{x'y} = r_{xy}$, for example. Also, the tests of significance that are applied to means, variances, and correlations—F and t tests—remain numerically invariant. However, the effects of making an arbitrary monotonic transformation are unpredictable, and the effect of making a systematic mathematical transformation such as the logarithmic, exponential, square root, reciprocal, etc., may be virtually so. If the data are "only ordinal," such transformations are "allowable."

This means that, at least in principle, a mean that was originally near one end of the scale could conceivably be near the other one after the transformation; a correlation that was substantial before transformation become negligible, or vice versa, etc. Furthermore, two means whose difference is in one direction before transformation is in the other direction afterwards. For example, suppose that there are two sets of three scores each: One is 1, 2, and 9, and the other is 6, 7, and 8. If the scale is ordinal, then presumably it is legitimate to substitute x' for x according to the following table:

x:	1	2	3	4	5	6	7	8	9
x':	6.9	7.0	7.1	7.2	7.3	7.4	7.5	7.6	14.4

On the old scale, the means were 6.0 and 7.0, respectively; on the new one they are 9.0 and 7.5, opposite in difference, even though the order of the scores is the same of x' as for x. Naturally, one is not happy with such a turn of events and would like not to be at the mercy of whimsical but "legitimate" transformations of the data. Thus it is apparently true that a legitimate transformation of the data has had a radical effect on the way it looks. Therefore, one is urged to use an ordinal statistic such as the median here. If one does, then the original medians are 2 and 7 and the new medians are 7.0 and 7.5, rather close together by comparison but at least in the same order. Furthermore, the observations that have the median scores in the new scale are the same ones that had the median scores in the original.

This is less of a general problem than the example may make it appear to be, however, because there are common circumstances under which it is irrelevant, and its magnitude is likely to be quite small except under unusual circumstances. A common circumstance under which it is irrelevant is one where, by convention, an admittedly ordinal variable is never subjected to anything like a general monotonic transformation such as was used above. This is the essence of Lord's (1953) argument; he extends it to nominal scales. Course grades are a homely example. If the common letter grades A, B, C, D, and F are assigned the numbers 4, 3, 2, 1, and 0, there are few who would insist that there is any legitimately empirical sense in which the separations between them are equal. However, grade point average is a mean computed on this scale. This does not cause a problem as long as it is understood that any GPA that is reported has been computed by that convention, and myriads of parametric statistical analyses have been carried out on just that variable. Even though we know that this is an ordinal variable, it is treated as if the scale were fixed, although only conventionally, and as long as it remains fixed no difficulties arise.

It can be contended that this merely avoids the problem. What if a different form of the scale had been used? Would this have changed the results of the statistical analysis? Often not. For one thing, except when samples are very small and the distributions are very peculiar, as was the case in the little example preceding, monotonic transformations are likely to have only mild effects on such things as the correlation between variables or the relative order of a set of means. Thus, given a set of GPAs, suppose the grade scale is changed so that the spacing is no longer equal. This is likely to have surprisingly little effect in the sense that the correlation between the new "GPAs" and the original ones will be very high. This general principle was first demonstrated by Abelson and Tukey (1963), and also illustrated by Labovitz (1967), who showed that the effect of a monotonic transformation was likely to be rather small unless the transformation was a very bizarre one such as using 0; 0.1; 0.2; 0.3; 4,000,000, instead of 0, 1, 2, 3, 4.[2]

In this example, there are many who would be reluctant to apply such a transformation to the grade scale; they say that even though it is only ordinal, the transformation that has been made is too extreme. Thus, there is an instinctive feeling that although one cannot defend the scale as an interval one, neither is it a pure ordinal scale in the sense that *any monotonic transformation whatever* can be applied. Intuitively, it is an intermediate case where the "allowable" transformations are not limited to the linear ones, but neither is it extended to the full

---

[2]The fact that the points on the scale happen to be equally spaced is neither necessary nor sufficient for interval scale status. One could have a discrete interval scale on which the points were unequally spaced. It may be speculated that the equal spacing of the grade scale is some kind of an intuitive minimax solution. If the true spacing is unequal but unknown, then arbitrarily choosing equal spacing is likely to be least in error from the true spacing.

family of monotonic, although recent work by Narens (1981) indicates there is no scale form "between" the ordinal scale and the fully interval level.

Davison and Sharma (1988) presented a reasoned discussion of the relevance of measurement levels to testing hypotheses of zero mean differences and the like, showing that often scale type has little effect on Type I error probabilities. But this simple conclusion strictly holds only in cases such as using a t test to compare means where a full null hypothesis of sampling from the same or identically distributed populations is true. Similar results occur in testing for zero correlations in the case where the variables are independent. The only consequence of monotonic but nonlinear transformation then is to change the shape of the distribution, and this has long been known to have little effect on Type I error probabilities (e.g., Baker, Hardyck, & Petrinovitch, 1966). These cases represent only a very limited set of the possible circumstances where statistical inference takes place.

A different situation results if two distributions differ in shape or spread but have the same means (H_0 true). Here, the means will usually change by different amounts under monotonic transformation, so H_0 changes from true to false on a change of scale. Similar effects can occur with correlations.

Also, even the simple results described by these authors are limited to the null case. Effects of transformation on mean differences, and on confidence intervals for them, can be quite substantial and unpredictable. This is particularly relevant in factorial designs where changes of scale can have important effects on interactions. Correlations can likewise be affected by transformation, a consideration that is particularly relevant in complex applications like covariance structure analysis.

As was noted earlier, there is often a core of truth to a myth, and this is the case here: One should not dismiss the problem entirely. The form in which a variable should be used for statistical analysis can make some difference in a field as well as in an individual study. There is, for example, a long history of controversy in the area of electrodermal recording, summarized by Grings (1974), concerning just what the empirical definition of a galvanic skin response should be. This has apparently had appreciable empirical import. Also, although it is true that the simulation studies (e.g., Abelson & Tukey, 1963; Baker et al., 1966; Labovitz, 1967) show only small effects for transformation, they are sometimes not negligible and often might have been large enough to influence interpretations. Also, much of the reassurance concerning small effects is derived from cases where the null hypothesis is true, whereas scientific interest focuses more on cases in which it is false. Thus it is desirable that the scale status of the principle variables should be established empirically, at least in a field of research as a whole if not in every individual study.

On the other hand, there are reasons for preferring ordinal statistics. Cliff (1991) summarized some of these. For one, he noted that the verbal form of a hypothesis or conclusion is often ordinal, so ordinal analyses may be the most appropriate for testing the hypothesis or supporting the conclusion.

The foregoing arguments generally support a nonobsessive attitude toward the degree to which assumed scale type should influence choice of statistic. There is first the possibility that no confusion will arise because no transformation will be contemplated; even if it is allowable, a variable is defined conventionally and always studied in that form. Then there is the likelihood that a transformation would not affect the conclusions that the investigator makes even if it were made, due to the fact that ordinal transformations are likely to have only a small relative effect on the usual types of statistics computed, particularly if the null hypothesis is true. These effects are particularly mild if any contemplated transformation is limited to only moderately extreme forms. However, there can be an effect, particularly in non-null cases, and the establishment of the best-behaved form for a variable is an important scientific problem. Until this best form has been established, one may well be wise to employ ordinal statistics.

Review of Myths.   The burden of this section has been that there are a number of beliefs about psychological measurement that are at best exaggerations of the true state of affairs. The first of these was that psychological measurement is impossible, but it was pointed out that instances where psychological observations display the kind of regularity of relations which furnishes the evidence for measurement are not uncommon. The second one was that a variable's place in the nominal–ordinal–interval–ratio hierarchy is known a priori. It was argued that instead it depends on the existence or nonexistence of certain prescribed sets of regularities in large collections of data. In the next section, some of these requirements will be spelled out more explicitly. A third alleged myth was that there is no scale if any error or inconsistency is found.[3] It was argued that this was an impossible requirement, and that the scale properties are an idealization that is only approximated in practice. Errors of measurement will occur, and it is the scientist's job to reduce and/or explain them. Finally, the somewhat peripheral question of the appropriate statistical analysis as a function of the scale type was examined, and it was argued that this is not a question which should be of central concern to the investigator. Naturally, these views are not without controversy; otherwise, the beliefs which are here held to be myths would not be widely enough held to justify their discussion. Nonetheless, the views presented

---

[3]There are important instances of a synthesis of the two strategies. Falmagne (1978, 1979) has presented probabilistic versions of several axiomatic models. In a significant empirical application (Falmagne, Iverson, & Marcovici, 1979) a model of this kind is tested. The test includes the translation of the probabilistic model into a statistical model for data, including procedures for estimating parameters for various competing models and tests of significance of departure from them. This work gives all the indications of including the best features of both approaches.

here are offered as a rational position in the light of the overall nature of the scientific endeavor.

WHAT IS PSYCHOLOGICAL MEASUREMENT?

General Characteristics

Although it might be advantageous to provide a one-sentence definition of measurement that could be highlighted with a felt marker by students and memorized, a somewhat less succinct approach has advantages in terms of overall validity. To some extent, a definition has been sketched in the previous section, both directly and by contrast.

To begin with, for measurement to take place, there must be a web of empirical relations that supports the conclusion that well-behaved dependent and independent variables have been identified. This web involves at least two variables, and preferably more, and they should come from a variety of different sources. Examples where this seems to be the case include reactions to stimulus intensity and judgments concerning semantic aspects of words, of which the two studies cited earlier are examples. When this regularity is observed, it is possible to describe the relations by means of a mathematical model, which may take as its basis either an explicit system of axioms with an implied derivable system of equations (the axiomatic emphasis) or a system of equations with an implied, underlying set of axioms (equational emphasis). Once such a mathematical structure is imposed, numerical values can be attached to the empirical variables, both dependent and independent, and the argument here is that this system of equations or axioms is a necessary condition, not just a superstructure.

If it must be that there is something that can be isolated and called the measurement, it is these numbers that are assigned in accordance with the model that are the measurements. Once the web of relations has become established, and verified across a wide enough range of circumstances and time, showing under what conditions the measurements are invariant, then it is possible to adopt shortcuts. It is these shortcut procedures that we are employing when in some practical context we say we are *measuring* something. Often such routine measurements are at some remove from the central set of empirical relations defining the variable we say we are measuring.

Stevens (1959) states that "The reach of this concept measurement is becoming enlarged to include as measurement the assignment of numerals to objects or events according to rule—any rule [p. 19]." In the context, it does not appear that he is necessarily offering this as a definition but rather as the endpoint of a trend that he observes toward broader and broader definition of measurement. The contention here is that, although the definition has become very broad, it has not become this broad. Thus, although it is possible to use this, or any other definition of measurement, it is more useful to restrict the term to cases where number assignment is tightly bounded and supported by an empirical network of relations.

As stated earlier, it is the characteristics of this network or web which define the kind of scale one is dealing with, and it is here that some of the exciting developments have taken place because they have shown not only that certain qualitative empirical relations had to be satisfied before a scale could be defined but that they were *sufficient* to make this definition. Thus, for the first time it became clear how to convert qualitative relations into a quantitative scale. There were contributions here from both the axiomatic and equational emphases.

Conjoint Measurement

The two keystone papers, one from each point of view, were both published in the 1960s. Luce and Tukey (1964) show one set of conditions which were sufficient for the definition of an interval scale. More startlingly, they showed that if there were two qualitative variables—nominal scales—and one ordered variable, certain simple rules of consistency were sufficient to convert all three simultaneously into interval scales.

The Conjoint Axioms.   Space is limited here, but it may be worthwhile to try to describe the conditions and the results. First of all, it is simplest to think of the variable that is initially known to be ordinal as the dependent variable, here denoted x. (This is not necessary. See Krantz, 1964.) Then the other two must occur in all possible combinations, as in a two-factor analysis of variance, and we call them the factors A and B. It must also be in principle possible to subdivide these variables into more and more finely divided categories. Thus we have a two-way layout with a large number of levels on each variable.

Now in order for the analysis into three interval scales to work, the dependent variable must display certain very regular relations. First, within any row and within any column the order of values for x must be the same. This is called in the jargon here "independence" because the order in the row is independent of which column is considered and vice versa. Clearly, this consistent ordering will furnish a rather compelling basis for converting the originally nominal variables A and B into an *ordinal* scale for each.

The interval properties for the three variables may be thought of as resting on two additional properties that the data must have. One of the properties is that there is an essential equivalence between the two factors A and B; whenever we pick a cell $a_1 b_1$ and a second level on one of the variables (e.g., a_2), it is possible to find a level on the other variable, call it b_2, such that $a_2 b_1$ is equivalent to $a_1 b_2$ on the variable x. That is, for every cell, there is a cell in every other row and every other column that matches it in effect. The second aspect is that if we pick any *pair* of levels on *one* factor, say a_1 and a_2, there are compensatory levels on

B, such that a_1b_j has the same effect as a_2b_{j+1}, and furthermore there is an unlimited number of these different levels on *b* such that the difference in their effects just compensates for the difference in the effects of a_1 and a_2. These two ways in which it must be possible to find the equivalent combinations of levels in the two factors are called "solvability" and the "Archimedean" property, respectively. They are illustrated in Fig. 3.1.

The other property that the data must have is a somewhat more refined kind of consistency beyond the ordinal one called independence. Again, it has to do with the comparison of the effects of different levels on the two factors. This requirement has been formulated in several ways that accomplish the same ends (e.g., Holman, 1971; Krantz, 1964; Luce & Tukey, 1964). All amount to showing that putting together two changes on one factor (a_1 to a_2 to a_3, say) has an effect equivalent to putting together two changes on the other. The informal presentation used here follows the original (Luce and Tukey) formulation.

It goes as follows. Start with a base level on the two factors, a_1b_1, say. Suppose we move up a step on *A*, holding *B* at b_1, and observe *x* at a_2b_1, and then do the opposite, observing *x* at a_1b_2, and it turns out that x_{21} is greater than x_{12}. That is, the step on *A* has had a larger effect than the step on *b*. Now we observe also the effect of a third level of *A* in combination with the second level of *B*, a_3b_2 and also observe a_2b_3 for a third level of *B* with the second level of *A*, and suppose we find x_{32} greater than x_{23}. These two comparisons are in effect showing that the first step on *A* was larger than the first step on *B* and that the second step on *A* was also larger than the second one on *B*. Now, we compare the effect of *both* steps on *A* to the effect of both steps on *B* by comparing x_{13} to x_{31}. One would expect that two larger steps were greater than two smaller ones, finding x_{31} greater than x_{13}. If this is true for all possible combinations of these variables—it need not be—then the final requirement is satisfied. This final requirement is called "double cancellation," and the name is a reflection of the original way in which the requirement was arrived at (Luce & Tukey, 1964).

That this requirement is not necessarily satisfied even when independence is can be seen from Fig. 3.2. The left portion is a table showing the three levels of *A*

FIG. 3.1. Schematic illustration of solvability condition for additive conjoint measurement. In order for additivity to hold, it must be possible to find pairs of conditions such that the equalities among the indicated diagonals hold. This also determines the intervals on the scales because of the equating of intervals on one with those on the other.

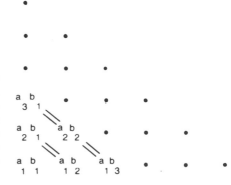

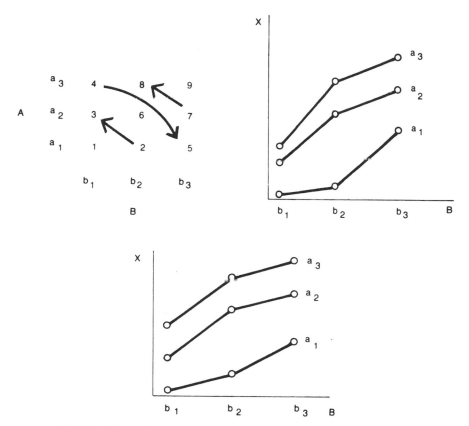

FIG. 3.2. Illustration of the effect of failure of the double-cancellation axiom. The upper left section shows the rank order of elements with the contradiction. The upper right section graphs this as would be done in illustrating the effects in a 3 × 3 analysis of variance; the lines do not cross, but they are far from parallel and cannot be made parallel by transforming the scale of the dependent variable. The lower figure is the same as the upper right except that the order of a_3b_1 and a_1b_3 has been reversed; the figure is somewhat less irregular than the previous one; moreover, monotonic transformation of the scale of the dependent variable will make the lines parallel.

and of B and the entries are the rank order of the cells. Note that within each row the order of the column and the order of the rows is also 1, 2, 3 (independence). In the table, it can be seen that while a_2b_1 is greater than a_1b_2, and a_3b_2 is greater than a_2b_3, a_1b_3 is greater than a_3b_1, contradicting the double cancellation requirement. What this looks like when graphed as one would in illustrating a two-factor analysis of variance is shown on the right of the figure. The lines do not cross; that would only happen if independence were violated. However, the lines are not parallel; there is a rather distinct irregularity in their shape. If the order of

a_3b_1 and a_1b_3 had been reversed and double cancellation thus satisfied, then the more regular figure at the bottom would result. In the latter case it is possible, by a suitable transformation of x, to make the three lines parallel, but when double cancellation is violated it is not.

Now, if these requirements are satisfied (i.e., if there is independence, equivalence of gradations of the two variables, and no violations of double cancellation), then interval scales are defined for all three variables in the following sense. It is possible to find a monotonic transformation of the dependent variable such that it is a simple, additive function of what in analysis of variance terminology is called main effects for the two factors. That is, the interaction can be reduced to zero. Then this form of the dependent variable is the obvious one to choose for it as opposed to any monotonically related alternative. Stated in terms of symbols, x is the ordinal version of the original dependent variable, and $y \stackrel{m}{=} f(x)$, where $\stackrel{m}{=}$ means "is a monotonic function of" (Young, 1972). The fact that it is a simple additive function of the two factors can be stated as $y_{ij} = \alpha_i + \beta_j$. It seems obvious that α should be used as the scale for the A factor and β for the B factor, even if this is different from the scale for the original levels. The variable y is defined to be an interval scale because anything other than a linear transformation of it will destroy the additive dependence on A and B. The effects α and β can only be transformed by linear functions because any more general transformation will either violate the linear model or contradict one or more of the ordinal relations in the data. On the other hand, linear transformations of one of the three variables can always be compensated by transformations of the other two. Thus the data define interval scales for all three *when the conditions are met*, and because *we choose the additive representation of the relations among them*.

In the years since the conjoint measurement principles were established, the system has been refined and extended, and alternative interpretations of the requirements have been made. Narens and Luce (1986) provided a modern summary of these results, which not only give a solid basis for measurement in behavioral science but establish a far-reaching framework for measurement in all of science.

The important lessons seem to be that there need to be (a) observations that are at least trivariate, (b) the demonstration of equivalences in the effects of the variables, and (c) a fine-grained property for each. When these requirements are met, then the variables can earn the status of interval scales. If, in addition, a variable can be combined in a consistent way with itself, then a ratio scale can result.

These fundamental requirements for measurement have been formulated in a highly abstract and general way, but there are more concrete special cases that demonstrate intervalness. When a set of variables are found to interrelate in an *additive* way, in the analysis-of-variance sense of the independent variables showing clear main effects and zero interactions on a dependent one, then this is evidence for the interval status of all the variables involved (Anderson, 1970; Cliff, 1971).

This principle may account in part for the adoption of response time as the dominant dependent variable in cognitive science. The pioneering study by Sternberg (1969) showed clearly additive effects on response time for a number of combinations of variables, supporting the status of differences in response time as a variable that directly reflects differences in processing. The evidence supports the interpretation that there is a direct comparability between the differences of 400 and 500 milliseconds and that between 600 and 700 milliseconds in physics as well as in cognition. Given this very positive start, it is regretable that cognitive scientists are not more often moved to use it as a basis for establishing scales for the *other* variables in their studies. They seem satisfied to demonstrate qualitative effects for those variables rather than employing the multiple levels of them that would enable the field to establish cognitively equal values for a number of variables that affect processing.

Thus variables achieve interval scale status by virtue of empirical demonstration of equality of units, and modern measurement theory specifies the essential aspects of such demonstration. The "units" on variable A are equal because it can be shown that a given change in A has the same effect as a whole list of connected changes in B, and a second change in A is equal to the first because it is equivalent to the same list of changes in B. The same thing is true of changes in B. This means that the equivalence of differences in one variable is demonstrated indirectly, by showing that each has the same effect as a difference in the other variable. The more independent variables that can be locked together in this fashion into designs with more and more factors, the more amply is their interval scale status confirmed.[4] If we wish to follow a strict definition, to say some variable A forms an interval scale is to say that the axioms of conjoint measurement theory have been satisfied by it when it is varied in combination with a wide variety of other variables.

One way of thinking about the way in which the axioms provide a sufficient basis for the scales is to realize that the proliferation of ordinal relations of a particularly consistent kind is analogous to a piece of cloth that may start out as a few widely separated threads but is being woven more and more tightly by the multiplicity of consistent relations of the specified kind. Eventually, the cloth is a solid sheet, and then the only way it could be altered is by changing scale units and origins.

The foregoing is a rather sketchy and informal overview of what is called *additive conjoint measurement*. A much more thorough account is given by Krantz et al. (1971, especially pp. 245–261). Many variations and elaborations

---

[4]There is an added bonus if there are three or more factors. In that case, the double-cancellation requirement need not be checked separately; whenever independence is satisfied for all subsets of these factors, the double-cancellation requirement will be satisfied also.

of conjoint measurement are possible. In addition to that volume, Krantz and Tversky (1971) and Tversky (1967) provide interesting alternative axiom systems wherein the observations of different consistencies lead to models other than the additive one, and also show how certain requirements can be relaxed. A particularly interesting observation is that there seems to be only a relatively small number of qualitatively different but general axiom systems for interval scales which can be differentiated and which lead to models other than the additive one but are of comparable simplicity and power.

Axioms for Orders and Ratios.   Ordinal and ratio scales are also axiomatizable. That is, it is also possible to set up sets of qualitative conditions which must be satisfied if it is to be possible to define these types of scales, and, conversely, if these conditions are met then the empirical relations are sufficient to define the scales. The axioms tell us what we should be looking for in the way of empirical relations if scales of a certain type are to be definable and also tell us that if relations of these kinds are observed, then they do form the basis for a scale. The axioms for ordinal scales were touched on briefly in an earlier section here.

Equational Emphasis

What was earlier termed the "equational emphasis" takes a stance quite different from the axiomatic. Rather than trying to isolate the qualitatively defined relations that provide the basis for a certain type of model and consequently the scales that provide definitions for the relevant variables, it starts from a model as a descriptor of a certain collection of observations. The model consists of a set of equations, or perhaps inequalities, which relate observations to underlying variables, at least in the ideal case of perfect consistency. Rather than requiring perfect consistency, however, the typical attack from this orientation assumes that there will be at least some degree of observational error, and it attempts to find values of the underlying variables that are least inconsistent in some sense with the observations.

Nonmetric Multidimensional Scaling.   This strategy is the approach that has characterized psychophysics since Weber and psychometrics since Spearman, but beginning in the early 1960s there was a quantum jump in the power and generality with which it has been applied. This jump consisted in showing how, from this point of view also, a sufficiency of apparently ordinal information can define higher-level scales. The papers by Shepard (1962a, b) on "nonmetric" multidimensional scaling are singled out as providing the pre-eminent example of this approach.[5]

---

[5]This emphasis is to some degree unfair. Torgerson and Meuser (1962) and Guttman and Lingoes (Guttman, 1967, 1968; Lingoes, 1965a, b), in the multidimensional scaling field itself, and Anderson

In the case of multidimensional scaling (MDS), the typical observations are the judged similarity or dissimilarity of all possible pairs of stimuli. The model specifies, in the case that is most commonly treated, that psychological distance is a Euclidean distance in k-dimensional space. If this is true, and if distance is proportional to judged dissimilarity, then it is possible to analyze the distances (e.g., Torgerson, 1958) to recover the values of the stimuli on the underlying scales or dimensions. However, it is more plausible to assume that the dissimilarities are only monotonically related to psychological distance, and that this monotonic relation is unknown a priori. The procedures for analyzing dissimilarity under this assumption are what is known—rather inaccurately—as *nonmetric* multidimensional scaling (nMDS).

The breakthrough that occurred in this period was the widespread realization, of which we take Shepard's (1962a, b) as the clearest example, that the model itself could provide the means of defining the relation between the ordinal scale of dissimilarity and psychological distance. The approaches to this problem differ in their details, but in general what is done is to assume some initial estimate of the relation between dissimilarity and the true psychological distance. Most simply we begin by assuming psychological distance equal to the dissimilarities (Young & Torgerson, 1967). Hereafter, such *estimates* of psychological distance will be called *disparities*. These disparities are analyzed by any of a variety of methods (e.g., Guttman, 1968; Kruskal, 1964a, b; Takane, Young, & DeLeeuw, 1977; Young & Torgerson, 1967) to arrive at estimated values on the underlying dimensions for the stimuli. The Euclidean distance formula

$$d_{ij} = \left[\sum_m (x_{im} - x_{jm})^2 \right]^{1/2}$$

relates distance (not disparity) to the projections x_{im} of point i on the dimension m. Having estimated the projections from the disparities, one can compute the distances. If the model fits exactly, the disparities and the distances would be equal, but in general they are not, at least if the number of dimensions is less than the number of points.

But it is assumed initially that the disparities are only ordinally related to psychological distance; therefore, they could be transformed ordinally. In nMDS this is done, and it is done so as to make the differences between the original disparities and the distance computed from the dimensions smaller. That is, the disparities are compared to the distances, and adjusted to make the two as nearly equal as possible without distorting the disparities' rank order. This new version of the disparities can be analyzed again to yield a new set of projections on

---

(1962) and Kruskal (1965), for other models, have proposed that fit to a model could be used to define the appropriate interval or ratio-scale definition for a variable that otherwise was defined only ordinarily. However, Shepard's was the earliest actual publication (publication dates on the other papers postdate the actual methods), and it provided a clear rationale, striking examples, and a computer program for performing the analysis. Thus it is felt to have been the most influential.

dimensions, which are in turn compared to the latest version of the disparities. These again are ordinally adjusted to bring the two sets more nearly in line, and the whole procedure starts again. Eventually, a place is reached where no further adjustment makes any appreciable improvement, and the process stops.

The interesting thing is that this ordinal treatment of the dissimilarities works not only in the sense that the process converges to a result but that the dimension loadings of the stimuli are meaningful and often simpler than the ones that result when dissimilarity is treated as a ratio scale. Moreover, simulations (e.g., Shepard, 1974) have shown that the process will recover a true configuration, provided there are enough stimuli relative to the number of dimensions. Even in the presence of measurement error a close approximation to the true configuration will be achieved.

At the conclusion of an nMDS analysis, initially qualitative and ordinal data has been converted to interval scales. Before the analysis, the stimuli were defined only qualitatively—no mean feat in itself—and the dissimilarity measure was an ordinal variable. Now, the stimuli have been located as points on one or more interval variables, the multidimensional scales, and the final disparities are defined in a ratio form.

This has been accomplished by assuming that a particular model, Euclidean distance, explains the degree of dissimilarity judged between stimuli. Then, the locations of the stimuli on dimensions and the form of the disparity-dissimilarity relation are chosen in such a way as to make the data most consistent with the equations in the model. That is why this is called here the "equational emphasis." "Measurement" takes place by assuming that the model is a valid one and by solving a set of observations for the values of the assumed underlying variables that are implied by the model.

Axiomatic Versus Equational.   The latter is true also in the case of the axiomatic emphasis. The difference is that in the axiomatic emphasis it is assumed that all the axioms are satisfied, and in that case a wide variety of computational procedures will arrive at exactly the same results for the scale values, and so exactly how it is done is not of central concern. If the axioms are not satisfied, then there is no solution in the sense that there is no set of values for the variables such that the model holds. For example, if independence fails in a two-way factorial design, it is obvious that there is no way that the curves can be made parallel by any ordinal adjustment of x. It is not so obvious, but equally true, that neither is it possible if double cancellation is violated. Failure of other axioms may instead result in the solution being nonunique. If the axioms are not satisfied, the scales are not defined.

By contrast, a modeling orientation to data where the additive model is assumed to hold, as in additive conjoint measurement, would attempt to find an ordinal transformation of x and values of the "effects" α and β such that the additive model fits as closely as possible (see Anderson, 1962, 1974; Kruskal,

1965). If the fit is close enough by some statistical criterion, then the model and the three scales are accepted as valid. If not, then all are rejected or at best questionable.

It is possible to provide an axiomatic treatment of multidimensional scaling (Beals, Krantz, & Tversky, 1968; Tversky & Krantz, 1970), but by far the greater emphasis in practice has been on data analysis (i.e., a modeling emphasis). The fits to the data are not perfect, indicating that some axiomatic property has been violated in the data, but only rarely has there been any concern about this specifically, as long as the overall fit of the distance model is satisfactory.

Application of the equational emphasis, for which Anderson (1962, 1970) has coined the term *functional measurement,* requires several ingredients. The basic one is data; another is the model itself, stated in a form specific enough to allow its implementation. The other essential ingredient is an algorithm for converting the data into the scales, a computational procedure, which finds the numerical scale values that fit the data. Implicitly or explicitly, such an algorithm is based on a goodness-of-fit criterion (see Guttman, 1971; Kruskal, 1964a, b; Shepard & Carroll, 1966). That is, the scale values associated with observable events are solved for so as to optimize the criterion, and so they are to some extent influenced by the particular criterion that is used. Least squares, or some variation on it, is by far the most common one employed, but many others are possible. (Shepard & Carroll [1966] provide an interesting example of the sophisticated definition of such criteria).

In the modeling emphasis, there is an unfortunate tendency toward lack of attention to what the errors of fit are and where they occur. Such attention might lead to the formulation of a more valid model.

The computer has become increasingly involved in the application of the modeling emphasis because it permits the carrying out of solution procedures that are otherwise impossible. This is particularly the case when monotonic transformation of the data is involved, but is not a necessary device. Cliff (1971) was quite successful in an application in which it was carried out by hand. There, disparities (using the terminology of nMDS stated earlier even though the problem was one of an additive model) were plotted against distances, and the monotonic transformation was found by drawing a curve through the scatter diagram by hand and reading the transformation off the scale.

One final aspect of both types of emphases may bear comment. This is the necessity of giving the model opportunity, ample opportunity, to fail. This essentially means that enough data points must be observed so that there are surplus degrees of freedom. By nMDS, n points can always be fit into $n - 2$ dimensions. Double cancellation has no opportunity to fail if one factor is only observed at two levels, so the additive model can be made to fit unless independence is violated. In addition, statistical considerations imply that the scale values become more valid as they are determined using more and more points, and the model becomes more and more plausible as it fits more and more data. Thus, it is highly desirable to use a number of levels on each variable if one is to establish firm scales.

Routine Measurement

The discussion above places measurement, the attachment of numbers to observations, very firmly in an empirical–theoretical context. It is necessary that the empirical relations display a high degree of consistency, and consistency is always defined by conformity with a relatively simple theory or model. The nature of these consistencies implies the underlying model, or at least greatly restricts the models that are appropriate, and scale values are actually the values of empirical variables derived through an analysis which is made in terms of the model. (The status of "measurements" derived through an incorrect model is questionable.)

It often seems to us that we measure things without invoking a model or going through any elaborate verification of consistency of observations, and indeed this is often the case, even in psychology. What makes this possible?

All the physical measuring that we do in everyday life seems to be of this kind, simply involving a *measuring* procedure without involving anything more elaborate. We use a tape measure, micrometer, or radar beam; a bathroom scale or a balance; a speedometer; a light meter. We can do this because it has been established that the observations—here the readings—*have been shown in the past* either to satisfy by themselves models and/or axiom systems or to be in direct correspondence to observations which do. Furthermore, they are known to do so with a degree of accuracy which is adequate for the purpose at hand.

In addition, there is often at least some degree of skill involved in the performance of such measurements, and the skill boils down to carrying out operations in such a way as to increase the likelihood that the numbers would show the required consistency. Thus we measure length in both directions, confirm it by triangulation, etc., or calibrate a device at each use by comparing it to a standard. Although we do not carry out a full model verification and solution for variables in each application, if we are prudent we do make some verification that the procedure is still firmly connected to the empirical–theoretical structure on which it is based. Thus routine measurement does take place in the empirical–theoretical context which has been the subject of this discussion.

Routine Psychological Measurement. The same thing takes place within the more or less purely psychological context also, albeit with a considerably smaller degree of precision. Two homely examples are the rating scale and the multi-item test, although neither has much more than ordinal status. Countless applications have shown that if one asks people—at least literate, Westernized people—to apply a rating scale to a collection of stimuli, they will do so in a manner that displays a good deal of consistency unless the task is in some way ambiguous or the stimuli are very complex or amorphous. The consistency may be with respect to the same task, what we call test-retest and interjudge reliability, or with respect to other behaviors, what we call validity. The amount of apparently random error involved is much larger than in physical measurement, but this is partly due to the likelihood that the ratings are applied to a rather narrow range. (After all, when subjects rate the utility of various objects, the collection does not include either a pinch of dirt or a working Aladdin's lamp.) The known influence of various context effects as well as individual idiosyncrasies in the use of the scale make it doubtful that more than ordinal information is valid. In any application of rating scales the prudent user makes at least a reliability check. Crude as they are, rating scales constitute a workable measurement technology because there has been repeated observation that numbers assigned in this way display the appropriate kinds of consistency, or at least have done so in the past in contexts similar to the one in which application is contemplated.

A similar argument can be made for mental tests. Dichotomous test items display a modest but nontrivial degree of consistency in the way they order persons; at least some collections of them do. Thus, they reinforce each other's ordering properties. Total scores arrived at by summing sets of such items display a more substantial degree of ordinal consistency with other variables. Therefore, we are justified in concluding that there is "something there," of a noisy sort if not a pure one. However, one is dubious that any convincing evidence exists, such as provided by conjoint measurement, that would allow the equating of intervals along the score variable. Either it is treated ordinally, or as a *pro forma* interval scale. There exist, of course, models that attempt to convert the ordinal test data provided by test items into some more strictly defined scale (e.g., Birnbaum, 1968; Lord & Novick, 1968; Rasch, 1966), but the evidence that supports the interval-scale status of the derived variables is not compelling because of the amount of error involved.[6] The point here is that there is an underlying web of relationships for mental tests that has been demonstrated repeatedly to justify their status as measurements, at least ordinal ones.

Therefore, we expect that fairly routine activities by a reasonably sophisticated person making up items and administering a test will similarly result in numbers that would show the same or similar degree of consistency if the required checks were carried out. For reasons of practicality, the complete set of

---

[6]The situation is more complex here than was originally thought. The axiomatic approach puts the emphases—rightly, I feel—on data relations as the primary grounds for establishing a certain kind of scale. Simply proposing a model and finding that it can be fit to data is not sufficient grounds for defining scales in terms of the variables or parameters of the model. There can be an arbitrariness in such applications: Even though a given model fits, there are bound to be other models that fit just as well. Their variables (and parameters) may be nonlinear transformations of those in the first model. Both sets cannot be interval scales of the same empirical variables. It has been argued (e.g., Cliff, 1989; Mislevy, 1987) that something like this arbitrariness of choice has occurred in the case of the item response theory that underlies many large-scale modern applications of testing.

relation–verification procedures is not performed, although it is prudent to perform some partial verification, such as a reliability check, in order to ensure that something has not gone haywire in the given application.

The argument here is that routine measurement takes place when there is a substantial body of experience that an elaborated and well-articulated structure of theory and data exists that supports the measurement status of the observations that make up this routine measurement. Examples of this exist in psychology as well as physical sciences, the use of rating scales and mental tests being examples, although their precision is much lower than is attained for physical variables. Routine measurement, as opposed to observation of the relations among variables in a theory-related context, is by far the most common form in which measurement is encountered, even though it must rest on such relations somewhere, and this may explain why one tends to think of measurement as separate from science.

CONCLUSION

The purpose here has been to show that measurement is not an activity that is separate from the scientific enterprise. Scales, whether of velocity or pleasantness, do not survive if they are excised from a supporting matrix of empirical and theoretical relations. The example of length measurement by concatenating rods was used to show that a measurement process, however its seeming elegance, that attempted to stand by itself in isolation from a larger theoretical context was of doubtful value. It cannot sustain itself without a larger framework.

The nature of this framework is what determines the kind of scale that is being dealt with. The major problem in a science is just the identification of what the principal variables are, the demonstration of what things are the same and what are different, and what makes them different (i.e., nominal scale definition). Eventually, such variables become established, and it is these which are called nominal scales if no more stringent requirements are met.

The elevation of variables to ordinal, interval, or ratio scale status is also an empirical matter. Certain kinds of regularity must be present in the relations between variables if they are to have this status, and one of the major contributions of the axiomatic emphasis in measurement is the specification of just what these requirements are. A general characteristic of these requirements is that they entail relations among collections of elements, and not just individual pairs of them, and not just the relation between pairs of variables, but ones involving three or more of them. A scale is ordinal, interval, or ratio because the application of a more general family of transformations would contradict certain of the empirical relations observed, and if the empirical relations are left undisturbed when a transformation at that level is applied.

One of the foci of concern in the establishment of the scale type of a variable is the type of statistics that are appropriate. Under many circumstances, this is less of a problem than is sometimes stated because statistics may be relatively invariant with respect to scale transformation and because it may be that no transformation is contemplated. This is not to say that the scale type is to be ignored in considering statistics but rather that it is not necessarily a cause for obsessive concern.

Intimately attached to observation is error. Thus, one cannot expect any empirical system of relations to be perfectly consistent. This means that an axiom system is an ideal that one hopes to approach, but never achieves in practice. Apparent inconsistencies may be resolved by theoretical insights, and the amount of inconsistency can usually be reduced by technical innovation and expertise. Certainly this is an objective in sciences in general and should also be so in psychology.

A scale is a theoretical variable in a model, and "scaling" or measurement is the attachment to empirical events of values of the variables in a model. This can be done from an axiomatic point of view, but for the most part it is the domain of the "equational emphasis" in quantitative psychology. Here, the approach is to assume that a certain model is descriptive of a set of observations, and then to calculate the values of the theoretical variables in the model which are most consistent with the observations. This is done, explicitly or implicitly, through the optimization of some measure of fit of the scale values to the observations.

This optimization process may also serve to define the scale status of a variable in the sense that, for example, some particular transformation of an ordinal variable permits the best fit of a model. In that case, the transformed version of the ordinal variable is an interval or ratio scale in the sense that transformations of it would worsen the degree of fit. For a single set of data, this definition is rather arbitrary, but insofar as similar kinds of transformations are repeatedly required for similar kinds of data, and scales derived from the transformed version show improved parsimony and external validity (e.g, Cliff, 1971), the interval scale status of the variable in its transformed form gains credence. Here again, it is a question of the extent to which empirical relations support the form of a scale that is the major concern.

If measurement is so intimately connected with webs of empirical and theoretical relationships, which are what we usually call science, it is puzzling that there is such a strong tendency to think of it as a separate process. The reason for this may lie in the fact that much of our contact is with "routine measurement," cases in which the connection with a rich structure are not readily apparent. With routine measurement, however, there *is* a strong connection with such a structure. It is just not made explicit or at most sketchily so, and so may not be noticed. Examples exist with psychological measurement as well as physical measurement.

In short, theory and data lead to measurement, and the general nature of the measurements as well as their specific values depend on the theory and the data.

ACKNOWLEDGMENT

This chapter was partially supported by a fellowship from the James McKeen Cattell Fund.

REFERENCES

Abelson, R. P., & Tukey, J. W. (1963). Efficient utilization of non-numerical information in quantitative analysis: General theory and the case of simple order. *Annals of Mathematical Statistics, 34,* 1347–1369.

American Psychiatric Association. (1968). *Diagnostic and statistical manual of mental disorders* (2nd ed.). Washington, DC: American Psychiatric Association.

Aschenbach, T. M., & Edelbrock, C. S. (1978). The classification of child pathology: A review and analysis of empirical efforts. *Psychological Bulletin, 85,* 1275–1301.

Anderson, N. H. (1962). On the quantification of Miller's conflict theory. *Psychological Review, 69,* 400–414.

Anderson, N. H. (1970). Functional measurement and psychophysical judgment. *Psychological Review, 77,* 153–170.

Anderson, N. H. (1974). Algebraic models in perception. In E. C. Carterette & M. P. Friedman (Eds.), *Handbook of perception* (Vol. 2). New York: Academic Press.

Anderson, N. H., & Shanteau, J. (1977). Weak influence with linear models. *Psychological Bulletin, 84,* 1155–1170.

Baker, B. O., Hardyck, C. D., & Petrinovich, L. F. (1966). Weak measurement vs. strong statistics: An empirical critique of S. S. Stevens' prescriptions on statistics. *Educational and Psychological Measurement, 26,* 291–309.

Beals, R., Krantz, D. H., & Tversky, A. (1968). Foundations of multidimensional scaling. *Psychological Review, 75,* 127–142.

Birnbaum, A. (1968). Some latent trait models and their use in inferring an examinee's ability. In F. M. Lord & M. R. Novick (Eds.) *Statistical theories of mental test scores.* Reading, Mass.: Addison-Wesley.

Birnbaum, M. H. (1973). The devil rides again: Correlation as an index of fit. *Psychological Bulletin, 79,* 239–242.

Birnbaum, M. H. (1974). Reply to the devil's advocates: Don't confound model testing with measurement. *Psychological Bulletin, 81,* 854–859.

Bronowski, J. (1973). *The ascent of man.* Boston: Little, Brown.

Campbell, N. R. (1920). *Physics: The elements.* London: Cambridge University Press.

Campbell, D. T., & Fiske, D. W. (1959). Convergent and discriminant validity in the multitrait-multimethod matrix. *Psychological Bulletin, 56,* 81–105.

Cliff, N. (1959). Adverbs as multipliers. *Psychological Review, 66,* 27–44.

Cliff, N. (1971). Consistencies among judgments of adjective combinations. In A. K. Romney, R. N. Shephard, & S. B. Nerlove (Eds.), *Multidimensional scaling: Theory and application in the behavioral sciences* (Vol. 2). New York: Seminar Press.

Cliff, N. (1972). Psychometrics. In B. B. Wolman (Ed.), *Handbook of psychology.* New York: Prentice-Hall.

Cliff, N. (1988). Adverbs and adjectives: A model-based approach. *Chance, 1,* 32–36.

Cliff, N. (1989). Ordinal consistency and ordinal true scores. *Psychometrika, 54,* 75–91.

Cliff, N. (1991). Ordinal methods in the study of change. In L. M. Collins & J. Horn (Eds.) *Best methods for the study of change.* Washington, DC: American Psychological Association.

Cliff, N., Collins, L. M., Zatkin, J., Gallipeau, D., & McCormick, D. J. (1988). An ordinal scaling method for questionnaire and other ordinal data. *Applied Psychological Measurement, 12,* 217–230.

Coombs, C. H. (1964). *A theory of data.* New York: Wiley.

Cronbach, L. J., Gleser, G. C., Nanda, H., & Rajaratnam, N. (1972). *The dependability of behavioral measurements: Theory of generalizability of scores and profiles.* New York: Wiley.

Curtis, D. W., & Rule, S. J. (1978). Binocular processing of brightness information: A vector sum model. *Journal of Experimental Psychology, Human Perception and Performance, 4,* 132–143.

Davison, M. L., & Sharma, A. R. (1988). Parametric statistics and levels of measurement. *Psychological Bulletin, 104,* 137–144.

Eisler, H., & Montgomery, H. (1974). On theoretical and realizable ideal conditions in psychophysics: Magnitude and category scales and their relation. *Perception and Psychophysics, 16,* 157–168.

Ellis, B. (1966). *Basic concepts of measurement.* London: Cambridge University Press.

Falmagne, J. C. (1979). On a class of probabilistic conjoint measurement models: Some diagnostic properties. *Journal of Mathematical Psychology, 19,* 73–88.

Falmagne, J. C. (1978). A representation theorem for finite random scale systems. *Journal of Mathematical Psychology, 18,* 52–72.

Falmagne, J. C., Iverson, G., & Marcovici, S. (1979). Binaural "loudness" summation: Probabilistic theory and data. *Psychological Review, 86,* 25–43.

Fishburn, P. C. (1970). Intransitive indifference with unequal intervals. *Journal of Mathematical Psychology, 7,* 144–149.

Grings, W. W. (1974). Recording of electrodermal phenomena. In R. F. Thompson & M. M. Patterson (Eds.), *Bioelectric recording techniques, Part C: Receptor and effector processes.* New York: Academic Press.

Guilford, J. P. (1954). *Psychometric methods* (2nd ed.). New York: McGraw-Hill.

Guttman, L. (1967). The development of nonmetric space analysis: A letter to John Ross. *Multivariate Behavioral Research, 2,* 71–82.

Guttman, L. (1968). A general nonmetric technique for finding the smallest coordinate space for a configuration of points. *Psychometrika, 33,* 469–506.

Guttman, L. (1971). Measurement as structural theory. *Psychometrika, 36,* 329–347.

Hall, J. L. (1978). Stabilized lasers and precision measurements. *Science, 202,* 147–156.

Holman, E. W. (1971). A note on conjoint measurement with restricted solvability. *Journal of Mathematical Psychology, 8,* 489–494.

Krantz, D. H. (1964). Conjoint measurement: The Luce–Tukey axiomatization and some extensions. *Journal of Mathematical Psychology, 1,* 248–277.

Krantz, D. H. (1972). A theory of magnitude estimation and cross-modality matching. *Journal of Mathematical Psychology, 9,* 168–199.

Krantz, D. H., Luce, R. D., Suppes, P., & Tversky, A. (1971). *Foundations of measurement* (Vol. 1). New York: Academic Press.

Krantz, D. H., & Tversky, A. (1971). A conjoint-measurement analysis of decision rules in psychology. *Psychological Review, 78,* 152–169.

Kruskal, J. B. (1964a). Multidimensional scaling by optimizing goodness of fit to a non-metric hypothesis. *Psychometrika, 29,* 1–27.

Kruskal, J. B. (1964b). Non-metric multidimensional scaling: A numerical method. *Psychometrika, 29,* 115–129.

Kruskal, J. B. (1965). Analysis of factorial experiments by estimating monotone transformations of the data. *Journal of the Royal Statistical Society, Series B, 27,* 251–264.

Labovitz, S. (1967). Some observations on measurement and statistics. *Social Forces, 46,* 151–160.

Levine, M. V. (1970). Transformations that render curves parallel. *Journal of Mathematical Psychology, 7,* 410–443.

Lingoes, J. C. (1965a). An IBM 7090 program for Guttman–Lingoes smallest space analysis—I. *Behavioral Science, 10,* 183–184.

Lingoes, J. C. (1965b). An IBM 7090 program for Guttman–Lingoes smallest space analysis—II. *Behavioral Science, 10,* 487.

Lord, F. M. (1953). On the statistical treatment of football numbers. *American Psychologist, 8,* 750–751.

Lord, F. M. (1980). *Applications of item response theory to practical testing problems.* Hillsdale, NJ: Lawrence Erlbaum Associates.

Lord, F. M., & Novick, M. R. (1968). *Statistical theories of mental test scores.* Reading, MA: Addison-Wesley.

Luce, R. D. (1972). What sort of measurement is psychophysical measurement? *American Psychologist, 27,* 96–106.

Luce, R. D., & Tukey, J. W. (1964). Simultaneous conjoint measurement: A new type of fundamental measurement. *Journal of Mathematical Psychology, 1,* 1–27.

Michell, J. (1990). *An introduction to the logic of psychological measurement.* Hillsdale, NJ: Lawrence Erlbaum Associates.

Milsevy, R. J. (1987). Recent developments in item response theory with implications for teacher certification. *Review of Educational Research, 14,* 239–275.

Mislevy, R. J. (1989). Foundations of a new test theory (ETS Research Report No. RR-89-52-ONR). Princeton, NJ: Educational Testing Service.

Narens, L. (1981). On the scales of measurement. *Journal of Mathematical Psychology, 24,* 249–275.

Narens, L., & Luce, R. D. (1986). Measurement: The theory of numerical assignments. *Psychological Bulletin, 99,* 166–180.

Poulton, E. C. (1968). The new psychophysics: Six models for magnitude estimation. *Psychological Bulletin, 69,* 1–19.

Rasch, G. (1966). An individualistic approach to item analysis. In P. F. Lazarsfeld & N. W. Henry (Eds.), *Readings in mathematical social science.* Chicago: Science Research Associates.

Roberts, F. S. (1970). On nontransitive indifference. *Journal of Mathematical Psychology, 7,* 243–258.

Roberts, F. S. (1971). Homogeneous families of semiorders and the theory of probabilistic consistency. *Journal of Mathematical Psychology, 8,* 248–263.

Scott, J. P. (1973). Comparative social psychology. In D. A. Dewsbury & D. A. Rethlingshafer (Eds.), *Comparative psychology: A modern survey.* New York: McGraw-Hill.

Shavelson, R. J., Webb, N. M., & Rowley, G. L. (1989). Generalizability theory. *American Psychologist, 44,* 922–932.

Shepard, R. N. (1962a). Analysis of proximities: Multidimensional scaling with an unknown distance function. I. *Psychometrika, 27,* 125–140.

Shepard, R. N. (1962b). Analysis of proximities: Multidimensional scaling with an unknown distance function. II. *Psychometrika, 27,* 219–246.

Shepard, R. N. (1974). Representation of structure in similarity data: Problems and prospects. *Psychometrika, 39,* 273–421.

Shepard, R. N., & Carroll, J. D. (1966). Parametric representation of nonlinear data structures. In P. R. Krishnaiah (Ed.), *Multivariate analysis* (Vol. 2). New York: Academic Press.

Siegel, S. (1956). *Nonparametric statistics.* New York: McGraw-Hill.

Siegel, S., & Castellan, N. J. (1988). *Nonparametric statistics for the behavioral sciences* (2nd ed.). New York: McGraw-Hill.

Sternberg, S. (1969). The discovery of processing stages: Extensions of Donder's method. *Acta Psychological, 30,* 276–313.

Stevens, S. S. (1951). Mathematics, measurement and psychophysics. In S. S. Stevens (Ed.), *Handbook of experimental psychology*. New York: Wiley.

Stevens, S. S. (1957). On the psychophysical law. *Psychological Review, 64*, 153–181.

Stevens, S. S. (1959). Measurement, psychophysics, and utility. In C. W. Churchman & P. Ratoosh (Eds.), *Measurement: Definitions and theories*. New York: Wiley.

Stevens, S. S. (1971). Issues in psychophysical measurement. *Psychological Review, 78*, 426–450.

Stevens, S. S. (1974). Perceptual magnitude and its measurement. In E. C. Carterette & M. P. Friedman (Eds.), *Handbook of perception* (Vol. 2). New York: Academic Press.

Stevens, S. S., & Galanter, E. H. (1957). Ratio scales and category scales for a dozen perceptual continua. *Journal of Experimental Psychology, 54*, 377–411.

Swets, J. A. (1986). Form of empirical ROCs in discrimination and diagnostic tasks: Implications for theory and measurement of performance. *Psychological Bulletin, 99*, 181–198.

Takane, Y., Young, F. W., & de Leeuw, J. (1977). Nonmetric individual differences multidimensional scaling: An alternating least squares method with optimal scaling features. *Psychometrika, 42*, 7–67.

Teghtsoonian, R. (1971). On the exponent in Stevens' law and the constant in Ekman's law. *Psychological Review, 78*, 71–80.

Torgerson, W. S. (1952). Multidimensional scaling: I. Theory and method. *Psychometrika, 17*, 401–419.

Torgerson, W. S. (1958). *Theory and methods of scaling*. New York: Wiley.

Torgerson, W. S., & Meuser, G. (1962). Informal notes on Torgerson and Meuser's program for multidimensional scaling. Department of Psychology, The John Hopkins University, mimeographed report.

Treisman, M. (1964). Sensory scaling and the psychophysical laws. *Quarterly Journal of Experimental Psychology, 16*, 11–22.

Tversky, A. (1967). A general theory of polynomial conjoint measurement. *Journal of Mathematical Psychology, 4*, 1–20.

Tversky, A., & Krantz, D. H. (1970). The dimensional representation and the metric structure of similarity data. *Journal of Mathematical Psychology, 7*, 572–596.

Wainer, H., Fairbank, D. T., & Hough, R. L. (1978). Predicting the impact of simple and compound life change events. *Applied Psychological Measurement, 2*, 313–322.

Weitzenhoffer, A. M. (n.d.). *Measurement, mathematics and reality*. Unpublished manuscript.

Young, F. W. (1972). A model for polynomial conjoint analysis algorithms. In R. N. Shepard, A. K. Romney, & S. B. Nerlove (Eds.), *Multidimensional scaling: Theory and applications in the behavioral sciences* (Vol. 1). New York: Seminar Press.

Young, F. W., & Torgerson, W. S. (1967). TORSCA, A FORTRAN IV program for Shepard–Kruskal multidimensional scaling analysis. *Behavioral Science, 12*, 498.

Zinnes, J. L. (1969). Scaling. *Annual Review of Psychology, 20*, 447–478.

4 Multidimensional Scaling

Lawrence E. Jones
Laura M. Koehly
University of Illinois at Urbana-Champaign

The inherent complexity of psychological processes and phenomena requires theories and methodologies that recognize and address this complexity. Decades of overreliance on univariate analysis of variance, unidimensional item analysis techniques, and unidimensional scaling methods has, in our opinion, led to oversimplified and incomplete understandings of social, cognitive, developmental, and behavioral processes and phenomena. Although conventional multivariate data analysis methods, for example factor analysis, have aided the definition and delineation of constructs measured via explicit item domains (e.g., personality and attitude), these methods have been of limited use in the measurement and modeling of domains where subjects' perceptions of stimuli and stimulus relationships have been the focus. For this class of problems, multidimensional scaling and related models are potentially very useful. They can be used to reveal and quantify the structure of complex stimulus domains, isolate and identify individual differences in perception, cognition, and preference, and measure changes in perceived structure over time, across subject populations, and experimental interventions.

Multidimensional scaling (MDS) techniques, including specialized methods for scaling of proximities and preferences and methods for the analysis of individual differences in perception and preference, are concerned with the spatial (or, more generally, geometric) representation of stimuli, individuals, and the relationships between stimuli and individuals. In the graphical depiction of the stimulus configuration (*map*) derived via scaling of proximities data, stimuli are represented as points in a space defined by a set of coordinate axes (*dimensions*), and perceived stimulus attributes are represented as directions or vectors through the spatial representation. In the case of multidimensional preference models, individuals are represented as points (*ideal points*) or vectors in the same space as the stimuli—a *joint space*. Other properties of, or responses to, the stimuli, including measurements of physical attributes (e.g., size, price, chemical composition), rated attributes (e.g., attractiveness, utility, taste qualities), and behavioral responses (e.g., choice frequency, discrimination accuracy, voting), may be related to the MDS-derived spatial representation using linear and nonlinear multiple regression and/or clustering procedures that locate these properties as vectors, planes, or subregions in the space. Likewise, for models that parameterize individuals, information about judges or respondents (e.g., attitudes, personality variables, behavioral responses to the stimulus domain) may be related to these model parameters, thereby identifying the correlates or sources of such differences.

In *The Theory of Data* (1964), Coombs started with the (deceptively) simple proposition that "data may be viewed as relations between points in a space" (p. 1); the taxonomy of data and data generation models that Coombs proposed served as an organizing and heuristic framework for extant psychometric and stimulus scaling models, as well as the wide variety of multidimensional proximity and preference scaling models that would be developed during the ensuing 25 years. Coombs' "data theory" provided formal definitions of similarity, preferential choice, and dominance data, the primary types of data that serve as input to the models considered in the present chapter. Also, he introduced the notion of a joint space wherein subjects and stimuli could be represented simultaneously. Coombs' work provided a general, formal framework that encouraged multidimensional modeling and spatial representation of stimulus domains, individual differences, and the conjunction of the two. Coombs' book, more than any other single source, provides a valuable introduction to the fundamental concepts and insights that underlie the models and methods covered in the present chapter.

OVERVIEW

This chapter introduces multidimensional scaling models, associated methods for selecting and interpreting solutions, and offers general advice on how to design and conduct research employing MDS methods. Recognizing that there are 20 or so texts and reference volumes covering the technical underpinnings of MDS models,[1] we decided to focus on conceptual and methodological issues surrounding the use of MDS models and to illustrate some of these models via a detailed account of the application of selected MDS methods to an empirical problem. In the exposition and discussion of this example, we detail and otherwise explore

---

[1]Texts that do a good job of presenting the technical aspects of MDS models include Kruskal and Wish (1978, two-way models), Arabie, Carroll, and DeSarbo (1987, three-way models), Coxon (1982), and Green, Carmone, and Smith (1989).

some considerations and issues that are rarely discussed in most texts or in typically abbreviated published accounts of research applying MDS methodology.

Before considering the example, however, we discuss (a) some of the basic ideas underlying MDS models; (b) two widely used models, nonmetric MDS and the weighted Euclidian model for INdividual Differences SCALing (INDSCAL); and (c) several methodological topics and problems that arise in research employing MDS techniques. These topics are introduced and discussed in the chronological order that the investigator would encounter them, starting with substantive, theoretical considerations, progressing through stimulus sampling and research design, data collection, and concluding with methods for systematic interpretation of results. Following the example, an application of MDS techniques to similarity judgments of schematic faces, the chapter concludes with brief reviews of a few specialized topics in scaling and a discussion of the strengths and limitations of MDS methodology.

BASIC CONCEPTS

Proximity and Similarity

The basic data for MDS are measures of proximity between pairs of objects or stimuli. The proximity measure reflects how closely the members of each pair of stimuli are psychologically related. In his seminal papers introducing nonmetric multidimensional scaling techniques for "the analysis of proximities," Shepard (1962a, 1962b) subsumed several types of data under the generic term *proximity,* including direct similarity ratings of stimulus pairs, measures of pairwise substitutability, confusion, association, mutual choice, disjunctive reaction time, and other indices based on rating, sorting, ranking, identification, and discrimination tasks. Likewise, indices of correlation, association, and co-occurrence derived from other types of data or tasks can be treated as (indirect) proximity measures.

In this chapter, δ_{ij} will be used to denote the proximity measure for any pair of stimuli (i, j), $i,j = 1, 2, \ldots n$ (number of stimuli). If the measure is constructed or scored so that the highest values of δ_{ij} correspond to stimulus pairs that are psychologically most alike or "closest," then δ_{ij} is a *similarity measure.* If the δ_{ij} is scored so that the highest values correspond to pairs that are least alike, then δ_{ij} is a measure of *dissimilarity.* For clarity and convenience, we typically use δ_{ij} to refer to dissimilarity data.

Extended treatments of the concept of (dis)similarity, and methods for assessing similarity, are given by Coombs (1964), Gregson (1975), Tversky (1977), and Davison (1983). Discussions of measures of similarity, association, and so forth, based on score profiles, sorting data, and joint/conditional probability measures, are provided by Cronbach and Gleser (1953), Arabie and Boorman (1973), Rosenberg (1982), Weisberg (1974), and Anderberg (1973).

Distance Functions

Multidimensional scaling models rely on the notion of a metric space in which relations on pairs of points, that is pairs of distances, are used to represent corresponding psychological measures of proximity between pairs of stimuli. MDS models capitalize on an analogy between the psychological concept of dissimilarity and the geometric concept of distance. Formally, the distance model for dissimilarity can be stated:

$$\delta_{ij} \simeq d_{ij} = \sqrt{\sum_{r=1}^{R} (x_{ir} - x_{jr})^2} \tag{1}$$

where

δ_{ij} is a measure of dissimilarity defined over all (i,j) pairs of stimuli,

d_{ij} is the distance between points i and j, and

x_{ir} and x_{jr} are the scale values of the stimuli along each of the R coordinate axes defining the space.

If the $(x_{ir} - x_{jr})$ differences are known, it is a simple matter to compute the distances between pairs of points. MDS methods, however, are concerned with the reverse problem: Given subjects' judgments about the dissimilarities between pairs of objects (δ_{ij}), MDS techniques work backward to discover both the number and the nature of the stimulus attributes or dimensions that were used to make those judgments, and to estimate the locations of the stimuli along those dimensions. The scale values are estimated by the MDS algorithm, and R, the dimensionality of the Euclidean space, is determined by the data analyst, based on model fit and interpretability considerations.

The coordinate axes defining the MDS-derived space are referred to as *dimensions,* with the scale values of a stimulus reflecting the quantities of these dimensions or attributes characterizing that stimulus. Equation 1 should be recognizable as the Euclidean distance function. Distances between pairs of points in a Euclidean space are invariant under translation of the origin of the space, reflection of axes, and rotation. Interpretation of MDS solutions/configurations is based on the ordinal and interval properties of stimulus scale values, thus the rotational invariance property implies that *any* direction through the space is potentially meaningful. Although other distance functions (e.g., the Minkowski metrics[2]) can be assumed in nonmetric MDS (Kruskal 1964a, 1964b), in practice such metrics are rarely used. Hubert and Arabie (1988) developed a method employing combinatorial optimization for fitting the city block metric in the unidimensional case, that is when $R = 1$.

MDS MODELS

Following the terminology introduced by Tucker (1960) and elaborated by Carroll and Arabie (1980) in their review of MDS and related models, scaling techniques can be classified according to the order, identities, and number of the data matrices input to the analysis. A single, symmetric, matrix of dissimilarities ($_n\Delta_n$) is *two-way* because it has rows and columns for its two "ways." It is one *mode* because both ways correspond to the same set of stimuli. Thus, an MDS model with Δ as input can be said to involve the analysis of "one-mode, two-way" data. If each of N subjects judges all pairs of stimuli, we will have a set of dissimilarity matrices, Δ_k, $k = 1, 2, \ldots, N$, or a data "cube." The addition of the extra mode, that is subjects, gives us a two-mode, three-way data array.

A typical MDS analysis starts with one or more matrices of proximities data and derives from these data a spatial (usually Euclidean) representation wherein points represent stimuli, and distances between pairs of points reflect perceived dissimilarities between the corresponding pairs of stimuli. The number and identities of the coordinate axes defining the space, and the projections of stimulus points on these axes (the scale values) often reveal something about the attributes that the respondents utilized in perceiving and judging the stimuli, as well as insights about the parent population from which the stimuli were sampled. As noted earlier, other kinds of information about the stimuli may be collected and then related to the derived configuration. The results of these auxiliary analyses can be used for informing a decision about the dimensionality of the configuration and interpreting the component dimensions underlying the configuration. Generalizations and elaborations of the basic MDS model

---

[2]The Euclidean distance function (Equation 1) is a special case of the Minkowski distance function:

$$d_{ij} = \left(\sum_{r=1}^{R} |x_{ir} - x_{jr}|^p \right)^{1/p} \qquad p \geq 1.$$

When $p = 1$, we have the *city block* metric; when $p = 2$, we have the familiar Euclidean metric; and when $p = \infty$, the distance between points i and j equals the largest dimension-wise difference, i.e.,

$$d_{ij} = \max_r |x_{ir} - x_{jr}|.$$

have been developed to investigate individual differences in perception and cognition, changes in perception over time, situations, and so forth, and relationships of the derived stimulus structure to other types of judgments, for example, preferences.

In subsequent sections, we present applications of two widely used MDS programs: the KYST (Kruskal, Young, & Seery, 1977) implementation of nonmetric MDS, and the SINDSCAL (Pruzansky, 1975) implementation of the Individual Differences Scaling (INDSCAL) or weighted Euclidean model. Before discussing the examples, we consider the models themselves, their assumptions, and some problems related to estimation of model parameters.

Metric MDS

Building on earlier work by Richardson (1938) and Klingberg (1941), Torgerson (1952) developed a metric multidimensional scaling technique. His method starts with ratings or other estimates of the psychological distances (δ_{ij}'s) among pairs of stimuli and assumes that these data are linearly related to the model-derived distances (d_{ij}'s). Depending on the data collection task, an *additive constant* estimation procedure is used to convert the original data into quantities that are more like distances. The resulting quantities are converted to an $n \times n$ matrix of scalar products (see footnote 4) between the points, interpreted as vectors emanating from the geometric centroid of the points. On the basis of the Young and Householder (1938) theorems, the scalar products matrix is factored into its eigenvalues and eigenvectors. The number of large, positive eigenvalues is taken as the dimensionality of the Euclidean space of the stimuli and the corresponding eigenvectors are the estimates of the stimulus scale values. Although the metric MDS model is rarely used by itself, some modern MDS programs, including KYST, can use a modified metric scaling solution as a starting point for the iterative estimation procedures they employ.

Nonmetric MDS

Nonmetric multidimensional scaling, as originally proposed by Shepard (1962a, 1962b) and refined by Kruskal (1964a, 1964b), refers to a model that assumes a monotonic relationship between the input dissimilarity measures (δ_{ij}) and the interpoint distances (d_{ij}) derived by the solution algorithm. Most computer programs available for estimating these distances, and associated scale values (x_{ir}'s), use an iterative procedure, the method of steepest descent, that systematically adjusts the coordinates of the (stimulus) points to achieve a progressively closer approximation to the underlying monotonic function. The fit measure ordinarily employed by KYST-2A, the program used herein, is Kruskal's "Stress-1," a measure of departure from monotonicity:

$$S_1 = \sqrt{\frac{\sum_{i<j} (d_{ij} - \hat{d}_{ij})^2}{\sum_{i<j} d_{ij}^2}} \qquad (2)$$

Stress is a "badness-of-fit" measure, with the numerator being a residual sums-of-squares of departures of model-derived distance estimates (i.e., the d_{ij}'s) from the $\hat{d}_{ij}$'s, a set of quantities that are monotonically related to the original data, that is, the δ_{ij}'s. The denominator normalizes the measure by a scaling factor representing the size of the configuration. When $S_1 = 0$, the (monotonic or ordinal) agreement between model parameters and the data is perfect. Values larger than 0 reflect ordinal disagreement between the data and the model distances, that is, departure from monotonicity. The derived solution for a given dimensionality R (i.e., set of scale values, $_nX_r$, and corresponding distances, $_nD_n$) is the one that yields the smallest stress. The desired overall solution is the one with dimensionality R such that solutions at dimensionalities $R + 1$ and higher lead to no appreciable improvement in stress.

Normally the input to KYST is a single symmetric, two-way, one-mode proximity matrix containing data collected from one individual, or group data that have been averaged (or otherwise aggregated) to form a single matrix. Alternatively, several matrices may be input, but KYST treats these as replications, differing only in terms of measurement error.

Other features and options available in KYST include: (a) the ability to handle missing data; (b) choice among various continuous functions relating distances to proximities (including linear, which constitutes the traditional metric MDS model); (c) choice among members of the family of distance functions subsumed by the Minkowski metric; and (d) ability to perform unfolding analysis based on preferential choice or other preference strength measures. The application presented later illustrates the most common use of KYST, for nonmetric scaling of a single proximity matrix using the Euclidean spatial distance model.

INDSCAL

For some classes of problems, the investigator may wish to explore and identify individual differences in perceptions of the stimulus domain. The desired representation of stimulus structure, identification of the dimensions underlying subjects' perceptions of the stimuli, and estimates of the relative saliences of these dimensions, are given by individual differences multidimensional scaling analysis of the set of the three-way, two-mode (dis)similarities data. The INDSCAL model (Carroll & Chang, 1970) is the most widely used procedure of this type. In the representation of the perceived stimulus structure derived by INDSCAL, stimuli are represented by points embedded in a R-dimensional space, where distances between points represent perceived dissimilarities among the stimuli. The coordinate axes defining this space are assumed to correspond to fundamental attributes underlying subjects' perceptions or judgments of the stimuli. Also, the analysis derives for each individual judge, a set of weights representing the relative *saliences* of the R dimensions for that judge. The matrix of weights summarizes information about differences among judges in a quantitative form that can be related to independently assessed demographic, sociometric, personality, or other individual differences variables.

More formally, the INDSCAL model assumes (a) a set of R dimensions underlying all subjects' perceptions of the n stimuli (the *group stimulus space*), and (b) a particular subject k's dissimilarity judgments (or more generally, a set of proximities arising from data "source" k) are linearly related to a weighted Euclidean distance in the group space. Specifically, for the kth judge, the weighted Euclidean distance between stimuli i and j is given by

$$d_{ij}^{(k)} = \sqrt{\sum_{r=1}^{R} w_{kr}(x_{ir} - x_{jr})^2} \qquad (3)$$

where

w_{kr} is the salience weight assigned by subject k to dimension r,

x_{ir} and x_{jr} are the scale values of stimuli i and j along coordinate axis r,

$i, j = 1, 2, \ldots, n$, and

$k = 1, 2, \ldots, N$.

This formula is the same as the formula for Euclidean distance (Equation 1) except for the presence of the weighting term w_{kr}. Looking at this space in a slightly different way, it is an ordinary Euclidean space with coordinates:

$$y_{jr}^{(k)} = \sqrt{w_{kr}}\, x_{jr}. \qquad (4)$$

It is a space in which the configuration has been expanded or contracted differentially for each judge, but only along the directions defined by the coordinate axes.

The x_{jr}'s in Equations 3 and 4 are the coordinates of the *group stimulus space*, ${}_n\mathbf{X}_r$. The *dimensions* (columns of $\mathbf{X}$) of this space indicate those characteristics of the stimuli that were used in making (dis)similarity judgments. It is important to realize that the orientations of the coordinate axes of this space are not arbitrary as in Euclidean space, but are fixed. No rotation is permitted because of the judges' weights; any rotation would require solving for a new set of weights and would decrease the goodness of fit of the model to the data. For this reason the scale values along each component dimension of the solution space should be directly interpretable.[3]

---

[3]In practice, "mild" rotations of the coordinate axes may lead to more interpretable dimensions, with a negligible effect on overall model fit.

A second important aspect, as noted earlier, is the several individual stimulus spaces ($\mathbf{Y}^k$). Each of these individual stimulus spaces is the group space as "seen" by subject k. Each $\mathbf{Y}^k$ space is related to the underlying group stimulus space $\mathbf{X}$ by subject weights $\mathbf{W}$. Conceptually the individual stimulus space $\mathbf{Y}^k$ differs from the group stimulus space $\mathbf{X}$ in having each of its axes stretched or shrunk. The order of the stimuli on each dimension of each individual space is the same as the order for corresponding dimensions of the group space. The spacing of the stimuli varies, but the order does not. This does not, however, imply that the order of the distances among stimuli in the various individual spaces is fixed. The order of the distances depends on the weights involved, and these may vary from judge to judge.

A third important aspect of the INDSCAL model is the matrix of subject weights $\mathbf{W}$. This matrix represents the importance or salience of the various dimensions to the various judges. The weights range from 0 to 1. If a particular dimension is not used by judges in their perceptions, they will have a weight of 0 for that dimension. If, on the other hand, a dimension is very important for a certain judge, the *ratio* of that dimension's weight to the other weights will be large. Each judge's set of weights corresponds to a vector in the weight space extending from the origin of the space. The distance of the judge's point from the origin approximately corresponds to the amount of variance accounted for in the judge's data. If a judge's weights are all zero, then no variance is accounted for. That judge's data do not correspond to the model at all. The other extreme is where the sum of squared weights for a given judge is unity. That judge's data correspond perfectly to the model. Note, however, that the direction of judge k's weight vector determines the structure of individual space $\mathbf{Y}^k$. If two judges' weight vectors are perfectly aligned, though not the same length, then the structure of their individual spaces will be identical, except for size.

The input for INDSCAL (and other individual differences scaling models) consists of a set of N symmetric matrices of dissimilarity judgments, each $n \times n$. The output consists of estimates of scale values, x_{jr} for stimuli, each reflecting the amount of attribute r attributed to stimulus j; and estimates of subject weights, w_{kr}, interpreted as reflecting the saliences or importances of the r attributes.

The fit statistic used by the INDSCAL algorithm is essentially a (squared) correlation between $b_{ij,k}$, the scalar products computed from the data,[4] and $\hat{b}_{ij,k}$, the scalar products based on the point coordinates estimated by the model. Specifically, the VAF (Variance Accounted For) measure is

---

[4]The scalar product (b_{ij}) between any two points i and j is defined as:

$$b_{ij} = \sum_{r=1}^{R} x_{ir}x_{jr}$$

where x_{ir} and x_{jr} are coordinates of the points, as defined previously. Geometrically, a scalar product is the cosine of the angle between two vectors emanating from the origin of the coordinate system and terminating at points i and j, multiplied by the product of their lengths.

$$VAF = 1 - \frac{\sum_i \sum_j \sum_k (b_{ij,k} - \hat{b}_{ij,k})^2}{\sum_i \sum_j \sum_k (b_{ij,k} - b_{...k})^2}, \tag{5}$$

where $b_{...k}$ is the mean of all scalar products between objects i and j ($i \neq j$) for source k. Thus, when $VAF = 0$ the model does not fit the data at all, and when $VAF = 1$ the fit is perfect. In contrast to STRESS, a badness-of-fit measure, VAF indexes goodness-of-fit, and increases as the fit to the data improves.

RESEARCH DESIGN, DATA COLLECTION, AND INTERPRETATION

A typical multidimensional scaling study involves the collection of three or four types of data: (a) (dis)similarity judgments, or another type of proximity measure, for all pairs of stimuli; (b) objective measures of the stimuli, when feasible, for example, price, physical measurements, and so forth; (c) ratings of the stimuli, along unidimensional attribute (or "property") scales, for example, traits, sensory or perceptual attributes, affective reactions, and so forth; and (d) information about the respondents, for example, personality traits, attitudes, demographic characteristics, and familiarity or experience with the stimuli. Information of the last three types is used as an aid to interpretation of the dimensions and configuration derived via MDS of the dissimilarities data, and to explore or identify individual and group differences in perception or construal of the stimuli.

Stimulus Selection

Unless it is feasible to incorporate an entire population of stimuli into the design of an MDS study, decisions about their number (n) and method of selection are crucial. Most scaling studies employ pairwise combinations of stimuli, and the number of pairs increases geometrically with n, that is, the number of distinct pairs is $[n(n-1)/2]$, so it is desirable to keep the number of stimuli small ($n = 10$–25) to hold judges' interest. On the other hand, n must be sufficiently large to include a representative sample of the parent stimulus domain. Also, if the (anticipated) number of dimensions is large, n must be proportionately larger to result in a stable solution. It is important to realize that in the multiple regression procedures that are used to identify the dimensions resulting from the scaling analysis, the number of stimuli (n) not the number of judges (N), is the effective sample size for the analysis, and the basis for determining degrees of freedom for the associated significance test. Finally, the selected sample of stimuli has a strong influence on the number and identities of the dimensions resulting from the scaling analyses. Thus, if the selected sample is not representative of the parent population, conclusions about the dimensions underlying perceptions of the stimuli will be invalid, or at least incomplete. The requirement here is completely parallel to that dictating careful selection of test items in factor analytic research on domains such as attitudes, abilities, or personalities.

In exploratory research where the emphasis is on identification of the major dimensions underlying perceptions of the stimulus domain, and where the population of stimuli is well defined, random selection of stimuli is a reasonable approach. In investigations where both the number and identities of stimulus dimensions are well established by prior research, and the purpose of the research is precise calibration of stimuli or confirmation of a predicted structure, a more systematic stratified or cluster sampling approach should be used.

Number of Stimuli

The most common method for collecting proximities data involves presentation of the $n(n-1)/2$ pairwise combinations of the n stimuli, omitting pairings of stimuli with themselves. Typically, each pair is judged along a 5- to 20-point category scale ranging from "Very Similar" to "Very Dissimilar." These data are entered into a square, symmetric matrix, one for each subject (or other data source), with the diagonal missing. The cells of each subject's data matrix will contain measures of proximity or dissimilarity, δ_{ij}, for each pair of stimuli. The data are assumed to be symmetric (i.e., $\delta_{ij} = \delta_{ji}$), thus only the lower triangular portion of the full matrix is required for input to most MDS programs.

In general, n should be large relative to the number of dimensions to be retained. Specifically, the number of data points, ($[n(n-1/2]$, if all distinct pairs are presented) should be large relative to the number of parameters estimated, that is, there are $R \times n$ scale values estimated in a one-mode, two-way MDS, where R is the number of dimensions. Green, Carmone, and Smith (1987), based on a review of other investigators' recommendations, concluded that 4 to 6 stimuli per dimension may be adequate. Kruskal and Wish (1978) suggested that the number of dimensions, R, should not exceed $(n-1)/4$. Davison (1983) recommended that n should be equal to or larger than $40 \times [R/(n - 1)]$.

In the example presented later, results of a nonmetric MDS of 12 stimuli in 4 dimensions is reported, a situation where the number of stimuli is less than the prescribed numbers dictated by these authors (Davison, $n \geq 15$; Kruskal and Wish, $n \geq 17$; Green et al., $n = 16-24$). Although these authors' guidelines may be reasonable for typical applications, we believe that under certain conditions (e.g., extremely reliable dissimilarities data) their prescriptions may be too conservative.

Data Collection Tasks

Once researchers have selected the stimuli, they must decide which data collection technique to use. If the stimulus set is relatively small, presenting all pairwise comparisons to the subject is feasible and desirable. However, when the stimulus set is large, researchers must consider (a) task length—for example, 40 stimuli will yield $40(39)/2 = 780$ pairwise comparisons; (b) subjects' capabilities and responses to the task—for example, fatigue and boredom; and (c) nature of the stimuli—for example, auditory, semantic, or geographic stimuli may suggest different task considerations. A discussion of the many types of tasks that have been proposed is beyond the scope of this chapter. However, a few of the most widely used data collection methods are presented.

Sorting.   Sorting is a data collection technique that allows subjects to partition a set of stimuli into categories based on their similarity, or relatedness. This procedure provides co-occurrence data that can be used as a direct measure of similarity, or from which indirect estimates of psychological distances between the stimuli can be calculated. Sorting techniques can be grouped according to three dichotomies (Rosenberg, 1982): (a) single sort versus multiple sort, (b) restricted sort versus unrestricted sort, and (c) fixed sort versus free sort.

A *single sort task* allows the subject to group the stimuli only once. *Multiple sorts,* on the other hand, permit the subject to sort the stimuli more than once using different criteria on each sort. On each sort, the subject begins the procedure anew, so that the previous partition should not directly affect the subject's subsequent grouping. *Restricted sorting* tasks confine the subject to using each stimulus only once. In contrast, *unrestricted sorting* permits the subject to place a stimulus in more than one group. Finally, in a *fixed sort* procedure, the subject is asked to sort objects into a specified number of categories. The *free sort* allows subjects to sort the objects into as many categories as they wish. The experimenter may or may not choose to place an upper limit on the number of categories that may be used by the subject.

The major advantage to using sorting procedures over other dissimilarities data collection techniques is efficiency. Subjects can make judgments about a large set of objects in a relatively short period of time. Collecting data through the direct rating of a large number of pairs can severely test subjects patience and motivation. Thus sorting tasks may be advantageous when large stimulus sets are required. The preparation of the data collection paraphernalia when using sorting methods is simpler than for other data collection techniques (i.e., pairwise comparisons, method of triads, etc.). Furthermore, sorting, just as pairwise comparison tasks, does not involve prior specification of the dimensions or attributes of the stimuli to be used as a basis for judgments. In other words, subjects' categorizations are uncontaminated by the researcher's theory or preconceptions.

However, sorting may not be the ideal data-gathering tool for all possible structures or in all situations. It has been found that there is good agreement between sorting and pairwise comparisons only in lower dimensions of a multidimensional scaling solution (Rosenberg, 1982). Sorting data are not generally appropriate for examination of individual differences; the data for any single subject are too sparse in information about the magnitude of stimulus similarities and differences. An example of when sorting tasks are appropriate is in the area of kinship terminology. Rosenberg's results (1982) suggest that kinship terms can easily and quickly be sorted into distinct categories. Sorting methods may be difficult to use and inappropriate in some situations; for example, sorting auditory stimuli would be virtually impossible. Interactive ordering algorithms (Young & Cliff, 1972; Young, Null, Sarle, & Hoffman, 1982) or cyclic designs (David, 1963), which select a manageable subset of pairs to be presented, may be more appropriate in circumstances where large stimulus sets are concerned.

Cyclic Designs.   If pairwise comparisons for large stimulus sets are needed, some manageable subset of the $n(n-1)/2$ pairs must be presented to subjects. Young and Cliff (1972) designed an interactive scaling program that obtains a subset of judgments, not determined a priori, but selected according to subjects' previous responses. However, this method of data collection is constrained on the subjects' mode of response. Spence and Domoney (1974) suggested that a subset of stimulus pairs should be chosen in advance according to an explicit experimental design. They examined four types of stimulus designs: random designs, overlapping clique designs, and two varieties of cyclic designs. A high efficiency cyclic design outperformed all other designs; however, random selection of stimulus pairs performed almost as well.

A simple method of constructing cyclic paired comparison designs was proposed by David (1963). David's algorithm involves three steps:

1. Designate the stimuli 0, 1, 2, 3, 4, . . . , $(n-1)$, where n is the number of stimuli.
2. Consider the cyclic sets $\{s\}$: (0, s), (1, $s + 1$), (2, $s + 2$), . . . , (t, $s + t$), . . . ($n - 1$, $s + n-1$), where $t = 0, 1, 2, . . . , (n-1)$. Each cyclic set contains n pairs of stimuli.
3. Combine the desired number of cyclic sets to form a cyclic design.

With $n = 12$ as an example,

1. The stimuli are numbered 0, 1, 2, 3, . . . , 11.
2. The cyclic sets $\{1\}$, $\{3\}$, and $\{5\}$ are:

$\{1\} = \{(0,1), (1,2), (2,3), (3,4), (4,5), (5,6), (6,7), (7,8), (8,9), (9,10),$
$(10,11), (11,0)\}$

$\{3\} = \{(0,3), (1,4), (2,5), (3,6), (4,7), (5,8), (6,9), (7,10), (8,11), (9,0),$
$(10,1), (11,2)\}$

$\{5\} = \{(0,5), (1,6), (2,7), (3,8), (4,9), (5,10), (6,11), (7,0), (8,1), (9,2),$
$(10,3), (11,4)\}$

3. All the pairwise comparisons in the sets $\{1\}$, $\{3\}$, and $\{5\}$ are included in the resulting cyclic design; that is, $\{1, 3, 5\} = \{1\} + \{3\} + \{5\}$.

When creating a cyclic design, the number of cyclic sets to be included in the design must be determined. Spence (1982) suggested that the minimum number of pairs in the design should be $3 \times n \times R$. This number depends on the unknown dimensionality of the space; therefore, the investigator must make a conservative estimate of the number of dimensions (R) that is expected. The minimum number of judgments ($3nR$) implies that the cyclic design consists of at least $6R$ cyclic sets. The conjunction of the cyclic sets may exhibit a perceptible pattern, so the entire sequence should be randomly permuted before presentation to the subjects.

Once the number of sets to be included in the cyclic design is established, the investigator needs to create a design with high *global connectedness*. Connectedness can be indicated by design efficiency and the number of triangles in the design graph (Spence, 1982). Efficiency represents the proportion of variance in the complete stimulus design which is explained by the incomplete design. Monte Carlo studies suggest that higher efficiency designs, or designs with fewer triangles, outperform others. Algorithms for high efficiency designs can be found in Spence (1982).

Reliability. Inasmuch as individual differences multidimensional scaling models, and especially multidimensional unfolding models, are sensitive to unreliability in judgments, it is important to provide for assessments of reliability of similarity and preference judgments in the research design. A simple and conservative reliability estimate is given by the correlation between judgments of 10 to 15 repeated pairs of representative stimuli (e.g., Nygren & Jones, 1977). These estimates may then be used to screen subjects and as a basis for inferring the relative contributions of systematic individual differences versus unreliability to total variance accounted for by the model. For sorting or ranking methods, there is no efficient method for checking reliability, short of asking the subjects to replicate their rankings or sorts.

Monte Carlo Methods for Assessing Dimensionality

Monte Carlo simulation methods are employed to solve statistical problems where a complete mathematical solution would be impractical or impossible. Monte Carlo studies involve the process of analyzing several sets of data generated randomly, or according to some a priori distribution. The hypotheses being tested via the Monte Carlo study guide the experimental design. For example, if the effects of measurement error in the dissimilarities to be scaled are being investigated, then different levels of error would be introduced into the simulated data. However, being designed experiments, simulation studies are susceptible to various pitfalls, such as inadequate experimental design, sloppy execution, or inappropriate or invalid data analysis.

Spence (1983) reviewed Monte Carlo simulation studies of both two-way and three-way multidimensional models. The mathematics behind two-way multidimensional scaling in the metric situation (Torgerson, 1952) are well understood, and analytically feasible. Thus, few simulation studies examining the two-way metric model have been conducted. Nonmetric two-way scaling, however, involves an iterative procedure which is subject to local optimum problems and sensitive to ties in the data. Thus, Monte Carlo methods have been used to investigate the behavior of these models with different "starting configurations" (Arabie, 1973) and proportions of ties. In the three-way scaling model, both the metric and the nonmetric problems involve iterative processes; thus, these models are not analytically solvable and simulation studies have been used to understand their properties. The bulk of simulation research examines empirical sampling distributions of fit indices, such as Stress (Klahr, 1969; Spence, 1979; Spence & Olgivie, 1973), compares algorithms of computer programs (Lingoes & Roskam, 1973; Ramsey, 1977; Spence, 1972), or explores basic features of MDS methods, such as the effects of error, dimensionality, and/or the number of stimuli (Carroll & Chang, 1970; Cohen & Jones, 1974; MacCallum, 1977; MacCallum & Cornellus, 1977; Young, 1970).

A perfect nonmetric MDS solution, with a Stress value of zero, is obtained when the number of dimensions retained is equal to two less than the number of objects being scaled. Stress should always decrease as the number of dimensions increases. So, how does one assess what Stress value is best? The smallest value does not necessarily indicate the best solution. Spence and Olgivie (1973) examined this question via Monte Carlo methodology. They studied the behavior of Stress-1 under the null hypothesis that the observed dissimilarities are essentially random. Unfortunately, this null hypothesis is a rather weak one; in practice, the dissimilarities will rarely possess the properties of random data. Consequently, the null hypothesis may be rejected even though the resulting configuration may be neither good nor useful. Nevertheless, results from these studies provide a conservative, useful baseline for evaluating model fit and solution dimensionality.

Multidimensional scaling can be thought of as a descriptive technique for representing data. In order to use this methodology, the correct dimensionality of the structure must be ascertained. Stress by dimension plots can be examined for indications of an "elbow", that is, the point on the plot where subsequent changes in Stress are relatively small. The obtained "badness-of-fit" measure at the elbow can be compared with appropriate Monte Carlo baseline values for the relevant number of stimuli using, for example, tables produced by Spence and Olgivie

(1973). However, Stress is not the only means available for assessing solution dimensionality. The configuration of points should be examined and interpreted; are the dimensions meaningful? Property Vector Fitting may aid in the interpretation of the dimensions. Besides interpretability, ease of use is an important factor in determining how many dimensions to retain. A seven-dimensional solution is impossible to visualize, difficult to comprehend, and generally not very useful. Finally, the solution must be stable. Can the findings be replicated? If one subject's judgments are withheld from analysis, will the same configuration of points emerge? Jackknifing and bootstrapping techniques (Efron, 1979; Tukey, 1958; Weinberg, Carroll & Cohen, 1984) can be used to establish whether the solution is stable. Goodness-of-fit, interpretability, ease of use, and stability are all important considerations in determining the dimensionality of a MDS solution.

Property Vector Fitting

Social and behavioral science theories often postulate one or more specific dimensions whereby subjects perceive, construe, judge, classify, or discriminate among stimuli. For example, the James–Lange theory of emotion postulates that emotion is primarily a form of instinctive behavior where bodily reactions are accompanied by emotion-producing perceptions, be they sights, sounds, or ideas. This theory suggests that the appraisal of some situation and the resulting bodily arousal yield the emotion. Thus, one might expect two dimensions representing appraisal and arousal to emerge in a multidimensional scaling of schematic faces. As predicted by the James–Lange theory, two dimensions have consistently emerged as defining the multidimensional space of the perception of emotion from faces, namely Pleasantness ("Appraisal") and Level of Arousal (Abelson & Sermat, 1962; Schlosberg, 1952, 1954). Similarly, in psychophysical research involving complex stimuli, the investigator typically postulates a correspondence between psychological attributes of the stimuli (e.g., brightness, hue) and corresponding physical characteristics (e.g., luminance, wavelength). Property Vector Fitting (PVF) can be used to verify the presence and relevance of these hypothesized dimensions.

In property vector fitting, the investigator's hypotheses or hunches about stimulus attributes that should be relevant (or irrelevant) to judges in general, individuals, or to subgroups of judges, are represented by appropriately designed category rating scales, a set of nominal categories (e.g., male, female), or variables describing objective characteristics of the stimuli. If the construct embodied in a property scale is salient for the designated individual or subgroup, and assuming that stimulus differences along the attribute are taken into account in judging or assessing similarity, then ratings of stimuli on that scale should be predictable from the MDS-derived configuration. As a special case, if a coordinate axis of a solution is psychologically meaningful, then an appropriate, independently measured property scale should have a high zero-order correlation with the projections of stimuli (i.e., scale values) on that axis.

As described later, multiple regression procedures are used to test the hypothesis and to describe the nature and strength of the linear relationship between the perceived stimulus structure and the attribute scale(s).[5] The regression analysis locates a vector corresponding to each property scale in the stimulus space, such that projections of points representing stimuli on that vector and ratings of those stimuli are maximally correlated. If the correlation is high, then there is a close relationship between mean ratings on the attribute and projections of points representing stimuli; a low correlation indicates that no (linear) direction through the space corresponds to the obtained ratings. Thus, the multiple correlation associated with each vector can be considered as an indirect measure of the salience or relevance of the independently measured attribute for the subgroup or individual whose ratings were used to locate the vector. The location of the vector relative to dimensions of the MDS space, and its position relative to other vectors, provide important information for interpreting the meaning of an MDS configuration for the subject(s). When the construct of interest is represented by nominal categories rather than ordinal or interval attribute measures, a multiple discriminant analysis (Tatsuoka, 1971), with the MDS solution coordinates matrix as "predictors" and the category memberships of stimuli as the "grouping" variable, would be used instead. This analysis locates regions in the MDS space corresponding to stimulus categories and, like the regression-based PVF method, allows inferences about subgroup differences.

Although PVF procedures have been employed in a wide variety of investigations as a means of interpreting MDS solutions, their utility for testing hypotheses about individual and subgroup differences in construct salience has not been widely recognized. Using PVF procedures, it is possible to locate vectors for two or more subgroups of subjects whose attribute scale values refer to the same rating scale, but where the meaning or interpretation of the scale might differ across individuals or groups. For example, in a study of Black-White differences in face perception (Jones & Hirschberg, 1975), separate scales of face attractiveness were derived for Black and White subjects; vectors corresponding to these scales ran in different directions through the (common) MDS-derived stimulus space. This result reflected the fact that the criteria for judging attractiveness by Blacks and Whites were systematically different.

Thus, PVF methods can be used to: (a) interpret MDS solutions, (b) help decide how many dimensions to retain, and (c) investigate hypotheses about individual and subgroup differences in perception and judgment. The correlation

---

[5]Discussions of methods for fitting property vectors and other methods for systematic interpretation of MDS solutions are given by Kruskal and Wish (1978), Shepard (1972), and Borg and Lingoes (1979). Early examples of the application of property vector fitting to test psychological theories include Cliff and Young (1968), and Hanno and Jones (1973).

and regression procedures used to fit property vectors employ the $n \times R$ matrix (**X**) of MDS-derived scale values as predictors and one (or more) column vectors of stimulus attribute ratings or other measurements (the "properties") as the criterion variable(s).

The relationships between the MDS configuration and a property scale can be represented geometrically by locating a vector corresponding to the scale such that the stimulus projections, P_i, on the vector, correspond as closely as possible, in a least-squares sense, to the mean ratings of the stimuli on the external scale. The location of the desired vector is established by a linear regression of the form:

$$P_i = w_1 x_{i1} + w_2 x_{i2} + \cdots + w_r x_{ir} + \cdots + w_R x_{iR} + a \qquad (6)$$

$$i = 1, 2, \ldots, n \text{ (stimuli)}$$

where

x_{ir} is the coordinate value of the ith stimulus on the rth coordinate axis,

w_r is the regression weight of the rth axis (dimension), and

a is an additive constant.

If the mean attribute ratings are transformed to deviation scores and if the scale values (i.e., columns of **X**) are centered at zero, then (a) the vector corresponding to the property scale will intersect the origin of the MDS space, and (b) the direction cosines of the desired vector are given by:

$$c_r = \frac{w_r}{\sqrt{\displaystyle\sum_{r=1}^{R} w_r^2}} \qquad (7)$$

where c_r is the desired cosine of the angle between the vector and the rth coordinate axis. A detailed example, applying PVF methods to KYST and SINDSCAL solutions, is presented in the next section.

The Chang and Carroll (1968) PROFIT program can be used for property vector fitting via linear multiple regression, as well as by a more general method based on optimizing an index of nonlinear correlation. PROFIT has plotting facilities that plot property vectors against one another and against the coordinate axes of the stimulus space.

SCHEMATIC FACES EXAMPLE

Schematic faces have been widely used as stimuli in research on judgment (Tversky, 1977), perception (Brunswik, 1956), concept formation, and memory because their physical features can be designated, controlled, and manipulated very easily. Statisticians have employed schematic faces to portray variation and covariation in multivariate (e.g., objects × variables) data sets (Chernoff, 1971). There is a close psychophysical correspondence between physical features of these faces and certain judged attributes (e.g., variations in mouth curvature correspond to judged differences in happiness), consequently the first author used schematic face data in class data collection and analysis exercises to illustrate the application of MDS to problems in multidimensional psychophysics and social judgment. The similarity and attribute data that are utilized in the following examples were collected from members of the first author's graduate seminar in multidimensional scaling during the last several years.

Methods

Stimuli. Twelve faces were constructed to vary on three attributes: (a) face shape: oval, round; (b) eye color: light, dark; and (c) mouth curvature: down-turned, flat, upturned. The combinations of these three attributes (i.e., 2 × 2 × 3) formed a product set of 12 distinct faces as shown in Fig. 4.1. Other than noting that these features correspond to generally salient characteristics of human faces, and they typify the sort of faces used in other perceptual research, not much else can be said about the parent stimulus population. However, the feature levels were chosen to be clearly discriminable and to represent a wide range along corresponding psychological dimensions, for example, happiness.

Data Collection. The experimental session consisted of three parts: (a) in-

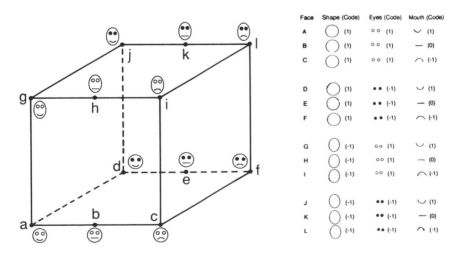

FIG. 4.1. Stimulus design matrix for the 12 schematic faces.

structions and preview; (b) pairwise dissimilarities judgments; and (c) ratings of faces on specific unidimensional attribute scales.

The instructions for the similarity judgment task were as follows:

Dissimilarity Rating Instructions

This experiment concerns how people perceive facial expressions. You will be presented with pairs of simple, schematic faces. Your task is to rate how similar or dissimilar each pair of faces seems to you using the following nine-point scale:

```
    1       2       3       4       5       6       7       8       9
 / -------- / -------- / -------- / -------- / -------- / -------- / -------- / -------- /
   Very                                                              Very
  Similar                                                          Dissimilar
```

The most similar pair(s) should be rated "1" and the most dissimilar pair(s) should be rated "9." Try to use all the numbers, "1" through "9." You should base your judgments of similarity on any characteristics that seem relevant, but you should use the same attributes for judging all pairs. Do not spend too much time on any one pair; instead, form an overall impression of the similarity or dissimilarity of the faces in each pair and then promptly make your judgment.

Before beginning the task, you will be presented with fifteen preview pairs that include the entire set of faces. These example pairs contain some of the most similar and most dissimilar pairs and should give you an idea of the range of differences you will encounter.

Each preview pair will be presented for five seconds. Although you will not record ratings for these pairs, you should form a general impression of how similar or dissimilar each pair of faces is. When you are ready to view the preview pairs, press "Enter."

Following the instructions, subjects were shown a representative subset of 15 pairs. The preview pairs were selected to: (a) contain all 12 stimuli; (b) be representative of the whole set of pairs; and (c) to span the range of anticipated similarity-dissimilarity, that is, anchor the subject's rating scale.

Then, subjects were given all 66 possible pairwise combinations of the 12 schematic faces and asked to rate each pair along the nine-point category scale. Pairs were presented in a "Ross order" (Ross, 1934), an ordering and arrangement of pairs that controls for time and space effects by locating each stimulus so that (a) it is equally spaced relative to its other occurrences throughout the ordering, and (b) each stimulus appears as the first member in one-half of the pairs and as the second member of the remaining pairs.

The schematic faces were presented, one pair at a time, on a monochrome, high-resolution CRT display. Subjects entered their ratings using the "1" through "9" keys on the numeric row of the computer keyboard. Following each judg-

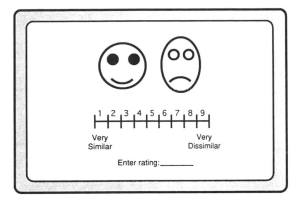

FIG. 4.2.   Dissimilarity rating display for the schematic faces example.

ment, the stimulus display disappeared and the next pair of faces was presented. Figure 4.2 shows an example of the screen displayed on each trial.

After collection of dissimilarity judgments, subjects rated each individual face in turn on several five-point "trait" scales: Sad-Happy, Attractive-Unattractive, Unintelligent-Intelligent, Weak-Strong, and Unemotional-Emotional. Figure 4.3 shows the screen display used to elicit these judgments.

The dissimilarities data collected in this experiment can be arranged in a 12 × 12 × 46 (stimuli × stimuli × subjects) two-mode, three-way data matrix. The data for each subject, a "slice" of the three-way matrix, is symmetric (by assumption) with zeroes on the diagonal, that is, judges were not asked to rate the dissimilarities of the stimuli paired with themselves.

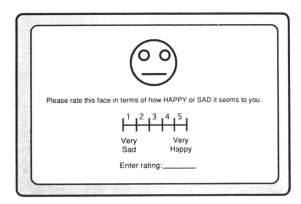

FIG. 4.3.   Unidimensional judgment display for the schematic faces example.

TABLE 4.1
Mean Dissimilarity Judgments for Paired Comparisons
of 12 Schematic Faces

(face)	4.29										
(face)	5.54	4.29									
(face)	3.91	5.45	6.99								
(face)	6.32	4.35	6.43	4.00							
(face)	6.89	6.94	3.94	5.24	4.49						
(face)	3.56	6.09	7.29	5.81	7.94	8.74					
(face)	6.12	4.01	6.34	7.67	6.18	8.14	4.33				
(face)	6.82	6.30	4.88	8.20	7.99	5.88	5.35	4.43			
(face)	6.10	7.61	8.87	3.71	6.35	6.95	3.91	6.12	7.21		
(face)	8.16	5.75	7.74	6.26	4.44	6.96	6.19	3.66	6.45	4.20	
(face)	8.55	8.30	6.18	7.01	6.78	4.27	6.48	6.88	3.84	5.10	4.81
	(face)	(face)	(face)	(face)	(face)	(face)	(face)	(face)	(face)	(face)	(face)

Nonmetric MDS: KYST

The nonmetric MDS analyses described in this section were based on the 12×12 aggregated dissimilarity matrix Δ. Each element, δ_{ij}, was computed as the arithmetic mean of the 46 judgments of the i,jth pair of stimuli. The resulting matrix, in lower triangular form, is shown in Table 4.1. Likewise, the unidimensional attribute ratings were averaged across subjects resulting in a 12 (faces) $\times$ 5 (scales) matrix (see Table 4.4). The mean ratings of faces along these scales were used to locate property vectors in both the KYST and SINDSCAL stimulus spaces.

The data were analyzed using KYST-2A (Kruskal, Young, & Seery, 1977), a very versatile program that can fit a variety of metric and nonmetric MDS models.[6] Figure 4.4 shows the input file for a nonmetric MDS of the aggregated

---

[6]The KYST-2A, SINDSCAL, PROFIT, and PREFMAP programs and user's manuals are available from Bell Laboratories Computing Information Laboratory, 600 Mountain Avenue, Murray Hill, NY 07974.

TORSCA PRE-ITERATION=3	a "quasi non-metric" analysis stage to generate an initial starting configuration
DIMAX=6 DIMIN=1	compute solutions starting at six dimensions progressing down to a one-dimensional solution
COORDINATES=ROTATE	orient the coordinate axes so that they are principal axes of the configuration
ITERATIONS=100	terminate computations at the 100th iteration if convergence has not been achieved by then
REGRESSION=ASCENDING	treat data values as dissimilarities
PRINT=DATA	print out the input data matrix
DATA LOWERHALFMATRIX DIAGONAL=ABSENT	form of the data matrix
FACE DATA - COLLECTED 1987-89 - 46 SUBJECTS	title information
12 1 1	order of data matrix; number of stimuli; number of replications per subject; number of subjects (matrices)
(11F5.3)	floating point FORTRAN format for the longest row of data matrix

[Data matrix inserted here]

COMPUTE

STOP

FIG. 4.4. Input file for KYST MDS analysis of aggregated dissimilarities data.

dissimilarities of the 12 schematic faces, based on the mean dissimilarity matrix shown earlier. The input file contains information about the form of the input data matrix, analysis control parameters, and output specifications.

The COMPUTE statement initiates the analysis and STOP marks the end of the job. Several analyses may be performed within the same run by including control information and (optionally) new data sets between COMPUTE commands.

With only 66 (i.e., $[12 \times 11]/2$) data points, a six-dimensional solution with 72 estimated scale values is clearly unjustified, and even a five-dimensional solution (60 estimated parameters) or four-dimensional solution (48 parameters) would seem to represent overfitting of the data. Under these conditions, a near perfect fit of the data is virtually guaranteed (Spence & Olgivie, 1973). Applying Kruskal and Wish's (1978) guideline ($[12 - 1]/4 = 2.75$), even fitting a three-dimensional solution is skating on thin ice. But rules are made to be broken.

Students analyzing these data usually select a three-dimensional solution, recognizing that the construction of the faces involved only three physical features or attributes, and configurations in three (let alone four) dimensions are difficult to visualize and interpret. In this connection, Shepard (1974) advised: "Always try for a solution in a space of three, or preferably, fewer dimensions where the spatial structure of the entire configuration can be seen and interpreted

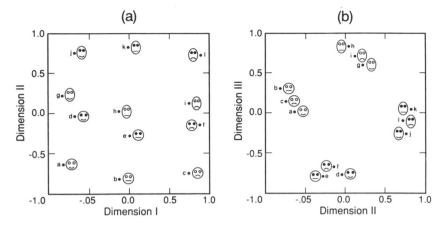

FIG. 4.5.   Three-dimensional configuration obtained by the KYST program for perceived similarity among 12 schematic faces. (a) Dimensions I and II (b) Dimensions II and III

directly" (p. 382). The three-dimensional solution for the data at hand is displayed in Fig. 4.5. The frowning faces are located at the right end of Dimension I, the smiling faces are at the left end, and the faces with straight mouths are in the middle. Locations of faces along this dimension are closely related to mean judgments of Happiness and Attractiveness, as is documented later. Students viewing this configuration for the first time often notice that the faces with the open or "light-colored" eyes have lower scale values (along Dimension I) relative to the corresponding dark-eyed faces, suggesting that the open-eyed faces are happier and more attractive.

Turning to the second dimension, the faces with oval shapes have high positive scale values and round faces have low (i.e., negative) scale values. However, the open-eyed faces, regardless of shape, have lower scale values than the corresponding dark-eyed faces. Students often interpret this dimension as Intelligence and hypothesize that face shape and eye type (or color) "interact," such that oval-shaped, dark-eyed faces appear more intelligent than oval, open-eyed faces, and so forth. Dimension III (Fig. 4.5) contrasts faces with open eyes to faces with closed eyes, although locations along the dimension reflect differences in head shape as well, again suggesting some sort of complex interaction.

All interpretations of the aforementioned solution postulating that "interactions" between physical features of the faces combine to produce psychological differences on attributes such as Happiness and Intelligence are, of course, wrong. The source of the confusion is a failure to realize that the obtained three-dimensional configuration almost exactly matches the stimulus design configuration (Fig. 4.1). An appropriate orthogonal rotation of the obtained configuration (**X**), using the transformation matrix in Table 4.2, produces a new, recognizable

TABLE 4.2
Transformation Matrix Applied
to Rotate KYST Three-dimensional Solution
to Maximum Congruence with Stimulus
Design Configuration

−.4431	.0122	.0560
.0196	−.4616	.2482
−.0494	−.2554	−.4694

configuration that conforms to the stimulus design. Nonmetric MDS solutions (in Euclidean space) are invariant under translations, reflections, and (orthogonal) rotations of the coordinate axes. Consequently the rotated solution fits the data just as well as the original configuration, but it has a much simpler form and interpretation.

The "Correct" Solution

Figure 4.6 shows the plot of stress against solution dimensionality for KYST nonmetric MDS solutions, using a Euclidean distance function, obtained for dimensionalities six through one, inclusive. The six-, five-, and one-dimensional solutions were included only to provide a context for evaluating model fit. The stress plot in Fig. 4.6 suggests that a four-dimensional solution is the best choice. We now examine the four-dimensional solution in detail.

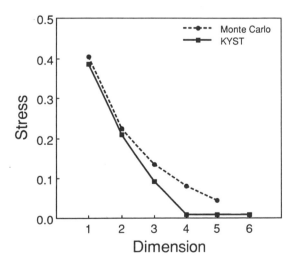

FIG. 4.6. Stress plots of dimensions I through VI for the solution obtained by the KYST program and with corresponding Monte Carlo (mean) values based on scalings of random rankings.

The clear "elbow" at four dimensions indicates that adding a fifth dimension yields no noticeable improvement in the fit of the solution. But the reduction of .084 in stress resulting from addition of a fourth dimension may or may not be "significant," pending attempts to interpret the four-dimensional configuration and its component dimensions. It is noted that the stress for the four-dimensional solution was .009. Spence and Olgivie (1973) suggested that the null hypothesis of random data can be rejected when all obtained stress values are at least three standard deviations ($\hat{\sigma}$ = .0091) below (expected) values derived from Monte Carlo methods. Mean stress values for random rankings scaled in five through one dimensions, along with the values obtained from the solutions under consideration, are also given in Fig. 4.6. By this criterion, we can conclude that the four-dimensional solution probably did not arise from totally random data, a reassuring conclusion, or not, depending on one's beliefs about the attentiveness and motivations of respondents.[7]

KYST Four-dimensional Stimulus Space.   Figure 4.7 contains the third page of the printed output for the four-dimensional KYST solution. The "Satisfactory Stress Was Reached" message tells us that the (default) criterion used in KYST to terminate the iterative estimation process was satisfied. The matrix labeled "Final Configuration" contains the scale values of the 12 faces on each of the four dimensions.

Figure 4.8 contains the "Shepard diagram" corresponding to the four-dimensional solution; this diagram plots model-derived distances (d_{ij}'s) against the corresponding data values (δ_{ij}'s). The monotonic function (relating the $d's$ and $\delta's$) is represented by the dashes ("----"), which have been connected to provide a better rendition of the monotonic function. The plotted values (D's) represent paired $d's$ and $\delta's$ that are not well fit by the monotonic function; the further (along the direction of the ordinate) the plotted point is from the function, the more that discrepancy contributes to the badness-of-fit (Stress) of the solution. In Fig. 4.8 only 19 of the D's appear, indicating that the remaining 47 values fall on (or nearly on, within the accuracy of a line printer generated character plot) the underlying function. For the data and solution at hand, the fit is exceptionally good, as would be expected from the obtained Stress (Formula 1) of .009 for the four-dimensional solution. Note that the monotone function derived for these data is approximately linear, a result that is relevant later on for deciding how appropriate the INDSCAL model is for these data.

Figure 4.9 shows the Shepard diagram for the three-dimensional solution (discussed in a previous section) for these same data. Although the decrease in

---

[7]Inasmuch as the data under consideration came from students in a graduate-level scaling course, and because they were informed before the experimental session that they would be analyzing the data and interpreting the results, there was little reason to doubt their attentiveness or the quality of the resulting data.

Schematic Faces PSYCH 409 Spring 1991 (N=46)

INITIAL CONFIGURATION COMPUTATION. NO. PTS.= 12 DIM= 4

PRE-ITERATION   STRESS

0   0.0244
1   0.0204
2   0.0183
3   0.0172

MAXIMUM NUMBER OF PRE-ITERATIONS 3, REACHED.

THE BEST INITIAL CONFIGURATION OF 12 POINTS IN 4 DIMENSIONS HAS STRESS 0.017 FORMULA 1

HISTORY OF COMPUTATION. N= 12.   THERE ARE 66 DATA VALUES, SPLIT INTO 1 LISTS.   DIMENSION = 4

ITERATION	STRESS	SRAT	SRATAV	CAGRGL	COSAV	ACSAV	SFGR	STEP
0	0.017	0.800	0.800	0.000	0.000	0.000	0.0006	0.0003
1	0.017	0.994	0.860	1.000	0.660	0.660	0.0006	0.0007
2	0.017	0.983	0.899	1.000	0.884	0.884	0.0006	0.0024
3	0.016	0.942	0.913	0.999	0.960	0.960	0.0005	0.0087
4	0.013	0.821	0.881	0.951	0.954	0.954	0.0003	0.0308
5	0.011	0.870	0.878	-0.593	-0.067	0.716	0.0003	0.0167
6	0.009	0.819	0.858	-0.693	-0.480	0.701	0.0002	0.0070

SATISFACTORY STRESS WAS REACHED

THE FINAL CONFIGURATION HAS BEEN ROTATED TO PRINCIPAL COMPONENTS.

THE FINAL CONFIGURATION OF 12 POINTS IN 4 DIMENSIONS HAS STRESS 0.009 FORMULA 1

LABEL FOR CONFIGURATION PLOTS   FINAL CONFIGURATION

		1	2	3	4
A	1	-0.065	-0.837	-0.273	0.479
B	2	-0.340	-0.561	-0.429	-0.495
C	3	-0.943	0.125	-0.484	0.117
D	4	-0.031	-0.615	0.691	0.280
E	5	-0.383	-0.280	0.609	-0.599
F	6	-0.786	0.369	0.481	0.289
G	7	0.769	-0.273	-0.441	0.419
H	8	0.417	0.047	-0.637	-0.551
I	9	0.007	0.694	0.694	-0.259
J	10	0.797	0.021	0.549	0.265
K	11	0.503	0.366	0.335	-0.673
L	12	0.055	0.987	0.293	0.250

FIG. 4.7. Four-dimensional solution output obtained by the KYST PROGRAM: Iteration history and "final configuration."

121

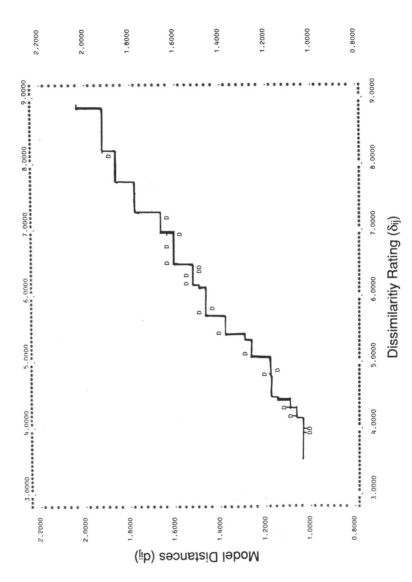

FIG. 4.8. Four-dimensional KYST solution: Shepard diagram.

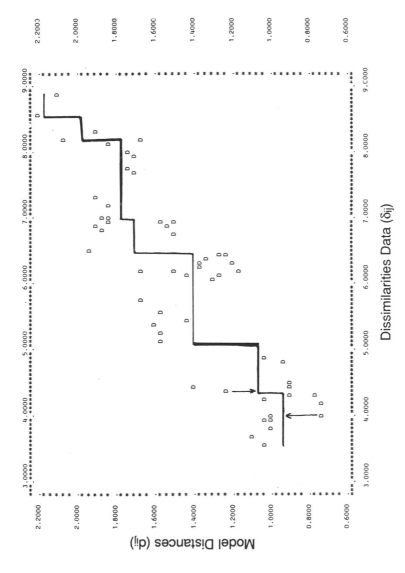

FIG. 4.9. Three-dimensional KYST solution: Shepard diagram.

123

stress from three- to four-dimensions is small, the difference in "scatter" between the diagrams for the two solutions appears substantial.

Returning to the four-dimensional configuration, its coordinate system has been rotated into *principal axes* orientation, a rotation that partitions the total variance of the coordinates in such a way that the first axis lies in the maximum variance direction through the configuration and so that each successive (orthogonal) axis will account for the greatest possible fraction of that variance not accounted for by all preceding axes.[8]

Figure 4.10 shows all six planar projections or "views" of the KYST four-dimensional solution. Each panel of the figure contains a projected view of the four-dimensional configuration on a plane defined by a pair of the four coordinate axes. A good starting point for visualizing the structure of the stimulus configuration is to examine the I–II and III–IV planes, because these are, in a sense, mutually exclusive—even though, of course, each represents only a different view of the same configuration of points. Inspection of the I-II plot (upper, left panel), concentrating first on the projections of the stimuli on axis I, reveals smiling faces toward the right end of the dimension, faces with "straight" or expressionless mouths in the center, and frowning faces at the left end. Tentatively, the ordering of stimuli along this dimension reflects perceived differences in Happiness-Unhappiness.

The second (vertical) dimension is more complex and difficult to interpret; oval faces with dark eyes have the highest scale values, followed by oval faces with light (or "open") eyes, round heads with dark eyes, and round faces with light eyes. A student who recently analyzed these data speculated that "dimension 2 appears to depict an interaction between face shape and eye color, . . . some type of happiness dimension."

Likewise, as already noted, the orderings of the faces along dimensions III and IV suggest somewhat complex interactions among features. PVF analyses would be helpful in locating meaningful directions in the stimulus space and, in general, interpreting dimensions that are not readily interpretable based on intuition alone. However, as the reader may have guessed by now, the orientation of the four-dimensional solution is also incorrect, with an orientation whereby the first dimension corresponds to the diagonal of a four-dimensional hypercube. Table 4.3 contains both the transformation matrix that rotates the four-dimensional solution into the "correct" orientation along with the scale values of the faces on these transformed dimensions.

---

[8]Most MDS programs rotate (by default, or as an option) their solutions to principal axes orientation, a convention whereby (a) the geometric center of gravity of the configuration is at the origin of the coordinate axes (i.e., [0, 0, 0, . . .]), (b) the axes are mutually orthogonal (i.e., the vectors of point coordinates are uncorrelated), and (c) the variance of the projections of the stimulus points on the coordinate axis decreases for each successive axis.

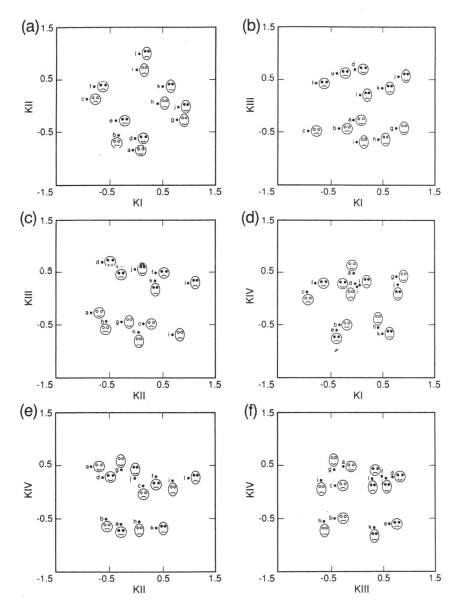

FIG. 4.10. Four-dimensional configuration obtained by the KYST program for perceived similarity among 12 schematic faces: (a) I-II Plane, (b) I-III Plane, (c) II-III Plane, (d) I-IV Plane, (e) II-IV Plane, and (f) III-IV Plane.

TABLE 4.3
(a) Transformation Matrix Aplied to Rotate KYST
Four-dimensional Solution to Maximum Congruence
with Stimulus Design Configuration
(b) Transformed KYST Four-dimensional Solution
Using Transformation Matrix in (a)

(a)

−.3101	.4424	−.0020	.1081
.4325	.3091	−.1255	−.0728
−.1087	−.0760	−.5427	−.1359
−.0550	−.0101	.0226	−.5377

(b)

Stimulus	Dimension			
	I	II	III	IV
A	−.3385	−.2715	.2642	−.1665
B	−.0632	−.2862	.2927	.3286
C	.3929	−.3429	.2515	−.1082
D	−.3469	−.2591	−.2914	−.2031
E	−.0355	−.2962	−.3081	.2183
F	.3353	−.2731	−.2992	−.3327
G	−.3318	.2851	.2815	−.0623
H	−.0701	.2418	.3514	−.1680
I	.3614	.1681	.2945	−.0732
J	−.3307	.3017	−.2909	−.1294
K	.0028	.3170	−.2440	.3441
L	.3642	.3046	−.2773	−.2402

Property Vectors.   Table 4.4 contains the mean ratings of the 12 faces on the five bipolar attribute scales as well as variables that encode the face features (i.e., head, eye, and mouth type). These variables were used, one at a time, as criterion variables in PVF analyses, with the four-dimensional KYST solution scale values (Table 4.5) as predictors.

Table 4.6 summarizes the results of these analyses. The Rs index how well the four-dimensional solution predicts or explains each of the external face rating scales and feature codes. The KYST scale values are uncorrelated, thus the betas (standardized regression weights)[9] from the multiple regression equal the zero-order correlations (between each set of scale values and the property in question), and the sum of these squared betas equals R^2. Each R^2 summarizes the fit of a vector in the four-dimensional KYST space corresponding to the scale. An R^2 of 1.0 would indicate a perfect relationship between projections of the stimulus points on that vector and the mean ratings of the faces.

Figure 4.11 shows the Happy, Strong, Attractive, Intelligent, and Emotional

---

[9]The weights presented in Table 4.6, however, are the unstandardized ("raw") weights.

TABLE 4.4
Mean Unidimensional Trait Ratings for the 12 Schematic Faces

	Happy	Strong	Unattractive	Intelligent	Emotional
	1.273	−.194	−.751	−1.543	.536
	−.316	−1.985	.529	−.864	−1.556
	1.103	−.493	1.276	−.932	.949
	1.352	1.060	−1.071	.559	.897
	−.096	.164	−.325	.763	−1.091
	−1.087	.164	.796	−.119	.820
	1.116	−.134	−1.018	.492	.407
	.172	−1.149	.316	.085	−1.737
	−1.260	−.731	.529	−1.204	.717
	1.367	1.955	−1.872	2.187	.588
	−.316	.642	−.058	.763	−1.143
	−1.103	.702	1.649	−.186	.613

vectors in the I–II plane (left panel) and III–IV plane (right panel) of the KYST four-dimensional stimulus space. Notice that the property vectors are not collinear with the coordinate axes of the solution space, indicating that the axes of the stimulus space (in principal axes orientation) are not interpretable.[10]

When appropriate (orthogonal) rotations are performed (Table 4.3), the expected configuration, a rectangular prism corresponding to the stimulus design, is recovered in the subspace of the first three dimensions. The fourth dimension,

---

[10]In the obtained orientation, the first (principal) axis (i.e., Dimension I) corresponds approximately to the *diagonal* of the rectangular prism comprising the stimulus design matrix (see Fig. 4.1). Although this is a *maximum variance* direction, it is not a psychologically relevant direction through the stimulus space; also, as a consequence of the incorrect placement of the first coordinate axis, the locations of the other three axes are "wrong" as well.

TABLE 4.5
Four-dimensional KYST Solution Scale Values Matrix

Stimuli		*Dimensions* I	II	III	IV
A		−.065	−.837	−.273	.479
B		−.340	−.561	−.429	−.495
C		−.943	.125	−.484	.117
D		−.031	−.615	.691	.280
E		−.383	−.280	.609	−.599
F		−.786	.369	.481	.289
G		.769	−.273	−.441	.419
H		.417	.047	−.637	−.551
I		.007	.694	−.694	.219
J		.797	−.021	.549	.265
K		.503	.366	.335	−.673
L		.055	.987	.293	.250

Emotional-Unemotional, which has no simple counterpart in the stimulus design, is a contrast between faces with straight mouths (unemotional) and faces with upturned or downturned mouths (happy or sad = emotional). The I–II and III–IV planes of the rotated four-dimensional KYST solution are given in Fig. 4.12. The structure expected from the stimulus design is evident, and the Happy, Attractive, and Emotional property vectors are now collinear with appropriate coordinate axes. Table 4.7 contains direction cosines and fit statistics (i.e., *R*s) for the property vectors. These four dimensions, and the configuration of the 12 faces contained within them, also resulted from a SINDSCAL analysis of the three-way, two-mode (Faces × Faces × Subjects) data set. These results, and a detailed discussion of the corresponding property vectors, are presented in the next section.

TABLE 4.6
Property Vector Analyses: Four-dimensional KYST Predicting Face
Feature Codes and Unidimensional Trait Scale (Mean) Ratings

Property	Regression Weights				R
	I	II	III	IV	
Mouth type	.915	−1.188	.296	.262	.998
Head shape	−1.484	−1.092	.375	.066	.999
Eye type	−.093	−.491	−1.880	.182	.999
Mouth contrast*	.170	−.386	.120	−3.277	.988
Happy-	1.067	−1.383	.511	.554	.988
Strong-	.842	−.133	1.537	.372	.922
Unattractive-	−1.018	1.445	−.346	−.504	.971
Intelligent-	1.340	−.134	.852	−.138	.842
Emotional-	−.493	.300	.376	2.094	.952

*straight mouth vs. smile or frown

Individual Differences MDS: INDSCAL Model

SINDSCAL solutions were obtained at dimensionalities six through two, thereby
bracketing the four-dimensional solution that was expected to give the best
account of the data. The control and format cards for this analysis are shown in
Fig. 4.13. Figure 4.14 plots the INDSCAL "overall" fit statistic, VAF, for each

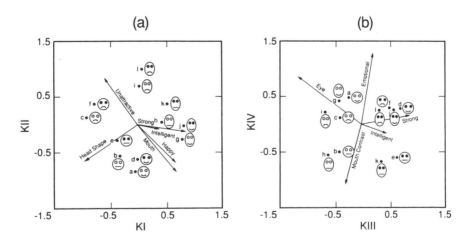

FIG. 4.11.   Four-dimensional configuration obtained by the KYST program for perceived similarity among 12 schematic faces. Dimensions I
and II along with relevant property vectors are plotted in (a), while
Dimensions III and IV along with relevant property vectors are shown
in (b).

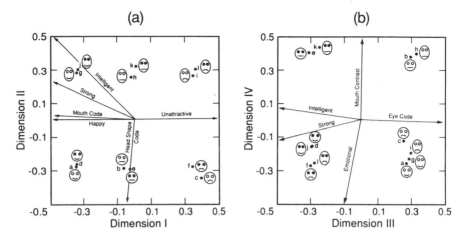

FIG. 4.12.   Four-dimensional rotated KYST solution for perceived similarity among 12 schematic faces. I-II Plane along with relevant property vectors is plotted in (a), while III-IV Plane, with relevant property vectors is plotted in (b).

solution against solution dimensionality numbers. If the plot exhibits an elbow at some dimensionality, this is an indication that additional dimensions beyond the dimensionality specified by the elbow contribute negligible improvement to overall fit. The plot exhibits a clear elbow at four dimensions, so we examine the dimensions of this solution to see if they are interpretable.

The VAF measure (Equation 5) summarizes the overall fit of the model to all data sources, that is, subjects in this application. The overall VAF is comprised of the VAF's of individual subjects; SINDSCAL computes and prints out a

TABLE 4.7
Property Vector Analyses: Four-dimensional Rotated KYST Predicting
Face Feature Codes and Unidimensional Trait Scale (Mean) Ratings

Property	Regression Weights				R
	I	II	III	IV	
Mouth type	−2.821	.048	−.032	−.133	.998
Head shape	−.125	−3.450	−.199	−.008	.999
Eye type	−.009	−.184	3.450	−.121	.999
Mouth contrast*	.039	−.002	.046	4.807	.988
Happy-	−3.397	.010	−.300	−.520	.988
Strong-	−1.683	.722	−2.571	−.518	.922
Unattractive-	3.368	.086	−.003	.435	.971
Intelligent-	−1.867	1.655	−1.443	.271	.842
Emotional-	.358	−.592	−.561	−3.114	.952

*straight mouth vs. smile or frown

```
 6    2   46   12                                              Card #1
15    2    0    0    0                                         Card #2
Schematic Faces Data; 46 Subjects, 12 Stimuli                 Card #3
(12F3.2)                                                      Card #4
              [Insert N cards for the data matrices]         Card #5
                                                                 .
                                                                 .
                                                                 .
                                                    Card #(4+N)
              [Insert one blank card after data]    Card #(5+N)
```

CARD LAYOUT

<u>Card #1</u>

```
field 1 = Maximum dimensionality
field 2 = Minimum dimensionality
field 3 = Number of subjects
field 4 = Number of stimuli
```

<u>Card #2</u>

```
field 1 = Maximum number of iterations
field 2 = Data type: similarities, dissimilarities, correlations
field 3 = Punch option: normalized solution, scalar products
field 4 = Plot option: no plotting, plot all pairs of planes
field 5 = Starting configuration: user inputs, random start
```

<u>Card #3</u>

Title card -- can be one line only, with maximum of 72 characters

<u>Card #4</u>

Fortran format for the data matrices

<u>Cards #5 through (N+4)</u>

Data matrices

<u>Card #(N+5)</u>

Columns 1-20 must be blank

FIG. 4.13.   Input file for SINDSCAL MDS analysis.

correlation, r_k, summarizing the model fit for each subject. These subject fit indices can be plotted against solution dimensionality as well, providing additional relevant information useful for deciding which dimensionality solution to adopt.

Figure 4.15 exhibits plots of these fit correlations[11] for a subset of five

---

[11]When the columns of **X** (the object space scale values matrix) are uncorrelated,

$$r_k = \sum_{r=1}^{R} w_{kr}^2$$

where w_{kr} is the salience weight for subject k for dimension r.

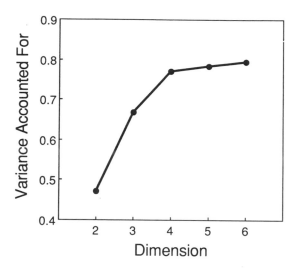

FIG. 4.14. Goodness of fit indices for INDSCAL solutions, Dimension I
through Dimension VI.

subjects. The functions for subjects A and S increase up to four dimensions and
then level off, indicating that a four-dimensional stimulus space captures most of
the systematic variance in their data. The pattern of fit statistics for subject U
suggests that a three-dimensional solution would be adequate to account for his
data. Subject I's goodness of fit function suggests a two-dimensional stimulus
configuration is appropriate for his data. Finally, the function for subject 5
increases gradually up through six dimensions, but this pattern was unique in the
sample and was considered an insufficient basis for adopting a five- or six-
dimensional solution. In general, examination of individual fit functions can
point to the existence of "minor" dimensions, salient for a few subjects, that
might be overlooked if the decision rested entirely on examination of the aggregate (VAF) fit measure. Pending a check of the interpretability of its component
dimensions, a four-dimensional solution was selected for further examination.

Salience Weights.   Table 4.8 contains the entire "SUBJECTS WEIGHT
MATRIX" for the four-dimensional SINDSCAL solution. Figures 4.16 and 4.17
show plots of the I–II and III–IV planes of the subject space. With the exception
of subjects Z and 8, salience weights for all subjects were positive. Subject Z's
and 8's negative weights, and their low fit statistics (0.395 and .477, respectively) suggest that their data were unreliable or may violate model assumptions;
in any case, these subjects' data are not well fit by the model. The salience
weights for each subject are related to model fit,[12] so locations of subjects in the

---

[12]The length of the vector from the origin to the subject point is approximately equal to the fit of
the model to the subject's data.

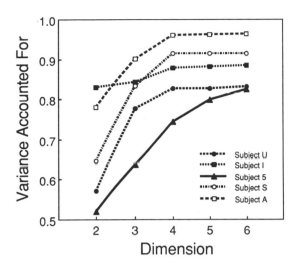

FIG. 4.15. Goodness of fit indices of subjects U, I, 5, S, and A for INDSCAL solutions, Dimensions I through Dimension VI.

space should not be interpreted directly. Ordinarily, subject weights should be transformed (normalized) so that the distance of each point from the origin of the space is the same (Arabie et al., 1987).

The second panel of Table 4.8 contains relative weights resulting from the following transformation:

$$w_{kr}^* = \frac{w_{kr}}{\sqrt{\sum_r w_{kr}^2}} \qquad (8)$$

which removes the effect of variations in subject fit (Young & Lewyckyj, 1979).

Examination of the subject salience weight patterns reveals substantial individual differences in perception of the schematic faces. Most, but not all, subjects attach high importance to the Happy-Unhappy dimension; this pattern is reflected by the overall salience (VAF) for that dimension (Table 4.8, last row). Dimension II has relatively high salience for subjects E, N, U, 2, and 19, whereas Dimension III was most salient by a small margin for subjects T, 4, 7, and 17. Lacking a significance test, inferences about whether or not a dimension is salient, in an absolute sense, for a particular subject, cannot be made.

Group Stimulus Space. The SINDSCAL four-dimensional stimulus space for the 12 schematic faces is presented in the panels of Fig. 4.18. The three-dimensional subspace defined by Dimensions I, II, and III (Fig. 4.19) contains a configuration of points that matches, almost exactly, the physical stimulus design

TABLE 4.8

Subject Weight Matrix for Four-dimensional Solution
by SINDSCAL Program and Proportion of Total Variance
Accounted for by Each Dimension

	Obtained				Normalized			
	I	*II*	*III*	*IV*	*I*	*II*	*III*	*IV*
A	.437	.559	.559	.323	.455	.583	.583	.337
B	.427	.517	.337	.205	.549	.665	.433	.264
C	.772	.180	.175	.347	.874	.204	.198	.393
D	.479	.410	.441	.339	.570	.488	.525	.403
E	.307	.565	.172	.223	.437	.805	.245	.318
F	.445	.406	.448	.372	.531	.485	.535	.444
G	.488	.482	.335	.396	.579	.560	.389	.460
H	.335	.663	.522	.348	.344	.682	.537	.358
I	.813	.210	.128	.217	.927	.240	.146	.248
J	.602	.544	.406	.287	.633	.572	.427	.302
K	.547	.511	.520	.301	.570	.532	.542	.314
L	.430	.601	.528	.314	.448	.625	.549	.327
M	.489	.454	.519	.346	.535	.497	.568	.389
N	.266	.706	.499	.171	.289	.767	.542	.186
O	.760	.327	.769	.294	.828	.356	.293	.320
P	.448	.440	.565	.304	.499	.490	.629	.538
Q	.376	.447	.454	.550	.408	.485	.492	.597
R	.760	.297	.181	.383	.827	.323	.197	.417
S	.385	.520	.529	.369	.422	.570	.580	.405
T	.248	.421	.610	.334	.344	.486	.704	.386
U	.116	.556	.560	.215	.191	.915	.922	.354
V	.515	.524	.128	.493	.576	.586	.143	.551
W	.662	.185	.379	.218	.813	.227	.465	.268
X	.524	.378	.455	.332	.611	.441	.531	.387
Y	.697	.305	.133	.469	.771	.338	.147	.519
Z	−.265	−.029	.284	−.065	−.658	−.072	.706	−.161
1	.309	.519	.656	.392	.338	.567	.617	.428
2	.304	.747	.402	.311	.319	.784	.422	.326
3	.528	.550	.363	.366	.574	.598	.394	.398
4	.460	.445	.569	.305	.506	.489	.626	.335
5	.299	.424	.371	.381	.402	.571	.499	.513
6	.336	.639	.555	.302	.351	.668	.580	.316
7	.292	.380	.635	.417	.325	.423	.707	.464
8	.312	.293	.218	−.015	.646	.610	.454	−.031
9	.248	.421	.610	.334	.294	.499	.724	.396
10	.589	.272	.492	.304	.678	.313	.566	.352
11	.469	.363	.429	.392	.565	.437	.517	.472
12	.527	.414	.474	.318	.598	.472	.538	.361
13	.521	.583	.498	.250	.542	.608	.518	.260
14	.486	.535	.606	.199	.504	.555	.629	.206
15	.772	.257	.174	.361	.851	.283	.192	.398
16	.645	.421	.429	.295	.694	.453	.461	.317

(*continued*)

TABLE 4.8
(*Continued*)

	Obtained				Normalized			
	I	*II*	*III*	*IV*	*I*	*II*	*III*	*IV*
17	.324	.496	.603	.229	.370	.566	.688	.261
18	.500	.587	.300	.273	.574	.674	.344	.313
19	.243	.714	.528	.268	.253	.745	.551	.279
20	.685	.250	.215	.205	.870	.317	.273	.260
VAFs:	.246	.223	.197	.104				

(Fig. 4.1), a cube with vertices corresponding to various combinations of mouth, eye, and head shape features comprising the faces. The left panel of Fig. 4.20 shows the projection of the stimulus configuration onto the I–II plane and the right panel shows the III–IV plane. Dimension IV (bottom panels) represents a contrast between faces with straight mouths at one extreme, with smiling and frowning mouths at the other extreme. The approximate proportions of the total VAF for these dimensions were .252, .208, .167, and .118, respectively. Figure 4.21 illustrates the I–II plane of the four-dimensional SINDSCAL solution Individual Stimulus spaces for Subjects I and U. It is apparent that Dimension I is more salient than Dimension II to Subject I as indicated by the elongation in the direction of Dimension I. Subject U, on the other hand, weights Dimension II more than the first dimension.

Table 4.9 contains the matrix of correlations for all pairs of dimensions, that is, stimulus scale values. Although the INDSCAL model assumes that the stimulus dimensions are orthogonal, and although the coordinate axes are, by definition, orthogonal, the estimated scale values may be correlated. If observed correlations are substantially larger or smaller than zero, either model assumptions have been violated or the dimensionality of the solution in question is too high. For the present data the largest correlation is only − .05, suggesting that the four dimensions underlying perception of the schematic faces are essentially orthogonal.

Beyond the interpretations made on the basis of resemblance between the (physical) stimulus design matrix and the configuration of stimulus points revealed by the SINDSCAL analysis, inferences about psychological responses and attributions to these faces were also of interest. As noted in an earlier section, specific hypotheses about a variety of such dimensions can be tested by PVF methods utilizing specific unidimensional ratings of the stimuli. Table 4.10 summarizes the results of several PVF analyses relating the four-dimensional SINDSCAL stimulus space to (a) four "dummy variables" encoding the physical features of the faces, and (b) mean ratings on five unidimensional attribute scales representing a priori hypotheses about perception of the faces.

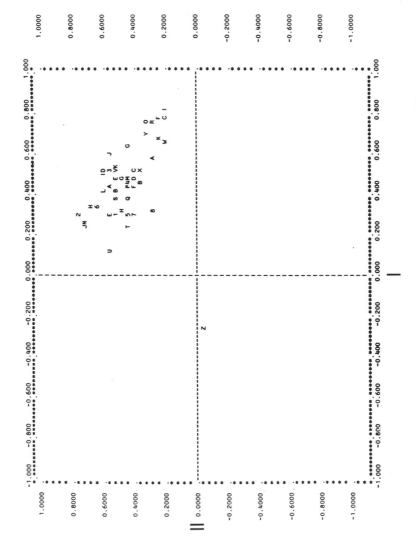

FIG. 4.16. Subject weight space obtained by SINDSCAL program: I-II Plane.

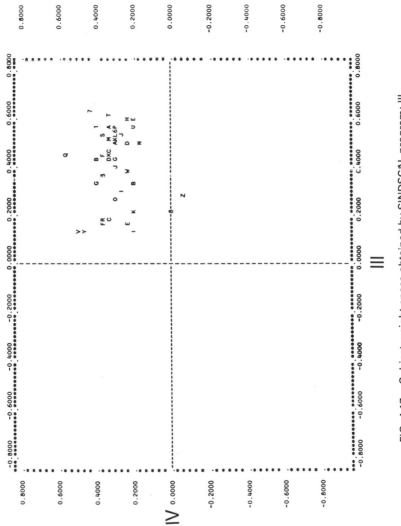

FIG. 4.17. Subject weight space obtained by SINDSCAL program: III-IV Plane.

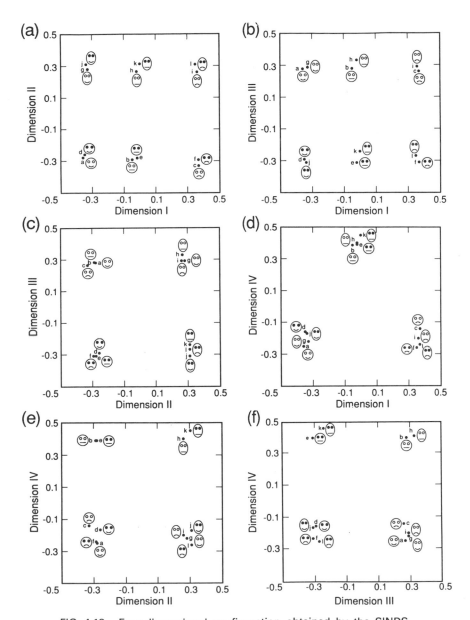

FIG. 4.18. Four-dimensional configuration obtained by the SINDS-CAL program for perceived similarity among 12 schematic faces: (a) I-II Plane, (b) I-III Plane, (c) II-III Plane, (d) I-IV Plane, (e) II-IV Plane, and (f) III-IV Plane.

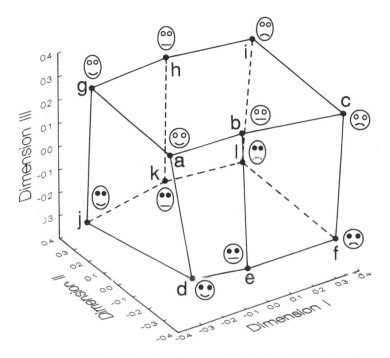

FIG. 4.19. Four-dimensional SINDSCAL solution for perceived similarity of schematic faces: Rotated three-dimensional subspace formed by Dimensions I-III.

Property Vectors.   The fifth column of Table 4.10 contains the multiple correlations between four SINDSCAL dimensions and each of the nine attribute or property scales. All of the multiple correlations are significant at the .01 level, and all but one of the Rs (for the scale Intelligent-Unintelligent) exceed .90.[13] Kruskal and Wish (1978) suggested that multiple correlations in the .90's are desirable for "a good interpretation of a dimension" but that correlations in the high .70's and in the .80's may suffice, as long as they are significant at the .01 level or better (pp. 37–9).

The first four columns of the table contain the regression weights that were used to locate the property vectors in the SINDSCAL group stimulus space (Fig. 4.20). For example, the endpoint of the "Happy-Sad" vector projected into the I–II plane of the solution is located by the coordinates (-3.14, .01), resulting in a property vector that virtually coincides with the first coordinate axis. Examining the regression weights for dimensions III and IV, it can be seen that the Happy-

---

[13]Because the n for each of the PVF regression analyses is only 12, and because the analyses involve five variables, the obtained R's are spuriously high. Although these R's could be "corrected" by standard formulas, we do not believe that such corrections are warranted or informative.

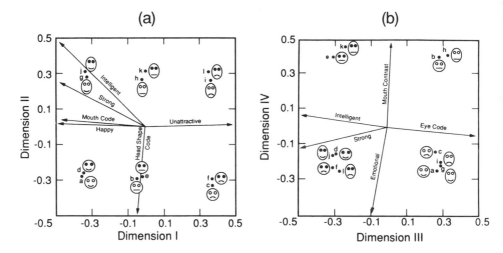

FIG. 4.20. Four-dimensional configuration obtained by the SINDS-CAL program for perceived similarity among 12 schematic faces. Dimensions I and II, along with appropriate property vectors are plotted in (a), while Dimensions III and IV, with relevant property vectors, are shown in (b).

Sad vector has essentially no projection into this plane of the solution. Examining projections of the faces onto the vector in the I–II plane of the solution, it is evident that perceived Happiness or Sadness is determined entirely by curvature of mouth. However, notice that the happy (◡) and "sober" (—) faces are slightly closer together than the sober and frowning (◠) faces; this result is interesting because the mouths of the smiling and frowning faces were formed using the same arc, differing only in orientation. Also note that the locations of the faces in this subspace are determined by mouth type and head shape only, with faces of differing eye type being approximately coincident. (A small rotation of the configuration would probably make the dark-eyed and light-eyed faces coincide.)

For these faces and these subjects, Happiness and Attractiveness of the faces are very similar constructs as evidenced by the fact that vectors corresponding to these two scales are approximately collinear. As shown in Table 4.10, the zero-order correlations between these scales and Dimension I are .98 and .97, respectively.

The second dimension is Head Shape, with a correlation of -1.0 with the dummy variable (see Fig. 4.1) representing that feature. Although none of the trait attributions is closely related to Head Shape, both Intelligence ($r = .50$) and Strong($-$Weak) ($r = .23$) are positively correlated with this dimension; elongated or oval faces are judged as Stronger and more Intelligent than round faces. By examining the location of the Intelligent vector in Fig. 4.20 (or the corre-

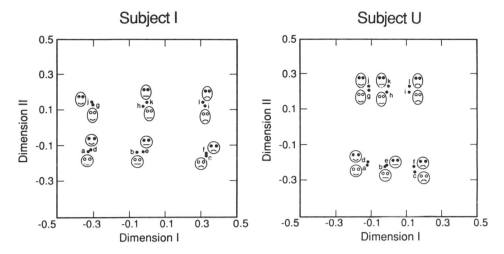

FIG. 4.21. Four-dimensional SINDSCAL solution individual stimulus spaces for Subjects I and U (I-II Plane).

sponding regression weights in Table 4.10), it can be seen that judged Intelligence is jointly determined by Mouth Type, Head Shape, and Eye Type, with all three features having approximately equal weights; an Intelligent face is elongated, dark-eyed, and smiling. A similar pattern is seen for Strong, but Mouth Type is less important than Head Shape and Eyes; a strong face is elongated and dark-eyed.

Turning to the right panel of Fig. 4.20, it can be seen that Dimension III is Eye Type, with light or open eyes having positive scale values on that dimension. The fourth, and overall least salient dimension, is "Emotionality," defined by a contrast between faces with a straight mouth (no emotion) versus faces that are smiling or frowning ("emotional"). The correlation between the dummy variable representing this contrast and judgments of Emotionality was .93.

The PVF method just illustrated represents a powerful tool not only for substantiating interpretations of stimulus spaces derived from MDS methods, but

TABLE 4.9
Four-dimensional SINDSCAL Solution
Dimension Correlations

	I	II	III	IV
I	1.000			
II	−.018	1.000		
III	−.017	.001	1.000	
IV	−.056	.000	.021	1.000

TABLE 4.10
Property Vector Analyses: Four-dimensional SINDSCAL Predicting
Face Feature Codes and Unidimensional Trait Scale (Mean) Ratings

Property	Regression Weights					Pearson Correlations			
	I	II	III	IV	R	I	II	III	IV
Mouth type	−2.82	.05	−.03	−.13	.990	−1.00	.03	.00	.01
Head shape	−.13	−3.45	−.20	−.01	.999	−.02	−1.00	−.05	.00
Eye type	−.01	−.18	3.45	−.12	.999	−.01	−.06	1.00	−.01
Mouth contrast*	.05	−.01	.05	4.82	.984	−.05	.00	.04	.99
Happy-	−3.41	.01	−.30	−.52	.991	−.98	.02	−.08	−.09
Strong-	−1.71	.73	−2.56	−.53	.925	−.48	.23	−.79	−.14
Unattractive-	3.37	.08	.01	.44	.974	.97	.01	−.01	.07
Intelligent-	−1.86	1.68	−1.46	.25	.848	−.55	.50	−.42	.10
Emotional-	.33	−.58	−.55	−3.14	.958	.16	−.17	−.18	−.93

*straight mouth vs. smile or frown

also for testing hypotheses about the relative salience or importance of psychological and psychophysical attributes in perception and judgment of complex stimuli. Likewise, a modification of the PVF method can be used to test hypotheses about individual and subgroup differences in attribute salience.[14]

Taken together, well-designed plots of the MDS spaces, with property vectors located in appropriate subspaces, represent very efficient and informative graphical tools for summarizing large amounts of information. However, such plots will be readily interpretable only when the stimulus configuration has been rotated to a psychologically meaningful orientation, especially when the dimensionality of the solution is high—that is, greater than three. SINDSCAL solutions have the endearing characteristic that the orientations of the dimensions are usually "correct," or psychologically meaningful, just as advertised (Carroll & Chang, 1970).

Too Good to Be True?   Students (and the occasional journal editor) sometimes express disbelief at the large zero-order and multiple correlations obtained in studies of the sort just described. Their skepticism stems from the fact that whole subdisciplines of social and behavioral science are built on correlational results (or comparable effect sizes in experimental research) in the .20 to .50

---

[14]Briefly, a useful variation on the PVF method involves computing mean ratings on property scales for separate subgroups of subjects and then locating the corresponding vectors in either (a) the SINDSCAL group stimulus space, or (b) in SINDSCAL "subgroup" spaces constructed by applying the mean salience weights for each subgroup to the group space (i.e., Equation 4). This approach recognizes the possibility of individual (or subgroup) differences in *both* proximity judgments and (unidimensional) attribute judgments. If for a given attribute, different R's and/or vector locations are obtained for the various subgroups, these results can be used to draw conclusions about group differences in the salience or meaning of the attribute.

range. The explanation for the large correlations and effect sizes often obtained in property vector fitting and external preference modeling in MDS studies has two components: (a) in well-designed MDS studies, the estimates of stimulus scale values are based on large amounts of "rich" data, so that the scale values are overdetermined and very stable, in a statistical sense; (b) in PVF analyses, the vector of mean judgments constituting the measure of the stimulus attribute is usually based on many replications, that is, subjects. When combined in a multiple regression analysis, with the MDS-derived scale values serving as predictors, and the attribute judgments as the criterion, the net result is often a strong relationship (i.e., a high R), with little or no attenuation ascribable to unreliability of the variables involved in the analysis. Of course, the high correlations will be obtained only when the property scales or other measures are, in fact, relevant.

SPECIALIZED METHODS

Conventional multidimensional scaling methods alone may not fully address the specific research problem at hand. However, some specialized methods in MDS may be appropriate. For example, the researcher may be interested in creating a joint subject-stimulus preference space, in which case Multidimensional Preference Scaling would be the appropriate method to employ. Or, perhaps theory or past research suggest a well-defined stimulus dimension. Constrained MDS methods could be used to determine whether the solution will yield the hypothesized dimension and to minimize the number of parameters estimated. These two special topics in MDS are discussed in the following pages.

Multidimensional Preference Models

Unfolding models are used to create a joint subject-stimulus space that reflects subjects' preference orders for the stimuli under investigation. These models look at the relationship between individuals' perceptions of the stimuli under study with their preferences for those stimuli. Subjects' preferences can be represented in two basic ways: (a) as *distances* between the object points and a subject "ideal point" embedded in the perceptual space or (b) as the *projections* of the object points onto a subject vector. These two preference representations have been incorporated (Carroll, 1980) into a hierarchial set of preference models; these are (in order of complexity): the Vector Model, the Simple Unfolding Model, the Weighted Unfolding Model and the General Unfolding Model.

Carroll (1980) distinguished between two broad classes of methods for preference modeling: internal analysis and external analysis. *Internal modes of analysis* are based entirely on the preference judgments for a set of individuals. Internal methods use only the preference data, typically for a number of different subjects, to develop simultaneously the stimulus space and the subject (i.e., individual difference) parameters, either subject vectors or ideal points depending on the model used. In contrast, *external modes of analysis* relate several subjects' preference judgments to an a priori set of stimulus dimensions. The set of dimensions used for external analysis may come from a prior multidimensional scaling solution of independently measured similarities data, or it could result from a physical or other "rational" dimensionalization of the stimuli, like the stimulus design in Fig. 4.1.

Vector Model.   The vector model, first proposed by Tucker (1960), is the simplest model in the hierarchy. The model assumes a set of stimulus points embedded in a multidimensional space, where subjects are represented by distinct vectors through the space. The direction of the subject vector indicates increasing preference strengths for the stimuli. Therefore the predicted preference order of the objects is given by the projections of object points onto the subject vector. The cosines of the angles that the subject vector forms with the coordinate axes indicate the relative importance of the corresponding dimensions to the preference judgments; these importance parameters represent coefficients in a linear combination of dimensions. When the multidimensional configuration is orthonormal,[15] then the relative importance of a dimension is equal to the correlation between the subject vector and the coordinate axis.

Algebraically, this model states that

$$\pi_{kj} = F_k(p_{kj}) = \sum_{r=1}^{R} b_{kr} x_{jr} \tag{9}$$

where

π_{kj} = "true" preference strengths

F_k = function for subject k; if it is a linear function then the metric model is assumed. A monotonic function implies a "nonmetric" solution.

p_{kj} = observed preference strength measure of the jth stimulus for the kth subject,

x_{jr} = scale value of the jth stimulus on the rth dimension,

---

[15]The multidimensional configuration is orthonormal if

$$\sum_{j=1}^{n} x_{jk} x_{jl} = \begin{cases} 1 & \text{when } k = l \\ 0 & \text{when } k \neq l \end{cases}$$

for $k, l = 1, 2, \ldots, R$. In other words, the dimensions are orthogonal and have unit length.

b_{kr} = importance of dimension r for subject k (r_{kr} if orthonormal), and

R = number of dimensions.

When the vector model is fit via an internal analysis, both the b_{kr}'s and the x_{jr}'s are estimated from the data using an Eckart–Young (1936) decomposition of the observed preferences. The nonmetric problem is solved by performing a nonmetric factor analysis on the p_{kj}'s. The computer program, MDPREF (Chang & Carroll, 1969), will solve both the nonmetric and the metric internal vector fitting problems.

For the external vector model, the x_{jr}'s are known, and multiple regression methods are used to solve for the b_{kr}'s. PREFMAP-3 (Meulman, Heiser, & Carroll, 1986) can be used to estimate the parameters of the external vector model.

For the schematic faces example, an external analysis for the vector model with two subjects might yield the two vectors indicated in Fig. 4.22. Projections of the faces onto the vectors give the subjects' predicted preference orders. Subject 1 appears to prefer faces that have dark eyes, with round-shaped faces being slightly more preferred to the oval faces. Subject 2, on the other hand, prefers the frowning and smiling mouths over the straight mouth. Again, Subject 2, like Subject 1, prefers the round face slightly more than the oval face. Notice that if we superimpose the property vectors onto the figure, there is a strong correspondence between Subject 1's vector and the Intelligence property vector, suggesting that this subject prefers intelligent looking faces. Subject 2's vector

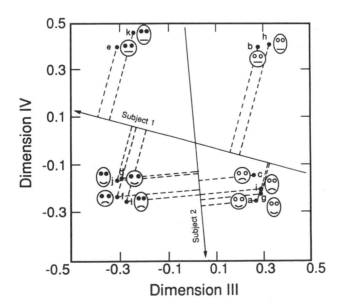

FIG. 4.22. Vector model: Schematic faces hypothetical example.

appears to be closely related to the Emotional property vector; thus this subject prefers emotional faces to nonemotional faces.

The vector model, both internal and external versions, is fit using standard techniques, that is, through factor analysis or multiple regression. For the previous hypothetical example, the SINDSCAL solution was used in a multiple regression analysis to solve for the subjects' relative importance weights. Subjects' preference rankings for the 12 schematic faces would be used as the dependent variables; the dimension scale values are the independent variables. The resulting regression weights represent the vector coordinates for each subject, indicating importance weights of each stimulus dimension for each subject. Note that this is identical to property vector fitting except that the "property" is a set of preference strength, or other dominance, measures.

Simple Unfolding Model. In 1950, Coombs introduced the unidimensional unfolding model. In Coombs's model, a subject is represented by an *ideal point*, which indicates the subject's optimal value on that stimulus dimension. A subject's preference order and preference "magnitude" for the stimuli are reflected by the position of the subject ideal point and the distances between the ideal point and the object points, respectively (see Fig. 4.23). This model is called the "unfolding" model because an individual's judged preference order can be found by "folding" the stimulus scale at that individual's ideal point. By simultaneously unfolding the preference scales for each subject, the unidimensional, common stimulus space is recovered.

The unidimensional unfolding model was generalized to the multidimensional case by Bennett and Hays (1960). In the multidimensional unfolding model, the stimuli and subjects are represented as points in a space, where a subject's preference order and stimulus preference strengths are indicated by the Euclidean distance between the object points and the subject's ideal point. The larger the distance between an object point and the subject's ideal point, the less the individual prefers that object.

Algebraically, the model states

$$\pi_{kj} = F_k (p_{kj}) = d_{kj}^2 \qquad (10)$$

with

$$d_{kj}^2 = \sum_{r=1}^{R} (y_{kr} - x_{jr})^2$$

where

y_{kr} is the *r*th coordinate of the ideal point for the *k*th subject, and

x_{jr} is defined the same as in the vector model (as are π_{kj}, F_k, p_{kj} and *r*).

FIG. 4.23.   Unidimensional unfolding.

Notice that $d_{kj}{}^2$ represents the squared Euclidean distance between subject k's ideal point and the jth stimulus point. In this model, π_{kj} is a squared Euclidean distance. Using the schematic faces example to illustrate the unfolding model (see Fig. 4.24), we can see that the preference order is given by the distances between the subject ideal point and the stimulus points. The smaller the distance, the more preferred the object. Again Subject 1 prefers the dark-eyed faces. However, in the vector model example the straight mouth faces were preferred over the frowning or smiling faces. The ideal point model yields a different ordering than the vector model for Subject 1. Now the smiling faces are preferred to the straight mouth faces and the frowning face, respectively, and the dark eyes are preferred to the light eyes. For Subject 2, the frowning and smiling mouths are also preferred to the straight mouth. However, now the light-eyed "emotional" faces are preferred over the dark-eyed faces. This relatively complex preference ordering cannot be accommodated by *any* vector model, in a space of the same dimensionality.

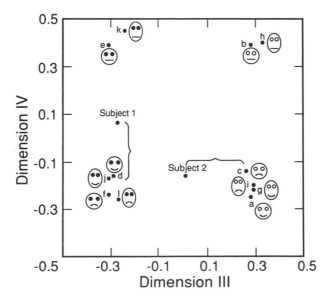

FIG. 4.24.   Simple unfolding model: Schematic faces hypothetical example.

When will the vector model and the unfolding models produce the same preference orders? The vector model is essentially a special case of the simple unfolding model. If the ideal points are located well outside the stimulus configuration, the distances between the stimulus points and the subjects' ideal points will reflect a preference order approaching that of the vector model. If the ideal points for Subject 1 and Subject 2 are extended beyond the periphery of the stimulus space, then the preference orders derived from the "extended ideal points" will correspond to the order predicted by the vector model.

Weighted Unfolding Model.   The weighted unfolding model, similar to the simple unfolding model, depicts the individual as a point in the multidimensional space; but the weighted model allows each individual to weight the dimensions differently. A dimension that is very important to one individual may not be important at all in the judgments of another individual. In place of the usual Euclidean distance, a formula including a weight parameter, w_{kr}, is employed:

$$d_{kj}^2 = \sum_{r=1}^{R} w_{kr}(y_{kr} - x_{jr})^2 \qquad (11)$$

The weighting factor w_{kr} can be thought of as the salience of the rth dimension for subject k. It can be seen that the simple unfolding model is a special case of the weighted model where the weights for all the subjects on each dimension are equal. A large weight value ($-1 < w_{kr} < 1$) reflects the fact that preference along the rth dimension decreases more rapidly than for a less heavily weighted axis (Carroll, 1980). For example, Fig. 4.25 suggests that Subject 1 weights Dimension III more heavily than Dimension IV. The dark eyes versus light eyes characteristic is more important to Subject 1 and this importance is reflected in the preference ratings. Subject 2, however, does not give dimension III any more weight than Dimension IV. Thus the eye characteristic and the mouth contrast are of equal importance to Subject 2.

General Unfolding Model.   The General Unfolding Model, sometimes called the general Euclidean model, allows the assumption that the same basic set of dimensions is involved in the judgments of all individuals to be relaxed. Although all individuals are assumed to share a common stimulus space, they are allowed to choose different sets of "reference axes" within that space. Thus, each individual is allowed to rotate the reference frame of the perceptual space and then to weight the dimensions defined by this new frame of reference. Remember, Euclidean distances are invariant under orthogonal rotations. Therefore it is not the rotation alone that differentiates this model from the simple unfolding model. It is the rotation along with the differential weighting of these "new" rotated dimensions that make this model unique. Figure 4.26 illustrates the general unfolding model for the schematic faces example. Subject 1 still prefers

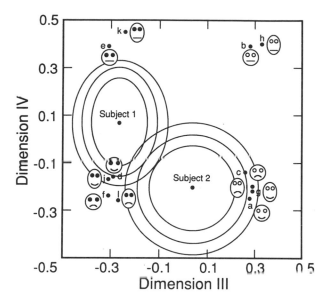

FIG. 4.25. Weighted unfolding model: Schematic faces hypothetical example.

the dark-eyed faces, but only a subset of them, namely, the emotional dark-eyed faces. Now, however, the light-eyed straight-mouthed faces are preferred to the dark-eyed straight-mouth faces. The straight-mouth faces are preferred over the light-eyed "emotional" faces. Subject 2's preferences for the "emotional" faces remain unchanged. However, the dark-eyed straight-mouth faces are now preferred to the light-eyed straight-mouth faces. This example illustrates that a group of individuals can show differences in three respects: ideal point location, axis orientation, and weighting of the reoriented axes (Meulman, Heiser, & Carroll, 1986).

Solving the Unfolding Problem.   The nonmetric internal unfolding problem can be formulated as nonmetric multidimensional scaling of an $N \times n$ rectangular matrix, **P**. KYST-2A (Kruskal, Young, & Seery, 1977) and ALSCAL (Young & Lewyckyj, 1979) allow input of an upper (or lower) corner matrix and treat the matrix as though it were a submatrix **P** of a larger one with large blocks of missing data. These programs have a split-by-rows option, which has the effect of treating an input matrix as row conditional.[16] A nonmetric unfolding of any

---

[16]If p's are proximities and d's distances, the matrix $\mathbf{P} = \{p_{ij}\}$ is row conditional if and only if $p_{ij} > p_{ik}$ implies that $d_{ij} < d_{ik}$. However, $p_{ij} > p_{lk}$ (where i and l are different rows) implies nothing about the order of d_{ij} and d_{lk}. The values in one row of the matrix give no information about the values in a different row of the matrix. Thus the $N \times n$ rectangular proximity matrix used to solve the nonmetric internal unfolding problem is row conditional. One subject's set of proximity judgments gives no information about a different subject's set of judgments.

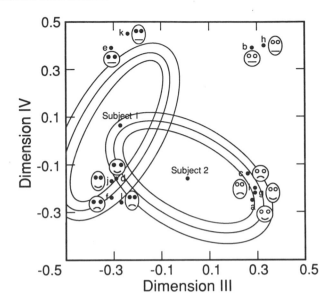

FIG. 4.26. General unfolding model: Schematic faces hypothetical example.

off-diagonal matrix should be done by using the split by rows option (treat the matrix as conditional, even if it is not), performing nonmetric multidimensional scaling, and using Stress-2, where

$$S_2 = \sqrt{\frac{\sum\limits_{j}^{R} (d_{ij} - \hat{d}_{ij})^2}{\sum\limits_{j}^{R} (d_{ij} - \bar{d}_i)^2}}. \tag{12}$$

KYST-2A or ALSCAL can be used to perform metric internal unfolding by replacing the monotone regression option with linear or polynomial regression. The matrix can be treated as conditional or unconditional, in the metric case. Stress-2 should be used, however, unless the regression is without the constant term in which case Stress-1 can be used (Carroll, 1980).

An alternative approach to internal metric unfolding is Schönemann's (1970) "metric unfolding" procedure. Schönemann's approach treats **P** as an unconditional matrix and assumes p_{kj} to be linearly related to d_{kj}^2. Under these conditions, an Eckart-Young decomposition of the doubly centered matrix[17] of prefer-

---

[17]A doubly centered matrix is a matrix where the mean of each column is zero and the mean of each row is zero.

ence scale values should yield both the stimulus space and the subject ideal points space. PREFMAP-2 (Chang & Carroll, 1972) will also solve the internal unfolding model using a two–stage process. First, the stimulus configuration is obtained from the preference data by factoring either the singly or doubly centered matrix of preferences. Then, the ideal points for the subjects are fit into the derived object space (Carroll, 1980).

PREFMAP-3 can be used to fit the external unfolding models. The subject $\times$ stimulus preferences matrix and the stimulus $\times$ dimension solution matrix are used to solve the unfolding problem. The PREFMAP approach translates an external analysis of the unfolding model into a regression problem, where $F_k(p_{kj})$ = d_k^2 with F_k assumed to be linear. Thus:

$$p_{kj} = F_k^{-1}(d_{kj}^2) = a_k d_{kj}^2 + c_k \tag{13}$$

where

$$d_{kj}^2 = \sum_{r=1}^{R} w_{kr}(y_{kr} - x_{jr})^2.$$

This is a multiple linear regression problem, with the preference scale values p_{kj} for subject k as the dependent variable and the x_{jr}'s as $r + 1$ independent variables. For the simple unfolding model, all w_{kr} are equal. The general unfolding model uses transformed y_{kr}'s and x_{jr}'s, which represent a subject's rotation of the axes. PREFMAP-3, in Phase III, with the monotonic regression option, will result in a nonmetric external unfolding solution.

Constrained Models

Interpretability of a multidimensional scaling solution is paramount. Sometimes, however, the configuration that maximizes a goodness-of-fit function is not interpretable. A more meaningful multidimensional space may result by constraining, or systematically altering, the configuration to satisfy a priori criteria. External information about the stimuli, the expected configuration, or the underlying theory involved can be used to constrain the scaling model, refine the resulting solution, and possibly yield a more meaningful configuration. For example, an investigator scaling the schematic face data might expect a Pleasantness dimension, based on theory or past research in face perception. One may expect this Pleasantness dimension to be represented by the mouth characteristic in the stimulus design. When using the unconstrained model, it may be difficult to locate this hypothesized dimension, as was illustrated by the schematic faces KYST solution discussed earlier. Thus, the investigator may constrain the model such that the stimuli with smiling mouths will project on the high end of the Pleasantness dimension, the straight mouth in the middle, and the frowning face on the low end, representing Unpleasantness. The restricted model estimates the stimulus configuration while at the same time constraining the model in a way appropriate to the stimulus design or other a priori structural hypothesis (Bloxom, 1978).

The constrained model estimates model parameters "with the options that each parameter can be fixed to equal some a priori value, constrained to be equal to any other parameter, or free to take on any value in the parameter space" (Bloxom, 1978, p. 398). The general unconstrained multidimensional scaling model is one where each parameter is free to take on any value. In the unconstrained situation, the only way to achieve a better fit is by adding another dimension with its full set of parameters. However, by constraining model parameters, there may exist models that can represent the data with greater or almost equal accuracy, but with far fewer parameters than required by the unconstrained method (Bentler & Weeks, 1978). The general multidimensional scaling model states:

$$\delta_{ij} = d_{ij} + a + e_{ij} \tag{14}$$

with

$$d_{ij}^z = (\mathbf{x}_i - \mathbf{x}_j) \, \mathbf{S} \, (\mathbf{x}_i - \mathbf{x}_j)'$$

where

$\mathbf{x}_i$ = scale value vector of stimulus i,

a = additive constant, and

$\mathbf{S}$ = covariance matrix for the dimensions (allows for oblique rotation).

A variety of restricted multidimensional scaling models arise immediately with the recognition that some of the parameters of the general model may be restricted to take on only certain values, or ranges of values. Generally, the restricted model consists of constraining some of the x_{ir} such that $x_{ir} = c$, some fixed known constant c, or $x_{ir} = wx_{jr}$, some known constant proportion w of some free parameter x_{jr} (Bentler & Weeks, 1978). Prior analyses, theory, or other considerations will indicate which constraints should be placed on the model. For example, theory suggests that the schematic faces should result in a Pleasantness dimension represented by the mouth shape. Thus the x_{i1} might be constrainted to equal 1, 0, or -1 depending on the mouth shape of stimulus i. An upturned mouth would be set to have a scale value of 1 on dimension I, a straight mouth constrained to 0, and a downturned mouth to -1.

Asymmetric Proximities.   Asymmetric distancelike data can occur in several situations, such as confusions of one stimulus with another, migration rates, frequencies of journal citations, or initiation of contact by members of a social group. The simplest method used to analyze asymmetric distances ignores the asymmetry, by averaging responses δ_{ij} and δ_{ji}, yielding a symmetric matrix. Then a conventional multidimensional scaling method is applied to the symmetric matrix. However, there is the possibility that the asymmetry may contain important information.

Any square nonsymmetric matrix can be decomposed into a symmetric and a skew-symmetric matrix $\mathbf{P} = \mathbf{Q} + \mathbf{R}$, where $\mathbf{Q}$ is symmetric [$q_{ij} = q_{ji} = (p_{ij} + p_{ji})/2$] and $\mathbf{R}$ is skew symmetric, $\mathbf{R} = \mathbf{P} - \mathbf{Q}$, $r_{ij} = -r_{ji}$ (Bentler & Weeks, 1982). The asymmetric multidimensional scaling model states:

$$\delta_{ij} = d_{ij} + a + k_i - k_j + e_{ij} \tag{15}$$

At least one constraint must be placed on k; generally one element of k is set to equal zero. The model parameters can then be restricted according to stimulus design or theoretical considerations. The asymmetric model introduces a new set of model parameters, namely k, that need to be estimated.

Constrained MDS Versus Confirmatory MDS. Heiser and Meulman (1983) drew a distinction between constrained multidimensional scaling and confirmatory multidimensional scaling. "Constraints refer to the translation of either theoretical or data analytical objectives into computational specifications. Confirmation refers to a study of the balance between systematic and random variation in the data for modeling of the systematic part" (p. 381). The rotation of the schematic faces KYST solution to match the implied stimulus design is an example of confirmatory multidimensional scaling. Model parameters were not constrained to equal a certain constant before estimation, as in the case of the Pleasantness dimension alluded to earlier in this section. Rather, the estimated configuration was rotated toward the stimulus design target configuration (see Fig. 4.1) to verify, or confirm, that the solution did indeed match the physical stimulus design.

PROBLEMS AND PROSPECTS

Davison (1983) distinguished among three general types of MDS applications: (a) *dimensional applications,* in which the researcher is primarily interested in the number and identities of the stimulus dimensions employed by the subjects in perceiving and judging a stimulus domain; (b) *data reduction,* where the interest is to reduce the complex interrelationships between stimuli represented in one or more proximity matrices to a simpler, more visualizable form; and (c) *configural verification* studies, which begin with a theory or hypothesis about the pattern or shape of the MDS-derived configuration. In verification studies, both the number and identities of the stimulus dimensions might be known in advance, with the research focus on the ordering and/or interval properties of the stimuli. A fourth type of application involves using MDS and related methods to assess *structural change* in the perception or construal of stimuli resulting from an experimental manipulation, developmental changes, or some other type of intervention, for example, psychotherapy, education, or additional exposure to the stimuli. The majority of MDS applications to date has been of the first two types. Although these types of studies have provided valuable descriptive information about a wide variety of stimulus domains, more applications of the latter two types need to be made if the full promise and power of the MDS modeling framework is to be fully realized.

For many problem areas in the social and behavioral sciences (e.g., perception, cognition, social structure), MDS procedures and the associated methodology have important advantages compared to other approaches commonly used to investigate these problems. Also, MDS methods have some inherent limitations; some are at the level of model assumptions whereas others concern task, subject, and stimulus matters. The latter can often be alleviated by careful research design, task selection, instructions to subjects, and appropriate caution in interpretation of results. A brief discussion of these advantages and limitations follows.

Advantages

Similarity Judgments.   For most stimulus domains and subjects, judgment of pairwise similarities is a simple, nonreactive, and. natural task. Important attributes, which might not be readily accessible to directed judgment methods (i.e., unidimensional attribute ratings on scales specified by the investigator), are tapped in these similarities judgments. With the generalized similarity judgment task the selection of relevant attributes is up to the subject not the experimenter, which is its most important feature. Within broad limits, this aspect of the methodology guarantees that the MDS-derived dimensions will be psychologically relevant. However, certain types of similarity judgment tasks can produce data that violate model assumptions (Tversky, 1977).

Individual Differences.   Individual differences scaling techniques (e.g., SINDSCAL, PREFMAP, MDPREF) quantify individual differences at the level of dimension "weights" or saliences. These quantities allow inferences about interindividual variation (or intraindividual variation with repeated measures data) in the degree to which respondents rely on the stimulus dimensions in judging similarity or forming preferences. These salience weights can then be related to independently assessed attributes of the judges via regression or discriminant analysis. These external measures may be personality or attitude measures, demographic characteristics, or other information about the judges' psychological, physical, or experiential characteristics. These model-derived salience measures are not plagued by the types of response biases that typically contaminate self-reports about attribute importance and other measures derived from unidimensional judgment data. Assessment and identification of individual differences at the level of salience weights represents a potentially important, theoretically interesting methodology. For example, in the Davison and Jones (1976) study of a military unit, hypotheses about the relationship between members' status in the unit and salience of status in their construal of others were investigated. We found that members who were seen by others (and themselves) as low in status, attached high salience to status in judging others.

Although few published examples exist, it is feasible to perform one-mode, two-way, metric or nonmetric MDS on similarities data generated by a single subject. In a well-designed study, with a motivated subject, the data from a single judge are ordinarily reliable, numerous, and "rich" enough to support such an analysis. A related possibility would involve collection of similarities data from a single judge on numerous occasions, say over the course of psychotherapy or during a semester-long college course. The resulting two-mode, three-way data could be modeled using SINDSCAL, with occasions replacing subjects as the second mode. These possibilities, along with the standard options for analysis of individual differences, point to the fact that MDS methods span the entire idiographic-nomothetic continuum. On the one hand, methods such as INDSCAL permit detailed comparisons among judges and identification of communalities and differences in their perceptions or construals of the stimulus domain under investigation; on the other, some of these methods can be used to summarize group-level data.

Structure and Process.   In her preface to a book on applications of multivariate models to social science phenomena (Hirschberg & Humphreys, 1982), Hirschberg discussed the distinction between structural and process models of cognition. She noted that whereas structural models "deal with states of mind, process models attempt to account for changes in these states; put in this simplified way, it is clear that structural models have a certain logical priority" (p. 2). Taking this line of argument one step further, it has been proposed (Jones, 1983) that meaningful studies of social and other types of information processing should be based on domains where stimulus structures have already been delineated and calibrated by previous empirical investigations. MDS, cluster analysis and related methods, for example, correspondence analysis and conjoint measurement, are well suited for this purpose. Although these methods are not designed to model dynamic processes, important insights about the selection, encoding, and organization of stimulus domains can be achieved from informed application of MDS methods.

Shoben and Ross (1987) made a related point in arguing that results from MDS and related methods can provide constraints for theorizing about cognitive process, and specifically, distinguishing between competing theories. For example, they suggested that the dispute between proponents of unitary theories of memory (e.g., Anderson & Ross, 1980) and advocates of "dual-store" accounts (e.g., Tulving, 1983) might be resolved by careful application of MDS and related methods to the stimulus domains employed in these investigations.

Shoben and Ross (1987) provided a thorough and insightful review of applications of MDS in cognitive psychology, with an emphasis on work where MDS results were subsequently used to predict behavior in cognitive tasks (e.g., latencies in a categorization task) as well as investigations of structural change over time and stimulus context effects. Nosofsky's work (1990, 1991) on perceptual classification and recognition memory is an excellent example of how MDS results can be used as a basis for further modeling and as a source of constraints for theorizing.

Study of Pre- or Nonverbal Subjects.   Certain choice/discrimination tasks, for example the *same-different paradigm,* yield confusion and/or reaction time data that can be interpreted and analyzed as proximities data. Likewise, some types of sociometric data, for example dyad-level measures of interaction frequency, can be treated as proximities data. Thus it becomes possible to analyze the perceptual or cognitive structure of a stimulus domain for preverbal infants, nonhuman animals, or any organism capable of discrimination or interaction with others of its kind. Recognizing this possibility, Schneider (1972) used a "percentage of correct choices" measure derived from a same-different task to investigate the dimensionality and structure of color-space for pigeons.

Limitations and Cautions

In most problem areas where MDS methods have been employed, the promise of these methods for providing important insights about substantive issues has yet to be realized. The majority of published research employing MDS methods has been exploratory and descriptive, with relatively few examples of investigations exploiting the power of MDS to address broader theoretical and methodological issues.

As with any versatile data analysis or modeling framework, MDS methods are well suited to certain types of research questions or purposes, and less appropriate, or even unsuited, to other kinds of questions. MDS methods can be applied to virtually any type of data (see Shepard, 1972), but simply because a data matrix can be analyzed using these methods does not mean that it should be. Here we provide a brief discussion of the limitations of conventional MDS methods.[18]

---

[18]Broadly defined, MDS methods include correspondence analysis, discriminant functions, principal components analysis, factor analysis, conjoint and functional measurement methods, and certain types of clustering techniques. Our discussion is confined to MDS methods narrowly defined to include only techniques that require as input a one-mode, two-way or two-mode, three-way (dis)similarities matrix, or in the case of multidimensional preference models, a two-mode, two- or three-way matrix of preference-strength measures.

Data Collections Issues.   Acquisition of direct, generalized similarity judgments, the most common data type for MDS, requires pairwise comparisons. Thus, the subjects' judgment task can be repetitious and tedious, especially when the number of stimuli is large. A related problem occurs when the stimuli are lengthy (e.g., paragraphs), complex, or unfamiliar. The time required for subjects to process and judge pairs of such complex stimuli often exceeds that available. Sorting and ranking methods, and pair-reduction schemes, can be used to increase task interest and efficiency.

When the stimuli are differentially familiar, the corresponding proximities will be differentially reliable. Under these conditions, degenerate or distorted MDS solutions may occur. To alleviate these problems, the investigator should assess familiarity via direct ratings or some other means; for example, Nygren and Jones (1977) asked subjects to identify the party affiliations of the political candidates that were used as stimuli in their experiments. The resulting measures can be used to screen the data or employed as weights in the monotone regression stage of the KYST-2A estimation algorithm.

Process Assumptions.   In general, MDS models involve fairly elaborate assumptions about the nature of the similarity judgments (or other proximity measures) employed as input (Beals, Krantz, & Tversky, 1968), the perceptual-judgmental processes of the subjects generating the data (Attneave, 1950; Tversky, 1977; Tversky & Gati, 1978), and, in the case of INDSCAL, the nature of individual differences. The perceptual-judgmental model implicitly assumed is dimensional and continuous. In contrast, the processes involved in assessing similarity in many stimulus domains are probably more categorical and discontinuous, and ideally should be modeled with procedures that both mirror this sort of process and yield representations that are nonspatial and/or categorical in form. Tversky (1977) challenged the distance models underlying the methods considered herein with a variety of demonstrations questioning the minimality ($d_{ii} = 0$) and symmetry ($d_{ij} = d_{ji}$) conditions underlying the metric distance axioms. His proposed "contrast model" expresses the similarity between stimuli as a linear combination of their common and distinctive *discrete features*, a framework that can account for asymmetric data and some types of stimulus context effects.

When the assumption of a spatial distance model for MDS is untenable, a variety of nonspatial models for proximities data are available. In addition to the vast array of clustering methods (Sneath & Sokal, 1973), several nonspatial models have been proposed in the last decade; these include ADCLUS (Shepard & Arabie, 1979), ADDTREE (Sattath & Tversky, 1977), and INDCLUS (Carroll & Arabie, 1983). Discussion of these and other alternative models is beyond the scope of this chapter. An excellent overview and taxonomy of these models, along with 30 or so other multidimensional scaling and tree structure procedures is provided by Carroll and Arabie (1980).

A Diagnostic Method. With such a wide diversity of scaling models and procedures available, how should an investigator choose the optimum method for the research problem and data at hand? Pruzansky, Tversky, and Carroll (1982) applied both an additive tree model (Sattath & Tversky, 1977) and a conventional MDS model, that is KYST, to numerous artificial and actual data sets. They developed two empirical measures, skewness and elongation, which when applied to 20 sets of proximities data, were successful in "diagnosing" which model would provide the best fit to the data. Their analysis showed that data sets arising from *perceptual* stimuli (e.g., colors, forms) were better fit by nonmetric MDS, whereas data sets for *conceptual* stimuli (e.g., exemplars from semantic categories) were better fit by ADDTREE. Examining these results, Shoben and Ross (1987) suggested that the difficulty that conventional MDS procedures have with categorical data sets "may be a result of the way people judge similarities in this context and not an indication of the nature of the underlying representation" (p. 249). They argued that when a stimulus set contains both the category name and its exemplars, for example bird-goose, all members of the category tend to be rated as highly similar to their category name. On the other hand, two exemplars, for example robin and goose, would be judged dissimilar to each other. The net result is a "conflict" between the exemplar distances and the exemplar-superordinate (i.e., category name) distances, leading to poor fit of the MDS solution.

Hubert and Golledge (1981) developed a methodology for evaluating the adequacy of reconstructed matrices. Their technique can be utilized to compare the original proximity matrix to matrices containing distances derived from MDS, clustering, or other scaling solutions. The reconstructed distance matrices can represent solutions derived from two different scaling models or two solutions obtained from a single method, but with different dimensionalities. The Hubert and Golledge technique assesses the degree of fit of the reconstructed distance matrix (or matrices) to a data matrix, A, by examining the nature and the magnitude of

$$r_{A,B-C} = \frac{r_{AB} - r_{AC}}{\sqrt{2(1 - r_{BC})}} \qquad (r_{BC} \neq 1) \qquad (16)$$

where

r_{AB}, r_{AC}, and r_{BC} are the simple correlations between corresponding entries in proximity matrix A and the reconstructed matrices, B and C.

A reference distribution for $r_{A,B-C}$ is constructed using randomization methods.

This heuristic can be employed to choose the best model for the problem or data set being investigated. For example, a clustering solution and a multidimensional scaling solution can be compared to the raw proximities in an attempt to assess which method best reconstructs the data. Such an application may lend validity to the Pruzansky, Tversky, and Carroll (1982) criteria. Perhaps an investigator is interested in evaluating whether treatment effects exist. A clinical psychologist may want to ascertain whether depressed subjects' perceptions of social attitudes change significantly following therapy. The before treatment and after treatment multidimensional spaces can be compared via the Hubert and Golledge technique. A variety of applications are discussed by Hubert and Golledge (1981).

At their worst, when applied to inappropriate types of data or stimulus domains, or applied carelessly without regard for model assumptions, MDS methods can misrepresent, mislead, and even detract from our understandings of psychological phenomena or processes. At their best, multidimensional scaling models and related techniques are powerful, versatile tools for: (a) investigating perceptual, cognitive, and behavioral domains; (b) extracting the structure underlying these domains from large amounts of multivariate data; (c) aiding the representation and visualization of the derived structure; (d) modeling complex relationships between perceptions, preferences, and other types of judgments or behaviors; and (e) accomplishing the first four objectives without obscuring important individual or group differences.

REFERENCES

Abelson, R. P., & Sermat, V. (1962). Multidimensional scaling of facial expressions. *Journal of Experimental Psychology, 63*(6), 546–554.

Anderberg, M. R. (1973). *Cluster analysis for applications*. New York: Academic Press.

Anderson, J. R., & Ross, B. H. (1980). Evidence against a semantic-episodic distinction. *Journal of Experimental Psychology: Human Learning and Memory, 6,* 441–466.

Arabie, P. (1973). Concerning Monte Carlo evaluations of nonmetric multidimensional scaling algorithms. *Psychometrika, 38,* 607–608.

Arabie, P., & Boorman, S. A. (1973). Multidimensional scaling of measures of distance between partitions. *Journal of Mathematical Psychology, 10,* 148–203.

Arabie, P., Carroll, J. D., & DeSarbo, W. S. (1987). *Three-way scaling and clustering*. Beverly Hills, CA: Sage Publications.

Attneave, F. (1950). Dimensions of similarity. *American Journal of Psychology, 63,* 516–556.

Beals, R., Krantz, D. H., & Tversky, A. (1968). Foundations of multidimensional scaling. *Psychological Review, 75,* 127–142.

Bennett, J. F., & Hays, W. L. (1960). Multidimensional unfolding: Determining the dimensionality of ranked preference data. *Psychometrika, 25,* 27–43.

Bentler, P. M., & Weeks, D. G. (1978). Restricted multidimensional scaling models. *Journal of Mathematical Psychology, 17,* 138–151.

Bloxom, B. (1978). Constrained multidimensional scaling in N spaces. *Psychometrika, 43,* 397–408.

Borg, I., & Lingoes, J. C. (1979). Multidimensional scaling with side constraints on the distances. In J. C. Lingoes, E. E. Roskam, & I. Borg (Eds.)., *Geometric representations of relational data* (2nd ed.). Ann Arbor, MI: Mathesis.

Brunswik, E. (1956). *Perception and the representative design of psychological experiments*. Berkley, CA: University of California Press.

Carroll, J. D. (1980). Models and methods for multidimensional analysis of preferential choice (or other dominance) data. *Psychometrika, 35*(3), 283–319.

Carroll, J. D., & Arabie, P. (1980). Multidimensional scaling. In Rosenzweig, Mr. R. & Porter, L. W. (Eds.), *Annual review of psychology* (Vol. 31, pp. 607–649). Palo Alto, CA: Annual Reviews.

Carroll, J. D., & Arabie, P. (1983). INDCLUS: An individual differences generalization of the ADCLUS model and the MAPCLUS algorithm. *Psychometrika, 48*, 157–169.

Carroll, J. D., & Chang, J. J. (1970). Analysis of individual differences in multidimensional scaling via an N-way generalization of Eckart-Young decomposition. *Psychometrika, 35*, 283–319.

Chang, J. J., & Carroll, J. D. (1972). *How to use PREFMAP and PREFMAP-2—Programs which relate preference data to multidimensional scaling solutions.* Unpublished manuscript, Bell Telephone Labs, Murray Hill, NJ.

Chang, J. J., & Carroll, J. D. (1968). *How to use PROFIT, a computer program for property fitting by optimizing nonlinear or linear correlation.* Unpublished manuscript, Murray Hill, NJ, AT&T Bell Laboratories.

Chang, J. J., & Carroll, J. D. (1969). *How to use MDPREF, a computer program for multidimensional analysis of preference data.* Murray Hill, NJ: Bell Laboratories.

Chernoff, H. (1971). *The use of faces to represent points in n-dimensional space graphically* (Tech. Rep. No. 71). Palo Alto: Stanford University, Department of Statistics.

Cliff, N., & Young, F. W. (1968). on the relation between unidimensional judgments and multidimensional scaling. *Organizational Behavior and Human Performance, 3*, 269–285.

Cohen, H. S., & Jones, L. E. (1974). The effects of random error and subsampling of dimensions on recovery of configurations by nonmetric multidimensional scaling. *Psychometrika, 39*, 69–90.

Coombs, C. H. (1950). Psychological scaling without a unit of measurement. *Psychological Review, 57*, 148–158.

Coombs, C. H. (1964). *A theory of data.* New York: Wiley.

Coxon, A. P. M. (1982). *The user's guide to multidimensional scaling.* Exeter, NH: Heinemann Educational Books.

Cronbach, L. J., & Gleser, G. C. (1953). Assessing similarity between profiles. *Psychological Bulletin, 50*, 456–473.

David, H. A. (1963). The structure of cyclic paired-comparison designs. *Journal of the Australian Mathematical Society, 3*, 117–127.

Davison, M. L. (1983). *Multidimensional scaling.* New York: Wiley.

Davison, M. L., & Jones, L. E. (1976). A similarity-attraction model for predicting sociometric choice from perceived group structure. *Journal of Personality and Social Psychology, 33*(5), 601–612.

Eckart, C., & Young, G. (1936). The approximation of one matrix by another of lower rank. *Psychometrika, 1*, 211–218.

Efron, B. (1979). Bootstrap methods: another look at the jackknife. *Annals of Statistics, 7*, 1–26.

Green, P. E., Carmone, F. J., & Smith, S. M. (1987). *Multidimensional scaling: Concepts and applications.* Boston, MA: Allyn & Bacon.

Gregson, R. A. M. (1975). *Psychometrics of similarity.* New York: Academic Press.

Hanno, M., & Jones, L. E. (1973). Effects of a change in reference person on the multidimensional structure and evaluations of trait adjective. *Journal of Personality and Social Psychology, 28*(3), 368–375.

Heiser, W. J., & Meulman, J. (1983). Constrained multidimensional scaling, including confirmation. *Applied Psychological Measurement, 7*(4), 381–404.

Hirschberg, N., & Humphreys, L. G. (1982). *Multivariate applications in the social sciences.* Hillsdale, NJ: Lawrence Erlbaum Associates.

Hubert, L. J., & Arabie, P. (1988). Relying on necessary conditions for optimization: unidimensional scaling and some extensions. In H. H. Bock (Ed.), *Classifications and related methods of data analysis* (pp. 463–472). Amsterdam: North Holland.

Hubert, L. J., & Golledge, R. G. (1981). A heuristic method for the comparison of related structures. *Journal of Mathematical Psychology, 23,* 214–226.

Jones, L. E. (1983). Multidimensional models of social perception, cognition, and behavior. *Applied Psychological Measurement, 7*(4), 451–472.

Jones, L. E., & Hirschberg, N. (1975). *What's in a face? Individual differences in face perception.* Paper presented at the American Psychological Association Convention, Chicago, IL.

Klahr, D. (1969). A Monte Carlo investigation of the statistical significance of Kruskal's nonmetric scaling procedure. *Psychometrika, 34,* 319–330.

Klingberg, F. L. (1941). Studies in measurement of the relations between sovereign states. *Psychometrika, 6,* 335–352.

Kruskal, J. B. (1964a). Nonmetric multidimensional scaling: A numerical method. *Psychometrika, 29*(2), 115–129.

Kruskal, J. B. (1964b). Multidimensional scaling by optimizing goodness of fit to a nonmetric hypothesis. *Psychometrika, 29*(1), 1–27.

Kruskal, J. B., Young, F. W., & Seery, J. B. (1977). *How to use KYST-2A, A very flexible program to do multidimensional scaling and unfolding.* Murray Hill, NJ: Bell Telephone Laboratories.

Kruskal, J. B., & Wish, M. (1978). *Multidimensional scaling.* Beverly Hills, CA: Sage Publications.

Lingoes, J. C., & Roskam, E. E. (1973). A mathematical and empirical analysis of two multidimensional scaling algorithms. *Psychometrika Monograph Supplement, 38* (4, Pt. 2, Monograph No. 19).

MacCallum, R. C. (1977). Effects of conditionality on INDSCAL and ALSCAL weights. *Psychometrika, 42,* 297–305.

MacCallum, R. C., & Cornelius, E. T. (1977). A Monte Carlo investigation of recovery of structure by ALSCAL. *Psychometrika, 42,* 401–428.

Meulman, J., Heiser, W. J., & Carroll, J. D. (1986). *PREFMAP-3 user's guide* (Document No. 11229-860918-08TMS File No. 25952). Murray Hill, NJ: Bell Telephone Laboratories.

Nosofsky, R. M. (1990). Relations between exemplar-similarity and likelihood models of classification. *Journal of Mathematical Psychology, 34*(4), 393–418.

Nosofsky, R. M. (1991). Tests of an exemplar model for relating perceptual classification and recognition memory. *Journal of Experimental Psychology: Human Perception and Performance, 17*(1), 3–27.

Nygren, T. E., & Jones, L. E. (1977). Individual differences in perception and preferences for political candidates. *Journal of Experimental Social Psychology, 13,* 182–197.

Pruzansky, S. (1975). *How to use SINDSCAL: A computer program for individual differences in multidimensional scaling.* Murray Hill, NJ: Bell Telephone Laboratories.

Pruzansky, S., Tversky, A., & Carroll, J. D. (1982). Spatial versus tree representations of proximity data. *Psychometrika, 47*(1), 3–24.

Ramsey, J. O. (1977). Maximum likelihood estimation in multidimensional scaling. *Psychometrika, 42,* 241–266.

Richardson, M. W. (1938). Multidimensional psychophysics. *Psychological Bulletin, 35,* 659–660.

Rosenberg, S. (1982). The method of sorting in multivariate research with applications selected from cognitive psychology and person perception. In N. Hirschberg & L. G. Humphreys (Eds.), *Multivariate applications in the social sciences* (pp. 4–66). Hillsdale, NJ: Lawrence Erlbaum Associates.

Ross, R. T. (1934). Optimum orders for the presentation of pairs in the method of paired comparisons. *Journal of Educational Psychology, 25,* 375–382.

Sattath, S., & Tversky, A. (1977). Additive similarity trees. *Psychometrika, 42,* 319–345.

Schlosberg, H. (1952). The description of facial expressions in terms of two dimensions. *Journal of Experimental Psychology, 44*(4), 229–237.

Schlosberg, H. (1954). Three dimensions of emotion. *Psychological Review, 61*(2), 81–88.

Schneider, B. (1972). Multidimensional scaling of color difference in the pigeon. *Perception and Psychophysics, 12,* 373–378.

Schönemann, P. H. (1970). On metric multidimensional unfolding. *Psychometrika, 35,* 349–366.

Shepard, R. N. (1962a). The analysis of proximities: Multidimensional scaling with an unknown distance function. I. *Psychometrika, 27*(2), 125–140.

Shepard, R. N. (1962b). The analysis of proximities: Multidimensional Scaling with an unknown distance function. II. *Psychometrika, 27*(3), 219–246.

Shepard, R. N. (1972). A taxonomy of some principal types of data and of multidimensional methods for their analysis. In R. N. Shepard, A. K. Romney, & S. Nerlove (Eds.), *Multidimensional scaling: Theory and applications in he behavioral sciences: Vol. 1. Theory* (pp. 24–47). New York: Seminar Press.

Shepard, R. N. (1974). Representation of structure in similarity data: Problems and prospects. *Psychometrika, 39*(4), 373–421.

Shepard, R. N., & Arabie, P. (1979). Additive clustering: representation of similarities as combinations of discrete overlapping properties. *Psychological Review, 86,* 87–123.

Shoben, E. J., & Ross, B. H. (1987). Structure and process in cognitive psychology using multidimensional scaling and related techniques. In R. R. Ronning, J. A. Glover, J. C. Conoley, & J. C. Witt, (Eds.), *The influence of cognitive psychology on testing* (pp. 229–266). Hillsdale, NJ: Lawrence Erlbaum Associates.

Sneath, P. H. A., & Sokal, R. R. (1973). *Numerical taxonomy.* San Francisco: W. H. Freeman.

Spence, I. (1982). Incomplete experimental designs for multidimensional scaling. In R. G. Golledge & J. N. Rayner (Eds.), *Proximity and preference* (pp. 29–46). Minneapolis, MN: University of Minnesota Press.

Spence, I. (1972). A Monte Carlo evaluation of three nonmetric multidimensional scaling algorithms. *Psychometrika, 37,* 461–486.

Spence, I. (1983). Monte Carlo simulation studies. *Applied Psychological Measurement, 7*(4), 405–425.

Spence, I. (1979). A simple approximation for random rankings stress values. *Multivariate Behavioral Research, 14,* 355–365.

Spence, I., & Domoney, D. W. (1974). Single subject incomplete designs for nonmetric multidimensional scaling. *Psychometrika, 41,* 43–64.

Spence, I., & Olgivie, J. C. (1973). A table of expected stress values for random rankings in nonmetric multidimensional scaling. *Multivariate Behavioral Research, 8,* 511–517.

Tatsuoka, M. (1971). *Multivariate analysis.* New York: Wiley.

Torgerson, W. S. (1952). Multidimensional scaling: I. Theory and method. *Psychometrika, 17*(4), 401–419.

Tucker, L. R. (1960). Intra-individual and inter-individual multidimensionality. In H. Gulliksen & S. Messick (Eds.), *Psychological scaling: Theory and applications* (pp. 155–161). New York: Wiley.

Tukey, J. W. (1958). Bias and confidence in not-quite so large samples. *Annals of Mathematical Statistics, 29,* 614.

Tulving, E. (1983). *Elements of episodic memory.* London: Oxford Press.

Tversky, A. (1977). Features of similarity. *Psychological Review, 84*(4), 327–351.

Tversky, A., & Gati, I. (1978). Studies of similarity. In E. Rosch & B. B. Lloyd (Eds.), *Cognition and categorization* (pp. 79–98). Hillsdale, NJ: Lawrence Erlbaum Associates.

Weinberg, S. L., Carroll, J. D., & Cohen, H. S. (1984). Confidence regions for INDSCAL using the jackknife and bootstrap techniques. *Psychometrika, 49,* 475–491.

Weisberg, H. F. (1974). Models of statistical relationship. *The American Political Science Review,* *68,* 1638–1655.

Young, F. W. (1970). Nonmetric multidimensional scaling: Recovery of metric information. *Psychometrika, 35,* 455–473.

Young, F. W., & Cliff, N. (1972). Interactive scaling with individual subjects. *Psychometrika, 37,* 385–415.

Young, F. W., & Lewyckyj, R. (1979). *ALSCAL users guide.* Carrboro, NC: Data Analysis and Theory Associates.

Young, F. W., Null, C. H., Sarle, W. S., & Hoffman, D. L. (1982). Interactively ordering the similarities among a large set of stimuli. In R. G. Golledge & J. N. Rayner (Eds.), *Proximity and preference* (pp. 10–28). Minneapolis, MN: University of Minnesota Press.

Young, G., & Householder, A. S. (1938). Discussion of a set of points in terms of their mutual distances. *Psychometrika, 3,* 19–22.

5 Can the Various Meanings of Probability Be Reconciled?

Glenn Shafer
School of Business, University of Kansas

AN AGREEMENT TO DISAGREE

For over 50 years, there has been a consensus among philosophers, statisticians, and other probabilists about how to think about probability and its applications. According to this consensus, probability is first of all a theory in pure mathematics, based on Kolmogorov's axioms and definitions. Different interpretations of these axioms are possible, and the usefulness of each interpretation can be debated, but the mathematical theory of probability stands above the debate. As the historian Lorraine Daston (1988) put it, "The mathematical theory itself preserves full conceptual independence from these interpretations, however successful any or all of them may prove as descriptions of reality" (pp. 3–4).

The consensus is depicted in Fig. 5.1. The subjectivists, who interpret probability as degree of belief, and the frequentists, who interpret it as relative frequency, have only the purely mathematical theory as common ground. Both subjectivists and frequentists find applications for probability, but these applications are separated from the common ground by the opposing philosophies. They are based on different meanings for probability.

In practice, this consensus is an agreement to disagree. The two camps, the frequentists and the subjectivists, agree on the mathematics of probability, but they also agree that everyone has a right to give whatever interpretation they please to this mathematics. Though they continue to debate the fruitfulness of their different interpretations, they have come to realize that they are talking past each other. They have no common language beyond the mathematics on which they agree so perfectly.

The consensus has become so ingrained in our thinking that it seems natural

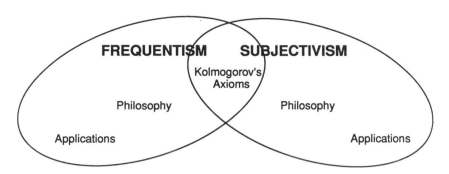

FIG. 5.1. The consensus.

and unavoidable. All mathematics has been axiomatic since the work of David Hilbert, and any axiomatic system, as Kolmogorov (1950) pointed out, admits "an unlimited number of concrete interpretations besides those from which it is derived" (p. 1). So every branch of pure mathematics can declare its conceptual independence of its applications. As Daston (1988) put it, "For modern mathematicians, the very existence of a discipline of applied mathematics is a continuous miracle—a kind of prearranged harmony between the 'free creations of the mind' which constitute pure mathematics and the external world" (p. 4).

We should remember, however, that not all fields that use mathematics have ceded primacy to pure mathematics the way probability has. In physics, for example, axioms are secondary to physical theory, which melds mathematics and meaning in a way that goes beyond any single set of axioms. The physicist is usually interested in a physical theory that can be axiomatized in different and sometimes incompatible ways, not in a single axiomatic theory that can be interpreted in incompatible ways.

I remember vividly a lecture by one of my own physics teachers, in which he derived one physical relation from another and then gave a second derivation that went more or less in the opposite direction. When a student pointed out the near circularity, he launched into a passionate discussion of the difference between physicists and mathematicians. This blackboard is the world, he said. Mathematicians want to find a single starting place—a particular dot of chalk—from which to derive everything else. Physicists take whatever starting point is convenient for getting where they want to go. Sometimes physicists go from here to there, sometimes from there to here—at this point in the lecture, he drew arrows all over the blackboard. The point is to see how things hang together and to understand parts not understood before, not to get everywhere from one place.

My purpose in this chapter is to urge looking at probability the way physicists look at a physical theory. Probability is not a physical theory, but it does have an object. The axioms are about something. This something is an unusual situation—a situation that occasionally occurs naturally, sometimes can be contrived, and often can only be imagined. In this unusual situation, *probability* is not devoid of meaning. It has many meanings, just as *energy* or *work* have many meanings within the situation described by the theory of mechanics. The numerical probabilities in the unusual situation described by the theory of probability are simultaneously fair prices, warranted degrees of belief, and frequencies.

The unusual situation the theory of probability describes occurs infrequently and may be imperfect even when it does occur, so I call it "the ideal picture of probability."

Outline of the Chapter

The chapter first describes informally the simplest case of the ideal picture of probability, the case where a fair coin is flipped repeatedly. We see there how the ideal picture ties frequencies, fair prices for gambles, and warranted degrees of belief together in a circle of reasoning, any point of which can be used as a starting point for an axiomatic theory.

The chapter then refines this informal account into a mathematical framework and formulates axioms for fair price and probability that resemble Kolmogorov's axioms yet capture aspects of the ideal picture that are left outside Kolmogorov's framework.

Next the chapter relates the ideal picture to the philosophical history of mathematical probability. The ideas that make up the ideal picture had been developed and even unified to some extent by the end of the 18th century, but this unity fell victim to the extreme empiricism of the 19th century, which saw frequency as an acceptable basis for a scientific theory but rejected fair price and warranted degree of belief as metaphysical fictions. In the 20th century, the subjectivists have matched the frequentists' empiricism with a story about personal betting rates that sounds like an empirical description of people's behavior. Both the frequentist and subjectivist foundations for probability have elements of truth, but they become fully cogent only when they are brought back together and seen as alternative descriptions of the same ideal picture.

The mistake that 19th-century empiricists made about the mathematical theory of probability was to suppose that it could be used only by fitting it term-by-term to some reality. They believed that using the theory meant finding numbers in the world—frequencies or betting rates—that followed the rules for probabilities. In the late 20th century, however, we can take a more flexible view of the relation between theory and application. We can take the view that the mathematical theory of probability is first of all a theory about an ideal picture, and applying the theory to a problem means relating the ideal picture to the problem in any of several possible ways.

The final section discusses some of the ways the ideal picture can be used. Some statistical modeling uses the ideal picture as a model for reality, but much statistical modeling uses it only as a standard for comparison. Another way to use the ideal picture is to draw an analogy between the evidence in a practical problem of judgment and evidence in the ideal picture. We can also use simulations of the ideal picture—sequences of random numbers—to draw samples and assign treatments in experiments, so that probabilities in the ideal picture become indirect evidence for practical judgments.

AN INFORMAL DESCRIPTION
OF THE IDEAL PICTURE

The ideal picture of probability is more subtle than the pictures drawn by most physical theories, because it involves knowledge as well as fact. Probability, in this picture, is *known* long-run frequency. The picture involves both a sequence of questions and a person. The person does not know the answers to the questions but does know the frequencies with which different answers occur. Moreover, the person knows that nothing else she knows can help her guess the answers.

This section briefly describes the ideal picture informally, with an emphasis on its intertwining of fact and knowledge. It deals with the simplest case, the fair coin repeatedly flipped. This simple case is adequate to demonstrate how the ideal picture ties three ideas—knowledge of the long run, fair price, and warranted belief—in a circle of reasoning. We can choose any point in this circle as a starting point for an axiomatic theory, but no single starting point does full justice to the intertwining of the ideas.

The picture of the fair coin generalizes readily to biased coins and experiments with more than two possible outcomes, and to the case where the experiment to be performed may depend on the outcomes of previous experiments.

For a more detailed description of the ideal picture, see Shafer (1990a).

Flipping a Fair Coin

Imagine a coin that is flipped many times. The successive flips are called *trials*. Spectators watch the trials and bet on their outcomes. The knowledge of these spectators is peculiarly circumscribed. They know the coin will land heads about half the time, but they know nothing further that can help them predict the outcome of any single trial or group of trials. They cannot identify beforehand a group of trials in which the coin will land heads more than half the time, and the outcomes of earlier trials are of no help to them in predicting the outcomes of later trials. And they know this.

Just before each trial, the spectators have an opportunity to make small even-money bets on heads or on tails. But because they are unable to predict the outcomes, they cannot take advantage of these opportunities with any confidence. Spectators know they will lose approximately half the time. A net gain, small relative to the amount of money bet, is possible, but a comparable net loss is also possible. No plan or strategy based on earlier outcomes can assure a net gain. For all these reasons, the spectators consider even-money bets on the individual trials fair.

Spectators begin with only a limited stake, so they may be bankrupted before they can make as many bets as they want. They can avoid bankruptcy by making the even-money bets smaller when their reserves dwindle, but this will make it even harder to recover lost ground. Consequently, they can hope only for gains comparable in size to their initial stake. No strategy can give them any reasonable hope of parlaying a small stake into a large fortune. This is another aspect of the fairness of the even-money bets.

The spectators also bet on events that involve more than one trial. They may bet, for example, on the event that the coin comes up heads on both of the first two trials, or on the event that it comes up heads on exactly 500 of the first 1,000 trials. They agree on fair odds for all such events. These odds change as the trials involved in the events are performed. They are fair for the same reasons that the even odds for individual trials are fair. A spectator betting at these odds cannot be confident of any gain and has no reasonable hope of parlaying a small stake into a large fortune. Moreover, if they make many small bets involving different trials, they will approximately break even.

Fairness has both long- and short-run aspects. The statement about bets involving many different trials is strictly a statement about the long run. But the other statements apply to the short run as well. No way of compounding bets, whether it involves many trials or only a few, can make spectators certain of gain or give them a reasonable hope of substantially multiplying their stake.

Precise statements about the long run are themselves events to which the spectators assign odds. They give great odds that the coin will land heads on approximately half of any large number of trials. They give 600 to 1 odds, for example, that the number of heads in the first 1,000 tosses will be between 450 and 550. They also give great odds against any strategy for increasing initial capital by more than a few orders of magnitude. They give at least 1,000 to 1 odds, for example, against any particular strategy for parlaying $20 into $20,000. Thus the knowledge of the long run that helps justify the fairness of the odds is expressed directly by these odds.

Just as very great odds seem to express knowledge,[1] less great but substantial odds seem to express guarded belief. The spectators' degree of belief in an event is measured numerically by the odds they give. The odds are warranted by knowledge of the short and long runs, thus this numerical degree of belief is not a matter of whim; it is a warranted partial belief.

The spectator's numerical degrees of belief express quantitatively how war-

---

[1]There is a consensus in philosophy that knowledge is justified true belief. We cannot know something unless it is true. By equating knowledge with mere great odds, I may appear to challenge this consensus. The spectators can know something that might not be true. It is not my intention, however, to enter into a debate about the nature of knowledge. I merely ask leave to use the word in an ordinary sloppy way.

ranted belief becomes knowledge or practical certainty as the risky shot is stretched into the long shot, or as the short run is stretched into the long run. The spectators' certainty that long shots, or very ambitious gambling strategies, will fail is a limiting case of their skepticism about all gambling strategies, more ambitious and less ambitious. They give at least k to 1 odds against any strategy for multiplying initial capital by k—2 to 1 odds against doubling initial capital, 1,000 to 1 odds against increasing initial capital a thousandfold, and so on. Similarly, their certainty that heads will come up half the time in the long run is a limiting case of their belief that the proportion of heads will not be too far from one-half in the shorter run. The degree of belief and the degree of closeness expected both increase steadily with the number of trials.

A Circle of Reasoning

Our description of the ideal picture traced a circle. We started with knowledge of the long run. Then we talked about the odds warranted by this knowledge. Then we interpreted these odds as a measure of warranted belief—that is, as a measure of probability. And we noted that the knowledge of the long run with which we began was expressed by certain of these odds.

This circle of description can be refined into a circle of reasoning. The spectators can reason from their knowledge of the long run to the assignment of fair odds to individual trials. They can argue from the odds for individual trials to odds for events involving more than one trial. They can argue that all these odds should be interpreted as degrees of warranted belief (or probabilities). Then they can deduce very high probabilities for events that express the knowledge of the long run with which they began.

This circle of reasoning is depicted by Fig. 5.2. The first step is represented by the arrow from "Knowledge of the Long Run" to "Fair Odds." The spectators move along this arrow when they argue that even odds for individual trials are sensible and fair, because these odds take all their relevant knowledge into account, and because someone who makes many bets at these odds will approximately break even, and so on.

The next step can be located inside "Fair Odds." This is the step from odds on individual trials to odds on all events. As it turns out, once we agree on odds on individual trials, and once we agree that these odds are not affected by the results of earlier trials, there is exactly one way of assigning odds to events involving more than one trial so that a person cannot make money for certain by compounding bets at these odds.

The next step, represented by the arrow from "Fair Odds" to "Probability," is to interpret fair odds as a measure of warranted belief. The spectators point out their own willingness to bet at the odds they call fair. Appealing to the natural tie between action and belief, they conclude that these odds measure their beliefs.

Within "Probability," the spectators deduce that their degrees of belief, or

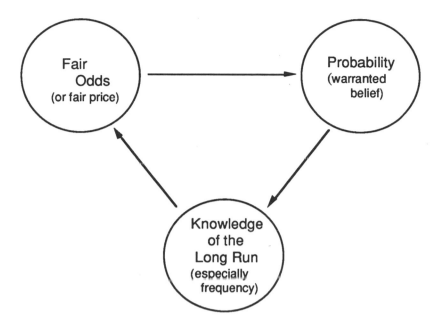

FIG. 5.2.   The circle of probability ideas.

probabilities, for complicated events include very high probabilities that the coin will land heads approximately half the time in any particular long run of trials and any particular scheme for parlaying small sums into large ones will not succeed. This allows them to travel the final arrow, from "Probability" back to "Knowledge of the Long Run."

Making the Picture into Mathematics

The reasoning we have just described is not axiomatic mathematics. Much of it is rhetorical rather than deductive. And it goes in a circle. This is typical of informal mathematical reasoning. When we axiomatize such reasoning, we choose a particular starting point. We then use the rhetorical reasoning to justify definitions, and the deductive reasoning to prove theorems.

In Fig. 5.2, the arrows represent the major rhetorical steps and hence the major potential definitions. The spectators can define odds on the basis of their long-run knowledge, they can define warranted belief in terms of odds, and they can define knowledge as very great warranted belief. The circles joined by the arrows represent the potential starting points. An axiomatic theory can be based on axioms for knowledge of the long run, axioms for fair odds, or axioms for warranted belief.

In deference to the weight of popular opinion in favor of the frequentist interpretation of probability, I began this description of the ideal picture with knowledge of the long run. But, as we will see later, it is actually easier to begin an axiomatic theory with fair odds or with warranted belief.

The fact that knowledge of the long run, fair odds, and warranted belief can each be used as a starting point for an axiomatic theory should not be taken to mean that any one of these ideas is sufficient for grounding the theory of probability in a conceptual sense. The axioms we need in order to begin with any one of these starting points can be understood and justified only by reference to the other aspects of the picture. The three aspects of the ideal picture are inextricably intertwined.

A later section supports this claim with the historical record. Historically, the three starting possible points are represented by Kolmogorov's axioms (probability), von Mises's random sequences (long-run frequency), and de Finetti's two-sided betting rates (odds or price). Kolmogorov's axioms were always intended as a formal, not a conceptual, starting point; everyone agrees they must be justified either by a frequency or betting interpretation. Von Mises did want to make long-run frequency a self-sufficient starting point, but his work, together with that of Wald and Ville, leads to the conclusion that knowledge of long-run frequency is only one aspect of the knowledge that justifies calling the odds in the ideal picture fair. De Finetti wanted to make odds or price a self-sufficient starting point, without any appeal to the long-run to justify the fairness of odds or prices, but this too fails to provide a full grounding for the ideal picture.

Conclusion

The situation described in this section is only one version of the ideal picture of probability. Like the situation described by any physical theory, the ideal picture has many variations, not all of which are strictly compatible with each other. It would be unwise, therefore, to claim too much for the story told here. But the intertwining of knowledge, fair odds, and belief described here occurs, in one way or another, in all the visions that have informed the growth of mathematical probability.

A FORMALIZATION OF THE IDEAL PICTURE

The preceding section pointed to several possible axiomatizations of the ideal picture. This section develops a formal mathematical framework in which some of these axiomatizations can be carried out.

The most fundamental feature of any mathematical framework for probability is its way of representing events. Kolmogorov represented events as subsets of an arbitrary set. The framework developed here is slightly less abstract. Events are subsets, but the set of which they are subsets is structured by a *situation tree*, which indicates the different ways events can unfold. This brings in the idea of a sequence of events and hence the possibility of talking about frequencies.

Using the idea of a situation tree, we develop axioms for fair price, and we translate them into axioms for probability. We show how knowledge of the long run can be deduced from these axioms. We conclude by briefly comparing the axioms with Kolmogorov's axioms.

To completely validate the claims made in the preceding section, we should also develop axioms for knowledge of the long run. This task was undertaken, in a certain sense, by von Mises, Wald, and especially Kolmogorov, in his work on complexity theory and the algorithmic definition of probability. This work is mentioned later on, but it would stretch this chapter too far, in both length and mathematical complexity, to review it in detail and relate it to the other ideas in Fig. 5.2.

The framework developed in this section is more general than the story about the fair coin. This framework permits biased coins, as well as experiments with more than two outcomes, and it also permits the choice of the experiment to be performed on a given trial to depend on the outcomes of preceding trials. It does not, however, encompass all versions of the ideal picture; for example, it does not allow the spectators to choose the sequence in which they see the outcomes of trials.

The Framework for Events

Situation trees provide a framework for talking about events, situations, expectations, and strategies.

Situation Trees. Figure 5.3 is one example of a situation tree. It shows the eight ways three flips of a fair coin can come out. Each of the eight ways is represented by a path down the figure, from the circle at the top to one of the eight stop signs at the bottom. Each circle and each stop sign is a *situation* that can arise in the course of the flips. The circle at the top is the situation at the beginning. The stop signs are the possible situations at the end. The circles in between are possible situations in which only one or two of the flips have been completed. Inside each situation are directions for what to do in that situation.

Figure 5.4 depicts another situation tree, one that involves several different experiments. The first experiment is a flip of a fair coin. Depending on how it comes out, the second is either another flip of a fair coin or a flip of a coin that is biased three to one for heads. Later experiments may include flipping another fair coin, flipping a coin biased four to one for heads, or throwing a fair die. Altogether, there will be three or four experiments, depending on the course of events. The odds for each experiment are specified in some way; we specify the bias or lack of bias for each coin, and we say that the die is fair.

The ideal picture involves a situation tree like Fig. 5.3 or Fig. 5.4, except that

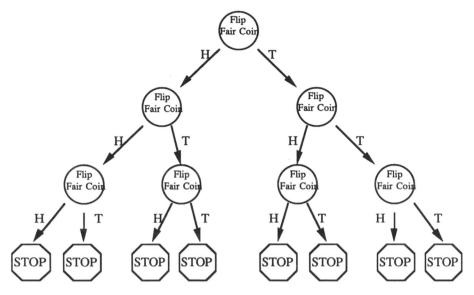

FIG. 5.3. A situation tree for three flips of a fair coin.

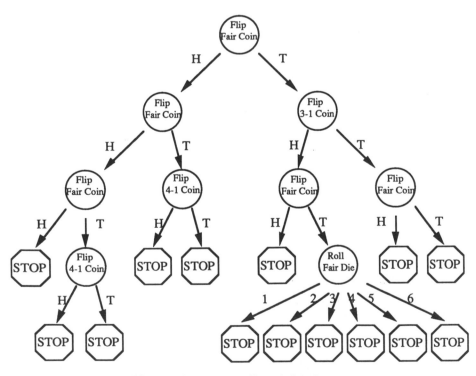

FIG. 5.4. A more complicated situation tree.

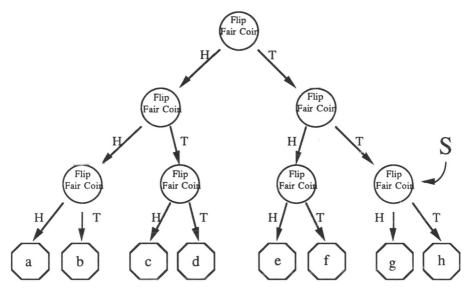

FIG. 5.5.   Events as sets of stop signs.

all the paths down the tree are very long. In each situation, we specify an experiment with a finite number of possible outcomes, and we specify in some way the odds for these outcomes.

Events.   An event is something that happens or fails as we move down the situation tree. Getting heads on the first flip is an event. Getting exactly two heads in the course of the first three flips is an event. Formally, we can identify an event with a set of stop signs—the set consisting of those stop signs in which the event has happened. This can be illustrated using the lettered stop signs of Fig. 5.5. Here the event that we get heads on the first flip is the set {a, b, c, d} of stop signs. The event that we get exactly two heads is the set {b, c, e}. And so on.

Notice that for each situation there is a corresponding event—the set of stop signs that lie below it. This is the event that we get to the situation. It is often convenient to identify the situation with this event. We identify the situation S in Fig. 5.5, for example, with the event {g, h}. Not all events are situations. The event {b, c, e} in Fig. 5.5, for example, is not a situation.

We say that the event A is *certain* in the situation S if S is contained in A. We say that A is *impossible* in S if the intersection of A and S is empty.

Expectations.   Let us call a function that assigns a real number—positive, zero, or negative—to every stop sign an *expectation*.[2] We call the numbers

---

[2]This is now usually called a *random variable*. I use the 18th-century term, *expectation*, in order to avoid evoking 20th-century presumptions about the meaning of randomness.

assigned by an expectation *payoffs*. A positive payoff is the number of dollars the holder of the expectation will receive in that stop sign; a negative payoff is the number of dollars the holder must pay. Figure 5.6 shows an expectation that pays the holder $1 for every head in three flips.

Let us use uppercase letters from the end of the alphabet—*X, Y, Z*, and so on—for expectations, and let us write $X(i)$ for X's payoff in the stop sign i. Expectations can be added; we simply add their payoffs in each stop sign. The expectation $X + Y$ has the payoff $X(i) + Y(i)$ in stop sign i. We can also add constants to expectation. The expectation $X + r$ has the payoff $X(i) + r$ in i.

An *$r ticket* on an event A is an expectation that pays $r if A happens and $0 if A does not happen. Figure 5.7 shows a $1 ticket on the event {b, c, e}. We write $\langle \$r, \text{A} \rangle$ for an $r ticket on A.

Suppose you bet $p on an event at odds p to $(1 - p)$, where $0 \leq p \leq 1$. This means that you pay $p, you will get a total of $1 back if the event happens, and you will get nothing back if the event fails. Thus you have paid $p for a $1 ticket on the event. So stating odds on an event is equivalent to setting a price for a ticket on the event. Saying that $p:(1 - p)$ is the fair odds on A is the same as saying that $p is the fair price for a $1 ticket on A.

The sum of two tickets is an expectation. It is not always a ticket; but sometimes it is; for example, $\langle \$r, \text{A} \rangle + \langle \$s, \text{A} \rangle = \langle \$(r + s), \text{A} \rangle$.

Every expectation is the sum of tickets, but a given expectation can be obtained as a sum of tickets in more than one way. The expectation in Fig. 5.6, for example, is the sum of a $3 ticket on {a}, a $2 ticket on {b, c, e}, and a $1 ticket

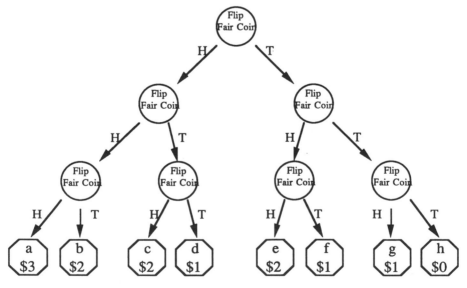

FIG. 5.6.   An expectation.

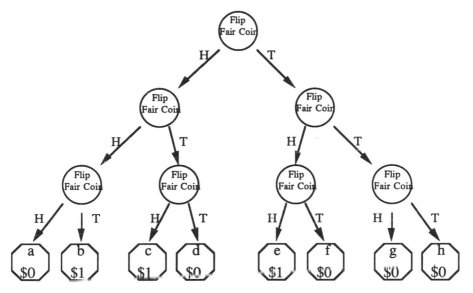

FIG. 5.7.   A $1 ticket on {b, c, e}.

on {d, f, g}, but it is also the sum of a $1 ticket on {a, b, c, d, e, f, g}, a $1 ticket
on {a, b, c, e}, and a $1 ticket on {a}.

In general, gambling means buying and selling expectations. We can think of
this in several ways. On the one hand, we can think of it in terms of tickets on
events. All expectations are sums of tickets, consequently gambling boils down
to buying and selling tickets. On the other hand, we can think in terms of the total
expectation we acquire by all our buying and selling. If we buy a collection Φ_1 of
tickets for r, and we sell a collection Φ_2 of tickets for s, then the net result is
that we have added the expectation

$$\sum_{X \in \phi_1} X - \sum_{X \in \phi_2} X - \$r + \$s$$

to whatever expectation we already had.

Strategies.   Spectators are free to buy and sell expectations at each step as
the sequence of experiments proceeds. In terms of the situation tree, this means
that they can buy and sell expectations in each situation. The only restrictions are
those imposed by their means and obligations. They cannot pay more for an
expectation in a given situation than they have in that situation, and they cannot
sell an expectation in a given situation if there is a stop sign below that situation
in which they would not be able to pay off on this expectation together with any
others they have already sold.

A *strategy* is a plan for how to gamble as the experiments proceed. To specify a strategy, we specify what expectations to buy and sell in each situation, subject to the restrictions just stated. An earlier section said that a strategy could take the outcomes of preceding experiments into account. This is explicit in the framework of a situation tree. A situation is defined by the outcomes so far, so when spectators specify what expectations they will buy and sell in a situation, they are specifying what they will do if these are the outcomes.

A strategy boils down, in the end, to an expectation. The spectators' initial capital, say r, and their strategy, say $\mathcal{S}$, together determine, for each stop sign i, the capital, say $X_{r,\mathcal{S}}(i)$, that the spectator will have in i. So the strategy amounts to trading the r for the expectation $X_{r,\mathcal{S}}$.

The strategy $\mathcal{S}$ is *permissible* in the situation S for a spectator with capital r in S (and no other expectations or obligations) only if $X_{r,\mathcal{S}}(i)$ is nonnegative for all i in S. Unlike businesspeople in real life, a spectator in the ideal picture is not allowed to undertake obligations that she may not be able to meet.

Axioms for Fair Price

Now let us use the framework provided by the situation tree to develop some of the possibilities for axiomatization mentioned earlier. It is convenient to begin with fair price. We formulate axioms for fair price and relate these axioms to the circle of probability ideas in the way suggested by Fig. 5.2. In other words, we informally justify the axioms by the knowledge we claim of the long run (this is the arrow from knowledge of the long run to fair price), we use the axioms to derive rules for probability (this is the arrow from fair price to probability), and then we deduce the knowledge of the long run that motivated the axioms (this is the arrow from probability to knowledge of the long run).

There are a number of ways to formulate axioms for fair odds or fair prices. For this brief exposition, it is convenient to emphasize fair prices for tickets on events.

Let us write $V_S(X)$ for the fair price of the ticket X in the situation S. We omit the parentheses when we use the bracket notation for a ticket; in other words, we write $V_S\langle\$r, A\rangle$ instead of $V_S(\langle\$r, A\rangle)$.

Here are our axioms for the ticket prices $V_S(X)$:

Axiom T1. If A is certain in S, then $V_X\langle\$1, A\rangle = 1$.

Axiom T2. If A is impossible in S, then $V_S\langle\$1, A\rangle = 0$.

Axiom T3. If A is possible, but not certain in S, then $0 < V_S\langle\$1, A\rangle < 1$.

Axiom T4. If $0 \leq r \leq t$, then $V_S\langle\$r, A\rangle \leq V_S\langle\$t, A\rangle$.

Axiom T5. If the sum of the tickets X and Y is also a ticket, then $V_S(X + Y) = V_S(X) + V_S(Y)$.

Axiom T6. If X and Y are tickets, S precedes T, and $V_T(X) = V_T(Y)$, then $V_S\langle X, T \rangle = V_S\langle Y, T \rangle$.

Axiom T6 extends our notation by using a ticket as a prize in another ticket. In other words, $\langle X, T \rangle$ is the ticket that pays X if T happens and nothing otherwise. This does not really extend what we mean by a ticket, because the compounded ticket $\langle X, T \rangle$ still boils down to a ticket that pays a certain amount of money if a certain event happens and nothing otherwise. If $X = \langle \$r, A \rangle$, for example, then $\langle X, T \rangle = \langle \langle \$r, A \rangle, T \rangle = \langle \$r, A \cap T \rangle$.

The derivation of these axioms from knowledge of the long run begins with an argument for the existence of fair prices for all tickets. This knowledge of the long run explicitly includes knowledge of fair odds for outcomes of each individual experiment, odds that do not change until that experiment is performed. So we can call $\$r \cdot p$ the fair price in situation S of a $\$r$ ticket on an outcome of an experiment that is to be performed in S or later and for which the fair odds are p to $(1 - p)$. (If the experiment is to be performed before S, or only in situations incompatible with S, then the fair price is either $\$0$ or $\$r$.) Fairness means that a person breaks even in the long run by betting on these events at these odds, and no one can compound bets, over the short run or the long run, to make money for certain. By buying tickets on various outcomes in various situations (this may involve buying a ticket in one situation to provide funds to buy a ticket in another situation), we can put together a ticket on any event, so we conclude that there are fair prices for all tickets.

The axioms then follow from the idea that one cannot make money for certain by compounding tickets. Axiom T1, for example, is justified because otherwise one could make money for certain in S merely by buying or selling the ticket $\langle \$1, A \rangle$. Axiom T5 holds because otherwise one could make money for certain in S by buying X and Y separately and selling $X + Y$, or vice versa. Axiom T6 holds because otherwise one could make money for certain in S by buying $\langle X, T \rangle$ and selling $\langle Y, T \rangle$ in S and then, if one arrives in T, selling X and buying Y (or vice versa).

Axiom T3 requires special comment. Strictly speaking, only the weaker statement that $0 \le V_S\langle \$1, A \rangle \le 1$ is justified, but the strict inequalities are convenient. Allowing equality would mean, in effect, allowing events to have zero probability even though they are possible. Our framework is finite—there are a finite number of experiments each with finite number of outcomes—so there is no need for this.

Axioms T1–T6 are only about tickets. But all expectations are sums of tickets, and the assumption of fairness implies that all ways of compounding an expectation from tickets yield the same total price. So every expectation has a fair price. As it turns out, we can deduce this from Axioms T1–T6 alone, without appealing to the background knowledge about fairness that justifies these axioms. More precisely, we can deduce from these axioms the existence of prices $E_S(X)$ for all situations S and all expectations X such that $E_S(X) = V_S(X)$ when X is a ticket. We can deduce that these prices add:

$$\text{If } Y = \sum_{X\in\phi} X, \text{ then } E_S(Y) = \sum_{X\in\phi} E_S(X).$$

We can also deduce that

$$\min_{i\in S} X(i) \le E_S(X) \le \max_{i\in S} X(i), \tag{1}$$

and more generally that if $\mathcal{P}$ is a partition of S into situations, then

$$\min_{T\in\mathcal{P}} E_T(X) \le E_S(X) \le \max_{T\in\mathcal{P}} E_T(X). \tag{2}$$

Equation 1 says that you cannot make money for sure by buying X in S and collecting on it when you get to a stop sign (or by selling X in S and paying it off when you get to a stop sign), and Equation 2 says that you cannot make money for sure by buying X in S and selling it when you get to a situation in $\mathcal{P}$ (or by selling X in S and buying it back when you get to a situation in $\mathcal{P}$).

We can also deduce that strategies are to no avail. More precisely, we can deduce that if the strategy $\mathcal{S}$ is permissible in S for a spectator with capital $\$r$ in S, then $E_S(X_{r,\mathcal{S}}) = r$. Thus a strategy accomplishes nothing that we cannot accomplish directly by paying the fair price for an expectation.

Axioms for Probability

We have completed our work inside the circle labeled "Fair Odds" in Fig. 5.2. Now we move along the arrow from fair odds to probability by using the fair odds on an event as a measure of warranted belief in the event.

Actually, we do not exactly use the odds $p:(1 - p)$ on A as the measure of our belief in A. We are accustomed to a scale from zero to one for belief, thus instead we use the price p. We write

$$P_S(A) = V_S\langle\$1, A\rangle, \tag{3}$$

and we call $P_S(A)$ the probability of A in S.

The following axioms for probabilities follow from Axioms T1–T6 for fair prices.

Axiom P1. $0 \le P_S(A) \le 1$.

Axiom P2. $P_S(A) = 0$ if and only if A is impossible in S.

Axiom P3. $P_S(A) = 1$ if and only if A is certain in S.

Axiom P4. If A and B are incompatible in S, then $P_S(A \cup B) = P_S(A) + P_S(B)$.

Axiom P5. If T follows S, and U follows T, then $P_S(U) = P_S(T) \cdot P_T(U)$.

Axioms P1–P5 are essentially equivalent to Axioms T1–T6. If we start with Axioms P1–P5 and define ticket prices by

$$V_S(\$r, A) = r \cdot P_S(A),$$

then we can derive Axioms T1–T6. It then turns out that

$$E_S(X) = \sum_{i \in S} X(i) \cdot P_S(\{i\}) \tag{4}$$

for every expectation X.

The fact that we can begin with Axioms P1–P5 does not, of course, make probability autonomous of the other ideas in the circle of reasoning. Like each of the other ideas, probability is caught in the circle of reasoning. It can serve as a formal starting point, but when it does, it uses axioms whose motivation derives from the other starting points. The only apparent justification for Axioms P1–P5 lies in the long-run and short-run fairness of odds that we used to justify Axioms T1–T6.

Axioms P1–P5 are quite similar to Kolmogorov's axioms. We return to this point later. First, let us travel one more step in our circle, from probability to knowledge of the long run.

Implications for the Short and Long Runs

The axioms we have just formulated capture the essential properties of fair price and probability in the ideal picture, and from them we can derive the spectators' knowledge of the long run. The details cannot be crowded into this chapter, but we can state the most basic results.

One aspect of the spectators' knowledge of the long run is their knowledge that no strategy, short- or long-run, can assure a net gain. As we have already seen, a strategy always boils down to buying an expectation, so it suffices to show that buying an expectation cannot assure a net gain. And this is easy. It follows from Equation 4 that for any expectation X and any situation S,

$$\text{if } P_S\{X > E_S(X)\} > 0, \text{ then } P_S\{X < E_S(X)\} > 0.$$

If X can pay more than its price, then it can also pay less.

Another aspect of the spectators' knowledge of the long run is that no strategy can give a reasonable hope of parlaying a small stake into a large fortune. Following a strategy in S boils down to using one's entire capital in S to buy a nonnegative expectation X, thus it suffices to show that the probability of a nonnegative expectation paying many times its price is very small. And this again is easy. It is easy to show that

$$P_S\{X \geq k \cdot E_S(X)\} \leq \tfrac{1}{k},$$

when X is nonnegative. The odds against a strategy for multiplying one's capital by k are at least k to one.

Finally, consider the frequency aspect of the spectators' knowledge of the long run. In the case of the fair coin, the spectators know that the proportion of heads is one-half in the long run. They know something similar in the general case. In order to derive this knowledge from our axioms, we need to formulate the idea of a spectator's successive net gains from holding an expectation.

Let Ω denote the initial situation in a situation tree, and suppose that spectators acquire an expectation X in Ω. They hold this expectation until they come to a stop sign, but every time they move down from one situation to the next, they take note of X's change in value. They call this change their net gain. Their first net gain is

$$G_1 = E_{S_1}(X) - E_\Omega(X),$$

where S_1 is the situation at which they arrive immediately after Ω. Their second net gain is

$$G_2 = E_{S_2}(X) - E_{S_1}(X),$$

where S_2 is the situation at which they arrive immediately after S_1. And so on. The net gains $G_1, G_2, \ldots$ depend on the path they take down the tree (because $S_1, S_2, \ldots$ depend on the path they take down the tree). In other words, the net gains are expectations. And we can prove the following theorem about them.

Theorem. Suppose the net gains G_j are uniformly bounded. In other words, there exists a constant κ such that $|G_j(i)| \leq \kappa$ for every j and every stop sign i. And suppose ϵ and δ are positive numbers. Then there exists an integer N such that

$$P_\Omega\left(\frac{\sum\limits_{j=1}^{n} G_j}{n} \leq \epsilon\right) \geq 1 - \delta$$

whenever $n \geq N$.

In other words, the average net gain in n trials is almost certainly (with probability $1 - \delta$) approximately (within ϵ of) zero. This theorem is one version of the law of large numbers, first proven by James Bernoulli. For a proof of this version, see Shafer (1985).

To see what this theorem means in the case of the fair coin, we can suppose the spectator chooses a number n and bets $1 on heads for each of the first n trials. Altogether she must pay n, and she will get back $2Y$, where Y is the total number of heads in the first n trials. So her net expectation is

$$X = 2Y - n.$$

We have $E_\Omega(Y) = \frac{n}{2}$ and $E_\Omega(X) = 0$. The jth net gain from X, G_j, is $1 if the jth trial comes up heads and $-$1 if it comes up tails. And

$$X = \sum_{j=1}^{n} G_j.$$

Hence

$$\frac{\sum_{j=1}^{n} G_j}{n} \leq \epsilon$$

is equivalent to

$$\left| \frac{X}{n} \right| \leq \epsilon$$

or

$$\left| \frac{Y}{n} - \frac{1}{2} \right| \leq \frac{\epsilon}{2}.$$

So the theorem says that $\frac{Y}{n}$, the frequency of heads, is almost certainly close to $1/2$.

The frequency aspect of the long run in a general situation tree is only a little more complicated. To derive it from the theorem, we assume that the spectators bet $1 in each situation on the outcome of the experiment to be performed in that situation. If we also assume that the probabilities of the events on which they bet never fall below a certain minimum, so that the possible gains for $1 bets are bounded, then the theorem applies, and it says that the frequency with which the spectators win is almost certainly close to the average of the probabilities for the events on which they bet.

The Role of Kolmogorov's Axioms

Kolmogorov's axioms are similar to Axioms P1–P5, but simpler. The simplicity is appropriate, because these axioms serve as a mathematical rather than conceptual foundation for probability.

Kolmogorov begins not with a situation tree, but simply with a set Ω of possible outcomes of an experiment. Events are subsets of Ω. We may assume, in order to make Kolmogorov's axioms look as much as possible like Axioms P1–P5, that Ω is finite. In this case, Kolmogorov assumed that every event A has a probability $P(A)$, and his axioms can be formulated as follows:

Axiom K1. $0 \leq P(A) \leq 1$.
Axiom K2. $P(A) = 0$ if A is impossible.
Axiom K3. $P(A) = 1$ if A is certain.
Axiom K4. If A and B are incompatible, then $P(A \cup B) = P(A) + P(B)$.

Here "A is impossible" means that A = $\varnothing$, "A is certain" means that A = Ω, and "A and B are incompatible" means that A $\cap$ B $\neq$ $\varnothing$. In addition to the axioms, we have several definitions. We call

$$P(A|B) = \frac{P(A \cap B)}{P(B)} \qquad (5)$$

the *conditional probability* of A given B, and we say that A and B are independent if $P(A|B) = P(A)$. We call a real-valued function X on Ω a *random variable*, we set

$$E(X) = \sum_{i \in \Omega} X(i) \cdot P(\{i\}), \qquad (6)$$

and we call $E(X)$ the *expected value* of X.

Axioms K1–K4 are basically the same as Axioms P1–P4. Equation 5 corresponds to Axiom P5, and Equation 6 is similar to 4. But the comparison brings out the sense in which Kolmogorov's axioms do not provide a conceptual foundation for probability. Kolmogorov himself was a frequentist, and yet the axioms do not involve any structure of repetition. This is something that must be added, through the construction of product probability spaces.

Kolmogorov's axioms are justly celebrated in their role as a mathematical foundation for probability. They are useful even in understanding situation trees, for probability spaces, sets with probability measures in Kolmogorov's sense, are needed to provide probabilities for the individual experiments in a situation tree. We should not try, however, to use these axioms as a guide to the meaning of probability. Doing so only produces conundrums. It makes us puzzle over the "probability of a unique event." It makes independence seem like a mysterious extra ingredient added to the basic idea of probability. It makes conditional probability equally mysterious, by making it seem completely general—a definition that applies to any two events. Independence and conditional probability have a role in the ideal picture of probability, and this role can give us guidance about their use, but all such guidance lies outside Kolmogorov's axiomatic framework.

The framework provided by situation trees and Axioms P1–P5 does not create these mysteries and confusions. This framework makes it clear that events do not have probabilities until they are placed in some structure of repetition. Independence has a role in this structure; events involved in successive trials are independent if the experiment performed in each situation does not depend on earlier outcomes. But we can relax this condition, for successive net gains are uncorrelated even when the experiment performed in each situation does depend on earlier outcomes. And we do not talk arbitrarily about the conditional probability of one event given another; we talk instead about the probability of an event in a situation.

HISTORICAL PERSPECTIVE

This section relates the ideal picture to the historical development of probability theory.

Remarkably, the early development of mathematical probability in the 17th and 18th centuries followed a path similar to the path we have followed through Fig. 5.2, except that it began with fair price as a self-evident idea, not one that had to be justified by an appeal to knowledge of the long run. By the end of the 18th century, the different elements of the ideal picture were relatively unified, but this unity was not well articulated, and it was broken up by the empiricism of the 19th century. This break-up persists in today's stand-off between frequentists and subjectivists. I argue, however, that the competing philosophical foundations for probability that these two groups have advanced are fully coherent only when they are reunified within the ideal picture.

The Original Development of the Ideal Picture

We can use Fig. 5.2, starting with fair odds, as an outline of the development of probability in the 17th and 18th centuries. The theory of fair price in games of chance was first developed by Pascal, Fermat, and Huygens in the 1650s. The step from fair price to probability was taken during the next 50 years, most decisively by James Bernoulli. Bernoulli also was the first to use ideas of probability to prove the law of large numbers, the central feature of our knowledge of the long run. The final step, from knowledge of the long run back to fair price, was apparently first taken only by Condorcet in the 1780s. I only sketch these developments here. For more information, see Hacking (1975) and Hald (1990).

The origins of probability theory are usually traced to the theory of fair price developed in the correspondence between Pierre Fermat and Blaise Pascal in 1654 and publicized in a tract published by Christian Huygens in 1657. The word probability did not appear in this work. It is an ancient word, with equivalents in all the languages these scholars spoke. A probability is an opinion, possibility, or option for which there is good proof, reason, evidence, or authority. But these authors were not talking about probability. They were talking about fair price. Essentially, they reasoned along the lines that we retraced earlier to deduce fair prices for some expectations from fair prices for others. They did not, however, use knowledge of long-run frequency to justify the existence of fair price. For them, it was self-evident that an expectation should have a fair price.

In fact, there was remarkably little talk about the long run in the 17th-century work. Many of the authors played and observed the games they studied, and we must assume that they all had the practical gambler's sense that fair bets would allow one to break even over the long run. But the connection between fairness and the long run was not used in the theory. On the other hand, the theory did involve repetition. There was always some sequence of play in prospect, and this ordering of events was used to relate fair prices to each other, just as we used it in an earlier section. Situation trees like Figs. 5.3 and 5.4 were implicit in the thinking of Pascal, and they were drawn explicitly by Huygens (see Edwards, 1987, p. 146).

From the very beginning of the theory of games of chance, people did want to use the theory in other domains. Pascal may have been the first to do so, in his famous argument for betting on the existence of God. Even when writing on this topic, Pascal did not use the word *probability,* but his friends Antoine Arnauld and Pierre Nicole used it in 1662 in their Port Royal *Logic.* In one justly famous passage, they explained how people who are overly afraid of thunder should apportion their fear to the probability of the danger. From this it is only a short step to probability as a number between zero and one, and a number of people took this step. In 1665, at the age of 19, Leibniz proposed using numbers to represent degrees of probability (Hacking, 1975, p. 85). The English cleric George Hooper, writing in 1689, used such numbers without hesitation, sometimes calling them probabilities and sometimes calling them credibilities (Shafer, 1986).

It was James[3] Bernoulli who made probability an integral part of the mathematical theory. In his book *Ars Conjectandi,* which was published in 1713, 5 years after his death, Bernoulli defined probability as degree of certainty. The theory of fair price could be applied to probability, Bernoulli explained, because conjecturing is like throwing dice, except that the stakes are certainty. Just as the rounds you win and lose in a game entitle you to a definite portion of the stakes, the arguments you find for and against an opinion entitle you to a definite portion of certainty. This portion is the opinion's probability.

By relating probability to the theory of fair price, Bernoulli set the stage for deriving properties of probability from properties of fair price. Fair price is additive, so probability must also be additive. Fair prices change as events unfold, so probabilities also change as events unfold. This is the substance of the arrow from fair price to probability in Fig. 5.2. Bernoulli did not work out these new properties of mathematical probability,[4] but this was quickly done by Abraham de Moivre. In *The Doctrine of Chances,* which first appeared in 1718, de Moivre established many of the ideas used in probability theory today. He talked about probabilities of events (rather than about probabilities of things, as Ber-

---

[3]His English contemporaries referred to Bernoulli as James, but it is now more common to use the German Jakob, because he grew up in German-speaking Basel. But he usually wrote in Latin, where his name is Jacob, or French, where his name is Jacques. We still call Bernoulli's country Switzerland in English, instead of choosing among Schweiz, Suisse, Svizzera, and Helvetia. In the same spirit, I call him James.

[4]It is not even quite fair to say that these properties are consequences of Bernoulli's work, for he made a looser connection between probability and fair price, one that permitted nonadditive probabilities such as those that appear in the theory of belief functions (Shafer, 1978, 1986).

noulli had) and formulated the idea that the probability of one event may change when another event happens; he also formulated versions of the rules of additivity and compound probability, our Axioms P4 and P5. The arguments that he gave for these rules in the third edition of his book (pp. 5–9) were essentially the same as the argument we used to derive Axioms T5 and T6. Similar arguments were given by Bayes (Shafer, 1982, 1985).

Bernoulli's second great contribution was his law of large numbers, a version of which we proved earlier. Bernoulli saw this theorem as a way to justify the use of observed frequencies as probabilities. This steps out of the ideal picture that we have been studying, for within that ideal picture, the spectators know the probabilities, and hence do not need to use frequencies to estimate them.

Within the ideal picture, the law of large numbers is part of the knowledge of the long run that can be used to justify the existence and derive the properties of fair prices. The fair price is the price that will break even in the long run. This use of the law of large numbers within the ideal picture did emerge in the 18th century, but only at the end. Apparently it was first formulated by Condorcet, in the 1780s (Todhunter, 1865, pp. 392–393)

The Disintegration of the Ideal Picture in the 19th Century

The 18th-century elements of the ideal picture that we have just reviewed were synthesized at the beginning of the 19th century in the work of the famous French mathematician Laplace, but this synthesis broke up in the course of the 19th century. The break-up can be attributed to the applied ambitions of the theory, together with the empiricism of the philosophy of science of the times. The mathematicians who studied the theory wanted to use it very widely, not just in games of chance, but the empiricism of the times demanded that the terms of a scientific theory have direct empirical reference. It is easy to imagine such a reference for frequency, but not for fair price or warranted belief.

Laplace worked on probability from the early 1770s until 1820, when the third edition of his famous treatise, *Théorie Analytique des Probabilités,* was published. His most important contributions to probability were mathematical advances, such as the central limit theorem, which facilitated the use of probability in the analysis of data. These contributions can be regarded as the beginning of mathematical statistics (Stigler, 1986). We are more concerned here, however, with Laplace's approach to the foundations of the subject. Here he emphasized probability itself, as if there were always warranted numerical degrees of belief that had the properties that De Moivre and Bayes had derived from the properties of fair price. Traces of those derivations remain in Laplace's work, but on the whole, he wrote as if probability were a self-sufficient starting point. One aspect of this de-emphasis of fair price was that the ordering of events, which was so prominent from Pascal to Bayes, was underplayed. Thus for 19th-century readers, who took Laplace as their authority, this ordering was not an important feature of the ideal picture.

Though he took warranted belief as basic, Laplace integrated it thoroughly with frequency. He had no qualms about Bernoulli's law of large numbers, which purported to prove that the frequency of an event will equal its probability. But as Porter (1986) and Hacking (1990) explained, many later 19th-century writers found the direction of this reasoning troublesome. Most were willing to accept it in games of chance, where rational beliefs are justified by the same symmetries that imply equal frequencies. But in other domains, where the probabilists now wanted to ply their craft, frequency itself seemed to be the only empirical basis for probability. Beginning in the 1840s, philosophers and philosophically minded mathematicians of an empiricist bent, especially Cournot, Ellis, Fries, Mill, and Venn, advanced the view that probability should be defined as frequency. For many of them, proving that frequency will equal probability was unnecessary and even silly.

According to the thesis of this chapter, a synthesis of frequency and rational belief is once again possible and desirable. This is because we can afford to go back to the idea that the theory of probability only applies, in the first instance, to settings such as games of chance. We can afford to do so because our empiricism is more flexible than 19th-century empiricism in the way it relates theory and application. We can now take the view that applying the theory of probability means relating the ideal picture of probability to reality, and there are many ways that this can be done.

The Foundations of Frequentism

Most probabilists resisted frequentism during the 19th century, if only because it seemed to take aim at the most interesting mathematics in their theory. By the end of the century, as positivism became dominant throughout science, probabilists had accepted the idea that probability would ultimately find its foundation in frequency, but they still struggled to reconcile this with the structure of the mathematical theory.

A solution of sorts was achieved in the early 20th century by Kolmogorov's axioms. This solution simply put a wall between the mathematical theory itself, which was to be treated axiomatically, and the interpretation and application of the theory. One could equate probability with frequency by definition in applications, while still deriving frequency from probability within the theory.

Few have been satisfied with this, however. There has been a continuing quest for a deeper frequentist foundation for probability. The most important milestones in this quest have been the work of von Mises on random sequences, the critique of his work by Ville and Wald, and the work by Kolmogorov on algorithmic complexity. (For an overview, see Martin-Löf, 1969. For related recent work, see Uspenskii, Semenov, and Shen', 1990.)

Von Mises, who began writing on probability in the 1920s, hoped to buttress the frequency interpretation by establishing the existence of infinite sequences of heads and tails, say, in which exactly half the entries are heads in the limit, both in the sequence as a whole and in subsequences. He proposed deriving the whole theory of probability from the properties of these random sequences.

Ville demonstrated that frequency is not a sufficient foundation for probability, even in von Mises's framework. The existence of limiting frequencies is not enough to rule out successful gambling schemes. We can construct an infinite sequence of heads and tails in which half the entries are heads in the limit (the limiting frequency of heads is one-half both in the whole sequence and in subsequences selected on the basis of preceding outcomes) and yet in which an observer can make money by betting on heads, because the number of heads is always slightly greater than the number of tails in any finite initial portion of the sequence.

Wald proved the existence of infinite sequences that (a) have a limiting frequency of heads equal to one-half for the whole sequence and for many subsequences, and (b) rule out many gambling schemes of the type suggested by Ville. In fact, given a countable number of subsequences and a countable number of other gambling schemes, there exists a sequence that cannot be beaten by a bettor that uses any of these subsequences or gambling schemes.

In the 1960s, Kolmogorov and others advanced a definition of randomness that applies to finite rather than infinite sequences. According to this definition, a sequence is random to the extent that it is complex, where complexity is measured by the length of the shortest computer program that will generate the sequence. Kolmogorov presented his complexity definition, just as he had presented his axioms many years earlier, as a foundation for an objective, frequency interpretation of probability. As he and others have shown, the complexity definition does imply the knowledge of the long run that is claimed in the ideal picture. It implies both the stability of frequency and the futility of gambling schemes.

Did Wald and Kolmogorov succeed in providing foundations for a purely objective conception of probability? The claim to pure objectivity is shaky, for there are obvious subjective elements in their results. In the case of Wald, the subjectivity lies in the choice of the countable number of properties that are demanded of the sequence. A countably infinite set of properties is surely all a person would want, but they do not make a sequence random from the perspective of someone else who chooses a property not in the set. In the case of Kolmogorov, the subjectivity lies in the choice of the computer. Some sequences can be generated by a short program on one computer but only by a very long program on another.

The viewpoint of this chapter suggests that rather than minimize these obvious subjective elements, we should acknowledge them. They too represent aspects of the ideal picture. They represent the relation between knowledge and fact in the ideal picture. The countable set of properties (for Wald) or the computer (for

Kolmogorov) represent the spectators. The fact that someone else may know more than these spectators is beside the point. But, these spectators' knowledge is limited to knowledge of long-run frequencies and knowledge of their own inability to devise successful betting schemes. Randomness is a property of the relation between fact and observer.

The Foundations of Subjectivism

Belief plays such an important role in the ideal picture that frequentism has never been universally persuasive, even among those who share the frequentists' empiricism. The most vigorous opponents of the frequentists in the 20th century have been the subjectivists, such as Ramsey, de Finetti, and Savage, who have sought an empirical foundation for probability in the ideas of personal (rather than fair) betting rates and personal (rather than warranted) degrees of belief. They have argued that a person's personal belief in an event can be measured by the amount that the person is willing to pay for a $1 ticket on the event.

From the viewpoint of this chapter, this represents an attempt to simplify the ideal picture. The simplification involves dropping the idea of fairness as well as the ordering of events that provides the link with frequency. Is this simplification successful? Can we establish the properties of probability—in the form of Kolmogorov's axioms and definitions, say—from the idea of personal betting rates alone? The subjectivists have argued that we can, but when we compare their arguments to the argument from fairness, the holes are apparent.

First, consider the rule of additivity, represented by Axioms T5, P4, and K5. They did not want to appeal to fairness, so Ramsey, de Finetti, and Savage had to use a very implausible assumption to derive this rule. They had to assume that the greatest price people are willing to pay for a $1 ticket on a given event is the same as the least price at which they are willing to sell such a ticket. This symmetry is inherent in the notion of fair price; a price cannot be fair unless it is fair to both the buyer and the seller. But it is not inherent in the idea of personal price. It is perfectly rational for a person to refuse both sides of some bets.

The possibility of one-sided betting rates and hence one-sided numerical degrees of belief opens a space for alternative theories of subjective probability, in which degrees of belief do not satisfy the usual axioms of probability. One such theory is the theory of belief functions (Shafer, 1990b). The followers of Ramsey, de Finetti, and Savage, have not neglected to denounce this and other one-sided theories as irrational, but there is no argument behind these denouncements.

Second, consider the rule for changes in probability, represented earlier by Axiom T6, Axiom P5, and Equation 5. They do not assume any ordering of events, thus the subjectivists do not explain this rule in terms of personal betting rates in successive situations. Instead, they talk about called-off bets; the conditional probability $P(A|B)$, according to de Finetti, is a personal betting rate for a bet on A that will be called off if B does not happen. This makes it possible to derive Equation 5, but it leaves unanswered the question of what rates for called-off bets have to do with changes in probability.

Here, as in the case of frequentism, the foundation advanced by the subjectivists is basically sound. But to make complete sense of it, we need to put it back into the ideal picture.

THE DIVERSITY OF APPLICATION

In the preceding pages, I repeatedly asserted that applying probability theory to a problem involves relating the ideal picture to that problem. This concluding section briefly reviews some of the ways this can be done.

Probability Models

In the frequentist view, the straightforward way to use probability is to make a probability model of a real repeatable experiment, a model that gives probabilities for the outcomes of that experiment. The model can then be tested by its fit with data from repetitions of the experiment, perhaps after using this data to estimate some of the probabilities in the model.

Such probability modeling is one instance of the thesis that applying probability to a problem means relating the ideal picture to the problem. We are using the ideal picture itself as a model. The question that must be debated is the extent to which the relation between knowledge and fact that is central to the ideal picture carries over to the reality being modeled. Do we really have a probability model, or merely a frequency model? The answer varies. In practice, we never have as much effective knowledge (knowledge of as many probabilities, for example) as the spectators in the ideal picture have, and in some cases we have relatively little. Often the statements we make in probability modeling relate to the knowledge of some idealized observer, not to our own knowledge. It is the negative aspects of the spectators' knowledge in the ideal picture—their inability to take advantage of bets at odds given by the frequencies—that seems to carry over most often to the practical problem.

It should be remembered that even within the ideal picture, not all probabilities are interpretable as frequencies. In a situation tree in which the same experiment is always repeated, we can interpret the probability for an outcome of that experiment as a frequency, and in general situation trees, we can interpret certain averages of probabilities as frequencies. But probabilities for events involving many trials, though they derive their status as fair prices from probabilities interpretable as frequencies, may not themselves be interpretable as frequencies. When we elaborate probability models mathematically by taking limits in the large (infinite numbers of trials) or in the small (continuous models), we tend to create probabilities that do not correspond to frequencies in the reality being modeled even if they do seem interpretable as frequencies in the ideal picture. Matheron (1989) pointed out that this gap between model and reality grows even wider when we insist on interpreting time-series and geostatistical models in terms of imaginary independent repetitions (see also Stein, 1990). By emphasizing that our model is the ideal picture rather the numerical probabilities, we can avoid this insistence.

Probability as a Standard of Comparison

We often use the ideal picture of probability as a standard of comparison. This is explicit in some cases, as when we test the performance of experts by comparing their success with random choice, or when we evaluate or compare judges who make probabilistic predictions (Bloch, 1990). It is less explicit in other cases, as when we use standard statistical tests to assess whether additional independent variables should be included in least-squares fits to nonobservational data.

Several authors, especially Beaton (1981) and Freedman and Lane (1983), have advanced "nonstochastic" interpretations for the standard F-tests in the case of nonobservational data. Their arguments involve the deliberate creation, through permutation of residuals, of populations of data to which the actual data can be compared. Without discussing these arguments in detail, I would like to suggest that their rhetoric can be simplified and strengthened if we think in terms of a comparison between the predictive accomplishment in the data of the variables being tested and the predictive accomplishment in the ideal picture of variables that are irrelevant.

Randomization

We are all accustomed to computer-generated random numbers. The programs that generate such numbers are as deterministic as any other computer programs, thus the numbers are often characterized as only "pseudo-random." From the viewpoint of this chapter, however, this derogation is inappropriate. Randomness is not a property of a sequence of numbers in itself; it is a property of the relation between these numbers and an observer. So the question is not whether or not a given sequence of numbers is truly random; it cannot be random in and of itself. The question is what observer we are talking about. A sequence of numbers generated by a certain program is not random relative to observers who are able to use the program to reproduce them. It may be more or less random relative to observers to whom we deny (or who deny themselves) this ability.

From the viewpoint of this chapter, we are deliberately creating an instance of the ideal picture when we generate a sequence of random numbers. When we use the sequence to choose a sample from a population or to assign treatments in an experiment, we are deliberately entangling the ideal picture with data bearing on a practical question, so that probabilities in the ideal picture come to bear, indirectly, on that question.

We cannot enter here into the debates about the validity of arguments contrived in this way. I would like to suggest, however, that by explicitly bringing the ideal picture into the story, we can make these arguments more persuasive. The ideal picture itself requires a certain form of ignorance, and creating it typically requires some enforcement of that ignorance (not using the program to regenerate the random numbers, not looking at them, etc.), and hence it is no additional paradox that entangling this ideal picture with a practical problem should involve ignoring certain information (which labels were sampled or assigned to which treatments).

Argument by Analogy to the Ideal Picture

The ideal picture, as described in this chapter, always involves some element of repetition, even if this repetition is not exact. There is some sequence of events that allows us to bring a frequency or long-run element into the discussion. How, then, can we apply probability to a problem for which we do not have a sequence of similar problems?

According to one answer to this question, using probability requires creating some such sequence—some reference class. This is a fair answer, and it has the virtue of making the deliberate nature of subjective probability judgment clear. When the reference class is almost completely imaginary, however, it may be more instructive to say that we are drawing an analogy between the question that interests us and a question in the ideal picture. We are saying that our knowledge (and ignorance) about this question is similar to our knowledge about a certain question in a certain version of the ideal picture. Our evidence about the question is similar in strength, and perhaps in structure, to knowing the probabilities in that version of the ideal picture.

Shafer and Tversky (1985) discussed how both Bayesian and belief-function probability arguments can be seen in this way.

Conclusion

We must relate the ideal picture to a problem in order to use probability. It is obvious from the examples that we have just discussed that the success we have in doing this in any particular instance will always be debatable. The ideal picture may or may not be good enough a model; it may or may not be relevant as a standard of comparison; it may or may not provide a convincing analogy. This is life. But the debate in each particular case need not be an empty debate. We can formulate criteria for judging the excellence of each of these kinds of probability argument.

As Meier, Sacks, and Zabell (1984, pp. 161–164) pointed out, the real debate in applied statistics is not between the formulas of the frequentists and the formulas of the Bayesians. The real debate is between "strict constructionists," who would limit the use of probability to those situations where frequentist assumptions are fully satisfied, and "Benthamites," who find the mathematical precision of probability useful no matter how little evidence they have at hand. The framework of this chapter is designed to focus this debate on examples and make it more productive. It provides a common language in which to criticize and praise both Bayesian and frequentist analyses. To use this language, frequentists must go beyond saying that assumptions are or are not satisfied; they must draw an analogy between their relation with their data and the spectator's relation with the outcomes in the ideal picture. Bayesians must go beyond saying that certain numbers represent their beliefs; they must defend the analogy by which these numbers are produced. This puts both the frequentist and the Bayesian in the position of discussing the quality of their analyses, not the ideology that underlies them.

The philosophy of probability advanced in this chapter unifies the frequentist and subjectivist approaches at a level deeper than the level of axioms. It allows

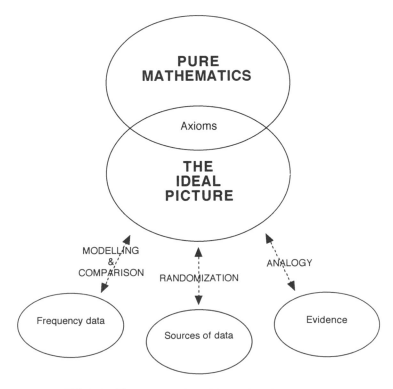

FIG. 5.8.   The constructive philosophy of probability.

us to bring together in one framework the unified 18th-century understanding of probability, the frequentist foundations of von Mises and Kolmogorov, and the subjectivist foundations of de Finetti. It also allows us to spell out explicitly the different ways we construct probability arguments. It merits the name given it in Fig. 5.8: the constructive philosophy of probability.

ACKNOWLEDGMENTS

Research for this chapter has been partially supported by the National Science Foundation through grant IRI8902444 to the University of Kansas and grant BNS8700864 to the Center for Advanced Study in the Behavioral Sciences. The author has benefited from conversations with Robert Fogelin, David Israel, Ali Jenzarli, Don Ylvisaker, and Joe VanZandt.

REFERENCES

Arnauld, A., & Nicole, P. (1662). *l'Art de penser*. Paris. (Widely used as a textbook, with many editions and translations, this book is often referred to as the Port Royal Logic.)

Beaton, A. E. (1981). *Interpreting least squares without sampling assumptions* (Report No. 81-38). Princeton, NJ: Educational Testing Service.

Bernoulli, Jacob. (1713). *Ars conjectandi*. Basil: Thurnisiorum.

Bloch, D. A. (1990). *Evaluating predictions of events with binary outcomes: An appraisal of the Brier score and some of its close relatives* (Tech. Report No. 135). Stanford, CA: Division of Biostatistics, Stanford University.

Daston, L. (1988). *Classical probability in the enlightenment*. Princeton, NJ: Princeton University Press.

De Moivre, A. (1718). *The doctrine of chances: Or, a method of calculating the probability of events in play*. London: W. Pearson.

Edwards, A. W. F. (1987). *Pascal's arithmetic triangle*. New York: Oxford University Press.

Freedman, D., & Lane, D. (1983). A nonstochastic interpretation of reported significance levels. *Journal of Business and Economic Statistics, 1*, 292–298.

Hacking, I. (1975). *The emergence of probability*. Cambridge, England: Cambridge University Press.

Hacking, I. (1990). *The taming of chance*. Cambridge, England: Cambridge University Press.

Hald, A. (1990). *A history of probability and statistics and their applications before 1750*. New York: Wiley.

Kolmogorov, A. (1950). *Foundations of the theory of probability*. (Nathan Morrison, Trans.). New York: Chelsea.

Laplace, P. S. (1812). *Théorie analytique des probabilités*. Paris: Courcier (3rd ed., 1820, with supplements).

Martin-Löf, P. (1969). The literature on von Mises' Kollektivs revisited. *Theoria, 35*(1), 12–37.

Matheron, G. (1989). *Estimating and choosing, An essay on probability in practice* (A. M. Hasofer, Trans.). Berlin: Springer-Verlag.

Meier, P., Sacks, J., & Zabell, S. L. (1984). What happened in Hazelwood: Statistics, employment discrimination, and the 80% rule. *American Bar Foundation Research Journal, 1984*, 139–186.

Porter, T. M. (1986). *The rise of statistical thinking, 1820–1900*. Princeton, NJ: Princeton University Press.

Shafer, G. (1978). Non-additive probabilities in the work of Bernoulli and Lambert. *Archive for History of Exact Sciences, 19*, 309–370.

Shafer, G. (1982). Bayes's two arguments for the rule of conditioning. *Annals of Statistics, 10*, 1075–1089.

Shafer, G. (1985). Conditional probability (with discussion). *International Statistical Review, 53*, 261–277.

Shafer, G. (1986). The combination of evidence. *International Journal of Intelligent Systems, 1*, 127–135.

Shafer, G. (1990a). The unity of probability. In G. von Furstenberg (Ed.), *Acting under uncertainty: Multidisciplinary conceptions* (pp. 95–126). Boston: Kluwer.

Shafer, G. (1990b). Perspectives on the theory and practice of belief functions. *International Journal of Approximate Reasoning, 4*, 323–362.

Shafer, G., & Tversky, A. (1985). Languages and designs for probability judgement. *Cognitive Science, 9*, 309–339.

Stein, M. (1990). Review of Matheron (1989). *Technometrics, 32*, 358–359.

Stigler, S. M. (1986). *The history of statistics: The measurement of uncertainty before 1900*. Cambridge, MA: Harvard University Press.

Todhunter, I. (1865). *A history of the mathematical theory of probability*. London: Macmillan.

Uspenskii, V. A., Semenov, A. L., & Shen', A. Kh. (1990). Can an individual sequence of zeros and ones be random? *Russian Mathematical Surveys, 45*, 121–189.

II METHODOLOGICAL ISSUES

Methodology in this book is interpreted in the broadest possible sense. Following Abraham Kaplan, it is conceived as the description, explanation, and the justification of the means by which scientific inquiry is conducted. It is therefore not restricted to specific procedures and techniques, but includes epistemological issues as well. Conventional methodology textbooks tend to present the different methods in a mechanical and technical manner. The aim of this section is to go beyond the technique, and examine fundamental issues (some which are still controversial) underlying the methodology employed in social sciences research.

Chapter 6, by Serlin and Lapsely, examines the suitability of psychological research as a scientific enterprise. In particular, they discuss philosophical issues related to two major questions: The extent to which psychological theories are sufficiently powerful to enable the derivation of precise hypotheses that can be rigorously tested, and the degree to which progress in the discipline is cumulative in nature.

Psychological research in the twentieth century has been strongly influenced by the school of British empiricists led by Hume, Berkeley, and Lock. In chapter 7, MacKay challenges this tradition and offers an alternative outlook. While not necessarily denouncing the importance of empirical tests for the confirmation of psychological theories, he presents some other criteria which he advocates as being of equal importance. While some of Mac-

Kay's proposals may be controversial, it may nevertheless be useful to reexamine the overwhelming role of empiricism in current psychological research.

Methodology, when interpreted in the narrower sense of being composed of experimental techniques and procedures, is deeply interrelated with the theoretical issues that are being examined and statistical analyses one wants to conduct. These interelationships are illustrated in chapter 8, which presents the relevant considerations for employing a between or within-subjects design.

Chapter 9, by Holland, carries a warning regarding the potential pitfalls associated with confusing cause and effect. Holland's main claim is that the analysis of causation should begin with studying the effects of causes, rather than the common approach which attempts to identify and define the cause of a given effect.

For most social scientists, the name of sir Ronald Fisher is associated with the analysis of variance (ANOVA) and the logic underlying experimental designs. Chapter 10, by Brenner-Golomb presents a broader perspective on Fisher's approach to inductive inference in science, and describes the logical developments underlying his important contributions.

6

Rational Appraisal of Psychological Research and the Good-Enough Principle

Ronald C. Serlin
University of Wisconsin-Madison

Daniel K. Lapsley
University of Notre Dame

INTRODUCTION

The extent to which psychological research can be suitably described as a scientific enterprise has long been a source of doubt, anxiety, and reflection. To those who are rightly impressed by the achievements in the physical sciences, the activity of psychological researchers seems inadequate and impoverished by comparison. In order to be described as a legitimate scientific enterprise it would seem that psychology must be able to satisfy some minimum standards of scientific adequacy. One should reasonably expect, for example, that psychology be capable of generating powerful theories that can be severely tested by precise hypothesis-testing procedures. It should further be expected that one be able to detect cumulative progress in the various theoretical domains of the discipline as a result of these theory-appraising methodologies. But the ability of psychological research to satisfy these twin expectations is precisely what is called into question. Indeed, psychological research is often said to be atheoretical, noncumulative, and saddled with a statistical hypothesis-testing methodology that is either deeply flawed or else ill-used by researchers.

Although there are numerous critics of significance testing (e.g., Morrison & Henkle, 1970; Spielman, 1974), Meehl (1967, 1978, 1986) effectively critiqued standard practices in the "softer" areas of social science research. He wrote, for example, that "the almost universal reliance on merely refuting the null hypothesis is a terrible mistake, is basically unsound, poor scientific strategy, and one of the worst things that ever happened in the history of psychology" (Meehl, 1978, p. 817). Meehl (1978) also faulted psychological research for its lack of cumulative progress. According to Meehl (1978), "It is simply a sad fact that in soft psychology theories come and go more as a function of baffled boredom than anything else; and the enterprise shows a disturbing absence of that cumulative character that is so impressive in disciplines like astronomy, molecular biology, and genetics" (p. 807). The lack of cumulative progress, and the poverty of null hypothesis testing, are not unrelated problems, as will become evident. If they prove to be intractable problems for psychology then the very rationality of the research enterprise is legitimately called into question. That is, if these criticisms are sustained, if it is true that psychological theories cannot in fact be subjected to severe testing and do not cumulate into well-corroborated empirical knowledge, then the scientific character of research in psychology might well be a delusion. The purpose of this chapter is to reexamine these issues. After first examining the Meehlian complaints against psychological research in more detail, we then propose a number of remedies. Against the claim that the significance test cannot be made to threaten a theory with refutation, we propose a "good-enough" methodology that claims to do precisely that. Against the claim that psychological research is not cumulative, we argue, following Lakatos (1978a), that progress in research is never plainly evident but must instead be excavated from historical reconstructions of the various literatures. Along the way we provide examples of how one uses "good-enough" hypothesis testing. We also argue that the comparison with physics is not always to our disadvantage when the good-enough methodology and certain Lakatosian considerations are kept in mind. Finally, we conclude with a discussion of what rational appraisal of psychological research might look like, and how this might have an impact on graduate training in psychology.

THE MEEHLIAN INDICTMENT OF PSYCHOLOGY

The Methodological Paradox

In Meehl's (1967) view, improved measurement precision in the behavioral sciences has the paradoxical effect of yielding weaker tests of substantive theories. This paradox hinges on the fact that the psychological point null hypotheses are always false. Insofar as psychological variables are invariably contaminated by a large number of "crud" factors, one would never expect any two populations to have literally equal means. It follows, then, that one would always expect to reject the point null hypothesis if statistical power is sufficiently great. Hence, because the null hypothesis is always false, improved precision in the behavioral sciences provides an easier hurdle for theories to overcome, which violates the Popperian (Popper, 1959) tenet that theories must be subjected to severe tests.

The implication of this argument is quite startling. In order for a theory to be corroborated, under a standard account, it must face the heat of refutation. It must be subjected to severe tests and be fairly confronted with the possibility of falsification. If a theory cannot be falsified, it fails the Popperian demarcation criterion as to what is to count as a meaningful scientific theory. Yet it would appear that psychological theories are not fairly confronted with the possibility of refutation. If the null hypothesis is always false, and if its rejection is thought to be an indication of the plausibility of the substantive alternative hypothesis, then it follows that one need never doubt the plausibility of the alternative hypothesis, because the rejection of the null hypothesis is guaranteed given sufficient power. But this hardly constitutes a severe test for the substantive theory, which suggests that the ritualistic rejection of null hypotheses and the corroboration of theories are two different matters in psychological research.

This state of affairs is contrasted with what is taken to be the standard case in physics (Meehl, 1967). According to Meehl (1967), the typical theory in physics predicts a point value or function form. That which corresponds to the point null hypothesis in psychology is a value derived as a consequence of a substantive theory. An increase in statistical power in physics has the effect of stiffening the experimental hurdle by "*decreasing* the prior probability of a successful experimental outcome if the theory lacks verisimilitude, that is, precisely the reverse of the situation obtaining in the social sciences" (Meehl, 1967, p. 113). If a physical theory has no merit, it will not survive an experimental test, given perfect precision. If a psychological theory has no merit, the logical probability of it surviving such a test is said to approach one.

The asymmetry in hypothesis testing between psychology and physics can be traced to the fact that in psychology, the point null hypothesis is not derived from a substantive theory. It is a "strawman" competitor whose rejection we interpret as increasing the plausibility of the substantive theory. But this interpretation is hazardous if the distinction between statistical hypotheses and substantive theories is to be respected (Bolles, 1962; Meehl, 1978). A substantive theory is a conjecture about the nature of psychological processes, entities, and phenomena. A statistical hypothesis is a conjecture about the value of a population parameter. If a null statistical hypothesis is not derived from substantive theoretical considerations, which seems the case in psychological research, then its rejection would not (necessarily) increase the plausibility of the substantive theory. Hence the chasm between statistical hypothesis and substantive theory is very wide in psychology. But in physics, theories that entail point predictions are the very ones that physicists take seriously and hope to confirm. The chasm between theory and statistical hypothesis is not terribly wide. Consequently, the asymmetry between psychology and physics has two features. First, physicists devolve subtantive point values for their statistical tests, whereas psychologists test for the strawman competitor, zero. Second, increased precision in physics gravely threatens a theory with refutation, whereas such precision in psychology decreases such a threat. It would appear, then, that significance testing in psychology is a vacuous exercise, neither corroborating nor refuting our substantive theories. If Meehl is correct, then there would indeed be little reason for anyone to embrace or discard a theory for reasons other than curiosity, stubbornness or "baffled boredom." Consequently, it should not be surprising that psychological research seems to lack that cumulative quality that we tend to associate with more developed sciences. We now turn briefly to this topic.

Slow Progress in Psychology

As already noted, much of the difficulty concerning progress in psychological research is laid at the door of significance testing, which Meehl (1978, p. 806) described as "a poor way of doing science." Yet there are perhaps special reasons why cumulative progress is a more elusive achievement for psychological researchers. Meehl (1978), for example, catalogued 20 features of our subject matter that would seem to make it difficult to pin down psychological knowledge with any confidence. Of particular interest is the claim that psychological constructs are typically awash in a sea of context-dependent "stochastologicals," which refers to the fact that rather than dealing with lawlike relationships for which a certain amount of nomic necessity exists, we tend to deal mostly with "correlations, tendencies, statistical clusterings, increments in probabilities, and altered stochastic dispositions" (Meehl, 1978, p. 813), all of which show strong context dependence. Furthermore, Meehl noted that we rarely can know the complete list of relevant contextual influences. If we do know some of them, we can rarely specify the function form of the context dependency, nor the numerical values of the parameters for the function forms that we do know. This context dependence tends to make theory appraisal problematic. "When the observational corroborators of the theory consist wholly of percentages, crude curve fits, correlations, significance tests, and distribution overlaps, it is difficult or impossible to see clearly when a given batch of empirical data refutes a theory or even when two batches of data are 'inconsistent'" (Meehl, 1978, p. 814).

A similar indictment is leveled against the nature of psychological theories. Theories are said to be only loosely situated within a nomological network, such that auxiliary theories are just as problematic as the theory under test. In the Popperian view, a theory is never directly put to the test. Rather, it is the theory, plus a set of auxiliary theories that are jointly tested. Hence negative empirical results could never decisively refute a theory because a researcher could always implicate one of the auxiliaries as being responsible for the putative refutation. Although this describes the case with theory appraisal in the hard sciences, the problem is said to be more severe for the soft sciences because of the looseness with which theories are connected with auxiliaries within the network. Not only is independent testing of auxiliaries harder to carry out in psychology, it is also claimed that there is no intimate connection, no sense of derivability, between auxiliary and substantive theories in the first place. Thus, according to Meehl (1978):

Almost nothing we know or conjecture about the substantive theory [T] helps us to an appreciable degree in firming up our reliance on the auxiliary (A). The situation in which A is merely conjoined to T in setting up our test of T makes it hard for us social scientists to fulfill a Popperian falsifiability requirement—to state before the fact what would count as a strong falsifier. (p. 819)

Hence it becomes clear, at least for Meehl, that slow progress is related to the fact that we cannot refute our theories, we cannot subject them to severe test via the *modus tollens*. And this is the result not only of certain peculiarities in significance testing (the asymmetry problem), but also because of the flabby nature of our theories, and the fact that we can never decisively bring data to bear on any one theory in particular.

We are now in a position to reconsider the Meehlian complaints against the standard practice of psychological researchers. We argue that a consideration of the Lakatosian reconstruction of science (Lakatos, 1978a) will take us some distance in restoring some semblance of rationality in our research practices, and in indicating how it might be possible to detect cumulative progress. We next describe a "good-enough" hypothesis-testing strategy that addresses the asymmetry problem noted by Meehl and allows a fortified test of a null hypothesis that is not always false.

SLOW PROGRESS RECONSIDERED: AN HISTORICIST APPROACH

One of the dogmas of positivism purported that there was a natural demarcation between observation ("facts") and theory. This view has long been discredited, as pointed out here. Although it is odd to hear anyone still try to maintain the distinction between facts and theories, it would be a mistake to assume that all vestiges of this dogma have been eliminated from our thinking about the scientific enterprise. Hardly anyone, for example, save the unreconstructed Baconian, would stare open-faced at nature waiting for the "facts" to make themselves evident. Rather, in order to make headway, in order to do science, one puts forward conjectures, one constructs theories, and within the context of theories, facts begin to emerge and to become *sensible*. We take it not to be controversial to assert that facts cannot exist outside the texture of theories. Yet if this formulation is readily accepted, as we take it to be, why should there also be an expectation that cumulative progress in scientific research is something that is plainly evident in the absence of suitable theory as to how science works? Just as one does not idly stare at nature waiting for "observations" to surface, one does not survey literatures waiting for progress to emerge unaided by theoretical considerations as to what "progress" amounts to. If evidence of progress is the "fact" that one is searching for, then one requires a theory that permits the excavation of the relevant data. One requires a theory that specifies how the history of science is to be reconstructed, by what criteria progress is to be ascertained, and the like. There are obviously numerous theories as to how science works, which suggests that, like all theories, conjectures about the scientific enterprise itself are fallible. But this need not lead to any thoroughgoing skepticism. Our approach has been to appeal to the work of Lakatos.

The Lakatosian Framework

According to Lakatos (1978a), the comparability of scientific results and the assessment of scientific progress must take on a historical character. When one takes a historical view of a research program one is often struck by the fact that theories are rarely abandoned. Indeed, theories are often tenaciously held even in the face of seemingly disconfirming evidence. Rarely, if ever, do scientists treat anomalies as falsifications of a theory. No theory is ever abandoned because of a "refuting" instance, because any negative result can always be attributed instead to extraneous factors that were provisionally treated as "unproblematic background knowledge," or to factors subsumed by the *ceteris paribus* clause that is (at least implicitly) appended to every theoretical deduction. Lakatos' (1978a) own view, which he called *sophisticated falsificationism,* attempted to account for this evident feature of science. In this view, one must distinguish between criticism of a theory and its abandonment. Mere criticism of a theory is never sufficient grounds for falsification. This is so because, in Lakatos' view, the "hard core" of a theory is protected from refutation by a "protective belt" of auxiliary theories, such that the arrow of the *modus tollens* must always be directed away from the core to the auxiliaries. Lakatos called this decision the *negative heuristic* of a research program. The negative heuristic specifies the path that the research program is not to take. That is, one decides to cordon off the core of the theory from the threat of refutation, insisting instead that the auxiliaries bear the brunt of the tests.

The direction that the research program should take is subsumed by the *positive heuristic* of the program. It specifies how one is to proceed in order to generate novel facts and thereby increase the empirical content of the program. It consists of models or suggestions on how to modify the refutable protective belt, on how to digest anomalies. Indeed, the positive heuristic of a research program bids one to proceed in the face of counterevidence and *refutation.* Empirical anomalies are never considered decisive, because "all theories are born refuted and die refuted" (Lakatos, 1978d, p. 5). Rather, these refutations are merely considered "inconclusive" until some later time when (it is hoped) the positive heuristic can turn the disconfirming evidence into corroborating evidence. In other words, the positive heuristic specifies how successive modifications and adjustments are to be developed within a research program so that anomaly and refutation are digested. Each successive modification yields a new theory, so the nature of scientific appraisal is shifted from the appraisal of isolated theories ("in light of the evidence") to the appraisal of a *series* of theories (research programs), "where each subsequent theory results from adding auxiliary clauses to the previous theory in order to accommodate some anomaly" (Lakatos, 1978a, p. 33). A research program (or "series of theories") is said to be *theoretically progressive* if it has excess empirical content over its predecessor. It is said to be *empirically* progressive if some of the excess content is also corroborated. Furthermore, a research program is said to be *scientific* if it is at least theoretically progressive, and *pseudoscientific* if it is not. There will, of course, be anomalies encountered at every step in the development of a program. But we may rationally decide not to allow these putative refutations to transmit falsity to the hard core if the corroborated content of the protecting belt of auxiliaries increases, that is, if the research program, under the aegis of the positive heuristic, is theoretically and empirically progressive. This account of the scientific enterprise clearly explains the relative autonomy of theoretical science and the tenacity by which theories are embraced even in the face of *counterevidence*. The methodology of research programs, according to Lakatos (1978c),

> is more tolerant [than naive falsificationism] in the sense that it allows a research program to outgrow infantile diseases, such as inconsistent foundations and occasional ad hoc moves. Anomalies, inconsistencies, and ad hoc strategems can be consistent with progress. [But the appraisal of research programs] is also more strict in that it demands not only that a research program should successfully predict novel facts but also that the protective belt of its auxiliaries should be largely built according to a preconceived unifying idea, laid down in advance in the positive heuristic of the research program. (p. 149)

But when should one abandon a theory? On the Lakatosian account, only when certain criteria are met. There must exist a rival program that is powerful enough to account for all of the facts of the former program and, importantly, also possess sufficient generative power to anticipate novel facts, some of which have been corroborated (Lakatos, 1978a). Although one is entitled to embrace a rival under these conditions, they do not constitute sufficient grounds as long as the former program is still *progressive,* that is, as long as its positive heuristic is still capable of anticipating novel facts. Lakatos (1978a) also noted that one may still cling to a *degenerating* research program so long as no rival program exists that satisfies the aforementioned criteria.

There are a number of implications of this view that should be noted. First, the empirical character of a scientific theory and scientific growth are mutually defining. What gives science its scientific character is not the fact that it generates theories capable of making testable assertions about the nature of reality, but rather the fact that successive theories generated by a science possess excess content and excess corroboration when compared against predecessor or competing theories (Lakatos, 1978b; Serlin & Lapsley, in press). It is the *progressive* character of a research program and the *growth of knowledge* that it represents, that determines whether or not a program is scientific. Indeed, a theory is never eliminated because it fails a test. The fate of a theory never depends on the results of experiments. Rather, *falsification* depends on the emergence of better theories, where "better theories" anticipate novel facts (excess content), some of which have been corroborated (excess corroboration). If a theory possesses these features, that is, if it represents growth, it is deemed *scientific*. If a theory does not contribute to growth, if it is ad hoc in one of the several senses described by Lakatos (1978a, see footnote 1, p. 88), it is deemed *pseudoscientific*. Consequently, in Lakatos' view, there can be no "instant rationality" in the appraisal of a research program, but rather appraisal must be guided by a consideration of the historical record of empirical successes and failures that are seen in the light of the track record of rival theories. That is to say, "there are no such things as crucial experiments, at least not if these are meant to be experiments which can instantly overthrow a research program. In fact, when one research program suffers defeat and is superceded by another, we may, with long hindsight, call an experiment crucial if it turns out to have provided a spectacular corroborating instance for the victorious program and a failure for the defeated one" (Lakatos, 1978a, p. 86).

With this brief review of the Lakatosian perspective we are now in a position to reexamine the slow progress issue in psychological research. In our view, as noted earlier, the progressive and cumulative character of a research program is not a self-evident fact that can be known in the absence of a theoretical perspective that directs our analysis of a literature. The "methodology of scientific research programs" articulated by Lakatos provides one way to conduct this analysis. It insists that evidential support be considered a comparative, historical matter, one that is to be excavated and *reconstructed* from the history of science. If the force of this analysis is granted, then one sees that slow progress is one of the defining features of science, and not an indictment. Indeed, "sophisticated falsificationism is a slower but possibly safer process" (Lakatos, 1978a, p. 40) than other theories of science (e.g., naive falsificationism), where there is an expectation that the content knowledge of science should grow linearly by means of a rapid succession of "conjectures and refutations" (Popper, 1963). But as we have seen, refutations are never decisive. When guided by a positive heuristic a theory forges ahead in almost complete disregard for refutations, for theories are tenaciously held even in the face of disconfirming evidence.

Consequently, if one of the complaints against psychological research is that we cannot seem to refute our theories, then perhaps the adoption of a Lakatosian perspective helps us see why this is an unreasonable expectation in the first place. It takes a long time to appraise a research program. Appraisal is not instant, based on the results of isolated experiments and the discovery of anomaly. Rather, as Lakatos (1978a, p. 35) pointed out, "There is no falsification before the emergence of a better theory. . . . Falsification is not simply a relation between a theory and the empirical basis, but a multiple relation between competing theories, the original 'empirical basis,' and the empirical growth resulting from the competition. Falsification can thus be said to have a '*historical character*'" (p. 35).

Unfortunately, the appraisal of psychological theories and the search for cumulative growth is rarely conducted under the aegis of the "methodology of scientific research programs." Meehl (1967) was correct in his criticism of the habit of literature reviewers, who seem content merely to "count noses," that is, merely to tally the empirical successes and failures of a research program. This is a defective way to review a literature not because (according to Meehl) reviewers undervalue refutations, but rather because it is done in a way that is *ahistorical*. The typical literature review, particularly of the narrative sort, is too expectant of "instant rationality," and therefore neglects the historical comparison against rivals and the requirements for continuous growth. As Feldman (1971, p. 86; see also Rosnow & Rosenthal, 1989) noted, deficient literature reviewing "might account in part for the relatively unimpressive degree of cumulative knowledge in many fields in the behavioral sciences." When reviewing is done from the perspective of the Popperian falsificationist, who expects theories to be overthrown given the slightest hint of recalcitrant evidence, then it is little wonder that "slow progress" and "lack of cumulative findings" should become an indictment of psychological research.

Fortunately, a number of papers have recently appeared that would seem to address the problem of literature reviewing in the social sciences (e.g., Cooper, 1989; Jackson, 1980; Ladas, 1980), and the emergence of meta-analysis as a tool for evaluating scientific literatures is of considerable significance (e.g., Hedges & Olkin, 1985). There are also a number of instances of the use of the methodology of scientific research programs in the literature that provide ready examples of how the methodology might be used to detect cumulative progress. Case (1985), for example, provided a masterful reconstruction of the cognitive development research program. Lapsley and Serlin (1984) and Phillips and Nicolayev (1978) subjected the Kohlbergian research program to such an analysis, and Urbach (1974a, 1974b) charted the progress and degeneration in the IQ debate.

Nothing that has been said thus far should be construed as absolving research psychologists of all of the indictments that are typically leveled against them. Meehl (1967) was undoubtedly correct when he complained about the ad hoc nature of much of what passes as theory-building in some areas of the social sciences. Lakatos (1978a) distinguished between three kinds of ad hoc propositions. What he called *ad hoc$_1$* are those propositions that do not increase the novel content of a theory. Theories are *ad hoc$_2$* when they propose novel content, but none of which is corroborated. *Ad hoc$_3$* strategems achieve "progress" with a "patched up, arbitrary series of disconnected theories" (Lakatos, 1978a, p. 88). Although all three kinds of ad hoc strategems are to be found in even the most mature sciences, that ad hoc$_3$ maneuvers are overrepresented in at least some domains of psychological research seems hard to deny. We would agree with Lakatos (1978a, see footnote 4, p. 89) that the "methodology of research programs," if rigorously adopted by researchers and reviewers, would go a long way to stem this form of "intellectual pollution."

Although the foregoing discussion explains the apparent lack of progress in psychology, we have not yet dealt with Meehl's asymmetry problem. If this issue is not successfully addressed, then there is no way for psychologists even to test their theories rationally, let alone appraise them via a Lakatosian perspective. That is, the problem is not so much that we inappropriately appraise the successes and failures and therefore fail to detect progress, but rather that our tests are uninformative either way, given the deficiencies noted by Meehl with regard to significance testing. To resolve these difficulties, we introduce a *good-enough principle,* which allows one to obtain usable information by fortifying the null hypothesis. This enables significance tests to provide stiff observational hurdles for theories to overcome.

THE GOOD-ENOUGH PRINCIPLE

The asymmetry problem posed by Meehl is solved by examining Meehl's (1978) own account of actual scientific practice. Based in part on this account, we propose a good-enough principle and describe its associated statistical methodology. The suggested methodology does not result, even with an infinite sample size, in an inevitable rejection of the null hypothesis, and it is based on Popper's demand that scientists agree, in advance, to what they define as a falsifying experimental outcome. Although we have briefly described the methodology elsewhere (Serlin & Lapsley, 1985), we feel that a detailed account here will prove useful.

As Meehl (1978, p. 825) pointed out, when a scientist evaluates the results of an experiment he or she "looks at the agreement, and comments that 'the results are in reasonably good accord with theory.'" Such a scientist has set Popperian standards that indicate what kinds of experimental results are *good enough,* so that the experiment would not be considered a falsification. By implication, the standards would also reveal when a falsification had occurred.

It is important to point out that it is because all theories are false that a perfectly precise experimental outcome will *never* exactly agree with theoretical prediction. In order for psychologists to conduct and evaluate experiments whose outcomes are not known in advance, a good-enough belt around the theoretical prediction must be employed. This requirement is necessary even for theoretical predictions that are point values or function forms.

The Popperian implications of the good-enough principle for the "straw man" point null hypothesis are direct. Let us say that a psychological theory predicts that the means of two populations will differ on some measure. The typical point null hypothesis would then state that the two population means are equal. But like all other theories, the conjecture posited by the point null hypothesis is false. This results in two problems. First, because the point null hypothesis is false, a large enough sample size will always lead to its rejection. And second, because the logical complement to the theoretical prediction comprises the null hypothesis, this inevitable rejection will lead to theoretical "support."

These deficiencies, however, can be corrected. First, a good-enough belt must surround the point value of zero, so that the theoretical prediction would now correctly state that the two population means differ by more than some good enough value, say Δ_S (here, Δ_S represents the *smallest* difference that would constitute a nontrivial effect). And second, the appropriate null hypothesis that is *derived* from this theoretical prediction would state that the two population means differ by Δ_S or less. In this way, with perfect precision, a null hypothesis that tests a theory that is good enough would always be rejected, and a null hypothesis testing a theory that is not good enough would never be rejected. The logic of the *modus tollens* at work here now parallels that used in physics, in that the theoretical prediction logically yields the conclusion to be drawn, and a rejection of the appropriate null hypothesis allows one to conclude that the substantive theory has been confirmed.

Thus, the good-enough principle allows psychologists to specify in advance of an experiment what they would consider to be a falsifying instance. A Popperian corollary to the good-enough principle states that the researcher must also specify in advance the Type I error rate to be allotted to the hypothesis test. As with all Popperian specifications, the Type I error rate assignment is a methodological decision that must be endorsed in order to put a theoretical proposition to the test. Allowing the Type I error rate to "float" would mean that even after the experiment a result would be uninformative as to the success or failure of the theoretical prediction. In this context, Cohen (1990, p. 1311) voiced an "amen" to Rosnow and Rosenthal's (1989, p. 1277), "Surely, God loves the .06 nearly as much as the .05." We merely wonder what She thinks about the .07?[1] At some point the researcher must decide on an appropriate Type I error rate, and it is Popperian to make the decision in advance of the experiment.

In addition, similar considerations apply to testing psychological point value or function form predictions. Let us assume here that a psychological theory predicts that two population means do not differ, or they differ by a specific amount, or the relationship in the population between two variables is linear. Using only the first example (the others follow parallel logic), the prediction that the means differ by zero will never be supported by a perfectly precise experiment, so that the prediction must be modified to state that the means will differ by less than some good-enough value, say Δ_M (here, Δ_M represents the *most* that the means should differ). The null hypothesis derived from this theoretical pre-

---

[1]This sentiment was originally uttered by Mike Seaman, University of South Carolina.

diction would state that the population means differ by Δ_M or more. With the Type I error rate decided in advance, a rejection of this null hypothesis would constitute a confirming instance for the theory.

It may seem that this emphasis on confirmation is contrary to the Popperian emphasis on falsification. This is not the case. First, as Lakatos (1978a) noted,

> Our considerations show that the positive heuristic forges ahead with almost complete disregard of "refutations": it may seem that it is the *"verifications"* rather than the refutations which provide the contact points with reality. Although one must point out that any "verification" of the $n + 1$-th version of the program is a refutation of the n-th version, we cannot deny that *some* defeats of the subsequent versions are always foreseen: it is the "verifications" which keep the program going, recalcitrant instances notwithstanding. (pp. 51–52)

And second, it is Popperian to demand that a theory overcome a stiff observational hurdle. Only the Type I error rate is controlled in a statistical test, and a confirmation of the $n + 1$-th version is a falsification of the nth version; consequently, the error of false theoretical support must be considered to be the error associated with a false rejection of the null hypothesis. Hence, the theoretical prediction, fortified by a good-enough belt, must define the alternative hypothesis, and the null hypothesis must be its logical complement.

We emphasize that these same considerations apply to experiments in the hard sciences. Nature is just as unkind to physicists as it is to psychologists. If theory predicts a point value or function form, and if no good-enough region is used, then because all theories are false, sufficient precision will *always* result in a falsification. In both the hard and soft sciences, with sufficient precision and without a good-enough region, the results of experiments are always known in advance. It is only with the aid of a good-enough specification that one can avoid the paradoxical conclusions made inevitable by the prospect of perfect precision. So although the asymmetry between psychology and physics is indeed real, it is only real in the sense that the nature of the point values typically tested under the null hypotheses are different. In other words, although the mathematical sophistication of psychological theories does not yet permit the derivation of quantitative predictions, as is more typically the case in physics, the logical form of hypothesis testing is the same in that the substantive theory allows the logical derivation of the alternative and null hypotheses.

Let us now examine the directional null hypothesis. Under the good-enough principle, one must specify both direction and magnitude in advance of the experiment. If the statistical test indicates a possible increase less than that which is specified as good enough, the directional null hypothesis is retained. This would be true even when the direction is chosen at random. Thus, with perfect precision and a good-enough belt, the null hypothesis will *never* be rejected unless the magnitude of the effect is good enough. Without the good-enough specification, random assignment of direction and perfect precision will result in a rejection half of the time. Thus, the good-enough principle does stiffen the observational hurdle in the case of a directional null hypothesis and perfect precision.

Admittedly, specifying good-enough values is difficult. As Walster and Cleary (1970) noted, "Regardless of the researcher's point of view, . . . he must make a judgement about the magnitude of effects of interest" (p. 248). The width of the good-enough belt depends on the state of the art of the theory and of the best measuring device available. It depends on the state of the art of the theory for two main reasons. First, a historical look at one's research program or an examination of a competing research program will help determine how accurately one's theory should predict in order that it be competitive with other theories. And second, in order to make predictions, one's theory may require parameters as input that themselves can only be predicted or measured to certain limits of accuracy. These limitations would need to be incorporated into the good-enough belt.

The width of the good-enough belt also depends on the best available measuring instrument. All "facts" are based on the theories of the measuring devices, theories that are false, so a certain amount of *systematic* error is liable to be present in any datum. The magnitude of this error will affect the width of the good-enough belt. *Random* error is not included in good-enough considerations, for such error is accounted for by the statistical hypothesis test.

Statistical Procedures

Over the last several years, researchers have shown increasing interest in testing hypotheses for and calculating confidence intervals about measures of effect size. For example, as Cohen (1990) wrote, "the primary product of a research inquiry is one or more measures of effect size. . . . You can attach a p value to it, but it is far more informative to provide a confidence interval" (p. 1310). Part of this emerging interest in effect sizes may be due to a broadening understanding that effect sizes are more indicative of substantive importance than is a p value, because the latter is strongly influenced by sample size. Another possible reason for the increased interest in effect sizes may be the relatively recent availability of meta-analytic techniques that often use effect sizes as data. A major reason for our interest is that our theories must make predictions that include a good-enough belt. These predictions are then used to specify statistical hypotheses that involve ranges, not point values, and range hypotheses concerning effect sizes can be tested using known statistical distributions. As Gigerenzer (chap. 11, this vol.) wrote, "We need rich theoretical frameworks that allow for specific predictions in the form of precise research hypotheses. The null hypothesis of zero difference (or zero correlation) is only one version of such a hypothesis—perhaps only rarely appropriate."

Our approach agrees with that ascribed by Gigerenzer to Neyman and Pearson. We state null and alternative hypotheses and discuss Type I error rate and power. We urge a thoughtful assignment of Type I error rate, and we feel that the assignment must be made in advance of the experiment. Each experimental result is one piece of the ongoing work in a research program.

Overall, we view the statistical test as if it were a scientific observational instrument, designed to ascertain whether or not a theoretical prediction is supported by "fact." The scientist states the prediction, includes a good-enough belt, and, knowing that the instrument has been designed to provide a certain resolution, specifies in advance that if the data support the theory, the instrument should be able to reveal the support. The whole world then peers into the instrument, and the theory either is or is not supported. The results are then made part of the historical record of the research program. If necessary, the positive heuristic is invoked to account for the anomaly. Regardless, the work of the research program continues, even if the program is replaced by a successful competing research program, until the replaced program is considered to be hopelessly degenerating.

Methods are available that are applicable to the problem of testing the range null hypotheses required by the good-enough principle. Hodges and Lehmann (1954) provided a procedure for showing in the one- and two-sample model that the magnitude of the effect exceeded a specified minimum value and for obtaining a confidence interval for the population effect. Hedges (1981) described methods for performing tests and obtaining confidence intervals for Glass' (1976) standardized effect size measure (the standardized effect size is the difference between two means expressed in standard deviation units). These were based on a normal approximation to the noncentral t distribution. Kraemer (1983) provided a central t approximation that could be used to the same end.

Seemingly, then, procedures are available that would allow the researcher to make decisions regarding the magnitude of an effect and, thereby, to test the range null hypotheses of the good-enough principle. Unfortunately, the Hodges and Lehmann (1954) test requires the use of their charts, from which accuracy is somewhat difficult to obtain, or a specialized computer program that is not available in the literature. In addition, the calculation of their confidence interval would also require a similar computer program, and as yet no one has solved the problem of showing that the effect was less than a specified magnitude.

Here we concentrate on test and confidence interval procedures involving Glass' standardized effect size, the correlation ratio in analysis of variance, and the square of the multiple correlation coefficient in regression analysis. There are two reasons for this specialization. First, the distributions of these effect size measures are known, and second, computer programs are available in the literature for performing the required calculations. We focus throughout on using the tests and confidence intervals for the purpose of determining when a confirming instance has occurred, and we show that the approximations of Hedges and Kraemer are inadequate to this task under certain circumstances.

The One- and Two-Sample Cases

Various notation has been used to refer to the sample and population standardized mean difference in the two-sample case. For example, Hedges (1981) denoted these as g and δ, respectively, whereas Kraemer (1983) referred to them as d and δ. Some confusion can arise with either choice because, as discussed by these authors, the distribution of the sample standardized effect size is that of the noncentral t, whose noncentrality parameter is often denoted as δ. We adopt here Kraemer's notation, including using λ to refer to the noncentrality parameter of the noncentral t distribution.

In the one-sample case, the range null hypothesis will specify that the population mean will lie within (or outside of, depending on prediction) a specified range, here specified in population standard deviation units, of a predicted value. The sample statistic, d_1, is the difference between the sample mean and the specified value, expressed in sample standard deviation units. Similarly, in the two-sample case, the range null hypothesis will state that the population mean difference will lie within (or outside of, again depending on prediction) a range, again expressed in population standard deviation units, of a predicted value. Here, the sample statistic, d_2, expresses how far the difference in sample means is from the predicted value, expressed in sample standard deviation units.

Distribution Theory

In the one-sample case, let N observations be drawn from a normally distributed population with mean μ and variance σ^2. Then the sample mean $\bar{Y}$ will be normally distributed with mean μ and variance σ^2/N. Let the sample variance S^2 be an unbiased estimate of σ^2, and let the theoretically predicted value of the population mean be denoted μ_0. Then the theoretical prediction will state that $\delta_1 = (\mu - \mu_0)/\sigma$ is good enough. δ_1 is estimated in the sample by $d_1 = (\bar{Y} - \mu_0)/S$. Under the range null hypothesis, $t = \sqrt{N}\, d_1$ follows a noncentral t distribution with $N - 1$ degrees of freedom and noncentrality parameter $\lambda = \sqrt{N}\, \delta_1$.

In the two-sample case, let n_1 and n_2 observations be drawn from two normally distributed populations with means μ_1 and μ_2 and common variance σ^2. Then the sample mean difference $\bar{Y}_1 - \bar{Y}_2$ will be normally distributed with mean $\mu_1 - \mu_2$ and variance $N\sigma^2/n_1 n_2$, where N is the total sample size. Let the pooled within-group sample variance S^2 be an unbiased estimate of σ^2, and let the theoretically predicted value of the population mean difference be denoted μ_0. Then the theoretical prediction will state that $\delta_2 = [(\mu_1 - \mu_2) - \mu_0]/\sigma$ is good enough. δ_2 is estimated in the sample by $d_2 = [(\bar{Y}_1 - \bar{Y}_2) - \mu_0)]/S$. Most often in the two-sample case, psychologists are interested in estimating the population standardized mean difference from the sample standardized mean difference; if so, then $\mu_0 = 0$ in the formulas for δ_2 and d_2. Under the range null hypothesis, $t = \sqrt{n_1 n_2/N}\, d_2$ follows a noncentral t distribution with $N - 2$ degrees of freedom and noncentrality parameter $\lambda = \sqrt{n_1 n_2/N}\, \delta_2$.

Good-Enough Methodology

We describe the good-enough hypothesis-testing and confidence interval procedures in the two-sample design, first in the directional case where theory predicts that the effect will exceed a minimum. We then examine the method when a directional effect less than a maximum is predicted. We next describe the procedure for testing that the population standardized effect is within a good-enough range in either direction of prediction, and finally we describe the method for testing the prediction that the effect is outside a good-enough range in either direction of prediction. The one-sample case follows similar logic in all respects.

The first prediction to be examined, then, is that the effect is larger than Δ_S, the smallest magnitude of an effect, expressed in standard deviation units, that would be considered good enough. An effect smaller than this would constitute a falsifying instance. Then the null hypothesis would be

$$H_0: \delta_2 \leq \Delta_S.$$

This null hypothesis specifies a range for δ_2. Given the relationship between δ_2 and λ, the null hypothesis also specifies a range for the noncentrality parameter of the underlying noncentral t distribution of the sample d_2. Small values of the sample test statistic are consistent with the null hypothesis, thus only large values of the sample test statistic will lead to rejection of the null hypothesis. The critical value is chosen so that, under H_0, the sample test statistic will exceed the critical value no more than $100\alpha\%$ of the time. This Type I error rate depends on the true value of λ in the population.

Of course, there is only one true value of λ, and if it were known, the experiment would be unnecessary. The value of λ is unknown, thus the critical value for the test must be chosen so as to ensure that the Type I error rate does not exceed α for any value of λ allowed under the null hypothesis. The larger the true λ is, the greater the probability that the sample test statistic will be greater than any particular fixed value. Therefore, if the critical value is chosen so that the Type I error rate equals α when λ is at the limit allowed under H_0, then because all other values of λ under the null hypothesis are smaller than this upper limit, the Type I error rate under H_0 is guaranteed to be at most α. For the present directional null hypothesis, then, the critical value, denoted $CV_{1-\alpha}$, is chosen as the $100(1 - \alpha)$ percentile of the noncentral t distribution with $N - 2$ degrees of freedom and with noncentrality parameter $\lambda = \sqrt{n_1 n_2/N}\ \Delta_S$. A computer program provided by Cooper (1968) and modified by Chou (1985) can be used to determine the critical value, or the normal approximation used by Hedges (1981) or the central t approximation used by Kraemer (1983) will yield an approximation to the critical value.

In order to find a confidence interval for δ_2, both Hedges (1981) and Kraemer (1983) solved for δ_2 in the equations approximating $CV_{1-\alpha}$. The results are approximate confidence intervals. An alternative would be to use the method described by Venables (1975) and the program of Cooper (1968) and Chou (1985) to solve for a confidence interval for λ, which then yields an exact confidence interval for δ_2. The procedure can be conceptualized in the following manner (see Kendall & Stuart, 1967, p. 206): Let θ denote the parameter for which the confidence interval is desired. Envision that a test of the hypothesis H_0: $\theta = \theta_0$ is to be performed, where θ_0 is one particular value of θ. Determine whether the observed sample statistic would fall into the acceptance region or the rejection region of the hypothesis test. Repeat this determination for all possible values of θ_0. If we aggregate the "acceptable" values of the parameter, we obtain the confidence interval.

For the hypothesis under consideration, the parameter of interest is the noncentrality parameter. Given the observed value of the test statistic, say t_{obs}, we ask for which values of λ_0 would we accept the null hypothesis H_0: $\lambda \leq \lambda_0$? This null hypothesis would be accepted for large values of λ_0 and rejected for small values of λ_0, thus the cutoff between these sets of λ values is that value of the noncentrality parameter for which t_{obs} equals the critical value of the test. If the value of λ that makes $CV_{1-\alpha}$ equal to the observed test statistic is denoted $\lambda_{1-\alpha}(t_{\text{obs}})$, then the confidence interval for λ is given by $\lambda \geq \lambda_{1-\alpha}(t_{\text{obs}})$. The confidence interval for δ_2 can be found from the confidence interval for λ by dividing by $\sqrt{n_1 n_2/N}$.

The next test to be examined is that of the prediction that the effect is smaller than Δ_M, the largest magnitude of an effect, expressed in standard deviation units, that would be considered good enough. Now the null hypothesis is

$$H_0: \delta_2 \geq \Delta_M.$$

Large values of the sample test statistic are consistent with the null hypothesis, so only small enough values of the sample test statistic will lead to rejection. The critical value, denoted CV_α, is chosen as the 100α percentile of the noncentral t distribution with $N-2$ degrees of freedom and with noncentrality parameter $\lambda = \sqrt{n_1 n_2/N}\ \Delta_M$. If the value of λ that makes CV_α equal to the observed test statistic is denoted $\lambda_\alpha(t_{\text{obs}})$, then the confidence interval for λ is given by $\lambda \leq \lambda_\alpha(t_{\text{obs}})$. The confidence interval for δ_2 can be found from the confidence interval for λ by dividing by $\sqrt{n_1 n_2/N}$.

We next examine the procedure for testing the prediction that the population standardized effect is within a good-enough range in either direction of prediction. This time the null hypothesis is

$$H_0: |\delta_2| \geq \Delta_M.$$

Large absolute values of the sample test statistic are consistent with the null hypothesis; consequently, only small absolute values of the sample test statistic will lead to rejection. Two critical values, denoted $CV_{\alpha/2}$ and $CV_{1-\alpha/2}$, could be chosen equal to the $100\alpha/2$ and the $100(1 - \alpha/2)$ percentiles of the noncentral t distribution with $N - 2$ degrees of freedom and with noncentrality parameter $\lambda = \sqrt{n_1 n_2/N}\,\Delta_M$. In the case of this hypothesis, however, it is perhaps easier to deal with the hypothesis expressed in terms of the square of δ_2 and the square of Δ_M, because then only one critical value derived from the noncentral F distribution is required. In addition, the procedure considered here can then be extended to other measures of association, presented later. The present null hypothesis is equivalent to

$$H_0: (\delta_2)^2 \geq (\Delta_M)^2.$$

Under this latter range null hypothesis, $F = (n_1 n_2/N)(d_2)^2$ follows a noncentral F distribution with 1 and $N - 2$ degrees of freedom and noncentrality parameter $\lambda = (n_1 n_2/N)(\delta_2)^2$. Large values of F are consistent with the null hypothesis, so the 100α percentile of the noncentral F distribution with 1 and $N - 2$ degrees of freedom and noncentrality parameter $\lambda = (n_1 n_2/N)(\Delta_M)^2$ is chosen as the critical value for the test, CV_α. If the value of λ that makes CV_α equal to the observed test statistic is denoted $\lambda_\alpha(F_{obs})$, then the confidence interval for λ is given by $\lambda \leq \lambda_\alpha(F_{obs})$. The confidence interval for the absolute value of δ_2 can be found from the confidence interval for λ by dividing by $n_1 n_2/N$ and taking the square root. A computer program written by Narula and Weistroffer (1986) can be used to find the critical value and the limit to the confidence interval.

Finally, the method for testing the prediction that the population effect is outside a good-enough range follows the same logic as the last procedure, with the upper tail probabilities of the noncentral F distribution substituted for the lower tail probabilities in the previous method. The null hypothesis

$$H_0: |\delta_2| \leq \Delta_S$$

is equivalent to

$$H_0: (\delta_2)^2 \leq (\Delta_S)^2.$$

The critical value, $CV_{1-\alpha}$, is equal to the $100(1 - \alpha)$ percentile of the F distribution with 1 and $N - 2$ degrees of freedom and noncentrality parameter $\lambda = (n_1 n_2/N)(\Delta_S)^2$. The confidence interval for λ is given as $\lambda \geq \lambda_{1-\alpha}(F_{obs})$, from which the confidence interval for the absolute value of δ_2 can be found by dividing by $n_1 n_2/N$ and taking the square root.

Power

For each of the good-enough tests, as for all standard null hypothesis tests, the power of the procedure depends on α, sample size, and how far the true population parameter is from that specified under the null hypothesis. For a given effect size specified under the null hypothesis and for a given sample size and Type I error rate α, a power curve can be drawn for the test by specifying effect size values under the alternative hypothesis and determining cumulative probabilities using the appropriate computer program.

Alternatively, one can specify the effect size under the null hypothesis, the Type I error rate α, and the desired power to detect a particular effect of interest under the alternative hypothesis and use the computer program to determine the required sample size. Note here that two effect sizes must be specified. In the cases in which it is desired to show that the effect size exceeds a particular value, we can indicate the nature of these two required effect sizes by using the terminology of Levin (personal communication, 1991): The limiting effect under the null hypothesis would be called the *maximum effect of noninterest,* whereas the effect specified for power calculations would be called the *minimum effect of interest.* As the true effect approaches the latter, matters get more and more interesting. Similarly, in cases in which it is desired to show that the effect size is less than a particular value, the terms become reversed: The limiting effect under the null hypothesis would be called the *minimum effect of noninterest,* and the effect specifed for power calculations would be called the *maximum effect of interest.*

Example

Let us illustrate the exact test and confidence interval procedures for a directional hypothesis and compare the confidence interval to the approximate intervals of Hedges (1981) and Kraemer (1983). Let us assume that theory-based considerations specify a directional good-enough prediction that the means should differ by at least 0.2 standard deviations, and let us also assume, as in an example provided by Kraemer (1983), that the sample sizes were $n_1 = n_2 = 10$. Based on these sample sizes and the hypothesized limit to the effect size, the hypothesized limit on the noncentrality parameter is calculated to be 0.4472. From the computer-generated cumulative percentiles of the noncentral t distribution with 18 degrees of freedom and noncentrality parameter 0.4472, $CV_{1-\alpha} = 2.229$. The power curve for this example is shown in Fig. 6.1. If, as in Kraemer's example, the observed effect size d_2 was 1.0, then the sample test statistic $t_{obs} = 2.236$. Hence, the directional null hypothesis is rejected, and it is concluded that a confirmation has occurred. In terms of a confidence interval, we find that for $\lambda_0 = 0.4538$, $CV_{1-\alpha}$ would equal $t_{obs} = 2.236$. Hence, the confidence interval for

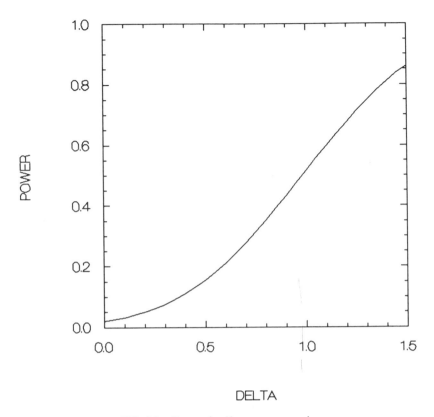

FIG. 6.1. Power for Kraemer example.

the noncentrality parameter is $\lambda \geq 0.4538$, from which is found the confidence interval for the effect size, $\delta_2 \geq 0.2029$. From Hedges's and Kraemer's respective approximations we would find for the confidence interval $\delta_2 \geq 0.1765$ or $\delta_2 \geq 0.2037$.

The adequacy of the approximations must be viewed from a Popperian perspective, recalling that the purpose of rigorous experimentation is to reveal possible confirming outcomes. If theory maintains that the effect size should be greater than 0.2 standard deviations, the Hedges approximation would not reveal the confirmation, whereas the Kraemer approximation and the exact approach would uncover it. In this sense, the Hedges approximation is conservative, here by about 13%. Unfortunately, although the Kraemer approximation typically yields a value close to the exact limit, it is slightly liberal. Whereas the Hedges approximation would miss some confirmations, the Kraemer approximation would typically "discover" too many. For these reasons, it is best to use the exact method.

Comparison with Cohen's (1988) Method
of "Proving the Null Hypothesis"

In using the present methodology to confirm the prediction that an effect is at most some particular magnitude, we are able to show that an outcome is effectively zero. Elaborating on this application may help to highlight the distinctive features of the good-enough methodology, especially when this methodology is compared to that suggested by Cohen (1988, pp. 16–17) for the problem often referred to as "proving the null hypothesis." It is well known that a nonrejection of the standard null hypothesis does not allow the same kind of conclusion to be drawn as would a rejection. If one wishes to confirm the prediction that an effect is trivial, then the logical complement must be set up as the null hypothesis. Cohen (1990), on the other hand, maintained that one could use the traditional null hypothesis testing methodology probabilistically to "prove the intended null hypothesis of no more than a trivially small effect" (p. 1309).

In Cohen's (1988) view, the investigator may validly conclude that an effect is trivial under certain circumstances. The experiment should be set up as if testing the standard null hypothesis, with a specified Type I error rate, which he called a. The sample size should be chosen so that the power of a standard null hypothesis test, which he called $(1 - b)$, is high for the detection of a specified *trivial* effect size, which he called i (for iota). Conceptually, if the power is very high and the null hypothesis is *still* not rejected, then the effect size is very likely to be less than i. "Thus," wrote Cohen (1988), "in using the same logic as that with which we reject the null hypothesis with risk equal to a, the null hypothesis can be accepted in preference to that which holds that [effect size] $= i$ with risk equal to b. Since i is negligible, the conclusion that the population [effect size] is not as large as i is equivalent to concluding that there is 'no' (nontrivial) effect" (p. 16).

There are certain difficulties with the Cohen approach. First, because Cohen indicated (1988, p. 104) that the null hypothesis for his procedure has been mitigated "to mean 'trivially small,'" the conclusion that the effect is trivially small is drawn from a nonrejection of the null hypothesis, rather than from a rejection of its logical complement. This seems to be at odds with standard statistical logic. In addition, some confusion results from using the same notation and terminology for this technique and for the standard null hypothesis test. If the risk in his procedure is now b, the power of the test cannot be $(1 - b)$, and it is not clear just what the role of a is. As suggested by Gigerenzer (chap. 11, this vol.), we should "point out the confused logic of the hybrid, and insist on consistency." The good-enough methodology allows us to do so.

As we described earlier, good-enough methodology provides a test that allows the conclusion that an effect is trivially small. In order to draw this conclusion, say in a two-sample test, the null hypothesis must be

$$H_0: (\delta_2)^2 \geq i^2,$$

so that the alternative hypothesis is

$$H_1: (\delta_2)^2 < i^2,$$

where we use i as the criterion for triviality, as in Cohen's procedure. The critical value for this test is the 100α percentile of the noncentral F distribution.

We can discuss the power and Type I error rate for this procedure in terms of Cohen's a and b (defined for his standard null hypothesis test). The value b is the probability that a sample F ratio will be less than Cohen's critical value (resulting in nonrejection of the standard test). Cohen's b is found by equating the Cohen critical value to the $100b$ percentile of the noncentral F distribution, with the noncentrality parameter based on the effect size being equal to i; but this is exactly how the critical value for the good-enough procedure is found. Hence, Cohen's b is equivalent to the Type I error rate, α, for our procedure. It is for this reason that Cohen called b the risk in his procedure. Thus, if the triviality cutoffs are the same in the two procedures, and if b is set equal to α, the critical values for the procedures are the same. Finally, because $(1 - a)$ is the probability of accepting Cohen's null hypothesis when the noncentrality parameter is zero, it is also the power of the good-enough test for that condition; that is, $(1 - a)$ is the maximum power of the test that allows the conclusion that the true effect is less than i. As described earlier, a power curve can be drawn for the test. Figure 6.2 shows the power curve for an example from Cohen (1988, p. 58) in which $a = .05$ and $b = .05$. Then the Type I error rate $\alpha = b = .05$ and the maximum power is $(1 - a)$, or 0.95, for detecting an effect size less than $i = 0.20$. Note that the power for the procedure is adequate only if the true effect were less than 0.06.

Other Applications

The methods based on the noncentral F distribution can be extended to the analysis of variance model, in which case the good-enough limits Δ_S and Δ_M would be expressed in terms of the population correlation ratio η^2 (the proportion of total variability explained by group membership) and to the regression model, in which case the good-enough limits would be expressed in terms of the population squared multiple correlation coefficient R^2. In fixed-effect analysis of variance, under a range null hypothesis the sample F statistic follows a noncentral F distribution with noncentrality parameter $\lambda = N\eta^2/(1 - \eta^2)$ (see Timm, 1975, p. 365), whereas if the values of the predictors in regression analysis are assumed fixed, the sample F statistic follows a noncentral F distribution with noncentrality parameter $\lambda = NR^2/(1 - R^2)$ (see Anderson, 1958, p. 93). Given these relationships between the good-enough limits and the noncentrality parameters, the methods described in the nondirectional two-sample case can be used to test hypotheses and calculate confidence intervals for the parameters of interest.

As an example, assume a researcher theorizes that three measures of mood

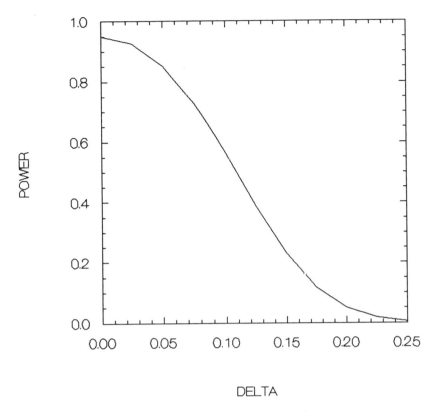

DELTA

FIG. 6.2. Power for Cohen example.

should not be related to a cancer patient's perception of pain. It is felt that the mood variables should be able to account for at most $\Delta_M = 25\%$ of the total variability in pain scores for the relationship to be considered substantially trivial. Hence, the null hypothesis would be

$$H_0: R^2 \geq .25.$$

Assume a sample of $N = 90$ patients is observed and the sample squared multiple correlation coefficient was equal to .15. In terms of the noncentrality parameter, the null hypothesis can be written

$$H_0: \lambda = NR^2/(1 - R^2) \geq 90(.25)/(1 - .25) = 30.$$

The critical value, 5.2837, is found from the computer program as the fifth percentile of the noncentral F distribution with 3 and 86 degrees of freedom and noncentrality parameter equal to 30. Because the F statistic of 5.0588 is smaller than the critical value, a confirmation of the theory has occurred. The confidence interval is given by $R^2 \leq .24$. Note that the standard F test would yield significance, with $p < .01$, allowing the conclusion that the population R^2 is nonzero, but that is of no interest in terms of theory confirmation and falsification.

PSYCHOLOGY AND PHYSICS RECONSIDERED

We have argued that significance-testing in psychology, when fortified with the good-enough principle, is not defective when compared with physics, and the methodological asymmetry noted by Meehl (1967) is more apparent than real. We would now like to reconsider the relationship between psychology and physics in this light. It would appear that nothing is so revealing of our inadequacies as a discipline than to compare our methodologies and achievements with that of physics. This is indeed a favorite strategem of those who are critical of the scientific pretensions of psychological research. In our view, however, this strategem is effective only when one adopts a view of physics that is overly optimistic and idealized, and one that is neglectful of the actual record of scientific practice in this discipline. Fortunately, more realistic appraisals of how to relate the two disciplines are beginning to emerge (e.g., D'Andrade, 1986). In a fascinating study, for example, Hedges (1987) was able to compare the empirical cumulativeness of research in both physics and psychology. By examining 13 quantitative reviews of the particle physics literature, and quantitative reviews of six domains of social science research, Hedges (1987) was able to conclude that psychological research is not disadvantaged in the cumulativeness of its findings when compared to this elite branch of physics. According to Hedges (1987),

> What is surprising is that the research results in the physical sciences are not markedly more consistent than those in the social sciences. The notion that experiments in physics produce strikingly consistent (empirically cumulative) results is simply not supported by the data. Similarly, the notion that experiments in the social sciences produce relatively inconsistent (empirically noncumulative) results is not supported by the data either. (p. 450)

Indeed, the rate of inconsistency and disagreement exhibited by the reviews was about 45% in either discipline, when no studies were eliminated from the reviews. (Consistency of findings improves in both disciplines when studies are omitted.) It would appear, then, that not only is there considerable similarity in hypothesis-testing methodologies between the two disciplines, as argued in the previous section, there is also considerable similarity evident in the empirical cumulativeness of research findings and in the quantitative methodologies used to detect it in the various literatures.

As Hedges (1987) noted, however, in the absence of similar kinds of studies, any firm generalization about the relative empirical cumulativeness of physics and psychology must be limited to the research domains sampled. But Hedges (1987) was able to show just what might result when one excavates and reconstructs a literature. At least with respect to the research domains sampled here, there is little reason for psychologists to bemoan their supposed unhappy lot, and little reason as well to idealize the consistency of findings in particle physics. One additional case study is reported to support this view. The point of this exercise is not, of course, to disparage the workings and achievements of physicists, but rather to point out that scientific activity, in either psychology or physics, is a difficult and often messy affair. Both disciplines have their own problems, to be sure, but matters are not improved and no useful end is served when we engage in idolatrous veneration of physics at our own expense.

The Problem of Solar Neutrinos

Pinch (1985) provided a case study of theory testing in physics that is illustrative of many of the issues that we have touched on, such as the requirements of good-enough hypothesis testing, the inconclusiveness of refutations, the necessity for operating with conventional assumptions, and the difficulty in testing auxiliaries and *ceteris paribus*. The *problem of solar neutrinos* emerged during the course of putting the nuclear astrophysical theory to a test. The theory attempts to account for the evolution and structure of stars. Its central tenet purports that stars burn hydrogen. Although this tenet had been widely accepted within the astrophysical research community, it proved difficult to subject to a severe test, at least until 1958. At that time it was suggested that one way to test the "hydrogen-burning" hypothesis was to construct an apparatus that made it possible to detect solar neutrinos, which are a by-product of hydrogen burning. This was a daunting challenge, because neutrinos are exceedingly difficult to detect. One method involved the use of a large (100,000 gallon) tank of dry-cleaning fluid that was sunk one mile into the earth in an abandoned mine shaft. The construction of the apparatus was begun in 1964 but was not completed until 1967. Exceedingly complex mathematical calculations, aided by numerous simplifying assumptions, initially determined that the astrophysical theory would be corroborated if the detection methodology captured 40 ± 20 SNUs (Solar Neutrino Units). Before the experiment was actually conducted, however, the prediction was downsized to 19 ± 11 SNUs. Clearly, "deriving" a prediction from the theory was quite difficult, and involved not a "point" prediction per se but a point prediction within a specified "good-enough" range. Indeed, according to Pinch (1985), "The prediction of a solar neutrino capture rate depends on a whole morass of theories and experimental data. These are not even drawn from one single area of science" (p. 175). Further, as Pinch (1985) told it, input parameters had to be juggled in order to provide a realistic model of the Sun. "It is difficult to see," wrote Pinch (1985, p. 176), "how the derivation of the final prediction could be described as a process of deduction."

By August 1967 the results of the study were available, and they did not appear to support the (good-enough) prediction of the theory. Indeed, so low was the signal that the result could only be reported at an upper limit of 6 SNUs, a value that is compatible with background radiation. A second experimental run, aided by technical improvements, reported an even lower rate of neutrino capture (upper limit of three SNUs). By all appearances, then, the astrophysical theory sustained a stunning refutation as a result of this "crucial experiment."

In spite of the putative refutation, however, the theory was not abandoned. Indeed, the hard core assumption that stars burn hydrogen was never in doubt. The refutation only invited appeals to *ceteris paribus*. According to Pinch (1985), "It should be emphasized that none of the revisions were to the basic theory itself, that remained largely unaltered. Rather it was amongst the large number of input parameters necessary for the calculation that the adjustments were made" (p. 180). New calculations of SNU capture rate, plus other recent findings, led to a new post hoc "prediction" of 7.5 ± 3 SNUs. Although the observed capture rate was still out of this good-enough range, it was thought that other refinements would bring the predicted SNU capture rate into line with what was actually observed. It is true to say, of course, that different members of a research community will evaluate the data and what is at stake theoretically in different ways. Critics of the astrophysical theory could see a refutation if strong doubts are expressed about the legitimacy of initial conditions, methodological and simplifying assumptions, parameter estimation, and the like. As Pinch (1985) pointed out:

> Initial conditions, like all basic statements, are themselves only accepted by con-ventional processes. There is nothing to stop scientists, if they so wish, from refusing to accept the new initial conditions. This means that they need not be bound by any apparent consistency or contradiction between theory and observa-tion statement. By refusing to accept the initial conditions, they, in effect, refuse to accept the outcomes of the test of theory based on those conditions. The conven-tional element at the heart of scientific practice allows for the possibility that agreement over consistency or contradictions cannot be reached during a crucial test. (p. 181)

This shows clearly, of course, that researchers are not bound by the tyranny of data. The failure of a prediction, held out on the eve of an experiment, does not automatically falsify a theory. Theories can be "juggled" so that support can be claimed if data merely satisfies, in some good-enough way, and sometimes after the fact, some anticipated consequence of the theory. But one can only claim support; it can never be compelled from the research community.

The solar neutrino example illustrates a number of themes. It shows, first of all, that the derivation of "point" predictions is a difficult affair, involving the juggling of parameters, simplifying assumptions, the uncertainty of derivations through the morass of auxiliary theories, and the specification of a good-enough range. It also shows that corroboration and refutation are only uncertainly and conventionally linked to the success or failure of predictions. Thirdly, the neutrino example illustrates how theories are clung to tenaciously and the appeal procedure by which theorists protect the hard core of the theory from refutation. Certainly, to the naive falsificationist, the solar neutrino example represents a serious departure from acceptable scientific method. Yet this brand of falsificationism does not credibly reconstruct the actual practice of working scientists. There is a lesson to be drawn for research psychologists: The difficulties of deriving testable predictions through the morass of uncertain auxiliary theories, the uncertainty involved in the estimation of parameters, the stubborn refusal to allow theories to be refuted, even to the point of pursuing after-the-fact strategems, should not be used as an indictment against the research practices of psychologists. All of this is well in evidence in astrophysics, and may well constitute standard practice for working scientists, whatever the discipline.

CONCLUSION

The purpose of this chapter was to respond to two popular criticisms of psychological research. It is claimed, for example, that theory appraisal in psychology is an impoverished affair, due to deficiencies in the use of significance testing. The criticism is then thought to be driven home by comparing the research practices of psychologists with what is taken to be the standard case in physics. In contrast, we have argued that hypothesis-testing in psychology, when fortified with the good-enough principle, is not rationally disadvantaged when compared against hypothesis testing in physics. We also argued that slow progress and lack of cumulative findings are not the indictments of psychology they are often made out to be. We showed, for example, by appealing to Hedges (1987), that the *empirical* cumulativeness of at least some domains of psychology is strikingly comparable to what is the case in particle physics. We also argued that evidence for *theoretical* cumulativeness is best sought by reconstructing the various literatures in light of the methodology of research programs as described by Lakatos (1978a). We complained about the tendency of critics to unfairly hold up an idealized vision of research practices in physics as a standard by which to indict psychological practices, and offered two case studies that should encourage not only a more realistic appraisal of what is actually the case in physics, but also a more charitable appraisal of what is the case in psychology.

Meehl (1990) suggested that one way to improve the prospects of psychological research was to increase the mathematical proficiency of our graduate students. This is an interesting proposal that merits serious consideration. We would like to add our own suggestion. In our view it is not simply enough to train graduate students to be conversant with various theories, and to be skilled users of statistical methodologies. What must also be inculcated is the view that theories are part of research programs that must be evaluated historically in light of certain criteria that help us appraise growth, progress, and cumulativeness. In other words, research programs must be rationally reconstructed. Meehl was more right than not when he complained about the amount of "naive guessing" that goes on in psychological research, much of which is embarassingly atheoretical. Many readers of this volume undoubtedly have sat on dissertation committees where the chief rationale for doing a particular study is sheer novelty, and absent any larger concern for how the anticipated results might constitute growth in a research program. Typically the literature review goes back only a handful of years, or else touches on only that part of the relevant literature that addresses some local concern of interest. It is not enough to simply "know" a literature. One must also reconstruct it in such a way that it can be seen to reveal the cumulative character of the enterprise. The methodology of research programs provides an impressive armamentum of tactics to this end. The general procedure, according to Lakatos (1978a), is to first provide a rational reconstruction: "One tries to compare this rational reconstruction with actual history, and try to criticize both one's rational reconstruction for lack of historicity and the actual history for lack of rationality" (p. 53). Whether or not one finds the Lakatosian framework congenial, and it is not without its critics, the main point is that we will never find cumulative progress in our research until we look for it. And rational appraisal of psychological research, and our appreciation of its scientific character, will always hinge on how we appraise growth in knowledge.

REFERENCES

Anderson, T. W. (1958). *An introduction to multivariate statistical analysis*. New York: Wiley.

Bolles, R. (1962). The difference between statistical hypotheses and scientific hypotheses. *Psychological Reports, 11*, 639–645.

Case, R. (1985). *Intellectual development: Birth to adulthood*. Orlando, FL: Academic Press.

Chou, Y. (1985). A remark on algorithm AS5: The integral of the noncentral *t*-distribution. *Applied Statistics, 34*, 102.

Cohen, J. (1988). *Statistical power analysis for the behavioral sciences*. Hillsdale, NJ: Lawrence Erlbaum Associates.

Cohen, J. (1990). Things I have learned (so far). *American Psychologist, 45*, 1304–1312.

Cooper, B. H. (1968). Algorithm AS5: The integral of the noncentral *t*-distribution. *Applied Statistics, 17*, 193–194.

Cooper, H. (1989). *Integrating research: A guide for literature reviews*. Newbury Park, CA: Sage Publications.

D'Andrade, R. (1986). Three scientific world views and the covering law model. In D. Fiske & R. Shweder (Eds.), *Metatheory in social science: Pluralisms and subjectivities* (pp. 19–41). Chicago: University of Chicago Press.

Feldman, K. (1971). Using the work of others: Some observations on reviewing and integrating. *Sociology of Education, 44*, 86–102.

Glass, G. V. (1976). Primary, secondary, and meta-analysis of research. *Educational Researcher, 5*, 3–8.

Hedges, L. V. (1981). Distribution theory for Glass's estimator of effect size and related estimators. *Journal of Educational Statistics, 6,* 107–128.

Hedges, L. (1987). How hard is hard science, how soft is soft science? The empirical cumulativeness of research. *American Psychologist, 42,* 443–455.

Hedges, L., & Olkin, I. (1985). *Statistical methods for meta-analysis.* Orlando, FL: Academic Press.

Hodges, J., & Lehmann, E. (1954). Testing the approximate validity of statistical hypotheses. *Journal of the Royal Statistical Society (B), 16,* 261–268.

Jackson, G. (1980). Methods for integrative reviews. *Review of Educational Research, 50,* 438–460.

Kendall, M., & Stuart, A. (1967). *The advanced theory of statistics* (Vol. 2). New York: Hafner.

Kraemer, H. C. (1983). Theory of estimation and testing of effect sizes: Use in meta-analysis. *Journal of Educational Statistics, 8,* 93–101.

Ladas, H. (1980). Summarizing research: A case study. *Review of Educational Research, 50,* 597–624.

Lakatos, I. (1978a). Falsification and the methodology of scientific research programs. In J. Worrall & G. Currie (Eds.), *The methodology of scientific research programs: Imre Lakatos philosophical papers* (Vol. 1, pp. 8–101). Cambridge, England: Cambridge University Press.

Lakatos, I. (1978b). Changes in the problem of inductive logic. In J. Worrall & G. Currie (Eds.), *Mathematics, science, and epistemology· Imre Lakatos philosophical papers* (Vol. 2, pp. 128–210). Cambridge, England: Cambridge University Press.

Lakatos, I. (1978c). Popper on demarcation and induction. In J. Worrall & G. Currie (Eds.), *The methodology of scientific research programs: Imre Lakatos philosophical papers* (Vol. 1, pp. 139–167). Cambridge, England: Cambridge University Press.

Lakatos, I. (1978d). Introduction: Science and pseudoscience. In J. Worrall & G. Currie (Eds.), *The methodology of scientific research programs: Imre Lakatos philosophical papers* (Vol. 1, pp. 1–7). Cambridge, England: Cambridge University Press.

Lapsley, D., & Serlin, R. (1984). On the alleged degeneration of the Kohlbergian research program. *Educational Theory, 34,* 157–169.

Meehl, P. (1967). Theory-testing in psychology and physics: A methodological paradox. *Philosophy of Science, 34,* 103–115.

Meehl, P. (1978). Theoretical risks and tabular asterisks: Sir Karl, Sir Ronald, and the slow progress of soft psychology. *Journal of Consulting and Clinical Psychology, 46,* 806–834.

Meehl, P. (1986). What social scientists don't understand. In D. Fiske & R. Shweder (Eds.), *Metatheory in social science: Pluralisms and subjectivities* (pp. 315–329). Chicago: University of Chicago Press.

Meehl, P. (1990). Appraising and amending theories: The strategy of Lakatosian defense and two principles that warrant it. *Psychological Inquiry, 1,* 108–141.

Morrison, D., & Henkel, R. (Eds.). (1970). *The significance test controversy.* Chicago: Aldine.

Narula, S., & Weistroffer, H. (1986). Computation of probability and non-centrality parameter of a non-central F-distribution. *Communications in Statistics B, 15,* 871–878.

Phillips, D. C., & Nicolayev, J. (1978). Kohlbergian moral development: A progressing or degenerating research program? *Educational Theory, 28,* 286–301.

Pinch, R. (1985). Theory testing in science—the case of solar neutrinos: Do crucial experiments test theories or theorists? *Philosophy of Social Science, 15,* 167–187.

Popper, K. (1959). *The logic of scientific discovery.* New York: Basic Books.

Popper, K. (1963). *Conjectures and refutations.* London: Routledge & Kegan Paul.

Rosnow, R., & Rosenthal, R. (1989). Statistical procedures and the justification of knowledge in psychological science. *American Psychologist, 44,* 1276–1284.

Serlin, R. C., & Lapsley, D. K. (1985). Rationality in psychological research: The good-enough principle. *American Psychologist, 40,* 73–83.

Serlin, R. C., & Lapsley, D. K. (1990). Meehl on theory appraisal. *Psychological Inquiry, 1,* 169–172.

Spielman, S. (1974). The logic of tests of significance. *Philosophy of Science, 41,* 211–226.

Timm, N. (1975). *Multivariate analysis.* Monterey, CA: Brooks/Cole.

Urbach, P. (1974a). Progress and degeneration in the "IQ debate" (I). *British Journal for the Philosophy of Science, 25,* 99–135.

Urbach, P. (1974b). Progress and degeneration in the "IQ debate" (II). *British Journal for the Philosophy of Science, 25,* 235–259.

Venables, W. (1975). Calculation of confidence intervals for noncentrality parameters. *Journal of the Royal Statistical Society (B), 37,* 406–412.

Walster, G. W., & Cleary, T. A. (1970). Statistical significance as a decision rule. In E. Borgatta & C. Bohrnstedt (Eds.), *Sociological Methodology* (pp. 246–254). San Francisco: Jossey-Bass.

7

The Theoretical Epistemology: A New Perspective on Some Long-Standing Methodological Issues in Psychology

Donald G. MacKay
University of California, Los Angeles

Psychology has developed an impressive array of methods over the last 120 years and it is widely maintained that methodology represents our area of greatest accomplishment. In contrast, our failure to develop general and plausible theories is seen as our greatest shortcoming. For example, as Royce (1984) pointed out, "Despite 100 years of data gathering, psychology has not evolved into a mature, scientific discipline. . . . Psychology's greatest deficiency . . . lies in its failure to develop viable theory" (pp. vii–ix).

Even in the methodological arena, however, unsolved problems and signs of discontent are easy to find. I begin by examining some unsolved problems that are widely believed to concern empirical methodology. I then review attempts to solve these problems over the past 75 years and examine why these attempts at solution have failed.

UNSOLVED METHODOLOGICAL ISSUES

Ecological Validity and Applicability

Psychology is currently witnessing a reaction against experiments that have only tenuous relevance to how people behave in everyday life outside the lab (see e.g., Ceci & Bronfenbrenner, 1991; Neisser, 1991). For example, psychologists such as Tulving (1979) expressed frustration over the artificiality and inapplicability of current psychological knowledge. What applications there have been are quite unlike the sophisticated theory-based applications one sees from advanced sciences such as physics and biology, and are often difficult to distinguish from common sense. To address this problem, some researchers have argued that we should set aside our concern for rigorous control, precise measurement of responses, and standardization of materials and presentation procedures in order to develop more naturalistic observations (e.g., Neisser, 1985). However, such proposals remain controversial. Some psychologists (e.g., Banaji & Crowder, 1989; Cohen, 1983, p. 16) feel that naturalistic studies may at best describe the characteristic habits and strategies of people, but do not help with the goal of determining underlying mechanisms, their limitations, and the causal interactions of structures and processes. Other psychologists (e.g., Conway, 1991) have called for attempts to integrate ecological and laboratory-based approaches and findings.

Unresolvability of Issues Deemed Important

Among the issues deemed most important for research in psychology have been those bearing on "images of humanity" (see Thorngate & Plouffe, 1987). These images characterize the underlying nature of our species in terms of dimensions such as basically active rather than passive or reactive, basically good rather than evil, basically cooperative rather than competitive, basically flexible rather than rigid, basically industrious rather than lazy, basically thoughtful rather than irrational, and basically masters rather than victims of circumstance. And vice versa, of course, or any possible combination of values on these dimensions. The resulting images consitute loosely defined ideologies that are similar in some respects to the paradigms or fuzzy schemas for how nature behaves that Kuhn (1970; 1977) described in other sciences (see also Bechtel, 1988). And because dimensions underlying such images of humanity are unlimited in number, research and debate on these images can in principle continue indefinitely.

Although images of humanity have implicitly or explicitly guided debates on the implications of our data and have inspired some of the most rigorous research in the behavioral and brain sciences (see Thorngate & Plouffe, 1987), issues associated with such images have turned out to be unresolvable. There is a problem because the meaning of predicates such as "are good" or "are evil", and so forth, lack fixed definition and can shift in either direction depending on what results are obtained. And although this problem of "meaning invariance" has been widely recognized since the early days of behaviorism, no generally acceptable solution has been proposed or adopted (see Bechtel, 1988; Feyerabend, 1988).

Noncumulative Aspects of Psychological Knowledge

Even when psychological issues have proven resolvable and our facts reliable and robust, old experiments, concepts, and phenomena have often been forgotten, and have been reinvented or reduplicated out of ignorance (see Cole &

Rudnicky, 1983). Perhaps, as some have complained, our ability to gather facts in psychology has outstriped our ability to make use of and build on these facts. Or perhaps the rapid pace of technological change encourages neglect of earlier work. Or perhaps time has tended to obscure the purpose of earlier experiments. As Baars (1986) noted, experiments carried out, say, 50 years ago must have seemed worthwhile at the time but now in retrospect often seem irrelevant or trivial.

However, relatively recent work has also been subject to neglect. As Bower and Hilgard (1981, p. v) pointed out, psychology seems to be in a "constant state of ferment and change, if not turmoil and revolution," with disorientation on the part of students, and confusion on the part of researchers as to where current results fit in. Paradigmatic shifts, together with the forgetting of earlier concepts, phenomena, and procedures, have disrupted the cumulative development of knowledge, and as Tulving (1979) noted, even the most sophisticated research activity runs the risk of resembling Brownian motion in such a situation.

The relevance of psychology to cultural values may also contribute to the transitory nature of psychological knowledge. For example, historical or geopolitical factors are known to limit the durability of psychological knowledge by influencing the acceptability of hypotheses such as "Human beings are basically rational." Within this larger social context, "images of humanity" can change rapidly and capriciously and relegate related empirical work to the dustbin (see Thorngate & Plouffe, 1987).

Irreplicability and Confirmation Bias

Irreplicability is a problem with a long history in psychology (see MacKay, 1988a, 1988b), and from the turn of the century to the present day, the problem has been attributed to confirmation bias, a tendency to selectively report results that favor one's hypotheses, or to repeatedly modify one's experimental procedures until supporting results are obtained (see e.g., Greenwald, Pratkanis, Leippe, & Baumgardner, 1986). Perhaps psychologists have placed greater reliance on the correctness of their empirical hypotheses than on the suitability of procedures used to test them (as Greenwald et al., 1986, p. 227, suggest); or perhaps the scientific reward system in psychology has encouraged researchers to become "ego-involved advocates" of their hypotheses and to publish irreplicable results (see Greenwald et al., 1986, p. 227). Or perhaps confirmation bias is a built-in component of "normal science," where, according to Kuhn (1970), researchers apply an accepted paradigm to new contexts in order to obtain results that comport with the paradigm. Whatever its cause, confirmation bias and irreplicability have been considered so pervasive and so serious as to call for radical change in the fundamental methodological underpinnings of psychology and science in general (see Greenwald et al., 1986, p. 226). So far, however, none of the attempted solutions have succeeded in solving the problem.

Observational Fragility

Although the advent of experimental paradigms (discussed later) has enabled some areas of psychology to achieve a high standard of replicability, this replicability often depends on exactly duplicating procedures in the original study (see Broadbent, 1987): If one varies the prescribed procedure only slightly, very different results are likely to emerge. This problem of observational fragility reflects the vagueness of current theories according to Broadbent: If theoretical statements that sum up results of experiments are sufficiently vague, one cannot determine whether some seemingly minor change of conditions is crucial. As a result, one is left unclear about what sort of experimental data will invalidate a theory, or whether the theory is even intended to apply to some new experimental situation (see Broadbent, 1987).

CURRENT ATTEMPTS
TO SOLVE THESE PROBLEMS

The aforementioned problems are not new, and psychology has made concerted efforts to solve them. In the following pages I evaluate the effectiveness of three such efforts that extend over the past 30 to 70 years.

The Divide-and-Conquer Strategy and Its Effects

To help with the division of scientific labor, and perhaps also to make large issues such as "Are humans basically rational?" more manageable, psychology has followed what might be called a divide-and-conquer strategy over the past several decades (see MacKay, 1982). Under this strategy, a subdomain is segregated on practical or intuitive grounds in order to develop one or more unique empirical approaches for generating a coherent body of facts and insights within the subdomain. For example, rather than attempting to understand skill in general, one can specialize in a skill that has been labeled "typical" (e.g., discus throwing; see Holding, 1981), and ignore skills that have been labeled "atypical" (e.g., speech production; see MacKay, 1982).

This strategy has had unfortunate side effects. First, important generalizations that happen to cross the largely arbitrary or accidental divisions between subdomains have been missed (see MacKay, 1982). In addition, there is fragmentation of knowledge. Taken one at a time, facts in most current surveys and textbooks are interesting and perhaps even enlightening, but taken together they often resemble a kaleidoscope of unintegrated puzzle pieces. For example, even chapters reviewing the same topic and published within the same edited volume often contain no overlapping references whatsoever (Lachman, Lachman, & Butterfield, 1979; see also Dale & Cochran, 1989).

Experimental Paradigms and Their Effects

To ensure replicability, and to enhance their technical competence, many modern psychologists have restricted their frame of reference to narrow experimental paradigms such as the memory search and lexical decision paradigms (see Grossberg, 1982). The implicit goal of researchers adopting such paradigms is to explore effects of a limited number of well-known factors on behaviors of subjects in the paradigmatic situation. Once these factors have been mined, the depleted paradigm is often abandoned as its members move on to a new one (see, e.g., Battig & Bellezza, 1979).

Methodological paradigms have introduced a number of undesirable consequences. Psychology has become splintered into progressively more narrow and diverging pockets of interest, a fragmentation process that could continue indefinitely because procedural paradigms are unlimited in number. Moreover, another undesirable consequence has been the sometimes mechanical character of paradigmatic fact gathering for the sake of fact gathering (see Hyland, 1981; Toulmin & Leary, 1985). For example, even the best psychologists sometimes seem to assume that experiments can proceed in absence of theory, the number of possible experiments is finite, and the psychologist's job is to do them all. (See e.g., Anderson, 1980, p. 16: "Psychological research, extensive as it is, has only scratched the surface of the experiments possible.")

Perhaps the most serious consequence is that paradigmatic fact gathering tends to interfere with rather than promote development of theories for integrating available knowledge. Paradigm-specific experiments have tended to take on an inwardly directed, puzzle-solving character that is more responsive to earlier experimental procedures rather than to fundamental theoretical questions (Baddeley & Wilkins, 1984). Often variables examined in one paradigm have already been explored in previous paradigms, and because procedural variations per se rarely provide new insights, conflicting interpretations of effects of a factor in one paradigm usually remain unresolved when the factor is examined again in the next paradigm (see, e.g., Anderson, 1976).

The Failure of Miniature Models

To address Broadbent's fragility problem and to increase the fit between data and theory, researchers have been trying deliberately to develop "miniature models" in recent decades. Miniature models are closely tied to a specific experimental paradigm, and sometimes even to results of a single experiment. The generally accepted goal is not just to develop small-scale models, based on specific experimental paradigms, but ultimately to integrate a large number of these paradigm-specific models into a single general theory. However, it is an interesting historical fact that this hoped-for integration has not been happening: So far miniature models have only proliferated rather than merged (MacKay, 1988a). Even paradigm-specific models confined to the information-processing approach have not been converging into ever larger theories (see Newell, 1973).

Why has this not happened? Why does the miniature models strategy seem to be getting nowhere? More generally, why have we been unable to solve methodological problems such as irreplicability, noncumulativity, and observational fragility? And why have our attempted solutions made matters worse? I argue that tacit adoption and exclusive reliance on an "empirical epistemology" during the past 75 years of research in psychology has contributed to such problems. And because the empirical epistemology has also provided the basis for attempts to solve these problems, these attempted solutions have had the opposite effect. However, problems such as ecological validity, irreplicability, observational fragility and noncumulative, inapplicable and fragmented knowledge in psychology[1] can be constructively solved by adopting a "theoretical epistemology" for use in combination with the empirical epistemology.

I begin with a general overview of the theoretical and empirical epistemologies, paying special attention to their contrasting views on methodology. I then return in the end to implications of these contrasting views for the methodological issues already discussed.

THE TWO EPISTEMOLOGIES
IN GENERAL OVERVIEW

The theoretical and empirical epistemologies are two general frameworks for the pursuit of scientific understanding. Each viewpoint is coherent and contrasts systematically and categorically with the other: The two frameworks do not just represent the extremes of a set of continuous dimensions.

The main goal of the empirical epistemology is to develop a body of reliable facts and real-world applications, whereas the main goal of the theoretical epistemology is to develop theories that explain available facts, facilitate practical applications, and predict new facts for future tests. Both epistemologies therefore seem to share goals such as "practical applications" and concepts such as "facts" and "theories," but these surface similarities are deceptive because the two epistemologies differ in how they approach and interpret these goals and concepts. For example, on the *surface,* both epistemologies define *theory* as a

---

[1]Aspects of the two epistemologies have been labeled concrete versus abstract, earthy versus airy (Robinson, 1984), and empirical versus rational (MacKay, 1988ab, 1989, 1990). This chapter summarizes the full set of contrasts using the terms *theoretical* versus *empirical* in order to avoid confusion with the philosophical terms *empiricism* (the view that all knowledge is derived from experience) versus *rationalism* (the view that certain types of knowledge can be known prior to experience (i.e., some general truths can be discovered or formulated via logical reasoning alone, e.g., inferences from axioms in mathematics; Pavio, 1990). The author thanks Asa Kashir for pointing out this potential confusion resulting from use of the labels empirical vs. rational.

relatively small set of interrelated and logically consistent propositions containing theoretical terms that can be related to existing and yet-to-be-observed empirical phenomena. This surface definition cannot be taken at face value, however, because the two epistemologies mean very different things by, for example, *theoretical terms*. Moreover, by using terms such as *theory* in fundamentally different ways, the two epistemologies end up differing on how theories are created, evaluated, and revised, and how they relate to observations and experimental procedures.

Although each epistemology takes the entire field as its scope, and can potentially encompass a psychologist's entire endeavor, it is a mistake to characterize one approach as correct, and the other as incorrect or misguided. The two approaches are complementary rather than mutually exclusive, and within the field at large, success with one approach does not depend on suppressing the other. Indeed, I argue that each approach can benefit from the success of the other. That said, the goal of this chapter is clearly not to lay out virtues of the theoretical epistemology alongside vices of the empirical epistemology. However, because thinking in psychology has been largely confined to the empirical epistemology since about 1915 (MacKay, 1988a), I take the virtues of this epistemology to be self-evident, and focus instead on some less obvious shortcomings that stem from exclusive reliance on this empirical framework. Also, because almost no psychologists currently adhere solely to the theoretical epistemology, my descriptions focus more on the potential assets rather than the well-known limitations of this epistemology. Finally, I emphasize how the theoretical epistemology differs from the empirical epistemology because the distinction between empirical and theoretical science has been either discounted or denied within the empiricist tradition (see e.g., Robinson, 1984, p. 29): The empirical epistemology has often been represented as synonymous with science itself (see e.g., Ceci & Bronfenbrenner; 1991, p. 28: "Science is an epistemology whose disciples have agreed to basic principles regarding replicability.")

To illustrate the empirical epistemology and its continuing popularity in psychology, I cite statements from the recent literature. However, authors of these statements have not deliberately intended to espouse the empirical epistemology as spelled out here: Psychology has been following the empirical epistemology implicitly rather than explicitly, and it is conceivable that no one will admit to holding all aspects of this empirical framework. Many may even find the contrasts between the two epistemologies incomprehensible (the problem of incommensurability is discussed later).

Theories Under the Empirical Epistemology

As defined within the empirical epistemology, theories can be and often are fundamentally empirical and descriptive rather than oriented toward underlying mechanism. The distinction is nicely illustrated in Bruce (1991, p. 46), who contrasts mechanistic explanations of memory (how memory works, i.e., underlying mechanisms) with functional explanations (descriptions of the everyday uses of memory). Both types of explanation would constitute theory under the empirical epistemology.

In general, however, the empirical epistemology defines theories by exclusion: Theories are anything other than data, operations, or observations. This definition is extremely broad: MacKay (1988b; 1989) documented examples of recent use where the term *theory* embraces concepts, conceptual statements, assumptions, methodologies, empirical hypotheses, empirical generalizations, guiding ideas, opinions, frameworks, approaches, experimental paradigms, and metatheories, in addition to what falls under the special definition of theories within the theoretical epistemology.

Empirical epistemology definitions of theory are also extremely loose. For example, even unique and in principle irreplicable observations have been referred to as theories within the recent literature (see MacKay, 1988a). Moreover, such looseness in use of the term *theory* is neither new (see Underwood, 1957, pp. 175–180) nor unique to psychology; for example, a recent introductory text on the philosophy of science (O'Hear, 1989) uses the term to refer to claims that are clearly descriptive rather than explanatory or derived from underlying mechanism, for example, "All swans are white." Of course, O'Hear's (1989) example "theory" is also inaccurate (e.g., some swans are black), a dimension worth noting because theories generally receive negative characterization within the empirical epistemology (see MacKay, 1988a).

The definition of theory within the empirical epistemology is open to logical, psycholinguistic, and epistemological criticisms. The logical criticism is that concepts and data or operations are impossible to separate: Even data obtained via the simplest of operations require conceptual classification. Consider counting for example. As Gaukroger (1978, p. 45) pointed out, "If I am counting the number of things in a room, I must restrict myself to a single system of classification. I cannot include a chair, wood, legs, molecules, and oblong shapes in the same total." (For other examples of the inseparability of concepts, operations and data, see MacKay, 1988a).

The psycholinguistic criticism is that the term *theory* is used so broadly and imprecisely within the empirical epistemology as to present a real danger that both bathwater and baby (genuine theory) will be discarded, as occurred during the behaviorist revolution (see MacKay, 1988a). The broad definition of theory has also hampered development of the theoretical epistemology in psychology, and paradoxically, may be hampering development of the empirical epistemology as well by conflating distinctions that are central to its goals. For example, empirical generalizations have been conflated with programmatic statements concerning what to investigate, and how, even though this distinction is important for evaluating research programs within the empirical epistemology (see MacKay, 1988a, 1989; see also Royce, 1988). To address this psycholinguistic criticism and to minimize confusion within the present chapter, I distinguish whenever necessary between *theory(E),* the broad definition in the empirical epistemology, and *theory(T),* the more specific definition used within the theoretical epistemology. This more specific definition is discussed later.

According to the epistemological criticism (developed in the next section), the negative connotation attributed within the empirical epistemology to theory(T) is counterproductive.

Theories Under the Theoretical Epistemology

The *sine qua non* of theories within the theoretical epistemology is mechanistic explanation: Theories(T) are not just descriptive, but explain phenomena in terms of underlying mechanisms. These mechanistic explanations derive from the logic of how a small number of conceptually simple theoretical constructs such as hidden units (McClelland, Rumelhart, & the PDP Research Group, 1986) and nodes (MacKay, 1987) interact (e.g., alter their linkage strength).[2]

The postulated interactions between the theoretical entities in theories(T) purport to explain how things (e.g., language perception and production) universally and inevitably work for all time, space, *and hypothetical or Gedanken examples* (Kuhn, 1977). Such theoretical universals cannot be directly tested. Nor can they be found by examining their applicability within a range of ecological settings (as Neisser, 1991, p. 35 suggested). Moreover, the call for theoretical(T) universals within the theoretical epistemology should not be confused with a search for *empirical universals:* As Ceci and Bronfenbrenner (1991) correctly pointed out, "Humans respond differentially to diverse cultural and physical settings. There are no empirical universals in psychology that hold across all physical and cultural settings, times and age groups" (p. 30). However, this empirical fact is irrelevant to how theoretical science should go about developing theories(T).

Theoretical(T) explanations are not tied to particular situations, experimental, cultural, or otherwise, and are meant to capture empirical generalizations and their exceptions (see Hempel, 1966). A typical empirical generalization is the

---

[2]Although well-developed theories(T) exhibit additional characteristics missing in these two psychological theories, it must be kept in mind that the theoretical epistemology required for developing such theories has been underdeveloped or neglected in the history of psychology: As a result, very few well-worked-out, familiar, and generally accepted theories(T) exist in the field for purposes of illustration.

Thus, I have been forced at several key points in this chapter to resort to some clearer and better-known examples from chemistry, physics, and biology in order to illustrate familiar mechanistic explanations and theories(T). This appeal to examples from theoretically more advanced fields is irrelevant to the obvious differences between, for example, chemical reactions versus human behavior noted by Conway (1991) and others. Although the theories(T) that have been developed in chemistry will undoubtedly differ from those that will be developed in psychology, the process of developing theories(T) in the physical and behavioral sciences is likely to be the same.

law of speed-accuracy trade-off, a regularity emerging from many experiments and thousands of observations of the relationships between two or more empirically defined variables. The greater the number, scope, and diversity of the empirical laws that such a theory explains, the greater its power and importance.

The theoretical epistemology does not define theories in relation to operations or observations: Theoretical constructs such as hidden units and nodes enjoy purely hypothetical or presumptive status, and so do well-established theoretical constructs such as electrons, atoms, and molecules. How such constructs interact can be inferentially related to certain observable phenomena, but in principle one cannot observe an electron (Carnap, 1966). As Robinson (1984) noted, "The entities of theoretical science cannot be perceived, by anyone, ever" (p. 26).

Of course theoretical terms such as *electron* sometimes become so useful and comport so well with detailed observations that they become adopted as observational or descriptive terms for researchers working within the empirical epistemology. However, such hypothetical-to-observational shifts are neither part of the theoretical epistemology, nor generally considered desireable within it. For example, if it were possible to observe a "theoretical entity" such as an electron, perpetuating the hypothetical or theoretical status of this concept would still be advisable from a theoretical perspective. First of all, purely hypothetical terms are, by definition, open to change and enable theories(T) to remain flexible in a way that empirical observations cannot. For example, because theories(T) are meant to go beyond the realm of current observation, it must be possible to alter a theoretical term in scope and empirical correspondence rules to encompass not just new observations, but new types of observations, and hypothetical status makes this flexibility possible.

Predictions within the Two Epistemologies

Both the empirical and theoretical epistemologies engage in predictions, but of radically different types (see Robinson, 1984). Empirical science uses empirical laws to make *summary predictions,* for example, generalizations from observed values of correlated empirical variables to intermediary, unobserved values. However, in addition to summarizing a range of existing regularities, theories(T) make *discovery predictions;* they predict new variables or previously unexamined regularities in relationships between variables.

Quantification Under the Two Epistemologies

Under the empirical epistemology, precisely quantified descriptions of the relation between empirical variables are especially likely to be labeled theory, and mathematical expression or simulation is often taken as essential for theoretical statements. However, quantitative expressions for theoretical terms are desirable but not essential under the theoretical epistemology, where mechanistic explanation rather than description is the *sine qua non* for theories(T). Qualitative statements describing how hypothetical constructs such as nodes relate, interact, or change over time, in the absence of mathematical descriptions or simulations of these phenomena, still qualify as theoretical rather than empirical statements (MacKay, 1982, 1987). Indeed, a progression from qualitative to quantitative expression of theoretical concepts characterizes all major scientific theories. Examples are the wave theory of sound and the atomic theory of matter: Both began in Roman times as qualitative analogies before acquiring their current mathematical form (Holland, Holyoak, Nisbett, & Thagard, 1986). Interestingly, however, the original qualitative concepts have remained and provided the basis for understanding and using these theories long after the more quantitative expressions were developed (Thagard & Holyoak, 1985).

However, the original qualitative statements in these theories were never vague or inaccurate versions of empirical statements. Moreover, not all quantitative statements are theoretical under the theoretical epistemology: For example, Massaro's (1987, 1989) use of fuzzy set mathematics to describe empirical data is nonexplanatory or unenlightening as to underlying mechanism and would not constitute theory(T) under the theoretical epistemology (see MacKay, 1989).

Meaning Invariance and Operationalism Under the Two Epistemologies

Holding the meaning of empirical terms constant across different contexts of use is especially important to the empirical epistemology. If the meaning of an empirical hypothesis can shift depending on the outcome of an experiment, the hypothesis becomes unfalsifiable and vacuous. For example, consider the hypothesis that chimps are (or are not) capable of learning language, claims that underlie a great deal of recent research in psycholinguistics: This chimp learning hypothesis can be characterized as unfalsifiable because the notion of what language is can change depending on what chimps are in fact shown to do.

The traditional approach to solving the meaning invariance problem within the empirical epistemology is to insist on operational definitions. Observations become definitive if operational definitions for the terms of a hypothesis can be agreed on, and this basic fact may go a long way toward explaining how the empirical epistemology has come to dominate research in psychology for so long and why psychologists have continued to adhere to operationalism long after its rejection in physics and philosophy of science alike (Hyland, 1981; see also Leahey, 1980). Perhaps the nature of hypotheses that often have guided psychological research (e.g., the "images of humanity" discussed previously) has also intensified the appeal of meaning invariance and operational definitions within psychology's empirical epistemology.

The theoretical epistemology, on the other hand, views meaning invariance as important for empirical terms, but as unnecessary and undesireable for theoretical terms. Within the theoretical epistemology, the meaning of theoretical terms varies with the theory or theoretical context in which they are used: Theoretical terms change their meaning depending on the theory in which they are embedded. For example, both Newton and Einstein used the term *mass* in their theories, but in fundamentally different ways (see Feyerabend, 1988).

Operational definitions are likewise desirable for empirical terms but not for theoretical terms under the theoretical epistemology, and insisting on an operational definition will reduce a theoretical term to an empirical one. If an important theoretical claim that has been tied to some operational definition is in jeopardy, a standard strategy within the theoretical epistemology is to reject or modify the operational definition (Bechtel, 1988). Indeed, theoretical claims can always be protected within the theoretical epistemology by modifying auxilliary assumptions and definitions (see, e.g., Quine, 1961).

The theoretical epistemology replaces operational definitions for theoretical terms with rules of correspondence. These rules map theoretical constructs onto empirical generalizations, but are modifiable and open to extension. This flexible character of correspondence rules enables theoretical constructs to outlast existing means of observation, and to suggest future observations, lines of research, and practical applications that are currently unimaginable. For example, by altering rules of correspondence and adding new ones, the theoretical term *sound wave* has survived for 1,800 years, explaining thousands of originally unimagined observations of an ever more direct and precise nature (Holland et al., 1986). The fact that correspondence rules are loose and variable means that full operational definitions for a theoretical construct are impossible: Unlike empirical terms, theoretical terms cannot be completely and immutably defined (see Hempel, 1970, pp. 205–206). Such conceptual flexibility is seen as a shortcoming under the empirical epistemology but is considered essential to scientific progress under the theoretical epistemology. And as Hempel (1970) pointed out, it is a noteworthy historical fact that *theoretical* entities, and not inflexible observations, have stimulated the greatest conceptual and empirical advances in science.

The Origins of Theory Under the Two Epistemologies

Although the origins of theory are not of serious concern to the empirical epistemology (see MacKay, 1988a), it nevertheless recognizes the importance of developing theories(E) and has definite views on how such theories originate or should originate. According to a standard claim within the empirical epistemology, data come first and drive theories, which emerge spontaneously when a large enough body of data has been amassed and calls for explanation. Thus, empirical domains that have not led to discovery of new theories(E) or theoretical principles have been labeled bankrupt within the empirical epistemology (see Banaji & Crowder, 1991, p. 1185). Similarly, Underwood (1957, p. 186) argued that many areas of psychology were unready for theory(E) at that time because their stock of preliminary data fell below the critical mass assumed necessary for theory construction.

Greenwald and colleagues (1986, p. 226) contributed a new twist to the critical mass idea, suggesting that reversing familiar findings or establishing their limits by manipulating situational variables will force theory to develop faster. Neisser (1976, pp. 141–142) added qualitative prerequisites to the critical mass idea, suggesting that theories are premature until more ecologically valid data become available. Finally, Massaro (1987, p. 24) suggested a better way of achieving critical mass, arguing that theory development is best stimulated by organizing empirical hypotheses into a binary tree and testing them in a systematic fashion resembling a game of "20 questions."

The theoretical epistemology has developed epistemological, hypothetical, and historical critiques that apply to all versions of the critical mass view of theory construction. The epistemological critique states that theories(T) cannot originate by amassing data or paradigm-specific descriptions: Observations cannot in principle extend across all time, space, and hypothetical examples, as is required for theoretical constructs in the theoretical epistemology. The hypothetical critique holds that it is difficult to imagine how well-established scientific theories could have originated solely as a result of collecting more and more data, no matter how precise, extensive, or qualified the data might be. Under the theoretical epistemology, data are unnecessary for creating and revising theories(T), and observations often play less of a role in developing such theories than factors such as parsimony, consistency, and "making sense." Consider, for example, the observation that uranium is yellow whereas hydrogen is a colorless gas: It is difficult to imagine how specifying conditions under which these observations do or do not hold could lead in principle to the theoretical concepts that uranium atoms have about 238 electrons, whereas hydrogen atoms have only one. The historical critique purports that such theoretical concepts did not originate in this way whatever it is imagined to be. In the actual history of science, theorists have often developed highly successful theoretical constructs—for example, atoms, sound waves—long before any experimental data whatsoever have accumulated (see Holland et al., 1986).

Theories(T) originate as conceptual inventions. Carnap (1966) provided an early summary of this theories-as-inventions view:

> We observe stones and trees and flowers, noting various regularities and describing them by empirical laws. But no matter how long or how carefully we observe such things, we never reach a point at which we observe a molecule or an electron. The term "molecule" never arises as a result of observations. For this reason, no amount of generalization from observations will ever produce a theory of molecular processes. Such a theory must arise in another way. (p. 230)

As Robinson (1984, p. 28) noted, "Theoretical science is invented," a product of creative cognition rather than situation-specific observation: Collection of more and more observations cannot automatically facilitate development of theory(T) and can actually retard it. Theories(T) cannot originate in ways suggested within the empirical epistemology, for example, by determining the potentially infinite set of conditions under which particular experimental findings do or do not obtain (MacKay, 1988a).

Theory Revision Under the Two Epistemologies

A typical view of theory revision under the empirical epistemology is that theories(E) are revised or abandoned if and only if contradicted by experimental data (as per Hull's hypothetico-deductive program). Indeed, the failure of Hull's program is often taken as justification for a stance that is both antitheoretical and antiexperimental: For example, according to Neisser (1985, pp. 272–273), both theories and theory testing have been tried and found wanting in Hull, and should be replaced, at least for the time being, by straightforward descriptions of behaviors emitted in everyday life. The theoretical epistemology criticizes this stance on historical and epistemological grounds: According to the historical critique, neither a theoretical epistemology nor theories(T) have been tried or found wanting in psychology (see MacKay, 1988a, 1988b). For example, Thorngate and Plouffe (1987) argued that tests of causal theories have less often served to motivate empirical studies in psychology than personal experience and vague, unstated empirical hypotheses such as "You catch more flies with honey than vinegar."

The epistemological critique states that Hull's method is neither necessary nor usually sufficient for revision of theories(T) (see MacKay, 1988a). Researchers working within the empirical epistemology often misunderstand this crucial point, as when Bruce (1985, p. 86) criticized Neisser for failing to appeal to empirical tests both when accepting echoic memory as a theoretical construct in 1967 and when rejecting it in 1983. Empirical tests are unnecessary for revision of theories(T), so these criticisms of Neisser are irrelevant from the standpoint of the theoretical epistemology.

Evaluating Theories Under the Two Epistemologies

Under the empirical epistemology, "objective considerations" such as testability and compatibility with available observations are the main criteria for evaluating theories(E). However, theories(T) are evaluated on other dimensions besides compatibility with observation and are in general considered false and open to revision. Theories(T) also enable sophisticated applications, summarize a broad range of observations, and stimulate advances in knowledge. Moreover, predictions derived from theory(T) are testable in principle but not necessarily in practice: When theory(T) is first proposed, demanding the possibility of immediate test is counterproductive (see e.g., Carnap, 1966; Feyerabend, 1988).

More important under the theoretical epistemology are subjective criteria for evaluating theories(T). When summarizing empirical laws, for example, theories(T) must make existing observations easier to remember, and this introduces subjective factors such as parsimony into evaluation of theory(T). Theory(T) must be elegant and simple so that users can easily remember it and think about its implications as well as the data it summarizes. Theories that reduce the complexity observed in nature to a few general principles are highly valued within the theoretical epistemology.

"Making sense" is another subjective factor contributing to evaluating theories(T), but not, one hopes, to reporting empirical observations (the goal of the empirical epistemology). Theorists generally revise or reject theory(T) not because it proves difficult or impossible to test, but because it no longer makes sense to them (see Brandt, 1984). Similarly, theories(T) are valued not just for the number of empirical laws they explain but for the diversity and apparent disconnectedness of these laws. The more diverse and seemingly disconnected the empirical relationships, the more highly valued the theory(T) that explains them. These and other subjective factors underlying evaluation of theory(T) (e.g., "depth of penetration"; Royce, 1988) help to explain why theories(T) are valued and used long after they have proven inadequate or insufficient for explaining all of the available facts. As Kuhn (1970) pointed out, "It is possible to maintain a theory as a whole even though it has been falsified by single experiments or other observations. . . . Theories are only rejected when all their important propositions must be revised and/or a new and better theory arises." Theories that facilitate recall of facts will be used until a new theory comes along that makes recall of the facts easier. Needless to say, other subjective factors such as the effort required in learning to use a new theory can also play a role in resistance to theoretical change.

METHODOLOGY
UNDER THE TWO EPISTEMOLOGIES

Falsificationism Under the Two Epistemologies

Under the empirical epistemology, falsification, the elimination of "alternate explanations of behavior" (Popper, 1959) is the "business at hand" (Massaro, 1987, p. 281) and has been equated with science itself. For example, Ceci and Bronfenbrenner (1991, p. 28) defined science as "a strategy of 'proof by disproof.'"

However, the theoretical epistemology rejects all aspects of falsificationism: If theories(T) were rejected as soon as they became falsified, no new theories could be developed because at least some existing evidence invariably contradicts new theories. For example, evidence based on the Aristotelian view of astronomical motion contradicted Galileo's earth-in-motion theory when first proposed; an example is the fact that objects dropped from a height fall directly to a spot below, and not to a spot behind, as "would surely happen" if the earth had moved during the fall (Feyerabend, 1988). Under the theoretical epistemology, new ideas that have not had a chance to devise their own methods of support must be protected against the premature dismissal that falsificationism seems to demand.

Verificationism Under the Two Epistemologies

Under the empirical epistemology, tests of theory(E) cannot be aimed at verification or demonstrations of how it fits particular empirical situations or explains particular experimental findings, and theories(E) should be accepted until contradicted by empirical data (Popper, 1959).

In contrast, verificationism is acceptable as one of many strategies within the theoretical epistemology, and theoretical development often proceeds a long way by examining how a theory(T) works in a variety of particular instances. Moreover, the theoretical epistemology rejects the idea that theories(T) should be accepted *until* they have been falsified. Creation of new and alternative theories is often necessary in order to discover, seek, or bring to light new data that would falsify or delimit an established theory. As Feyerabend (1988) pointed out, Brownian motion was only discovered after a new theory (the kinetic theory of gasses) was proposed as an alternative to aspects of the second law of phenomenological thermodynamics, and would never have been discovered by pursuing direct tests of the original law.

Hypothetical and Naturalistic Observations Under Two Epistemologies

The goal of the empirical epistemology is to provide the best possible observations under the best possible conditions, that is, controlled experiments rather than naturalistic observations (Roediger, 1991). Hypothetical or Gedanken rather than actual observations are seen as andecdotal at best, not to be taken seriously, and in general anathema to the empirical epistemology. An example Gedanken observation is the following description from Hinde (1966) of a hypothetical male chaffinch as it wakes from its roosting place:

> It may sing for a while, patrolling its teritory intermittently between bouts of singing. During this period it is likely to attack or threaten any other male it sees. It may then fly down from the tree and feed on the ground for a while: often it feeds in close proximity to other males, whom it tolerates at a distance of a few feet. After a period of feeding, it is likely to fly up into a bush to preen and then return to singing.

Under the theoretical epistemology, naturalistic observations are highly valued because the goal of the theoretical epistemology is to integrate all knowledge, independent of its origins, procedures or means of acquisition. Moreover, the theoretical epistemology not only seriously entertains naturalistic Gedanken observations such as those mentioned earlier but considers them central to its enterprise. The power of Gedanken observations lies in their apparent generality, typicality, and simplicity: Hinde's Gedanken observations assume that these hypothetical phenomena are so powerful as to characterize the behavior of any individual of any species (including our own) at any time, and so commonplace that they could be observed by a child under natural conditions, as well as under controlled conditions if anyone cared to carry out the experiments and to rule out the potential experimental artifacts. Any theory that contradicts such simple, typical, and readily made observations is open to unlimited empirical contradiction under the theoretical epistemology, and requires revision.

Circularity Under the Two Epistemologies

To call a theoretical concept *circular* is equivalent to calling it untestable, and constitutes a devastating criticism under the empirical epistemology. However, under the theoretical epistemology, where testing theories(T) against observations is not such a central concern, circularity is seen as necessary at least sometimes, and in general, not devastating. Thus, arguments within the theoretical epistemology are often circular. A classic example (from Feyerabend, 1988) is Galileo's use of circular arguments to promote his "earth-in-motion theory." To support his hypothesis that the moon was a physical body like the earth, Galileo invoked telescopic evidence of the mountainous lunar landscape. However, this evidence was unacceptable to the Aristotelians who maintained that the telescope introduced optical distortions because of the very different "etherial medium" through which light had to pass from celestial bodies such as the moon. To counter this neo-Aristotelian argument, Galileo invoked a new theory of optics, in effect, justifying (unacceptable) empirical results in terms of his theory and using these same results to justify his theoretical claims. As Bechtel (1988) pointed out, Galileo was only able to establish his new (astro)physics via circular arguments, "packaging his alternative view as a whole and insisting on answering all objections on grounds internal to his new conception" (p. 59).

Not just the use and evaluation of circularity, but the core concept of circularity itself differs within the two epistemologies: Statements within the empirical epistemology that take the form "X is circular or untestable" can, under the theoretical epistemology, be synonymous with three different readings: "X is descriptive, X is theoretical, or X cannot promote observations using current technology." By way of example, consider the problem of explaining probabilistic (nondeterministic) sequences in a general theory of serial order in behavior. Probabilistic sequences abound in behavior, and the sequential behavior of

Hinde's hypothetical chaffinch can be used for purposes of illustration. What determined the sequence of activities in Hinde's Gedanken observations? Why did the bird first sleep, then wake, then sing and patrol, threatening or attacking other males, next fly down to feed, then fly up to a bush to preen, and finally to sing again?

The traditional behaviorist account of sequential behavior attributes such sequences to changing stimuli in the external environment, but as Chomsky (1959) pointed out, this argument is circular if stimuli for, for example, preening, are defined in terms of the preening response, as was indeed the case in available behaviorist accounts. Now compare this account with MacKay's (1980) account of probabilistic sequences. MacKay proposed that a set of "motivational nodes" determines probabilistic sequences involving sleeping, waking, singing, patrolling, flying, threatening, feeding, and preening in chaffinches. Like all other nodes, one and only one motivational node can become activated at any one time because nodes become activated under a "most-primed-wins principle": Whatever node in a given set receives the most priming will be the one that gets activated and determines the output. What class of action occurs at any given time therefore depends on which motivational node receives greatest priming from both internal and external sources.

Like the behaviorist account, MacKay's account can be labeled circular within the empirical epistemology because he provided no objective procedure for specifying what motivational node has received most priming in any given case: One can currently only look at what behavior is dominant and infer that the corresponding motivational node must have been activated so as to control the output. Being circular and untestable, theoretical concepts such as motivational nodes should not be published in a regular journal under the empirical epistemology. And if published, such concepts should be ignored, just as the behaviorist account of such probabilistic sequences has been ignored following Chomsky.

The theoretical epistemology takes a different view of the circularity in these two accounts. Under the theoretical epistemology, the circular nature of the two accounts is not a central problem, and the empirical epistemology is applying the term *circular* to two quite different problems, conflating a fundamental distinction between unlimited empirical contradiction versus untestability under current technology. Specifically, vast (unlimited) amounts of already available and readily observable phenomena directly contradict the behaviorist account, whereas the correspondence rules and empirical technology required to test MacKay's account have not yet been developed. Moreover, these two problems differ in seriousness under the theoretical epistemology: As discussed later, the problem of technological advance is not beyond remedy, whereas unlimited empirical contradiction is.

To illustrate the problem of unlimited empirical contradiction, note how the behaviorist account of probabilistic sequences contradicts Hinde's Gedanken observations. For example, because stimuli (however defined) for patroling and preening were presumably present throughout the hypothetical episode that Hinde reported, the behaviorist account fails to explain why these activities occurred in the order that they did (patrol then preen). Moreover, the stimulus of a nearby male (however defined) was clearly present while the bird was searching for food, so why did the chaffinch threaten the male earlier but not then? The behaviorist account fails to explain why a hungry male chaffinch continues to search for food despite the presence of a stimulus that normally elicits territorial rather than feeding behavior.

By way of contrast, what MacKay's account requires is definition of its central constructs (motivational nodes, priming and activation) at a neural level. The fact that no such definitions for these theoretical concepts have been worked out and accepted is a relatively minor shortcoming under the theoretical epistemology. And so is the fact that electrodes have never been placed on and recordings taken from motivational nodes for preening, but only those for feeding, attacking, sleeping, and waking (see e.g., von Holst & von St. Paul, 1963). If acceptable definitions of nodes and priming at a neural level are eventually worked out and if motivational nodes underlying preening are eventually localized in this species, then the theoretical explanation is not circular: It predicts, among other things, that whatever motivational node has acquired greatest priming at any point in time will be the next node to determine behavior. Unlike the problem of unlimited empirical contradiction, untestability under current technology and correspondence rules is unfortunate but not devastating under the theoretical epistemology.

The Evaluation of Facts
Under the Two Epistemologies

The two epistemologies differ strikingly on the issue of what constitutes a fact and what makes a fact interesting. Under the empirical epistemology, empirical hypotheses constitute facts if observed events or relations are sufficiently unlikely to have occurred by chance, and such facts are considered interesting in and of themselves. Under the theoretical epistemology, however, theories(T) influence how interesting a fact is: Empirical findings become especially interesting when they fail to fit a well-established theory, or when they fit a newly proposed theory, and most spectacularly, both. Indeed, observations do not count as scientific facts within the theoretical epistemology until a plausible theoretical mechanism for explaining them is proposed. For example, science at large refused to consider the sizable body of well-known observations on selective breeding as scientific facts until Darwin proposed a plausible theoretical mechanism for explaining these observations. Similarly, observations suggesting the occurrence of extrasensory perception currently fall outside the realm of fact in the behavioral and brain sciences not necessarily because researchers on psychic phenomena have let theory(E) bias their observations, but on the contrary, because no plausible theoretical mechanism has been proposed for explaining the available data (see MacKay, 1990). Here then is a case where the two epistemologies come to the same conclusion but for different reasons, the empirical epistemology because theories(E) are connotatively undesirable, and the theoretical epistemology because observations independent of theory(T) cannot be taken at face value.

In summary, the empirical and theoretical epistemologies use many of the same terms in fundamentally different ways. It is as if the two epistemologies employ the same words to speak incommensurable languages that are designed for use in fundamentally different intellectual worlds (Kuhn, 1977, pp. xii–xiii). And according to Kuhn, the ability to communicate one viewpoint to adherents of another, incommensurable viewpoint depends on a process of translation that is problematic in general, and impossible without the intervention of "bilinguals" who are conversant in both viewpoints. Thus, developing or even just comprehending the theoretical epistemology may be particularly difficult in psychology because most psychologists are adherents of the empirical epistemology, and few, if any, are sufficiently conversant in both epistemologies to undertake this translation process.

WHY PREVIOUS SOLUTIONS FAILED: THE VIEW FROM THE THEORETICAL EPISTEMOLOGY

Strategies such as divide-and-conquer, experimental paradigms, and the development of miniature theories(E) serve a logical function within the empirical epistemology where the primary goal is to make observations. Like the empirical epistemology itself, however, these strategies cannot possibly solve problems such as narrow, fragmented, and easily ignored or forgotten facts, reduplicative rather than cumulative research efforts, and lack of viable theory (see e.g., Conway, 1991). In fact, strategies developed within the empirical epistemology will augment these problems unless offset by development of a theoretical epistemology that aims to integrate available knowledge. For example, Greenwald and colleagues (1986) called for result-centered methods, which can likewise be predicted to aggravate the problems they are intended to solve if carried out within a strictly empirical epistemology (see MacKay, 1988a).

The Divide-and-Conquer Strategy

As an approach to theory construction, the strategy of segregating a field of inquiry into subdomains represents a direct offshoot of the empirical epistemology: The fragmentation of knowledge entailed by the divide-and-conquer strategy hinders discovery of both theories(T) and empirical generalizations (see MacKay, 1982), and is anathema to the theoretical epistemology.

Experimental Paradigms

The idea of exploring a set of variables in some paradigmatic situation is of course foreign to the theoretical epistemology where the goal is to integrate knowledge derived from as wide a range of procedures as possible, including naturalistic and hypothetical observations. The idea of abandoning a problem area once some limited set of factors has been explored is likewise foreign to the theoretical epistemology where the goal is general understanding rather than fact gathering for the sake of fact gathering. Within the theoretical epistemology, theoretical problems are not abandoned until an acceptable solution is found; and often not even then, because alternate and especially, more general theories (see Feyerabend, 1988) are highly valued within the theoretical epistemology.

The Failure of Miniature Models

The "miniature model" approach to theory construction has failed according to the theoretical epistemology because general and viable theories cannot in principle grow out of miniature or paradigm-specific models. Theories(T) are not cumulative or generalized descriptions of facts, observations, or empirical laws, and cannot be discovered, developed, or evaluated by concatenating descriptions of different experimental paradigms. Although theories(T) summarize a wide range of empirical generalizations, they do not directly describe events specific to particular experimental paradigms or situations. If we restrict ourselves to data-specific curve-fitting, our goal of developing a general and viable theory(T) of mind will continue to elude us forever.

A NEW PERSPECTIVE
ON METHODOLOGICAL ISSUES

Confirmation Bias and Its Remedy
Under Two Epistemologies

Historically, the empirical epistemology has been quick to suggest and adopt radical methodological solutions to the problem of confirmation bias (see Mac-Kay, 1988a). Viewed from the theoretical epistemology, however, confirmation bias is not susceptible to methodological solution, and recently proposed methodological solutions will introduce further problems that are at least as serious as confirmation bias (see MacKay, 1988a).

A more feasible, didactic rather than methodological solution to confirmation bias is possible within either epistemology to ensure that future experimenters acquire greater confidence in the suitability of their procedures, and do not become "ego-involved advocates" of their empirical hypotheses. Experimenters should be trained to avoid empirical confirmation bias as automatically as not driving a car through a red light. And as in the case of traffic violations, sophisticated procedures should be developed for detecting and remedying confirmation bias, if possible before it becomes expressed in the literature.

Yet another solution to the confirmation bias problem would be available once the behavioral sciences develop a theoretical epistemology that can serve as a counterweight to the empirical epistemology: That is, person(s) testing a theory(T) could be different and presumably less "ego-involved" than person(s) developing the theory(T). Under this proposal, experimenters should never test empirical hypotheses that have been derived from a theory(T) that they themselves have developed, a division-of-labor solution that has already been adopted in theoretically advanced sciences such as biology.

Turning now to the theoretical epistemology, confirmation bias is not as serious a problem as is often supposed within the empirical epistemology: Conservatism with regard to theory(T) is in fact desirable under the theoretical epistemology. Newly discovered empirical phenomena that fail to fit established theory(T) do not and should not "discredit" or bring "disapproval" on the theory because theories(T) should not be overthrown lightly, and because falsifying a prediction is not a straightforward affair (see Duhem, 1953; Quine, 1960). That is, predictions cannot be tested in isolation from the network of (sometimes implicit) theoretical assumptions in which they are embedded, and often fail not because the theory(T) per se is at fault, but because the situation of test has violated some all-other-factors-being-equal assumptions of the theory. (For dramatic examples from astronomy and neuropsychology, see Churchland, 1986). Novel observations or judgments "from the hurly-burly of the laboratory" (Churchland, 1986, p. 264) only become really secure and unimpeachable when explained by some theory(T), the unavailability of viable theoretical alternatives further adds to the bias against rejecting established theory within the theoretical epistemology. Finally, a strong case can be made that developing viable theories in psychology would greatly reduce the likelihood of confirmation bias rather than increase it. Established theories highlight unpredicted findings as not just surprising and difficult to understand given the pattern of prior knowledge within the theory's presumed domain, but also as challenging, important, and essential to pursue and eventually, publish rather than ignore or suppress.

Irreplicability and Observational Fragility Under the Two Epistemologies

Whereas failures to replicate have been blamed on theories(E) within the empirical epistemology (see e.g., Greenwald et al., 1986, p. 222), some nonreplications result from failures to know, understand, or communicate the conditions essential to reproducing a result, and under the theoretical epistemology, reflect lack of theory(T) for summarizing available knowledge. Faced with the task of summarizing a mass of unintegrated findings and experimental details, investigators often ignore or downplay the seemingly minor procedural events that can completely change the outcome of an experiment and make replication difficult. The writers of secondary sources add to this unprincipled selectivity, not because they are "ego-involved theory advocates," as Greenwald and colleagues (1986, p. 227) maintained, but ironically, because a strictly empirical epistemology has hindered development of theory(T) in psychology. As already noted, the fragility of current results may likewise reflect a lack of theory(T), due again to over-reliance on a strictly empirical epistemology.

Ecological Validity and Applicability Under the Empirical Epistemology

The desire to address everyday behavior has a long history in psychology, and recent expressions of frustration over the inapplicability of current experimental knowledge are understandable. The empirical epistemology has blamed theories for the relative inapplicability of current psychological facts. For example, Greenwald and colleagues (1986, p. 227) maintained that the social reward system in psychology has encouraged researchers to become "ego-involved advocates of theory" and to publish observations that are overgeneralized and unreliable, and thus, inapplicable and ecologically obtuse. Within the empirical epistemology, this ecological validity problem can only be solved by designing experiments that apply directly to real-world problems (see, e.g., Conway, 1991).

The theoretical epistemology rejects the assumption that experimental findings can or should apply directly to the real world. Real-world problems that require creative solution are never as simple as laboratory situations, which are, of necessity, carefully and deliberately contrived. The goal of applied work is to think flexibly about a real-world problem, to come up with as many courses of action as possible, and to try out the best ones, often in tentative, small-scale fashion until an acceptable solution is found. Experimental observations cannot directly help in this process. As Neisser (1985) noted, "impoverished laboratory environments" cannot in principle directly reflect the complexity of everyday life. The very fact that experimental observations originate in rigidly controlled and (one hopes) well-understood laboratory situations restricts the applicability of experimental observations to unsolved real-world problems. If an experimental observation applies directly to some real-world problem, the problem has already been solved and does not, by definition, require creative solution.

Ecological Validity and Applicability Under the Theoretical Epistemology

Under the theoretical epistemology, sophisticated applications and characterizations of everyday phenomena must derive from theories(T) rather than from experimental observations. Theories(T) are flexible and general, and can thus apply across a broad range of everyday situations, unlike experimental observations, which by definition and design are restricted to a limited range of controlled conditions. However, even theories(T) sometimes lack sufficient flexibility and generality for handling the complexity of real-world problems, so that specialized practitioners must often use their experience, intuition, and ingenuity when applying theory(T) to practical ends.

The simplicity of theories(T) is also essential to applied work. Theories(T) reduce a large number of complex empirical generalizations and their exceptions to a small number of conceptually simple hypothetical constructs. For example, mental nodes (MacKay, 1987) and the simple ways they interact are easier to think about than the many empirical phenomena that they summarize. Such simplicity can help the practitioner come up with sophisticated solutions to applied problems. Unintegrated scientific observations, on the other hand, are not simple: Empirical factors and the potentially unlimited interactions between them are difficult to keep in mind, let alone apply. The theoretical epistemology attributes the relative inapplicability of knowledge in psychology primarily to the lack of theory(T), and warns that discovering additional facts without developing theory(T) can bring diminishing practical returns (see MacKay, 1988a).

Lacking theories(T), the behavioral sciences currently lack a scientifically based technology. As Gergen (1988) pointed out, most applications in the behavioral sciences derive from overgeneralized empirical hypotheses or assumptions such as "individuals are responsible for their actions" or "the environment controls behavior." These hypotheses or assumptions translate directly into general recommendations such as "the aberrant psychological processes of an individual should be treated directly" or "change defective groups such as the educational system, family, or society that are responsible for aberrant psychological processes." Lacking a more sophisticated approach to applications, psychology has introduced such vague and conflicting recommendations into manuals for child rearing, therapy, courtroom procedures, screening, and hiring (see Gergen, 1988).

In summary, the ecological validity issue illustrates in miniature a major limitation to metatheoretical debates currently ongoing in the behavioral sciences (e.g., Bruce, 1985; Massaro, 1989; Neisser, 1985) and related disciplines (e.g., Alcock, 1987; Rao & Palmer, 1987): The debates have been entrenched within a strictly empirical epistemology (see MacKay, 1988a, 1988b). However, dissatisfaction with research as it applies to everyday problems is best directed toward developing the theoretical epistemology as a supplement to the empirical epistemology.

CONCLUSION

I have argued that the methodological and theoretical shortcomings outlined in the introduction are interrelated: Both stem from exclusive reliance on the empirical epistemology over the past 75 years of psychological research. I have argued that developing the theoretical epistemology, as a complement to and collaborator with the empirical epistemology, is essential in psychology for solving problems such as ecological validity, irreplicability, observational fragility, a noncumulative knowledge base, and inapplicable and fragmented knowledge. What is needed in the end is a balance between the two epistemologies: Virtually all major advances in modern physics and chemistry can be traced to collaborative interactions between highly developed empirical and theoretical epistemologies in these fields (Robinson, 1984).

Finally, in addition to providing new insights into methodological problems, the theoretical epistemology has suggested a new perspective on some of the metatheoretical debates currently ongoing in psychology and related disciplines. Moreover, recognizing the fundamental differences in orientation, rules, and contributions of these two epistemologies may be necessary for seeing science as anything more than a fundamentally irrational enterprise in which anything goes (Feyerabend, 1988; Laudan, 1981): As we have seen, things that "go" in one epistemology often do not "go" in the other, and vice versa.

REFERENCES

Alcock, J. E. (1987). Parapsychology: Science of the anomalous or search for the soul? *Behavioral and Brain Sciences 10*, 539–643.

Anderson, J. R. (1976). *Language, memory and thought*. Hillsdale, NJ: Lawrence Erlbaum Associates.

Anderson, J. R. (1980). *Cognitive psychology and its implications*. San Francisco: W. H. Freeman.

Baars, B. J. (1986). *The cognitive revolution in psychology*. New York: Guilford Press.

Baddeley, A. D., & Wilkins, A. J. (1984). Taking memory out of the laboratory. In J. E. H & P. E. Morris (Eds.), *Everyday memory, actions and absent-mindedness* (pp. 1–18). London: Academic Press.

Banaji, M., & Crowder, R. (1989). The bankrupcy of everyday memory. *American Psychologist, 44*, 1185–1193.

Battig, W. F., & Bellezza, F. S. (1979). Organization and levels of processing. In C. R. Puff (Ed.), *Memory organization and structure* (pp. 321–346). New York: Academic.

Bechtel, W. (1988). *Philosophy of science: An overview for cognitive science*. Hillsdale, NJ: Lawrence Erlbaum Associates.

Bower, G. H., & Hilgard, E. R. (1981). *Theories of learning*. Englewood Cliffs, NJ: Prentice-Hall.

Brandt, L. W. (1984). Logic and psycho-logic of science. *Annals of Theoretical Psychology, 2*, 203–210.

Broadbent, D. (1987). Simple models for experimentable situations. In P. Morris (Ed.), *Modeling cognition* (pp. 169–186). New York: Wiley.

Bruce, D. (1985). The how and why of ecological memory. *Journal of Experimental Psychology: General, 114*, 78–90.

Bruce, D. (1991). Mechanistic and functional explanations of memory. *American Psychologist, 46*, 46–48.

Carnap, R. (1966). *Philosophical foundations of physics*. New York: Basic Books.

Ceci, S. J., & Bronfenbrenner, U. (1991). On the demise of everyday memory. *American Psychologist, 44*, 27–33.

Chomsky, N. (1959). Review of Skinner's *Verbal behavior. Language, 35,* 26–58.

Churchland, P. S. (1986). *Neurophilosophy.* Cambridge, MA: MIT Press.

Cohen, G. (1983). *The psychology of cognition.* London: Academic Press.

Cole, R. A., & Rudnicky, A. I. (1983). What's new in speech perception? The research and ideas of William Chandler Bagley, 1874-1946. *Psychological Review, 90,* 94–101.

Conway, M. A. (1991). In defence of everyday memory. *American Psychologist, 46,* 19–26.

Dale, R. H. I., & Cocran, B. P. (1989). Do cognitive psychologists share a paradigm? *Bulletin of the Psychonomics Society,* 325–326.

Duhem, P. (1953). *The aim and structure of physical theory.* (P. Weiner, Trans.) Princeton, NJ: Princeton University Press.

Feyerabend, P. K. (1988). *Against method.* London: Verso.

Gaukroger, S. (1978). *Explanatory structures.* Atlantic Highlands, NJ: Humanities Press.

Gergen, K. J. (1988). The concept of progress in psychological theory. In W. J. Baker, L. P. Mos, H. V. Rappard, & H. J. Stam (Eds.), *Recent trends in theoretical psychology* (pp. 1–14). Berlin: Springer-Verlag.

Greenwald, A. G., Pratkanis, A. R., Leippe, M. R., & Baumgardner, M. H. (1986). Under what conditions does theory obstruct research progress? *Psychological Review, 93,* 216–229.

Grossberg, S. (1982). *Studies of mind and brain: Neural principles of learning, perception, development, cognition and motor control.* Boston: Reidel.

Hempel, C. G. (1966). *Philosophy of natural science.* Englewood Cliffs, NJ: Prentice-Hall.

Hempel, C. G. (1970). *Aspects of scientific explanation.* New York: Macmillan.

Hinde, R. A. (1966). *Animal behaviour: A synthesis of ethology and comparative psychology.* New York: McGraw-Hill.

Holding, D. H. (1981). *Human skills.* New York: Wiley.

Holland, J. H., Holyoak, K. J., Nisbett, R. E., & Thagard, P. R. (1986). *Induction: Processes of Inference, Learning, and Discovery.* Cambridge, MA: MIT Press.

Holst, E. von, & St. Paul, U. von (1963). On the functional organization of drives. *Animal Behavior, 11,* 1–20.

Hyland, M. (1981). *Introduction to theoretical psychology.* London: Macmillan.

Kuhn, T. S. (1970). *The structure of scientific revolutions.* (2nd ed.). Chicago: University of Chicago Press.

Kuhn, T. S. (1977). A function for thought experiments. In P. N. Johnson-Laird & P. Wason (Eds.), *Thinking: Readings in cognitive science.* Cambridge: Cambridge University Press.

Lachman, R., Lachman, J. L., & Butterfield, E. C. (1979). *Cognitive psychology and information processing: An introduction.* Hillsdale, NJ: Lawrence Erlbaum Associates.

Laudan, L. (1981). The pseudo-science of science. *Philosophy of the Social Sciences, 11,* 173–198.

Leahey, T. H. (1980). The myth of operationism. *Journal of Mind and Behavior, 1,* 127–143.

MacKay, D. G. (1980). *A general theory of serial order in behavior.* Unpublished manuscript, UCLA.

MacKay, D. G. (1982). The problems of flexibility, fluency, and speed-accuracy trade-off in skilled behavior. *Psychological Review, 89,* 483–506.

MacKay, D. G. (1987). *The organization of perception and action: A theory for language and other cognitive skills.* New York: Springer-Verlag.

MacKay, D. G. (1988a). Under what conditions can theoretical psychology survive and prosper?: Integrating the rational and empirical epistemologies. *Psychological Review, 95,* 559–565.

MacKay, D. G. (1988b). Practical applications and theories of memory: A new epistemology to supplement the old. In M. M. Gruneberg, P. E. Morris, & R. N. Sykes (Eds.), *Practical aspects of memory* (Vol. 2, pp. 441–446). Chichester, England: Wiley.

MacKay, D. G. (1989). Is *Paradigm* a new and general paradigm for psychological inquiry? Read my lips. *Behavioral and Brain Sciences, 12,* 770–772.

MacKay, D. G. (1990). Why facts neither speak for themselves nor resolve the psi controversy: The view from the rational epistemology. *Behavioral and Brain Sciences, 13,* 385–386.

Massaro, D. W. (1987). *Speech perception by ear and eye: A paradigm for psychological inquiry.* Hillsdale, NJ: Lawrence Erlbaum Associates.

Massaro, D. W. (1989). Speech perception by ear and eye: A paradigm for psychological inquiry. *Brain and Behavior Sciences, 12,* 741–794.

McClelland, J. L., Rumelhart, D. E., & the PDP Research Group. (1986). *Parallel distributed processing. Explorations in the microstructure of cognition: Vol. 2. Psychological and biological models.* Cambridge, MA: MIT Press.

Neisser, U. (1976). *Cognition and reality.* San Francisco: W. H. Freeman.

Neisser, U. (1985). The role of theory in the ecological study of memory: Comment on Bruce. *Journal of Experimental Psychology: General, 114*(2), 272–276.

Neisser, U. (1991). A case of misplaced nostalgia. *American Psychologist, 46,* 34–36.

Newell, A. (1973). You can't play 20 questions with nature and win: Projective comments on the papers of this symposium. In W. E. Chase (Ed.), *Visual information processing* (283–308). New York: Academic Press.

O'Hear, A. (1989). *An introduction to the philosophy of science.* Oxford: Clarendon.

Pavio, A. (1990). *Mental representations: A dual coding approach.* New York: Oxford University Press.

Popper, K. R. (1959). *The logic of discovery.* London: Hutchinson.

Quine, W. V. O. (1960). *Word and object.* Cambridge, MA: MIT Press.

Quine, W. V. O. (1961). Two dogmas of empiricism In W. V. O. Quine (Ed.), *From a logical point of view* (2nd ed., pp. 20–46). New York: Harper & Row.

Rao, K. R., & Palmer, J. (1987). The anomaly called psi: Recent research and criticism. *Behavioral and Brain Sciences 10,* 539–643.

Robinson, H. J. (1984). A theorist's philosophy of science. *Physics Today, 37,* 24–32.

Roediger, H. L. (1991). They read an article? A commentary on the everyday memory controversy. *American Psychologist, 46,* 37–40.

Royce, J. R. (1984). Preface. In J. R. Royce, & L. P. Mos (Eds.), *Annals of theoretical psychology, 1.* New York: Plenum.

Royce, J. R. (1988). The implications of differential theory appraisal and the context of discovery for advancing theory in psychology. In W. J. Baker, L. P. Mos, H. V. Rappard, & H. J. Stam (Eds.), *Recent trends in theoretical psychology* (pp. 59–64). Berlin: Springer-Verlag.

Thagard, P., & Holyoak, K. (1985). Discovering the wave theory of sound: Induction in the context of problem solving. *Proceedings of the ninth international joint conference on artificial intelligence.* Palo Alto: William Kaufmann.

Thorngate, W., & Plouffe, L. (1987). The consumption of psychological knowledge. In H. J. Stam, T. B. Rogers, & K. J. Gergen (Eds.), *The analysis of psychological theory: Metatheoretical perspectives* (pp. 61–92). Washington: Hemisphere Publishing.

Toulmin, S., & Leary, D. E. (1985). The cult of empiricism in psychology, and beyond. In S. Koch & D. E. Leary (Eds.), *A century of psychology as science* (pp. 594–516). New York: McGraw-Hill.

Tulving, E. (1979). Memory research: What kind of progress? In L. G. Nilsson (Ed.), *Perspectives on memory research: Essays in honor of Upsala University's 500th anniversary* (pp. 19–34). Hillsdale, NJ: Lawrence Erlbaum Associates.

Underwood, B. J. (1957). *Psychological research.* New York: Appleton-Century-Crofts.

8 Between- or Within-Subjects Design: A Methodological Dilemma

Gideon Keren
Free University of Amsterdam

A common question, frequently faced by researchers, concerns the use of a between- or within-subjects experimental design. In the between design each subject is exposed to a single treatment, whereas in the within (or repeated measures) design, subjects are exposed to several or all the treatments that are included in the study. Faced with the choice of manipulating the independent variable in a between- or within-subjects design, which one should the investigator use? The purpose of this chapter is to discuss the considerations that should guide researchers in making their choice.

A brief glance at the experimental psychological literature suggests that studies in perception, psychophysics, memory, and learning virtually all employ a within-subjects design. In contrast, studies in areas such as social psychology, personality, and decision making tend to use a between-subjects design. The adoption (in different research areas) of one or the other design, implies certain implicit assumptions that may be crucial in interpreting empirical results. Moreover, there is evidence that the two experimental designs do not always yield the same pattern of results (see Erlebacher, 1977, for some illuminating examples). It is therefore imperative that researchers will use the appropriate considerations in making their choice of design, and be aware of the assumptions underlying the chosen design in the process of interpreting experimental results.

The different relevant considerations, although intertwined, can be classified into three groups. First are *statistical considerations* reflecting the different analysis associated with each design. Although we do not elaborate here on subtle statistical issues associated with between- or within-subjects design,[1] several

---

[1]A detailed exposition of the statistical characteristics of within-subjects design is presented in chap. 3, Vol. 2. Meyers (1979, chap. 7) also offers a lucid discussion on the topic.

notes are made in the following section, and potential misconceptions are pointed out.

A second class of considerations are *methodological issues*. The concern here is with potential (and usually unwanted) side effects that are solely due to the choice of design. Much of the debate regarding the appropriate choice of design has focused on the type of issues presented in the following section.

Finally, the third type of consideration that should be taken into account are *theoretical issues*. These relate to the particular questions the researcher wants to answer. Although this aspect has received relatively little attention, a later section purports that the theory and particular hypotheses one wants to test should be an essential determinant in the choice of design.

As mentioned, the empirical results obtained from within- and between-subjects designs are often incompatible. For theoretical or methodological reasons, the researcher may be interested in testing the difference in the patterns of results obtained from the two different designs, in which case the design type explicitly plays the role of an independent variable. The appropriate methods for analyzing such experiments (e.g., Erlebacher, 1977; Rosenthal & Rubin, 1980) and some representative empirical results are presented in a later section. The major issues to be taken into account in the process of choosing a within- or between-subjects design are summarized in the final section.

STATISTICAL ASPECTS

It is often claimed that the advantage of the within-subjects design is based on the fact that differences observed among conditions are not confounded with individual differences. Consequently, the claim goes on, the exclusion of individual differences results in a higher degree of sensitivity to treatment effects or, in other words, yields a substantial increase in power as compared with a between-subjects design. This statement is somewhat simplistic and may lead to misunderstanding. To make our point clear, consider a simple experiment with i subjects ($i = 1, \ldots, n$) and two different treatments $j = 1, 2$,[2] which can be modeled by

$$y_{ij} = \mu + \alpha_i + \beta_j + \alpha\beta_{ij} + e_{ij} \tag{1}$$

where α_i represent subject differences, β_j stands for the treatment effect, and $\alpha\beta_{ij}$ is the interaction between subjects and treatment. To estimate the difference between the two treatments in a *within-subjects* design, we calculate

$$
\begin{aligned}
y_{i1} - y_{i2} &= \mu + \alpha_i + \beta_1 + \alpha\beta_{i1} + e_{i1} - (\mu + \alpha_i + \beta_2 + \alpha\beta_{i2} \\
&\quad + e_{i2}) \\
&= (\beta_1 - \beta_2) + (\alpha\beta_{i1} - \alpha\beta_{i2}) + (e_{ii} - e_{i2}) \tag{2}
\end{aligned}
$$

---

[2]Although the discussion here is limited to two treatment groups, the generalization to K treatment groups is straightforward.

and averaging across subjects we obtain

$$\bar{y}_{.1} - \bar{y}_{.2} = (\beta_1 - \beta_2) + (\overline{\alpha\beta}_{.1} - \overline{\alpha\beta}_{.2}) + (\bar{e}_{.1} - \bar{e}_{.2}). \tag{3}$$

Note that the first term in Equation 3 represents fixed effects, the second term contains interactions that are correlated (with $\overline{\alpha\beta}_{.1} = -\overline{\alpha\beta}_{.2}$, and thus the second term can be expressed as $2\alpha\beta_{.1}$), and the third term is comprised of two uncorrelated error terms. The variance associated with $\bar{y}_{.1} - \bar{y}_{.2}$, which is the variance of the estimate in a within-subjects design with n subjects is

$$\begin{aligned} \sigma^2_{WS} &= \text{var}[\Sigma(y_{i1} - y_{i2})/n] \\ &= 4\,\text{var}(\alpha\beta_{i1})/n + [\text{var}(e_{i1}) + \text{var}(e_{i2})]/n. \end{aligned} \tag{4}$$

The comparable estimate of the difference between the two treatments in a *between-subjects* design is

$$\begin{aligned} y_{i1} - y_{i'2} &= \mu + \alpha_i + \beta_1 + \alpha\beta_{i1} + e_{i1} - (\mu + \alpha_{i'} + \beta_2 + \\ \alpha\beta_{i'2} + e_{i'2}) &= (\alpha_i - \alpha_{i'}) + (\beta_1 - \beta_2) + (\alpha\beta_{i1} - \alpha\beta_{i'2}) \\ &\quad + (e_{i1} - e_{i'2}) \end{aligned} \tag{5}$$

(where the prime ′ is used to distinguish between the two groups). Averaging across subjects in each group we obtain

$$\begin{aligned} \bar{y}_{.1} - \bar{y}_{.2} &= (\bar{\alpha}_. - \bar{\alpha}_{.'}) + (\beta_1 - \beta_2) + (\overline{\alpha\beta}_{.1} - \overline{\alpha\beta}_{.'2}) \\ &\quad + (\bar{e}_{.1} - \bar{e}_{.'2}). \end{aligned} \tag{6}$$

Note that in contrast to Equation 3, $\bar{\alpha}_.$ and $\bar{\alpha}_{.'}$ are uncorrelated because they represent different subjects, so that we now have three sources of uncorrelated errors. The variance of the estimate of the treatment for a between-subjects design (with n subjects for each treatment) is

$$\begin{aligned} \sigma^2_{BS} &= \text{var}[\Sigma y_{i1}/n - \Sigma y_{i'2}/n] = 2\text{var}(\alpha_i)/n + 2\text{var}(\alpha\beta_{i1})/n + \\ &\quad [\text{var}(e_{i1}) + \text{var}(e_{i'2})]/n. \end{aligned} \tag{7}$$

There are several important conclusions to be derived from the previous analysis. First, as far as the comparison between treatments is concerned, both the within- and between-subjects designs provide unbiased estimates (Equations 3 and 6 respectively) of the treatment effect ($\beta_1 - \beta_2$). The difference between the two designs lies in the precision by which the treatment effect is estimated, namely by the variance of the estimate (Equations 4 and 7). Moreover, it is not necessarily the case that the within-subjects design will always result in a better precision. To make this point clear we can compare the variance of estimate for the two designs and obtain

$$\sigma^2_{WS} - \sigma^2_{BS} = (2/n)*[\text{var}(\alpha\beta_{ij}) - \text{var}(\alpha_i)] \tag{8a}$$

or alternatively

$$\sigma^2_{BS} - \sigma^2_{WS} = (2/n)*\text{cov}(y_{i1}, y_{i2}). \tag{8b}$$

The conclusion from Equation 8b is that a within-subjects design is more powerful whenever $\rho_{12} > 0$, that is there is a positive correlation between the treatments. In practice this correlation is usually (but not necessarily always!) positive, which accounts for the fact that the error term for a within-subjects design is typically smaller than the comparable error term of a between-subjects design.[3] In summary, the within-subjects design usually entails a larger power but not necessarily under all circumstances.

The within-subjects design contains two additional appealing characteristics: One concerns the obvious advantage derived from the larger number of degrees of freedom associated with the within-subjects design. The other is related to the saving in the number of subjects required to complete the experiment. Indeed, this economical aspect often serves as the major appeal of a within-subjects design.

METHODOLOGICAL ISSUES

It is important to distinguish between two types of within-subjects designs. In one type, the same subject is exposed to different conditions and there is a substantial difference between stimuli employed in different experimental conditions. Thus, in this sort of design the subject is never exposed to the same (or a similar) stimulus more than once. A major reason to employ a within-subjects design under such circumstances is the claim that subjects serve as their own control, which enables a direct and unconfounded comparison between the different conditions. Additional advantages are the gain in statistical power and economy in use of subjects.

In the other type of design, the same subject may experience the same (or a very similar) stimulus on several trials. Such a design is certainly appropriate when the researcher's explicit goal is to investigate learning effects due to repeated trials (where trials, or blocks of trials are treated as an independent variable). If practice and learning effects are not desired, such a design can be used only if there are sufficient reasons to assume that (at least) for all practical purposes, the different trials are independent (in the psychological sense[4]).

A major concern with regard to the adoption of a within-subjects design is the lack of independence between different trials or different treatments administered

---

[3]An analysis similar to the one already described is offered by Hays (1973) in the context of paired observations. Hays showed that for groups matched by pairs, the variance of a difference between means is

$$\sigma^2_{diff} = \sigma^2_{M_1} + \sigma^2_{M_2} - 2cov(M_1, M_2)$$

where M_1 and M_2 are the means of the two groups. Hays noted that "in general, for groups matched by pairs, this covariance is a positive number, and thus the variance and standard error of a difference between means will usually be *less* for matched than for unmatched groups.

[4]One should distinguish between *statistical* independence and the *psychological* independence. The latter implies that the behavior of a subject on trial n is not influenced by the behavior of the same subject on trial $n - 1$. Although the two concepts are related, they are not identical.

to the same subject. Such dependencies among trials or treatments may introduce undesired interactions between the particular treatment under study and unwanted exogenous influences that cannot be separated. The potential presence of contaminated effects can appear in different forms.

Consider first the case, as frequently used in psychophysics or reaction time studies, in which the same or very similar stimuli are presented on a large number of trials. Literally, every event can occur only once and thus, from a strict point of view, one can argue that even two trials in which exactly the same stimulus is presented are not the same. Adopting a slightly looser approach, there are often sufficiently strong reasons to assume (for all practical purposes) independence among the different trials. A typical example is psychophysics, in which the same stimulus is presented a large number of times. Even in this case, doubts may be raised about the independence assumption, in particular the effect of practice (discussed later) and the buildup of potential expectations in the course of presenting repeated trials cannot be ignored.

Potential dependencies may also exist in a design in which a subject is exposed to a single trial in each of several conditions or treatments. Memory of previous trials cannot be erased nor can we prevent subjects from forming any hypotheses about the nature of the experiment (e.g., Rothenthal, 1976), thus any inferred relations among the different treatments may result in subjects' responses that are not necessarily independent. Responses to trials in previous conditions may affect, directly or indirectly, the subject's response in the present condition.

The concern about possible dependencies that are not always transparent is thus a major argument usually raised against the use of within-subjects designs. It should be noticed that the extent to which potential dependencies may exist could be judged on different dimensions: Similarity between stimuli, potential inferred relations between different items, the range of potential responses, and others. Poulton (1973) referred to such dependencies as *range effects* and provided a long list of experimental examples[5] in which subjects' responses are influenced by the range of stimuli, by the range of responses or by both. According to Poulton, such effects are always present when stimuli or responses can be ordered in a consistent manner, and where such an ordering implies explicit or implicit (derived) dependencies among different items and different experimental conditions. One customary remedy against such possible dependencies is to randomize items and conditions in order to avert the construction of a consistent structure. Randomization, however, may not always be effective: Subjects may search for dependencies even when stimuli are presented randomly, because they are unable to distinguish between random and nonran-

---

[5]Rothstein (1974) suggested that most of the examples drawn by Poulton concern magnitude estimation and motor performance studies (which indeed are particularly vulnerable to range effects), and questioned the generality of Poulton's sample.

dom series (see Rosenthal, chap. 20, this vol.). This is illustrated by the probability matching phenomenon (e.g., Estes, 1964), in which subjects attempt to match their response probabilities to experimental probabilities even though stimuli are presented randomly.

Greenwald (1976) referred to the possible contaminations arising from the use of a within-subjects design as *context* effects, and classified them in three categories that he termed practice, sensitization, and carry-over effects.

1. *Practice effects* are frequently present in psychophysical, motor performance, and attention studies that require a large number of trials. If the different experimental treatments are administered on different days, or even in blocks of trials in the same experimental session, the possibility that treatment effects are confounded with practice cannot be ruled out. One possibility to minimize such effects is *counterbalancing,* namely, equal use of all the possible combinations by which the treatments can be ordered (alternatively, if the number of combinations is too large, one may use a balanced subset of combinations such as employing a latin square design). However, as Greenwald pointed out, such a solution is not always satisfactory, because various treatments may be differently effective at different levels of practice. Remember that the possible interactions of treatment and practice in a within-subjects design cannot be removed: The only effect of counterbalancing is to spread the unwanted variance arising from such interactions among the different treatments, with the hope that it is equally spread. An alternative, and perhaps better, method for preventing the contamination of practice effects is to provide extensive training prior to the experimental tests, assuming that performance has reached asymptote by the end of the training period.

2. *Sensitization* refers to the possibility of perceived dependencies (regardless of whether or not they are justified) between trials or treatments that may lead subjects to form hypotheses about the treatment effect and respond accordingly.

For example, consider the experiments conducted by Keren and Wagenaar (1987), which were designed to investigate whether subjects' preferences concerning choice among gambles when played a single time (unique condition) or many times (the repeated condition) are the same. For purposes of comparison the gambles in the two conditions had to be the same and there was one difference: In the unique condition subjects were told that the gamble of their choice will be played only once, whereas subjects in the repeated condition were told that the chosen gamble will be played 10 times. The similarity between the unique and repeated conditions was so transparent (because the stimuli in the two conditions were in fact identical), that if a within-subjects design had been used, whatever subjects' preferences were, they would probably make sure their choices in the two conditions were not contradictory. In other words, the preferences exhibited in such a design would have been highly correlated.[6]

3. *Carry-over effects* result when the effect of a specific treatment persists in one way or the other, and thus contaminates the measurements at the time that the effect of other treatments is tested. Practice effects are an instance of carry-over effects; drug treatments that may leave a trace for a period of time serve as another example.

As with practice effects, the use of counterbalancing provides only a partially adequate remedy. A more effective way according to Greenwald is to separate the relevant treatments by sufficiently long time intervals, though this may not always be feasible.

Though the possible contaminations of within-subjects designs due to context effects are certainly real and can at best be only partially controlled, the question is whether a between-subjects design provides an adequate safeguard against context effects. Even Poulton (1973), who is certainly the most outspoken researcher regarding the deficiencies of within-subjects designs, admitted that potential context effects cannot always be prevented by reverting to a between-subjects design. Mainly, even in a between-subjects design context effects may be present, though they may be of a different nature compared with those arising from a within-subject design.

The claim that context effects will also influence a between-subjects design, is based on two (plausible) assumptions (Birnbaum, 1982; Greenwald, 1976) namely that (a) context is also provided by a single treatment, and (b) that subjects do not enter the experimental laboratory as tabula rasa but rather with extralaboratory experience that may leave some residue of context. It is the interaction of these two sources that may lead to effects that the researcher cannot completely control (by either experimental or statistical methods). Demonstrations of potential context effects in between-subjects design are reported in Birnbaum (1982) and Birnbaum and Mellers (1983).

Effects of stimulus range, stimulus spacing, and frequency, all of which are potential sources for contextual effects in perception, have been studied by Parducci and incorporated in his range-frequency theory (e.g., Parducci, 1965, 1983). Some methods, which may potentially help to identify the locus of such context effects in judgments, have been proposed by Wedell (1990). If both within- and between-subjects designs are vulnerable to context effects (even if of somewhat different natures), how should a researcher proceed in making his selection of design? Notwithstanding the different considerations discussed up to

___

[6]One could ask whether in a between-subjects design (as indeed employed by Keren and Wagenaar), the comparison of choices made by different subjects is a meaningful one. This question is addressed in a later section.

now, the decision of which design to adopt should also be determined by the theoretical framework in which the research is conducted and the particular hypotheses one wants to test.

EXTERNAL VALIDITY
AND THEORETICAL FRAMEWORK

The methodological considerations discussed up to now refer mainly to what may be termed *internal validity,* that is, the extent to which valid inferences can be derived from the particular experiment at hand. Two additional major concerns are (a) whether the particular design chosen also has external validity, and (b) whether the inferences that can indeed be logically drawn by using a particular design, are also the most relevant for enhancing the broader research program in which the study is being conducted.

External Validity

Greenwald (1976) correctly pointed out that the *external validity* of an experiment, namely the extent to which the results can be generalized beyond the specific experiment that is being conducted, is an important aspect in deciding which type of design one should use. Considerations of external validity are to a large extent determined by contextual effects. As mentioned earlier, contextual effects may be present in either a between- or a within-subjects design, so it is important to consider and weigh such potential effects before making a final decision on the design to be employed. Potential contextual effects should also not be ignored in the process of interpreting experimental results.

Considerations Prescribed
by the Theoretical Framework

What design to use should in many cases be determined by the underlying theory and the particular hypotheses one would like to test. Unfortunately, this type of consideration has frequently been neglected by researchers, perhaps because no general guidelines can be outlined in this respect, and the relevant deliberations will be unique for each case. I believe, however, that this type of consideration has been often overlooked, so I try to highlight its importance by using an elaborated example from the decision-making literature.

Kahneman and Tversky (1979) recently offered an axiomatic alternative to traditional utility theory, which they termed *prospect theory.* The prospect $A = (x_i, p_i, y_i)$ is defined as a contract that yields outcome x_i with probability p_i, and an outcome y_i with probability $1 - p_i$. A specific hypothesis obtained from prospect theory is the so-called reflection effect: According to this hypothesis, given the choice between two prospects people prefer the more risky prospect (smaller probability and higher gains) when negative outcomes are involved, and the less risky prospect when positive outcomes are involved. In other words, risk seeking in the negative domain is accompanied by risk aversion in the positive domain. Thus, preferences among prospects in the negative domain are a reflection (mirror image) of their preferences among the corresponding positive prospects.

Empirical support for the reflection hypothesis is obtained from experimental data reported by Kahneman and Tversky (1979). Employing a between-subjects design, they used five separate problems to demonstrate significant reversals of preference between gain and loss prospects. Hershey and Schoemaker (1980) presented an interesting challenge to the experimental evidence provided by Kahneman and Tversky, and argued that the evidence based on a between-subjects design was not conclusive for supporting the reflection hypothesis.

In order to understand the reasoning of Hershey and Schoemaker, consider Table 8.1, which represents the four (hypothetical) preference combinations subjects may exhibit in an experiment testing the reflection effect. The options A_1 and A_2 are the less risky ones compared with B_1 and B_2, respectively. The cell entries n_1 through n_4 denote the percentage of subjects corresponding to each preference combination, such that $\Sigma n_i = 100$. Using a between-subjects design, the column totals c and d represent subjects' choices among the positive prospects, and the row totals a and b represent subjects' choices among the negative prospects, such that $a + b = c + d = 100$.

In terms of Table 8.1 (using a between-subjects design) the reflection effect is exhibited if the row total "a" and the column total "d" (or alternatively "b" and "c" respectively) are each significantly larger than 50%. This is indeed the type of evidence provided by Kahneman and Tversky (1979). Hershey and Schoemaker (1980) however, questioned whether a between-subjects design provides an adequate test of the reflection effect. They argue that a given pattern of overall preferences (derived from a between-subjects design) could be consistent with a varying numbers of individual reversals.

Consider the experimental outcomes portrayed in the two matrices of Table 8.2. The marginals (i.e., row and column totals) are taken from Kahneman and Tversky (1979, problem 4) and show the reflection effect according to the criteria

TABLE 8.1
The Possible Preference Combinations in a 2 × 2 Design

		Positive prospects		
		A_1	B_1	
Negative prospects	A_2	n_1	n_2	a
	B_2	n_3	n_4	b
		c	d	100

TABLE 8.2
Two Different Patterns of Results for a Hypothetical Within-Subjects Experiment,
with Identical Marginals of a Between-Subjects Design

		(A) Positive prospects				(B) Positive prospects		
		A_1	B_1			A_1	B_1	
Negative prospects	A_2	42	0	42	A_2	7	35	42
	B_2	23	35	58	B_2	58	0	58
		65	35	100		65	35	100

previously mentioned. Suppose, however, that the results were obtained from a within-subjects design. Hershey and Schoemaker pointed out that several values of n_1, n_2, n_3, n_4 (obtained from a within-subjects design) could underlie a given set of marginals a, b, c, d. Note, that the number of individuals who exhibit reflection in a within-subjects design is given by $n_2 + n_3$. According to this criterion, using the numbers in the left table (A) of Table 8.2 only 23% (0 + 23) of the individual subjects exhibit reflection. In contrast, 93% (58 + 35) of the individuals exhibit reflection in Table 8.2B (note that the margins in both tables A and B are the same). Thus, the results from a between-subjects design can be compatible with a mere 23% reflections, and at the time compatible with as much as 93% reflections.[7] Consequently, according to Hershey and Schoemaker (1980), the results from a between-subjects design are inconclusive.

Notwithstanding the claim of Hershey and Schoemaker, there are two important problems that remain open. First, the use of a within-subjects design for testing the reflection effect would be seriously hindered by unwanted contaminations discussed in the previous section. In particular, because the stimuli for the negative and the positive prospects are so similar, they may evoke the subjects' awareness to provide consistent responses (even if they do not reflect the true preferences). The use of a within-subjects design should be seriously questioned, because of the high likelihood of sensitization and carry-over effects in this case.

There is a second important consideration, related to the underlying theory and the particular hypotheses one would like to test. Without loss of generality, one may consider three different hypotheses concerning the outcomes of a hypo-

---

[7]Hershey and Schoemaker showed that given a pattern of results obtained from a between-subjects design (i.e., the values of a, b, c, d), the percentage of Individual Reversals (IR) that is compatible with a within subjects-design can be as small as

$$IR_{min} = 100 - \min\{a, c\} - \min\{b, d\}$$

and as large as

$$IR_{max} = \min\{a, d\} + \min\{b, c\}.$$

thetical experiment as illustrated in Table 8.1. To simplify the notation, let $P(A_1)$ denote the probability of choosing A_1 given the choice between A_1 and B_1. Similarly, for $P(B_1)$, and so forth. The three hypotheses one may contemplate are:

$$H1: \qquad\qquad\qquad P(A1) > 1/2 \quad \text{and} \quad P(B2) > 1/2$$
$$\text{or alternatively} \quad P(B1) > 1/2 \quad \text{and} \quad P(A2) > 1/2$$
$$H2: \qquad\qquad\qquad P(A2|A1) < P(A2|B1)$$

$$\text{or equivalently} \quad P(B2|A1) > P(B2|B1)$$
$$H3: \qquad\qquad\qquad P(A1 \cap B2) + P(A2 \cap B1) > 1/2$$

It is important to emphasize that $H1$, $H2$, and $H3$ are examples of three different classes of hypotheses: $H1$ is formulated in terms of marginals or average group preferences and, as such, may naturally be tested in a between-subjects design. $H2$ is formulated in terms of conditional probabilities (testing statistical dependencies). It clearly refers to individuals and consequently should be examined by a within-subjects design. Finally, $H3$ is explicitly phrased in terms of the number of individual reversals, and strictly speaking can accurately be tested only with a within-subjects design. It should be realized that despite the similarity among the three hypotheses, they are distinct and no one hypothesis implies either of the other two (a proof is given in Keren & Raaijmakers, 1988).

The previous analysis suggests that the design to use would depend on the particular hypothesis the researcher wants to test. If hypothesis H_1 is of interest, then a between-subjects design would be the most natural one to be used, whereas for testing hypotheses H_2 or H_3, a within-subjects design should be preferred. Which of the three hypotheses then is the most appropriate one to describe the reflection effect, would depend on how one interprets the reflection hypothesis and prospect theory. For instance, if prospect theory would allege the existence of a cognitive hypothetical construct that we may term the *reflection mechanism,* according to which the preferences of an individual in the negative domain are obtained by reflecting preferences in the positive domain, then certainly $H3$ would be the most natural hypothesis to test. On the other hand, if the reflection effect is only a label that conveniently describes a certain *pattern* of results (as is suggested by a careful reading of Kahnaman & Tversky, 1979), then the most appropriate hypothesis to test would be $H1$.

A lengthy exploration of possible interpretations of the reflection hypothesis is beyond the scope of this chapter (for more details, see Keren & Raaijmakers, 1988). The intention of the earlier discussion was only to demonstrate that the theoretical considerations and the exact formulation of the hypothesis one wants to test are crucial elements in the decision of what experimental design one wants to adopt.

DIRECT COMPARISONS OF BETWEEN-
VERSUS WITHIN-SUBJECTS DESIGNS

Between- and within-subjects designs may often yield different patterns of results, so the researcher may sometimes be interested in comparing the results
obtained from the two different designs. Such an undertaking may be expensive
and time consuming, and the researcher should have good reasons for conducting
such a test.

When a comparison between the two designs is desired, the design type
becomes an explicit independent variable, and the question is whether design
type interacts with any of the other substantive independent variables. Rosenthal
and Rubin (1980) provided a lucid presentation of how to conduct such tests, and
the following discussion borrows heavily from their article. As pointed out by
Rosenthal and Rubin, there are at least two kinds of comparisons to be considered: comparison of the variabilities and comparison of means.

Consider an experiment in which subjects are tested on general knowledge
items and are asked on each item to choose between two alternatives (e.g., The
capital of Turkey is: 1. Istanbul. 2. Ankara.), and then provide a confidence
rating (between 50% and 100%) that their chosen answer is indeed the correct
one. Furthermore, suppose that items are divided into two categories, easy items
with a high percent of correct answers, and difficult items for which the percent
of correct responses is relatively low. The major question is whether subjects can
distinguish between the difficult and easy items as reflected in their confidence
ratings.

Table 8.3 presents hypothetical results of such an experiment. The first two
columns contain the mean confidence ratings for 20 subjects who were tested on
the easy items and 20 different subjects who were tested on the difficult items (a
between-subjects design). Columns 3 and 4 contain the scores from an experiment in which subjects were exposed to both the easy and the difficult items (a
within-subjects design), where easy and difficult items were randomly mixed.
We start by comparing variabilities with each design separately. For the between-
subjects design, the independently estimated variances are compared by employing an F test (e.g., Glass & Stanley, 1970):

$$F(19, 19) = S_D^2/S_E^2 = 45.40/38.37 = 1.18 \qquad (9)$$

where S_D^2 and S_E^2 are the variance estimates for the difficult and easy conditions,
respectively. The ratio is obviously not significant. For the within-subjects design in which the variances are not independent, the following test statistic (e.g.,
Glass & Stanley, 1970) is employed:

$$t(18) = \frac{S_D^2 - S_E^2}{4S_D^2 S_E^2 (1 - r_{DE}^2) / (N - 2)} = 1.098 \qquad (10)$$

TABLE 8.3
Hypothetical Results for Two Experiments on Confidence Ratings
Using a Between- and Within-Subjects Design

Subject Number	Mean Confidence Ratings			
	Between Design		Within Design	
	Easy Items	Difficult Items	Easy Items	Difficult Items
1	86	72	84	80
2	80	64	68	68
3	89	80	76	72
4	76	66	82	80
5	70	68	76	70
6	84	76	74	73
7	82	64	82	80
8	90	73	72	75
9	70	67	76	70
10	84	76	80	78
11	76	01	76	69
12	82	75	84	78
13	82	76	68	75
14	73	61	86	84
15	84	72	81	76
16	80	76	79	80
17	76	76	70	76
18	82	62	71	67
19	74	85	87	83
20	69	78	78	80
$\bar{X}$ (MEAN)	79.45	72.40	77.50	75.70
S_{N-1} (SD)	6.19	6.74	5.80	5.09

where r_{DE} is the correlation coefficient between the mean confidence ratings for difficult and easy items calculated on the 20 paired means. The difference is not significant.

We now proceed to comparisons among means. For the between-subjects design we use the t test for independent samples

$$t(38) = (79.45 - 72.40)/2.046 = 3.44,$$

which is highly significant ($p < .005$). The difference between means for the within-subjects design is tested by means of a t test for correlated samples, which yields

$$t(19) = (77.5 - 75.7)/.884 = 2.03$$

suggesting a significant difference ($.025 < p < .05$). An eyeball inspection suggests that the difference between the easy and the difficult items is much larger in the between design as compared with the within design (the latter difference was nevertheless significant due, as mentioned below, to the controlled between-subjects variance).

Finally, we want to compare the variance of estimates across the two designs, that is the precision of the estimates of the two designs. The purpose of such a comparison is related to the question of whether the design had an effect. Using the same F test for independently estimated variances used in (10), we obtain

$$F(38, 19) = (2.046/.884)^2 = 5.36$$

which is significant at the .05 level. The reason that the precision of the within-subjects design is significantly larger (i.e., the standard error of the within design is smaller) is due to the fact that the scores on the easy and difficult items are positively correlated, thus suggesting that under those circumstances (see Equation 8) individual differences in the within design are better controlled.

The difference between the easy and the difficult items obtained by the between- and the within-subjects designs (i.e., the interaction between item difficulty and design) is tested by a t test

$$t = (7.05 - 1.8)/\sqrt{2.046^2 + .884^2}$$

where the denominator consists of the pooled standard errors of the two designs. Unfortunately, as noted by Rosenthal and Rubin (1982), this statistic is distributed neither normally nor exactly as a t distribution, though it is quite similar to the latter. When the df for both studies are sufficiently large, we may use the standard normal distribution that will provide an adequate estimate for all practical purposes.

When the samples for both studies are rather small, the appropriate number of df will lie somewhere between the df of the smaller of the two studies and the df of the two studies added together. Zwick (chap. 2, vol. 2) shows how the number of degrees of freedom in such cases can be approximated, and cites several statistical packages in which such an approximation procedure is built in.

Returning to our example and using Equations 9 and 10 in the chapter by Zwick (in vol. 2), yields an approximation of 19 df, and thus the t statistic computed earlier ($t = 2.35$) suggests that the difference between easy and difficult items was significantly larger ($p = .015$) in the between-subjects design compared with the within-subjects design.

In general, two different sorts of explanations can account for cases where treatment effects of between- and within-subjects designs differ significantly (as has been the case in our example). One class of explanations is *methodological* in nature; Rosenthal and Rubin discussed three possibilities under this category:

• *Sampling effects:* Occur when subjects are not assigned randomly to each of the two designs. Under such circumstances subjects assigned to one design may differ from subjects in the other design on a relevant factor.

- *Laboratory effects:* These may occur if the two design studies have been conducted in different places or with different experimental procedures.

- *Sequence effects:* Can occur under within-subjects designs, as mentioned. Counterbalancing order of presentation is not necessarily a sufficient safeguard against such effects.

A second sort of explanation is more *substantive* in nature and relates to the particular hypothesis or theory being tested. For example, the results in our example can be interpreted to mean that subjects tend to anchor on a certain subset of confidence ratings, and each rating is assessed relative to this anchor. In the between-subjects design, according to this interpretation, there is a different anchor for the easy and difficult items, whereas in the within-subjects design where items are mixed, the anchor is based on a mixture of easy and difficult items. The explanation based on an alleged process of anchoring can be classified as a context effect. According to the claim, in this example, the context effect was different under the two designs yielding different patterns of results.

CONCLUSIONS

The decision of whether to use a within- or between-subjects design has many facets and as such constitutes a multiattribute decision. There is obviously no algorithm that will provide the researcher with a definitive answer. The purpose of this chapter was to briefly review the different considerations (some of which have often been neglected) that should be taken into account. Under certain circumstances one may seriously consider using both designs despite the additional costs associated with such a decision. It is important to remember that often within- and between-subjects designs are simply addressing a different question. The first step therefore should always be an unambiguous statement of the research questions to be answered. Subsequent decisions regarding the appropriate design should take into account the different dimensions discussed in this chapter, though the final judgment will often remain subjective.

REFERENCES

Birnbaum, M. H. (1982). Controversies in psychological measurement. In B. Wegner (Ed.), *Social attitudes and psychological measurement* (pp. 401–485). Hillsdale, NJ: Lawrence Erlbaum Associates.

Birnbaum, M. H., & Mellers, B. (1983). Bayesian inference: Combining base rates with reports of sources. *Journal of Personality and Social Psychology, 45,* 792–804.

Erlebacher, A. (1977). Design and analysis of experiments contrasting the within- and between-subjects manipulations of the independent variable. *Psychological Bulletin, 84,* 212–219.

Estes, W. K. (1964). Probability learning. In A. W. Melton (Ed.), *Categories of human learning*. New York: Academic Press.

Glass, G. V., & Stanley, J. C. (1970). *Statistical methods in education and psychology*. Englewood Cliffs: Prentice-Hall.

Greenwald, A. G. (1976). Within-subjects design: To use or not to use. *Psychological Bulletin, 83*, 314–320.

Hays, W. L. (1973). *Statistics for the social sciences* (2nd ed.). New York: Holt, Rinehart & Winston.

Hershey, J. C., & Schoemaker, P.J.H. (1980). Prospect theory's reflection hypothesis: A critical examination. *Organizational Behavior and Human Performance, 25*, 395–418.

Kahneman, D., & Tversky, A. (1979). Prospect theory: An analysis of decision under risk. *Econometrica, 47*, 263–291.

Keren, G., & Raaijmakers, J.G.W. (1988). On between-subjects versus within-subjects comparisons in testing utility theory. *Organizational Behavior and Human Decision Processes, 41*, 233–247.

Keren, G., & Wagenaar, W. A. (1987). Violation of utility theory in unique and repeated gambles. *Journal of Experimental Psychology: Learning, Memory, and Cognition, 13*, 387–391.

Meyers, J. L. (1979). *Foundations of experimental design* (3rd ed.). Boston: Allyn & Bacon.

Parducci, A. (1965). Category judgment: A range frequency model. *Psychological Review, 72*, 407–418.

Parducci, A. (1983). Category ratings and the relational character of judgment. In H. G. Geissler, H.F.J.M. Buffart, E.L.J. Leeuwenberg, & V. Saris (Eds.), *Modern issues in perception* (pp. 89–105). Berlin: VEB Deutche Verlag der Wissenschaften.

Poor, D.D.S. (1973). Analysis of variance for repeated measures designs: Two approaches. *Psychological Bulletin, 80*, 113–121.

Poulton, E. C. (1973). Unwanted range effects from using within-subjects experimental designs. *Psychological Bulletin, 81*, 201–203.

Rosenthal, R. (1976). *Experimenter effects in behavioral research*. New York: Appelton-Century-Crofts.

Rosenthal, R., & Rubin, D. (1980). Comparing within- and between-subjects studies. *Sociological Methods and Research, 9*, 127–136.

Rothstein, L. D. (1974). Reply to Poulton. *Psychological Bulletin, 81*, 199–200.

Wedell, D. (1990). Methods for determining the locus of context effects in judgments. In J. P. Caverni, J. M. Fabre, & M. Gonzalez (Eds.), *Cognitive biases* (pp. 285–302). Amsterdam: North Holland.

9 Which Comes First, Cause or Effect?

Paul W. Holland
Educational Testing Service, Princeton, NJ

THE CAUSE OF AN EFFECT
VERSUS THE EFFECT OF A CAUSE

Even though it might not seem significant to separate the question of "what is the cause of a given effect?" from that of "what is the effect of a given cause?", I believe that this simple verbal distinction reflects the wide gulf between most philosophical discussions of causation and the practice of experimental science. Aristotle began it all by identifying various notions of the meaning of a thing's cause: its *material* cause, its *efficient* cause, its *formal* cause, and its *final* cause. Hume's three criteria—constant conjunction, temporal succession, and spatial contiguity—all refer to what he believed we must observe before we conclude that A is the cause of B. Other examples are easily cited. The "principle of causality" asserts that every phenomenon has a cause.

An yet what can experimental science actually do? It does nothing more (nor less) than establish that a particular effect is the consequence of some specified cause. It does not start with effects and figure our causes, rather it starts with causes and measures their effects. John Stuart Mill wrote this of the role of experiments.

> Observation, in short, without experimentation (supposing no aid from deduction) can ascertain sequences and co-existences, but cannot prove causation. (p. 253)

> We have not yet proved that antecedent to be the cause until we have reversed the process and produced the effect by means of that antecedent artificially, and if, when we do so, the effect follows, the induction is complete. (p. 252)

I am sure that statistics have been used and misused to prove causation ever since they were first gathered. In 1861, Farr cautioned Florence Nightingale that "I must repeat my objections to intermingling Causation with Statistics" (Porter, 1986, p. 36). This admonition fell on mostly deaf ears then as it probably would today. Even Bayes' theorem is sometimes couched in causal language. Probabilities of effects given causes are turned into probabilities of causes given observed effects. What a theorem!

However, the most substantial contributions of the field of statistics to causal inference are unquestionably those of the design of comparative experiments. Randomized experiments have transformed many areas of investigation and are the original products of a few statistical giants. In this view of the contributions of statistics to causal inference it is a simple step to propose that the fundamental ideas of causal inference ought to build on the known success of experiments, that is, on the measurement of effects, rather than on the deduction of causes. Rubin's model for causal inference is an attempt to do just this (Holland, 1986, 1988a, 1988b; Holland & Rubin, 1983, 1988; Rosenbaum, 1984a, 1984b, 1984c; Rubin, 1974, 1977, 1978, 1980, 1986). My short answer to the question: Measuring effects is logically prior to discovering causes, so "effect" comes first!

RUBIN'S MODEL

I think it is useful to start with an abstract statement of Rubin's model and then to interpret it in terms of concrete types of studies. The logical elements of this model, in its simplest version, form a quadruple (U, K, s, Y) in which U and K are sets, s is a mapping of U to K (its value denoted s_i), and Y is a real-valued function defined on the Cartesian product $K \times U$ (its value denoted Y_{ki}). The elements of the quadruple are interpreted as follows.

U = a population of units, denoted as $i \in U$,

K = a set of causes or treatments to which the elements of U may all be exposed, denoted as $k \in K$,

$s_i = k$, if k is the cause to which unit $i \in U$ is actually exposed,

Y_{ki} = the value of the response that would be observed for unit i if $i \in U$ were exposed to cause $k \in K$.

The elements of the quadruple are the primitives of this model and serve as the undefined terms. All other concepts are defined in terms of these primitives. The most basic quantity that needs definition is the *observed* response on each unit in U. This is given by

$$y_i = Y_{s_i i}. \tag{1}$$

In Equation 1 y_i is the value of Y that is actually observed for unit i. Note that y is a real-valued function defined on U such that $y_i = Y_{ti}$ if $s_i = t$ and $y_i = Y_{ci}$ if $s_i = c$. In general, t and c refer to two distinct elements of K, but in our usual experimental language they stand for the "treatment" and the "control" causes or experimental conditions.

Causes are taken as undefined primitives in this model, thus *effects* are defined in terms of them. The *causal effect* of cause t relative to cause c on unit i is the value

$$T_i = Y_{ti} - Y_{ci}. \tag{2}$$

Thus, T_i is the increase in the value of Y that would be observed for i if i were exposed to t over the value that would be observed for i if i were exposed to c. In this notation I have adopted the convention that variables not necessarily directly observable are denoted by capital letters whereas observations are denoted by lowercase letters. I have used subscripts to denote the arguments of functions in order to depart as little as possible from standard statistical notation, that is, y_i and s_i, and so forth.

Probably the aspect of Rubin's model that people have the most trouble with is the explicit notation for the potential response Y_{ki} for each cause-unit combination rather than simply the observed response y_i for each unit. However, this use of "potential responses" goes back at least as far as Neyman (1935) and is a standard tool for the analysis of randomization distributions in experimental design. One of Rubin's important contributions was to see that this idea is important for all problems of causal inference.

There is a *fundamental problem with causal inference* because it is impossible in principle to simultaneously observe both of the values, Y_{ti} and Y_{ci}, on a single unit, i. Thus, the causal effect T_i is in principle not directly observable. Many techniques of experimental science are aimed at overcoming this fundamental problem. In Holland (1986) I discuss some of these techniques more extensively than I can here, however, I briefly mention two familiar ones—unit homogeneity and randomization—that, in my opinion, are the twin pillars that support causal inference in controlled experimentation.

Unit Homogeneity

In a scientific laboratory care is exercised to prepare homogeneous samples of material (i.e., units) for study. This allows the experimenter to assume (at some level of accuracy) that $Y_{ki} = Y_{kj}$ for all experimental units i and j and all relevant causes or treatments, k in K. This implies that the value of T_i defined in Equation 2 equals the difference $Y_{ti} - Y_{cj}$ for a pair of distinct units i and j. We can observe Y_{ti} for i and Y_{cj} for a second unit, j, so the causal effect becomes directly measurable—all because of the assumed homogeneity of the experimental units.

However, the assumption of unit homogeneity is an assumption that cannot be verified directly. Of course, experience may lead a scientist to believe that it is valid for some purposes but this never proves the validity of an assumption, only its utility.

Randomization

When we examine the difference in average Y-values between groups of units, one group exposed to t and the other to c, we are estimating the quantity

$$\text{FACE} = E(y|s = t) - E(y|s = c). \tag{3}$$

The FACE is the *prima facia average causal effect* and can always be estimated by the differences between the treatment and control group average y-values. The FACE must be distinguished from the *average causal effect* (ACE) defined by

$$\text{ACE} = E(Y_t - Y_c|s = t) = E(T|s = t). \tag{4}$$

The ACE is the average of the causal effects T_i over those units in the population U who were exposed to t. The ACE, being an average of causal effects, is a causal parameter, whereas the FACE describes the association between the observed variables y_i and s_i. The ACE describes causation whereas the FACE describes "mere association."

We may express the FACE in terms that more closely relate it to the ACE as follows.

$$\begin{aligned} \text{FACE} = E(y|s = t) - E(y|s = c) &= E(Y_s|s = t) - E(Y_s|s = c) \\ &= E(Y_t|s = t) - E(Y_c|s = c) \\ &= E(Y_t|s = t) - E(Y_c|s = t) + E(Y_c|s = t) - E(Y_c|s = c) \end{aligned}$$

so

$$\text{FACE} = \text{ACE} + \text{BIAS}, \tag{5}$$

where

$$\text{BIAS} = E(Y_c|s = t) - E(Y_c|s = c). \tag{6}$$

The term *BIAS* involves the "counterfactual expectation" $E(Y_c|s = t)$, which is the average value of Y that would have been observed in the treatment group had those units all been exposed to the control treatment, instead. It is *counterfactual* because the event in the conditioning, $s = t$, precludes observing the variable being averaged, Y_c—see Glymour (1986) for more discussion of Rubin's model and counterfactuals.

When a large number of units are randomly assigned to treatments, s_i becomes a random variable that is statistically independent of each Y_{ki} considered as functions on U, for each k in K. In this case the counterfactual expectation $E(Y_c|s = t)$ equals the value $E(Y_c|s = c)$ and, in Equation 6, BIAS = 0 so that the

ACE and the FACE are equal. The equality of the FACE and the ACE under randomization is one reason why randomization is such a powerful tool for causal inference. Even when units are not homogeneous, randomization creates equality between a causal parameter (ACE) and an associational parameter (FACE). Note, however, that knowledge of the causal effect T_i for unit i is sacrificed for knowledge of the average of T_i over all $i \in U$ exposed to t.

BEYOND EXPERIMENTS

The desire to make causal inferences in controlled and/or randomized experiments is only the first step. Many branches of science cannot do such studies and yet the measurement of causal effects is still a goal of researchers in these fields. One purpose of Rubin's model is to show how the experimental paradigm can shed light on causal inference in such fields. This model carries the general message that the counterfactual expectation, $E(Y_c|s = t)$, is the key quantity about which we must make critical assumptions that, in the absence of randomization, are often untested or even untestable. This section briefly covers three topics that arise once we leave the relative intellectual safety of controlled experiments—prospective observational studies, retrospective case-control studies, and posttreatment concomitant variables.

Prospective Observational Studies

This category includes many types of studies in which the active *experimenter,* who controls the assignment of causes to units, is replaced by a passive *observer* who can only record which unit turned out to be exposed to each relevant cause or treatment.

Rubin's model can express this by the lack of the plausibility of the assumption that s_i is independent of the variables Y_{ki} for k in K and hence, in Equation 6, BIAS $\neq 0$. A technique that may sometimes replace the independence assumption, and that has been studied the most so far, concerns "generalized covariate adjustments." When randomization is absent, the FACE and the ACE are no longer equal, so that the mean difference in responses between the treatment and control groups is no longer an unbiased estimate of the ACE. Suppose that, in addition to the variables y_i and s_i, we also observe the value of a "covariate" x_i on each unit i in U. In order for the notation x_i to be appropriate, the value x_i must not be influenced by the particular cause or treatment to which i is exposed. This assumption might be plausible in some circumstances (i.e., a drug treatment will not change your sex or age). In other cases we can only insure that it is true by measuring x_i prior to the exposure of units to causes. When x_i does not depend on the value of s_i, x_i is a covariate. The assumption that s_i is *independent* of all relevant variables (i.e., randomization) is stronger than the weaker assumption that Y_{ki} and s_i are *conditionally independent* given the value of x_i. This weaker, conditional independence assumption is often made in observational studies and leads to the estimation of the *covariate-adjusted, prima facia average causal effect* defined as

$$C\text{-FACE} = E[E(y|s = t, x) - E(y|s = c, x)|s = t]. \tag{7}$$

We have

$$E(y|s = t, x) = E(Y_t|s = t, x), \tag{8}$$

and under the conditional independence assumption

$$\begin{aligned} E(y|s = c, x) &= E(Y_c|s = c, x) \\ &= E(Y_c|s = t, x). \end{aligned} \tag{9}$$

From these equalities it follows that $C\text{-FACE} = \text{ACE}$. Thus, under the conditional independence assumption estimates of the $C\text{-FACE}$ are estimates of the ACE. When $E(y|s, x)$ is estimated using a linear regression model, the coefficient of s has a causal interpretation, that is, as an estimate of an ACE, whereas the coefficients of the other independent variables in x do not necessarily have a causal interpretation.

Retrospective Case-Control Studies

Medical studies have made increasing use of the case-control design. In such studies, the elements of Rubin's model have the following interpretation. $y_i = 1$ or 0 as patient i is a *case* (has the disease under study) or a *control* (does not have the disease). U is the population of patients under study and K is the level of exposure of the causative agent being investigated (e.g., amount of smoking, use of oral contraceptives, etc.). In case-control studies the data often consist of y_i, s_i, and a vector of covariates, x_i. Care must be taken to insure that the values of the covariates are not affected by exposure to the levels of the causative agent.

Case-control data are gathered in a retrospective way, so all that can be guaranteed in such studies is the observation of data from the joint distribution of s_i and x_i given either $y_i = 1$ or $y_i = 0$. Thus, we can observe data on the conditional distribution $p(k, x|y) = P(s = k, x|y)$. When K has two elements, t and c, the population probabilities underlying these data may be arrayed into a series of 2×2 tables of the form

	$y = 1$	$y = 0$
$s = t$	$p(t, x|1)$	$p(t, x|0)$
$s = c$	$p(c, x|1)$	$p(c, x|0)$

$$\tag{10}$$

one for each value of x. The crossproduct ratio of the table in Equation 10 is

$$\alpha(x) = \frac{p(t, x|1) \, p(c, x|0)}{p(c, x|1) \, p(t, x|0)}. \tag{11}$$

By Bayes' theorem, the 2×2 table in Equation 10 has the same crossproduct ratio as this one

	$y = 1$	$y = 0$
$s = t$	$\pi(1|t, x)$	$\pi(0|t, x)$
$s = c$	$\pi(1|c, x)$	$\pi(0|c, x)$

$$\tag{12}$$

where $\pi(y|k, x) = P(Y_k = y|s = k, x)$.

The primary tools used in the analysis of retrospective studies are various types of covariate adjustments (Breslow & Day, 1980) that all make the conditional independence assumption discussed earlier. That assumption implies the equality

$$\pi_k^*(y|x) = \pi(y|k, x)$$

where $\pi_k^*(y|x) = P(Y_k = y|s = t, x)$. The corresponding 2×2 table is obtained by replacing π by π^* in Equation 12. This substitution results in the crossproduct ratio

$$\alpha^*(x) = \frac{\pi_t^*(1|x) \, \pi_c^*(0|x)}{\pi_t^*(0|x) \, \pi_c^*(1|x)}. \tag{13}$$

Hence, standard log-linear model techniques (Bishop, Fienberg, & Holland, 1975) may be used to study $\alpha^*(x)$ by analysis of the data in Equation 10 in case-control studies when the conditional independence assumption is plausible.

Note that $\alpha^*(x)$ compares the distribution (conditional on x) of Y_t to that of Y_c among those exposed to t; but neither $\alpha^*(x)$ nor its average over x is an ACE describing the average of T_i over some part of U. However, $\alpha^*(x)$ is still a useful "causal" parameter because it describes how the *distribution* of Y-values changes in response to exposure of units to t or c. The ACE is a stronger causal parameter because it describes how the average unit is changed by exposure to t or c. In this sense, causal inferences in case-control studies are inherently weaker than those available in prospective observational studies satisfying exactly the same conditional independence assumption. Case-control studies are discussed more extensively from this point of view in Holland and Rubin (1988).

When Is a Covariate Not a Covariate?

Rubin's model can help one make important distinctions that are sometimes unknowingly swept under the rug. A good example is the use of *posttreatment concomitant variables*. When a second variable, X (besides Y), enters the system,

Rubin's model must be expanded to (U, K, s, Y, X) where the new element, X, is also a function (possibly vector-valued) on $K \times U$. X_{ki} is defined on $K \times U$ to reflect the fact that the value of X_{ki} can depend both on k and i. However, as mentioned earlier, a covariate is a function of i alone, that is, $X_{ki} = x_i$. Rosenbaum (1984b) discussed the role of posttreatment concomitant variables in experimental and observational studies. A posttreatment concomitant is a variable whose value is measured after the unit i has been exposed to the cause s_i, and is not a covariate in the sense used here if it is possible that X_{ki} is affected by k as well as by i. Rosenbaum showed that adjustments for posttreatment concomitant are usually more of a problem than a solution when one is estimating an average causal effect and should not be done without a great deal of care. When X_{ki} depends strongly on k, the bias introduced by adjusting for X may overwhelm any other advantage such an adjustment might have had.

WHAT ABOUT PATH ANALYSIS?

Much of what Rubin's model tells us is simply common sense to statisticians steeped in a tradition of experimentation. Although its goal is to help us understand how to analyze nonexperimental data, there is no magic. We are left with the problem of contemplating a series of untestable but plausible assumptions about our data and checking the sensitivity of our conclusions to these assumptions. That is the message of the model, pure and simple. But the model goes beyond this platitude because it focuses our attention on crucial quantities such as the counterfactual expectation, $E(Y_c|s = t)$, or on basic assumptions such as the stability assumption or the stable unit-treatment value assumption SUTVA (Rubin, 1980, 1986). How much less attractive is such an approach than the promise of path analysis! In path analysis, the cold bones of correlation are turned into the warm flesh of causation with direct, indirect, total, and partial causal pathways. Diagrams emerge; papers can now be written about unseen causal mechanisms winding their ways through latent variables and finally emerging as the potent explanation of observed correlations. However, it is all the same data so it may be hard to understand how there is such a gulf between the dreary analyses of Rubin's model and the artistic appeal of path diagrams. It is, I fear, another manifestation of that unbridgeable gulf between the measurement of the effects of causes and the identification of the causes of given effects. What can pass for a cause in path analysis might never get a moment's notice in an experiment. Students' scores on a test can cause their future action (Saris & Stronkhorst, 1984). Gender or race are just as good as anything else as causes in path analysis, although no experimenter would know how to manipulate them. Holland (1988a) gave a detailed description of the indirect causes in path analysis using an expansion of Rubin's model for research designs in which we cannot directly manipulate the causes of interest. Holland (1988b) also used Rubin's model to address the causal status of gender in the application of statistics to employment discrimination.

Statistical science has made strong contributions to issues of causal inference when it has addressed the problem of measuring the effects of causes. It does less useful things when its methodology claims to identify the causes of effects. Rubin's model focuses our attention on what we can do well rather than on what we might like to do, however poorly.

ACKNOWLEDGMENT

This chapter is based on an earlier version published in 1986 in *The New York Statistician,* 38, 1–6, a publication of the New York Area Chapter of the American Statistical Association.

REFERENCES

Bishop, Y. M. M., Fienberg, S. E., & Holland, P. W. (1975). *Discrete multivariate analysis: Theory and practice.* Cambridge, MA: MIT Press.

Breslow, N. E., & Day, N. E. (1980). *Statistical methods in cancer research: Vol. 1. The analysis of case-control studies.* Lyon: International Agency for Research on Cancer.

Glymour, C. (1986). Statistics and Metaphysics. Journal of the American Statistical Association, *81,* 964–966.

Holland, P. W. (1986). Statistics and causal inference. *Journal of the American Statistical Association, 81,* 945–960.

Holland, P. W. (1988a). Causal inference, path analysis, and recursive structural equations models. In C. Clogg (Ed.), *Sociological Methodology* (pp. 449–484). Washington, DC: American Sociological Association.

Holland, P. W. (1988b). Causal mechanism or causal effect: Which is best for statistical science? *Statistical Science, 3,* 186–188.

Holland, P. W., & Rubin, D. B. (1983). On Lord's paradox. In H. Wainer & S. Messick (Eds.), *Principals (sic) of modern psychological measurement* (pp. 3–25). Hillsdale, NJ: Lawrence Erlbaum Associates.

Holland, P. W., & Rubin, D. B. (1988). Causal inference in retrospective studies. *Evaluation Review, 12,* 203–231.

Mill, J. S. (1843). *A System of logic.*

Neyman, J. (1935). Statistical problems in agricultural experimentation (with discussion). *Journal of the Royal Statistical Society,* Suppl. *2,* 107–80.

Porter, T. M. (1986). *The rise of statistical thinking 1820–1900.* Princeton, NJ: Princeton University Press.

Rosenbaum, P. R. (1984a). From association to causation in observational studies: The role of tests of strongly ignorable treatment assignment. *Journal of the American Statistical Association, 79,* 41–48.

Rosenbaum, P. R. (1984b). The consequences of adjustment for a concomitant variable that has been affected by the treatment. *Journal of the Royal Statistical Society* (A), *147,* 656–666.

Rosenbaum, P. R. (1984c). Conditional permutation tests and the propensity score in observational studies. *Journal of the American Statistical Association, 79,* 565–574.

Rubin, D. B. (1974). Estimating causal effects of treatments in randomized and nonrandomized studies. *Journal of Educational Psychology, 66,* 688–701.

Rubin, D. B. (1977). Assignment of treatment group on the basis of a covariate. *Journal of Educational Statistics, 2,* 1–26.

Rubin, D. B. (1978). Bayesian inference for causal effects: The role of randomization. *Annals of Statistics, 6,* 34–58.

Rubin, D. B. (1980). Discussion of "Randomization analysis of experimental data: The Fisher randomization test." *Journal of the American Statistical Association, 75,* 591–593.

Rubin, D. B. (1986). Which ifs have causal answers. *Journal of the American Statistical Association, 81,* 961–962.

Saris, W., & Stronkhorst, H. (1984). *Causal modeling in nonexperimental research.* Amsterdam: Sociometric Research Foundation.

10 R. A. Fisher's Philosophical Approach to Inductive Inference

Nancy Brenner-Golomb
University of Utrecht, The Netherlands

A SHORT BIOGRAPHY

Fisher was born in East Finchley, England, in 1890. When he completed his secondary education in Harrow in 1909, he got an open scholarship to Caius College, Cambridge, and got his degree in mathematics in 1912. A further grant enabled him to spend an additional year studying statistical mechanics, quantum theory, and the theory of errors, which greatly influenced his scientific outlook. After leaving Cambridge he worked as a statistician with the Mercantile and General Investment Company in London. With the outbreak of World War 1, because his services were rejected due to poor eyesight, Fisher chose to fulfill his patriotic duty by replacing recruited teachers of mathematics and physics in public schools. After the war he rejected a permanent appointment in the Galton Laboratory in favor of a 6-month appointment in Rothampsted Experimental Station of Agriculture, where, in view of his disagreement with Karl Pearson, he hoped to have greater freedom of research. He was confident that his work would prove its usefulness and his appointment would be extended. And indeed he remained in Rothampsted until 1933. In 1933 he followed K. Pearson as a professor of Eugenics in the Galton Laboratory and as editor of the *Annals of Eugenics*. In 1943 he was appointed professor of genetics in Cambridge. With these two appointments he came into close collaboration with various scientists. Among the 294 articles in his *Collected Papers* (Bennett, 1974), there are many written in response to particular scientists who asked him to solve their mathematical or methodological problems.

The wide recognition of Fisher's work came only after World War 2, with several awards, honorary degrees, and membership in academic organizations.

283

But more important, by then, his innovations had their effect wherever research did not allow large samples.[1] After his retirement in 1957 he visited the division of mathematical statistics of the Commonwealth Scientific and Industrial Research Organization in Adelaide, Australia, where he remained as research fellow until his death in 1962.

EVOLUTION, EUGENICS, AND GENETICS—CAMBRIDGE

Fisher's interest in statistics arose from his preoccupation with *Eugenics,* a sort of "applied genetics" directed to the study, the maintenance, and the improvement of the genetic potential of the human species. In his opinion, the solutions for the problems of genetics were also the key for understanding evolution.

When Fisher came to Cambridge, Darwin's Theory of Evolution presented the community of biologists with more problems than explanations. One problem was Darwin's rejection of Lamarck's thesis about the inheritance of acquired properties. Lamarck (1744–1829) thought that properties acquired during the lifetime of an organism are transmitted to its offspring. In simple organisms, he explained, changes in the environment mechanically affected the motion of fluids in their bodies and this motion controlled their adaptation to the environment. In complex organisms, the feeling of needs intervened in the process: When their environment changes, these complex organisms feel new needs that affect the motion of fluids in the particular organs that may satisfy these needs. For example, where only trees were available as a source of food, a giraffe felt the need to reach the branches that were higher than its body, and its efforts affected the motion of the fluids responsible for the structure of its neck, so that it became a little longer, and this change was transmitted to its offspring. In Lamarck's opinion, environmental pressures of this kind were responsible for *progressive evolution,* that is, for an increasing variety of organisms, adapted to live under changing circumstances.

Darwin (1809–1882) also thought that species vary in response to environmental pressures, but he claimed that a process of natural selection (independent of the animals' behavior) operated on these variations. He thought that if Lamarck was right, structural changes in animals would be gradual and cumulative, because small adaptive changes would be inherited by their offspring. But the observation of breeding animals in agriculture, according to Darwin, supplies evidence that this was not the case. He also thought there were theoretical reasons against Lamarck's idea of progressive evolution, which he derived from

---

[1]This acceptance in psychology is described in Rucci and Tweney (1980). The recognition of his contribution, however, does not mean that his ideas were accepted without reservation or rival methodological suggestions. For this aspect of Fisher's influence see Vol. 1, chap. 11.

Malthus (1776–1834): Where limited food resources are not sufficient to sustain competing species, only those species survive that possess more suitable characteristics to adapt themselves to their environment. However, Darwin could not suggest a mechanism to explain how this natural selection led to organic changes in species.

A solution to this problem was to grow out of Mendel's discoveries. But although his work was published in 1869, it remained unknown until the turn of the century to Darwin as well as to most biologists. Mendel's work dealt with the inheritance of color in the flowers and the wrinkliness in the seeds of peas. His theory suggested the existence of a unit factor of inheritance—the gene. Initially, this was not supposed to be a material entity but merely a theoretical construct implied by the way inheritance functioned. However, Bateson (1861–1926), who initiated the subject of genetics in Cambridge in 1909, showed (in 1894) that discontinuity, that is, sharp rather than gradual variations, was significant in evolution, thus supporting both Mendel's and Darwin's ideas. In contrast, Hugo de Vries (1848–1935), one of the three people who rediscovered Mendel's laws, opposed the idea that natural selection was the cause of evolution. He also attributed all genetic change to mutations caused by environmental influence. But according to him, any mutations *within* a species would cancel each other by interbreeding. A mutation, in his opinion, created a new species from the start, and this prevented interbreeding. In other words, by mutation, he did not mean what is meant today, except for the idea that variation was discrete and hereditary.

The plausibility of the modern idea of mutations depended on the credibility of the real existence of the genes. In 1910 Morgan (1866–1945) connected these units of inheritance to his work on chromosomes, and in 1927, Muller (1890–1968) confirmed the existence of mutations and their effect on heredity by means of localized X ray radiation of chromosomes. Only then did natural evolution appear to be a process totally dependent on the way genes can be transmitted from parents to offspring. However, in 1909, when Fisher came to Cambridge, these questions were far from settled (Allen, 1978, chaps. 1 & 3; Box-Fisher, 1978, pp. 21–28).

Of particular importance for Fisher was the fact that these new ideas in genetics were rejected by the eugenic movement. The science of Eugenics originated with Francis Galton (1822–1911). He believed that the future of mankind depended on its hereditary composition. He thought that this composition could be shown by applying statistical methods to population research; and because the Royal Society did not accept papers applying mathematics to biology, he sponsored the journal *Biometrika* in order to promote research in this direction. He also started what in 1909 became the Galton Laboratory of Eugenics at University College London. The first professor in this laboratory and the first editor of *Biometrika* was Karl Pearson. Pearson accepted Darwin's original theory of evolution by natural selection but rejected both Mendelism and the theories of de

Vries on the grounds that his biometrical work showed many instances of continuous (as opposed to discrete) variation.

The way each of these scientists developed his theory made them mutually exclusive: Morgan and Muller, like Bateson, thought that Mendel's theory of variation within species provided a successful explanation of discontinuity of inheritance, and thus excluded the possibility of continuous evolution; Pearson's conviction that variation was continuous suggested to him that Mendel was wrong; and de Vries's theory of mutations excluded the possibility that the discontinuity of Mendel's theory of variation *within* species can account for the evolution of the species, suggested by natural selection.

As a student, Fisher was already convinced that Mendelism did not exclude continuous variation and did provide the explanation for progressive evolution. He felt this could be shown by applying the methods of statistics. In order to do so he turned to probability theory.

In 1911, at the age of 21, Fisher addressed the second meeting of the Eugenic Society in Cambridge. The title of his speech was "Mendelism and Biometrics." In this 15-minute talk he tried to convince his fellow students that these two sciences were not only compatible but their combination was the only way to understand inheritance: Genetics, he said, was the mechanism of this inheritance, and statistics was the appropriate way of thinking about it. Moreover, he argued, in this combination lies the hope of improving the hereditary material of mankind. These ideas culminated in 1930 in a book, *The Genetical Theory of Natural Selection* (1958), in which he succeeded in describing the missing mechanism in Darwin's theory.

Fisher was convinced that the dominant reform movements of his time—those that hoped to put an end to alcoholism, to mental retardation, and to other disabilities, by environmental changes—were misled by the neo-Lamarckian theories of evolution. According to Fisher, the only way to ensure progressive improvement of the nation was to ensure that the better qualities of mankind should be represented in a generation of children in a slightly greater proportion than they had been represented in the generation of their parents, and this could happen wherever people of higher attainment had on the average slightly more children than those who were less successful. According to his daughter, he considered himself and his wife to be practicing eugenicists: Their eight (surviving) children formed a reservoir of valuable genetic stock, because the low birthrate of the upperclasses to which he belonged was, in his opinion, the main reason for the deterioration of the nation. He thought that this was also the reason for the fall of prosperous civilizations in the past and the fate awaiting Western civilization if nothing was done to prevent it.

It is worth noting that initially the science of eugenics was not related to racist ideas. Both K. Pearson and Muller, for example, were socialist eugenicists. Eugenics was discredited by fascism, but Fisher was insensitive to the change. He never abandoned either his faith in the predominance of genetic over cultural factors in determining the fate of people, or his hope to utilize genetics for changing it. When working in the Galton Laboratory, for example, he collaborated with the serological department in their RH-factor research. His colleagues in this department appreciated his methodological and experimental contributions to their work but were embarrassed by his hopes for finding in it a key to the improvement of human inheritance. Fisher was disappointed but did not abandon his beliefs (Box-Fisher, 1978, pp. 338–344).

In 1956, when the *British Medical Journal* published the results of investigations showing a correlation between smoking and lung cancer, he argued that a correlation between two phenomena did not prove that one is the cause of the other. He suggested there might be a genetic factor that caused both cancer and the tendency to smoke. He argued further that if the medical profession settled with their unfounded explanation, the badly needed inquiry into the real (i.e., genetic) causes of cancer would be neglected. He suggested the public money that the medical profession wished to devote to a campaign against smoking should better be invested in research to provide real knowledge about the causes of cancer. His own line of research was to compare smoking habits of identical and nonidentical twins. He found that although the latter did not differ from ordinary brothers, the smoking habits of identical twins were more consistently similar. This supported his hypothesis that there might be a genetic factor in determining the tendency to smoke.[2]

CHANCE AND DETERMINISM

In 1932 Fisher was invited to present The Herbert Spencer Lecture in Oxford, and he chose the subject *The Social Selection of Human Fertility*. The laws of nature known to us as the mathematical expressions of experimental classical physics, he argued, seem to imply that the universe is governed by exact and necessary laws of causation as if it were a deterministic mechanism. The regularity and predictability of heavenly motions, and the refinement of measuring techniques that enabled the extension of predictability to other spheres of reality, suggested the idea that determinism might be complete and with adequate information it may even be extended to the biological and the social sciences. The laws of chance seemed to represent a mere illusionary causelessness, a product of human ignorance. But developments in physics since the late 19th century, he said, do not support such a view. Maxwell (1831–1879) talked of the theory of

---

[2]In 1956, Fisher was statistical consultant to tobacco manufacturers and therefore was open to suspicion of serving their interests. He was very indignant that his well-known attitude to inference, and his requirement that it be carefully related to the information actually given by the data, be discredited by the fact that he got a small fee for his consultancy.

probability as being the logic of this world, and Boltzmann (1844–1906) used it in his theory of gases.

The reliability of a physical theory, Fisher concluded, is not derived from the reliability of the behavior of its ultimate components but quite the opposite: It is derived from the fact that these components were very numerous and largely *independent*. In his own words: "The only reason known to us for such reliability is that its properties are in some sort the average or total of a large number of independent items of behaviour" (Fisher, 1932, p. 11).

The discovery of the Uncertainty Principle by Heisenberg in 1930 presented a disturbing philosophical problem to most physicists. It undermined the established relation between their deterministic view of nature and their explanation of predictability. But Fisher saw in it a support for his view.

In classical physics, particles are conceived as entities with sharp coordinates, and two particles cannot occupy the same coordinates at the same time. Particles collide and exchange exact and calculable quantities of energy. A wave, in contrast, spreads boundlessly throughout a medium: It *is* this moving medium. Thus, one wave can never be in one point, and two waves can be at the same place at the same time. In many ways these two concepts were the opposite of each other. Therefore the idea that an entity could be described as both a particle and a wave amounted to a contradiction: The idea was unthinkable.

However, between 1887 and 1927 various physical phenomena involving radiation could be explained only by attributing to each participating entity properties of both particles and waves. Hence, the so-called Copenhagen Interpretation of Quantum Theory introduced the idea that a wave-particle duality is a fundamental nature of microentities (e.g., electrons). As a result, the classical idea that a particle's energy state is completely defined as a function of its position, that is, in terms of its (x, y, z) coordinates at time t, had to be abandoned, because positions are properties of (pointlike) particles, whereas the energy of these particle-wave entities is a function of their wave structure.

With this view in mind, Heisenberg's principle of uncertainty can be metaphorically understood as follows. In order to locate an electron, say, we must "squeeze" it into precise coordinates (x, y, z, t). But by doing so we loose the possibility to observe its energy level because the latter is a function of the amplitude and the frequency of the destroyed wave. In contrast, if we want to measure its energy, we must allow the electron-wave to occupy its whole natural space, but then no information is available about its position. In other words, increasing the possibility of predicting a position is inextricably related to decreasing the possibility of predicting the energy level, and vice versa. As a result, the new Copenhagen Interpretation maintained that in the micro domain nothing can be discovered that may bring us back to the deterministic theories.

The disturbing question that engaged physicists at the time was the following: Can the uncertainty principle mean that electrons in fact lack a simultaneous position and energy level? Surely the fact that we cannot measure them simultaneously can reflect only our crude techniques, rather than such an incredible idea that in any real entity these properties are not essentially related?

The opponents of indeterminism maintained that the explanation given to it should not be taken to be more than a metaphor. The nonpredictability described by Heisenberg's uncertainty relations, and the fact that only statistical methods could help overcome them, were similar, in their opinion, to the difficulties encountered in calculating levels of energy of gases: We cannot measure the positions and velocities of all molecules in a gas in order to calculate its total energy. But statistical thermodynamics makes such measurement superfluous, by relating measurable quantities, like pressure, volume, and temperatures, to average velocities of the molecules. In other words, an improved inferential technique solved the problem of *apparent* indeterminism, and therefore of nonpredictability. This comparison is possible, however, only if we do not abandon determinism.

The supporters of the new view argued that the comparison was faulty: The use of statistics in the theory of gases rests on the assumption that we understand the real structure of gas molecules, and the real relation between their behavior as individuals and as an aggregate. In other words, we have reasons to believe that everything we calculate with the help of our statistical techniques is equivalent to the calculations we would obtain had it been possible to measure the velocities of all the individual molecules. But the fact that elementary entities seem to have both properties of particles and properties of waves, does not allow us to make such an assumption. The microtechniques indicate that a conceptual change is necessary in order to understand microreality. We cannot pretend that the position is the same as in thermodynamics.

Physicists who clung to the classical conceptions (including Einstein) felt that methods that merely allow prediction, without being related to an understandable explanation of nature, cannot be satisfactory. The opponents argued that this implies that because there is no escape from suspecting that nature may be fundamentally indeterministic, this realization improves our understanding of the real foundations of predictability.

Fisher thought that this conclusion was a natural extension of his statistical philosophy. In his "Indeterminism and Natural Selection," published in *Philosophy of Science* (Fisher, 1934), he argued that because all laws of natural causation were essentially laws of probability, the predictability of a system has the same basis in the natural as in the social sciences. Causal relations are discovered, he explained, because explanations rely on implicit statistical simplifications. For example, we can ask why a pebble is round and how it came to be so. We accept the explanation that the pebble is rounded by the abrasive action of the surf because we recognize that such action is the result of a total effect, irrespective of any particular scratching or chipping that may have been the result of any particular impact. We cannot hope to specify in detail how more complicated geometrical configurations of masses of matter had come about. This is equally so in social phenomena. Births are independent events in the sense that the heredity of each individual is independent of any other. But it is exactly due to this independence that if in a population of 20 million to a generation, say, it is consistently the case that one half of the people reproduce about two thirds of their number and the other half—four thirds, it is as certain as a natural law that the inheritable qualities of these halves will appear in the next generation in the ratio 1:2 rather than 1:1.

In other words, far from being contradictory, the notions of probability and determinism are intrinsically related: The first concerns the frequencies of independent (and often indeterminate) events, and the second is the consequence of their aggregates. According to Fisher, predictability depends on this intrinsic relation: Any organization of the components of an aggregate, rendering them not independent of each other, may actually reduce the predictability of the system. For example, for the commander in an army, who has no control over the enemy's battalion moving "as one man," the behavior of this organized battalion is less reliably predictable than the behavior of a mere aggregate of men.

The introduction of indeterminism to *all* science, in Fisher's opinion, solves grave difficulties that arise on the assumption of a deterministic point of view. The first is the "classical" difficulty: Because every phenomenon that is a cause must itself have a cause, there is no end to the sequence of causes, unless one postulates a First Cause extraneous to the logical system. This difficulty is resolved with the indeterministic view, which alters the very conception of causation: "Only in an indeterministic system has the notion of causation restored to it that creative element, that sense of bringing something to pass which otherwise would not have been, which is essential to its commonplace meaning" (Fisher, 1934, p. 100).

In his *Creative Aspects of Natural Law* (The Eddington Memorial Lecture), Fisher explained this idea: In connection with human affairs, for a work to be creative, it must have aesthetic, moral, or social value; but in science *creative* means a qualifying change. The evolutionary process has been creative because new things came into being—"growth; voluntary movement; appetite, striving and effort; joy and pain; consciousness and, in man at least, self criticism" (Bennett, 1974, Vol. 5, p. 241). In other words, a causal relation is a complex result of innumerable events, whether these events are as described by the example of the pebble or as described by the theory of natural selection. The fact that each of these innumerable events is indeterminate, that is, that it is an open question whether it will or will not occur, is irrelevant: The creativity of the aggregate of these events lies in the irreversibility of the result. This irreversibility represents a new phenomenon, which can be described by a causal law, and is due to the fact that the preceding events were independent of each other.

Closely connected to this conception of causation, as a creative factor of basically nondeterminable change, are the other two difficulties about a deterministic view. First, it cannot explain the phenomena of evolution. In an indeterministic view, certain events entail systems of probabilities for various consequences. Statistically speaking, a chance event is a deviation from the expected. Such an event is casual with respect to its preceding causes, but the aggregate of all such casual components becomes a creative cause due to the consequences that it entails. A genetic mutation is of this sort: It is casual because in itself it is incapable of propelling the organism in any particular direction, but in the aggregate, under natural selection, it has irreversible consequences that could not have been foreseen. This process explains evolution.

The second related difficulty is the explanation of the human experience of time, that is, that we can remember but not foretell. With a deterministic view, this fact seems to be an arbitrary constraint on systematic knowledge, because the instantaneous state of such a system must be related to its subsequent states by equations identical with those that relate it to its previous states. That this is not so with states of the human mind is universally verified by subjective experience. An indeterminate system, however, allows the existence of consciousness of the creative aspect of causation: consciousness of that which will probably happen, as opposed to the memory of that which had already happened. This possibility makes sense of the unidirectional experience of time.

Similarly, in the deterministic view, the experience of purpose and choice must appear an illusion. Any organism that was to perform certain activities connected with survival and reproduction would have to have evolved so that it behaved as if its actions were purposeful, but the illusion itself would be of no selective advantage because it could not affect action. In particular, the appearance of such illusion in mankind would seem to be a pure accident that could have appeared equally in the lowest and highest organisms. In contrast, Fisher argued, in an indeterminate world, purposeful action of an organism as a whole is a stage of an evolutionary process by which relatively large masses of living matter have come to achieve an irreversible unity of structure and cooperation of its parts. In particular, where the cooperation of all parts includes memory of causal relations, consciousness of possible results, and the purposeful actions based on them, the irreversible unity of structure is what we call *human individuality*.

Fisher ended his lecture with the remark: "For us, creation is still going on." The life and actions of individuals may be of unique consequence, and we must accept the responsibility of this creative role because "it appears to be unquestionable that the activity of the human race will provide the major factor in the environment of almost every evolving organism" (Bennett, 1974, Vol. 5, p. 241). This statement could easily be made today. But the confirmation of Fisher's views about the unforeseen effects of the creative aspects of human actions, can be seen in the concluding sentence of his Herbert Spencer Lecture given in 1932: "It is, as it seems to me, part of our business as scientists to distinguish between what is inevitable and what is subject to control; but it is our business as citizens to see that the possible control is exercised" (Fisher, 1932, p. 32). By "the possible control" he meant the improvement of the species by policies of birth control. He was unable to foresee the effect that these eugenic ideas could, and did, have on the growth of fascism.

MATHEMATICS AND INDUCTION

In his address to the Royal Dublin Society in 1932, Fisher expressed the opinion that

> it is the method of reasoning, and not the subject matter, that is distinctive of mathematical thought. A mathematician, if he is of any use, is of use as an expert in the process of reasoning, by which we pass from a theory to its logical consequences, or from an observation to the inferences which must be drawn from it. (Bennett, 1974, Vol. III, p. 98)

Mathematics, then, ought to deal with both deductive and inductive reasoning.

An experimental scientist, he argued, always assumes that it is possible to draw valid inferences from the results of experiments, that is, that it is possible to argue from consequences to causes; from observations to hypotheses; from the particular to the general; from samples to the populations from which they were drawn. In short, the validity of induction is taken for granted. Mathematicians, in contrast, refuse to discuss inductive inference, on the grounds that unlike deduction it always involves a degree of guesswork. They fail to realize that the fact that uncertainty is traditionally being connected only to induction is a historical accident. They fail to distinguish between a subjective degree of uncertainty, involved in all inferential knowledge, and an objective uncertainty due to a real variability of a measured quantity. They fail to realize that in these cases of objective variability, prediction based on inductive inference can be as rigorous as deduction because "the nature and degree of the uncertainty may itself be capable of rigorous expression" (Fisher, 1947, p. 4).

These failures are explained by Fisher as follows. Traditionally, those mathematicians who did try to deal with the uncertainties of induction, did so by applying the theory of probability developed from the consideration of games of chance. The first attempt was made by Thomas Bayes, whose *Theorem of Inverse Probability* was published in 1763.[3] The assumptions made in the formulation of this theorem are that if H_i is an event that precedes E (for example a postulated cause of E) then the set of H_i for all i is exhaustive, that is, it includes all the possible events that can relevantly precede E (e.g., all possible causes of E), and they are mutually exclusive (e.g., only one H can be the cause). It is also clear that the theorem is applicable only when the initial probabilities of the H_i

---

[3]See Winkler's exposition of the theorem in Vol. 2, chap. 7.

are known a priori, that is, in advance of the observation of E. Dealing with games of chance, these assumptions are not problematic. But the theorem was intended to provide a corrected a posteriori value of the probability of H_i/E, in cases where H_i for a particular value of i was a postulated cause of E, taking the fact into account that E has been observed. And in these cases, even if we ignore the other assumptions, it is not a simple matter of calculation to assign them initial probabilities. Bayes suggested that we could postulate equal initial probability to each cause. According to Fisher, Bayes was aware of the nonacceptability of such a postulate (known as the Principle of Insufficient Reason) and, therefore, he did not publish his theorem.

The theorem was, in fact, published by Price 2 years after Bayes' death, and Laplace turned the postulate into an axiom. The axiom was attractive because it seemed to have solved the problem of induction. Ignoring details of calculation, the argument runs as follows. Writing p for the probability that E will happen, the probability that E will be observed r times out of n trials can be calculated for any value of p. Laplace took p to be a variable, and by applying the axiom, he assumed that we can take the distribution of p to be rectangular, that is, that it could have any value between 0 and 1 with equal probability. Adjusting Bayes' theorem to a continuous function he got

$$P(p_i/r) = \frac{P(p_i) \cdot P(r/p_i)}{\displaystyle\int_0^1 P(r/p_i) \cdot P(p_i)\, dp_i}$$

and the expected value of this expression is $\dfrac{r+1}{n+2}$. This is now taken to be the a posteriori probability of p. It follows that if an event is consistently observed, that is, if $r = n$, then for increasingly large values of n, p tends to 1. In other words, when induction is based on a very large number of observations, probable inference approaches certainty.

The argument, said Fisher, was based on a confusion between "probability," taken to mean an objective quantity (p), the estimation of which ought to be dependent on the nature of the data, and "probability" interpreted as a measure of a degree of belief, that is, of a psychological tendency to accept a hypothesis, and thus dependent on the state of our knowledge. As a result of this confusion, ignorance (rather than theoretical knowledge about the data in question) was considered to be a good reason for assigning probabilities to unknown events. Fisher made his point by an example from genetics.

Suppose we have a litter of black mice, born to parents one of which is black and the other brown. We can use Bayes' theorem to calculate the probability that the black parent is homozygote or heterozygote provided we know the litter from which it has come: The event E is an observed litter of black mice, born to parents, one brown (bb) and one black (BB or Bb), where b = brown and B = Black and Black is dominant. The probabilities required are H_1 = P(BB) and H_2 = P(Bb) of the black parent. There are three possibilities, as shown in Fig. 10.1.

If we know that the black parent was the offspring of two black parents that gave birth to at least one brown mouse, then we know that they were both heterozygote. Therefore we know that in this experiment the a priori probability of the black parent to be homozygote is a third and its probability to be heterozygote is two thirds. But according to Laplace's axiom, if we do not know the history of the litter, then merely on the basis of this ignorance, we are entitled to assume a probability half for each case!

According to Fisher, there were two (historical) reasons why Laplace, in spite of being the great mathematician that he was, could make such a mistake. First, he dealt mainly with games of chance. This may be explained as follows. At the gambling table, the probability that in a long sequence of throws of a dice a sixth of the faces will show a six, say, is an objective quantity. Nevertheless, the actual observation of such a frequency does depend on the fact that the players cannot know in advance whether their own subsequences will show more or less than this expected number of sixes. If particular players could know this, they would play only when their expectations were higher, and this would affect the total number of observed sixes. Therefore, the ignorance of the players is a factor in the determination of frequencies: It affects the randomness on which fair gambling depends. This explains why subjective ignorance was included in the conception of probability in Laplace's time. The mistake, then, is in the extension of this conception to the domain of scientific hypotheses, as if our ignorance, or our inability to distinguish between them, was relevant for the validity of these hypotheses.

The second reason why Laplace could make this mistake was his, and his contemporaries', conviction that only deduction was valid reasoning. The classical theory of probability, including Bayes' theorem, was a deductive form of reasoning. Those mathematicians who dealt with statistical problems at that time tried to force a deductive form of inference on scientific problems that were essentially inductive. However, says Fisher, it is well to remember that the principles and methods of *deductive* reasoning were probably unknown for thou-

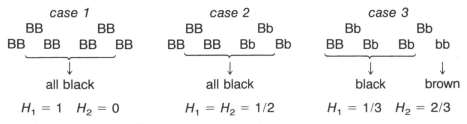

FIG. 10.1.   Inheritance of color in mice.

sands of years after the establishment of prosperous and cultured civilizations. It is true that the importance of the development of deductive reasoning that followed the construction of Euclidian geometry in the third century B.C. cannot be exaggerated. With well-defined concepts, the intellect found itself capable of acting with unprecedented efficiency. Nevertheless, it is certainly something of a historical accident that his particular discipline should have become fashionable in the Greek academies and later be embodied in the curricula of secondary education. We take the knowledge of the principles of deduction for granted only because geometry is universally taught at schools and because we cannot make any progress in that subject without thoroughly familiarizing ourselves with the requirements of precise deductive arguments. However, he adds, it is also a noted fact that inductive inference is the only process known to us by which essentially new knowledge comes into existence. To make clear the authentic conditions of its validity is the kind of contribution to the intellectual development of mankind that we should expect of a theory of experimental science. As the art of experimentation advances, the principles should become clear by virtue of which the planning and designing of experiments achieve their purpose. The liberation of the human intellect must remain incomplete so long as it is free only to work out the consequences of a prescribed body of dogmatic data and is denied access to unsuspected truths, which only direct observation can give. As it happened, he concluded, this great step toward the full exercise of intellectual liberty has been reserved for biometry (Introduction to Fisher, 1947; Bennett, 1974, Vol. 5, p. 224).[4]

We may summarize Fisher's argument as follows. The concept of probability involves two distinct meanings: a subjective notion expressing our uncertainty whether our beliefs are true, and an objective notion that measures a real distribution of a variable. Concerning the subjective notion, according to the traditional argument, because we are entitled to say that we *know* a proposition *p* if and only if we are certain of its truth, only deduction leads to knowledge because only logical inference preserves truth: If we know *q* and we also know that *p* logically follows from *q,* we are entitled to say that we know *p* with the same degree of confidence we have for *q.* However, if *p* follows from *q,* knowledge of *p* does not add new knowledge. We are only made aware of something that we could have known the moment we knew *q.* In contrast, induction seems to increase our

---

[4]In 1929, Fisher was elected to a fellowship of the Royal Society as a mathematician on the basis of his work on estimation theory and probability distributions. On that occasion he wrote to his teacher at Harrow:

> It is great luck to be recognized by mathematicians because academically speaking, statistics has scarcely been discovered yet . . . I wish I knew what sort of organization would suit the subject, for it would be deadly to it to be isolated as a self contained study . . . what we need is a fairly intensive mathematical training together with very wide scientific interests, not so much in established knowledge as in the means of establishing it. (J. Box-Fisher, 1978, p. 239)

knowledge: From limited observations we pass to general laws. Unfortunately, however, induction does not preserve truth. If we know that all observed swans are white and we conclude that all swans are white, we have no guarantee that the conclusion is as true as the premises. Therefore, traditionally, the subjective notion of probability has been related only to induction.

In fact, however, this element of uncertainty is ultimately present in the acquisition of all inferential knowledge, irrespective of it being inductive or deductive. If we know p due to its being deduced from q, the uncertainty is simply pushed back to q. The problem known as the problem of induction, then, is the realization that all knowledge involves a gap between the known evidence and the believed generalizations (hypotheses, or theses). The difference is in the location of the gap, that is, whether it appears with an isolated generalization, or with the premises of a system of statements. Hume's insight was the realization that we cannot have either evidence or logically valid reasons to justify our natural intuition that knowledge of facts extends beyond direct inspection. But this insight applies equally to Newton's laws of motion and to a statement like "$7/8$ of the population is likely to vote"; it applies equally to any of them when stated in isolation, and where they appear together with their logical conclusions within systems of statements. In short, the realization applies to all articulated knowledge.

In Fisher's opinion, the distinction between this element of uncertainty and the objective notion of probability is important not only because it leads to the conclusion that statements and predictions based on the notion of objective probabilities are as rigorous as those based on causal laws. It is also important because the failure to make it led to the idea that rigor is obtainable only by deduction, and this idea had a very damaging result: The insistence on deduction no longer acted as an incentive for perfecting our methods; it was now an obstacle to the acquisition of new knowledge. It prevented the acceptance of the fact that in its first steps, new knowledge must be speculative and insecure. His active support for the theory of continental drift in the 1950s sprang from this view.

In 1912, Alfred Wegener put this hypothesis forward. It was widely debated in the 1920s and 1930s, but on the whole it was dismissed. In 1956 Fisher compared the scientific atmosphere around the geomagnetic investigations that revived the interest in the theory of continental drift to the scientific controversy about organic evolution in the 19th century. Then as now, he explained, debates about early speculations led scientists to commit themselves to such impossible positions that, in spite of accumulated evidence, nobody dared revive these early speculations. In his opinion, this was the reason why Darwin worked almost secretly and reluctantly published in 1859, and also of the fact that it took another 50 years until his work was understood.

The purpose of a scientific career, he argued, is to increase knowledge. In this process, it is inevitable that some previously established ideas prove to be false or obsolete. The task of the mathematician is not to impose constraints on thought, but to find the suitable tools for dealing with each problem. Problems have individual features and these must be taken into account, both when scientific experiments are designed and when statistical methods are devised. The solutions of the problems must go hand in hand with the improvement of the tools. Only in this way can a genuine and comprehensive formulation of the process of inductive reasoning come into existence.

MATHEMATICAL STATISTICS

This chapter is not intended to deal with the details of Fisher's contributions to this subject. It is, however, worthwhile to note the new direction he gave to it.

Fundamental to the subject of statistics is the fact that the properties investigated are of aggregates rather than of individuals. Hence the elementary part of the theory is concerned with describing the frequency distributions of these properties and with summarizing them in such measurements as means and deviations from them. Such calculated measurements, derived from samples of larger populations are, of course, themselves variables, and their aggregates also form frequency distributions.[5] The basic sorts of questions that arise when using this method are the following:

1. Does a calculated statistic differ significantly from the estimated corresponding parameter? How do we test such significance?
2. Does an observed frequency distribution differ significantly from a theoretical one? Or, does a mathematical curve fit the observations?
3. How can we best use calculated statistics for estimating the corresponding parameters?

When Galton and K. Pearson introduced the application of statistics to biology and population studies, the central theoretical concept was the distribution of errors, introduced by Gauss (1777–1855) a century earlier. They considered statistics to be different from parameters as errors differ from true measurements. Therefore, only large samples were theoretically interesting because only then could the normal curve serve as a mathematical tool for answering the first and third questions. The second question did not differ from the first. When Pearson realized, for example, that his calculated correlation coefficients (a statistic he introduced) were far from being normally distributed, his problem was to find out how many observations would be needed in order to bring their distribution

---

[5]Incidentally, the distinction between measurements being applied to the population as a whole and to a sample, that is, between parameters and statistics, first made clear by Fisher, is by now so familiar that it hardly receives the appreciation it deserves.

to "normality." In contrast, Fisher's first paper in statistics, published in *Biometrika* in 1915 (see Bennett, 1974) dealt with the exact mathematical distribution of the correlation coefficient (r).

According to Fisher, the variability of sample values of a parameter is itself a phenomenon to be studied, and it cannot be compared to the distribution of errors. When we find the exact mathematical distribution of various statistics, he argued, we learn something about a real phenomenon, for example, about the real distribution of observed values of r, given that the correlation coefficient in the population is ρ.

Fisher's personal interest in the properties of r was due to the fact that the distribution of its measurements was one of the reasons why Pearson rejected Mendelism: Assuming the property of dominance, his calculated correlations of these properties between relatives were consistently too low. Fisher's study of this phenomenon led to his concept of the variance, first introduced in his second article, as the Correlation to Be Expected Between Relatives on the Supposition of Mendelian Inheritance. This new concept had merit because (as opposed to r) it could be divided into additive components: He showed how variation in inheritance could be broken down into hereditary and nonhereditary fractions, and how the first could be further broken down into variation due to dominance and gene interaction. Thus explaining both the reduced effect of dominating genes and the apparent contradiction between the Mendelian discrete variation due to mutations and the continuous variation observed by Pearson.[6]

The use of analysis of variance in experimentation is discussed in the next section. One general effect of both innovations was the support they gave to experimentation as opposed to observation[7]: By finding the exact distributions of statistics, he argued, we need not resort anymore to the accidental fact that, when the number of observations is large, their distributions are similar to that of errors. Hence, we need not insist on large samples, a demand that usually cannot be met under the constraints of the laboratory.

By 1930 Fisher published a variety of papers concerning the exact mathematical distribution of various statistics, and tests of significance were devised for each case, giving an answer to the first question.

For answering the second question, it was also K. Pearson who introduced a method: the χ^2 test of "goodness of fit." But in this case too, the method was

---

[6]The pioneering nature of his work can be seen in the following anecdote, told in his daughter's biography. The paper was submitted to the Royal Society in 1916 and was sent, as was the custom, to two referees. To K. Pearson as statistician and to R. C. Pennett as geneticist. Each of them discarded the article as a contribution to his own discipline while suggesting that it might be of interest to the other.

[7]Rucci and Tweney (1980) claimed that ANOVA "enabled researchers to fill the void that existed in experimental methodology" (p. 172). They pointed out, however, that, because observation is as widely used in psychology as experimentation, the correlation coefficient is used as frequently as ANOVA even after the incorporation of the latter into psychological research.

found inaccurate where the number of frequency-entries was small. Fisher introduced the concept of "degrees of freedom," that is, the number of observations that could be considered independent of each other. The correction was important, of course, only for small samples.

The procedures proposed in the early stages of the development of statistics were based on intuitive arguments and therefore, where the answer to the third question was concerned, a new dilemma was added to the old mistrust of induction: How is it possible that by using different logical methods we reach different conclusions from the same data? For example, we get different estimates of the variability in the population if we use the *mean deviation* instead of the *standard deviation*. In order to solve this problem Fisher asked himself: Is there a method of calculation that we may be justified to call *the best,* with superiority that could be derived from the structure of the problem itself? His research in this direction yielded his theory of estimation,[8] in which he introduced the concepts of (statistical) *consistency*—that is, the value of the calculated statistic must tend to that of the parameter being estimated when the number of observations is indefinitely increased—and *efficiency*—that is, the variance of the calculated statistic (at least when based on large samples) should not exceed that of any other consistent statistic used for estimating the same parameter. He reintroduced the neglected method of *maximum likelihood* (first introduced by Gauss) that gives the most efficient choice of calculated estimates. And he introduced the concept of *sufficiency:* A statistic is sufficient when any additional information available in the sample is irrelevant for estimating the parameter in question. For example, he showed that the arithmetic mean is not only the most consistent and efficient statistic for estimating the population's mean, but also if we use a formula for this estimate that includes the mode, say, the estimate is worse than if we use the arithmetic mean alone.

Fisher's theory of estimation involved an interesting controversy related to what he saw as a confusion between the subjective and the objective concepts of probability.[9] Within his theory of estimation was included the concept of fiducial limits. At the same time (1925–1935) Neyman and E. S. Pearson developed their theory of confidence limits. The mathematical expression of both was the same. But Fisher insisted there was an important conceptual difference between them, which can be put as follows.

We may discredit a hypothetical value of a parameter (e.g., the population

---

[8]See, for example, "On the Mathematical Foundations of Theoretical Statistics" (1922) and "Theory of Statistical Estimation" (1925) in Fisher (1950b, chaps. 10, 11).

[9]The purpose of this chapter is to show the philosophical origins of Fisher's work, and not to describe its contribution to the history of statistics. For such a description, see (for example) chapter 3 in Gigerenzer et al. (1989). For the same reason I ignore Fisher's long-standing disagreement with Neyman and E. S. Pearson, and his fierce objections to the work of all others, which arose out of different interpretations of the subject matter to which statistical methods were applied. For this topic see chapter 11 in this book.

mean) when, given this value, the expected distribution of its sample values (e.g., of the means of samples) shows that the probability that an observed value should occur is small, for example, 5%. This is Fisher's "Null hypothesis": We assume that a calculated statistic is a chance-deviation from the postulated parameter, and we reject this assumption only when the deviation is significant, where "significant" means more than we are ready to ascribe to chance alone. Neyman did not deny the argument, but pointed out that by doing so we introduce a practice that necessarily leads to two types of error: When relying on the same expected distribution it is clear that, if a large number of such tests are performed, about 5% of them will lead to the rejection of a correct hypothesis. Similarly, assuming that the tested hypothesis is false, it is clear that the real value of the parameter may yield a sample value that lies within the acceptable range of variability of the hypothetical one, leading to the acceptance of a false hypothesis. This observation led Neyman to the development of methods designed to determine the low probability we ought to accept as a good reason for rejecting an estimated parameter (e.g., 1% or 5%) according to the type of error we wish to prevent.

According to Fisher, Neyman confused two facts with his concept of confidence limits. First, the concept of probability involved in his two types of error expresses the fact that neither the rejection nor the acceptance of a hypothesis is irreversible, and, by applying tests of significance, there remains an inevitable degree of uncertainty concerning our *decisions*. This subjective concept, however, does not allow us to make any statement about the parameter in terms of objective probabilities.

Second, when we estimate a parameter, he says, the variability of available data is inherent in the nature of the world. Therefore, the data always present us with variable values of calculated statistics on different occasions. It is, therefore, an inevitable fact that the data lead us to the possible formulation of a series of hypothetical values. But the data do not contradict our knowledge that only one of these values can be true; and the selection among them must be made on statistical grounds. There is no reason to doubt the validity of our method, provided the fiducial limits of an estimated value are based on, and tested by, the available evidence. The logical arguments for the establishment of the limits of the possible variability of an estimated parameter have nothing to do with measuring our confidence in our decisions.

Fisher wanted to point out that although these two concepts, namely confidence limits and fiducial limits, were mathematically similar, this must not be allowed to blur their real difference. In his opinion, the case was similar to the confusion that arose due to the mathematical similarity between a normal curve that reflects real variability, and a normal curve that reflects the distribution of errors. In both cases, it was the blurring of the real difference between the concepts used, that led to incorrect interpretations of the data and to mistaken procedures of research.

THE DESIGN OF EXPERIMENTS—ROTHAMPSTED

Fisher accomplished his most important work in Rothampsted. He founded his new approach to scientific research, which he called *The Theory of Experimentation* (including the design and analysis of experiments); he wrote some of his most important papers on theory of estimation, and also his book *Statistical Methods for Research Workers* (1925/1950a). This book was his most influential work in most diverse fields of study, in making research workers familiar with the application of statistical methods, and in persuading them to adopt a statistical attitude to science. When the book first appeared it received hostile reviews.[10] In particular, statisticians disliked the attention given to small samples because, in their opinion, these were of little theoretical importance. But, as pointed out earlier, Fisher was convinced that the biometry of that time concentrated on large samples for mistaken theoretical reasons, and more important, that this constraint rendered it insufficient for practical research. In his opinion, only an attempt to tackle small sample problems as they occurred in experimentation could lead to accurate solutions for practical problems (Fisher, 1925/1950a, preface).

His adoption of available methods, which were not so common at the time (like Gosset's *t* test), and his correction of others that were common in Rothampsted before his arrival, were motivated by this conviction, and led to the new theory of experimentation previously mentioned.

The readers of this book do not need an exposition of the methods Fisher introduced. It is sufficient to remind ourselves of the main principles that guided him while introducing these methods to agricultural research at Rothampsted, and enabled him and other researchers to generalize these methods for other branches of research. These principles were the following:

1. An experiment itself must furnish an estimate of the nonremovable variability to which the quantities measured are subject.

2. The statistical analysis of the results must be determined by the way in which the experiment was conducted.

3. An experiment that tests the effect of one factor at a time is not better than one that studies many factors simultaneously. On the contrary, the latter may answer questions that the first cannot. For example, it gives the interaction of factors.

All three principles can be clarified by simple examples. First, suppose we have four seed varieties to be compared. It is obvious that if we try them on four plots

---

[10]A review in *Nature* (Dec. 1925) said, "In the present work, the absence of proof goes rather far, and we fear that the readers with little knowledge of the more recent statistical work will find the book as a whole difficult to follow, while those unfamiliar with the terms used in biological research will have trouble with some examples" (quoted from J. Box-Fisher, 1978, p. 482).

```
A    B    C    D
B    C    D    A
D    A    B    C
C    D    A    B
```

FIG. 10.2.   An example of a Latin Square design.

of land and then compare their measured yields, we have no way of telling whether the obtained differences in yield were due to the differences in the quality of the seeds, due to soil variety, or due to any other factor. The solution found in Rothampsted was replication: The field was divided into 16 plots, say, arranged in a Latin Square design, as shown in Fig. 10.2, where each seed variety tested is denoted by a letter. Each variety of seeds appears once and only once in each column and in each row. The measurements to be compared were the average yields of the four varieties.

The experimenters thought that they could prevent the effect of heterogeneity of the soil by avoiding likely coincidence of design with soil composition. For example, the Latin Square in the figure may coincide with a factor of soil variation that appears along and parallel to its diagonal. Hence they tried to choose Latin Squares where letters were dispersed without pattern. Fisher objected to this design of systematic field arrangement because the estimates of variability within each seed variety and between the varieties, as well as the variability due to the irremovable circumstances of experimentation, are based on the assumption that each experiment is a random event. In the example, this means that it is one of all possible Latin Squares of that size—*chosen at random*.[11] He argued that even if by chance such a procedure would lead to a pattern that may increase or decrease the estimates of error, the result of the experiment will be more accurate than otherwise, because in this case an estimate is based on the real distribution of the statistic in question, and it is by the properties of this distribution that its significance is tested. If we consistently choose an arrangement because it seems to be lacking a pattern, we render our methods of analysis incapable of detecting any bias we might introduce. In other words, we are not to confuse intuitive confidence with theoretically based accuracy. The only way we have for estimating the irremovable variability of the soil (or of any other factor that is *not* being tested) is based on the assumption that it reflects chance variation, so accuracy means satisfying the conditions under which this assumption is justified. And these conditions can be satisfied only if the experiment is designed accordingly.

The second principle can be illustrated by his well-known analysis of variance, which in the previous example can test the effect of the four varieties of seed by disentangling it from, and comparing it with, the effects of other sources of variation. All estimates required can be derived from the same experiment if

---

[11]For this purpose, Fisher studied the theory of combinations and found all possible 5 × 5 and 6 × 6 Latin Squares.

its design and analysis are parallel in structure: The analysis is based on the mathematical identity

$$\sum_i \sum_j (x_{ij} - \bar{x})^2 = n \sum_i (\bar{x}_i - \bar{x})^2 + n \sum_j (\bar{x}_j - \bar{x})^2$$

$$+ n \sum_l (\bar{x}_l - \bar{x})^2 + \sum_i \sum_j z_{ij}$$

where

$\bar{x}_i$ = the average of the *i*th row;

$\bar{x}_j$ = the average of the *j*th column;

$\bar{x}_l$ = the average of the *l*th letter (seed variety);

n = the number of rows, columns and letters, and

$z_{ij} = (x_{ij} - \bar{x}) - (\bar{x}_i - \bar{x}) - (\bar{x}_j - \bar{x}) - (\bar{x}_l - \bar{x}) = x_{ij} - \bar{x}_i - \bar{x}_j - \bar{x}_l + 2\bar{x}$

that is, z_{ij} gives "the rest" of the variability after removing the variability due to the factors specified. If the requirement of randomization is satisfied, we may test the *Null Hypothesis* that the variation between seed varieties is as much a variation due to chance as that observed within rows, columns or "the rest": If the Null Hypothesis is correct, each sum of squares on the right-hand side of the identity, divided by the number of its degrees of freedom, gives an estimate of the variation in the field. The *F* test (so called in honor of Fisher), was designed to test these estimates in pairs, so that the Null Hypothesis could be rejected only if the probability of *F* was shown to be too small—the idea being that the small value was due to seed variation being significantly different from the others. Irrespective of the controversies about such tests, the point in this context is the illustration of the principle that the experimental design and the analysis of its results are intrinsically related to each other.

The third principle can be illustrated by a simple case of the method developed according to it—Factorial Design. Suppose we try the effect of nitrogenous (N) and phosphate (P) fertilizers on the yield of a crop. We may use the same design as in the earlier example, where the letters indicate a treatment: N, P, NP (i.e., both) and Control (i.e., none). If we write $\bar{x}_0$ for the average crop of all control plots; $\bar{x}_n$ for the N plots; $\bar{x}_p$ for the P plots, and $\bar{x}_{np}$ for the NP plots, the effect of N can be estimated by the average of $(\bar{x}_n - \bar{x}_0)$ and $(\bar{x}_{np} - \bar{x}_p)$; and the effect of P by the average of $(\bar{x}_p - \bar{x}_0)$ and $(\bar{x}_{np} - \bar{x}_n)$. These are the *main effects*. The effect of N on the response to P can be obtained from $[(\bar{x}_{np} - \bar{x}_n) - (\bar{x}_p - \bar{x}_0)]$; and of P on the response to N from $[(\bar{x}_{np} - \bar{x}_p) - (\bar{x}_n - \bar{x}_0)]$. These are the *interaction effects*.

If we were to test the (main) effect of N alone, the same number of plots would give the same accuracy, and similarly for P. Hence, by testing them together we double the efficiency of the experiment even without considering their mutual (i.e., the interaction) effect. But, of course, the effect of interaction is usually of great interest, and this information cannot be obtained at all when we try the (main) effects of factors one at a time. In Fisher's own words, the point is the following.

> The modifications possible to any complicated apparatus, machine or industrial process, must always be considered as potentially interacting with one another, and must be judged by the probable effects of such interactions. If they have to be tested one at a time this is not because to do so is an ideal procedure but because to test them simultaneously would sometimes be too troublesome or too costly. (Fisher, 1947, p. 89)

However, he added, these constraints do not hold for all experiments. In fact, in a wide class of cases, as the experimental investigation is made more comprehensive, it can be also made more efficient "if by more efficient we mean that more knowledge and a higher degree of precision are obtainable by the same number of observations" (p. 89).

A CONCLUDING REMARK

Most theories that involved the introduction of a new method brought with them a question whether, or to what extent, the method reflects human reasoning. For example, utilitarianism involves the method of measuring the maximization of utility. Various experiments have been designed in order to find out, not only how people can maximize their utility, but also whether they actually do so. And if they do, the question arises whether this reflects a property of natural rationality, or a general acceptance of the invented method. Similarly, with the invention of the theory of games, experiments have been designed to test whether people actually reason in this way, and if they do, whether this reflects a natural "mental calculus" or a cultural phenomenon.

The same questions occur concerning epistemology. Descartes's method of introspection presupposes that human beings possess correct intuitions about validity. And empirical methods of research, which mistrusted this presupposition, could not refrain from assuming that people have correct intuitions about the uniformity of nature, because only in this way could they justify inductive generalizations.

An ultimate reliance on intuitions in epistemology is basically justified by the impossibility to do without them. Although Descartes's method of deducing knowledge about the world from reason alone has been discarded, empirical science could not do without accepting some mathematical or logical principles (in addition to the principle mentioned previously), on purely intuitive grounds.[12] And, then, a common explanation of its acceptance is that it describes human reason. The controversy that remains is whether the intuitive knowledge of such a principle is a natural (innate) property of the human mind, or a deep-rooted (psychological) product of cultural conditioning.

The idea that a natural way of reasoning has been discovered is justified by observing that the claim that a method of reasoning is a cultural product usually involves the assumption that a significant change in such a method is accepted when it is taken to be an improvement on previously accepted methods. At the time of change, people always have reasons for considering an innovation to be an improvement, and this consideration justifies their acceptance of the change. For a later observer, the process is an explanation of a historical event. It follows that if some universal principles are discovered, which are accepted by everybody without ever having had such a justification, these must be taken to be a natural basis of reasoning.

However, although some principles of reason had to remain without justification, the development of empirical science went hand in hand with the development of methods that emphasized the aspect of improving knowledge and minimizing the reliance on (unjustified) intuitions. And most important, epistemology separated the task of finding better (valid) methods for achieving such knowledge, and a psychological theory of the mind. In my opinion, we should read Fisher today with this approach in mind.

Fisher claimed that it was a historical accident that deduction has been considered more respectable than induction. However, if methodological changes are to be improvements, there must be a criterion for deciding what is an improvement. Concerning deduction there has never been any doubt: The criterion is *preservation of truth*. In contrast, because its purpose is the *establishment of truth*, the problem of induction is that it is necessarily an ad hoc method. Pragmatists pointed out that this is so because its only criterion of acceptability is success, and according to them, success means increased adaptation to the ever-changing circumstances of human life. Their argument, then, involves the idea that induction is the natural way by which we acquire the knowledge needed for this adaptation. In other words, induction describes the acquisition of knowledge.

Of course, pragmatists were aware of the fact that this description did not solve Hume's problem. On the contrary, the ad hoc nature of all knowledge only increased the suspicion that what we take to be objective knowledge may not be more than well-argued beliefs. Peirce found a way out of this suspicion by

---

[12]For example, if Modus Ponens (i.e., if A is true and A implies B then B must be true) appears in a theory of logic as an axiom, this means that it cannot be justified by other principles.

postulating that human beings have an instinct to guess true hypotheses.[13] The reluctance to accept this new version of reliance on innate intuitions, led to the conclusion that generalizations are accepted on the basis of intersubjective agreement. Unfortunately, this conclusion brought back the confusion between justification and a theory of mind, only in a different form.

This is not the place to discuss these ideas. I only want to point out that what is called the Bayesian approach,[14] reflects this new development. It seems to have a double purpose: to assess how people in fact accept their beliefs, and how they can correct them. In their opinion, the main attraction of Bayes' theorem lies in the fact that, except in the extreme cases where $P(H_i) = 0$ or $P(H_i) = 1$, people who start with very different prior probabilities end up with similar estimates when exposed to the same evidence. This explains the emergence of intersubjectivity (compare with the already discussed attraction of the theorem for solving the problem of induction). Hence, it is not necessary to require knowledge of prior probabilities.

According to Bayesians, these facts, including the exceptions mentioned, are confirmed by our experience. In other words, the method describes our natural way of reasoning. It provides a (psychological) explanation of the possibility of (public) science. The question remains whether the theorem provides also an improved methodology. The same reluctance of empirical science throughout history to rely on feelings of certainty is justified also in this case. First consider that intersubjectivity can be reached also when people in a particular group are exposed to false evidence, provided it is the same for all of them. In other words, if the application of the theorem describes our methods of reasoning, it need not necessarily improve it. At best it describes how people are conditioned to believe a hypothesis by being exposed to what is taken to be evidence. This possibility may be taken to be the reason why Fisher thought that, because the purpose of science is to improve knowledge, Bayes' theorem ought to be used only in cases where an a posteriori probability can be shown to be an improvement on an a priori one. In other words, only when we have reasons for assigning a priori probabilities, and when we can see that the theorem in fact yields an improvement. At least we ought to learn from him that the fact that similar mathematical tools, like Bayes' theorem, can be used for this purpose as well as for explaining intersubjectivity should not lead us to the confusion of the purpose and the premises of these different research projects.

---

[13]In Peirce's opinion (see Buchler, 1955, p. 215), only the postulation of such an instinct could justify the idea that true knowledge was destined to be accepted by all people who used their reason for acquiring it, and hence the acquisition of true knowledge was not dependent on accidental circumstances of life (p. 264). See also pp. 126–128 for his views on induction.

[14]See Vol. 2, chap. 7, in this book, and Salmon (1966, pp. 79–83).

ACKNOWLEDGMENT

This is a revised version of an article, "Ronald A. Fisher: wiskundige, statisticus en eugeneticus" which appeared in Dutch in *Intermediair*, 18 June 1982, authored by Nancy Brenner-Golomb and Ireneus Spit.

REFERENCES

Allen, G. (1978). *Life Science in the Twentieth Century*, Cambridge: Cambridge University Press.

Bartlett, M. S. (1968). R. A. Fisher, in the *International encyclopedia of the social sciences*, New York: MacMillan.

Bennett, J. H. Ed. (1974). *Collected papers of R. A. Fisher*, Adelaide, Australia: University of Adelaide.

Box-Fisher, J. (1978). *R. A. Fisher, the life of a scientist*, New York: Wiley.

Buchler, J. (1955). Philosophical writings of Peirce. New York: Publications, Inc.

Fisher, R. A. (1932). *The Social Selection of Human Fertility*, Oxford: Clarendon Press.

Fisher, R. A. (1934). Indeterminism and natural selection. *Philosophy of Science, 1*, 99–117.

Fisher, R. A. (1947). *The Design of Experiments*, Edinborough, London: Oliver and Boyd. (Original work published 1935).

Fisher, R. A. (1950a). *Statistical Methods for Research Workers*, Edinborough, London: Oliver and Boyd. (Original work published 1925)

Fisher, R. A. (1950b). *Contributions to Mathematical Statistics*, New York: Wiley.

Fisher, R. A. (1958). *The Genetical Theory of Natural Selection*, New York: Dover. (Original work published 1930)

Gigerenzer, G., Swijtink, Z., Porter, T., Daston, L., Beatty, J., & Krüger, L. (1989). *The Empire of Chance*, Cambridge: Cambridge University Press.

Rucci, A. J., and Tweney, R. D. (1980). Analysis of variance and the "second discipline" of scientific psychology: A historical account. *Psychological Bulletin, 87* (1), 166–184.

Salmon, W. C. (1966). *The Foundations of Scientific Inference*. Pittsburgh: University of Pittsburgh Press.

INTUITIVE STATISTICS

As mentioned in the introduction to the previous section, we adopt a broad definition of methodology including the epistemological facet. A fundamental question in this regard concerns our ability to assess and evaluate our methodological knowledge. Any scientific inquiry is undoubtedly dependent, among other things, on insights and intuitions. But how good are our intuitions? Can we properly assess them and identify when they are wrong?

During the last two decades a growing body of research has been accumulated on the topic of intuitive statistics. Apparently, as is indicated by this research we are not always as good intuitive statisticians as we would like to believe. The present section contains a sample (hopefully representative) of studies that document some pervasive flaws in intuitive statistical reasoning. A first step in providing an eventual remedy is to identify potential deficiencies of our intuitive reasoning, which is the main purpose of the present section.

The section starts with an overview written by Gigerenzer (chapter 11), of how statistical methodology was introduced into psychology. He points to some erroneous beliefs and misunderstandings that have been prevalent for years without being questioned.

Chapter 12 is a reprint of a paper by Tversky and Kahneman, in which they first pointed out the insensitivity (even of trained psychologists) to the role of sample size. Evidently, the normative law of large numbers is transformed to the law of small numbers when peoples' intuitions are involved.

Paul Meehl was one of the first researchers to point out the existence of overconfidence in our intuitive statistical capabilities, specifically in making predictions. In his seminal book published in 1954, Meehl presented evidence showing that simple linear combinations of cues (predictors) outperform the predictions of experts. The publication of the book has led to a longlasting debate, among other things because it demonstrated that experts have overstated their abilities. Chapter 13, by Dawes, Faust, and Meehl, is a summary of the current state of the art on the clinical vs. statistical prediction controversy.

Another notorious and pervasive characteristic of intuitive reasoning concerns the misunderstanding of randomness. The failure to comprehend the meaning of randomness is widespread and exhibits itself under different circumstances, the most well-known of which is the gambler's fallacy. Chapter 14 (did the number of this chapter occur randomly?), by Bar-Hillel and Wagenaar, offers an extensive review of the research conducted on the perception (and misperception) of randomness. It portrays the biases associated with the judgment of randomness and the possible underlying mechanisms that lead to these biases.

Randomness is a property of the generating process rather than the outcome. Consequently, there is no absolute way to determine if a sequence is random unless the process by which it was generated is known. Nonetheless, statistical methods exist that enable one to determine the likelihood that a sequence was formed by a random generator, and these are described in chapter 15, by Pashley.

11

The Superego, the Ego, and the Id in Statistical Reasoning

Gerd Gigerenzer
University of Chicago

Piaget worked out his logical theory of cognitive development, Köhler the Gestalt laws of perception, Pavlov the principles of classical conditioning, Skinner those of operant conditioning, and Bartlett his theory of remembering and schemata—all without rejecting null hypotheses. But, by the time I took my first course in psychology at the University of Munich in 1969, null hypothesis tests were presented as *the* indispensable tool, as the sine qua non of scientific research. Post–World War 2 German psychology mimicked a revolution of research practice that had occurred between 1940 and 1955 in American psychology.

What I learned in my courses and textbooks about the logic of scientific inference was not without a touch of morality, a scientific version of the 10 commandments: Thou shalt not draw inferences from a nonsignificant result. Thou shalt always specify the level of significance before the experiment; those who specify it afterward (by rounding up obtained *p* values) are cheating. Thou shalt always design thy experiments so that thou canst perform significance testing.

THE INFERENCE REVOLUTION

What happened between the time of Piaget, Köhler, Pavlov, Skinner, and Bartlett and the time I was trained? In Kendall's (1942) words, statisticians "have already overrun every branch of science with a rapidity of conquest rivalled only by Attila, Mohammed, and the Colorado beetle" (p. 69).

What has been termed the *probabilistic revolution in science* (Gigerenzer et al., 1989; Krüger, Daston, & Heidelberger, 1987; Krüger, Gigerenzer, & Morgan, 1987) reveals how profoundly our understanding of nature changed when concepts such as chance and probability were introduced as fundamental theoretical concepts. The work of Mendel in genetics, that of Maxwell and Boltzmann on statistical mechanics, and the quantum mechanics of Schrödinger and Heisenberg that built indeterminism into its very model of nature are key examples of that revolution in thought.

Psychology did not resist the probabilistic revolution, and psychologists in turn actively contributed to the growth of statistics. But psychology is nonetheless a peculiar case. In psychology and in other social sciences, probability and statistics were typically not used to revise the understanding of our *subject matter* from a deterministic to some probabilistic view (as in physics, genetics, or evolutionary biology), but rather to mechanize the *experimenters'* inferences—in particular, their inferences from data to hypothesis. Of course, there have been several attempts to revise our theories as well—for example, to transform Piaget's logical determinism into a more Darwinian view, where variability and irregularity are seen as the motor of evolution rather than as an annoyance (Gruber, 1977; Gruber & Vonèche, 1977), or to transform Skinner's theory into a probabilistic learning theory (Estes, 1959). But the real, enduring transformation came with statistical inference, which became institutionalized and used in a dogmatic and mechanized way. This use of statistical theory contrasts sharply with physics, where statistics and probability are indispensable in theories about nature, whereas mechanized statistical inference such as null hypothesis testing is almost unknown.

So what happened with psychology? David Murray and I described the striking change in research practice and named it the *inference revolution* in psychology (Gigerenzer & Murray, 1987). It happened between approximately 1940 and 1955 in the United States, and led to the institutionalization of one brand of inferential statistics as *the* method of scientific inference in university curricula, textbooks, and the editorials of major journals.[1]

---

[1]The ground for the inference revolution was prepared by a dramatic shift in experimental practice. During the 1920s, 1930s, and 1940s, the established tradition of experimenting with *single* subjects—from Wundt to Pavlov—was replaced in the United States by the *treatment group experiment,* in which group means are compared. For instance, between 1915 and 1950, the percentage of empirical studies reporting only group data in the *American Journal of Psychology* rose from 25% to 80%, and the reporting of only individual data decreased from 70% to 17% (Danziger, 1990). Danziger argued that this shift was in part due to the pressure felt by United States academic psychologists to legitimize their work through showing its practical utility. The Wundtian type of experiment was useless to educational administrators, the largest market for psychological products. The treatment group experiment, however, appeared to fit their needs exactly, for example, by allowing them to compare mean performance in two classrooms that were using different instruction methods. After this change in experimental practice, null hypothesis testing of group means appeared to be tailor-made to the new unit of research, the group aggregate. Consistent with Danziger's argument, the institutionalization of both the treatment group and null hypothesis testing spread from

The figures are telling. Before 1940, null hypothesis testing using analysis of variance or *t* test was practically nonexistent: Rucci and Tweney (1980) found only 17 articles in all from 1934 through 1940. By 1955, more than 80% of the empirical articles in four leading journals used null hypothesis testing (Sterling, 1959). Today, the figure is close to 100%. By the early 1950s, half of the psychology departments in leading U.S. universities had made inferential statistics a graduate program requirement (Rucci & Tweney, 1980). Editors and experimenters began to measure the quality of research by the level of significance obtained. For instance, in 1962, the editor of the *Journal of Experimental Psychology*, A. W. Melton (1962, pp. 553–554), stated his criteria for accepting articles. In brief, if the null hypothesis was rejected at the .05 level but not at the .01 level, there was a "strong reluctance" to publish the results, whereas findings significant at the .01 level deserved a place in the journal. The *Publication Manual of the American Psychological Association* (1974) prescribed how to report the results of significance tests (but did not mention other statistical methods), and used, as Melton did, the label *negative* results synonymously with "not having rejected the null" and the label *positive* results with "having rejected the null."

It is likely that Piaget's, Köhler's, Bartlett's, Pavlov's, and Skinner's experimental work would have been rejected under such editorial policies—these men did not set up null hypotheses and try to refute them. Some of them were actively hostile toward institutionalized statistics. For his part, Skinner (1972) disliked the intimate link Fisher established between statistics and the design of experiments: "What the statistician means by the design of experiments is design which yields the kind of data to which his techniques are applicable" (p. 122). And, "They have taught statistics in lieu of scientific method" (p. 319). Skinner continued to investigate one or a few pigeons under well-controlled conditions, rather than run 20 or more pigeons under necessarily less well-controlled conditions to obtain a precise estimate for the error variance. In fact, the Skinnerians were forced to found a new journal, the *Journal of the Experimental Analysis of Behavior*, in order to publish their kind of experiments (Skinner, 1984, p. 138). Their focus was on experimental control, that is, on minimizing error beforehand, rather than on large samples, that is, on measuring error after the fact.

This is not an isolated case, nor one peculiar to behaviorists. The *Journal of Mathematical Psychology* is another. One of the reasons for launching this new

---

the applied fields to the laboratories (Lovie, 1979). The contrast with Germany is telling. German academic psychologists of the early 20th century had to legitimize their work before a different tribunal, the values of a well-entrenched intellectual elite (Danziger, 1990). In contrast to the United States, the German educational system, run by tradition rather than by experimentation, provided only a limited market for psychologists. No comparable shift in experimental practice happened in German psychology. It was only after World War II that a new generation of German psychologists began to assimilate the methodological imperatives imported from their colleagues in the United States.

journal was again to escape the editors' pressure to perform institutionalized null hypothesis testing.[2] One of its founders, Luce (1988), called the institutionalized practice a "wrongheaded view about what constituted scientific progress" and "mindless hypothesis testing in lieu of doing good research: measuring effects, constructing substantive theories of some depth, and developing probability models and statistical procedures suited to these theories" (p. 582).

Who is to blame for the present state of mindless hypothesis testing? Fisher was blamed by Skinner, as well as by Meehl: "Sir Ronald has befuddled us, mesmerized us, and led us down the primrose path. I believe that the almost universal reliance on merely refuting the null hypothesis . . . is . . . one of the worst things [that] ever happened in the history of psychology" (Meehl, 1978, p. 817).

I share the sentiments expressed by Luce and Meehl. But to blame Fisher, as Meehl and Skinner did, gives us at best a spurious understanding of the inference revolution. Fisher declared that a significance test of a null hypothesis is only a "weak" argument. That is, it is applicable only in those cases where we have very little knowledge or none at all. For Fisher, significance testing was the most primitive type of argument in a hierarchy of possible statistical analyses (see Gigerenzer et al., 1989, chap. 3). In this chapter I argue the following points:

1. What has become institutionalized as *inferential statistics* in psychology is not Fisherian statistics. It is an incoherent mishmash of some of Fisher's ideas on one hand, and some of the ideas of Neyman and E. S. Pearson on the other. I refer to this blend as the "hybrid logic" of statistical inference. Fisher, Neyman, and Pearson would all have rejected it, although for different reasons.

2. The institutionalized hybrid carries the message that *statistics is statistics is statistics,* that is, that statistics is a single integrated structure that speaks with a single authoritative voice. This entails the claim that the problem of inductive inference in fact *has* an algorithmic answer (i.e., the hybrid logic) that works for all contents and contexts. Both claims are wrong, and it is time to go beyond this institutionalized illusion. We must write new textbooks and change editorial practices. Students and researchers should be exposed to different approaches (not one) to inductive inference, and be trained to use these in a constructive (not mechanical) way. A free market of several good ideas is better than a state monopoly for a single confused idea.

3. Statistical tools tend to turn into theories of mind. We can find the dogma "statistics is statistics is statistics" reappearing in one of the most interesting research areas in cognitive psychology: intuitive statistics and judgments under uncertainty. One statistical theory is confused with rational inductive inference per se.

---

[2]R. Duncan Luce, personal communication, April 4, 1990. See also Luce's (1989) autobiography, on p. 270 and pp. 281–282.

THE "PARENTS" AND THEIR CONFLICTS

In order to understand the structure of the hybrid logic that has been taught in psychology for some 40 years, I briefly sketch those ideas of Fisher, on the one hand, and Neyman and Pearson on the other, that are relevant to understanding the hybrid structure of the logic of inference.

Fisher's first book, *Statistical Methods for Research Workers,* published in 1925, was successful in introducing biologists and agronomists to the new techniques. It had the agricultural smell of issues like the weight of pigs and the effect of manure, and, such alien topics aside, it was technically far too difficult to be understood by most psychologists.

Fisher's second statistical book, *The Design of Experiments,* first published in 1935, was most influential on psychology. At the very beginning of this book, Fisher rejected the theory of inverse probability (Bayesian theory) and congratulated the Reverend Bayes for having been so critical of his own theory as to withhold it from publication (Bayes' treatise was published posthumously in 1763). Bayes' theorem is attractive for researchers because it allows one to calculate the probability $p(H/D)$ of a hypothesis H given some data D, also known as *inverse probability.* A frequentist theory, such as Fisher's null hypothesis testing or Neyman–Pearson theory, however, does not. It deals with the probabilities $p(D/H)$ of some data D given a hypothesis H, such as the level of significance.

Fisher was not satisfied with an approach to inductive inference based on Bayes' theorem. The use of Bayes' theorem presupposes that a prior probability distribution over the set of possible hypotheses is available. For a frequentist, such as Fisher, this prior distribution must theoretically be verifiable by actual frequencies, that is, by sampling from its reference set. These cases are rare. But if we are ignorant and have no a priori distributional information, then every researcher can express that ignorance in different numbers leading, for Fisher, to an unacceptable subjectivism. As we shall see, however, Fisher wanted to both reject the Bayesian cake and eat it, too.

Fisher proposed several alternative tools for inductive inference. In *The Design of Experiments,* he started with *null hypothesis testing,* also known as *significance testing,* and he gave that tool the most space in his book. It eventually became the backbone of institutionalized statistics in psychology. In a test of significance, one confronts a null hypothesis with observations, to find out whether the observations deviate far enough from the null hypothesis to conclude that the null is implausible. The specific techniques of null hypothesis testing, such as the t test (devised by Gossett, using the pseudonym "Student", in 1908) or the F test (F for Fisher, e.g., in analysis of variance) are so widely used that they may be the lowest common denominator of what psychologists today do and know.

The topic of this chapter is the *logic* of inference rather than specific techniques. Just as with Bayes' theorem, the problems we encounter do not concern the formula—the theorem is a simple consequence of the definition of conditional probability. The problems arise with its application to inductive inference in science. To what aspect of inductive inference does a particular algorithm, or technique, refer? What do the calculations mean? These are questions that pertain to what I call the *logic* of inference.

Concerning my account of Fisher's logic of significance testing, one thing must be said in advance: Fisher's writings and polemics had a remarkably elusive quality, and people have read his work quite differently. During Fisher's long and acrimonious controversy with Neyman and Pearson, which lasted from the 1930s to his death in 1962, he changed, and sometimes even reversed, parts of his logic of inference. Thus, the following brief account of Fisher's logic of inference represents one possible reading (for a more detailed analysis, see Gigerenzer et al., 1989, chap. 3).

How Do We Determine the Level of Significance?

In the *Design,* Fisher suggested that we think of the level of significance as a *convention:* "It is usual and convenient for experimenters to take 5 per cent as a standard level of significance, in the sense that they are prepared to ignore all results which fail to reach this standard" (1935/1951, p. 13). Fisher's assertion that 5% (in some cases, 1%) is a *convention* that is adopted by all experimenters and in all experiments, and nonsignificant results are to be ignored, became part of the institutionalized hybrid logic.

But Fisher had second thoughts, which he stated most clearly in the mid-1950s. These did not become part of the hybrid logic. One of the reasons for that revision was his controversy with Neyman and Pearson, and Neyman's (e.g., 1950) insistence that one has to specify the level of significance (which is denoted as α in Neyman–Pearson theory) *before* the experiment, in order to be able to interpret it as a long-run frequency of error. Neyman and Pearson took the frequentist position more seriously than Fisher. They argued that the meaning of a level of significance such as 5% is the following: If the null hypothesis is correct, and the experiment is repeated many times, then the experimenter will wrongly reject the null in 5% of the cases. To reject the null if it is correct is called an *error of the first kind* (Type I error) in Neyman–Pearson theory, and its probability is called *alpha* (α). In his last book, *Statistical Methods and Scientific Inference* (1956), Fisher ridiculed this definition as "absurdly academic, for in fact no scientific worker has a fixed level of significance at which from year to year, and in all circumstances, he rejects hypotheses; he rather gives his mind to each particular case in the light of his evidence and his ideas" (p. 42). Fisher rejected the Neyman–Pearson logic of repeated experiments (repeated random sampling from the same population), and thereby rejected his earlier proposal to have a conventional standard level of significance, such as .05 or .01. What researchers should do, according to Fisher's second thoughts, is to publish the *exact level of significance*, say, $p = .03$ (not $p < .05$), and communicate this result to their fellow research workers. This means that the level of significance is determined *after* the experiment, not, as Neyman and Pearson proposed, *before* the experiment.

Thus the phrase "level of significance" has three meanings: (a) the *standard level of significance*, a conventional standard for all researchers (early Fisher), (b) the *exact level of significance*, a communication to research fellows, determined after the experiment (late Fisher), and (c) the *alpha level, the relative frequency of Type I errors in the long run*, to be decided on using cost-benefit considerations *before* the experiment (Neyman & Pearson). The basic difference is this: For Fisher, the exact level of significance is a property of the data (i.e., a relation between a body of data and a theory); for Neyman and Pearson, alpha is a property of the test, not of the data. Level of significance and alpha are not the same thing.

Neyman and Pearson thought their straightforward long-run frequentist interpretation of the significance test—and the associated concepts of power and of stating two statistical hypotheses (rather than only one, the null)—would be an improvement on Fisher's theory and make it more consistent. Fisher disagreed. Whereas Neyman and Pearson thought of mathematical and conceptual consistency, Fisher thought of ideological differences. He accused Neyman, Pearson, and their followers of confusing technology with knowledge: Their focus on Type I and Type II errors, on cost-benefit considerations that determine the balance between the two, and on repeated sampling from the same population has little to do with scientific practice, but it is characteristic for quality control and acceptance procedures in manufacturing. Fisher (1955, p. 70) compared the Neyman-Pearsonians to the Soviets, their 5-year plans, and their ideal that "pure science can and should be geared to technological performance." He also compared them to Americans, who confuse the process of gaining knowledge with speeding up production or saving money. (Incidentally, Neyman was born in Russia, and went to Berkeley, CA, after Fisher made it difficult for him to stay on at University College in London).

What Does a Significant Result Mean?

The basic differences are these: Fisher attached an epistemic interpretation to a significant result, which referred to a particular experiment. Neyman rejected this view as inconsistent and attached a behavioral meaning to a significant result that did not refer to a particular experiment, but to repeated experiments. (Pearson found himself somewhere in between.)

In the *Design*, Fisher talked about how "to disprove" a null hypothesis (e.g., pp. 16–17). Whatever the words he used, he always held that a significant result affects our confidence or degree of belief that the null hypothesis is false. This is what I refer to as an *epistemic interpretation:* Significance tells us about the truth or falsehood of a particular hypothesis in a particular experiment. Here we see very clearly Fisher's quasi-Bayesian view that the exact level of significance somehow measures the confidence we should have that the null hypothesis is false. But from a more consistent frequentist viewpoint, as expressed by Neyman, a level of significance does not tell us anything about the truth of a particular hypothesis; it states the relative frequency of Type I errors in the long run.

Neyman (1957) called his frequentist interpretation *behavioristic:* To accept or reject a hypothesis is a decision to take a particular action. Imagine a typical application of Neyman–Pearson theory: quality control. Imagine you have chosen the probability of Type I errors (false alarms) to be .10 and that of Type II errors (misses) to be .01, because misses are much more costly to your firm than false alarms. Every day you take a random sample from the firm's production. Even if the production is normal, you will expect a significant result (false alarm) in 10% of all days. Therefore, if a significant result occurs, you will act as if the null hypothesis were false, that is, stop the production and check for a malfunction; but you will not necessarily believe that it is false—because you expect a lot of false alarms in the long run.

Fisher rejected Neyman's arguments for "inductive behavior" as "childish" (1955, p. 75), stemming from "mathematicians without personal contact with the Natural Sciences" (p. 69). And he maintained his epistemic view: "From a test of significance . . . we have a genuine measure of the confidence with which any particular opinion may be held, in view of our particular data" (p. 74). For all his anti-Bayesian talk, Fisher adopted a very similar-sounding line of argument (Johnstone, 1987).

Does "Significant" Imply that There Is a Causal Effect?

Of course not. It is useful to distinguish between the *statistical* null hypothesis and the *substantive* null hypothesis.[3] Only the latter refers to the absence of a particular cause. What is rejected in significance testing is the statistical hypothesis, not the existence or absence of a cause. But in Fisher's writings we can read both "yes" and "no" as answers to the aforementioned question. Sometimes Fisher formulated the null hypothesis as "the treatment has no effect, period," whereas in other places he formulated it as a statistical null hypothesis (see Gigerenzer et al., 1989, pp. 95–97). In the famous Tea-Tasting Experiment in the *Design,* for instance, he stated clearly that we cannot conclude from a significant result (disproving the null) that the opposite hypothesis (which is not formulated

---

[3]On the distinction between statistical and substantive hypotheses, see Hager and Westermann (1983) and Meehl (1978).

as an exact statistical hypothesis in null hypothesis testing) is proven. (This experiment was designed to test a lady's claim that she could tell whether the milk or the tea infusion was first added to a cup.) That is, we cannot infer the existence of a causal process from a significant result—here, that the lady can discriminate between whether the milk or the tea infusion was first added to the cup. For instance, there exist other causal mechanisms (someone told the lady in which cups the tea infusion had been poured first) that are consistent with rejecting the null hypothesis.

What Does a Nonsignificant Result Mean?

In the *Design*, Fisher proposed asymmetry: A null hypothesis can be disproved, but "never proved or established" (p. 16), so "experimenters . . . are prepared to ignore all [nonsignificant] results" (p. 13). This has been understood by many textbook writers as saying that no conclusions can be drawn from a nonsignificant result. And several textbook authors laid down the commandment that I was taught "Thou shalt not draw inferences from a nonsignificant result." This made nonsignificance appear a negative, worthless, and disappointing result. In Neyman–Pearson theory, in contrast, there is symmetry, and a conclusion is drawn from nonsignificance: Act as if the null hypothesis were true. The reason is that Neyman and Pearson start with a disjunction of two symmetric hypotheses (either H_0 or H_1 is true), and proceed by induction through elimination.

Fisher (1955) again had second thoughts: "It is a fallacy . . . to conclude from a test of significance that the null hypothesis is thereby established; at most it may be said to be confirmed or strengthened" (p. 73). Thus, although nonsignificant results cannot establish null hypotheses, according to his second thoughts, we can do more than just "ignore" them: We may say that a nonsignificant result "confirms," but does not "establish," the null hypothesis. Now Fisher suggested that a nonsignificant result might indeed support the null hypothesis, but he did not explain how.

Power

In null hypothesis testing, only one kind of error is defined: rejecting the null hypothesis when it is in fact true. In their attempt to supply a logical basis for Fisher's ideas and make them consistent (see Gigerenzer et al., 1989, pp. 98–106), Neyman and Pearson replaced Fisher's single null hypothesis by a *set* of rival hypotheses. In the simplest case, two hypotheses, H_0 and H_1, are specified, and it is assumed that one of them is true. This assumption allows us to determine the probability of both Type I errors and Type II errors, indicated in Neyman–Pearson theory by α and β respectively. If H_1 is rejected although H_1 is true, a Type II error has occurred. α is also called the *size* of a test, and $1 - \beta$ is called its *power*. The power of a test is the long-run frequency of accepting H_1, if it is true. The concept of power makes explicit what Fisher referred to as "sensitivity."

In the *Design,* Fisher pointed out two ways to make an experiment more sensitive: by enlarging the number of repetitions, and by qualitative methods, such as experimental refinements that minimize the error in the measurements (pp. 21–25). Nevertheless, he rejected the concept of Type II error and calculations of power on the grounds that they are inappropriate for scientific induction. In his view, calculations of power, although they look harmless, reflect the "mental confusion" between technology and scientific inference (Fisher, 1955, p. 73). If someone designs a test for acceptance procedures in *quality control,* where the goal is to minimize costs due to decision errors, calculations of power based on cost-benefit considerations in situations of repetitive tests are quite appropriate. But *scientific inference* and discovery, in Fisher's view, are about gaining knowledge, not saving money.

Fisher always rejected the concept of *power.* Neyman, for his part, pointed out that some of Fisher's tests "are in a mathematical sense 'worse than useless,'" because their power is less than their size (see Hacking, 1965, p. 99). Even in the Tea Tasting Experiment, used by Fisher to introduce the logic of null hypothesis testing in the *Design,* the power is only a little higher than the level of significance (.05), or cannot be calculated at all, depending on the conditions (see Neyman, 1950).

Random Sampling from Known Populations?

Acceptance procedures involve random sampling from a known population (say, a firm's daily production). They also allow for repeated random sampling (every day a random sample may be taken). Recall that Neyman and Pearson based their theory on the concept of repeated random sampling, which defined the probability of Type I and Type II errors as long-run frequencies of wrong decisions in repeated experiments.

Fisher, in contrast, held that in scientific applications there is no known population from which repeated sampling can be done. There are always many populations to which a sample may belong. "The phrase 'repeated sampling from the same population' does not enable us to determine which population is to be used to define the probability level, for no one of them has objective reality, all being products of the statistician's imagination" (Fisher, 1955, p. 71). Fisher proposed to view any sample (such as the sample of subjects in a typical psychological experiment, which is not drawn randomly from a known population) as a random sample from an *unknown hypothetical infinite population.* "The postulate of randomness thus resolves into the question, 'Of what population is this a random sample?' which must frequently be asked by every practical statistician" (Fisher, 1922, p. 313). But how can the practical statistician find out? The concept of an unknown hypothetical infinite population has puzzled many: "This is, to me at all events, a most baffling conception" (Kendall, 1943, p. 17).

Mechanical Scientific Inference

One reading of the *Design* is that null hypothesis testing is a fairly mechanical procedure: Set up a null hypothesis, use a conventional level of significance, calculate a test statistic, and disprove the null hypothesis, if you can. Fisher later made clear that he did not mean it to be so. For instance, he pointed out that the choice of the test statistic, and of deciding which null hypotheses are worth testing, cannot be reduced to a mechanical process. You need constructive imagination and much knowledge based on experience (Fisher, 1933). Statistical inference has two components: informed judgment and mathematical rigor.

Similarly, Neyman and Pearson always emphasized that the *statistical* part has to be supplemented by a *subjective* part. As Pearson (1962) put it: "We left in our mathematical model a gap for the exercise of a more intuitive process of personal judgment in such matters—to use our terminology   as the choice of the most likely class of admissible hypotheses, the appropriate significance level, the magnitude of worthwhile effects and the balance of utilities" (pp. 395–396).

In Neyman and Pearson's theory, once all judgments are made, the decision (reject or accept) falls out mechanically from the mathematics. In his later writings, Fisher opposed these mechanical accept/reject decisions, which he believed to be inadequate in science where one looks forward to further data. Science is concerned with communication of information, such as exact levels of significance. Again, Fisher saw a broader context, the freedom of the Western world. Communication of information (but not mechanical decisions) recognizes "the right of *other* free minds to utilize them in making *their own* decisions" (Fisher, 1955, p. 77).

But Neyman reproached Fisher with the same sin—mechanical statistical inference. As a statistical behaviorist, Neyman (1957) looked at what Fisher actually did in his own research in genetics, biology, and agriculture, rather than at what he said one should do. He found Fisher using .01 as a conventional level of significance, without giving any thought to the choice of a particular level dependent on the particular problem or the probability of an error of the second kind; he accused Fisher of drawing mechanical conclusions, depending on whether or not the result was significant. Neyman urged a thoughtful choice of the level of significance, *not* using .01 for all problems and contexts.

Both camps in the controversy accused the other party of mechanical, thoughtless statistical inference, thus I conclude that here at least they agreed— statistical inference should not be automatic.

These differences between what Fisher proposed as the logic of significance testing and what Neyman and Pearson proposed as the logic of hypothesis testing suffice for the purpose of this chapter. Both have developed further tools for inductive inference, and so did others, resulting in a large toolbox that contains maximum likelihood, fiducial probability, confidence interval approaches, point estimation, Bayesian statistics, sequential analysis, and exploratory data analysis, to mention only a few. But it is null hypothesis testing and Neyman–Pearson hypothesis-testing theory that have transformed experimental psychology and part of the social sciences.

THE OFFSPRING: HYBRID LOGIC

The conflicting views presented earlier are those of the parents of the hybrid logic. Not everyone can tolerate unresolved conflicts easily and engage in a free market of competing ideas. Some long for the single truth or search for a compromise that could at least repress the conflicts. Kendall (1949) commented on the desire for peace negotiations among statisticians:

> If some people asserted that the earth rotated from east to west and others that it rotated from west to east, there would always be a few well-meaning citizens to suggest that perhaps there was something to be said for both sides, and maybe it did a little of one and a little of the other; or that the truth probably lay between the extremes and perhaps it did not rotate at all. (p. 115)

The denial of the existing conflicts and the pretense that there is only one statistical solution to inductive inference were carried to an extreme in psychology and several neighboring sciences. This one solution was the *hybrid logic of scientific inference,* the offspring of the shotgun marriage between Fisher and Neyman and Pearson. The hybrid logic became institutionalized in experimental psychology (see Gigerenzer, 1987), personality research (see Schwartz & Dangleish, 1982), clinical psychology and psychiatry (see Meehl, 1978), education (see Carver, 1978), quantitative sociology (see Morrison & Henkel, 1970), and archaeology (see Cowgill, 1977; Thomas, 1978), among others. Nothing like this happened in physics, chemistry, or molecular biology (see Gigerenzer et al., 1989).

The Hybrid Logic Is Born

Before World War 2, psychologists drew their inferences about the validity of hypotheses by many means—ranging from eyeballing to critical ratios. The issue of statistical inference was not of primary importance. Note that this was not because techniques were not yet available. On the contrary; already in 1710, John Arbuthnot proved the existence of God by a kind of significance test, astronomers had used them during the 19th century for rejecting outliers (Swijtink, 1987), and Fechner (1897) wrote a book on statistics including inference techniques—to give just a few examples. Techniques of statistical inference were known and sometimes used, but experimental method was not yet dominated by and almost equated with statistical inference.

Through the work of the statisticians Snedecor at Iowa State College, Hotelling at Columbia University, and Johnson at the University of Minnesota, Fisher's ideas spread in the United States. Psychologists began to cleanse the Fisherian message of its agricultural smell and its mathematical complexity, and to write a new genre of textbooks featuring null hypothesis testing. Guilford's *Fundamental Statistics in Psychology and Education,* first published in 1942, was probably the most widely read textbook in the 1940s and 1950s. In the preface, Guilford credited Fisher for the new logic of hypothesis testing taught in a chapter that was "quite new to this type of text" (p. viii). The book does not mention Neyman, E. S. Pearson, or Bayes. What Guilford teaches as the logic of hypothesis testing is Fisher's null hypothesis testing, deeply colored by "Bayesian" terms: Null hypothesis testing is about the probability that the null hypothesis is true. "If the result comes out one way, the hypothesis is probably correct, if it comes out another way, the hypothesis is probably wrong" (p. 156). Null hypothesis testing is said to give degrees of doubt such as "probable" or "very likely" a "more exact meaning" (p. 156). Its logic is explained via headings such as "Probability of hypotheses estimated from the normal curve" (p. 160).

Guilford's logic is not consistently Fisherian, nor does it consistently use "Bayesian" language of probabilities of hypotheses. It wavers back and forth and beyond. Phrases like "we obtained directly the probabilities that the null hypothesis was plausible" and "the probability of extreme deviations from chance" are used interchangeably for the same thing: the level of significance. And when he proposed his own "somewhat new terms," his intuitive Bayesian thinking becomes crystal clear. A p value of .015 for a hypothesis of zero difference in the population "gives us the probability that the true difference is a negative one, and the remainder of the area *below* the point, or .985, gives us the probability that the true difference is positive. The odds are therefore .985 to .015 that the true difference is positive" (p. 166). In Guilford's hands, p values that specify probabilities $p(D/H)$ of some data (or test statistic) D given a hypothesis H turn miraculously into Bayesian posterior probabilities $p(H/D)$ of a hypothesis given data.

Guilford's logic is not an exception. It marks the beginning of a genre of statistical texts that vacillate between the researcher's "Bayesian" desire for probabilities of hypotheses and what Fisher is willing to give them.

This first phase of teaching Fisher's logic soon ran into a serious complication. In the 1950s and 1960s, the theory of Neyman and E. S. Pearson also became known. How were the textbook writers to cope with two logics of scientific inference? How should the ideological differences and personal insults be dealt with? Their solution to this conflict was striking. The textbook writers did not side with Fisher. That is, they did not go on to present null hypothesis testing as scientific inference and add a chapter on hypothesis testing outside science, introducing the Neyman–Pearson theory as a logic for quality control and related technological problems. Nor did they side with Neyman and Pearson, teaching their logic as a consistent and improved version of Fisher's and dispensing entirely with Fisherian null hypothesis testing.

Instead, textbook writers started to add Neyman–Pearsonian concepts on top of the skeleton of Fisher's logic. But acting as if they feared Fisher's revenge, they did it without mentioning the names of Neyman and Pearson. A *hybrid logic* of statistical inference was created in the 1950s and 1960s. Neither Fisher nor Neyman and Pearson would have accepted this hybrid as a theory of statistical inference. The hybrid logic is inconsistent from both perspectives and burdened with conceptual confusion. Its two most striking features are (a) it hides its hybrid origin and (b) it is presented as *the* monolithic logic of scientific inference. Silence about its origin means that the respective parts of the logic are not identified as part of two competing and partly inconsistent theoretical frameworks. For instance, the idea of testing null hypotheses without specifying alternative hypotheses is not identified as part of the Fisherian framework, and the definition of the level of significance and the power of a test as long-run frequencies of false and correct decisions, respectively, in repeated experiments is not identified as part of the Neyman–Pearson framework. And, as a consequence, there is no mention of the fact that each of these parts of the hybrid logic were rejected by the other party, and why, and what the unresolved controversial issues are.

The Structure of Hybrid Logic

In order to capture the emotional tensions associated with the hybrid logic, I use a Freudian analogy.[4]

The Neyman–Pearson logic of hypothesis testing functions as the Superego of the hybrid logic. It demands the specification of precise alternative hypotheses, significance levels, and power in advance to calculate the sample size necessary, and it teaches the doctrine of repeated random sampling. The frequentist Superego forbids epistemic statements about particular outcomes or intervals, and it outlaws the interpretation of levels of significance as the degree of confidence that a particular hypothesis is true or false.

The Fisherian theory of significance testing functions as the Ego. The Ego gets things done in the laboratory and gets papers published. The Ego determines the level of significance after the experiment, and it does not specify power nor calculate the sample size necessary. The Ego avoids precise predictions from its

---

[4]Here I am elaborating on a metaphor suggested by Acree (1978). In a different context, Devereux (1967) talked about the relation between anxiety and elimination of subjectivity by method.

research hypothesis; that is, it does not specify the exact predictions of the alternative hypothesis, but claims support for it by rejecting a null hypothesis. The Ego makes abundant epistemic statements about particular results. But it is left with feelings of guilt and shame for having violated the rules.

Censored by both the frequentist Superego and the pragmatic Ego are statements about probabilities of hypotheses given data. These form the Bayesian Id of the hybrid logic. Some direct measure of the validity of the hypotheses under question—quantitatively or qualitatively—is, after all, what researchers really want.

The Freudian metaphor suggests that the resulting conceptual confusion in the minds of researchers, editors, and textbook writers is not due to limited intelligence. The metaphor brings the anxiety and guilt, the compulsive and ritualistic behavior, and the dogmatic blindness associated with the hybrid logic into the foreground. It is as if the raging personal and intellectual conflicts between Fisher and Neyman and Pearson, and between these frequentists and the Bayesians were projected into an "intrapsychic" conflict in the minds of researchers. And the attempts of textbook writers to solve this conflict by denying it have produced remarkable emotional, behavioral, and cognitive distortions.

Anxiety and Guilt

Editors and textbook writers alike have institutionalized the level of significance as a measure of the quality of research. As mentioned earlier, Melton, after 12 years editing one of the most prestigious journals in psychology, said in print that he was reluctant to publish research with significance levels below .05 but above .01, whereas $p < .01$ made him confident that the results would be repeatable and deserved publication (1962, pp. 553–554). In Nunnally's *Introduction to Statistics for Psychology and Education* (1975) the student is taught similar values and informed that the standard has been raised: "Up until 20 years ago, it was not uncommon to see major research reports in which most of the differences were significant only at the 0.05 level. Now, such results are not taken very seriously, and it is more customary today to see results reported only if they reach the 0.01 or even lower probability levels" (p. 195). Not accidentally, both Melton and Nunnally show the same weak understanding of the logic of inference and share the same erroneous belief that the level of significance specifies the probability that a result can be replicated (discussed later). The believers in the divinatory power of the level of significance set the standards.

The researcher's Ego knows that these publish-or-perish standards exist in the outside world, and knows that the best way to adapt is to round up the obtained p value after the experiment to the nearest conventional level, say to round up the value $p = .006$ and publish $p < .01$. But the Superego has higher moral standards: If you set alpha to 5% before the experiment, then you must report the same finding ($p = .006$) as "significant at the 5% level." Mostly, the Ego gets its way, but is left with feelings of dishonesty and of guilt at having violated the rules. Conscientious experimenters have experienced these feelings, and statisticians have taken notice. The following comment was made in a panel discussion among statisticians; Savage remarked on the statisticians' reluctance to take responsibility for once having built up the Superego in the minds of the experimenters:

> I don't imagine that anyone in this room will admit ever having taught that the way to do an experiment is first carefully to record the significance level then do the experiment, see if the significance level is attained, and if so, publish, and otherwise, perish. Yet, at one time we must have taught that; at any rate it has been extremely well learned in some quarters. And there is many a course outside of statistics departments today where the modern statistics of twenty or thirty years ago is taught in that rigid way. People think that's what they're supposed to do and are horribly embarrassed if they do something else, such as do the experiment, see what significance level would have been attained, and let other people know it. They do the better thing out of their good instincts, but think they're sinning. (Barnard, Kiefer, LeCam & Savage, 1968, p. 147)

Statistics has become more tolerant than its offspring, the hybrid logic.

Denial of the Parents

The hybrid logic attempts to solve the conflict between its parents by denying its parents. It is remarkable that textbooks typically teach hybrid logic without mentioning Neyman, E. S. Pearson, and Fisher—except in the context of technical details, such as specific tables, that are incidental to the logic. In 25 out of 30 textbooks I have examined, Neyman and E. S. Pearson do not appear to exist. For instance, in his *Statistical Principles in Experimental Design* (1962; 2nd ed., 1971), Winer credited Fisher for the "logic of scientific method" (p. 3), and a few pages later, introduced the Neyman–Pearson terminology of Type I error, Type II error, power, two precise statistical hypotheses, cost-benefit considerations, and *rejecting* and *accepting* hypotheses. Nowhere in the book do the names of Neyman and E. S. Pearson appear (except in a "thank you" note to Pearson for permission to reproduce tables), although quite a few other names can be found in the index. No hint is given to the reader that there are different ways to think about the logic of inference. Even in the exceptional case of Hays's textbook (1963), where all parents are mentioned by their names, the relationship of their ideas is presented (in a single sentence) as one of cumulative progress, from Fisher to Neyman and Pearson (p. 287).[5] Both Winer's and Hays's are among the best texts, without the confusions that abound in Guilford's, Nunnally's, and a

---

[5]In the 3rd edition (1981), however, Hays's otherwise excellent text falls back to common standards: J. Neyman and E. S. Pearson no longer appear in the book.

mass of other textbooks. Nevertheless, even in these texts the parents' different ways of thinking about statistical inference and the controversial issues are not pointed out.

Denial of Conflicts Between Parents

Thus the conflicting views are almost unknown to psychologists. Textbooks are uniformly silent. (Some statistics teachers protest that airing these disputes would only confuse students. I believe that pointing out the conflicting views would make statistics much more interesting to students who enjoy thinking rather than being told what to do next.) As a result of this silence, many a text muddles through the conflicting issues leaving confusion and inconsistency in its wake—at least, among the more intelligent and alert students. For instance, Type I and Type II errors are often defined in terms of long-run frequencies of erroneous decisions in repeated experiments, but the texts typically stop short of Neyman's behavioral interpretation, and fall back to epistemic interpretations of the two errors as levels of confidence about the validity of the hypotheses. In fact, the poorer texts overflow with amazing linguistic contortions concerning what a level of significance means. For instance, within three pages of text, Nunnally explained that "level of significance" means all of the following: (a) "If the probability is low, the null hypothesis is improbable" (p. 194); (b) "the *improbability* of observed results being due to error" (p. 195); (c) "the probability that an observed difference is real" (p. 195); (d) "the *statistical confidence* . . . with odds of 95 out of 100 that the observed difference will hold up in investigations" (p. 195); (e) the degree to which experimental results are taken "seriously" (p. 195); (f) "the danger of accepting a statistical result as real when it is actually due only to error" (p. 195); (g) the degree of "faith [that] can be placed in the reality of the finding" (p. 196); (h) "the null hypothesis is rejected at the 0.05 level"; and (i) "the investigator can have 95 percent confidence that the sample mean actually differs from the population mean" (p. 196). And, after the last two versions, the author assured his readers: "All of these are different ways to say the same thing" (p. 196).

Nunnally did not spell out the differences between the logics of Fisher, Neyman and Pearson, and the Bayesians. He avoided the conflicting interpretations by declaring that everything is the same. The price for this is conceptual confusion, false assertions, and an illusory belief in the omnipotence of the level of significance. Nunnally was a pronounced but not an atypical case.

Obsessive-Compulsive and Mechanical Behavior

As previously mentioned, statisticians have emphasized the indispensable role of personal judgment, although with respect to different parts of their logics. For Fisher, informed judgment was needed for the choice of the statistical model, the test statistics, and a null hypothesis worth investigating. For Neyman and Pearson, personal judgment was needed for the choice of the class of hypotheses (two hypotheses, in the simplest case), and the cost-benefit considerations that lead to the choice of Type I error, power, and sample size. For Bayesians such as de Finetti, finally, "subjectivism" and "relativism" are the very cornerstones of 20th-century probability theory (de Finetti, 1931/1989; Jeffrey, 1989).

The need for these kinds of informed judgments was rarely a topic in the textbooks. Rather, a mass of researchers must have read the textbooks as demanding the mindless, mechanical setting up of null hypotheses and recording of p values. Journals filled with p values, stars, double stars, and triple stars that allegedly established replicable "facts" bear witness to this cookbook mentality.

Guilford's misunderstanding that to set up a null hypothesis means to postulate a *zero* difference or a *zero* correlation was perpetuated. "Null" denotes the hypothesis to be "nullified," not that it is necessary to postulate a zero effect. Rarely were null hypotheses formulated that postulated something other than a zero effect (such as "the difference between the means is 3 scale points"). Rarely were precise alternative hypotheses stated, and even if there were two competing precise hypotheses, as in Anderson's information integration theory, only one of them was tested as the null hypothesis, sometimes resulting in tests with a power as low as .06 (Gigerenzer & Richter, 1990). Reasons for using a particular level of significance were almost never given, and rarely was a judgment about the desired power made and the sample size calculated. As a result, the power of the tests is typically quite low (below .50 for a medium effect), and pointing this out (Cohen, 1962) has not changed practice. Two-and-a-half decades after Cohen's work, the power of the null hypothesis tests was even slightly worse (Sedlmeier & Gigerenzer, 1989). Rather, null hypotheses are set up and tested in an extremely mechanical way reminiscent of compulsive handwashing. One can feel widespread anxiety surrounding the exercise of informed personal judgment in matters of hypothesis testing. The availability of statistical computer packages seems to have reinforced this mechanical behavior. A student of mine once tested in his thesis the difference between two means, which were numerically exactly the same, by an F test. Just to say that the means are the same seemed to him not objective enough.

The institutionalization of the hybrid logic as the sine qua non of scientific method is the environment that encourages mechanical hypothesis testing. The *Publication Manual of the American Psychological Association,* for instance, called "rejecting the null hypothesis" a "basic" assumption (1974, p. 19) and presupposes the hybrid logic. The researcher was explicitly told to make mechanical decisions: "Caution: Do not infer trends from data that fail by a small margin to meet the usual levels of significance. Such results are best interpreted as caused by chance and are best reported as such. Treat the result section like an income tax return. Take what's coming to you, but no more" (p. 19; this passage was deleted in the 3rd ed., 1983). This prescription sounds like a Neyman–

Pearson accept–reject logic, where it matters for a decision only on which side of the criterion the data fall, not how far. Fisher would have rejected such mechanical behavior (e.g., Fisher, 1955, 1956). Nevertheless, the examples in the manual that tell the experimenter how to report results use p values that were obviously determined *after* the experiment and rounded up to the next conventional level, such as $p < .05$, $p < .01$, and $p < .001$ (pp. 39, 43, 48, 49, 70, 96). Neyman and Pearson would have rejected this practice: These p values are not the probability of Type I errors—and determining levels of significance after the experiment prevents determining power and sample size in advance. Fisher (e.g., 1955, 1956) would have preferred that the exact level of significance, say $p = .03$, be reported, not upper limits, such as $p < .05$, which look like probabilities of Type I errors but aren't.

Distorted Statistical Intuitions

Mechanical null hypothesis testing seems to go hand-in-hand with distorted statistical intuitions. I distinguish distorted statistical intuitions from the confusion and inconsistency of the hybrid logic itself. The latter results from mishmashing Fisher and Neyman and Pearson without making the conflation explicit, as I argued earlier. The conceptual confusion of the hybrid logic provided fertile ground for the growth of what I call *distorted statistical intuitions*. The distortions all seem to go in one direction: They exaggerate what can be inferred from a p value.

The framework of distorted intuitions makes the obsessive performance of null hypothesis testing seem quite reasonable. Therefore, distorted intuitions serve an indispensable function. These illusions guide the writings of several textbook authors and editors, but they seem to be most pronounced in the users of null hypothesis testing, researchers in psychology and neighboring fields. Some distorted intuitions concern the frequentist part of the hybrid logic, others the Bayesian Id. I give one example of each (there is a larger literature on distorted statistical intuitions taught in statistical textbooks and held by experimenters; see Acree, 1978; Bakan, 1966; Brewer, 1985; Carver, 1978; Guttman, 1977, 1985; Lykken, 1968; Pollard & Richardson, 1987; Rozeboom, 1960; Tversky & Kahneman, 1971).

Replication Fallacy. Suppose α is set as .05 and the null hypothesis is rejected in favor of a given alternative hypothesis. What if we replicate the experiment? In what percentage of exact replications will the result again turn out significant? Although this question arises from the frequentist conception of repeated experiments, the answer is unknown. The α we chose does not tell us, nor does the exact level of significance.

The *replication fallacy* is the belief that the level of significance provides an answer to the question. Here are some examples: In an editorial of the *Journal of*

Experimental Psychology, the editor stated that he used the level of significance reported in submitted papers as the measure of the "confidence that the results of the experiment would be repeatable under the conditions described" (Melton, 1962, p. 553). Many textbooks fail to mention that the level of significance does not specify the probability of a replication, and some explicitly teach the replication fallacy. For instance, "The question of statistical significance refers primarily to the extent to which similar results would be expected if an investigation were to be repeated" (Anastasi, 1958, p. 9). Or, "If the statistical significance is at the 0.05 level . . . the investigator can be confident with odds of 95 out of 100 that the observed difference will hold up in future investigations" (Nunnally, 1975, p. 195). Oakes (1986, p. 80) asked 70 university lecturers, research fellows, and postgraduate students with at least 2 years' research experience what a significant result ($t = 2.7$, $df = 18$, $p = .01$) means. Sixty percent of these academic psychologists erroneously believed that these figures mean that if the experiment is repeated many times, a significant result would be obtained 99% of the time.

In Neyman and Pearson's theory the level of significance (alpha) is defined as the relative frequency of rejections of H_0 if H_0 is true. In the minds of many, $1 -$ alpha erroneously turned into the relative frequency of rejections of H_0, that is, into the probability that significant results could be replicated.

The Bayesian Id's Wishful Thinking.   I mentioned earlier that Fisher both rejected the Bayesian cake and wanted to eat it, too: He spoke of the level of significance as a measure of the degree of confidence in a hypothesis. In the minds of many researchers and textbook writers, however, the level of significance virtually turned into a Bayesian posterior probability.

What I call the *Bayesian Id's wishful thinking* is the belief that the level of significance, say .01, is the probability that the null hypothesis is correct, or that $1 - .01$ is the probability that the alternative hypothesis is correct. In various linguistic versions, this wishful thinking was taught in textbooks from the very beginning. Early examples are Anastasi (1958, p. 11), Ferguson (1959, p. 133), Guilford (1942, pp. 156–166), and Lindquist (1940, p. 14). But the belief has persisted over decades of teaching hybrid logic, for instance in Miller and Buckhout (1973, statistical appendix by Brown, p. 523), Nunnally (1975, pp. 194–196), and the examples collected by Bakan (1966) and Pollard and Richardson (1987). Oakes (1986, p. 82) reported that 96% of academic psychologists erroneously believed that the level of significance specifies the probability that the hypothesis under question is true or false.

The Bayesian Id has got its share. Textbook writers have sometimes explicitly taught this misinterpretation, but more often invited it by not specifying the difference between a Bayesian posterior probability, a Neyman–Pearsonian probability of a Type I error, and a Fisherian exact level of significance.

Dogmatism

The institutionalization of *one* way to do hypothesis testing had its benefits. It made the administration of the social science research that exploded since World War 2 easier, and it facilitated editors' decisions. And there were more benefits. It reduced the high art of hypothesis construction, of experimental ingenuity and informed judgment, into a fairly mechanical schema that could be taught, learned, and copied by almost anyone. The informed judgments that remain are of a low-level kind: whether to use a one- or a two-tailed significance test. (But even here some believed that there should be no room for judgment, because even this simple choice seemed to threaten the ideal of mechanical rules and invite cheating.) The final, and perhaps most important, benefit of the hybrid logic is that it provides the satisfying illusion of *objectivity:* The statistical logic of analyzing data seemed to eliminate the subjectivity of eyeballing and wishful distortion. To obtain and maintain this illusion of objectivity and impartiality, the hybrid logic had to deny its parents—and their conflicts.

The danger of subjective distortion and selective reading of data exists, to be sure. But it cannot be cured by replacing the distortions of particular experimenters by a collective distortion. Note that the institutionalized practice produces only selective and limited objectivity, and hands other parts of scientific practice over to rules of thumb—even parts for which the statistical methods would be applicable. For example, during the 19th century, astronomers used significance tests to reject *data* (so-called outliers), assuming, at least provisionally, that their hypothesis was correct (Swijtink, 1987). Social scientists today, in contrast, use significance tests to reject *hypotheses,* assuming that their data are correct. The mathematics does not dictate which one the scientists should trust and which one they should try to refute. Social scientists seem to have read the statistical textbooks as saying that statistical inference is indispensable in selecting good from bad hypotheses, but not for selecting good from bad data. The problem of outliers is dealt with by rules of thumb.[6]

The dogmatism with which the hybrid logic has been imposed on psychology researchers by many textbook writers and editors and by researchers themselves has lasted for almost half a century. This is far too long. We need a knowledgeable use of statistics, not a collective compulsive obsession. The last two decades suggest that things are, although very slowly, changing in the right direction.

---

[6]So is the problem of how many replications (subjects) an experiment should use. Sedlmeier and Gigerenzer (1989) found no use of Neyman–Pearsonian calculations of sample size in published work. Some statistical texts have explicitly encouraged this: "Experienced researchers use a rule of thumb sample size of approximately twenty. Smaller samples often result in low power values while larger samples often result in a waste of time and money" (Bruning & Kintz, 1977, p. 7).

BEYOND DOGMATISM:
TOWARD A THOUGHTFUL USE OF STATISTICS

Here are a few first principles: Do not replace the dogmatism of the hybrid logic of scientific inference by a new, although different one (e.g., Bayesian dogmatism). Remember the obvious: The problem of inductive inference has no universal mathematical solution. Use informed judgment and statistical knowledge. Here are several more specific suggestions:

1. *Stop teaching hybrid logic as the sine qua non of scientific inference.* Teach researchers and students alternative theories of statistical inference, give examples of typical applications and teach the students how to use these theories in a constructive (not mechanical) way. Point out the confused logic of the hybrid, the emotional, behavioral, and cognitive distortions associated with it, and insist on consistency (Cohen, 1990). This will lead to recognizing the second point.

2. *Statistical inference (Fisherian, Neyman–Pearsonian, or Bayesian) is rarely the most important part of data analysis.* Teach researchers and students to look at the data, not just on p values. Computer-aided graphical methods of data display and exploratory data analysis are means toward this end (Diaconis, 1985; Tukey, 1977). The calculation of descriptive statistics such as effect sizes is a part of data analysis that cannot be substituted by statistical inference (Rosnow & Rosenthal, 1989). A good theory predicts particular curves or effect sizes, but not levels of significance.

3. *Good data analysis is pointless without good data.* The measurement error should be controlled and minimized before and during the experiment; instead one tends to control it after the experiment by inserting the error term in the F ratio. Teach researchers and students that the important thing is to have a small real error in the data. Without that, a significant result at any level is, by itself, worthless—as Gosset, who developed the t test in 1908, emphatically emphasized (see Pearson, 1939). Minimizing the real error in measurements may be achieved by an iterative method: First, obtain measurements and look at the error variance, then try methods to minimize the error (e.g., stronger experimental control, investigating each subject carefully in a single-case study rather than in a classroom), then go back and obtain new measurements and look at the new error variance, and so on, until improvements are no longer possible. Axiomatic measurement theory that focuses on ordinal rather than numerical judgments may help (Krantz, Luce, Suppes, & Tversky, 1971). It is all too rarely used.

4. *Good data need good hypotheses and theories to survive.* We need rich theoretical frameworks that allow for specific predictions in the form of precise research hypotheses. The null hypothesis of zero difference (or zero correlation) is only one version of such a hypothesis—perhaps only rarely appropriate. In

particular, it has become a bad habit not to specify the predictions of a research hypothesis, but to specify a different hypothesis (the null) and to try to reject it and claim credit for the unspecified research hypothesis. Teach students to derive competing hypotheses from competing theoretical frameworks, and to test their ordinal or quantitative predictions *directly,* without using the null as a straw man.

EPILOGUE: MORE SUPEREGOS

Around 1840, the classical theory of probability dissolved and the frequentist interpretation of probability emerged (Daston, 1988; Porter, 1986). Today, teaching in statistics departments is still predominantly in the frequentist tradition, and Fisher's and Neyman and Pearson's theories are two variants thereof. But this century has witnessed the revival of subjective probability, often referred to as *Bayesian statistics,* largely through the writings of the Italian actuary de Finetti and the English philosopher Ramsey in the 1920s and 1930s, and in the 1950s by the American statistician Savage. For a Bayesian, probability is about subjective degrees of belief, not about objective frequencies. A degree of belief of $1/10$ that the next president of the United States will be a woman can be interpreted as the willingness to take either side of a nine to one bet on this issue. Bayesians are still a minority in statistics departments, but the Bayesian model of rationality has found a role in theoretical economics (mainly microeconomics), cognitive psychology, artificial intelligence, business, and medicine.

In 1963, Edwards, Lindman, and Savage argued that psychologists should stop frequentist null hypothesis testing and do Bayesian statistics instead (their counterparts in Europe were, among others, Kleiter, 1981; Tholey, 1982). Edwards and his colleagues also started a research program on whether intuitive statistical judgments follow Bayes' theorem. Their suggestion that psychologists should turn Bayesian fell on deaf ears, both in the United States and in Europe. Researchers already had their hybrid logic, which seemed to them the objective way to do scientific inference, whereas Bayesian statistics looked subjective. And given the distorted statistical intuitions of many, there was actually no need; the level of significance already seemed to specify the desired Bayesian posterior probabilities.[7]

The second of Edwards's proposals, in contrast, caught on: To study whether and when statistical intuitions conform to Bayes' theorem (e.g., Edwards, 1968). More than in Edwards's research, the heuristics and biases program of the 1970s and 1980s (e.g., Tversky & Kahneman, 1974) focussed on what were called *fallacies* and *errors* in probabilistic reasoning: *discrepancies* between human judgment and Bayes' formula.

---

[7]I know of only a handful of studies published in psychological journals where researchers used Bayesian statistics instead of the hybrid logic. Even Hays, who included a chapter on Bayesian statistics in the second edition of his statistics text, dropped it in the third edition.

The New Bayesian Superego

The Bayesian Id of the hybrid logic had turned into the new Superego of research on intuitive statistics. Frequentist theories were suppressed. Bayesian statistics (precisely, one narrow version thereof) was seen as *the* correct method of statistical reasoning, whether it was about the subjective probability that a particular person was an engineer (Kahneman & Tversky, 1973) or that a cab involved in a hit-and-run accident at night was blue (Tversky & Kahneman, 1980). However, if one applies Neyman–Pearson theory to the cab problem, or alternative Bayesian views, one obtains solutions that are strikingly different from Tversky and Kahneman's Bayesian calculations (Birnbaum, 1983; Gigerenzer & Murray, 1987, pp. 167–174; Levi, 1983). The objections of Fisher and Neyman to the universal use of Bayesian statistics seemed to be buried below the level of consciousness, and so was the most basic objection of a frequentist: Probability is about frequencies, not about single events (such as whether a particular cab was blue or Linda is a bank teller).

A striking result demonstrates the importance of that objection: So-called fallacies frequently disappear when subjects are asked for frequency judgments rather than for single-event probabilities (Gigerenzer, 1991a, 1991b; Gigerenzer, Hoffrage, & Kleinbölting, 1991). Within the heuristics and biases program, the frequentist Superego of the hybrid logic, who had banned probability statements about particular events or values, was no longer heard. Nor was the frequentist Barnard (1979), who commented thus on subjective probabilities for single events: "If we accept it as important that a person's subjective probability assessments should be made coherent, our reading should concentrate on the works of Freud and perhaps Jung rather than Fisher and Neyman" (p. 171).

Suddenly, the whole psychic structure of statistical reasoning in psychology seemed to be reversed. Now Bayesian statistics (precisely, a narrow version thereof) was presented as the sine qua non of statistical reasoning, as *the* normative standard. Against this standard, all deviating reasoning seemed to be a fallacy. Neyman had warned of "the *dogmatism* which is occasionally apparent in the application of Bayes' formula" (1957, p. 19). He meant the conviction "that it is possible to devise a formula of universal validity which can serve as a normative regulator of our beliefs" (p. 15). Similarly, for Fisher, only some uncertain inferences, but not all kinds, can be adequately dealt with by probability theory. Bayesian theory "is founded upon an error, and must be wholly rejected" (Fisher, 1925, p. 9).

Good statistical reasoning has been once more equated with the mechanical application of some statistical formula.

It seems to have gone almost unnoticed that this dogmatism has created a strange double standard. Many researchers believe that their subjects must use Bayes' theorem to test hypotheses, but the researchers themselves use the hybrid logic to test their hypotheses—and thus themselves ignore base rates. There is the illusion that one kind of statistics normatively defines objectivity in scientific inference, and another one rationality in everyday inference. The price is a kind of "split brain," where Neyman–Pearson logic is the Superego for experimenters' hypothesis testing and Bayesian statistics is the Superego for subjects' hypothesis testing.

CONCLUSIONS

Statistical reasoning is an art and so demands both mathematical knowledge and informed judgment. When it is mechanized, as with the institutionalized hybrid logic, it becomes ritual, not reasoning. Many colleagues of mine have argued that it is not going to be easy to get researchers in psychology and other sociobiomedical sciences to drop this comforting crutch unless one offers an easy-to-use substitute. But this is exactly what I want to avoid—the substitution of one mechanistic dogma for another. It is our duty to inform our students about the many good roads to statistical inference that exist, and to teach them how to use informed judgment to decide which one to follow for a particular problem. At the very least, this chapter can serve as a tool in arguments with people who think they have to defend a ritualistic dogma instead of good statistical reasoning. Making and winning such arguments is indispensable to good science.

ACKNOWLEDGMENTS

This chapter was written while I was a Fellow at the Center for Advanced Study in the Behavioral Sciences, Stanford, CA. I am grateful for financial support provided by the Spencer Foundation and the Deutsche Forschungsgemeinschaft (DFG 170/2-1). Leda Cosmides, Lorraine Daston, Raphael Diepgen, Ward Edwards, Ruma Falk, Gideon Keren, Duncan Luce, Kathleen Much, Zeno Swijtink, and John Tooby helped to improve the present chapter.

REFERENCES

Acree, M. C. (1978). *Theories of statistical inference in psychological research: A historicocritical study.* Ann Arbor, MI: University Microfilms International. (University Microfilms No. H790 H7000)

Anastasi, A. (1958). *Differential psychology* (3rd ed.). New York: Macmillan.

Arbuthnot, J. (1710). An argument for Divine Providence, taken from the constant regularity observ'd in the births of both sexes. *Philosophical Transactions of the Royal Society, 27,* 186–190.

Bakan, D. (1966). The test of significance in psychological research. *Psychological Bulletin, 66,* 423–437.

Barnard, G. A. (1979). Discussion of the paper by Professors Lindley and Tversky and Dr. Brown. *Journal of the Royal Statistical Society* (A), *142,* 171–172.

Barnard, G. A., Kiefer, J. C., LeCam, L. M., & Savage, L. J. (1968). Statistical inference. In D. G. Watts (Ed.), *The future of statistics* (p. 147). New York: Academic Press.

Bayes, T. (1763). An essay towards solving a problem in the doctrine of chances. *Philosophical Transactions of the Royal Society, 53,* 370–418.

Birnbaum, M. H. (1983). Base rates in Bayesian inference: Signal detection analysis of the cab problem. *American Journal of Psychology, 96,* 85–94.

Brewer, J. K. (1985). Behavioral statistics textbooks: Source of myths and misconceptions? *Journal of Educational Statistics, 10,* 252–268.

Bruning, J. L., & Kintz, B. L. (1977). *Computational handbook of statistics* (2nd ed.). Glennview, IL: Scott, Foresman.

Carver, R. P. (1978). The case against statistical significance testing. *Harvard Educational Review, 48,* 378–399.

Cohen, J. (1962). The statistical power of abnormal-social psychological research: A review. *Journal of Abnormal and Social Psychology, 65,* 145–153.

Cohen, J. (1990). Things I have learned (so far). *American Psychologist, 45,* 1304–1312.

Cowgill, G. L. (1977). The trouble with significance tests and what we can do about it. *American Antiquity, 42,* 350–368.

Danziger, K. (1990). *Constructing the subject.* Cambridge: Cambridge University Press.

Daston, L. (1988). *Classical probability in the Enlightenment.* Princeton, NJ: Princeton University Press.

Devereux, G. (1967). *From anxiety to method in the behavioral sciences.* Paris: Mouton.

Diaconis, P. (1985). Theories of data analysis: From magical thinking through classical statistics. In D. C. Hoaglin, F. Mosteller, & J. W. Tukey (Eds.), *Exploring data tables, trends and shapes* (pp. 1–36). New York: Wiley.

Edwards, W. (1968). Conservatism in human information processing. In B. Kleinmuntz (Ed.), *Formal representation of human judgment* (pp. 17–52). New York: Wiley.

Edwards, W., Lindman, H., & Savage, L. J. (1963). Bayesian statistical inference for psychological research. *Psychological Review, 70,* 193–242.

Estes, W. K. (1959). The statistical approach to learning theory. In S. Koch (Ed.), *Psychology: A study of a science* (Vol. 2, pp. 380–491). New York: McGraw-Hill.

Fechner, G. T. (1897). *Kollektivmasslehre* (G. F. Lipps, Ed.). Leipzig: W. Engelmann.

Ferguson, L. (1959). *Statistical analysis in psychology and education.* New York: McGraw-Hill.

Finetti, B. De (1989). Probabilism. *Erkenntnis, 31,* 169–223. (Original work published 1931)

Fisher, R. A. (1922). On the mathematical foundations of theoretical statistics. *Philosophical Transactions of the Royal Society of London,* A, *222,* 309–368.

Fisher, R. A. (1925). *Statistical methods for research workers* (8th ed., 1941). Edinburgh: Oliver & Boyd.

Fisher, R. A. (1933). The contributions of Rothamsted to the development of the science of statistics. *Annual Report of the Rothamsted Station,* 43–50. (Reprinted in *Collected papers,* Vol. 3, 84–91)

Fisher, R. A. (1935). *The design of experiments* (5th ed., 1951; 7th ed., 1960; 8th ed., 1966). Edinburgh: Oliver & Boyd.

Fisher, R. A. (1955). Statistical methods and scientific induction. *Journal of the Royal Statistical Society* (B), *17,* 69–77.

Fisher, R. A. (1956). *Statistical methods and scientific inference.* Edinburgh: Oliver & Boyd.

Gigerenzer, G. (1987). Probabilistic thinking and the fight against subjectivity. In L. Krüger, G. Gigerenzer, & M. S. Morgan (Eds.), *The probabilistic revolution. Vol. 2. Ideas in the sciences* (pp. 11–33). Cambridge, MA: MIT Press.

Gigerenzer, G. (1991a). From tools to theories. A heuristic of discovery in cognitive psychology. *Psychological Review, 98,* 252–267.

Gigerenzer, G. (1991b). How to make cognitive illusions disappear: Beyond "heuristics and biases". *European Review of Social Psychology, 2*, 83–115.

Gigerenzer, G., Hoffrage, U., & Kleinbölting, H. (1991). Probabilistic mental models: A Brunswikian theory of confidence. *Psychological Review, 98*, 506–528.

Gigerenzer, G., & Murray, D. J. (1987). *Cognition as intuitive statistics*. Hillsdale, NJ: Lawrence Erlbaum Associates.

Gigerenzer, G., & Richter, H. R. (1990). Context effects and their interaction with development: Area Judgments. *Cognitive Development, 5*, 235–264.

Gigerenzer, G., Swijtink, Z., Porter, T., Daston, L., Beatty, J., & Krüger, L. (1989). *The empire of chance. How probability changed science and everyday life*. Cambridge: Cambridge University Press.

Gruber, H. E. (1977). The fortunes of a basic Darwinean idea: Chance. In R. W. Rieber & K. Salzinger (Eds.), *The roots of American psychology: Historical influences and implications for the future* (pp. 233–245). New York: New York Academy of Sciences.

Gruber, H. E., & Vonèche, J. J. (Eds.). (1977). *The essential Piaget*. New York: Basic Books.

Guilford, J. P. (1942). *Fundamental Statistics in Psychology and Education* (3rd ed., 1956, 6th ed., 1978, with B. Fruchter). New York: McGraw-Hill.

Guttman, L. (1977). What is not what in statistics. *The Statistician, 26*, 81–107.

Guttman, L. (1985). The illogic of statistical inference for cumulative science. *Applied Stochastic Models and Data Analysis, 1*, 3–10.

Hacking, I. (1965). *Logic of statistical inference*. Cambridge: Cambridge University Press.

Hager, W., & Westermann, R. (1983). Zur Wahl und Prüfung statistischer Hypothesen in psychologischen Untersuchungen. *Zeitschrift fur experimentelle und angewandte Psychologie, 30*, 67–94.

Hays, W. L. (1963). *Statistics for psychologists* (2nd ed.). New York: Holt, Rinehart & Winston.

Jeffrey, R. (1989). Reading Probabilismo. *Erkenntnis, 31*, 225–237.

Johnstone, D. J. (1987). Tests of significance following R. A. Fisher. *British Journal of the Philosophy of Science, 38*, 481–499.

Kahneman, D., & Tversky, A. (1973). On the psychology of prediction. *Psychological Review, 80*, 237–251.

Kendall, M. G. (1942). On the future of statistics. *Journal of the Royal Statistical Society, 105*, 69–80.

Kendall, M. G. (1943). *The advanced theory of statistics* (Vol. 1). New York: Lippincott.

Kendall, M. G. (1949). On the reconciliation of theories of probability. *Biometrika, 36*, 101–116.

Kleiter, G. D. (1981). *Bayes Statistik*. Berlin: De Gruyter.

Krantz, D. H., Luce, R. D., Suppes, P., & Tversky, A. (1971). *Foundations of measurement* (Vol. 1). New York: Academic Press.

Krüger, L., Daston, L., & Heidelberger, M. (Eds.). (1987). *The probabilistic revolution: Vol. 1. Ideas in history*. Cambridge, MA: MIT Press.

Krüger, L., Gigerenzer, G., & Morgan, M. S. (Eds.). (1987). *The probabilistic revolution: Vol. 2. Ideas in the sciences*. Cambridge, MA: MIT Press.

Levi, I. (1983). Who commits the base rate fallacy? *Behavioral and Brain Sciences, 6*, 502–506.

Lindquist, E. F. (1940). *Statistical analysis in educational research*. Boston: Houghton Mifflin.

Lovie, A. D. (1979). The analysis of variance in experimental psychology: 1934-1945. *British Journal of Mathematical and Statistical Psychology, 32*, 151–178.

Luce, R. D. (1988). The tools-to-theory hypothesis. Review of G. Gigerenzer and D. J. Murray, "Cognition as intuitive statistics." *Contemporary Psychology, 33*, 582–583.

Luce, R. D. (1989). Autobiography. In G. Lindzey (Ed.), *Psychology in autobiography* (Vol. 8, pp. 245–289). Stanford: Stanford University Press.

Lykken, D. T. (1968). Statistical significance in psychological research. *Psychological Bulletin, 70*, 151–159.

Meehl, P. E. (1978). Theoretical risks and tabular asterisks: Sir Karl, Sir Ronald, and the slow progress of soft psychology. *Journal of Consulting and Clinical Psychology, 46,* 806–834.

Melton, A. W. (1962). Editorial. *Journal of Experimental Psychology, 64,* 553–557.

Miller, G. A., & Buckhout, R. (1973). *Psychology: The science of mental life.* New York: Harper & Row.

Morrison, D. E., & Henkel, R. E. (Eds.). (1970). *The significance test controversy.* Chicago: Aldine.

Neyman, J. (1950). *First course in probability and statistics.* New York: Holt.

Neyman, J. (1957). Inductive behavior as a basic concept of philosophy of science. *International Statistical Review, 25,* 7–22.

Nunnally, J. C. (1975). *Introduction to statistics for psychology and education.* New York: McGraw-Hill.

Oakes, M. (1986). *Statistical inference: A commentary for the social and behavioral sciences.* New York: Wiley.

Pearson, E. S. (1939). "Student" as statistician. *Biometrika, 30,* 210–250.

Pearson, E. S. (1962). Some thoughts on statistical inference. *Annals of Mathematical Statistics, 33,* 394–403.

Pollard, P., & Richardson, J. T. E. (1987). On the probability of making Type I errors. *Psychological Bulletin, 102,* 159–163.

Porter, T. M. (1986). *The rise of statistical thinking, 1820-1900.* Princeton, NJ: Princeton University Press.

Publication Manual of the American Psychological Association. (1974) (2nd ed.). Baltimore: Garamond/Pridemark Press.

Rosnow, R. L., & Rosenthal, R. (1989). Statistical procedures and the justification of knowledge in psychological science. *American Psychologist, 44,* 1276–1284.

Rozeboom, W. W. (1960). The fallacy of the null hypothesis significance test. *Psychological Bulletin, 57,* 416–428.

Rucci, A. J., & Tweney, R. D. (1980). Analysis of variance and the "second discipline" of scientific psychology: A historical account. *Psychological Bulletin, 87,* 166–184.

Schwartz, S., & Dangleish, L. (1982). Statistical inference in personality research. *Journal of Research in Personality, 16,* 290–302.

Sedlmeier, P., & Gigerenzer, G. (1989). Do studies of statistical power have an effect on the power of studies? *Psychological Bulletin, 105,* 309–316.

Skinner, B. F. (1972). *Cumulative record.* New York: Appleton-Century-Crofts.

Skinner, B. F. (1984). *A matter of consequences.* New York: New York University Press.

Sterling, R. D. (1959). Publication decisions and their possible effects on inferences drawn from tests of significance—or vice versa. *Journal of the American Statistical Association, 54,* 30–34.

"Student" [W. S. Gosset]. (1908). The probable error of a mean. *Biometrika, 6,* 1–25.

Swijtink, Z. G. (1987). The objectification of observation: Measurement and statistical methods in the nineteenth century. In L. Krüger, L. Daston, & M. Heidelberger (Eds.), *The probabilistic revolution: Vol. 1. Ideas in history* (pp. 261–285). Cambridge, MA: MIT Press.

Tholey, P. (1982). Signifikanztest und Bayessche Hypothesenprüfung. *Archiv für Psychologie, 134,* 319–342.

Thomas, D. H. (1978). The awful truth about statistics in archaeology. *American Antiquity, 43,* 231–244.

Tukey, J. W. (1977). *Exploratory data analysis.* Reading, MA: Addison-Wesley.

Tversky, A., & Kahneman, D. (1971). Belief in the law of small numbers. *Psychological Bulletin, 76,* 105–110.

Tversky, A., & Kahneman, D. (1974). Judgment under uncertainty: Heuristics and biases. *Science, 185,* 1124–1131.

Tversky, A., & Kahneman, D. (1980). Causal schemas in judgments under uncertainty. In M. Fishbein (Ed.), *Progress in social psychology* (Vol. 1, pp. 49–72). Hillsdale, NJ: Lawrence Erlbaum Associates.

Winer, B. J. (1962). *Statistical principles in experimental design* (2nd ed., 1971). New York: McGraw-Hill.

12 Belief in the Law of Small Numbers

Amos Tversky
Daniel Kahneman
Hebrew University of Jerusalem

"Suppose you have run an experiment on 20 subjects, and have obtained a significant result which confirms your theory ($z = 2.23$, $p < .05$, two-tailed). You now have cause to run an additional group of 10 subjects. What do you think the probability is that the results will be significant, by a one-tailed test, separately for this group?"

If you feel that the probability is somewhere around .85, you may be pleased to know that you belong to a majority group. Indeed, that was the median answer of two small groups who were kind enough to respond to a questionnaire distributed at meetings of the Mathematical Psychology Group and of the American Psychological Association.

On the other hand, if you feel that the probability is around .48, you belong to a minority. Only 9 of our 84 respondents gave answers between .40 and .60. However, .48 happens to be a much more reasonable estimate than .85.[1]

---

*Amos Tversky is currently at Stanford University, and Daniel Kahneman is currently at The University of California at Berkeley.

[1]The required estimate can be interpreted in several ways. One possible approach is to follow common research practice, where a value obtained in one study is taken to define a plausible alternative to the null hypothesis. The probability requested in the question can then be interpreted as the power of the second test (i.e., the probability of obtaining a significant result in the second sample) against the alternative hypothesis defined by the result of the first sample. In the special case of a test of a mean with known variance, one would compute the power of the test against the hypothesis that the population mean equals the mean of the first sample. Since the size of the second sample is half that of the first, the computed probability of obtaining $z \geq 1.645$ is only .473. A theoretically more justifiable approach is to interpret the requested probability within a Bayesian framework and compute it relative to some appropriately selected prior distribution. Assuming a uniform prior, the desired posterior probability is .478. Clearly, if the prior distribution favors the null hypothesis, as is often the case, the posterior probability will be even smaller.

Apparently, most psychologists have an exaggerated belief in the likelihood of successfully replicating an obtained finding. The sources of such beliefs, and their consequences for the conduct of scientific inquiry, are what this paper is about. Our thesis is that people have strong intuitions about random sampling; that these intuitions are wrong in fundamental respects; that these intuitions are shared by naive subjects and by trained scientists; and that they are applied with unfortunate consequences in the course of scientific inquiry.

We submit that people view a sample randomly drawn from a population as highly representative, that is, similar to the population in all essential characteristics. Consequently, they expect any two samples drawn from a particular population to be more similar to one another and to the population than sampling theory predicts, at least for small samples.

The tendency to regard a sample as a representation is manifest in a wide variety of situations. When subjects are instructed to generate a random sequence of hypothetical tosses of a fair coin, for example, they produce sequences where the proportion of heads in any short segment stays far closer to .50 than the laws of chance would predict (Tune, 1964). Thus, each segment of the response sequence is highly representative of the "fairness" of the coin. Similar effects are observed when subjects successively predict events in a randomly generated series, as in probability learning experiments (Estes, 1964) or in other sequential games of chance. Subjects act as if *every* segment of the random sequence must reflect the true proportion: if the sequence has strayed from the population proportion, a corrective bias in the other direction is expected. This has been called the gambler's fallacy.

The heart of the gambler's fallacy is a misconception of the fairness of the laws of chance. The gambler feels that the fairness of the coin entitles him to expect that any deviation in one direction will soon be cancelled by a corresponding deviation in the other. Even the fairest of coins, however, given the limitations of its memory and mortal sense, cannot be as fair as the gambler expects it to be. This fallacy is not unique to gamblers. Consider the following example:

> The mean IQ of the population of eighth graders in a city is *known* to be 100. You have selected a random sample of 50 children for a study of educational achievements. The first child tested has an IQ of 150. What do you expect the mean IQ to be for the whole sample?

The correct answer is 101. A surprisingly large number of people believe that the expected IQ for the sample is still 100. This expectation can be justified only by the belief that a random process is self-correcting. Idioms such as "errors cancel each other out" reflect the image of an active self-correcting process. Some familiar processes in nature obey such laws: a deviation from a stable equilibrium produces a force that restores the equilibrium. The laws of chance, in contrast, do not work that way: deviations are not canceled as sampling proceeds, they are merely diluted.

Thus far, we have attempted to describe two related intuitions about chance. We proposed a representation hypothesis according to which people believe samples to be very similar to one another and to the population from which they are drawn. We also suggested that people believe sampling to be a self-correcting process. The two beliefs lead to the same consequences. Both generate expectations about characteristics of samples, and the variability of these expectations is less than the true variability, at least for small samples.

The law of large numbers guarantees that very large samples will indeed be highly representative of the population from which they are drawn. If, in addition, a self-corrective tendency is at work, then small samples should also be highly representative and similar to one another. People's intuitions about random sampling appear to satisfy the law of small numbers, which asserts that the law of large numbers applies to small numbers as well.

Consider a hypothetical scientist who lives by the law of small numbers. How would his belief affect his scientific work? Assume our scientist studies phenomena whose magnitude is small relative to uncontrolled variability, that is, the signal-to-noise ratio in the messages he receives from nature is low. Our scientist could be a meteorologist, a pharmacologist, or perhaps a psychologist.

If he believes in the law of small numbers, the scientist will have exaggerated confidence in the validity of conclusions based on small samples. To illustrate, suppose he is engaged in studying which of two toys infants will prefer to play with. Of the first five infants studied, four have shown a preference for the same toy. Many a psychologist will feel some confidence at this point, that the null hypothesis of no preference is false. Fortunately, such a conviction is not a sufficient condition for journal publication, although it may do for a book. By a quick computation, our psychologist will discover that the probability of a result as extreme as the one obtained is as high as $3/8$ under the null hypothesis.

To be sure, the application of statistical hypothesis testing to scientific inference is beset with serious difficulties. Nevertheless, the computation of significance levels (or likelihood ratios, as a Bayesian might prefer) forces the scientist to evaluate the obtained effect in terms of a *valid* estimate of sampling variance rather than in terms of his subjective biased estimate. Statistical tests, therefore, protect the scientific community against overly hasty rejections of the null hypothesis (i.e., Type I error) by policing its many members who would rather live by the law of small numbers. On the other hand, there are no comparable safeguards against the risk of failing to confirm a valid research hypothesis (i.e., Type II error).

Imagine a psychologist who studies the correlation between need for Achievement and grades. When deciding on sample size, he may reason as follows: "What correlation do I expect? $r = .35$. What N do I need to make the result significant? (Looks at table.) $N = 33$. Fine, that's my sample." The only flaw in this reasoning is that our psychologist has forgotten about sampling variation, possibly because he believes that any sample must be highly representative of its population. However, if his guess about the correlation in the population is correct, the correlation in the sample is about as likely to lie below or above .35. Hence, the likelihood of obtaining a significant result (i.e., the power of the test) for $N = 33$ is about .50.

In a detailed investigation of statistical power, Cohen (1962, 1969) has provided plausible definitions of large, medium, and small effects and an extensive set of computational aids to the estimation of power for a variety of statistical tests. In the normal test for a difference between two means, for example, a difference of $.25\sigma$ is small, a difference of $.50\sigma$ is medium, and a difference of 1σ is large, according to the proposed definitions. The mean IQ difference between clerical and semiskilled workers is a medium effect. In an ingenious study of research practice, Cohen (1962) reviewed all the statistical analyses published in one volume of the *Journal of Abnormal and Social Psychology,* and computed the likelihood of detecting each of the three sizes of effect. The average power was .28 for the detection of small effects, .48 for medium effects, and .83 for large effects. If psychologists typically expect medium effects and select sample size as in the above example, the power of their studies should indeed be about .50.

Cohen's analysis shows that the statistical power of many psychological studies is ridiculously low. This is a self-defeating practice: it makes for frustrated scientists and inefficient research. The investigator who tests a valid hypothesis but fails to obtain significant results cannot help but regard nature as untrustworthy or even hostile. Furthermore, as Overall (1969) has shown, the prevalence of studies deficient in statistical power is not only wasteful but actually pernicious: it results in a large proportion of invalid rejections of the null hypothesis among published results.

Because considerations of statistical power are of particular importance in the design of replication studies, we probed attitudes concerning replication in our questionnaire.

> Suppose one of your doctoral students has completed a difficult and time-consuming experiment on 40 animals. He has scored and analyzed a large number of variables. His results are generally inconclusive, but one before-after comparison yields a highly significant $t = 2.70$, which is surprising and could be of major theoretical significance.
>
> Considering the importance of the result, its surprisal value, and the number of analyses that your student has performed—
>
> Would you recommend that he replicate the study before publishing? If you recommend replication, how many animals would you urge him to run?

Among the psychologists to whom we put these questions there was overwhelming sentiment favoring replication: it was recommended by 66 out of 75 respondents, probably because they suspected that the single significant result was due to chance. The median recommendation was for the doctoral student to run 20 subjects in a replication study. It is instructive to consider the likely consequences of this advice. If the mean and the variance in the second sample are actually identical to those in the first sample, then the resulting value of t will be 1.88. Following the reasoning of Footnote 1, the student's chance of obtaining a significant result in the replication is only slightly above one-half (for $p = .05$, one-tail test). Since we had anticipated that a replication sample of 20 would appear reasonable to our respondents, we added the following question:

> Assume that your unhappy student has in fact repeated the initial study with 20 additional animals, and has obtained an insignificant result in the same direction, $t = 1.24$. What would you recommend now? Check one: [the numbers in parentheses refer to the number of respondents who checked each answer]
>
> (a) He should pool the results and publish his conclusion as fact. (0)
> (b) He should report the results as a tentative finding. (26)
> (c) He should run another group of [median = 20] animals. (21)
> (d) He should try to find an explanation for the difference between the two groups. (30)

Note that regardless of one's confidence in the original finding, its credibility is surely enhanced by the replication. Not only is the experimental effect in the same direction in the two samples but the magnitude of the effect in the replication is fully two-thirds of that in the original study. In view of the sample size (20), which our respondents recommended, the replication was about as successful as one is entitled to expect. The distribution of responses, however, reflects continued skepticism concerning the student's finding following the recommended replication. This unhappy state of affairs is a typical consequence of insufficient statistical power.

In contrast to Responses *b* and *c,* which can be justified on some grounds, the most popular response, Response *d,* is indefensible. We doubt that the same answer would have been obtained if the respondents had realized that the difference between the two studies does not even approach significance. (If the variances of the two samples are equal, t for the difference is .53.) In the absence of a statistical test, our respondents followed the representation hypothesis: as the difference between the two samples was larger than they expected, they viewed it as worthy of explanation. However, the attempt to "find an explanation for the difference between the two groups" is in all probability an exercise in explaining noise.

Altogether our respondents evaluated the replication rather harshly. This follows from the representation hypothesis: if we expect all samples to be very similar to one another, than almost all replications of a valid hypothesis should be statistically significant. The harshness of the criterion for successful replication is manifest in the responses to the following question:

> An investigator has reported a result that you consider implausible. He ran 15 subjects, and reported a significant value, $t = 2.46$. Another investigator has attempted to duplicate his procedure, and he obtained a nonsignificant value of t with the same number of subjects. The direction was the same in both sets of data.
>
> You are reviewing the literature. What is the highest value of t in the second set of data that you would describe as a failure to replicate?

The majority of our respondents regarded $t = 1.70$ as a failure to replicate. If the data of two such studies ($t = 2.46$ and $t = 1.70$) are pooled, the value of t for the combined data is about 3.00 (assuming equal variances). Thus, we are faced with a paradoxical state of affairs, in which the same data that would increase our confidence in the finding when viewed as part of the original study, shake our confidence when viewed as an independent study. This double standard is particularly disturbing since, for many reasons, replications are usually considered as independent studies, and hypotheses are often evaluated by listing confirming and disconfirming reports.

Contrary to a widespread belief, a case can be made that a replication sample should often be larger than the original. The decision to replicate a once obtained finding often expresses a great fondness for that finding and a desire to see it accepted by a skeptical community. Since that community unreasonably demands that the replication be independently significant, or at least that it approach significance, one must run a large sample. To illustrate, if the unfortunate doctoral student whose thesis was discussed earlier assumes the validity of his initial result ($t = 2.70, N = 40$), and if he is willing to accept a risk of only .10 of obtaining a t lower than 1.70, he should run approximately 50 animals in his replication study. With a somewhat weaker initial result ($t = 2.20, N = 40$), the size of the replication sample required for the same power rises to about 75.

That the effects discussed thus far are not limited to hypotheses about means and variances is demonstrated by the responses to the following question:

> You have run a correlational study, scoring 20 variables on 100 subjects. Twenty-seven of the 190 correlation coefficients are significant at the .05 level; and 9 of these are significant beyond the .01 level. The mean absolute level of the significant correlations is .31, and the pattern of results is very reasonable on theoretical grounds. How many of the 27 significant correlations would you expect to be significant again, in an exact replication of the study, with $N = 40$?

With $N = 40$, a correlation of about .31 is required for significance at the .05 level. This is the mean of the significant correlations in the original study. Thus, only about half of the originally significant correlations (i.e., 13 or 14) would remain significant with $N = 40$. In addition, of course, the correlations in the replication are bound to differ from those in the original study. Hence, by regression effects, the initially significant coefficients are most likely to be reduced.

Thus, 8 to 10 repeated significant correlations from the original 27 is probably a generous estimate of what one is entitled to expect. The median estimate of our respondents is 18. This is more than the number of repeated significant correlations that will be found if the correlations are recomputed for 40 subjects randomly selected from the original 100! Apparently, people expect more than a mere duplication of the original statistics in the replication sample; they expect a duplication of the significance of results, with little regard for sample size. This expectation requires a ludicrous extension of the representation hypothesis; even the law of small numbers is incapable of generating such a result.

The expectation that patterns of results are replicable almost in their entirety provides the rationale for a common, though much deplored practice. The investigator who computes all correlations between three indexes of anxiety and three indexes of dependency will often report and interpret with great confidence the single significant correlation obtained. His confidence in the shaky finding stems from his belief that the obtained correlation matrix is highly representative and readily replicable.

In review, we have seen that the believer in the law of small numbers practices science as follows:

• He gambles his research hypotheses on small samples without realizing that the odds against him are unreasonably high. He overestimates power.

• He has undue confidence in early trends (e.g., the data of the first few subjects) and in the stability of observed patterns (e.g., the number and identity of significant results). He overestimates significance.

• In evaluating replications, his or others', he has unreasonably high expectations about the replicability of significant results. He underestimates the breadth of confidence intervals.

• He rarely attributes a deviation of results from expectations to sampling variability, because he finds a causal "explanation" for any discrepancy. Thus, he has little opportunity to recognize sampling variation in action. His belief in the law of small numbers, therefore, will forever remain intact.

Our questionnaire elicited considerable evidence for the prevalence of the belief in the law of small numbers.[2] Our typical respondent is a believer, regardless of the group to which he belongs. There were practically no differences between the median responses of audiences at a mathematical psychology meet-

---

[2]Edwards (1968) has argued that people fail to extract sufficient information or certainty from probabilistic data; he called this failure conservatism. Our respondents can hardly be described as conservative. Rather, in accord with the representation hypothesis, they tend to extract more certainty from the data than the data, in fact, contain. The conditions under which people may appear conservative are discussed in Kahnemann, D., and Tversky, A. *Subjective probability: A judgment of representativeness.* (Tech. Rep.) Oregon Research Institute, 1971, 2 (2).

ing and at a general session of the American Psychological Association convention, although we make no claims for the representativeness of either sample. Apparently, acquaintance with formal logic and with probability theory does not extinguish erroneous intuitions. What, then, can be done? Can the belief in the law of small numbers be abolished or at least controlled?

Research experience is unlikely to help much, because sampling variation is all too easily "explained." Corrective experiences are those that provide neither motive nor opportunity for spurious explanation. Thus, a student in a statistics course may draw repeated samples of given size from a population, and learn the effect of sample size on sampling variability from personal observation. We are far from certain, however, that expectations can be corrected in this manner, since related biases, such as the gambler's fallacy, survive considerable contradictory evidence.

Even if the bias cannot be unlearned, students can learn to recognize its existence and take the necessary precautions. Since the teaching of statistics is not short on admonitions, a warning about biased statistical intuitions may not be out of place. The obvious precaution is computation. The believer in the law of small numbers has incorrect intuitions about significance level, power, and confidence intervals. Significant levels are usually computed and reported, but power and confidence limits are not. Perhaps they should be.

Explicit computation of power, relative to some reasonable hypothesis, for instance, Cohen's (1962, 1969) small, large, and medium effects, should surely be carried out before any study is done. Such computations will often lead to the realization that there is simply no point in running the study unless, for example, sample size is multiplied by four. We refuse to believe that a serious investigator will knowingly accept a .50 risk of failing to confirm a valid research hypothesis. In addition, computations of power are essential to the interpretation of negative results, that is, failures to reject the null hypothesis. Because readers' intuitive estimates of power are likely to be wrong, the publication of computed values does not appear to be a waste of either readers' time or journal space.

In the early psychological literature, the convention prevailed of reporting, for example, a sample mean as $\bar{X} \pm PE,$ where PE is the probable error (i.e., the 50% confidence interval around the mean). This convention was later abandoned in favor of the hypothesis-testing formulation. A confidence interval, however, provides a useful index of sampling variability, and it is precisely this variability that we tend to underestimate. The emphasis on significance levels tends to obscure a fundamental distinction between the size of an effect and its statistical significance. Regardless of sample size, the size of an effect in one study is a reasonable estimate of the size of the effect in replication. In contrast, the estimated significance level in a replication depends critically on sample size. Unrealistic expectations concerning the replicability of significance levels may be corrected if the distinction between size and significance is clarified, and if the computed size of observed effects is routinely reported. From this point of view, at least, the acceptance of the hypothesis-testing model has not been an unmixed blessing for psychology.

The true believer in the law of small numbers commits his multitude of sins against the logic of statistical inference in good faith. The representation hypothesis describes a cognitive or perceptual bias, which operates regardless of motivational factors. Thus, while the hasty rejection of the null hypothesis is gratifying, the rejection of a cherished hypothesis is aggravating, yet the true believer is subject to both. His intuitive expectations are governed by a consistent misperception of the world rather than by opportunistic wishful thinking. Given some editorial prodding, he may be willing to regard his statistical intuitions with proper suspicion and replace impression formation by computation whenever possible.

ACKNOWLEDGMENTS

This chapter is reprinted with permission from *Psychological Bulletin*, *76* (2), 105–110. We wish to thank the many friends and colleagues who commented on an earlier version, and in particular we are indebted to Maya Bar-Hillel, Jack Block, Jacob Cohen, Louis L. Guttman, John W. Tukey, Ester Samuel, and Gideon Shwarz.

Requests for reprints should be sent to Amos Tversky, Center for Advanced Study in the Behavioral Sciences, 202 Junipero Serra Boulevard, Stanford, California 94305.

REFERENCES

Cohen, J. (1962). The statistical power of abnormal-social psychological research. *Journal of Abnormal and Social Psychology, 65*, 145–153.

Cohen, J. (1969). *Statistical power analysis in the behavioral sciences.* New York: Academic.

Edwards, W. (1968). Conservatism in human information processing. In B. Kleinmuntz (Ed.), *Formal representation of human judgment.* New York: Wiley.

Estes, W. K. (1964). Probability learning. In A. W. Melton (Ed.), *Categories of human learning.* New York: Academic.

Overall, J. E. (1969). Classical statistical hypothesis testing within the context of Bayesian theory. *Psychological Bulletin, 71*, 285–292.

Tune, G. S. (1964). Response preferences: A review of some relevant literature. *Psychological Bulletin, 61*, 286–302.

13 Statistical Prediction versus Clinical Prediction: Improving What Works

Robyn M. Dawes
Carnegie Mellon University

David Faust
University of Rhode Island

Paul E. Meehl
University of Minnesota

In Pennsylvania, offenders sentenced to maximum prison terms of 2 years or longer are considered for parole under the authority of the Pennsylvania Board of Probation and Parole after they have completed half of their maximum sentence. The decision to grant or withhold parole is based on a four-step procedure beginning with a summary recommendation from the correctional staff, proceeding through a "parole case analyst" and then to a "parole interviewer." This interviewer is either a board member or a specialized hearing examiner who has access to the previous reports of the staff and the analyst, and who makes a final recommendation to the parole board, which has the ultimate responsibility for the decision. One thousand thirty-five prison inmates were interviewed for parole between October 1977 and May 1978, yielding 743 cases in which the parole board made final decisions, of which 84.7% were to grant parole. In all but one of these cases, the decision of the parole board was identical to the final recommendation of the interviewer, who also made four- or five-point ratings on: (a) prognosis for supervision, (b) risk of future crime, (c) risk of future dangerous crime, and (d) assaultive potential. On the basis of a 1-year follow-up study, J. Carroll, Wiener, Coates, Galegher, and Alibrio (1982) were able to compare the prediction of the parolee's behavior based on the interviewer ratings with its prediction based on simple background factors, such as number of previous convictions. (These factors also were available to the interviewers and were shown to be correlated with their clinical judgments.)

Approximately 25% of the parolees were considered "failures" by the board within a 1-year period—for reasons such as being recommitted to prison, absconding, committing a criminal act, being apprehended on a criminal charge, or committing a technical violation of parole. None of the interviewers' ratings predicted any of the outcomes, the largest correlation being .06. In contrast, a three-variable model based on offense type, number of convictions, and number of (noncriminal) violations of prison rules during the last year of prison did have (very) modest predictability, $R = .22$, a result consistent with earlier findings that actuarial predictions based primarily on prior record predict parole violation with a multiple R of approximately .30 (Gottfredson, Wilkins, & Hoffman, 1978). When parolees were convicted of new offenses, the seriousness of such crimes was correlated .27 with the interviewers' ratings of assaultive potential, but a simple dichotomous evaluation of past heroin use correlated .45. Parole revocation and violence are very difficult to predict, partly because offenses of record are a small minority of those committed, but these outcomes are better predicted on a statistical than a judgmental basis, as has been found in other studies examining criminal recidivism (Glaser, 1964).

J. Carroll et al.'s results illustrate the outcome of research comparing statistical to clinical prediction, where these two types of prediction refer to these two ways of combining data (not to its source). The purpose of this chapter is (a) to present a brief synopsis of this research; (b) to present a (possibly new) framework for interpreting this evidence; (c) to discuss the characteristics of the predictive problem that may be primarily responsible for the superiority of "formula over head"; (d) to discuss some of the objections to the research, and (e) to propose a way of implementing statistical models that overcomes a major objection to their use. The first topic has been discussed at length in previous books and papers (e.g., Dawes, 1988; Dawes, Faust, & Meehl, 1989; Meehl, 1954), as have the third (e.g., B. Carroll, 1987; Dawes, 1979), and the fourth (e.g., Faust, Meehl, & Dawes, 1990; Meehl, 1986). This chapter, therefore, focuses on the second and fifth.

THE RESEARCH

Here, we list 10 diverse areas in which studies have shown the superiority of statistical prediction. There are other areas as well, but we list these 10 so that the reader can have access to a representative set of studies on which we base our conclusions of superiority of statistical prediction. (We are omitting those covered in Meehl's 1954 book or Sawyer's 1966 review, except for areas in which we know no subsequent studies.) These areas are those that predict:

1. Academic success (Dawes, 1971; Schofield & Garrard, 1975; Wiggins & Cohen, 1971)
2. Business bankruptcy (Beaver's, 1966, and Deacon's, 1972, models compared to Libby's, 1976, experts)

3. Longevity (Einhorn, 1972)
4. Military training success (Bloom & Brundage, 1947)
5. Myocardial infarction (Goldman et al., 1988; Lee et al., 1986)
6. Neuropsychological diagnosis (Leli & Filskov, 1984; Wedding, 1983)
7. Parole violation (J. Carroll et al., 1982; Gottfredson, Wilkins, & Hoffman, 1978)
8. Police termination (Inwald, 1988)
9. Psychiatric diagnosis (Goldberg, 1965)
10. Violence (Miller & Morris, 1988; Werner, Rose, & Yesavage, 1983)

Some of the studies in some of these 10 areas can be summarized briefly.

Dawes (1971) compared clinical and statistical prediction of success in graduate school. Statistical methods, even those based on single variables (e.g., grade-point average), outperformed the clinical predictions of an admissions committee that had access to more extensive information. Using the statistical method, it would also have been possible to eliminate 55% of applicants that the admissions committee considered and later rejected, without eliminating any applicants the committee considered and later accepted.

Dawes and his colleagues at Oregon decided that this finding concerning automatic elimination was of sufficient importance that it be formally implemented—both to save the psychology faculty there from the meaningless work of evaluating applicants who had no chance of admission, and to save these applicants themselves the work, expense, and heartache of applying to a program into which they had no chance of being admitted. Before doing so, however, Dawes (1979) cross-validated this elimination procedure on the subsequent year, even though the ratio of observations to variables involved in the elimination were so large that there was little question of the statistical stability of the earlier results. The elimination procedure was, after all, "radical." What he did was to inform the other members of the Oregon admissions committee that the procedure was being implemented and they would be asked to examine only those applicants who passed the screening, but then deceptively pass on to them for evaluation any applicant who appeared to him to have any particular strengths not reflected in grade-point average or test scores. None of his colleagues noticed this deception. Nor were any of those applicants who would not have passed the screening given a rating by the other committee members high enough to have any chance of being admitted. The reason was that for every applicant below the cut-score who had a particular strength, there was one above this score who had a comparable strength, and there was no reasonable or ethical reason for admitting the former applicant rather than the latter. Subsequently, Goldberg (1977) informed potential applicants of a revised formula being used for screening: Average Graduate Record Exam score plus grade point average multiplied by 100. Not only were the applicants informed that potential applicants with a score less than

9.50 should not waste their time and energies applying, but the probability of being admitted with particular scores above that level was shared as well. Although this procedure was met with some cries of "dehumanization," the psychology professors at Oregon felt they were being perfectly open and honest with the applicants by providing them with as much information as possible about the chances of being admitted and therefore highly ethical. (Of course, the number of $25 admissions fees to the university went down.)

Einhorn (1972) studied the prediction of survival time following the diagnosis of Hodgkin's disease, a previously untreatable, and hence fatal form of cancer. Pathologists rated patients' biopsy slides along nine dimensions they deemed relevant in appraising disease severity and also formulated an overall rating of severity. Statistical formulae were first developed and then validated by examining relations between the pathologists' ratings and actual survival time. Although the pathologists' overall ratings of severity showed minimal relations to survival time, a statistical method achieved modest but significant relations. Of particular interest, the study shows that the pathologists' ratings did contain information of potential predictive value, but only the statistical combination method captured this potential.

Finally, Libby (1976) had loan officers from either relatively small or large banks predict which 30 of 60 firms about which financial information was available would go bankrupt within 3 years after issuing financial statements. Overall, the loan officers achieved 74% predictive accuracy, in comparison to the 82% accuracy achieved by the use of a statistical method (Beaver, 1966; Deacon, 1972).

There are some exceptions—particularly in the medical domain (e.g., Brannen, Godfrey, & Goetter, 1989; Sutton, 1989)—but the framework proposed in the next section of this chapter may yield some insight into why they occur. Overall, we reiterate Meehl's (1986) conclusion:

> There is no controversy in social science that shows such a large body of qualitatively diverse studies coming out so uniformly in the same direction as this one [the relative validity of statistical versus clinical prediction]. When you are pushing 90 investigations [now closer to 140], predicting everything from the outcome of football games to the diagnosis of liver disease and when you can hardly come up with a half dozen studies showing even a weak tendency in favor of the clinician, it is time to draw a practical conclusion. (pp. 372–373)

THE FRAMEWORK

In his 1954 book, Meehl proposed certain ground rules for the comparison of clinical versus statistical prediction. The most important of these were that the prediction should be based on exactly the same data, and the statistical prediction should avoid capitalization on chance due to overfitting a sample of data. The latter rule was followed either (a) by using crossvalidation (which might better be termed *validation*, with data on which the statistical rule is derived termed the *development sample*); or (b) by using unit weights (such an a priori weighting system being equivalent to a single predictor—as in a system using a validation sample), or (c) by using a sufficiently large sample that the stability of the statistical model was not in question. Since that time, both jackknife procedures (e.g., Drehmer & Morris, 1981; Gollob, 1967) and the use of the Wherry–Lord "prophecy" formula in multiple regression contexts have become common ways of dealing with the overfitting problem. The Wherry–Lord formula occurs in many different algebraic forms; in the simplest its numerator is equal to the actual squared multiple regression coefficient minus that expected on a chance basis (= $k/(n - 1)$, where k is the number of predictors and n is the sample size), while its numerator is equal to 1 minus this chance expectation, a form that happens to be isomorphic to almost all "correction" formulas. Simulations have shown this formula to be quite accurate (e.g., Schmitt, Coyle, & Rauschenberger, 1977); in fact, a formula identical to that of Wherry–Lord has been proposed as a method for determining how many variables to enter into a regression equation in order to maximize expected predictability of a new sample (Breiman & Freedman, 1983). Aware of the problems of overfitting, most researchers in this area have either followed Meehl's second ground rule, or have used one of the subsequent procedures.

The first ground rule, in contrast, has often been violated in studies purporting to investigate the clinical versus statistical prediction problem. In the studies assessing interviews, for example, the clinician often has access to more information than is used in the statistical prediction model. A larger information set is also available in the medical studies of which we are aware that show greater accuracy for clinical prediction; for example, in the study by Brannen, Gottfred, and Goetter (1989), the predictions of an acute physiological and chronic health scoring system (APACHE-II) were found to be inferior to those of "the critical care fellow," who was board certified in internal medicine and who "had seen the patient, obtained a history, and conducted a physical examination, as well as reviewed the pertinent laboratory and roentgenogran and data available" (p. 1083);[1] in the study by Sutton (1989), Bayes' formula was found to be inferior to the diagnosis of doctors who actually saw the patients. In both of these studies there is a possibility that valid predictors were noted in the live examination, predictors not available to the statistical systems (but—as is pointed out later—which might be integrated into such systems, to create predictions of equal or greater accuracy). A clear statement of the information problem in a comparison

---

[1]Following the completion of the present article, a new prediction system, APACHE-III, has been demonstrated to be superior to such judgment—specifically about survival before hospital discharge in an intensive care unit; see Knaus, Wagner, & Lynn (1991).

that violates Meehl's first rule can be found in a business context examined by Blattberg and Hoch (in press), in which they concluded that predictions should be made by "50% model and 50% manager." "Experts also had inside information, not the Machiavellian variety available to corporate officers, but they clearly had more information available to them than did the models. We have elected to label this inside information as intuition and see it as a valuable decision input."

Basically, we distinguish four types of relations between the information available to the statistical model and to the clinician. Based on Gergonne's (1817) naive set theory (which does not involve the paradoxes of material implication), these relations are illustrated in Fig. 13.1. The information sets are either exclusive (rarely the basis for a comparison thus far), identical (following Meehl's ground rules), inclusive—in which the information available to one method is a subset of that available to the other—or disjunctive. The vast majority of the studies in the "clinical versus statistical" field have been based on information sets that are either identical or inclusive, with the information on which the model is based being a subset of the information available to the clinician, not vice versa. In the studies mentioned earlier, for example, most involved a comparison of predictions based on the same data; in contrast, the

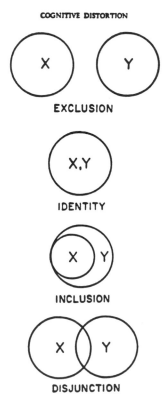

COGNITIVE DISTORTION

EXCLUSION

IDENTITY

INCLUSION

FIG. 13.1.   The Gergonne relations.

DISJUNCTION

studies on personnel selection by Bloom and Brundage (1947) and by Dawes (1971), on longevity by Einhorn (1972), on parole violation by J. Carroll et al., and on medical diagnosis by Lee et al. (1986) indicated superiority for statistical prediction even when the information on which it was based was a subset of the information on which the clinical prediction was based. For example, in the Lee et al. (1986) study "all baseline characteristics used in computing model predictions were among the descriptors listed on the one-page summary given to the doctors," (p. 555). The study by Goldman et al. (1988) predicting whether chest pain was due to myocardial infarction is unusual in that the data bases available to the computer simulation model and the clinicians (apparently) had a disjunctive relationship. We have found no studies in which the data available to the clinician is the subset of that available to the model, seemingly because one of the assumed benefits of the clinician is the ability to gather data that might not be considered relevant prior to the evaluation process (although that might be balanced by the ability to be distracted by irrelevant data; see Dawes, 1988, chaps. 5 and 6).

When the data bases are identical, the findings have been uniform in showing that statistical *combination* of data is superior to clinical combination. There are, as noted, a few exceptions when the information on which the model is based is included in the information available to the clinician; the problem with this structure is, however, that the conclusion can be unambiguous only if the statistical prediction is superior; in the event that the clinical prediction is superior, there is always the possibility that had the additional data been incorporated into the statistical model—so that if an identity relationship following Meehl's ground rules had been formed, the model might have turned out to be superior. Conversely, we have been able to discover no studies in which the data available to the clinician is a proper subset of that available to the model; given that structure, an outcome in favor of the clinician would be a particularly strong one in the context studied, but to the best of our knowledge no such outcomes have been observed. Finally, a study using the disjunctive structure is particularly difficult to interpret.

We recommend that if the researcher is interested in studying statistical versus clinical predictions as *general methods for combining data,* then any relationships between the data on which the model is based and on which the clinical or judgment is based should—as far as possible—be transformed to an identity relation. There are, of course, many important problems involved in such a transformation, particularly when the basis of clinical judgment is unclear—for example, some characteristics of a biopsy that are not included in coded ratings (as in the Einhorn study, in which the statistical model was still superior). Moreover, there are other ambiguities; should, for example, a "gestalt characteristic" be included as an input in a statistical model, or is it really an act of clinical integration? The latter position may appear obvious, until it is noted that virtually all inputs of statistical models involve some form of human information processing and coding (see Dawes & Corrigan, 1974), and it is not always clear where to distinguish coding from integration. Nevertheless, the "practical conclusion" of all these studies is quite clear.

Finally, there is one method of combining statistical information with clinical judgment that has been tested at least in a few contexts—and found wanting. The method is to inform the clinician of the output of a statistical model and then to allow the clinician to "improve" on it (Arkes, Dawes, & Christensen, 1986; Goldberg, 1968; Sawyer, 1966). In the few contexts studied, that combination does worse than the statistical models alone. For example, in the Arkes, Dawes, and Christensen study, people with and without expertise in baseball (as evaluated by a test dealing with rules and terminology) were (correctly) informed that among nonpitching candidates for "Most Valuable Player Award" in the National League between 1940 and 1961, the player on the team ending higher in the standings was chosen 70% of the time. The nonexpert group of subjects did better than the expert group, apparently because they employed the rule more often (according to self-report)—even though these subjects in the expert group may have been more likely to recall the award-winning player directly than those in the nonexpert group. (The average number of correct judgments in both groups fell short of the 14 correct judgments that would have been made were the rule applied "blindly!") Although these particular judgments of experts defined according to knowledge of rules and procedures of baseball may be of passing interest, the study was constructed specifically to be parallel to that of Goldberg (1968), in which experts were provided with a simple rule for differentiating psychiatric diagnoses of neurosis versus psychosis from Minnesota Multiphasic Personality Inventory (MNPI) profiles and proceeded to make judgments that were less valid than the rule itself; in fact, Arkes, Dawes, and Christensen chose a rule of 70% accuracy because the Goldberg (1965) rule has that accuracy. Unfortunately, the number of contexts studied is small.

CHARACTERISTICS OF THE PROBLEM

As Dawes (1979) and B. Carroll (1987) emphasized, these prediction problems involve many factors that are not assessed by either the model or the clinician, that often cannot be assessed because they are unknown, or cannot be assessed because their influence does not occur until after the prediction is made. Some of these (e.g., possible genetic dispositions tied to particular genes) may be capable of evaluation at some later point in time, whereas others (e.g., the nature of the old friends a parolee happens to meet the first few days out of jail) may be totally unpredictable. Such factors (either considered singly or in interactions with others), may be of a most ephemeral nature—but nevertheless of great importance in influencing outcomes. See, for example, Malmquist and Meehl (1978, p. 155) for a discussion of the role of luck in psychopathology. For the purposes of predicting future outcomes from *stable* predictors, these factors, however important, must be nevertheless considered as "noise," although not always of a random variety. How well do people perform in a context involving a great deal of such unpredictable noise?

Not well. Performance can be conceptualized by employing what is termed the *lens model analysis* of components of clinical inference (Hammond, Hursch, & Todd, 1964; Hammond & Summers, 1965; Tucker, 1964). When such inference is made on the basis of codable multivariable input, the resulting judgments can be broken down into three additive components: (a) a random component due to unreliability of judgment, (b) a component that can be predicted by a linear combination of the input variables, and (c) a reliable "residual" component (which presumably reflects "configurality," "intuition," and so on). The latter two components can then be correlated separately with both the criterion values and with the predicted criterion values based on a linear model of the input variables (the "ecological" linear model). The consistent finding is that only the second component of judgment, the linearly predictable one, is correlated with either the criterion values or the ecological model, more highly with the model values than with the actual ones. The finding that the residual component of judgment is unrelated to accuracy indicates why the clinical modification of the statistical model does not improve it when the statistical prediction is made in a linear manner. Moreover, the high correlation between the two models (of judgment and of reality) follows from the fact that any two linear models with weights of the same sign will correlate highly (Castellan, 1973); thus, it may simply reflect the fact that judges are weighting the variables in the appropriate directions.

In contrast to people, many statistical models are specifically designed to work in a context of unpredictable noise, which is most often captured by an "uncorrelated error" term in these models. The linear regression model is designed to achieve the best *relative* weighting of variables in order to maximize predictability from the resulting composite. There are many variants of this model (ordinary least squares, ridge regression, etc.), but they all are based on the same principle of attempting to maximize predictability—most usually for subsequent samples in the same population—in a context with an explicitly defined error component.

Linear models—again, those most commonly used in the contexts studied—also have the advantage that their predictions are often insensitive to differences in weights, provided all variables are weighted in the appropriate direction (Bloch & Moses, 1988; Dawes & Corrigan, 1974; Tukey, 1948; Wainer, 1976; Wilks, 1938). The output of linear models is particularly insensitive when the predicted variables form a positive manifold, as often occurs in the type of situation we reviewed; because many of the predictors (e.g., aptitude test score and grades, past arrest record, and number of prison violations) are related to the same sets of unobserved variables (e.g., intellectual competence and motivation, lack of impulse control, and sufficient cleverness not to get caught), they are often related positively to each other. It is, of course, always possible to *hypothesize* "suppressor relationships," in which the simple correlations with the dependent variable are in one direction while the weight in a regression equation is in another, as a result of the covariance structure between predictors. Such variables are typically not found in the context we have reviewed.

Finally, although incapable of forming some "gestalt" judgments, these models nevertheless are immune to many of the cognitive heuristics to which people are subject—for example, those stemming from availability, representative thinking, and framing. (For a review, see Dawes, 1988.) Research results indicate that even if the clinician, in contrast, may be capable of perceiving such gestalts, they are often not particularly important in predicting human outcomes in the "booming buzzing, confusion" of human adult life.

OBJECTIONS TO THE RESULTS

To state that the research results reported in the first section of this chapter do not arouse universal enthusiasm is an extreme understatement.

Some object that there is no well-specified population of prediction of human outcomes. Therefore, any sampling of particular ones in which the accuracies of clinical and actuarial predictions are compared cannot result in a general conclusion. Moreover, there could always be other contexts in which clinical prediction is superior (the reviewer's own often being the example). There is a problem with this objection because "could" is not equivalent to "are," and if such contexts do exist, they have not yet been discovered—and not for want of trying. As Meehl (1986) pointed out, when you discover such a uniform result across such diverse domains, you should reach, at minimum, a practical conclusion.

Individual studies can also be criticized. Whereas the results across contexts may be interpreted as supporting the superiority of actuarial prediction, each separate context, when considered in isolation, admits to an alternative interpretation or two. For example, in one context in which violence on a psychiatric ward was predicted (Werner, Rose, & Yesavage, 1983), the clinical predictions might have been superior, except that they served as a basis for taking precautions aimed at keeping patients from having any chance to become violent. (The additional finding that the trained clinicians made the same judgments as untrained high school students [Lierer, Warner, Rose, & Yesavage, 1985] could simply indicate that the students, too, would have achieved accuracy, were it not for the "self-negating" nature of the predictions.) Or in the J. Carroll et al. (1982) study of parole boards, actuarial predictions of who would succeed (based on variables such as number of past convictions and violations of prison rules) proved superior to predictions of parole interviewers (who had access to information about these variables). But perhaps the interviewers were nevertheless better at making the simple decision of who should or should not be let out on parole. So, if the interviewers' recommendations had not been followed, their assessments might have been revealed as superior—even though these assessments were shown to be inferior when they were in fact followed.

Perhaps. There is a problem with this kind of analysis, though, because it becomes necessary to concoct a new alternative explanation to "explain away" the findings in each separate context, rather than simply accept each replicable finding. And, as was true for the first objection, the alternatives are simply hypothesized, rather than supported by any data.

In contrast to these structural objections, Meehl (1986) speculated about some of the personal factors that lead to frequent, and often vehement, rejection of the research conclusion. These factors include simple ignorance, narcissistic belief about the validity of one's own judgment, and threat to professional status. There is an additional motivational factor that statistical prediction for human outcomes appears "dehumanized," and there is even a widespread belief that "statistics do not apply to the individual." (If so, there would be no point in conducting randomized trials on groups of people—such as the Salk vaccine experiment in 1954—in order to determine the validity or relative validity of various medical techniques, which must, of course, be applied to an individual person.)

Furthermore, there is the aversion to the lack of predictability of human life that is demonstrated in many of these studies; for example, the best statistical models in most appear to have maximal predictabilities expressed by correlation coefficients of .3 or .4, which can be threatening in such contexts as longevity, academic success, and parole violation. An unpredictable world cannot be a just one, and although predictability is not a sufficient condition for "justice," it is a necessary one. Thus, people who wish to believe that the world itself will give them certain "entitlements" (Lerner, 1980, 1987) are faced with the implication from these studies that "the race is not to the swift, . . . but time and chance," (Ecclesiastes, chap. 9, Verse 11).

There are, in addition, objections based on cognitive factors. First, the lack of predictability found in the studies appears to violate our belief that we really do "understand" the course of human life. As Dawes (in press) suggested elsewhere, this belief is based on the ability when given an outcome to identify important antecedent factors acting either singly or in monotonic interactions—for example, the success of "the right person at the right time." These factors are then identified as predictive. The problem, however, is they must predict as main effects combined with others when they are entered as variables of outcome studies; first, the effects of a single influence (variable) are vitiated by the effects of others; second, monotone "combinations of ingredients" are rare statistically; third, prediction must be made *to a specific point in time*—whereas retrospective examination of factors affecting outcome allows the analyst freedom in scanning across time for the existence of the important factors. Finally, and most importantly, even though the observer can create a monotone ("many-one") relationship when observing a consequence and searching for antecedents, the focus on consequences creates an "availability bias" whereby the fact that the same set of antecedents often leads to a different outcome (a "many-many" structure in reality) is unobserved. Knowing why something occurred therefore involves different cognitive processes than does predicting its occurrence, but the knowledge of "knowing why" is easily identified with knowledge that allows prediction. (See Dawes, in press, for further discussion.)

The last cognitive objection we discuss concerns the "rigidity" of statistical models. It is a clearly correct intuition that situations change. A model, however, is (or generally should be) based on a large sample of data and—the argument runs—once in place produces a determinant predicted value. As the situation changes, however, it is quite reasonable to postulate that the predictors will as well. The argument then runs that even though the statistical model may do better than clinical judgment on the data studied, it is not as capable as such judgment in "altering when it alteration finds." The extreme form of this objection is that no model should be proposed as a substitute for clinical intuition unless it was developed at one point in time and validated at a subsequent point.

This objection is based on a simple error, which is the belief that models cannot be modified from feedback. In fact, model parameters can be systematically altered by feedback, whereas clinical judges often do not have the feedback presented in a systematic manner, or at all. How many clinical psychologists, for example, carefully check the accuracy of their diagnoses and prognoses by evaluating their clients' lives years later? And if they do check, do they keep careful records of these judgments so they are not subject to hindsight biases (that "I knew it all along") or benign memories about these diagnoses and prognoses—or to the reconstructive nature of memory that leaves the past compatible with the present? (Pearson, Ross, & Dawes, in press.) "Every reminiscence is colored by today's being what it is, and therefore by a deceptive point of view" (Albert Einstein, referenced in Schilpp, 1949, p. 3).

IMPLEMENTATION

The statistical method has been demonstrated to be superior to the clinical method. In response, many people (not referenced here) have proposed that this finding mandates the improvement of clinical methods, perhaps by improving their reliability. But given that the statistical methods of prediction are not difficult to construct, are based on empirically observable relationships, and are far less expensive than clinicians making the same predictions, a reasonable alternative is to improve the models.

Those variables that clinicians believe to be important that are not captured in a particular model can be incorporated in it. Such variables may even include "gestalt judgments" based on clinical information-gathering techniques. (Recall that the basic question is one of how to combine data, given human involvement is always necessary in order to collect it; even an "objective" test depends on the efforts of a people to create it.) Once entered, the validity of these variables can be discovered rather than simply hypothesized.

Finally, statistical predictive models are easily modified as time or context demands. Although such models are derived and checked (e.g., "cross-validated") in particular contexts at certain points in time, it is possible—in fact desirable—to use feedback as the models are implemented to examine the validity of both their variables and the weighting of these variables. Even the most "subjective" variable thought to be important, such as overall rating of liking or disliking an interviewee, can be examined to determine its predictive validity. And we urge doing so—especially in contrast to postulating in the absence of evidence that such a variable may be predictive (and then often not even bothering to assess it in some reasonably reliable manner).

Many procedures exist for the type of "updating" we propose of models, particularly linear ones (e.g., Duncan & Horn, 1972; Kalman, 1960, 1963; Rumelhart, Hinton, & Williams, 1986). Perhaps the most relevant to predicting human outcomes (and the most easily understood) is *empirical Bayesian* updating. A prototypical example may be found in Rubin's (1980) analysis of optimal weighting for combining undergraduate grade-point averages and Law School Aptitude Test scores to predict academic performance across 82 law schools over 3 years. In effect, the weights computed for a particular school in a given year were regressed toward a common mean; this regression, however, was not total; as a consequence, particularistic information was retained. The empirical result was that with new data the regressed estimates generally outperformed both the weighting systems obtained for the same school the previous year and the overall mean estimates. (It should be pointed out again that this procedure is in no way limited to evaluating "objective" variables—although the degree to which a grade-point average is as objective a variable as it is often asserted to be consists simply of the fact that it is an average of multiple subjective judgments.)

Another method that may be used is modification of the Chow (1965) test. Suppose an investigator believes that at a certain point in time the best prediction equation has changed—through the introduction of new variables, new weightings of the same variables, or even interactions between variables; then, a dummy variable may be entered into the regression that indicates whether the prediction is made before or after this point. The *interaction* of this dummy variable with the predictor then indicates changes in the best prediction equation. Here, standard procedures of regression analysis can be employed—in particular, the incremental magnitude and significance of having the *set* of predictors involving interactions with this dummy variable.

In fact, the Bayesian and dummy variable interaction methods can be combined by having the analyst develop a prior distribution of belief about when and how the prediction equation might be best modified and then evaluating this belief in light of the data obtained. We present no simple, "canned," method of doing so. In fact, there is—and should be—an element of judgment in such modification. Are we then back to intuitive prediction? No, because the judgment is of the type that considers the prediction problem as a whole, and the individual predictions as elements of the set of predictions to be made; that is, the judgment adopts an "external" view of the prediction problem rather than an "internal" one focusing simply on the problem at hand; it views this problem as one of a similar set to which a solution is required (see Kahneman & Lovallo, 1990).

One goal that cannot be accomplished by such updating methods is that of allowing a clinician to make a judgment about a particular individual at a particular setting at a certain time in a manner that is unrelated to judgments about other people in other settings or at other times. Such judgments can be variously characterized as the exercise of expertise, or as "shooting from the hip" (Russo & Schoemaker, 1989, p. 143). In light of the research covered in this chapter and elsewhere, we see little reason for endorsing such judgments. (Even the expert claiming to make a clinical judgment on a "purely intuitive" basis attempts to substantiate its validity on the basis of experience with *people* [plural] similar to the person about whom the judgment is made.) Thus, for example, the conservative stance of Rubin's work in using regressed weighting coefficients is in our view a virtue, not a problem. The major point that statistical models are every bit as amenable to modification as is intuitive judgment is not vitiated by our recommendation to proceed cautiously in such modifications.

We suggest that there is no reason *not* to use available statistical techniques to maximize the predictability of models, when in fact models have been shown to be superior to clinical judgment. The research has been focussed primarily on demonstrating, or often questioning, this superiority, without a simultaneous consideration of how best to take advantage of it. Although others (e.g., Kleinmuntz, 1990) have urged that people combine their heads with their models in prediction, we urge that people use their heads to improve their models.

REFERENCES

Arkes, H. R., Dawes, R. M., & Christensen, C. (1986). Factors influencing the use of a decision rule in a probabilistic task. *Organizational Behavior and Human Decision Processes, 37,* 93–110. (Reprinted in J. Dowie and A. Elstein, Eds., *Professional judgment,* Cambridge, England: Cambridge University Press, 1987.)

Beaver, W. H. (1966). *Empirical research and accounting: Selective studies.* Chicago, IL: University of Chicago, Graduate School of Business, Institute of Professional Accounting.

Blattberg, R. C., & Hoch, S. J. (in press). Database models and managerial intuitions 50% model to 50% manager. *Management Science.*

Bloch, D. A., & Moses, L. E. (1988). Non-optimally weighted least squares. *The American Statistician, 42,* 50–53.

Bloom, R. F., & Brundage, E. G. (1947). Predictions of success in elementary school for enlisted personnel. In D. B. Stuit (Ed.), *Personnel research and test development in the Naval Bureau of Personnel* (pp. 233–261). Princeton, NJ: Princeton University Press.

Brannen, A. L., Godfrey, L. J., & Goetter, W. E. (1989). Prediction of outcome from critical illness: A comparison of clinical judgment with a prediction rule. *Archives of Internal Medicine, 149,* 1083–1086.

Breiman, L., & Freedman, D. (1983). How many variables should be entered into a regression equation? *Journal of the American Statistical Association, 78,* 131–136.

Carroll, B. (1987). Artificial intelligence expert systems for clinical diagnosis: Are they worth the effort? *Behavioral Science, 32,* 274–292.

Carroll, J. S., Winer, R. L., Coates, D., Galegher, J., & Alibrio, J. J. (1982). Evaluation, diagnosis, and prediction in parole decision making. *Law and Society Review, 17,* 199–228.

Castellan, N. J., Jr. (1973). Comments on the "lens model" equation and the analysis of multiple-cue judgment tasks. *Psychometrika, 38,* 87–100.

Chow, W. M. (1965). Adaptive control of the exponential smoothing constant. *Journal of Industrial Engineering, 16,* 314–317.

Dawes, R. M. (1971). A case study of graduate admissions: Application of three principles of human decision making. *American Psychologist, 26,* 180–188.

Dawes, R. M. (1979). The robust beauty of improper linear models. *American Psychologist, 34,* 571–582.

Dawes, R. M. (1988). *Rational choice in an uncertain world.* San Diego, CA: Harcourt Brace Jovanovich.

Dawes, R. M. (in press). The prediction of the future from the understanding of the past. *American Journal of Psychology.*

Dawes, R. M., & Corrigan, B. (1974). Linear models in decision making. *Psychological Bulletin, 81,* 95–106.

Dawes, R. M., Faust, D., & Meehl, P. E. (1989). Clinical versus actuarial judgment. *Science, 243,* 1668–1674.

Deacon, E. B. (1972). A discriminant analysis of predictors of business failure. *Journal of Accounting Research, 10,* 167.

Drehmer, D. E., & Morris, G. W. (1981). Cross-validation with small samples: An algorithm for computing Gollob's estimator. *Educational and Psychological Measurement, 41,* 195–200.

Duncan, D. B., & Horn, S. D. (1972). Linear dynamic recursive estimation from the viewpoint of regression analysis. *Journal of the American Statistical Association, 67,* 815–821.

Einhorn, H. (1972). Expert measurement and mechanical combination. *Organizational Behavior and Human Performance, 7,* 86–106.

Faust, D., Meehl, P. E., & Dawes, R. M. (1990). Clinical and actuarial judgment: Response. *Science, 247,* 146–147.

Gergonne, J. D. (1817). Essai de dialectique rationelle. *Annales des mathematiques pures et appliques, 7.*

Glaser, D. (1964). *The effectiveness of a prison and parole system.* Indianapolis: Bobbs-Merrill.

Goldberg, L. R. (1965). Diagnosticians versus diagnostic signs: The diagnosis of psychosis versus neurosis from the MMPI. *Psychological Monographs: General and Applied, 79* (No. 9).

Goldberg, L. R. (1968). Simple models or simple processes? Some research on clinical judgments. *American Psychologist, 23,* 483–496.

Goldberg, L. R. (1977). Admission to the Ph.D. Program in the Department of Psychology at the University of Oregon. *American Psychologist, 32,* 663–668.

Goldman, L., Cook, E. F., Brand, D. A., Lee, T. H., Rouan, G. W., Weisberg, M. C., Acampora, D. A., Stasiulewicz, C., Walshon, J., Terranova, G., Gottlieb, L., Kobernick, M., Goldstein-Wayne, B., Copen, D., Daley, K., Brandt, A. A., Jones, D., Mellors, J., & Jakubowski,

R. (1988). A computer protocol to predict myocardial infarction in emergency department patients with chest pain. *The New England Journal of Medicine, 318* (13), 797–802.

Gollob, H. F. (1967, September). *Cross-validation using samples of size one.* Paper presented at the American Psychological Association meetings, Washington, DC.

Gottfredson, D., Wilkins, L. T., & Hoffman, T. B. (1978). *Guidelines for parole and sentencing.* Lexington, MA: Lexington Books.

Hammond, K. R., Hursch, C. J., & Todd, F. J. (1964). Analyzing the components of clinical inference. *Psychological Review, 71,* 438–456.

Hammond, K. R., & Summers, D. A. (1965). Cognitive dependence on linear and nonlinear cues. *Psychological Review, 72,* 215–224.

Inwald, R. E. (1988). Five year follow-up study of departmental terminations as predicted by 16 pre-employment psychological indicators. *Journal of Applied Psychology, 73,* 703–710.

Kahneman, D., & Lovallo, D. (in press). Timid decisions and bold forecasts: A cognitive perspective on risk taking. *Journal of Strategic Management.*

Kalman, R. E. (1960). A new approach to linear filtering and prediction problems. *Transactions ASME Journal of Basic Engineering, 82,* 35–45.

Kalman, R. E. (1963). New methods in Wiener filtering theory. In J. L. Bodanoff & F. Kozin (Eds.), *Proceedings of the First Symposium on Engineering Applications of Random Function Theory and Probability* (pp. 270–388). New York: Wiley.

Kleinmuntz, B. (1990). Clinical and actuarial judgment. *Science, 247.*

Knaus, W. A., Wagner, D. P., & Lynn, J. (1991). Short-term mortality predictions for critically ill hospitalized adults: Science and ethics. *Science, 254,* 389–395.

Lee, K. L., Pryor, D. B., Harrell, F. E., Califf, R. M., Behar, V. S., Floyd, W. L., Morris, J. J., Waugh, R. A., Whalen, R. E., & Rosati, R. A. (1986). Predicting outcome in coronary disease. *The American Journal of Medicine, 80,* 553–560.

Leirer, V. O., Warner, P. D., Rose, T. L., & Yesavage, J. A. (1985, August). *Predictions of violence by high school students and clinicians.* Presented at the American Psychological Association Convention, Los Angeles.

Leli, D. A., & Filskov, S. B. (1984). Clinical deterioration associated with brain damage. *Journal of Clinical Psychology, 40,* 1435–1441.

Lerner, M. J. (1980). *The belief in a just world: A fundamental delusion.* New York: Plenum.

Lerner, M. J. (1987). Integrating societal and psychological rules of entitlement: The basic task of each social actor and fundamental problem for the social sciences. *Social Justice Research, 1,* 107–125.

Libby, R. (1976). Man versus model of man: Some conflicting evidence. *Organizational Behavior and Human Performance, 16,* 1–12.

Malmquist, C. P., & Meehl, P. E. (1978). Barabbas: A study in guilt-ridden homicide. *The International Review of Psycho-Analysis, 5,* 149–179.

Meehl, P. E. (1954). *Clinical versus statistical prediction.* Minneapolis, MN: University of Minnesota Press.

Meehl, P. E. (1986). Causes and effects of my disturbing little book. *Journal of Personality Assessment, 50,* 370–375.

Miller, M., & Morris, N. (1988). *Violence and victims, 3,* 263–328.

Pearson, R., Ross, M., & Dawes, R. M. (in press). Personal recall and the limits of retrospective questions in surveys. In J. Tanur (Ed.), *Questions about survey questions.* New York: Russell Sage.

Rubin, D. E. (1980). Using empirical Bayes techniques in the law school validity studies. *Journal of the American Statistical Association, 75,* 801–816.

Rumelhart, D. E., Hinton, G. E., & Williams, R. J. (1986). Learning representations by back-propagating errors. *Nature, 323,* 533–536.

Russo, J. E., & Schoemaker, P. J. H. (1989). *Decision traps.* New York: Doubleday.

Sawyer, J. (1966). Measurement and prediction, clinical and statistical. *Psychological Bulletin, 66,* 178–200.

Schilpp, P. A. (1949). *Albert Einstein: Philosopher-scientist.* Evanston, IL: Library of Living Philosophers.

Schmitt, N., Coyle, B. W., & Rauschenberger, J. (1977). A Monte Carlo evaluation of three formula estimates of cross-validated multiple correlation. *Psychological Bulletin, 84,* 751–758.

Schofield, W., & Garrard, J. (1975). Longitudinal study of medical students selected for admissions to medical school by actuarial and committee methods. *British Journal of Medical Education, 9,* 86–90.

Sutton, G. C. (1989). How accurate is computer-aided diagnosis? *Lancet,* October 14, 905–908.

Tucker, L. R. (1964). A suggested alternative formulation in the developments by Hursch, Hammond, and Hursch, and by Hammond, Hursch, and Todd. *Psychological Review, 71,* 528–530.

Tukey, J. W. (1948). Approximate weights. *Annals of Mathematical Statistics, 19,* 91–92.

Wainer, H. (1976). Estimating coefficients in linear models: It don't make no nevermind. *Psychological Bulletin, 83,* 312–317.

Wainer, H. (1978). On the sensitivity of regression and regressors. *Psychological Bulletin, 85,* 267–273.

Wedding, D. (1983). Clinical and statistical prediction in neuropsychology. *Clinical Neuropsychology, V,* 49–54.

Werner, P. D., Rose, T. L., & Yesavage, J. A. (1983). Reliability, accuracy, and decision making strategy in clinical predictions of imminent dangerousness. *Journal of Consulting and Clinical Psychology, 51,* 815–825. (Companion piece: Liere, V. O., Werner, P. D., Rose, T. L., & Yesavage, J. A. *Predictions of violence by high school students and clinicians.* Paper presented at the 1984 Oregon Psychological Association Spring Convention, Newport, Oregon.)

Wiggins, N., & Cohen, E. S. (1971). Man versus model of man revisited: The forecasting of graduate school success. *Journal of Personality and Social Psychology, 19,* 100–106.

Wilks, S. S. (1938). Weighting systems for linear functions of correlated variables when there is no dependent variable. *Psychometrika, 8,* 23–30.

14 The Perception of Randomness

Maya Bar-Hillel
The Hebrew University

Willem A. Wagenaar
University of Leiden

Randomness is a concept that somehow eludes satisfactory definition. Devices that are random by definition, such as fair coins, can nonetheless generate series of outcomes that lack the appearance of randomness (e.g., a very long string of Heads), whereas some digit series, although clearly patterned, define normal numbers, namely, numbers whose decimal form provably passes all tests for randomness (e.g., the infinite series obtained from writing down all the counting numbers in order:

$$1234567891011121314151617181920212223 \ldots).$$

In effect, randomness is an unobservable property of a generating process. Theory can assume this property, but in practice it can only be inferred indirectly, from properties of the generator's output. The inspection of outputs for "randomness" involves subjecting them to various statistical tests of these necessary, but not sufficient, properties. The conclusions based on these tests are thus inherently statistical in nature—there are no logical or physical proofs of randomness.

WHY STUDY THE PERCEPTION OF RANDOMNESS?

Where people see patterns, they seek, and often see, meaning. Regarding something as random is attributing it to (mere, or blind) chance. Perceiving events as random or nonrandom has significance for the conduct of human affairs, because matters of consequence may depend on it. The market price of stocks is essentially a random walk, but people see trends in it, with the help of which they attempt to predict future prices. People may be promoted (or demoted) for strings

369

of job-related successes (or failures) that are in effect no more than chance results. Coincidences are given significant, and often even mystical, interpretations, because their occurence seems to transcend statistical explanation.

The categorization of events into random or nonrandom is often done intuitively. Moreover, the emergence of "patterns" from what is essentially "noise" is so powerful, that people may reject the statistical analysis, even when it is available, in favor of the intuitive feeling. The perception, whether visual or conceptual, is so compelling as to withstand analysis. Much as the famous Müller-Lyer illusion is not dispelled by measurement (see Fig. 14.1), the perceived "clumping" of random events is not dispelled by statistical analysis (see Fig. 14.2). Indeed, it has led to the development of what statisticians call *clumping theory*.

One of the best-known examples of the misperception of randomness concerns the pattern of German flying-bombs that hit London during World War 2. "Most people believed in a tendency of the points of impact to cluster," though analysis showed the "fit of the Poisson distribution [to be] surprisingly good" indicating "perfect randomness . . . ; we have here an instructive illustration of the established fact that to the trained eye randomness appears as regularity or tendency to cluster" (Feller, 1950, p. 120). Another well-known example is people's incredulity at the fact that among a sample of 40 people, chances are in excess of 90% that two will share a birthday. A perhaps less well-known example is often exploited by so-called psychics, whose success at predicting people's supposedly random generations ("pick a number between 50 and 99, made of two different, and odd, digits") results from the combined facts that these generations are not really random, and that the probability of both the psychic and the medium choosing the same number, even if it were really done at random, is highly underestimated (Marks & Kammann, 1980). As a final example, clumping causes people's experience often to bear out the superstition that "bad luck comes in threes."

The motivation for studying perceptions of randomness could also come from an interest in intuition. Intuition is accorded an important and respectable role in many types of judgments. Modern linguistics regards (a competent native speak-

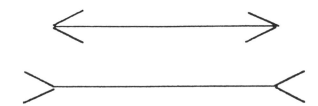

FIG. 14.1.   The Müller–Lyer illusion. The horizonal segments are of equal length.

FIG. 14.2. A 12 × 12 binary matrix with a 0.5 alternation rate. Notice the clumping of the black cells into "areas."

er's reflective) intuition to be the final arbiter of grammaticality. In aesthetics (e.g., judging the quality of a piece of art) or ethics (e.g., judging the fairness of an allocation rule) intuition is often all there is to go by. When judging the pitch of a tone, the temperature of a tub of water, or the mean of a set of data points—intuitive judgments are found to often provide acceptable, yet quick and ready, approximations to objective measurement. The study of *intuitive tests of randomness*, so to speak, thus acquires some interest also in comparison with normative tests thereof, even though—or because—there is no single statistical test sufficient to establish randomness.

This chapter examines some of the evidence collected by psychologists about people's intuitions regarding randomness. Psychologists have not themselves endeavored to define randomness. Rather, they have studied people's judgments of randomness, and their ability to "generate," or simulate, randomness. Often, though not always, they bypassed the problematics of the concept by omitting any mention of "randomness" in their instructions to subjects, and instead talking directly about standard and familiar *random devices*, such as coins or dies. For example, Bakan (1960) instructed subjects "to produce a series of 'heads' and 'tails' such as they might expect to occur if an unbiased coin were tossed in an unbiased manner" (p. 128). The subjects' output is then compared with either a formal analysis or a simulation of the device in question on the properties of choice.[1]

The chapter is organized according to (a) what—the descriptive properties of people's judgments and/or productions; (b) how—modeling the judgmental process and/or the cognitive production mechanism; (c) why—what sustains the erroneous subjective concept of randomness, and why it is not unlearned with experience.

---

[1]Occasionally, instructions have been biased. For example, Baddeley (1966) told subjects that the kind of random sequence they were expected to generate "would be completely jumbled and would not therefore be likely to comprise [meaningful patterns]" (p. 119). A critique of other instructions can be found in Ayton, Hunt, and Wright (1989).

WHAT?

It is perhaps unfortunate that early laboratory studies of the perception of randomness relied on production tasks ("do like a coin") rather than judgment tasks ("is this like a coin?"), and the former still form a majority of the existent studies. Insofar as systematic biases are found in such tasks, it is apparent that they could be either accurate reflections of biased notions of randomness, or biased reflections of accurate notions of randomness (or both). By analogy, people who have linguistic competence may still produce ungrammatical sentences in actual speech, and people who have a good musical ear may fail to carry a tune properly. Hence, judgment tasks are a purer way of studying the perception of randomness. Nonetheless, the basic biases in subjective perceptions of randomness were discovered already by the early production tasks.

The Basic Findings

Table 14.1 (from Wagenaar, 1972a) shows the many varieties of tasks that were used in several early studies of random productions (an even earlier review can

TABLE 14.1
Description of Ten Pre-1970 Random Production Studies

Author & Year	# of Symbols	Symbols	Length	Medium	Pace	N
Baddeley 1966	26	letters	2 × 100	saying	4,2,1,.5	12
"	26	letters	16 × 100	saying	2	12
"	2,4,8,16,26	letters	3 × 120	writing	1	124
"	2,4,8,16,26	letters	3 × ?	writing	—	120
"	2,4,8,16,26	digits	3 × ?	writing	—	92
Bakan 1960	2	H/T	2 × 150	writing	—	70
Chapanis 1953	10	digits	1 × 2520	writing	—	13
Rath 1966	2	digits	10 × 250	writing	.5	20
"	10	digits	10 × 250	writing	.75	20
"	26	letters	10 × 250	writing	1	20
Ross 1955	2	digits	1 × 100	stamping	?	60
Ross & Levy 1958	2	H/T	8 × 20	writing	?	15
"	2	H/T	4 × 20	writing	?	15
Teraoka 1963	5	digits	1 × 1252	saying	—	4
"	5	letters	1 × 1252	saying	—	4
"	5	nonsense syllables	1 × 251	saying	—	2
"	5	digits	1 × 751	saying	1	3
"	5	digits	1 × 752	saying	—	3
Warren & Morin 1965	2,4,8	digits	6 × 500	saying	.25,.5,.75	2
Weiss 1964	2	buttons	1 × 600	pushing	1	28
Wolitzky & Spence 1968	10	digits	1 × 45	writing	2.45	20

be found in Tune, 1964a, 1964b). These studies were startingly unsystematic. The number of alternatives varied from 2 (e.g., heads-tails, digits, card suits) to 26 (letters), produced in from 1 to 16 series per subject, of length from 20 up to 2,520 each. Mode of production (e.g., writing, calling out), as well as speed (from no limitation to 4 per second), availability of memory aids (from none to complete record), and other factors, also varied across the studies. With the exception of number of alternatives, and the required production rate, these variables were not varied within a single study.

Table 14.2 gives the measures or tests for nonrandomness that these studies employed. Deviations from randomness can appear in various forms. First, it is possible that the various alternatives be chosen with unequal frequencies. This is

TABLE 14.2
Results of Ten Pre-1970 Random Production Studies

Author & Year	Measure	Order	Results
Baddeley 1966	stereotyped and repeated digrams	1	stereotyped digrams unbalanced frequencies of
	redundancy	0	1- and 2-grams
Bakan 1960	number of runs	1	avoidance of symmetric
	alternation and		response patterns
	symmetry in trigrams	2	
	frequency of singletons	0	
Chapanis 1953	frequency of singletons	0	unbalanced frequencies of
	frequency of digrams		1,2, and 3-grams
	and trigrams	1,2	preference to decreasing
	autocorrelation	1,?	over increasing series
Rath 1966	frequency of singletons	0	preference for symbols
	frequency of digrams,		adjacent in the natural
	corrected; modified	1	order
	frequency of trigrams,		
	corrected	2	
Ross 1955	frequency of singletons	0	
	number of alternations	1	
Ross & Levy 1958	number of alternations	1	overuse of run length with
	occurence of runs	1–?	expected frequency ≥ 1
Teraoka 1963	frequency of singletons	0	stringing responses in their
	conditional probabilities	1	natural order
	frequency of digrams,		dependencies over gaps of 5
	modified	1	periodicity with cycle 5
	frequency of runs	1–4	
Warren & Morin 1965	redundancy	0–3	
Weiss 1964	frequency of n-grams,		
	corrected	1–9	preference for symmetric
	frequency of trigrams		trigrams
Wolitzky & Spence 1968	frequency of singletons	0	

called a *zero-order sequential effect*, because it does not involve any sequential property of the response series. Then, it is possible that the first-order transition probabilities reveal a sequential dependency. This first-order sequential dependency would appear as deviation from the expected frequencies of pair combinations (or, equivalently, from the expected number of either alternations or runs). First-order effects extend across a distance of one in the sequence. Higher-order effects test for dependencies between elements that are two, three, and so forth, places apart in the sequence. Some statistical measures of randomness confound effects of various orders (e.g., a paucity of runs of length *n* subsumes a first-order alternation effect), and some require longer sequences than others in order to apply meaningfully (e.g., testing runs of length *n* + *m* versus of length *n*). Statistically equivalent measures may correspond to different psychological processes, so the distinctions between them should be kept in mind for interpretative purposes.

The findings of these studies were reported in terms of the measures selected, and sometimes invented, by their authors (see Table 14.2). In spite of the variety of tasks and measures used, two fairly robust findings emerged from these studies, that have since withstood the test of time. The first concerns what are essentially motor biases, specific to the production task, and to the medium within which it is performed. It has no parallel in judgment tasks, and is not a reflection of notions of randomness. This is overpreponderance of short strings (two or three) of symbols that are adjacent in some "natural" sequence (e.g., consecutive numbers or letters) or some artifactual one (e.g., on the keyboard). This finding is not discussed further.

Second, "human produced sequences have too few symmetries and long runs, too many alternations among events, and too much balancing of event frequencies over relatively short regions" (Lopes & Oden, 1987, p. 392). The alternation bias is also called the *negative recency* effect, and it confirms a hypothesis that Reichenbach stated as early as 1934 (Reichenbach, 1949). The balancing over short regions is also called the *local representativeness* effect (Kahneman & Tversky, 1972). These closely related effects have been found to extend up to the sixth order of dependency. They are regarded as essentially cognitive biases, and as such, they have direct counterparts in judgment tasks.

In typical judgment tasks, sequences are presented to subjects, who are requested to select the sequence that is "more likely to have been produced by a fair coin" or "most random," or—conversely—which is "most patterned." Few researchers thought to study the perception of randomness in matched judgment and production tasks. An exception is Falk (1975), who asked subjects to rate for "randomness" exactly the same kinds of binary strings or binary matrices that her other subjects had been required to generate. In the production phase, Falk gave subjects 20 green and 20 yellow cards, and asked them to line them up "the way they would be if they were well shuffled."[2] She found the preferred alternation

---

[2]This is not, of course, a Bernoulli process.

rate to be not .5, but .6. Falk extended her study to two dimensional arrays—specifically, 10 × 10 matrices—instructing her subjects to color 50 of the 100 cells a single color "in a random way." She then generalized the notion of "alternation" to the matrix, defining it as two different-colored cells with a shared side. Falk found that the preferred alternation rate in the two-dimensional arrays was again .6, "equal to the 99th percentile in the mathematical sampling distribution of random binary tables" of this kind (Falk, 1981, p. 227). In the analogous one- and two-dimensional judgment tasks, Falk found the same alternation rate (i.e., .6) to be rated as most random, in preference even to strings (or matrices) with an alternation rate of .5—which is the statistically expected value (see Fig. 14.3). Indeed, ask yourself how random you find the matrix in Fig. 14.2, which was generated by coloring each cell of the array with $p = .5$.

Wagenaar (1970a) found the same bias. Presenting subjects with seven binary sequences at a time of white and black dots on a neutral gray background, he too found that "sequences with conditional probabilities [of repetition] around 0.4 were judged as most random" (p. 348). Some studies have reported higher alternation rates as subjectively "most random" (.7–.8 in Gilovich, Vallone, & Tversky's, 1985 "Hot hand" study described later).

In between-subject designs, the correlation between production biases and judgment biases is rather weak, around .3 for first-order deviation from randomness, dropping to about .2 for second-order effects, and virtually disappearing for higher-order effects (Wagenaar, 1972b; also Wiegersma, 1982a, 1982b). These tasks, however, were not as well matched as Falk's.

Other Judgment Studies

Detecting Random from Nonrandom Strings.   Lopes and Oden (1987) studied judgments of randomness within a totally different paradigm—that known as *signal detection*. Their stimuli were short binary strings (length 8)—much shorter than the strings that production tasks ask for. These strings were computer-generated on-line for each subject (so could be different for each subject). A subject viewed 250 strings generated by a Bernoulli process with $p = .5$. These were randomly interspersed with 250 strings generated by a process with an alternation probability of .8 (or, for other subjects, with an alternation probability of .2). On each trial, subjects guessed which process had generated the presented string, and were given a small monetary reward if they guessed correctly. Note that "correct" here is literal, not to be confused with "optimal."

Subjects' performance (i.e., percent correct) was compared with the actual (rather than expected) percent correct of an "optimal" rule based on maximum likelihood. The rule averaged about 82% correct. The subjects' hit rate depended on the conditions under which they were guessing, namely: Were they in the .8 or in the .2 alternation rate group? Were they informed about the direction of the alternation bias, or not? If not, did they get trial by trial feedback about the correct source of the string? The results appear in Table 14.3. All subjects

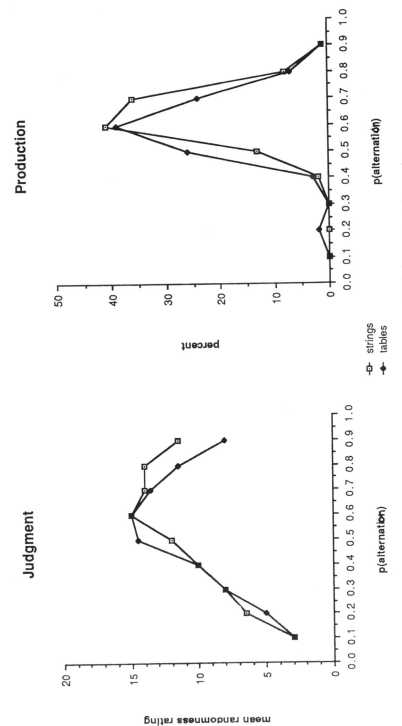

FIG. 14.3. Results of Falk's 1981 study, separated for the judgment and the production tasks.

TABLE 14.3
The Statistical Descriptors Used in Neuringer's (1986) Study

Probability of Making Correct Choice Between Random and Nonrandom Source			
uninformed; p(repetition) = .8	65%	uninformed; p(alternation) = .8	52%
informed; p(repetition) = .8	71%	informed; p(alternation) = .8	67%
feedback; p(repetition) = .8	71%	feedback; p(alernation) = .8	67%
[changed from 64% to 74%]		[changed from 56% to 76%]	

performed at better than chance level, and those operating under the most favorable conditions did not do much worse than the optimal rule. There was considerable variability in percent correct as a function of the type of string (i.e., did the string exhibit a cyclic or mirror symmetry, or had it no particular pattern?)—the hit rate was much higher for the nonpatterned strings, in line with familiar biases noted earlier. But even though performance for some types of strings fell considerably short even of chance, the ecological rarity of these "trick" strings prevented them from having much of an effect on overall performance. Lopes and Oden (1987) concluded that "biases in people's conceptions of randomness, although real enough, are less important to performance in the detection task than [whether or not judges know the direction of the bias in the non-Bernoulli process]" (p. 398). These results are compatible with previous findings (e.g., Cook, 1967) showing people to be more successful in correctly selecting the more "random" stimulus when the distractors happen to be highly patterned (e.g., regular or symmetric) or frequency biased (i.e., contain a preponderance of one of the two symbols).

The "Hot Hand" in Basketball.   A provocative judgment study, whose conclusions raised much passionate debate, was done by Gilovich et al. (1985). Rather than only manufacture artificial stimuli and ask subjects for their judgments, this study took as its point of departure a preexisting naturally formed judgment, and checked for its validity. The judgment in question is the belief, shared by basketball spectators and participants alike, in the existence of a "hot hand" or "streak shooting" phenomenon.

A corollary of the negative recency effect (and an example of the clumping effect) is that strings exhibiting the mathematically expected number of alternations will contain runs that appear to people inordinately long, hence "nonrandom." In a basketball context this could mean that a player's string of shots in a game will occasionally exhibit noticeable "streaks" of hits even if it is generated by a stationary process. Indeed, "analyses of the shooting records of the Philadelphia 76ers [including reputed streak shooter Andrew Toney] provided no evidence [for streak shooting]" (Gilovich et al., 1985, p. 295). Contrary to the belief of 100 basketball fans who were surveyed for their beliefs regarding sequential dependence among shots, the very data forming the basis for this belief shows unequivocally that the probability that a player will make a given shot is not higher after having made a previous shot than after having missed it. Significantly, when Gilovich et al.'s subjects were shown on paper strings of 11 X's and 10 O's that were created using an alternation probability of .5, they saw streaks there too. Apparently, the streaks that basketball aficionados report seeing in the game of some player are no more streaky than those exhibited by a random device whose p matches that player's hit rate. Hence players, even when they streak-shoot, are actually no "hotter" than random coins.

The Gambler's Fallacy.   The *gambler's fallacy* is another name for the negative recency effect. It refers to gamblers' reputed tendency in a game of roulette to gamble on red after a run of blacks. In an ingenious study, Gold and Hester (1989) demonstrated that this belief extends to an expectation that random devices somehow "intentionally monitor" their own output to make sure it balances out. Their subjects were shown a (secretly manipulated) sequence of coin tosses. On each trial, a "winning side" was specified, and subjects chose whether or not to gamble on it. If they did, they earned 100 points on the winning side, 0 otherwise. If they did not, they simply got 70 points. Seventy points was chosen because this is the value around which subjects usually split evenly between preferring the gamble or the sure thing. However, following a run of Heads (Tails), the subjects clearly preferred the gamble when the winning side was specified as Tails (Heads) and the sure thing when it was specified as Heads (Tails). This behavior is consistent with the gambler's fallacy. This was the case even for subjects whose verbally expressed beliefs countermanded the gambler's fallacy. Gold and Hester found that either switching coins before the target toss, or allowing the coin to "rest" awhile prior to it, reversed this preference for the gamble almost completely. It is as if subjects believe that the "mechanism" that "causes" the coin to exhibit negative recency is a memory-type one: It does not carry over from coin to coin, and it decays over time.

Other Production Studies

Production Tasks with a Large Number of Symbols.   Whereas judgments are not biased in terms of zero-order effects (i.e., relative frequencies), nor are productions that utilize a small number (e.g., two) of elements, production frequencies are seldom uniform when a large number of symbols is involved (see, e.g., Tables 14.1 and 14.2). As a case in point, Triesman and Faulkner (1987) found that when asked to produce random sequences of the digits subjects did not always produce uniform distributions. For example, 0 and 1 were typically underrepresented, whereas 3 was overrepresented (see Fig. 14.4). Moreover, this bias represents a consistent and systematic individual difference between subjects. The mean correlation between the distributions of digit frequencies given by subjects in two sessions conducted on different days was

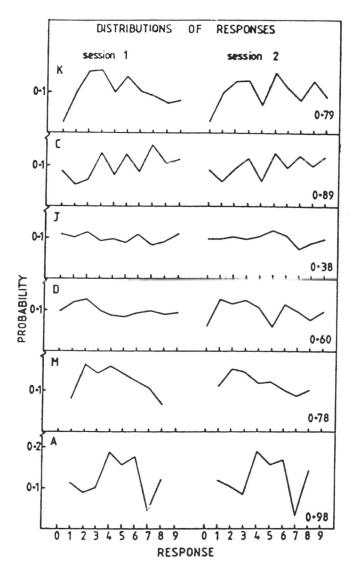

FIG. 14.4.   Distribution of responses for 6 subjects in Triesman and Faulkner's (1987) study. The numbers on the left are the cross-session correlations.

0.79. Other tasks where responses allegedly drawn at random from a uniform distribution are not uniformly distributed are mentioned in a later section.

Avoidance of Patterns.   Kubovy and Gilden (1990) gave subjects an answer sheet designed for multiple choice tests, and asked them to fill in the 240 circles in sequence, according to whether they imagine a coin coming up Heads or Tails.

They found their subjects careful to maintain a balance of 50%–50% within short sequences (4 to 11), but found little evidence that subjects avoid "patterned" sequences, such as 000111, or 010010. By their own admission, however, such patterns have low salience when embedded in larger series (e.g., how salient are these two patterns in the sequence: 101001000111011011?), and are harder to control than the short-range balance.

Stationariness in Production.   Budescu (1987) tested for, and found, stationariness in the series produced by his subjects. His subjects generated 60 series at most, however, and few if any of the subject-generated binary sequences extended to more than a few hundred elements. This is too short to test a hypothesis such that tolerance for, therefore the frequency of, longer runs or symmetric patterns will increase as the series extends, even if the rate of this increase will not be nearly enough. If this hypothesis is true, then the familiar biases can exist even in the absence of stationariness. Indeed, Wagenaar (1971) reported that "non-randomness decreases with time spent at the task" (p. 78).

Probability Learning: Predicting Random Sequences.   A paradigm that utilized production for purposes of prediction generated much research in the 1950s and 1960s (see Estes, 1964; Jones, 1971). Subjects predict a randomly generated binary sequence trial by trial, with feedback given after every trial. The proportions of the two symbols were typically not equal. The major finding in the probability learning paradigm is called *probability matching:* Subjects' prediction frequencies eventually came to match the observed frequency in the sequence. Though this is a clear manifestation that subjects learned the production probabilities, matching has a lower expected accuracy than merely predicting the majority category throughout (because $p \times p + (1 - p) \times (1 - p) < p$, for every $1/2 < p < 1$). More pertinent to present purposes, subjects' predictions "seemed to have preferences for patterns . . . reflecting their ideas of "chance"" (Tune, 1964a, p. 294), namely, avoidance of long runs.

A Learning Study

Although people's productions have failed many different types of tests for randomness, suitable feedback and training can apparently teach them how to overcome the biases they tend to exhibit. The most ambitious and thorough study of this kind was carried out by Neuringer (1986). In the Before phase, 11 students generated 60 series of 100 binary responses each (by self-paced typing of two digits on a computer keypad "as randomly as possible"). In the Feedback phase, feedback from several statistical descriptors was given just after each additional series of 100 responses was generated. There were two Feedback conditions, utilizing either 5 or 10 descriptors (with 7 subjects in the first, 4 in the second condition). The set of descriptors is described in Table 14.4.

Feedback was given as follows: For each descriptor, five equiprobable catego-

TABLE 14.4
Results of Lopes and Oden's (1987) Study

The first batch of five descriptors, in order of their introduction[a]

1. RNG1—based on the deviation of the observed frequencies of the 4 kinds of diagrams from their expectancies
2. RNG2—likewise, but alternate (rather than contiguous) responses are paired
3. C1—likewise, but response i of trial n is paired with response of i of $n + 1$
4. C2—likewise, but response i of trial n is paired with response i of $n + 2$
5. Number of alternations

The second batch of five descriptors, in order of their introduction

6. Relative frequency of the binary symbols
7. RUNS1—number of singletons
8. RUNS2—number of doubletons
9. RUNS3—number of triplets
10. RUNS4—number of quartets

[a]The notations and terminology are Neuringer's.

ries were found by computer simulation, and subjects were shown a tabulation of the quintile values that their series of 100 responses had scored on the descriptors. They were told to try to produce an equal number of series in each of the five categories (quintiles). Subjects were started out with feedback on descriptor 1 only. As soon as they had managed to generate at least one series in each quintile, feedback on the second descriptor was added, till the same criterion was achieved on it, too, at which point the third descriptor was added for feedback purposes, and so forth.

Sessions lasted about an hour, in which time subjects typically produced 60 series (100 long) each. Subjects were free to ask questions, and were given some explicit suggestions on how they might improve their performance (i.e., how they might generate a series whose appropriate descriptor would fall into a chosen category). Feedback sessions were piled up as long as was necessary for a subject to reach a criterion of 60 consecutive series (or 2×60, in the 10 descriptor condition), none of which deviated significantly (according to the Kolmogorov–Smirnoff statistic) from the computer-generated "random" series on any of the 5 (or 10) descriptors. Although there was considerable variance in learning speed, all subjects eventually reached this criterion (e.g., after a maximum of 483 feedback trials when 5 measures were used, and 1771 when 10 measures were used).[3]

The last 60 series were additionally analyzed according to eight new descriptors on which subjects had not been trained (e.g., binomial test, one-sample runs test, some chi-square tests, and some autocorrelations). These are tests that naive

---

[3]Needless to say, no such improvements were noted in a control group receiving no feedback.

subjects typically fail. However, two of the four trained subjects passed all eight new tests, and the other two passed six of them (though the *combined* responses of the last 60 series—that is, 6,000 responses per subject—failed some tests for all subjects).

In addition to these subjects, Neuringer himself served as a lone subject receiving feedback on 30 statistical descriptors in a 10-symbol generation task, and eventually achieved criterion performance (Neuringer, 1984).

Neuringer (1986) was quick to admit that "for both apriori and empirical reasons, we cannot conclude that subjects learned to behave 'truly randomly'" (p. 73). Moreover, whatever it was that subjects did learn was not permanent in that it seemed to deteriorate markedly as soon as feedback was discontinued.

HOW

Is There a Random Device in the Mind?

There is much evidence to show that people perform certain cognitive tasks by constructing or consulting mental images, little "pictures in the head," on which mental operations are performed in analogy to the operations that the represented object would have been subjected to in the physical world. For example, when asked on which side of his head George Bush parts his hair, many people report that they form a mental image of George Bush, and "look" at it to "see" the answer (Kosslyn, 1980); when asked what letter is formed when the letter N is rotated 90 degrees clockwise, they report "rotating" a little mental picture of N in their head (Cooper & Shepard, 1973); when asked at what speed a car was going when it crashed, people consult a mental video of the accident (Loftus, 1979).

It thus could, in principle, have been the case that when people are asked to produce "heads" and "tails" as if they were tossing a coin, they form a mental image of a coin in their head, "toss" it, and read out the observed results. Alas, that seems not to be the case. Might there, nonetheless, be some random device in the mind, or in the nervous system, that generates the responses subjects produce, but, unlike mental imaging, is opaque to introspection? The observed biases could be introduced at a later stage by the "reporter" of the random device's outcomes.

There are apriori grounds against the plausibility of "random generators in the mind." First, when good random devices are so notoriously difficult to find in the external physical world—why would there be any in the mind? Second, an internal random device subject to censorship, instead of accounting for the presence of biases, merely adds the question: How does the internal random generator work? Third, the model smacks of homunculism. It is a little like explaining the creations of a mediocre composer as the result of some unfortunate mental meddling in the creations of a little Mozart residing in the mediocre composer's head. Nonetheless, some have argued for this possibility (e.g., Triesman & Faulkner, 1987).

Kubovy and Gilden (1988) tested a production model according to which people have an internal random device that generates strings, but those strings that turn out insufficiently representative are blocked or censored. They subjected Bernoulli strings to various kinds of "representativeness filters" (such as, "eliminate strings with runs longer than 4"; "eliminate strings with perfect alternation"; etc.), and compared this truncated set to a set of human productions. The deviations between the simulation and the real thing was too large and systematic to be chalked to chance. Strangely, Kubovy concluded that the observed biases in "subjective randomness" cannot be the result of representativeness filters, rather than concluding that there cannot be a random generator in the head.

The Account by Local Representativeness

In the accompanying "Peanuts" strip (Fig. 14.5), Linus is taking a true-or-false exam. Linus is assuming, presumably, that true-or-false test developers randomize the order of correct answers to foil the testees, yet he attempts to predict this order. His paradoxical conclusion: "If you're smart you can pass a true or false test without being smart!" nicely captures the essence of the paradox of randomness: In order to be perceived as random, sequences cannot be afforded to be constructed at random.[4] "As a series of digits . . . comes closer and closer to satisfying all the tests for randomness it begins to exhibit a very rare and unusual type of statistical regularity that in some cases even permits the prediction of missing portions" (Gardner, 1977, pp. 164–165).

Linus's sequence of Trues (0) and Falses (1) is nicely compatible with Kahneman and Tversky's (1972) conclusion that, up to symbol exchange and left–right exchange, there is a single binary sequence of length 6 (01101-0) that is "ideally random." Indeed, Linus's string (01101-1000-10) exactly agrees with Kahneman and Tversky's in the first five places, an agreement also shared with Popper (1959), who proposed an algorithm for constructing binary strings that start "randomly" and stay "random" throughout (the first 11 symbols in Popper's string are 01101-0111-10).[5]

Kahneman and Tversky's series derives from their representativeness notion, according to which people judge the probability of events by the extent to which they represent the essential characteristics of their generating source (1972). People also believe in a "law of small numbers" (Tversky & Kahneman, 1971), namely, they expect even small samples to be representative. Combining these

---

[4]This brings to mind Richard's paradox: "The smallest number that is undescribable in less than twelve words."

[5]We leave it to the reader to judge how closely these "ideals" match each other—and the reader's. The strings were broken into segments to facilitate the comparison.

FIG. 14.5. The perfectly ordered true–false test, according to Linus.
(PEANUTS character © 1952, United Feature Syndicate, Inc.)

two yields the simplest and most intuitive account of subjective randomness, that
of local representativeness. By this account, when asked to judge which of a set
of sequences is "most random," people look to see which captures the essential
features of the random generating device best. In the case of a fair coin, say,
these features are equiprobability of the two outcomes, along with some irregularity in the order of their appearance; these are expected to be manifest not only
in the long run, but even in relatively short segments—as short as six or seven.
The flaws in people's judgments of randomness in the large is the price of their
insistence on its manifestation in the small.

Local representativeness readily accounts for the main results of the judgment
tasks, namely, the high alternation rate and the rejection of pattern and symmetry.
Nonetheless, some investigators have rejected it on the grounds that it is inconsistent with some of the production tasks results (e.g., the observation of nonuniform distributions in tasks using large numbers of alternatives), and because
of the weak correlation observed between judgment and prediction tasks.

Clearly, however, production tasks make different cognitive demands than
judgment tasks. For example, it takes a degree of musicality to hear with your
inner ear how a piece of piano music should sound, but playing it to sound that
way calls for technique as well. Thus, it is possible that in a judgment task, most
subjects would judge the productions of Triesman and Faulkner's subject J (see
Fig. 14.4) as more random than those of subject A—including subject A, their
producer, himself.

The Account by Elimination
of Alternative Nonrandom Hypotheses

Diener and Thompson (1985) asked their subjects to guess which of 50 binary
strings of 20 elements had been "produced by a random process similar to tossing
a fair coin [and which] were generated by some other, nonrandom, methods" (pp.
438–439), and later to give their probability that each string was generated by a
fair coin. The results showed that for strings classified as "nonrandom," reaction
time (i.e., the time it took to give the response) was shorter the lower the
subject's confidence in the string's randomness, whereas for strings classified as
"random," the reaction time was on average higher, but no such relationship was

found between it and the confidence ratings. The authors interpreted their results as showing that people compare each sequence to an ordered and fixed list of hypotheses that are alternative to randomness. Nonrandom agents high in the hierarchy produce both short reaction times (for saying "nonrandom") and low probabilities (for "random"). Only when all alternatives are eliminated is a judgment of randomness given. The absence of a correlation between reaction time and confidence for the strings classified as random was taken by the authors to disconfirm an account relying on direct judgments of representativeness. However, many methodological weaknesses in this study render this conclusion dubious.

Can People Generate a Single Response "Randomly"?

Of all the factors that can account for the biases that are unique to production tasks, we focus on the role played by memory, a purely cognitive variable. We examine the body of production-tasks results in light of the following hypothesis: People attempt to produce series that will match their subjective notion of randomness (the flaws in which are apparent from judgment tasks results), and the extra biases unique to production tasks are added by functional limitations on this attempt.

Memory for previous responses is as difficult to eradicate altogether as it is to stretch indefinitely. Nonrandom productions can be blamed on the fact that memory for previous responses is limited, as well as on the fact that previous responses are remembered at all. Both accounts uphold that productions are guided by a mental image of randomness. According to the former, if memory could be stretched indefinitely, people would not experience difficulty in keeping a mental tally of previous responses, and we would not get nonuniform (unrepresentative) distributions.[6] According to the latter, if previous responses were totally lost to memory, new ones could hardly be dependent on them, so we would not, for example, observe the high alternation rates. Memory operates differently on different measures of randomness.

The issue of previous responses is bypassed when we ask if people can produce a single response at random. This is hard to test directly, because it is not even clear how to instruct people what it is we want them to do. However, because lay people often assume that what comes to mind first does so at random, or that spontaneity is tantamount to unpredictability, it is worth looking at some of the evidence that demonstrates that people's first, or single, spontaneous responses cannot be treated as random.

In a pertinent study, Kubovy and Psotka (1976) asked people to report the first digit that came to their mind. The distribution of these digits is far from uniform.

---

[6]Our discussion throughout this chapter has assumed that all random variables are uniform, which of course they need not be, but everything said can be readily generalized to the nonuniform case.

By far the most popular response is 7, which is typically given by almost 30% of respondents. In contrast, 0, 1, 2, and 9 are each given by considerably less than 10% of the respondents. "Why does 7 appear spontaneous?", ask the authors, and reply:

> Perhaps it is unique among the numbers from 0 to 9 because it has no multiples among these numbers, and yet it is itself not a multiple of any of these numbers. The numbers fall into groups: 2, 4, 6, 8 form one group; 3, 6, 9 form another. Only 0, 1, 5, 7 remain. One can rule out 0 and 1 for being endpoints, and perhaps 5 for being a traditional midpoint. This leaves us with 7 in the unique position of being, as it were, the "oddest" digit. (Kubovy & Psotka, 1976, p. 294)[7,8]

Additional evidence that digits do not come to mind at random can be found in Triesman and Faulkner's (1987) results (Fig. 14.4), which showed high across-session within-subject correlations between digit frequencies.

Categories such as color, furniture, and fruits do not have a natural ordering, the way numbers do. For that reason, the determinants of the order in which they come to mind are opaque to naive respondents, who are therefore more compliant, and exercise less censorship, in reporting the first response that comes to their mind. Here again responses are highly predictable. When asked to say the first color, or piece of furniture, or fruit, that comes to mind, the most likely responses are, respectively, red, chair, and apple. These are also the most prototypical members of the respective category, as confirmed by other, independent, observations (Rosch, 1978). Moreover, in these categories and others, three to four prototypical category members account for 80% or more of the category responses (Battig & Montague, 1969).

In a related finding, about 80% of subjects give "heads" as their first response when simulating a coin (e.g., Bakan, 1960; Goodfellow, 1940). It is hard to argue that "heads" is more prototypical than "tails," so this is more likely a response bias reflecting the linguistic convention of preceding "heads" to "tails" in expressions such as "heads or tails?". Finally, Tiegen (1983) used a prediction task, rather than either a judgment or a production task, asking subjects to guess the outcome of a lottery where a number between 1 and 12 was allegedly

---

[7]Remember Linus?

[8]In this task, people might actually be disobeying the instruction. The first digit that comes to their mind may well be the first digit in the natural sequence of numbers. But it is censored (1 is the given answer in less than 3% of the cases) as not looking spontaneous enough. If so, then the reaction time of subjects responding with a "7" should be on average longer than that of subjects responding with a "1," because a higher proportion of the former than of the latter would have thought previously of some other digit and censored it. In Triesman and Faulkner's study, the second author, who served as one of the subjects (A, in Fig. 14.4), produced 7 with a frequency significantly lower than expected, and than that given by other subjects, presumably because "This is known to be a favored random response . . . and is therefore one a sophisticated subject [such as Faulkner] might be wary of overproducing" (Triesman & Faulkner, 1987, p. 341).

sampled at random. He too found a nonuniform distribution of guesses, with subjects clustering in the center, especially at 7, and avoiding the extremes.

The Role of Memory in Production Tasks

The previous section suggests that the role of memory in production tasks is by and large to assist people in producing sequences that capture their subjective notion of randomness. A well-known fact about short-term memory is that its span is 7 ± 2 items. This is also the span of immediate attention. This "Magical number 7" (Miller, 1956) may account for the size of the "windows" within which subjects try to achieve "representative randomness."

Subjects who wish to ensure that they are producing alternatives with equal frequencies must keep a mental tally of previous responses. For large sets of alternatives and long sequences this can be extremely difficult (as anyone who has tried to count cards at the blackjack table knows). One cognitive solution is to monitor the tally only within the limited segment of six or seven previous responses that can be readily remembered. Indeed, Wagenaar (1972b, chap. 6) reported a cycling tendency (i.e., a tendency to use each alternative once in a cycle of A responses, with A being the number of alternatives) that peaked for $A = 6$, and a tendency to match relative frequencies within segments of 6 to 7 items, which was independent of A. Cycling was virtually absent for smaller A's (e.g., $A = 2$), where local representativeness (i.e., frequency matching plus absence of "pattern") can take care of everything. For larger A's (e.g., the alphabet), where the number of alternatives far exceeds the short-term memory span, cycling is done over smaller subsets of letters at a time.

The strategies of cycling and matching in "moving windows" of size 6 or 7 can account also for some of the effects of the other factors that have been studied, factors such as the length of the sequence, the number and nature of the symbols, the rate of production, and the presence or absence of external aids for retaining previous responses. Unfortunately, only one study manipulated these various factors systematically (Wagenaar, 1972b). In that study, however, the effects were analyzed in terms of deviations from the *mathematical properties* of random variables, not in terms of deviations from the *subjective notion* of randomness, which is what interests us here. Be that as it may, the study suggests that factors that strain memory (larger A's; no aids for keeping a record of previous responses) bring about more randomness, presumably because they interfere with the attempt at local tallying, and introduce more "noise." Ironically, because the subjective "ideal" of a random sequence is flawed, obstructions to carrying it out turn out here to be beneficial.

Other factors that have been studied are monotony, age, intelligence, mathematical sophistication, speededness, and so forth (for a partial review see Tune, 1964b). Results, and especially conclusions, are mixed, no doubt because memory both aids the task (e.g., making it possible to keep a tally of first-order frequencies) and hinders it (making it possible for responses to rely on their predecessors). Thus, when writers describe the effects of various variables as increasing or decreasing randomness, it depends what particular property they are attending to.

Kubovy and Gilden's subjects (1990) also did their "bookkeeping" within windows, whose size varied (4–11—a range that slightly exceeds 7 ± 2). There were no memory requirements in that task, because all previous responses were available on a page, but the "windows" may have been necessitated by attention limitations.

WHY?

The opportunities for observing and experiencing randomness, or at least unpredictability, would seem to be myriad (stock market prices, newborns' sexes, accidents occurences, etc.), and the disadvantages of erroneous beliefs are self-evident. Yet in the course of time people either acquire an erroneous concept of randomness, or fail to unlearn it. In this section, we try to examine what in the nature of our experience, its observable properties, and the feedback it confers, might sustain people's erroneous concept of randomness, and why it is not unlearned. We also speculate what advantages, if any, accrue to this biased concept.

Is it Important to Have a Correct Notion of Randomness?

Insofar as being unpredictable is sometimes advantageous (as it demonstrably is, say, in various gaming and conflict situations) it would seem important to have a correct notion of randomness. Yet because one can use external aids to devise unpredictable strategic schemes, one need not rely on intuition for that goal. Moreover, though the kind of "unpredictability" that people regard as the epitomy of randomness differs *systematically* from the real thing, it does not differ *radically* from it. For example, a subjectively random binary sequence with an alternation rate of .6 rather than .5, can be predicted on average 52% of the time (60% × 60% + 40% × 40%), as compared to the 50% predictability of perfect chance. To have enough power (say, more likely than not) to detect a difference between 52% and 50% at customary significance levels (0.05 or less) requires large samples indeed—of at least 2,500 observations.

Another advantage of immediate ability to recognize randomness (or unpredictability) is economical, insofar as it saves one the (futile) effort of attempting prediction. On the other hand, (a) phenomena that yield phenotypically random observations can nonetheless be caused (in the common-sensical sense of the term), and hence potentially predicted, so the effort of seeking to explain or predict them can pay off. The distribution of newborns' sexes is nicely captured by the binomial distribution, but this is not to say that a newborn's sex cannot therefore be predicted at better than chance level; (b) the ability to make lay predictions and causal attributions comes very easily to people. Indeed, people readily, and spontaneously, engage in attempts to predict—even paradigms of randomness, such as coins (Gold & Hester, 1989) and roulette wheels (Wagenaar & Keren, 1988). Hence, the cognitive gain in obviating such attempts may be paltry.

The Biased Nature of Feedback

One reason why experience with random sequences does not teach us the true nature of randomness (or, to put it more modestly, the accurate statistical properties of random variables) is because once a sequence exhibits properties that differ from our internal prototype for randomness, we often cease to perceive it as random. Thus, when people encounter longer runs in a binary sequence than they expected to "by chance alone," rather than saying to themselves: "Aha! Long runs DO occur in random sequences," they say, "Aha! This seems NOT to be a random sequence" (recall, for example, the belief in the hot hand[9]; see also Dawes, 1988, p. 310).

The self-fulfilling nature of this biased belief is also apparent in the occasionally biased nature of the feedback generated by erroneous judgments. Consider a decision maker who has made, under conditions of uncertainty, a chain of normatively optimal, but practically unsuccessful decisions (namely, wise decisions that have turned out badly). The decision maker can be a business person, a physician, whatever. Decision making under uncertainty is tantamount to gambling, and in gambling there are no guarantees of success. Suppose the unfortunate outcomes were just a coincidence, namely, were brought about by chance. Though the decision maker cannot be faulted, this person's superiors erroneously perceive the long run of failures as evidence of incompetence. Unfair as this may sound, to the extent that it happens, it alters the nature of the distributions to which observers are then exposed: If decision makers are replaced after a bad run, they do not get the chance to have their bad run diluted by more typical future runs. Thus, their final track record, being based on a truncated career, is indeed poorer, on average, than that of a luckier, though not better, decision maker who did not have such a bad run. Thus, action based on a decision maker's possibly erroneous judgment generates evidence that ultimately confirms the erroneous judgment.

---

[9]A similar phenomenon was noticed by Wagenaar and Keren (1988), who showed that casino gamblers interpret long sequences of winning (losing) as streaks of good (bad) luck. As a consequence gambling acquires a skill aspect: A skillful player is one who recognizes a lucky streak when it occurs, exploits it, and can predict when it will end.

A different, though related, example of how actions based on erroneous judgments generate evidence confirming the judgment is discussed in Einhorn and Hogarth (1978). Imagine a waiter who prides himself on the ability to tell good from poor tippers at first sight. Having judged some customer to be a good tipper, the waiter gives this person prompt and friendly service. Another customer, judged to be a poor tipper, gets the corner table and curt service. Lo and behold—at the end of the meal, the first indeed tips more generously than the second (for further examples, see Cohen & March, 1974).

Arguably, the practice of removing random generators (decision makers, roulette wheels, ball players) after a bad run, though it confounds the nature of subsequent feedback, might ofttimes be a good idea, because truly poor performers are weeded out along with those who were just unlucky. Although there is a cost to removing a "good" generator because of an accident of bad performance, there is also a cost in holding on to a "bad" generator who gets the benefit of the doubt.[10] The point is, that in a typical real-life context, a judgment of randomness versus nonrandomness is made in the presence of an alternative source for the observed event, in a sense similar to Lopes and Odens's (1986) signal detection paradigm. Of course a string of 20 Heads *could* have been generated by a fair coin, and indeed, as theoreticians take glee in pointing out, is precisely as likely as any other ordered string of outcomes. On the other hand, it is even more likely to have been generated by a trick coin or a prankster—so much so, that in our kind of world, rejecting the hypothesis of "fair coin" on that kind of evidence could be a very sensible thing to do.

When randomizing is deemed important—for example, in experimental design, as when selecting subjects to serve in the treatment versus placebo groups of an experiment—the conscientious researcher uses a random device. But if the random device just happened, as a fluke occurence, to divide the subjects into groups in a patently unbalanced manner (e.g., all males in the control group, all females in the placebo), few researchers would serenely abide by that dictum. "The generation of random numbers is too important to be left to chance" (R. R. Coveyou, as quoted by Gardner, 1977, p. 169). In that sense, even sequences generated artifactually in real life by physical random devices end up, due to doctoring, as biased representatives of their source.

Advantages of the Subjective Notion of Randomness

The perception of events as random or nonrandom is most important when it serves as a guide to action in real life. The major bias in the subjective notion of

---

[10]If a roulette wheel in Las Vegas exhibits an unusual run of reds, the House does not wait to see if it will stop, but rather the wheel is changed. Wheels are changed more frequently than warranted, in the sense that some of the removed wheels are still operating fine ("randomly"); but then again, some are not—and it is too costly to wait till enough evidence is in to make a confident assessment.

randomness is the overpreponderance of alternations (or underpreponderance of runs). However, "to evaluate fairly whether [this bias is] helpful or harmful over a lifetime . . . , one would have to know whether in the world nonrandom events are more often biased towards alternation or towards repetition" (Lopes, 1982, p. 633). Although Lopes declined to speculate on the answer, Ayton, Hunt, and Wright (1989) were bolder.

> People's apparently biased concepts may perhaps be . . . "tuned" to capitalise on properties of our environment. So, from an ecological viewpoint, perhaps repetition of outcomes is actually *correctly* considered to be more likely that alternation in non-random sequences. Or, it may be that the utilities associated with non-random events are structured so that it is more cost-effective to notice those non-random processes biased towards repetition at the expense of missing some of those non-random processes that are biased towards alternation. (p. 223, italics in original)

Whereas the mathematical properties of random sequences are typically global properties, manifest in the limit of infinitely long runs, local representativeness is a local judgment—often the only kind that our cognitive apparatus can afford. Experience, after all, is finite, so the difference between local representativeness and the actual measures commonly employed by statisticians to test randomness would seem to be largely one of degree—local representativeness is a sort of poor man's goodness-of-fit, goodness-of-fit in the (very) small. Yet it is cheap, swift, widely applicable, and though slightly biased with respect to the normative standard, it "protects" against the gross departures from expectation that a fully honest and incorruptible randomizer must on rare occasions contend with.

ACKNOWLEDGMENT

We wish to thank David Budescu, Robyn Dawes, and Amos Tversky for useful and supportive comments on an earlier draft.

REFERENCES

Ayton, P., Hunt, A. J., & Wright, G. (1989). Psychological conceptions of randomness. *Journal of Behavioral Decision Making, 2,* 221–238.

Baddeley, A. D. (1966). The capacity for generating information by randomization. *Quarterly Journal of Experimental Psychology, 18,* 119–129.

Bakan, P. (1960). Response tendencies in attempts to generate random binary series. *American Journal of Psychology, 73,* 127–131.

Battig, W. F., & Montague, W. E. (1969). Category norms for verbal items in 56 categories: A replication and extension of the Connecticut category norms. *Journal of Experimental Psychology Monograph, 80,* (3, part 2).

Budescu, D. (1987). A Markov model for generation of random binary sequences. *Journal of Experimental Psychology: Human Perception and Performance, 13* (1), 25–39.

Chapanis, A. (1953). Random-number guessing behavior. *American Psychologist, 8,* 332.

Cohen, M. D., & March, J. G. (1974). *Leadership and ambiguity: The American college president.* New York: McGraw-Hill.

Cook, A. (1967). Recognition of bias in strings of binary digits. *Perceptual and Motor Skills, 24,* 1003–1006.

Cooper, L. A., & Shepard, R. N. (1973). Chronometric studies of the rotation of mental images. In W. G. Chase (Ed.), *Visual information processing* (pp. 75–176). New York: Academic Press.

Dawes, R. M. (1988). *Rational choice in an uncertain world.* New York: Harcourt Brace Jovanovitch.

Diener, D., & Thompson, W. B. (1985). Recognizing randomness. *American Journal of Psychology, 98,* 433–447.

Einhorn, H. J., & Hogarth, R. M. (1978). Confidence in judgment: Persistence in the illusion of validity. *Psychological Review, 85,* 395–416.

Estes, W. K. (1964). Probability learning. In A. W. Melton (Ed.), *Categories of human learning* (pp. 89–128). New York: Academic Press.

Falk, R. (1975). *The perception of randomness.* Unpublished doctoral dissertation, The Hebrew University (in Hebrew).

Falk, R. (1981). The perception of randomness. In *Proceedings of the Fifth International Conference for the Psychology of Mathematical Education* (pp. 222–229). Grenoble, France: Laboratoire I.M.A.G.

Feller, W. (1950). *An introduction to probability theory and its applications* (Vol. 1). New York: Wiley.

Gardner, M. (1977). *Mathematical carnival.* New York: Vintage.

Gilovich, T., Vallone, R., & Tversky, A. (1985). The hot hand in basketball: On the misperception of random sequences. *Cognitive Psychology, 17,* 295–314.

Gold, E., & Hester, G. (1989). *The gambler's fallacy and the coin's memory.* Unpublished manuscript, Carnegie Mellon University.

Goodfellow, L. D. (1940). The human element in probability. *Journal of General Psychology, 23,* 201–205.

Jones, M. R. (1971). From probability learning to sequential processing: A critical review. *Psychological Bulletin, 76,* 153–185.

Kahneman, D., & Tversky, A. (1972). Subjective probability: A judgment of representativeness. *Cognitive Psychology, 3,* 430–454.

Kosslyn, S. (1980). *Image and mind.* Cambridge, MA: Harvard University Press.

Kubovy, M., & Gilden, D. L. (1988). *More random than random: A study of scaling noises.* Paper presented at the Psychonomic Society Meeting, Seattle.

Kubovy, M., & Gilden, D. L. (1990). Apparent randomness is not always the complement of apparent order. In G. Lockhead & J. R. Pomerantz (Eds.), *The perception of structure.* Washington, DC: American Psychological Association.

Kubovy, M., & Psotka, J. (1976). Predominance of seven and the apparent spontaneity of numerical choices. *Journal of Experimental Psychology: Human Perception and Performance, 2*(2), 291–294.

Loftus, E. (1979). *Eyewitness testimony.* Hillsdale, NJ: Lawrence Erlbaum Associates.

Lopes, L. L. (1982). Doing the impossible: A note on induction and the experience of randomness. *Journal of Experimental Psychology: Learning, Memory and Cognition, 8,* 626–636.

Lopes, L. L., & Oden, G. C. (1987). Distinguishing between random and nonrandom events. *Journal of Experimental Psychology: Learning, Memory and Cognition, 13*(3), 392–400.

Marks, D. F., & Kammann, R. (1980). *The psychology of the psychic.* Buffalo, NY: Prometheus Books.

Miller, G. A. (1956). The magical number 7 plus or minus two: Some limits on our capacity in processing information. *Psychological Review, 63*, 81–97.

Neuringer, A. (1984). Melioration and self-experimentation. *Journal of the Experimental Analysis of Behavior, 42*, 397–406.

Neuringer, A. (1986). Can people behave "randomly"? The role of feedback. *Journal of Experimental Psychology: General, 115*, 62–75.

Popper, K. R. (1959). *The Logic of Scientific Discovery*. New York: Basic Books.

Rath, G. J. (1966). Randomization by humans. *American Journal of Psychology, 79*, 97–103.

Reichenbach, H. (1949). *The theory of probability*. Berkeley: University of California Press.

Rosch, E. (1978). Principles of categorization. In E. Rosch & B. B. Lloyd (Eds.), *Cognition and categorization* (pp. 27–48). Hillsdale, NJ: Lawrence Erlbaum Associates.

Ross, B. M. (1955). Randomization of a binary series. *American Journal of Psychology, 68*, 136–138.

Ross, B. M., & Levy, N. (1958). Patterned prediction of chance events by children and adults. *Psychological Reports, 4*, 87–124.

Teigen, K. H. (1983). Studies in ubjective probability: Prediction of random events *Scandinavian Journal of Psychology, 24*, 13–25.

Teraoka, T. (1963). Some serial properties of "subjective randomness". *Japanese Psychological Research, 5*, 120–128.

Triesman, M., & Faulkner, A. (1987). Generation of random sequences by human subjects: Cognitive operations or psychophysical process? *Journal of Experimental Psychology: General, 116*(4), 337–355.

Tune, G. S. (1964a). Response preferences: A review of some relevant literature. *Psychological Bulletin, 61*, 286–302.

Tune, G. S. (1964b). A brief survey of variables that influence random generation. *Perceptual and Motor Skills, 18*, 705–710.

Tversky, A., & Kahneman, D. (1971). The belief in the law of small numbers. *Psychological Bulletin, 76*, 105–110.

Wagenaar, W. A. (1970a). Appreciation of conditional probabilities in binary sequences. *Acta Psycologica, 34*, 348–356.

Wagenaar, W. A. (1970b). Subjective randomness and the capacity to generate information. *Acta Psycologica, 33*, 233–242.

Wagenaar, W. A. (1971). Serial non-randomness as a function of duration and monotony of a randomization task. *Acta Psycologica, 35*, 78–87.

Wagenaar, W. A. (1972a). Generation of random sequences by human subjects: A critical survey of the literature. *Psychological Bulletin, 77*, 65–72.

Wagenaar, W. A. (1972b). *Sequential response bias: A study on choice and chance*. Unpublished doctoral dissertation, Leiden University.

Wagenaar, W. A. (1988). *Paradoxes of gambling behavior*. Hillsdale, NJ: Lawrence Erlbaum Associates.

Wagenaar, W. A., & Keren, G. (1988). Chance and luck are not the same. *Journal of Behavioral Decision Making, 1*, 65–75.

Warren, P. A., & Morin, R. E. (1965). *Psychonomic Science, 3*, 557–558.

Weiss, R. L. (1964). On producing random responses. *Psychonomic Reports, 14*, 931–941.

Wiergesma, S. (1982a). A control theory of sequential response production. *Psychological Research, 44*, 175–188.

Wiergesma, S. (1982b). Can repetition avoidance in randomization be explained by randomness concepts? *Psychological Research, 44*, 189–198.

Wolitzky, D. L., & Spence, D. P. (1968). Individual consistencies in the random generation of choices. *Perceptual and Motor Skills, 26*, 1211–1214.

15 On Generating Random Sequences

Peter J. Pashley
Educational Testing Service

> *O! many a shaft at random sent*
> *Finds mark the archer little meant!*
> *And many a word, at random spoken,*
> *May soothe or wound a heart that's broken!*
> Sir Walter Scott, *The Lord of the Isles* (1815), Canto V, st. 18

> *Look at the subroutine library of each computer*
> *installation in your organization, and replace the*
> *random number generators by good ones. Try to*
> *avoid being too shocked at what you find.*
> Knuth, *The Art of Computer Programming* (1981), Vol. 2, p. 176, ex. 6

INTRODUCTION

Sir Walter Scott noted that shooting arrows or speaking words at random can produce unexpected and possibly dire results. Is the opposite also true? When one hopes for randomness, but unbeknownst actually receives nonapparent regularities, could the effect be serious? Most definitely. Today, experiments, simulations, sampling, and numerical methods often rely on random sequences, which, if not actually random, can distort results and mislead investigators.

Knuth, whose 1981 reference is still one of the best sources of detailed information in this field, cautioned students not to be shocked at the random number generators that were available at their schools. Is this warning still valid today? Absolutely. Although the state of affairs is improving with time, recent textbooks, journal articles, and computer trade magazines have prescribed, and computers from PCs to mainframes still provide, substandard random number generators.

How can investigators learn about good random number generators and safeguard themselves against poor ones, without investing too much time? Hopefully, this chapter will help show the way, in a concise but not too technical manner. At least that was the intent when written. But, do not be lulled into thinking this is a trivial subject. Consider the exercise quoted earlier, given by Knuth. This assignment was rated as difficult, lengthy, and suitable for a term paper. Fortunately, that level of undertaking should not be required from a pragmatic researcher who simply needs a reliable source of consistently random sequences.

Before one can adequately judge the worthiness of a random number generator (RNG), one should become acquainted with a number of related concepts: what exactly random sequences are; features a user would look for in a RNG; the different types of RNGs; distributional properties of RNGs; and how to assess the randomness of RNGs. In addition to discussing these topics, this chapter includes an Appendix containing BASIC code for setting up, running, and verifying an RNG suggested by Marsaglia, Zaman, and Tsang (1990).

There are times when experimenters only need the bare minimum of a RNG that can be used to produce "somewhat" random sequences. These threadbare RNGs can be easily programmed in a high-level language (such as FORTRAN) in just a few lines of code. An example of such a RNG is given in the section on *multiplicative linear congruential generators.*

For those who require or prefer a more in-depth and technical treatise of random numbers and their generation, beyond what is provided in this chapter, the writings of two authors are recommended. First, as already mentioned, Knuth's excellent coverage of this area still forms a sound basis for understanding this subject matter. Second, almost any article by Marsaglia is worth reading, as he has been on the cutting edge of this field for many years. If you are looking for the results of tests on RNGs commonly used with PCs, the trade magazines often contain reviews. Evaluations of mainframe RNGs can be found in the more technical journals. Be forewarned, though, that the quality of these latter two sources has been inconsistent to date.

WHAT ARE RANDOM SEQUENCES?

Does the sequence 0, 6, 2, 8, 6, 2, 0, 8, 9, 9, 8, 6, 2, 8, 0 constitute a set of random single-digit numbers? Can a computer generate truly random numbers? Could some tool other then a computer, such as a die, be used to generate truly random numbers? Is there a good reason for testing a sequence of numbers for randomness if we know beforehand that they are not truly random?

Clearly the answer to all of these questions is yes, well, maybe no, and come to think of it, it all depends. Why might there not be obvious and definitive answers to these seemingly basic queries? Well, lurking behind any scientific procedure, and certainly any statistical analysis, there are always disturbing philosophical quagmires. Fortunately (or unfortunately), most scientific techniques or constructs are so complex that any associated theoretical gremlins are well hidden. Unfortunately (or fortunately), this is not true with regard to the generation and testing of random numbers. In this case, there is little or nothing lying between a set of empirical results and the theoretical (or philosophical) constructs they represent.

In an attempt to de-fuzzify the situation, the questions posed at the beginning of this section are now discussed. (Note that the word *discussed* is used rather than *answered*.)

Does the Sequence 0, 6, 2, 8, 6, 2, 0, 8, 9, 9, 8, 6, 2, 8, 0 Constitute a Set of Random Single-Digit Numbers?

This sequence consists of 15 numbers, of which only 5 digits out of a possible 10 appear, and contains just one odd number, namely 9, which shows up twice and in succession. The ordered triple {6, 2, 8} is observed twice. The ordered pair {6, 2} appears three times, whereas {2, 8} and {8, 6} occur twice. Given these attributes, odds are most people would suspect the randomness of this sequence. However, this series of numbers constitutes a subsequence from the decimal expansion of π, which is generally regarded as very random (see "At the Limits," 1989 for an interesting discussion of the generation and randomness of π).

Whereas short sequences may not appear random, for evaluation purposes investigators should be most concerned with the behavior of a RNG over the long run. On the other hand, regardless of whether a sequence was generated in a truly random fashion, the result may not be useful in certain circumstances. To take an extreme example, consider flipping a fair coin to produce a sequence of 200 binary digits (0s and 1s). One outcome, which is as likely as any other, is 200 1s in a row. Although this occurrence may generate much excitement in the lab and disbelief elsewhere, such a series would be basically useless for almost any application.

Can a Computer Generate Truly Random Numbers?

Computer algorithms are inherently deterministic, ergo, computers cannot act in a random fashion (although they certainly seem to at times). So by definition, computers cannot generate truly random numbers. Fortunately, computers can be used to generate sequences of numbers that appear, for all intents and purposes, random. Some authors prefer to differentiate between truly random numbers and those generated by an algorithm by labeling the latter *pseudo-random* or *quasi-random*[1] numbers. This convention is not used here, but readers are encouraged to keep this difference in mind.

If we agree that computers can only generate sequences that appear random, one might ask whether the appearance of randomness is as good as the real thing. Empirically speaking, the answer to this question must surely be yes. The trick is to make sure that the computer algorithm you are using consistently yields sequences that appear random.

Could Some Tool Other than a Computer, Such as a Die, Be Used to Generate Truly Random Numbers?

Strictly speaking, no. No physical tool, no matter how finely crafted, works flawlessly. Ask casino owners who worry about the randomness of their gambling equipment, such as their roulette wheels. However, the effect of minuscule imperfections possessed by certain machines (like the ball mixing devices currently popular with lottery agencies) must certainly be infinitesimally small.

Why then are ball mixing devices not commonly used for generating random sequences for scientific purposes? First, though fun to watch, they are inconvenient to work with. Try picking, reading, and writing down 10,000 numbers. Second, the same sequences of numbers cannot be reused, say in an experimental replication or validation, unless they are all retained in some manner. Another inconvenience.

Computer RNGs, though perhaps less random than certain other random generating devices, produce sequences that are reproducible (usually with only one or two numbers being stored). They are also convenient to the extent that the random numbers they output can be input easily into subsequent analyses when both procedures exist in the same environment (i.e., computer memory).

Is There a Good Reason for Testing a Sequence of Numbers for Randomness if We Know Beforehand that They Are Not Truly Random?

Sure. In fact, people test hypotheses they know to be strictly false all the time. This is known as *statistical hypothesis testing*. How do people deal with this problem in practice? Some textbooks (whose authors will remain nameless) have gone as far as to suggest an experimental sample size should not be too big, so as

---

[1]Recently, some authors have applied the label quasi-random to a set of numbers that were generated with an emphasis on their distributional characteristics, rather than their randomness. Although these sequences can be useful in certain Monte Carlo integration calculations, they are not discussed in this chapter.

to avoid always rejecting the null hypothesis! This advice, of course, is nonsense. Estimating the effect size, rather than simply rejecting a hypothesis, should be the main goal of an experiment. The better you can estimate an effect size (i.e., the bigger the sample size) the better off you are.

The same is true for testing sequences of numbers for randomness. We all know beforehand that they are not truly random, but we still wish to know how badly nonrandom they are. The more numbers generated, the better our understanding of how good or bad the generator is in terms of randomness. Beside statistical hypothesis testing, one can also apply exploratory data analysis (EDA) techniques in order to try and uncover nonrandom aspects of the generated sequences.

FEATURES OF RANDOM NUMBER GENERATORS

Generating output with the appearance of randomness is, of course, a characteristic that all RNGs should possess. There are, however, other properties or attributes that we would like our RNG to exhibit. Some are very specific to certain applications and as such are not discussed here. What is discussed now are three features, common to all RNGs, which almost every user should be concerned with.

Period or Cycle

All RNGs start to repeat themselves, eventually. The length of a nonrepeating sequence is called the *period* or *cycle*. To illustrate this feature further, consider the class of very simple RNGs that calculate random numbers based on some operation performed on the previously generated element in the sequence. In general mathematical terms, these algorithms can be expressed as

$$x_{i+1} = f(x_i),$$

where x_i and x_{i+1} are consecutive random numbers, and $f(\cdot)$ denotes some function. An initial value or *seed* is required to start the process. In this simple case, every x_i will always be followed by the same x_{i+1}, when the sequence is repeated. For example, if the x_i's are constrained to be positive single-digit integers, the period of any generator of this type can be at most 9 (the number of alternative seeds), or possibly less. To illustrate, consider the algorithm

$$x_{i+1} = x_i - 4, \text{ if } x_i - 4 > 0, \text{ otherwise}$$
$$x_{i+1} = x_i + 5.$$

This will cycle through all possible digits, regardless of the seed used. On the other hand, the algorithm

$$x_{i+1} = x_i - 3, \text{ if } x_i - 3 > 0, \text{ otherwise}$$
$$x_{i+1} = x_i + 6,$$

has a period of 3, again, no matter which seed is employed. For other generators, the period can vary with the choice of seed values.

Naturally, one would like a long period. The longer the better, typically. Recently, some so-called *very long period* (VLP) algorithms have been proposed. For example, Marsaglia, Narasimhan, and Zaman (1990) developed an assembler program called ACARRYPC, which has a purported cycle of approximately 2^{1407}, or about 10^{160}. In contrast, earlier RNGs typically had periods between 10^8 and 10^9. Note, however, that a long period does not necessarily ensure randomness.

In practice, the application at hand should dictate which cycle sizes are sufficient. In all cases, though, the period should be significantly larger than the amount of random numbers needed.

Portability

With the proliferation of mainframes, minicomputers, and PCs, and the enhanced connectivity between them, there is an increasing need for generators that will give the same results after being run on a variety of computers. The main obstacles to portability reside in the way bits, bytes, and words are combined and used by different machines, and in some cases, different software. These characteristics determine the precision with which calculations can be performed to produce random numbers. For those not intimate with their computer hardware on this level, a (very) brief review of the relevant concepts is now given.

Most computers are digital (as opposed to analog) processors, operating with binary (base 2) data. The smallest storage unit is called a *bit,* containing one binary digit. A group of 8 bits is called a *byte,* and bytes can be combined to produce *words.* Common wordlengths for today's PCs are 16- and 32-bits.

Programmers are allowed, on most computers, to specify various *data types.* These include different wordlengths and stored number representations, including *integer* (or fixed point) and *real* (or floating point) formats. An integer representation is always exact and is usually two or four bytes in size (including one sign bit). Integer arithmetic is also exact, at least within the range defined by the wordlength, and given that division involves discarding remainders.

Real representations, on the other hand, are not necessarily exact representations. They usually include three components: a sign bit; a *mantissa,* which is an exact positive integer; and an exponent, which again is an exact positive integer. Typical sizes for a mantissa and exponent in a 32-bit machine are 23- and 8-bits, respectively. Arithmetic between reals is not necessarily exact, with the accuracy being machine dependent.

To assess the portability of a particular RNG, users must be cognizant of the attributes particular to their computers and whether they conform to the program specifications.

Computational Efficiency

At one time, providing a RNG that ran quickly was of prime importance. In fact, overzealous concern over this feature was, at least partially, responsible for some very bad RNGs (one such example, called the RANDU, is discussed later in the section on *checking randomness*). With the advent of much faster mainframes, and PCs that can be left on overnight, this concern has lessened. Just as the emphasis in computer programming has generally shifted from efficiency to readability, with the availability of faster machines, the emphasis in developing RNGs has shifted from efficiency to the quality of randomness. Of course, for some applications or impatient researchers, a very slow RNG can also be a hindrance. However, finding a happy medium between efficiency and randomness should not be an impossible task these days, regardless of the application, time constraints (within reason), or computer type.

SOME CLASSES
OF RANDOM NUMBER GENERATORS

Although RNGs should produce sequences that appear random, they themselves should not appear so. That is, randomly constructed algorithms often yield nonrandom results. There must be method to this madness. Discussed in this section are three common types of RNGs.

Multiplicative Linear Congruential Generators

Introduced by Lehmer (1951), this has been one of the most widely used and investigated random number generating algorithms. A general form of a Multiplicative Linear Congruential Generator (MLCG) is

$$x_{j+1} = (ax_j + c) \bmod m$$

where

m is called the modulus, with $m > 0$;

a is the multiplier, with $0 \le a < m$; and

c is the increment, with $0 \le c < m$.

The constant c is often chosen to be equal to zero. For those who have forgotten, the function "mod" finds a remainder as follows:

$$(x) \bmod m = x - m\mathrm{TRUNCATE}(x/m),$$

where the function "TRUNCATE($\cdot$)" reduces an argument to an integer. Note that the maximal period for these generators is m.

Due in part to the simplicity of this algorithm, associated theoretical results abound. For instance, good choices of m, a, c and seeds are well known. In particular, Fishman and Moore (1982, 1986) provided an exhaustive evaluation of MLCGs with modulus $2^{31} - 1$.

As the following FORTRAN code illustrates, MLCGs are easily programmed in most high-level languages:

```
IRANDOM = MOD(IRANDOM*DBLE(IA) + IC, DBLE(IM))
RANDOM = REAL(IRANDOM)/IM                        (1)
```

where IRANDOM, IA, IC, and IM are integer variables; and RANDOM is a real uniform deviate in the range $[0, 1)$. The IRANDOM, IA, IC, and IM variables must first be initialized before this code is processed in a program. IRANDOM should be first set to some seed value ranging from 1 to IM, and afterward, the current value of IRANDOM is used to calculate a subsequent value. The variables IA, IC, and IM should be initialized to corresponding a, c, and m values, respectively, which define a particular MLCG.

One MLCG, which has shown to yield fairly random sequences, has full period, and is at the same time quite portable, is defined by $a = 16807$, $m = 2^{31} - 1$, and $c = 0$. Park and Miller (1988) went as far as to claim this MLCG could constitute a "minimal standard" against which other RNGs should be compared. Fishman and Moore (1982, 1986), however, indicated that this generator may fail some of the more stringent tests of randomness. Regardless of whether Park and Miller's claim is a reasonable one or not, this simple generator may suit some experimenters who do not require a sophisticated and very random algorithm, but simply wish to "mix things up," so to speak, without going to much trouble.

Lagged-Fibonacci Generators

The Fibonacci sequence: $1, 1, 2, 3, 5, \ldots, t, s, t + s, \ldots$, named after the 13th-century mathematician, can be expressed as

$$t_i = t_{i-1} + t_{i-2}, \text{ for } i > 2, \text{ and } t_0 = t_1 = 1.$$

A generalized form of this sequence,

$$x_i = (x_{i-p} \Diamond x_{i-q}) \bmod m,$$

where $\Diamond$ is some operator, and p and q are called the *lags*, is known as a lagged-Fibonacci RNG.

A related subclass of algorithms, called the *shift register* or *Tausworthe* generators, are formed by setting $m = 2$ in order to produce individual bits. These bits are then joined into words, usually by applying a shift register procedure within a low-level programming language. The operator $\Diamond$, in this case, is inevitably taken to be a logical "exclusive-or," which unfortunately, has recently been shown to be suboptimal (Marsaglia, Narasimhan, & Zaman, 1990) for members of the lagged-Fibonacci family.

Perhaps a more promising variation of the lagged-Fibonacci type, suggested by Marsaglia, Narasimhan, and Zaman, is called the *subtract-with-borrow* generator. The general form of the algorithm is given by

$$x_i = (x_{i-p} - x_{i-q} - c_i) \bmod m,$$

where $p < q$, and

$$c_{i+1} = \begin{cases} 0 & \text{if } x_{i-p} - x_{i-q} - c_i \geq 0, \text{ and} \\ 1 & \text{otherwise.} \end{cases}$$

Marsaglia and Zaman (to appear) showed that this generator has a period of $m^q - m^p$, when $m^q - m^p + 1$ is a prime number with m as a primitive root. The size of these periods certainly qualify certain members of this class into the VLP group of generators. Consider a generator with $m = 2^{32} - 5, p = 22$ and $q = 43$. These parameters happen to satisfy the prime number and primitive root conditions, thus the associated period is approximately 2^{1376}, or about 10^{414}.

The advantages of lagged-Fibonacci generators are the possibilities of long periods, and demonstrated randomness for certain subclasses of algorithms. The disadvantage is the lack of many other theoretical results related to these generators, as compared to the amount available for MLCGs.

Composites

Most people's intuition would suggest that the sequences from a composite RNG, which is a combination of two or more RNGs, should be more random than those from the individual ones. In this case, their intuition seems to be right. Empirical observations seem to support this hypothesis and Marsaglia (1985) presented some theoretical findings that also lend credence to this notion.

A common approach to combining two RNGs is called *shuffling*. In this case, one of the generators is used to reorder the random sequence produced by the other. In an alternative scheme, the output of a single generator is reordered using a single shuffle table. This simpler technique was employed in the SAS (1985) function called "UNIFORM," which shuffles sequences from a MLCG using a 64-value table in an attempt to alleviate any autocorrelation problems. Note that combining a RNG with itself, through shuffling or some other method, is probably not a good idea. Problems, such as autocorrelations, may be exasperated, rather than alleviated.

Another approach to combining RNGs is by simple arithmetic operations. An example of this type, which uses modular subtraction, was suggested by Marsaglia, Zaman, and Tsang (1990). A BASIC version of this particular RNG is included in the Appendix.

DISTRIBUTIONS OF RANDOM NUMBERS

The primary random numbers calculated (internally) in generators are commonly integer values, due to efficiency considerations. These integers are usually converted to fractions, by dividing them by the largest possible random number value plus one, before being output. If the primary integer values follow a uniform distribution, as is usually the case, the output will also be uniform, but over the range (0, 1). To illustrate this procedure, consider a general MLCG:

$$x_{j+1} = (ax_j + c) \bmod m.$$

We may then produce uniform deviates, denoted by u_j, simply by calculating

$$u_{j+1} = x_{j+1}/m.$$

Note that the previous two equations were the ones that were converted into the FORTRAN code given in the *multiplicative linear congruential generators* section.

Although uniform deviates are probably the most commonly used random numbers, certain applications require sequences with other distributional properties. A general approach to this problem is to make use of the associated distribution function, or more specifically, the inverse distribution function. That is, if $F(\cdot)$ is the distribution function associated with the desired probability function $f(\cdot)$, then

$$y_i = F^{-1}(u_i)$$

maps a uniform random deviate (u_i) into one distributed as you would like. Unfortunately, the inverse distribution function is not always available. In these cases, approximations to this inverse, or other methods must be utilized.

For a case in point, consider the problem of generating standard normal deviates. Unfortunately, the inverse of the standard normal distribution function is analytically intractable. However, random numbers that are normally distributed can be obtained via the Box–Muller method (Box & Muller, 1958). This approach produces two independent normal deviates (n_1 and n_2) based on two random uniform deviates (u_1 and u_2), by assigning

$$n_1 = \sqrt{-2\ln u_1} \, \cos(2\pi u_2), \text{ and}$$
$$n_2 = \sqrt{-2\ln u_1} \, \sin(2\pi u_2). \tag{2}$$

For those who are uneasy with simple methods, more complex schemes for generating normal deviates are discussed by Knuth (1981).

Knuth also examined methods for generating deviates conforming to a wide variety of other distributions, both continuous and discrete. Press, Flannery, Teukolsky, and Vetterling in their 1986 book *Numerical Recipes,* also discussed these problems, and as a bonus, provided FORTRAN and PASCAL programs to solve them.

CHECKING RANDOMNESS

As discussed earlier, what exactly randomness is, is not obvious. Theoretically, a perfect device, such as a completely fair die, could produce truly random sequences. If the output from a RNG does not systematically and significantly differ from what would be expected from a truly random device, one could conclude that there is no evidence that particular RNG cannot produce sequences that appear random. Statistical tests and graphical techniques that could be used to investigate randomness are now briefly discussed.

Statistical Tests

The first, and most obvious, aspect of a random sequence, is the uniformity of the numbers (assuming uniform deviates were generated). This can be done by running either a Kolmogorov–Smirnov or chi-square test. The distributions of successive pairs, triples, quadruples, and so forth, can also be evaluated with a chi-square test. In addition, procedures for testing other attributes, such as runs, gaps, permutations, and serial correlations, are also available from various sources, including (of course) Knuth. IMSL (1987) is a good source of computer subroutines that can be used to evaluate the randomness of RNGs.

Note that the inherent problems with hypothesis testing do not go away when random numbers are the subject. As usual, if the sample size is large enough, every hypothesis will be rejected. Remember, though, that if a hypothesis is rejected, the effect size should then be considered. Also, if many tests are run, you should expect a number of them to fail. In fact, if your RNG never fails a statistical test of randomness, you should start to worry.

Graphical Techniques

Pictures really are worth a thousand words. Graphs can uncover striking properties of data that may otherwise go unnoticed. A favorite example, used by many authors to illustrate this point, is the infamous IBM SYSTEM/360 (1968) RANDU generator. This was a very popular MLCG, distributed widely by IBM and other companies. The multiplier and modulus were 65539 and 2^{31}, respectively. The algorithm was very efficient and thought to be quite random, at least initially. Simple plots, however, can uncover obvious nonrandom aspects of sequences generated by RANDU.

Consider the scatter plots in Fig. 15.1, in which point coordinates were determined from successive random numbers from RANDU. The first (Fig. 15.1a) indicates that the random numbers are fairly well dispersed in two-dimensions. Figure 15.1b shows the dispersion in three-dimensions, and again

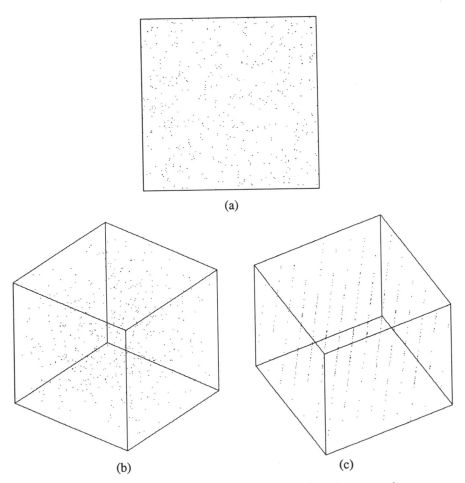

(a)

(b)   (c)

FIG. 15.1. Points whose coordinates are determined by successive random numbers obtained from the RANDU generator: (a) in two-dimensions; (b) in three-dimensions; and (c) the same points in three-dimensions, but after a rotation to expose the hyperplanes.

the scatter does not look too bad. But if the cube is rotated, 15 hyperplanes can be seen to appear, as in Fig. 15.1c. Marsaglia (1968) described this hyperplane phenomenon, common to all MLCGs, in an article amusingly entitled "The random numbers fall mainly in the planes." Fortunately, the number of hyperplanes associated with better MLCGs is high enough so that this inherent feature does not always create a problem.

Although the RANDU example is certainly an unusual case (i.e., finding such striking attributes), exploratory data analysis (EDA) techniques can be used effectively to investigate more subtle departures from randomness. Besides looking at data points (as in Fig. 15.1), other features might also be explored. For example, the distributes of runs and gaps can be plotted to evaluate their distributions. Probability graphs, such as Q–Q plots, can be used to check the basic distributional attributes of random deviates, especially at the extremes of the distributions where machine dependent numerical precision limitations may cause distortions.

Example.   The following is a brief illustration of the types of characteristics one might investigate while considering a RNG, and how these attributes might be presented. The RNG employed in this example was a MLCG with a, m, and c set to 16807, $2^{31} - 1$, and 0, respectively. The FORTRAN code given in (1) was used to calculate two consecutive samples of 3,000 uniform random variates each, which were then transformed into normal variates using the formula given in (2).

Empirical results for the two samples are shown in Fig. 15.2. Parts (a) and (b) are each comprised of a residual Q–Q plot with an associated confidence band, descriptive statistics, and significance test results. The residual Q–Q plot (described in detail by Chambers, Cleveland, Kleiner, & Tukey, 1983) indicates that the first generated sample lies comfortably within acceptable limits (i.e., the dotted lines defined as plus or minus 2 times the standard error of a normal quantile). None of the descriptive statistics suggest that the data were not sampled from a standard normal (i.e., with mean 0 and variance 1). In addition, all of the significance tests do not provide evidence to suggest that the data are not normal (given by the Kolmogorov-Smirnov result) or not random. Note that a inverse normal transformation was applied to the data before the tests for randomness (i.e., the pairs, triplets, runs, and d^2 tests) were run, as they are appropriate for random uniform variates. The first four significance tests are discussed in Knuth, and the d^2 procedure is found in Gruenberger and Mark (1951).

In contrast, the second sample (whose seed was the last number generated in the first sample) exhibits departures from both normality and randomness. The sample's corresponding descriptive statistics are less then inspiring, a non-trivial amount of points lie outside the residual Q–Q plot confidence band, and the

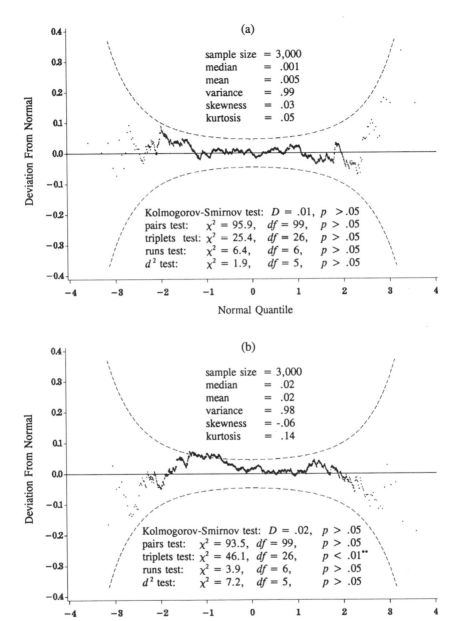

FIG. 15.2. Results from analyses of distributional and randomness properties performed on two samples produced by the same RNG: (a) residual Q–Q plot with standard error band, descriptive statistics (above the upper band) and tests of significance (below lower band) for the first sample; (b) associated results for the second sample.

sample failed the triplets test. Interestingly, the sample did pass the Kolmogorov-Smirnov test of normality.

Displays similar to those in Fig. 15.2 provide investigators with a quick and informative view of many of the important aspects of the generated samples using three important analytic tools: a plot of all the data (or grouped data when the sample is too large); descriptive statistics related to the distributional and randomness properties (although the latter was not shown here); and tests of significance related to these two properties. More of these analyses would be needed to determine whether the first or second sample was in fact the exception or the rule.

Of course, one should also consider any theoretical results that might be available for the generator used. As already mentioned, the combination of multiplier and modulus that was used here (i.e., 16807 and $2^{31} - 1$, respectively), was rated as poor by Fishman and Moore (1982, 1986). However, in our example the data was transformed into normal variates by combining successive uniform deviates. This last step may or may not have helped matters. The combination of two separate RNGs would have been preferable.

RECOMMENDATIONS

The field of random number generation has come a long way in the last 40-odd years. Unfortunately, we still are not at a point at which there exist universally acceptable RNGs. The following recommendations are given with this in mind:

- Do not blindly trust any RNG provided by a computer system.
- Ensure that the period associated with the RNG you use significantly exceeds the number of random values you will be needing.
- Combining independent RNGs will probably improve your results. This approach should, at least, not make matters worse.
- Test the RNG you will be using in proportion to the importance of your study and the effect nonrandom sequences may have on your results.

The RNG provided in the Appendix is a current state-of-the-art algorithm and should provide good random sequences. But remember, the generator RANDU, which seems so obviously bad now, was probably considered a state-of-the-art routine in its day. Perhaps the testing technology will also one day catch up with today's new RNGs, exposing their flaws more clearly. In spite of this potential eventuality, whether you are using a RNG to provide a haphazard sequence, or for serious randomization, use the most current methods. As Sir Walter Scott might say (if he were around today), a RNG at random snatched, may soothe or wound a theory that's hatched.

REFERENCES

At the limits of calculation: Pi to a billion digits and more. (1989, October). *Focus, 9,* 1, 3–4.

Box, G. E. P., & Muller, M. E. (1958). A note on the generation of random normal deviates. *The Annals of Mathematical Statistics, 29,* 610–611.

Chambers, J. M., Cleveland, W. S., Kleiner, B., & Tukey, P. A. (1983). *Graphical methods for data analysis.* Belmont, CA: Wadsworth.

Fishman, G. S., & Moore, L. R. (1982). A statistical evaluation of multiplicative congruential random number generators with modulus $2^{31} - 1$. *Journal of the American Statistical Association, 77,* 129–136.

Fishman, G. S., & Moore, L. R. (1986). An exhaustive analysis of multiplicative congruential random number generators with modulus $2^{31} - 1$. *SIAM Journal on Scientific and Statistical Computing, 7,* 24–45.

Gruenberger, F., & Mark, A. M. (1951). The d^2 test of random digits. *Mathematical Tables and Other Aids in Computation, 5,* 109–110.

Knuth, D. E. (1981). *The art of computer programming* (Vol. 2). Reading, MA: Addison-Wesley.

Lehmer, D. H. (1951). Mathematical methods in large-scale computing units. *Annual Computing Lab Harvard University, 26,* 141–146.

IMSL Stat/Library: FORTRAN Subroutines for Statistical Analysis. (1987). Houston, TX: IMSL.

Marsaglia, G. (1968). Random numbers fall mainly in the planes. *Proceedings of the National Academy of Science, 61,* 25–28.

Marsaglia, G. (1985). *Proceedings of Computer Science and Statistics: 16th Symposium on the Interface.* Amsterdam: Elsevier.

Marsaglia, G., Narasimhan, B., & Zaman, A. (1990). A random number generator for PC's. *Computer Physics Communications, 60,* 345–349.

Marsaglia, G., & Zaman, A. (to appear). *SIAM Journal of Scientific and Statistical Computing.*

Marsaglia, G., Zaman, A., & Tsang, W. W. (1990). Toward a universal random number generator. *Statistics & Probability Letters, 8,* 35–39.

Park, S. K., & Miller, K. W. (1988). Random number generators: Good ones are hard to find. *Communications of the ACM, 31,* 1192–1201.

Press, W. H., Flannery, B. P., Teukolsky, S. A., & Vetterling, W. T. (1986). *Numerical recipes: The art of scientific computing.* New York: Cambridge University Press.

SAS Language Guide for Personal Computers, Release 6.03 Edition. (1985). Cary, NC: SAS Institute Inc.

SYSTEM/360 Scientific Subroutine Package, Version III, Programmer's Manual. (1968). White Plains, NY: IBM.

APPENDIX

Marsaglia, Zaman, and Tsang (1990) described a RNG that they claim produces very random sequences, has a long period, and is portable. Although this algorithm is not extremely efficient (in terms of execution time and memory requirements), it should suffice for most applications. The authors have also provided FORTRAN code that can be used to implement the algorithm. Provided in this Appendix are brief descriptions of the algorithms suggested by Marsaglia, Zaman, and Tsang (corresponding to the RNG, a setup subroutine, and a verification program) and code for a BASIC implementation.

410

The RNG proposed by Marsaglia, Zaman, and Tsang is a composite lagged-Fibonacci and simple arithmetic type. The lagged-Fibonacci part combines sequence elements as follows:

$$\text{if } y_{n-97} \geq y_{n-33}, \text{ then } y_n = y_{n-97} - y_{n-33}, \text{ otherwise}$$
$$y_n = y_{n-97} - y_{n-33} + 1,$$

where the y_i's are 24-bit fractions on $[0, 1)$. The simple arithmetic part is calculated as:

$$\text{if } z_{n-1} \geq d, \text{ then } z_n = z_{n-1} - d, \text{ otherwise}$$
$$z_n = z_{n-1} - d + 16777213/16777216,$$

where $d = 7654321/16777216$. The two parts are combined in a similar manner:

$$\text{if } y_n \geq z_n, \text{ then } x_n = y_n - z_n, \text{ otherwise } x_n = y_n - z_n + 1.$$

The resulting sequence is also comprised of 24-bit fractions on $[0, 1)$.

A BASIC subroutine called UNIFORM, which implements this RNG, is given in Table A.1. Before UNIFORM can be called, though, a table of 97 values is needed. This can be provided by the subroutine SETUP, contained in Table A.2. Four integer seed values are required by SETUP, each ranging from 1 to 168, and not all 1. Readers interested in the reasoning behind the SETUP algorithm are referred to Marsaglia, Zaman, and Tsang's original paper.

In order to evaluate the portability of their RNG, Marsaglia, Zaman, and Tsang supplied a verification program (a BASIC version of which is given in Table A.3) that calls the setup and composite RNG routines. The output from this program, which consists of bit results, is given in Table A.4. If you implement these subroutines and the results are different, either you made a coding error or the RNG is not portable to your machine, at least in this present form.

TABLE A.1

BASIC Code for a Composite RNG Subroutine Called UNIFORM

```
300 ' ***********************************************************
301 '
302 ' Subroutine:   UNIFORM
303 '
304 ' Description:   A composite lagged-Fibonacci and simple
305 '                 arithmetic RNG.
306 '
307 ' Reference:   Marsaglia, Zaman and Tsang (1990).
308 '
309 ' Note:   UNIFORM requires starting values, which can be
310 '           initialized by the subroutine SETUP.
311 '
312 ' ***********************************************************
313 '
314 ' Calculate the lagged-Fibonacci generator part.
315 '
316       UNI = U(LAG1) - U(LAG2)
317           IF (UNI < 0) THEN UNI = UNI + 1
318       U(LAG1) = UNI
319 '
320 ' Reset the lags.
321 '
322       LAG1 = LAG1 - 1: IF (LAG1 = 0) THEN LAG1 = 97
323       LAG2 = LAG2 - 1: IF (LAG2 = 0) THEN LAG2 = 97
324 '
325 ' Calculate the simple arithmetic generator part.
326 '
327       C = C - CD: IF (C < 0) THEN C = C + CM
328 '
329 ' Combine the lagged-Fibonacci and simple arithmetic parts.
330 '
331       UNI = UNI - C: IF (UNI < 0) THEN UNI = UNI + 1
332 '
333       RETURN
```

TABLE A.2

BASIC Code for a Setup Routine (called SETUP) Which Provides Stating Values
for the Subroutine UNIFORM

```
200 '  ***********************************************************
201 '
202 ' Subroutine:  SETUP
203 '
204 ' Description:  Generates starting values to be used by the
205 '               subroutine UNIFORM.
206 '
207 ' Input:  Before this subroutine can be run, the four
208 '         seed variables (i.e., seed1, seed2, seed3, and
209 '         seed4), must be initialized to integer values,
210 '         ranging between 1 and 168, and not all 1.
211 '
212 ' Reference:  Marsaglia, Zaman and Tsang (1990).
213 '
214 '  ***********************************************************
215 '
216 ' Calculate a table of 97 values to be used by the lagged-
217 ' Fibonacci generator.
218 '
219       DIM U(97)
220 '
221       FOR INDEX1 = 1 TO 97
222           S = 0
223           T = .5
224           FOR INDEX2 = 1 TO 24
225               M = (SEED1*SEED2 MOD 179)*SEED3 MOD 179
226               SEED1 = SEED2: SEED2 = SEED3: SEED3 = M
227               SEED4 = (53*SEED4 +1) MOD 169
228               IF ((SEED4*M MOD 64) >= 32) THEN S = S + T
229               T = .5*T
230           NEXT INDEX2
231           U(INDEX1) = S
232       NEXT INDEX1
233 '
234 ' Initialize the two lag values.
235 '
236       LAG1 = 97
237       LAG2 = 33
238 '
239 ' Initialize values to be used by the simple arithmetic
240 ' generator.
241 '
242       C = 362436!/16777216#
243       CD = 7654321!/16777216#
244       CM = 16777213#/16777216#
245 '
246       RETURN
```

TABLE A.3

BASIC Code for a Routine (called VERIFY) Which May Be Used to Verify
the Portability of the Subroutines UNIFORM and SETUP

```
100 ' ************************************************************
101 '
102 ' Program:  VERIFY
103 '
104 ' Description:  Can be used to verify the portability of the
105 '               subroutines UNIFORM and SETUP.
106 '
107 ' Reference:  Marsaglia, Zaman and Tsang (1990).
108 '
109 ' ************************************************************
110 '
111 ' Initialize the four seed variables.
112 '
113       SEED1 = 12: SEED2 = 34: SEED3 = 56: SEED4 = 78
114 '
115 ' Call the subroutine SETUP.
116 '
117       GOSUB 200
118 '
119 ' Call the subroutine UNIFORM, 20000 times.
120 '
121       FOR INDEX1 = 1 TO 20000: GOSUB 300: NEXT INDEX1
122 '
123 ' Call the subroutine UNIFORM five more times, and print out
124 ' intermediate bit results.
125 '
126       FOR INDEX1 = 20001 TO 20005: GOSUB 300
127           FOR INDEX2 = 1 TO 7
128               TMP = INT(UNI*16^INDEX2)
129               TMP = TMP - (INT(TMP/16)*16)
130               PRINT USING "  ##"; TMP;
131           NEXT INDEX2
132           PRINT
133       NEXT INDEX1
134 '
135       END
```

TABLE A.4
Target Output from the Subroutine VERIFY

6	3	11	3	0	4	0
13	8	15	11	11	14	0
6	15	0	2	3	11	0
5	14	2	14	4	8	0
7	15	7	10	12	2	0

IV HYPOTHESIS TESTING, POWER, AND EFFECT SIZE

In the behavioral sciences, there is probably no more widely abused method for making statistical inferences than the testing of null hypotheses. It has been referred to as a misleading technique for answering an uninteresting question. The chapters in this section address some of the problems associated with the practice of hypothesis testing and describe procedures which may supplement or replace its use in various circumstances.

Chapter 16 is a reprint of a paper by Greenwald, in which he described the framework within which hypotheses are typically tested in psychological research. With the emphasis that is placed on rejecting the null hypothesis, the published literature can be expected to show systematic biases in both results and in the choice of studies. Consequently, it is likely that scientific progress is seriously impeded by these practices. To remedy this situation, Greenwald proposed that researchers conduct studies for which any possible outcome will be of interest, and that research be evaluated on its procedural adequacy and on the importance of the question studied, rather than in terms of the results of the study. Published in 1975, Greenwald's analysis is at least as relevant today as it was seventeen years ago.

Pollard, writing in chapter 17, builds on Greenwald's results, as well as those of Tversky and Kahneman in chapter 12, when he discusses the relation of the level of significance at which a null hypothesis is tested to the probability of a Type I error. After detailing a variety of confusions and misunderstandings regarding this relationship, Pollard concludes that, at the very least, hypothesis testing should be carried out with greater flexibility than is currently the case.

Rejecting the null hypothesis of no effect of an independent variable is quite different from concluding that the variable has a nontrivial effect. For this latter purpose, some assessment of effect size is necessary. Tatsuoka, in chapter 18, reviews a variety of ways which have been used to measure effect size in different research contexts, emphasizing the relationships among these measures. He concludes by describing an extension to effect sizes for the case of multiple dependent variables, which is also the topic of Cohen's chapter 6 in Volume II of this book.

With the emphasis in hypothesis testing on significance level, researchers often neglect questions of statistical power: What is the probability of detecting an effect, given that it exists? Chapter 19, written by Zimmerman and Zumbo, illustrates the fact that the impact of violations of various assumptions on the power of statistical test procedures can be substantial. The authors explain why nonparametric tests can sometimes help this situation and sometimes don't help at all. They also describe several alternatives to standard tests and point out when they might be useful.

The last chapter in this section (20), written by Rosenthal, addresses the general subject of meta-analysis. Working with significance levels, power, and effect sizes, he discusses how results of different studies can be both compared and combined. In doing so, he touches on a wide variety of issues, including the likelihood of replication of results, an assessment of the potential impact of unpublished nonsignificant studies, and ways of evaluating the practical importance of a given effect size. Its broad scope makes this chapter an appropriate ending for a section devoted to hypothesis testing, power and effect size.

16 Consequences of Prejudice Against the Null Hypothesis

Anthony G. Greenwald
Ohio State University

In a standard college dictionary (*Webster's New World*, College Edition, 1960), *null* is defined as "invalid; amounting to nought; of no value, effect, or consequence; insignificant." In statistical hypothesis testing, the *null hypothesis* most often refers to the hypothesis of no difference between treatment effects or of no association between variables. Interestingly, in the behavioral sciences, researchers' null hypotheses frequently satisfy the nonstatistical definition of *null*, being "of no value," "insignificant," and presumably "invalid." My aims here are to document this state of affairs, to examine its consequences for the archival accumulation of scientific knowledge, and lastly, to make a positive case for the formulation of more potent and acceptable null hypotheses as a part of an overall research strategy.

Because of my familiarity with its literature, most of the illustrative material I use is drawn from social psychology. This should not be read as an implication that the problems being discussed are confined to social psychology. I suspect they are equally characteristic of other behavioral science fields that are lacking in well-established organizing theoretical systems.

THE LOWLY NULL HYPOTHESIS

My paraphrasing of some widespread beliefs of behavioral scientists concerning the null hypothesis appears below. Some partial sources for the content of this listing are Festinger (1953, pp. 142–143), Wilson and Miller (1964), Aronson and Carlsmith (1969, p. 21), and Mills (1969, pp. 442–448).

1. Given the characteristics of statistical analysis procedures, a null result is only a basis for uncertainty. Conclusions about relationships among variables should be based only on rejections of null hypotheses.

2. Little knowledge is achieved by finding out that two variables are unrelated. Science advances, rather, by discovering relationships between variables.

3. If statistically significant effects are obtained in an experiment, it is fairly certain that the experiment was done properly.

4. On the other hand, it is inadvisable to place confidence in results that support a null hypothesis because there are too many ways (including incompetence of the researcher), other than the null hypothesis being true, for obtaining a null result.

Given the existence of such beliefs among behavioral science researchers, it is not surprising that some observers have arrived at conclusions such as:

Many null hypotheses tested by classical procedures are scientifically preposterous, not worthy of a moment's credence even as approximations. (Edwards, 1965, pp. 401–402)

It [the null hypothesis] is usually formulated for the express purpose of being rejected. (Siegel, 1956, p. 7)

REFUTATIONS OF NULL HYPOTHESIS "CULTURAL TRUISMS"

I am sure that many behavioral science researchers endorse the beliefs previously enumerated but would have difficulty in providing a rational defense for these beliefs should they be strongly attacked. That is, these attitudes toward the null hypothesis may have some of the characteristics of cultural truisms as described by McGuire (1964). Cultural truisms are beliefs that are so widely and unquestionably held that their adherents (a) are unlikely ever to have heard them being attacked and may therefore (b) have difficulty defending them against an attack. If I am correct, the reader will have difficulty defending the preceding beliefs against the following attacks (the numbered paragraphs correspond to those in the preceding listing.) Briefly stated, these attacks are:

1. The notion that you cannot prove the null hypothesis is true in the same sense that it is also true that you cannot prove *any* exact (or point) hypothesis. However, there is no reason for believing that an estimate of some parameter that is near a zero point is less valid than an estimate that is significantly different from zero. Currently available Bayesian techniques (e.g., Phillips, 1973) allow methods of describing acceptability of null hypotheses.

2. The point is commonly made that theories predict relationships between variables; therefore, finding relationships between variables (i.e., non-null results) helps to confirm theories and thereby to advance science. This argument ignores the fact that scientific advance is often most powerfully achieved by *rejecting* theories (cf. Platt, 1964). A major strategy for doing this is to demonstrate that relationships predicted by a theory are not obtained, and this would often require acceptance of a null hypothesis.

3. I am aware of no reason for thinking that a statistically significant rejection of a null hypothesis is an appropriate basis for assuming that the conceptually intended variables were manipulated or measured validly. The significant result (barring Type I error) does indicate that some relationship or effect was observed, but that is all it indicates. The researcher who would claim that obtained data show a relationship between two variables should be as clearly obliged to show that those variables are the ones intended as should the researcher who would claim that the data show the absence of a relationship.

4. Perhaps the most damaging accusation against the null hypothesis is that incompetence is more likely to lead to erroneous nonsignificant, "negative," or null results than to erroneous significant or "positive" results. There is some substance to this accusation—when the incompetence has the effect of introducing noise or unsystematic error into data. Examples of this sort of incompetence are the use of unreliable paper-and-pencil measures, conducting research in a "noisy" setting (i.e., one with important extraneous variables uncontrolled), unreliable apparatus functioning, inaccurate placement of recording or stimulating electrodes, random errors in data recording or transcribing, and making too few observations. These types of incompetence are often found in the work of the novice researcher and are proper cause for caution in accepting null findings as adequate evidence for the absence of effects or relationships. Some other very common types of incompetence are much more likely to produce false positive or significant results. These types of incompetence result in the introduction of *systematic* errors into data collection. Examples of such sources of artifact (cf. Rosenthal & Rosnow, 1969) are experimenter bias, inappropriate demand characteristics, nonrandom sampling, invalid or contaminated manipulations or measures, systematic apparatus malfunction (e.g., errors in calibration), or systematic error (either accidental or intentional) in data recording or transcribing. This latter category of incompetence is by no means confined to novices and may be quite difficult to detect, particularly because our existing customs encourage greater suspicion of null findings than of significant findings.

BEHAVIORAL SYMPTOMS OF ANTI-NULL-HYPOTHESIS PREJUDICE

We should not perhaps be very disturbed about the existence of the beliefs previously listed if those beliefs would prove to be unrelated to behavior. The following is a list of some possible behavioral symptoms of prejudice against null hypotheses: (a) designing research so that the personal prediction of the researcher is identified with rejection rather than acceptance of the null hypothesis; (b) submitting results for publication more often when the null hypothesis has been rejected than when it has not been rejected; (c) continuing research on a problem when results have been close to rejection of the null hypothesis ("near significant"), while abandoning the problem if rejection of the null hypothesis is not close; (d) elevating ancillary hypothesis tests or fortuitous findings to prominence in reports of studies for which the major dependent variables did not provide a clear rejection of the null hypothesis; (e) revising otherwise adequate operationalizations of variables when unable to obtain rejection of the null hypothesis and continuing to revise until the null hypothesis is (at last!) rejected or until the problem is abandoned without publication; (f) failing to report initial data collections (renamed as "pilot data" or "false starts") in a series of studies that eventually leads to a prediction-confirming rejection of the null hypothesis; (g) failing to detect data analysis errors when an analysis has rejected the null hypothesis by miscomputation, while vigilantly checking and rechecking computations if the null hypothesis has not been rejected; and (h) using stricter editorial standards for evaluating manuscripts that conclude in favor of, rather than against, the null hypothesis.

Perhaps the enumeration of the items on this list will arouse sufficient recognition of symptoms in readers to convince them that the illness of anti-null-hypothesis prejudice indeed exists. However, just as a hypochondriac should have better evidence of being ill than that symptoms just heard about seem familiar, so should we have better evidence than symptom recognition for making conclusions about the existence of prejudice against the null hypothesis.

A SURVEY TO ESTIMATE BIAS AGAINST THE NULL HYPOTHESIS

In order to obtain some more concrete evidence regarding the manifestations of anti-null-hypothesis prejudice, I conducted a survey of reviewers and authors of articles submitted to the *Journal of Personality and Social Psychology* (*JPSP*). The sample included the primary (corresponding) authors and the reviewers for all manuscripts that I processed as an associate editor of *JPSP* during a 3-month period in 1973. The sample thus consisted of 48 authors and 47 reviewers to whom I sent a questionnaire. Returns were obtained from 36 authors (75%) and 39 reviewers (81%). The major items in the questionnaire assessed behavior in situations in which bias for or against the null hypothesis could occur. These situations were (a) initial formulation of a problem, (b) setting probabilities of Type I and Type II error, and (c) deciding what action to pursue once results were obtained. All questions were stated with reference to a test of the "focal hypothesis" for a new line of research. The focal hypothesis test was further defined as "the one hypothesis test that is of greatest importance" to the line of investigation. Responses were indicated on probability scales that could range from 0 to 1.00. The major results are given in Table 16.1.

With the exception of responses to two questions, the results for authors and reviewers were quite similar. This was not terribly surprising because there was substantial overlap between the populations from which these two subsamples were drawn. From Questions 4a and 4d it can be seen that authors reported they were more likely to report null hypothesis rejections and less likely to abandon the problems following a null hypothesis rejection than were reviewers. Given these rather limited differences, the following discussion of these data treats only the overall responses for the combined sample.

The questionnaire results gave several strong confirmations of existence of prejudice against the null hypothesis. In the stage of formulation of a problem, respondents indicated a strong preference for identifying their own predictions with an expected rejection, rather than an acceptance of the null hypothesis. The mean probability of the researcher's personal prediction being of the null hypothesis rejection (Question 1: $\bar{X} = .81 \pm .04$) is substantially greater than .50.[1] This state of affairs is consistent with supposing that researchers set themselves the goal of confirming a theoretically predicted relation between variables more often than refuting one, despite good reason to believe that knowledge may advance more rapidly by the latter strategy (Platt, 1964).

In setting the probability of Type I error, respondents indicated relatively close adherence to the .05 alpha criterion (Question 2: $\bar{X} = .046 \pm .004$). Responses to Question 3 indicated a substantial lack of standard practice with regard to Type II errors (i.e., accepting the null hypothesis when in truth it should be rejected). About 50% of the respondents failed to answer the question requesting specification of a preferred Type II error (beta) criterion. Those who did indicate a Type II error criterion indicated much more tolerance for this type of error than for a Type I error, the resulting estimate of beta being approximately .30 (Question 3: $\bar{X} = .27 \pm .09$). This estimate, it should be noted, is in line with Cohen's (1962) conclusion that studies published in the *Journal of Abnormal and Social Psychology* were relatively low on power (probability of rejecting the null hypothesis when the alternative is true; power $= 1.00 -$ beta). In regard to tolerance for Type I and Type II errors then, the questionnaire respondents appeared biased *toward* null hypothesis acceptance in the sense that they reported more willingness to err by accepting, rather than rejecting, the null hypothesis. Such a conclusion would, I think, be quite misleading. Rather, responses to other questions not summarized in Table 16.1 and the frequency of nonresponse to Question 3 indicated that most respondents did not take seriously the idea of setting a

---

[1]The errors of estimates given are equal to the limits of 95% confidence intervals, approximately plus or minus twice the standard deviation of the estimated mean.

TABLE 16.1
Results of Survey of *JPSP* Authors and Reviewers to Determine Prejudice
Toward or Against the Null Hypothesis

Question	Mean Responses For			$SD_{M_{all}}$
	Reviewers	Authors	All	
1. What is the probability that your typical prediction will be for a rejection (rather than an acceptance) of a null hypothesis?	.790(39)	.829(35)	.803(74)	.021
2. Indicate the level of alpha you typically regard as a satisfactory basis for rejecting the null hypothesis.	.043(39)	.049(35)	.046(74)	.002
3. Indicate the level of beta you would regard as a satisfactory basis for accepting the null hypothesis.	.292(18)	.258(19)	.274(37)	.045
4. After an initial full-scale test of the focal hypothesis that allows rejection of the null hypothesis, what is the probability that you will				
(a) submit the results for publication before futher data collection,	.408(38)	.588(35)	.494(73)	.033
(b) conduct an exact replication before deciding whether to submit for publication,	.078(38)	.069(35)	.074(73)	.009
(c) conduct a modified replication before deciding whether to submit,	.437(38)	.289(35)	.366(73)	.027
(d) give up the problem.	.077(38)	.053(35)	.066(73)	.012
Total	1.000	1.000	1.000	
5. After an initial full-scale test of the focal hypothesis that does not allow rejection of the null hypothesis, what is the probability that you will				
(a) submit the results for publication before futher data collection,	.053(37)	.064(35)	.059(73)	.014
(b) conduct an exact replication before deciding whether to submit for publication,	.107(37)	.098(36)	.102(73)	.013
(c) conduct a modified replication before deciding whether to submit,	.592(37)	.524(36)	.558(73)	.025
(d) give up the problem.	.248(37)	.314(36)	.280(73)	.023
Total	1.000	1.000	1.000	

Note. Table entries are means of respondents' estimates of probabilities, based on the number of responses given in parentheses.

Type II error criterion in advance. For example, the responses to questions asking for probability of setting alpha and beta criterions in advance of data collection indicated a .63 ($\pm$.09) probability that alpha would be set in advance of data collection, compared with only a .17 ($\pm$.06) probability that beta would be set in advance. Rather than indicating a prejudice toward acceptance of the null hypothesis, then, I think the responses to the questions on alpha and beta indicate that acceptance of the null hypothesis is not usually treated as a viable research outcome.

In terms of what is done after completion of a full-scale data collection to test a focal hypothesis, a major bias is indicated in the .49 ($\pm$.06) probability of submitting a rejection of the null hypothesis for publication (Question 4a) compared to the low probability of .06 ($\pm$.03) for submitting a nonrejection of the null hypothesis for publication (Question 5a). A secondary bias is apparent in the probability of continuing with a problem and is computed conditionally upon the decision to write a report having *not* been made following data collection. This derived index has a value of .86 ($\pm$.05) when the initial result is a rejection of the null hypothesis, compared to .70 ($\pm$.05) when the initial result is a nonrejection of the null hypothesis, indicating greater likelihood of proceeding in the former case.[2]

In sum, the questionnaire responses of a sample of contributors to the social psychological literature gave self-report evidence of substantial biases against the null hypothesis in formulating a research problem and in deciding what to do with the data once collected. In the following section, the impact of these biases on the content of the archival literature is considered.

A MODEL OF THE RESEARCH-PUBLICATION SYSTEM

The alpha criterion most commonly employed in the behavioral sciences is .05. Without giving the matter much thought, one may guess on this basis that approximately 1 in 20 publications may be an erroneous rejection of a true null hypothesis. However, some thought on the matter soon brings the discovery that the probability of a published article being a Type I error depends on much more than (a) the researcher's alpha criterion. The other determinants include (b) the probability of accepting the null hypothesis when it is false (Type II error or beta), (c) the a priori probability of an investigator selecting a problem for which the null hypothesis is true or false, (d) the probability of rejections versus nonrejections of the null hypothesis being submitted for publication, (e) the probability of the researcher's giving up in despair after achieving a rejection versus a nonrejection of the null hypothesis, and (f) the probability of an editor's accept-

---

[2]In the case of a result rejecting the null hypothesis, this index is computed as $[(4b + 4c) \div (4b + 4c + 4d)]$, the numbers referring to the responses to the questions given in Table 16.1.

ing an article that reports a rejection versus a nonrejection of the null hypothesis. All of these probabilities represent opportunities for the occurrence of strategies that discriminate against the null hypothesis. The model I develop functions to derive consequences for the content of published literature from assumptions made about these strategies.

MODEL DESCRIPTION

In the model employed for the research-publication system (see Fig. 16.1), a critical notion is that of a *focal hypothesis test*. It is assumed that in any line of investigation, there is one statistical test that is of major interest. This may be a test for a main or interaction effect in an analysis of variance, a test of the difference between two groups or treatments, a test of correlation between two variables, and the like. This statistical test is assumed to be made in terms of a rejection or acceptance (nonrejection, if you prefer) of a null hypothesis of no main effect, no interaction, and so forth. In conducting this focal hypothesis test, the researcher is assumed to have formulated an extent of deviation from the null hypothesis (an alternative hypothesis, H_1) that the research should be able to detect with probability (power) $1 - \beta$. In practice, this formulation of H_1 may often be an implicit consequence of setting a critical region for rejection of the null hypothesis with a given risk, α, of Type I error. For example, assuming $\beta = \alpha$, the start of the critical region is effectively a midpoint between the null hypothesis and H_1.

In the model, the fate of a research problem is traced in terms of the probabilities of alternative outcomes at four types of choice points: (a) the researcher's formulation of a hypothesis, (b) collection of data, (c) evaluation of obtained results, and (d) an editor's judgment of a manuscript reporting the research results. At each of these points in the research-publication process, behavioral bias relating to the null hypothesis may enter. The model incorporates parameters that serve to quantify these biases, and these are listed here in their sequential order of occurrence in the research-publication process.

The Probability that the Null Hypothesis is True for the Focal Hypothesis. Specification of this parameter requires a clear definition of the null hypothesis. If by the null hypothesis one refers to the hypothesis of *exactly* no difference or *exactly* no correlation, and so forth, then the initial probability of the null hypothesis being true must be regarded effectively as zero, as would be the probability of any other point hypothesis. In most cases, however, the investigator should not be concerned about the hypothesis that the true value of a statistic equals exactly zero, but rather about the hypothesis that the effect or relationship to be tested is so small as not to be usefully distinguished from zero. For the purposes of the model then, the probability of the null hypothesis being true becomes identified with the probability that the true state of affairs underlying the focal hypothesis is within a *null range* (cf. Hays, 1973, pp. 850–853). In the model, the probability that the investigator's focal hypothesis is one for which truth is within such a null range is represented as h_0. The probability that truth is outside this range is $h_1 = 1.00 - h_0$. One would have to be omniscient to be assured of selecting accurate values for the h_0 and h_1 parameters. It seems, however, that the values of these parameters should be clearly weighted in the direction of starting with a false null hypothesis (i.e., $h_1 > h_0$). Some reasons for this are that (a) researchers identify their personal predictions predominantly with the falsity of the null hypothesis (see Table 16.1, Question 1), and there may often be good reason for them to make these predictions; and (b) as argued by McGuire (1973), there is usually at least a narrow sense in which most researchers' predictions are correct. For no outstandingly good reason, the values of .20 and .80 were selected for h_0 and h_1, respectively. To compensate for the difficulty of justifying this initial assumption, system results are given below for other values of these parameters.[3]

Outcome of Data Collection.   As used here *data collection* refers to the researcher's activities subsequent to problem formulation, up to and including the statistical analysis of results. It is assumed that any such data collection can be characterized by probabilities of Type I and Type II errors that are either explicitly chosen by the investigator or else follow implicitly (cf. Cohen, 1962) from choices of sample size, dependent measures, statistical tests, and the like. (Because investigators may often examine data midway in a planned piece of research and thereupon terminate or otherwise alter plans, the notion of a data collection is somewhat vague in practice and must necessarily be so in the model.) The outcome of a data collection will either be a rejection or a nonrejection of the null hypothesis. The probability of rejection if the null hypothesis is true is characterized in the model as r_0 and is approximately equivalent to the researcher's alpha criterion. Based on the questionnaire responses, r_0 is estimated at .05. If the null hypothesis is false, then the probability of its rejection is characterized as r_1 and this should be approximately 1.00 minus the researcher's beta criterion. This value is estimated at .70 based on the questionnaire responses. Probabilities of nonrejection of the null hypothesis are 1.00 minus r_0 (which equals .95) or 1.00 minus r_1 (which equals .30), respectively.[4]

---

[3]The equations for computing system output indexes have been prepared as a computer program in the BASIC language. This program generates system output indexes in response to values of the system input parameters entered at a terminal by the user. The program therefore permits ready examination of consequences of assumptions other than those made presently about values of the system's input parameters. A listing of this program may be obtained from the author.

[4]The .05 level is probably a conservatively low estimate of alpha employed by the researchers to whom questionnaires were sent. In response to a question that asked for an estimate of a level of alpha which "although not satisfactory for rejecting the null hypothesis, would lead you to consider

Probability of Writing a Report.   The model assumes that upon completing a data collection, the researcher examines the results and decides whether or not to write a report. The probability of deciding to write if the null hypothesis has not been rejected is represented as w_0 and is estimated at .06, based on the questionnaire results (see Table 16.1, Question 5a). When the null hypothesis has been rejected the probability of deciding to write is represented as w_1 and is estimated at .49, based on the questionnaire responses (Question 4a).

Probability of Editorial Acceptance.   In order for the result of a data collection to appear in print, it has to be accepted for publication by an editor. In the model, an editor accepts an article with probability e_0 if it reports a nonrejection of the null hypothesis and e_1 if it reports a rejection of the null hypothesis. The questionnaire data did not permit any estimates of these parameters and they have been estimated, somewhat arbitrarily, as both being equal to .25. Thus, although the model permits analysis of the consequences of editorial discrimination for or against the null hypothesis, no initial assumption has been made regarding the existence of such bias.

If at First You Don't Succeed.   The researcher who (a) has decided not to report the results or (b) has decided to report them but has been unable to obtain the cooperation of an editor, may be left holding a bagful of data. At this point, the model allows the researcher to decide whether to continue research or to abandon the problem. If the result of the preceding data collection was a nonrejection of the null hypothesis, the probability of continuing is represented as c_0; if the result was a rejection of the null hypothesis, the probability of continuing is represented as c_1. Estimates of these parameters have been derived from the questionnaire responses by computing the probability of continuations b and c in response to Questions 4 and 5, conditional on a decision to write *not* having been made. The resulting estimates are .70 for c_0 and .86 for c_1.

The model assumes that the researcher continues research by returning to the data collection stage, at which point the fate of the research is subject to the *r, w, e,* and *c* parameters as before. In carrying out computations based on the model,

---

that the null hypothesis is sufficiently likely to be false so as to warrant additional data collection before drawing a conclusion," the mean response was .11 ($\pm$.02). This suggests that researchers may be willing to treat "marginally sufficient" results more like null hypothesis rejections than like nonrejections. Further, the .05 estimate of r_0 is based on the classical hypothesis-testing assumption of an exact null hypothesis, rather than a range null hypothesis, as is employed in the model. The adoption of the range hypothesis framework has the effect of increasing alpha over its nominal level, the extent of the increase being dependent on the width of the null range in relation to the power ($1 - \beta$) of the research. Since full development of this point is beyond the scope of the present exposition, it shall simply be noted that the presently employed estimates of r_0 and r_1 are at best approximate. The estimates actually employed, as derived from the questionnaire responses, are conservative in the sense that they probably err by leading to an overly favorable estimate of system output.

a three-strikes-and-out rule was assumed. That is, if the researcher has not achieved publication after three data collections, it is assumed that the problem will be abandoned. With parameter values estimated for the present system, 62% of lines of investigation are published or abandoned after three attempts in any case. The limitation to three data collections is of little practical importance since the major output indices of the model (see below) change little with additional iterations.

The Figure 16.1 representation of the model portrays the researcher's choice points as spinners in a game of chance, the parameter values then being represented by the areas in which each spinner may stop. This illustration is intended to make it clear that the model parameters are conditional probabilities, each indicating the probability of a specific departure from a choice point once that

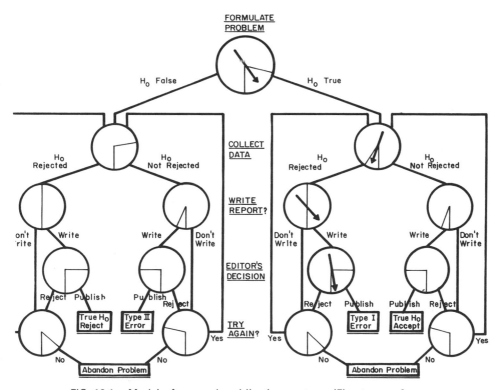

FIG. 16.1. Model of research-publication system. (Five types of sequential decision points in the research-publication process are represented by rows of circles that can be thought of as spinners in a board game, each spinner selecting one of two departures from the decision point. The spinners shown on four of the circles depict a published Type I error resulting from a researcher's first data collection on a problem.)

choice point has been reached, rather than being an attempted judgment of the research process.

LIMITATIONS OF THE MODEL

No pretense is made for this model providing anything more than a potentially useful approximation to the research-publication system. Limitations in the accuracy with which some central model parameters can be estimated have already been mentioned. Perhaps the most glaring weakness in the model is its assumption that the probability of editorial acceptance of a report is independent of the sequence of events that precede submission to a journal. The model considers all manuscripts that reject the null hypothesis to be equivalent before the editorial process regardless of the number of data collections in which the null hypothesis was rejected. Similarly, all manuscripts that report acceptance of the null hypothesis are regarded as equivalent. Perhaps even more importantly, the model assumes the editorial process to be insensitive to the actual truth-falsity of the null hypothesis. The performance of the system would be at least a little better, on the various output criteria to be reported, if the model assumed some success of the editorial process in weeding out Type I and Type II errors rather than these having a likelihood of acceptance equal to true rejections and acceptances of the null hypothesis, respectively. These modifications have not been made partly because they would add complexity and also because the elaboration of additional parameters for the editorial process would not seriously affect the relations between the model's input parameters and its output indices. (They would affect absolute values of the output indices.)

Note a general caution: The model parameter estimates based on questionnaire responses are certainly more appropriate to some areas of behavioral science research than to others. Particularly, they are appropriate to areas of research in which null hypothesis decision procedures (Rozeboom, 1960) are dominant. Further, given the use of null hypothesis decision procedures, assumptions made about the present state of the system are most appropriate for those areas of research in which measurement error is substantial in relation to the magnitude of theoretically or practically meaningful effects. These are areas in which investigators are prone to work with relatively high risks of Type I error and to proceed otherwise in ways that tend to discriminate against acceptance of the null hypothesis. Within psychology, for example, much research in psychophysics, neuropsychology, and operant behavior would not properly be considered in terms of the present model. On the other hand, much research in social, developmental, experimental, clinical, industrial, and counseling psychology would, I expect, be reasonably well simulated by the model.

MODEL OUTPUT INDICES

In order to illustrate how the model's output indices respond to change in model parameters, Figure 16.2 presents seven output measures as a function of the model parameter h_0 (probability that the null hypothesis is true for the focal hypothesis test). These results have been obtained with model parameters other than h_0 held constant at their previously described values (estimated from questionnaire responses).

If Type I and Type II errors are examined as a percentage of total journal content, it may be seen that these represent a gratifyingly small proportion of total published content (upper portion of Figure 16.2), given the estimated present-system value of $h_0 = .20$. It then becomes a bit disturbing to note that the Type I error rate of the system (system alpha) is rather high, .30. (System alpha is computed as the proportion of all publications on the right side of Figure 16.1 that are Type I errors.) System beta (the proportion of all publications on the left side of Figure 16.1 that are Type II errors) is quite low, .05.

It is somewhat coincidental, but nonetheless remarkable, that the system output levels of alpha (.30) and beta (.05) are exactly the reverse of the alpha ($r_0 = .05$) and beta ($1.00 - r_1 = .30$) levels used as estimates of model input parameters. The explanation for the discrepancy between the system alpha and system beta indices, on the one hand, and Type I and Type II errors considered as a percentage of all publications, on the other, can be found in an index giving the percentage of all publications in which the null hypothesis is reported as rejected for the focal hypothesis test (upper portion of Figure 16.2). This index has the quite high value of 91.5% when $h_0 = .20$. It is apparent then that the high value of system alpha, despite the low proportion of publications that are Type I errors, is a consequence of the fact that system output includes very few publications of true acceptances of the null hypothesis.

An Information Transmission Index. Because it is difficult to interpret the Type I and Type II percentage error indices or the system alpha and beta indices directly as measures of the quality of functioning of the research-publication system, it is desirable to have an index that better summarizes the system's accuracy in communicating information about the truth and falsity of researchers' null hypotheses to journal readers. An information transmission index, computed as shown in Table 16.2, can partially serve this purpose.

To interpret the information transmission index, assume that a journal reader is presented with a list of the focal hypotheses tested in an upcoming journal issue. Maximally, reading the journal might reduce the reader's uncertainty about the truth-falsity of the several focal hypotheses by an average of 1.00 bit. The information transmission index will approach this maximum value to the extent that (a) there is a fifty-fifty likelihood that the null hypothesis is true or false for

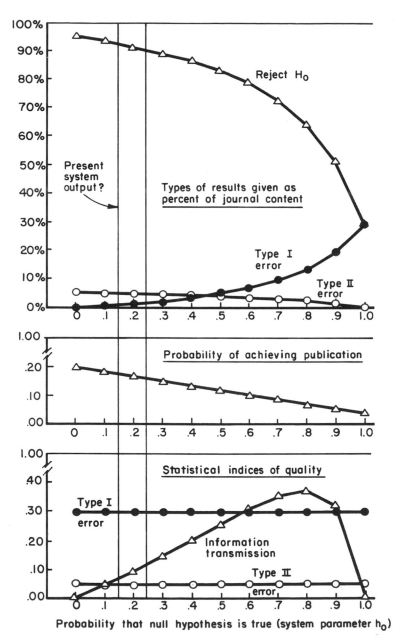

FIG. 16.2. Seven output indices for the research-publication system model. (To illustrate responsiveness of output indices to an input parameter, the seven indices are plotted as a function of system parameter h_0 [which equals the probability that the researcher formulates a problem for which the null hypothesis is, in fact, true].)

TABLE 16.2
Computation of Publication Information
Transmission Index

Truth of H_0	*Published Result*		Sum
	Not reject H_0	Reject H_0	
H_0 true	p_{00}	p_{01}	$p_{0.}$
H_0 false	p_{10}	p_{11}	$p_{1.}$
Sum	$p_{.0}$	$p_{.1}$	1.00

Note: Table entries are proportions of only those lines of investigation that have reached the stage of journal publication. The index is computed as (cf. Attneave, 1969, pp. 46 ff):

$$\left(-\sum_{i=0}^{1} p_{i.} \log_2 p_{i.} \right) + \left(-\sum_{j=0}^{1} p_{.j} \log_2 p_{.j} \right)$$

$$-\left(-\sum_{i=0}^{1} \sum_{j=0}^{1} p_{ij} \log_2 p_{ij} \right).$$

the published articles (i.e., the reader's uncertainty is maximal), (b) there is a fifty-fifty true-false reporting ratio for the null hypothesis in the published articles (i.e., the journal's content is maximally uncertain), and (c) the published conclusions are perfectly accurate (or perfectly inaccurate!) regarding the truth-falsity of the null hypothesis. It is important to note that this index bears little direct relation to the percentage of articles reporting a correct result. To appreciate this, consider that a journal may print nothing but correct rejections of the null hypothesis. By definition then, all of its content would be correct. However, the reader who had an advance list of the focal hypotheses of the to-be-published articles would gain *no* information regarding the truth-falsity of any focal null hypothesis from actually reading the journal, because this reader could know, by extrapolation from past experience, that the null hypothesis would invariably be rejected.

In Figure 16.2 (lower part), it is apparent that the information transmission index has a very low value (about .10 bits) given the present-system assumption that $h_0 = .20$. The fact that the information transmission index increases dramatically as h_0 increases reflects primarily some virtue in compensating, at the problem formulation stage, for biases against the null hypothesis residing elsewhere in the system.

Comment on the Information Transmission Index. A few of my colleagues have objected to the information transmission index as a summary of system functioning because it takes no account of their primary criterion for evaluating published research—the importance of the problem with which the research is concerned. These colleagues pointed out that archives full of confirmations and rejections of trivial null hypotheses would get high marks on the transmission index but would make for poor science. I am in full sympathy with this view and would not like readers to construe my preference for the information transmission index as a call for journals to catalog trivial results. Thus, it should be emphasized that the information transmission index is insensitive to several possible system virtues. Particularly, (a) it takes no account of the value to readers of the conceptual content of journal articles; (b) it ignores the information contained in tests of nonfocal hypotheses; and (c) by conceptualizing the test of the focal hypothesis as having just an accept-reject outcome, it ignores possible information in the direction or magnitude of effect shown by the focal hypothesis test. Further, the assumption implicit in the index—that readers can be aware in advance of articles' focal hypotheses—is obviously out of touch with reality. Despite these limitations, it is difficult to formulate an index that better summarizes functioning of the research-publication system.

There is an alternative form of the information transmission index that may seem preferable to the one shown in Table 16.2. This alternate index is based on *all* lines of investigation (not just those that reach the stage of publication) and classifies the outcomes of these lines as published rejection of the null hypothesis, published nonrejection, and also nonpublication. This index has the virtues of (a) summarizing activity in the whole system (rather than just the published portion) and (b) allowing nonpublication to provide information about the truth-falsity of the null hypothesis. Computations have been made for this index, the results indicating system functioning at about as poor a level as does the index described in Table 16.2. The alternate index has not been presented in Fig. 16.2 chiefly because its implicit assumption—that system output watchers can keep track of lines of research that do not achieve publication—seems too unreasonable.

A final index shown in Fig. 16.2, the probability of achieving a publication given embarcation on a research problem, is one that ought to be of practical concern to researchers. This index, plotted as a function of the h_0 parameter, indicates interestingly that the system "rewards" researchers with publications to the extent that they formulate a problem for which the null hypothesis is false.

A CHECK ON THE MODEL'S ACCURACY

One means of obtaining a rough check on the model's validity is to compare its predicted proportion of articles for which a focal null hypothesis is accepted against the actual content of the literature. With the assistance of John A. Miller and Karl E. Rosenberg, such a check was made for the *Journal of Personality and Social Psychology* for the year 1972. Every article published that year was read to determine, first, what the focal null hypothesis was and, second, whether the article concluded in favor of acceptance or rejection of that null hypothesis. Out of 199 articles for which a focal null hypothesis was identified, 24 reported acceptance (or nonrejection) of that hypothesis. A 95% confidence interval for the proportion of articles reporting null hypothesis acceptance (12.1% ± 4.5%) included the model's estimated value for the present system of 8.5%, providing some evidence supporting the model's validity. A similar check of four psychological journals in the mid 1950s by Sterling (1959) yielded a lower estimate of 8 out of 294 (which equals 2.7% ± 1.9%) articles that reported nonrejection of a focal hypothesis test. However, it is possible that Sterling may have used a more lenient criterion for declaring that an article rejected the null hypothesis for a focal hypothesis test (cf. Sterling, 1959, pp. 31–32).[5]

TOWARD A MORE SATISFACTORY SYSTEM

The foregoing results strongly suggest that the research-publication system is functioning well below its potential in research areas characterized by prejudice against the null hypothesis. With the system model it is easy to demonstrate the improvement in system functioning that is potentially possible if biases against the null hypothesis are eliminated. Figure 16.3 shows the consequences of step-by-step restoration of equal status to the null hypothesis, as reflected in values of the information transmission index. It is quite apparent from Figure 16.3 that unbiased behavior at the various stages of the research-publication process can have highly desirable effects on the informativeness of published research. The methods of achieving such unbiasedness are considered in more detail below.

SYSTEM EFFECT ON GENERALITY
OF RESEARCH FINDINGS

The information transmission and other system output indexes are insensitive to what may be the worst consequence of prejudice against the null hypothesis—the archival accumulation of valid results with extremely limited generality.

Consider the situation of Researcher R, who starts off with the hypothesis that an increase in variable x produces an increase in variable y. Because R is very convinced of the virtues of the theory that led to this prediction, R is willing to proceed through a number of false starts and pilot tests that involve the use of a few different experimenters to collect data, a few different methods of manipulat-

---

[5]It gives me pause, in reading over this paragraph, to consider whether or not I would have reported the results of the content check of *JPSP* if it had not been confirming of the model.

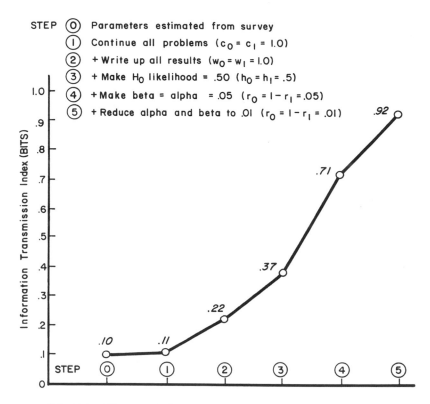

FIG. 16.3. Effects on information transmission index of step-by-step alterations in research-publication system parameters to reduce bias against the null hypothesis. (Present-system parameters estimated from survey results are given in the text. Hypothetical changed parameter values are indicated in parentheses in the legend, and characterize also all points to the right of the one in which the change is first indicated.)

ing variable x, a few different measures of variable y, and a few different settings to mask the true purpose of the experiment. At last, R obtains the result that confirms the expected impact of x on y but is properly concerned that the result may have been an unreplicable Type I error. To relieve this concern, R conducts an exact replication using the same combination of experimenter, operationalization of x, measure of y, and experimental setting that previously "worked," and is gratified to discover that the finding is replicated. Concerned about the validity of procedures and measures, R also obtains evidence indicating that the manipulation of x was perceived as intended and that the measure of y had adequate reliability and validity. R then publishes the research concluding that increases in x cause increases in y and, therefore, that the theory, which predicted this relationship, is supported.

The potential fault in this conclusion should be obvious from the way I have presented the problem, but it is not likely to be obvious to Researcher R. Because of R's investment in confirming a theory with a rejection of the null hypothesis, R has overlooked the possibility that the observed x-y relationship may be dependent on a specific manipulation, measure, experimenter, setting, or some combination of them. In eagerness to proclaim a general x-y relationship, R has been willing to attribute previous false starts to R's own (or, better, a research assistant's) incompetence and, on this basis, does not feel it either necessary or desirable to inform the scientific community about them.

This style of researcher's approach has been well described by McGuire (1973):

> The more persistent of us typically manage at last to get control of the experimental situation so that we can reliably demonstrate the hypothesized relationship. But note that what the experiment tests is not whether the hypothesis is true but rather whether the experimenter is a sufficiently ingenious stage manager. (p. 449)

For further discussion of situations in which findings of limited generality appear to be much more general, I refer the reader to Campbell's (1969, pp. 358–363) typology of threats to valid inference.

SOME EPIDEMICS OF TYPE I ERROR*

If the results generated by the model are to be believed, then the existing archival literature in the behavioral sciences should contain some blatant Type I errors. Although the absolute frequency of Type I error publications is not expected to be high, there should be some true null hypotheses for which only rejections of the null hypothesis have been published. About the only way to demonstrate the existence of Type I errors conclusively is to demonstrate that "established" findings cannot be replicated and that such failures to replicate cannot easily be regarded as Type II errors. As mentioned before, the fact that two of the three following cases are drawn from social psychology reflects only my familiarity with this field, not any belief that social psychology is more prone to such errors than are other areas of behavioral science research.

ATTITUDE AND SELECTIVE LEARNING

Between 1939 and 1958, approximately 10 studies (referenced in Greenwald & Sakumura, 1967) reported the consistent finding that subjects, when exposed to

---

*Note added in 1992: The conclusions about the three phenomena described in this section do not require alteration in light of subsequent research.

information on a controversial topic, more easily learned information that was agreeable rather than disagreeable to their existing attitude on the issue. This selective learning effect was regarded as sufficiently established to appear in many introductory psychology and social psychology textbooks, the study of Levine and Murphy (1943) particularly being regarded as somewhat of a classic.

Starting in 1963, however, almost all published studies that included a test of this hypothesis failed to confirm it (Brigham & Cook, 1969; Fitzgerald & Ausubel, 1963; Greenwald & Sakumura, 1967; Waly & Cook, 1966). In one study (Malpass, 1969) the hypothesis appeared to be confirmed in only one of three conditions in which it was tested. In general, the experiments reported since 1963 have been quite carefully done, each publication typically reporting the results of more than one replication of the hypothesis test and with careful attempts to control extraneous variables that might contaminate the tests. Therefore it does not seem reasonable to suggest that these recent findings should be regarded uniformly as Type II errors. Because the recent investigations have also made strenuous attempts, generally unsuccessful, to explain the earlier findings in terms of interactions with previously uncontrolled factors, the possibility that most of the earlier results were Type I errors is currently very plausible. This apparent epidemic of Type I error can be readily understood in terms of the hypothesized present research-publication system. Several of the earlier publications reported rejections of the null hypothesis with an alpha criterion greater than .05. After the selective learning effect had thus established some precedent in the literature, presumably researchers and editors were more disposed to regard a rejection of the null hypothesis as true than false. Possibly, also, investigators who could not obtain the established finding were content to regard their experiments as inadequate in some respect or other and did not even bother to seek publication for what they may have believed to be Type II errors, nor did they bother to conduct further research that might have explained their failure to replicate published findings.

THE SLEEPER EFFECT

The sleeper effect in persuasion is said to occur when a communication from an untrustworthy or inexpert source has a greater persuasive impact after some time delay than it does on original exposure. That is, the communication presumably achieves it effect while the audience "sleeps" on it. This result is established well enough so that it is described in most introductory social psychology texts. The research history of the sleeper effect demonstrates a variety of ways in which Type I publication errors may occur (if one assumes, that is, that the effect is not a genuine one).

The original report of a sleeper effect by Hovland, Lumsdaine, and Sheffield (1949) involved the use of an alpha criterion that was inflated by selective sampling from multiple post hoc tests of the hypothesis. That is, the effect was not predicted and was found on only a subset (not an a priori one) of the opinion items used by the investigators. In subsequent years, experimental investigators have chosen to look for the sleeper effect in terms of a comparison between the temporal course of opinion changes induced by the same communication from a trustworthy, versus an untrustworthy, source. That is, the increase in effect over time with the untrustworthy source should not be matched by a similar increase when the source is trustworthy. Significant interaction effects involving these two variables of source credibility and time since communication have been reported in a number of studies (e.g., Gillig & Greenwald, 1974; Hovland & Weiss, 1951; Kelman & Hovland, 1953; Shulman & Worrall, 1970; Watts & McGuire, 1964). However, in *none* of these studies was there reported a significant increase in impact, with passage of time since the communication, for subjects receiving the communication from an untrustworthy source. That is, the interaction effects were due primarily or entirely to loss of effects, with passage of time, for subjects receiving the communication from a trustworthy source.

The sleeper effect, it is clear, was established in the literature by a series of studies, each of which employed an ostensible alpha criterion of .05 but for which the effective alpha criterion was substantially higher. In the original Hovland et al. (1949) study, alpha was inflated through the selective reporting of post hoc significance tests; in the later studies, it was inflated by use of an inappropriate overall interaction effect test instead of the simple effect of the time variable within the untrustworthy source conditions. Evidence that the original and subsequent sleeper effect reports are likely to have been Type I errors has come recently from a series of seven investigations by Gillig and Greenwald (1974) involving a total of 656 subjects. With their procedures, a true sleeper effect (increase over time) of .50 points on the 15-point opinion measure they used would have been detected with better than .95 probability. A 95% confidence interval ($\pm.27$ scale points) around the observed mean change of $+.14$ clearly included the hypothesis of zero change.

QUASI-SENSORY COMMUNICATION

A perennially interesting subject for behavioral science research concerns the possibility of perception of events that provide no detectable inputs to known sensory receptors. Research on extrasensory perception or quasi-sensory communication (Clement, 1972; McBain, Fox, Kimura, Nakanishi, & Tirada, 1970) is so plagued with research-publication system problems that no reasonable person should judge that there exists an adequate basis for a true-false conclusion. This state of affairs is not due to lack of research. It would be difficult to estimate, on the basis of the published literature, the amount of research energy that has been invested in para-psychological questions, and this is precisely the problem. It is a certainty that the published literature, both in favor of and against quasi-sensory communication, represents only a small fraction of the total research effort. Two anecdotes in my own experience are illustrative:

1. A physicist at Ohio State University once described to me an investigation, conducted with a colleague as a digression at their laboratory, into the detection of human-expressed affect by plants.[6] They happened to have electronic apparatus of sufficient accuracy to detect electric potential charges of as small a magnitude as 10 nV between two points on the same or opposite surfaces of a leaf. This was approximately one part in 10^7 of the baseline voltage. They failed to detect responses of this magnitude reliably in a number of tests involving verbally and facially communicated threats to the plant. When I learned of this (at a cocktail party, of course) I asked if they had any intention either to publish their results or to repeat the experiment. The reply was negative, although I expect the scientific community would have been informed had their results been positive.

2. As an editorial consultant to a journal, I was asked to review an article that obtained an extrasensory perception effect that would reject the hypothesis of no effect if alpha were set at .10. I advised the editor that the result was one that had a higher probability of being Type I error than the ostensible .10, but the appropriate editorial response, because the study was competently done and the problem was interesting, was to guarantee to publish the results if the investigators would agree (a) to conduct a replication and (b) to publish the outcome of the replication (as well as the already submitted study). Two years later, the study was published (Layton & Turnbull, 1975; see also Greenwald, 1975) with the results of the replication *failing* to confirm the original findings.

Now we all know that anecdotes are unacceptable as scientific evidence because of the inflated probability that unusual events will be noticed and propagated as anecdotes. What is distressing is that the published literature on quasi-sensory communication (and other topics) also seems to be highly likely to detect and communicate relatively unlikely events. As it is functioning in at least some areas of behavioral science research, the research-publication system may be regarded as a device for systematically generating and propagating anecdotal information.

RATIONAL STRATEGIES REGARDING
THE NULL HYPOTHESIS

My criticisms of researchers' null-hypothesis-related strategies are not new. They have been expressed, in part, by several previous writers, the article by Bakan (1966) being perhaps closest to the approach I have taken. The point that Type I

---

[6]I am grateful to James T. Tough and James C. Garland for permission to give this informal report of their investigation.

publication errors are underestimated by reported alpha criteria has been made also in critiques of the use of significance tests in sociology (Selvin, 1966) and psychology (Sterling, 1959) (see also the anthology edited by Morrison & Henkel, 1970). What I have attempted to add to the previous critiques is a quantitative assessment of the magnitude of the problem as it exists, by means of (a) a questionnaire survey and (b) a system simulation employing system parameters derived from the survey results. The obtained quantitative estimates must be regarded as frightening, even calling into question the scientific basis for much published literature.

Previous critics have not been negligent in suggesting remedies for what they too have regarded as an undesirable situation. Some suggestions have been intended for use in conjunction with the standard significance testing approach. For example, Cohen (1962) has pointed out that social psychological experiments often have power adequate to detect only relatively large effects. His suggestion for higher powered experiments, if adopted, should be expected to result in an increase in the frequency of null hypothesis rejections relative to nonrejections. However, it is also possible that increased awareness of experimental power may lead to taking null results more seriously. Hays (1963) has suggested using estimates of magnitude of association to accompany the standard reports of alpha levels. This would help to assure that trivial effects associated with a rejection of the null hypothesis would be recognized as such, but might have no systematic effect on the treatment of null results.

Other writers have recommended departures from the significance testing framework. Particularly, suggestions for the use of interval estimation (Grant, 1962) or Bayesian analytic techniques (Bakan, 1966; Edwards, Lindman, & Savage, 1963) would help to avoid prejudice against the null hypothesis, because with these procedures, results need not be stated in terms of acceptance or rejection of a null hypothesis. Despite the good reasons for using interval estimation and Bayesian techniques that have been advanced by several writers, inspection of current journals makes it apparent that tests of significance against point null hypotheses remain the predominant mode of analysis for behavioral data. (Further, there is little evidence that behavioral researchers have given increased attention to the power of their research designs or to magnitude of association, in pursuit of the suggestions by Cohen, Hays and others.)

It would be a mistake, I think, to expect that a recommendation to adopt some analysis strategy other than (or in addition to) significance testing might, by itself, eliminate bias against accepting the null hypothesis. This is because, as has been shown here, *the problem exists as much or more in the behavior of investigators before collecting and after analyzing their data as in the techniques they use for analysis.* Further, because a research enterprise may often be directed quite properly at the determination of whether a given relationship or effect does or does not approximate a zero value, it seems inappropriate to urge the dropping of methods of analysis in which null hypotheses are compared with alternatives. As noted earlier, a research question stated in null hypothesis versus alternative hypothesis form is especially appropriate for theory-testing research. In such research, a result that can be used to accept a null hypothesis may often serve to advance knowledge by disproving the theory.

For these reasons, *my basic recommendation is a suggested attitude change of researchers (and editors) toward the null hypothesis. Support for the null hypothesis must be regarded as a research outcome that is as acceptable as any other.* I cannot leave this recommendation just baldly stated because I suspect that most readers will not know how to go about analyzing and reporting data in a fashion that can lead to the acceptance of the null hypothesis. I conclude, therefore, by considering some technical points related to acceptance of the null hypothesis. It should be clear to readers, as it is to me, that what follows is a rather low-level consideration of technical matters, directed at users around my own level of statistical naiveté but nonetheless accurate as far as I can determine through consultation with more expert colleagues.

HOW TO ACCEPT THE NULL
HYPOTHESIS GRACEFULLY

Use a Range, Rather than a Point, Null Hypothesis. The procedural recommendations to follow are much easier to apply if the researcher has decided, in advance of data collection, just what magnitude of effect on a dependent measure or measure of association is large enough not to be considered trivial. This decision may have to be made somewhat arbitrarily but seems better to be made somewhat arbitrarily before data collection than to be made after examination of the data. The minimum magnitude of effect that the researcher is willing to consider nontrivial is then a boundary of the null range. The illustrations that follow employ a "two-tailed" null range that is symmetric around the zero point of a test statistic.

Select N on the Basis of Desirable Error of Estimate of the Test Statistic. Assume, for example, that in an experiment with one treatment condition and a control condition, the researcher had decided that a treatment versus control difference of .50 units on the dependent measure is a minimum nontrivial effect. (Therefore, the null range is $(-.50, +.50)$ on this measure). It would seem inappropriate to collect data with N only large enough so that the estimate of the treatment effect would have a standard error of, say, .50. To appreciate this, consider that a 95% confidence interval based on this imprecise an estimate would encompass about twice the width of the null range. I can think of no hard and fast way of specifying a desirable degree of precision, but I would suggest that an error of estimate of effect on the order of 10%–20% of the width of the null range may often be appropriate. (A 95% confidence interval then would be

40%–80% of the null range's width.) More precision than this may often be desirable, but the researcher has to make such decisions based on the cost of obtaining such precision relative to the value of the knowledge obtained thereby.[7]

Have Convincing Evidence that Manipulations and Measures are Valid. Whether the data are to be used to accept or reject a null hypothesis or to make some other conclusion, it seems essential that the researcher be able to document the validity of procedures relative to the conceptual variables being studied. In the case of accepting the null hypothesis, the results are patently useless if the researcher has not defended against the argument that the research operations lacked correspondence with the variables that were critical to the hypothesis test. However, the researcher drawing a conclusion that rejects a null hypothesis should feel equal compulsion to demonstrate that the research procedures were valid.

Compute the Posterior Probability of the Null (Range) Hypothesis. I refer the reader to statistical texts (e.g., Hays, 1973, chap. 19; Mosteller & Tukey, 1969, pp. 160–183; Phillips, 1973) for an introduction to Bayesian methods (see also Edwards et al., 1963). Figure 16.4 offers a comparison of three modes of analysis—significance testing, interval estimation, and Bayesian posterior probability computation—for some hypothetical data. These hypothetical data are for the difference between two correlated means on a measure for which the researcher's null range is $(-.50, +.50)$. The standard deviation of the difference scores is assumed to be 1.00, and the obtained sample mean difference (M_D) is $+.25$, a point clearly within the null range. Each analysis method is presented for three sample sizes as an aid to comparing the different analysis procedures.

The first analysis employs a standard two-tailed significance test for a *point* (not range) null hypothesis. This would seem to be the analysis currently preferred by most behavioral scientists. At $\alpha = .05$, this analysis does not reject the null (point) hypothesis for the smallest sample size shown but does do so for the two larger sample sizes, despite (a) the observed data point being well within the null range and (b) the fact that with the larger sample sizes we should have more confidence in the accuracy of this estimate. Clearly, computation of the significance level of an obtained result relative to an exact null hypothesis is not a useful way of going about accepting a range null hypothesis. With a relatively large N it is, rather, a good means of exercising prejudice against the null hypothesis.

The second analysis shown in Fig. 16.4 presents 95% confidence intervals for the $M_D = +.25$ result for the three sample sizes. If we consider the containment of the 95% confidence interval within the null range as a criterion for accepting the null hypothesis, then we should accept the null hypothesis for the two larger

---

[7]Setting N to achieve a given level of precision requires some advance estimate of variability of the data. If such information is unavailable at the outset of data collection, it may then be necessary to determine this variability on the basis of initial data collection.

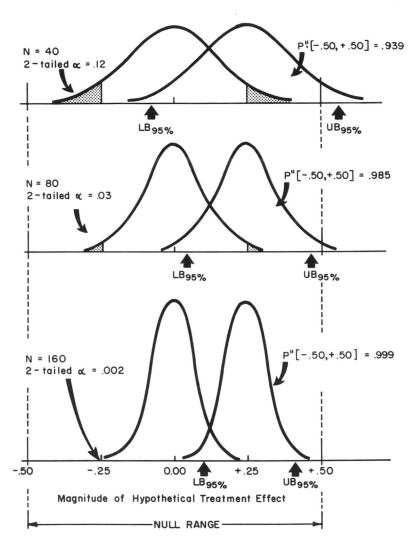

FIG. 16.4. Comparison of significance testing, confidence interval estimation, and posterior probability estimation for three sample sizes. (The example assumes a null hypothesis range of (−.50, +.50), a variance of 1.00, and an obtained sample estimate of +.25 for a hypothetical treatment effect. The distribution centered over 0.00 is the expected distribution of sample mean estimates of the effect if the point null hypothesis of 0.00 is true. This is used to compute significance levels [αs]. The distribution centered over +.25 is the Bayesian posterior likelihood distribution, the posterior probability [P″] estimate being computed as the fraction of the area under this distribution falling in the interval (−.50, +.50). LB and UB are lower and upper confidence interval boundaries.)

sample sizes. This is definitely an improvement over the significance test analysis, but it still has some drawbacks. Particularly, (a) we are at a loss to make direct use of the data for the smallest sample size, for which the 95% confidence interval overspreads the null range; and (b) the conclusion does not reflect the increase in confidence that should be associated with the result for $N = 160$ relative to that for $N = 80$. It is apparent that these drawbacks of the confidence interval procedure stem from the awkwardness of relating the interval estimation procedure to a decision relative to the null hypothesis (cf. Mosteller & Tukey, 1969, pp. 180–183).

The final procedure illustrated in Fig. 16.4 involves the computation of posterior likelihood distributions based on the obtained data. When in a Bayesian analysis one starts from ignorance (a "diffuse," "uniform," or "gentle" prior likelihood distribution), the posterior likelihood distribution is constructed directly from the mean and variability of the obtained data, much as is a confidence interval. A critical difference from the confidence interval analysis is that the assumptions underlying the Bayesian analysis facilitate drawing a conclusion about the acceptability of the null hypothesis. For the posterior distributions presented in Fig. 16.4, a uniform prior distribution is assumed. The resulting posterior probability statements have the desirable feature of allowing us to conclude that the (range) null hypothesis is considerably more likely than its complement for all three sample sizes, while at the same time allowing expressions of the increased certainty afforded by the larger sample sizes for the $M_D = +.25$ result.

To provide a more concrete illustration of a posterior probability computation used as the basis for accepting a null hypothesis, consider the data from the Gillig and Greenwald (1974) sleeper effect study described in the earlier section on Type I errors. In this study, Gillig and Greenwald were employing a 15-point opinion scale as the dependent measure. They considered that a change from an immediate posttest to a delayed posttest of less than .50 on this scale was a trivial effect (.50 was less than 25% of the standard deviation of the obtained difference scores). They employed 273 subjects to estimate this change, so that the standard error of their estimate of the effect was .134 (which equals 13.4% of the $(-.50, +.50)$ null range). Computation of the posterior likelihood distribution of the hypothesis, assuming a uniform prior distribution, indicated that 99.6% of the area under the posterior distribution was within the null range. The .996 figure can therefore be taken as a posterior probability measure of acceptance of the null (range) hypothesis for these data. This figure can be expressed alternatively as a posterior odds ratio of $.996/(1 - .996) = 249:1$ in favor of the null hypothesis. For comparison, an odds ratio of 19:1 ($\alpha = .05$) is frequently considered "significant" in rejecting a point null hypothesis (as contrasted with all possible alternatives).

Report All Results of Research for which Conditions Appropriate to Testing a Given Hypothesis have been Established. As has been demonstrated earlier, successful communication of information through archival publication is severely threatened by self-censorship on the part of investigators who obtain unpredicted (often meaning null) findings. The only justifiable basis for withholding a report of the results of a data collection should be that the hypothesis intended for testing was not actually tested. This could come about through failures of manipulation, measurement, randomization, and so forth. As previously noted the investigator should be prepared for these possibilities, meaning that a decision to withhold data should be supportable by demonstrating that such an invalidating condition obtained. Given a valid hypothesis test, the only justifiable procedure for reporting less than all of the data obtained is the decidedly dubious one of discarding portions of the data randomly; any nonrandom decision procedure with widespread application would result in publication being a biased sample of actual research results. Therefore, researchers should make a point of including at least brief mentions of findings of preliminary data collections, explaining why these results have been ignored (if they have), in reports of data on which more final conclusions have been based. It will be obvious that the admonition to publish all one's data fails to take into account the reality of editorial rejection. This point prompts a few final comments. First, it is a truly gross ethical violation for a researcher to suppress reporting of difficult-to-explain or embarrassing data in order to present a neat and attractive package to a journal editor. Second, it is to be hoped that journal editors will base publication decisions on criteria of importance and methodological soundness, uninfluenced by whether a result supports or rejects a null hypothesis.

CONCLUSIONS

As has, I hope, been clear there is a moral to all this. In the interest of making this moral fully explicit (and also for the benefit of the reader who has started at this point), I offer the following two boiled-down recommendations.

1. Do research in which any outcome (including a null one) can be an acceptable and informative outcome.

2. Judge your own (or others') research not on the basis of the results but only on the basis of adequacy of procedures and importance of findings.[8]

ACKNOWLEDGMENTS

Reprinted with permission from *Psychological Bulletin, 82*(1), 1–20. Preparation of this report was facilitated by grants from National Science Foundation

---

[8]Concluding note: Although I have not had occasion to cite their work directly in this report, the articles of Binder (1963), Campbell and Stanley (1963), Lykken (1968), and Walster and Cleary (1970) have stimulated some of the ideas developed here.

(GS-3050) and U.S. Public Health Service (MH-20527-02). Minor changes have been made in order for text written in the early 1970s not to appear archaic in the 1990s. Almost all of these changes undid the use of male pronouns for the generic third person.

REFERENCES

Aronson, E., & Carlsmith, J. M. (1969). Experimentation in social psychology. In G. Lindzey & E. Aronson (Eds.), *Handbook of social psychology* (2nd ed., Vol. 2), Reading, Mass: Addison-Wesley.

Attneave, F. (1959). *Applications of information theory to psychology.* New York: Holt.

Bakan, D. (1966). The test of significance in psychological research. *Psychological Bulletin, 66,* 432–437.

Binder, A. (1963). Further considerations of testing the null hypothesis and the strategy and tactics of investigating theoretical models. *Psychological Review, 70,* 107–115.

Brigham, J. C., & Cook, S. W. (1969). The influence of attitude on the recall of controversial material: A failure to confirm. *Journal of Experimental Social Psychology, 5,* 240–243.

Campbell, D. T. (1969). Prospective: Artifact and control. In R. Rosenthal & R. L. Rosnow (Eds.), *Artifact in behavioral research.* New York: Academic Press.

Campbell, D. T., & Stanley, J. C. (1963). Experimental and quasi-experimental designs for research on teaching. In N. L. Gage (Ed.), *Handbook of research on teaching.* Chicago: Rand McNally.

Clement, D. E. (1972). Quasi-sensory communication: Still not proved. *Journal of Personality and Social Psychology, 23,* 103–104.

Cohen, J. (1962). The statistical power of abnormal-social psychological research: A review. *Journal of Abnormal and Social Psychology, 65,* 145–153.

Edwards, W. (1965). Tactical note on the relation between scientific and statistical hypotheses. *Psychological Bulletin, 63,* 400–402.

Edwards, W., Lindman, H., & Savage, L. J. (1963). Bayesian statistical inference for psychological research. *Psychological Review, 70,* 193–242.

Festinger, L. (1953). Laboratory experiments. In L. Festinger & D. Katz (Eds.), *Research methods in the behavioral sciences.* New York: Holt.

Fitzgerald, D., & Ausubel, D. P. (1963). Cognitive versus affective factors in the learning and retention of controversial material. *Journal of Educational Psychology, 54,* 73–84.

Gillig, P. M., & Greenwald, A. G. (1974). Is it time to lay the sleeper effect to rest? *Journal of Personality and Social Psychology, 29,* 132–139.

Grant, D. A. (1962). Testing the null hypothesis and the strategy and tactics of investigating theoretical models. *Psychological Review, 69,* 54–61.

Greenwald, A. G. (1975). Significance, nonsignificance, and interpretation of an ESP experiment. *Journal of Experimental Social Psychology, 11,* 180–191.

Greenwald, A. G., & Sakumura, J. S. (1967). Attitude and selective learning: Where are the phenomena of yesteryear? *Journal of Personality and Social Psychology, 7,* 387–397.

Hays, W. L. (1963). *Statistics for psychologists.* New York: Holt, Rinehart & Winston.

Hays, W. L. (1973). *Statistics for social scientists* (2nd ed.). New York: Holt, Rinehart & Winston.

Hovland, C. I., Lumsdaine, A. A., & Sheffield, F. D. (1949). *Experiments on mass communication.* Princeton: Princeton University Press.

Hovland, C. I., & Weiss, W. (1951). The influence of source credibility on communication effectiveness. *Public Opinion Quarterly, 15,* 635–650.

Kelman, H. C., & Hovland, C. I. (1953). "Reinstatement" of the communicator in delayed measurement of opinion change. *Journal of Abnormal and Social Psychology, 48,* 327–335.

Layton, B. D., & Turnbull, B. (1975). Belief, evaluation, and performance on an ESP task. *Journal of Experimental Social Psychology, 11,* 166–179.

Levine, J. M., & Murphy, G. (1943). The learning and forgetting of controversial material. *Journal of Abnormal and Social Psychology, 38,* 507–517.

Lykken, D. T. (1968). Statistical significance in psychological research. *Psychological Bulletin, 70,* 151–159.

Malpass, R. S. (1969). Effects of attitude on learning and memory: The influence of instruction induced sets. *Journal of Experimental Social Psychology, 5,* 441–453.

McBain, W. N., Fox, W., Kimura, S., Nakanishi, M., & Tirado, J. (1970). Quasi-sensory communication: An investigation using semantic matching and accentuated affect. *Journal of Personality and Social Psychology, 14,* 281–291.

McGuire, W. J. (1964). Inducing resistance to persuasion: Some contemporary approaches. In L. Berkowitz (Ed.), *Advances in experimental social psychology* (Vol. 1). New York: Academic Press.

McGuire, W. J. (1973). The yin and yang of progress in social psychology: Seven koan. *Journal of Personality and Social Psychology, 26,* 446–456.

Mills, J. (1969). The experimental method. In J. Mills (Ed.), *Experimental social psychology.* Toronto: Macmillan.

Morrison, D. E., & Henkel, R. E. (Eds.). (1970). *The significant test controversy.* Chicago: Aldine.

Mosteller, F., & Tukey, J. W. (1969). Data analysis, including statistics. In G. Lindzey & E. Aronson (Eds.), *Handbook of social psychology* (2nd ed., Vol. 2). Reading, Mass: Addison-Wesley.

Phillips, L. D. (1973). *Bayesian statistics for social scientists.* New York: Crowell.

Platt, J. R. (1964). Strong inference. *Science, 146,* 347–353.

Rosenthal, R., & Rosnow, R. L. (Eds.). (1969). *Artifact in behavioral research.* New York: Academic Press.

Rozeboom, W. (1960). The fallacy of the null-hypothesis significance test. *Psychological Bulletin, 57,* 416–428.

Selvin, H. C., & Stuart, A. (1966). Data-dredging procedures in survey analysis. *American Statistician, 20,* 20–23.

Shulman, G. I., & Worrall, C. (1970). Salience patterns, source credibility, and the sleeper effect. *Public Opinion Quarterly, 34,* 371–382.

Siegel, S. (1956). *Nonparametric statistics for the behavioral sciences.* New York: McGraw-Hill.

Sterling, T. D. (1959). Publication decisions and their possible effects on inferences drawn from tests of significance—or vice versa. *Journal of the American Statistical Association, 54,* 30–34.

Walster, G. W., & Cleary, T. A. (1970). A proposal for a new editorial policy in the social sciences. *American Statistician, 24,* 16–19.

Waly, P., & Cook, S. W. (1966). Attitudes as a determinant of learning and memory: A failure to confirm. *Journal of Personality and Social Psychology, 4,* 280–288.

Watts, W. A., & McGuire, W. J. (1964). Persistency of induced opinion change and retention of the inducing message contents. *Journal of Abnormal and Social Psychology, 68,* 233–241.

Wilson, W. R., & Miller, H. (1964). A note on the inconclusiveness of accepting the null hypothesis. *Psychological Review, 71,* 238–242.

17 How Significant Is "Significance"?

Paul Pollard
Lancashire Polytechnic, Preston, U.K.

In many areas of psychological research, conclusions about the data are based on a test of significance. Typically if the significance level is 5% or less, it is concluded that a real effect has been observed. This chapter is concerned with certain problems with the logic of this procedure. In particular, the significance level is not related to the *probability of a Type I error* (i.e., the probability that a conclusion that a real effect has been observed is erroneous) in the way that it is normally assumed to be.

After a brief statement of the decision problem, I analyze the various alternative possible interpretations of the probability of a Type I error, and show that the significance level does not yield the value that would be the most useful, even though it is often interpreted as though it does. In later sections I discuss the possible sources of this confusion, both in terms of the training materials to which psychologists are typically exposed, and in terms of known fallacies in human reasoning. The confusion is interpreted in terms of both reasoning errors with conditional probabilities and faulty *modus tollens* reasoning. The latter analysis leads to the conclusion that the significance level cannot be used to make hypothetico-deductive conclusions about the falsification of a hypothesis. Next, I consider implications of these arguments for psychological practice, particularly in light of the bias in favor of *significant* results. As the significance level is at least partly arbitrary and, in any case, does not give the probability we would most wish to know, I suggest there is a need for a more flexible approach to significance testing with less dichotomous treatment of significant and nonsignificant results.

THE DECISION PROBLEM

Psychologists conduct empirical research that investigates relationships between variables. Relationships between independent and dependent variables are usually judged by consideration of differences in the dependent variables at different levels of the independent variable, whereas relationships between dependent variables are assessed by their correlation. Life would be considerably easier if it were the case that if no relationship existed, then observed differences or correlations would be zero. Unfortunately this is not the case. As a sample will rarely exactly reflect population parameters, practically all psychological research produces a nonzero difference or correlation. This leads to the decision problem as to whether the difference was due to chance fluctuation or represents a real effect. Henceforth, I simply refer to a difference, as the decision problem can always be seen as involving a difference (e.g., between the magnitude of an observed correlation and zero).

This problem is formulated in terms of establishing a null hypothesis (H_0) that there is no difference, and then deciding whether to reject it. It is assumed that, "in reality," H_0 is either true or false. If H_0 is true there is no real effect and the observed difference is a chance fluctuation. The decision whether or not to reject H_0 can be viewed as a situation in which the researcher makes a "best guess" about the nature of the world. There are a variety of pieces of information that could be considered germaine to the decision problem, but statistical testing yields just one—the probability that, if the null hypothesis were true, an effect as large or larger than that observed would occur. The decision has to be made on the basis of this probability.

If researchers reject the null hypothesis then they will be right if H_0 is indeed false, and wrong if H_0 is in fact true. In the latter case, the researcher has concluded that an effect exists when in fact it does not, which is referred to as a Type I error. Similarly, if the null hypothesis is not rejected, the researcher has either made a correct decision or has missed an effect if H_0 is in fact false. The latter is known as a Type II error. As we do not wish the research literature to be riddled with spurious effects, nor to encourage pointless experiments that build on such effects, we are more concerned with avoiding Type I errors. A significance level of 5% or below implies that the observed result is unlikely under the null hypothesis, and has been adopted as the criterion for rejection. However, this account glosses over exactly what the significance level tells us about the probability of a Type I error, which is examined in detail in the next section.

THE PROBABILITY OF A TYPE I ERROR

Pollard and Richardson (1987) pointed out that there are three possible meanings for this probability. Before considering these, it may be helpful to consider an analogy. Table 17.1 shows some imaginary data about defective widgits in a factory that makes red and green widgits. The figures are expressed in terms of the percentage of all widgets made, so that the four cells add to 100%. Please ignore, for the moment, the text in brackets. What is the probability of a defective red widgit?

The reader who answered this question may have correctly answered 3%, 5%, or 15%, depending on how they interpreted the question. Three situations of interest would lead to different answers, as follows:

1. Suppose that defective red widgits cause problems, but that defective green widgits are usable (a good thing as there are so many of them). If widgits come in both colors, then we are particularly interested in knowing the likelihood of a defective red one among all the widgits, and the required probability is 3%.

2. Suppose a checker can spot defective widgits, but is color blind. If again green widgits are usable, the interest is in the likelihood of a defective *red* widgit. The proportion of defective widgits that are red is derivable from the left-hand column of Table 17.1—3/60 = 5%.

3. If we only use red widgits, then our interest is in the probability of a defective red widgit, which is derivable from the top row of Table 17.1—3/20 = 15%. Of particular importance here is the fact that the probability of a widgit being defective, given that it is red, is not the same as the probability of a widgit being red, given that it is defective.

The reader is now asked to consider the bracketed text in Table 17.1, which forms the contingency table of the four possible situations of H_0 being true or false (T or F) crossed with a decision to reject or accept H_0. The top left-hand cell, which before represented defective red widgits, now represents the situation in which H_0 is actually true but is erroneously rejected (i.e., a Type I error). As before, the question about the probability of such a Type I error has three possible answers, depending on whether we consider only the left-hand column, only the top row, or the whole table.

Starting with question 2, consideration of the left-hand column alone yields the proportion of rejections among those cases in which H_0 is true. This yields

TABLE 17.1
Categorization of All Widgits as a Function
of Color and Defectiveness

	Color (H_0)	
	Defective (T)	O.K. (F)
Red (reject)	3	17
Green (accept)	57	23

the probability that *if H_0 is true,* it will be rejected. Pollard and Richardson referred to this as the *conditional prior probability* of a Type I error. It is conditional, because it is based on the situation of H_0 being true, and it is a *prior* probability because it exists before we run the experiment. We know beforehand that if H_0 is true, there is a 5% chance of making a Type I error.

We now consider question 1. What is the probability of making a Type I error across all experiments, irrespective of whether H_0 is true or false? From the table, this figure is derivable as 3%, as 3% of all tests will produce a situation in which a true H_0 is rejected. Pollard and Richardson referred to this as the *overall prior probability* of a Type I error. What can we say about this probability? It is important to note here that I have constructed the left-hand column of Table 17.1 to represent the situation when we adopt the 5% significance level. The conditional prior probability is always 5%, and thus the table represents a true state of the world of hypothesis testing in this respect. However, the remainder of the table does not do so in two respects: First, I have included 60% of cases in the H_0 true column but this could in principle vary between zero and 100% (i.e., we could in fact always, sometimes, or never test true null hypotheses). Second, the proportions of rejections and acceptances assigned to the right-hand column are arbitrary (although they do capture the basic idea that H_0 is presumably more likely to be rejected when it is false). Thus, although the conditional prior probability of a Type I error is 5% as in the table, I am obviously not suggesting that the overall prior probability of a Type I error is in actuality 3%.

However, we can determine the possible range of this probability by considering alternative numbers that could have been assigned to the table. If I had assigned higher proportions to the right-hand column, the proportion in the top left cell would have been reduced from 3% (as it has to remain as 5% of the left-hand column). In the extreme, if the right-hand column added to 100%, then the figure would be zero. Alternatively, if all proportions were assigned to the left-hand (H_0 true) column, the top left-hand cell would be 5%. As this is the worst case, we can see that the overall prior probability of a Type I error cannot exceed 5%. In Pollard and Richardson's terms, the significance level provides the conditional prior probability of a Type I error, and the *upper bound* to the overall prior probability of a Type I error.

Finally, we consider the third alternative, the equivalent of the probability of a widgit being defective, given that it is red. After we have run a significance test and found the result to lie in the rejection region, what is the probability that we have made a Type I error? Pollard and Richardson referred to this as the *conditional posterior probability* of a Type I error. It is conditional because it depends on rejection of H_0, and it is posterior because it is a probability that applies after we have assessed the empirical evidence. This is calculable from the top row concerning rejection of H_0, and on the example figures given in Table 17.1 we find that H_0 will be true on 15% of occasions on which it is rejected.

As before, I have made up the figures in Table 17.1 and thus do not argue that the posterior probability of a Type I error will be 15%. It is crucial to remember that, as with the widgit probabilities, the (posterior) probability of H_0 being true, given that it has been rejected, is not the same as the (prior) probability that H_0 will be rejected, given that it is true. As was the case for the overall prior probability, some idea of the possible range of posterior probability of a Type I error can be gained by considering possible alternative numbers that could have been assigned to Table 17.1. Unfortunately, this procedure does not produce as precise an answer as it does for the overall probability. In the best case, the right-hand column could add to 100% (i.e., we *always* test false null hypotheses), and the posterior probability of a Type I error would be zero. However, in the worst case the left-hand column could add to 100%, the top left cell would be 5% and the top right cell would be zero, and the posterior probability of a Type I error would be 100%. Also, at any intermediate split, varying the rejection/acceptance proportions in the right-hand column would change the posterior probability. In principle, then, the posterior probability of a Type I error could vary from zero to 100% and is thus incalculable.

CONFUSION BETWEEN THE PRIOR
AND POSTERIOR PROBABILITIES

Imagine hypothesis testing in a situation in which the widgit data of Table 17.1 applied. All defective widgits will cause problems and a particular person wishes to know whether a particular widgit is usable. This person sets up a null hypothesis that the widgit is defective, and decides whether to reject it on the basis of an empirical observation (consistent with usual conventions, an H_0 is adopted that is hoped *not* to be true). They know the conditional probability of a widgit being red, given that it is defective, but do not know the actual spread of proportions across the full table. The empirical observation reveals that the widgit is red. Under the null hypothesis, the probability of this (i.e., the proportion of defective widgits that are red) is 5%, and thus H_0 is rejected and it is concluded that the widgit is OK. From Table 17.1, we know that the probability of the red widgit actually being defective (i.e., the *posterior* probability of a Type I error) is 15%. Of course, as the person does not know the distribution of the numbers in the table, only that the conditional probability of a defective widgit being red is 5%, they do not know the posterior probability. The question is, although the person may be happy with a 5% chance, would they be equally happy with a 15% chance that the widgit will cause problems? Has the 5% got any relevance whatsoever to the confidence that this person should have that their widgit is not defective? Which probability would they prefer to know? I think it is surely indisputable that the person would prefer to know the posterior probability—the probability that a Type I error has been made. Unfortunately, as discussed earlier, this probability cannot usually be determined.

Note that achieving the 5% significance level does not mean that there is a 5% probability that our results were due to chance, in the same way that there was not a 5% probability that the red widgit was defective. If we knew the posterior probability that a decision to reject H_0 was wrong, this would allow us to have a legitimate level of confidence in our conclusion, and more generally to calculate the proportion of all significant results that would be expected to be Type I errors. Without this knowledge we can say nothing about the probability that we are right or wrong when we reject a null hypothesis, anymore than the person could say how likely their widgit was to be defective. In short, the 5% conditional prior probability of a Type I error is not the probability we really need. The *probability of a Type I error* that we need is the posterior probability that we are wrong when we reject the null hypothesis.

How is it that researchers tend to seem happy with this state of affairs? One answer is that many workers may actually assume they are determining the posterior probability of a Type I error. Both Pollard and Richardson (1987) and Falk (1986) reported that informally gathered data suggests that there is a widespread assumption among practicing psychologists that the probability of the null hypothesis being true, given that it has been rejected [which I henceforth refer to as $p(H_0|R)$] is the same as the (5%) probability that the null hypothesis will be rejected, given that it is true [$p(R|H_0)$]. Pollard and Richardson were not the first to make the point that these two probabilities are not the same (e.g., Bakan, 1966; Birnbaum, 1982; Carver, 1978; and other references given by Hill, 1990) and, in particular, I have since encountered a paper by Falk (1986) that made many of the same points as we did. However, given apparent prevalent misconceptions, restatement was presumably not redundant.

SOURCES OF CONFUSION:
STATISTICS TEACHING

The confusion between $p(H_0|R)$ and $p(R|H_0)$ has been traced to misleading expositions in both general psychology textbooks (Carver, 1978) and statistical texts used by psychologists (Falk, 1986; Pollard & Richardson, 1987). When hypothesis testing is introduced, the significance level is correctly identified as conditional on H_0 being true, and a Type I error is quite rightly defined as rejecting H_0 when it is true. However, later exposition tends to equate the significance level with the probability of a Type I error, while at the same time dropping reference to the conditional nature of this probability. This is done in several ways, often by presenting a table like Table 17.1 and associating probability of a Type I error with significance level by reference to both within the top left-hand cell. No indication is given that the probability in the top left cell is conditional on the left column. On other occasions, writers suggest that Type I errors will be made on 5% of occasions. They do not add *when H_0 is true*, and imply that they mean *when H_0 is rejected*.

For instance, Pollard and Richardson (1987) gave quotes from Siegel (1956), among several other examples, showing that the significance level is equated with a posterior probability about the null hypothesis. In brief, Siegel said that the probability that the results were due to chance is given by the significance level because "rejecting H_0 when in fact it is true is the Type I error" (p. 14). All reference to the conditional nature of the probability is removed and the probability of the conjunction of $p(H_0)$ and $p(R)$ is equated with $p(R|H_0)$, leading to the invalid inference that this gives the likelihood that a Type I error has been made. The recent update of this much used (and generally excellent) text includes identical treatment of the probability of a Type I error (Siegel & Castellan, 1988) and thus previous attempts to rectify confusion do not appear to have been universally successful.

The confusion may be encouraged at an undergraduate level, both via texts and orally. Personally I feel that it is very difficult to explain the logic of significance testing in a way that suppresses the confusion. As Falk (1986) pointed out, "Considering that one expects statistical inference to provide a decision accompanied by an evaluation of the probability of error, it is natural that one interprets the probability, associated with rejection of H_0, as that of having committed an error" (p. 87). When explaining significance, I take great care not to say anything that is wrong in that it directly implies that $p(H_0|R) = p(R|H_0)$, but still feel that many students will have concluded that this is the case. To try too hard to ensure that this assumption was not transmitted would lead to the danger of further confusing students, particularly as the rationale would make much more sense if the two probabilities were the same. I venture to believe that I am not alone in this and, in fact, as Falk suggested, many teachers may explicitly tell students that the significance level gives the probability that H_0 rejection was an error.

SOURCES OF CONFUSION: INFERENTIAL FALLACIES

Both Falk (1986) and Pollard and Richardson (1987) pointed out that there is a well-documented general tendency for people to confuse $p(A|B)$ with $p(B|A)$ (e.g., Kahneman & Tversky, 1973; Pollard & Evans, 1983). As professional psychologists have also been shown to suffer from biases in statistical inference (e.g., Tversky & Kahneman, 1971), it is thus not surprising that there is confusion between $p(H_0|R)$ and $p(R|H_0)$. Viewing the confusion as an example of a general confusion could be seen as adequately explaining why many people believe that the significance level yields the probability that we have made an error when we reject H_0. However, personally I prefer an alternative (although equivalent) formulation of the error proposed by Pollard and Richardson, in terms of faulty logical, rather than statistical, inference.

Under the hypothetico-deductive method, a prediction is generated from a theory and then tested. If the prediction fails, and was logically entailed by the theory, then the theory is falsified. The argument can be expressed as: "If T then P," "Not P," therefore we conclude "Not T." The conclusion is based on a modus tollens inference—if a conditional statement is true (e.g., if T really does entail P), then if the consequence is false, the antecedent must be false. If T is the null hypothesis, this method can allow for the adoption of the alternative hypothesis via falsification. In the case of statistical testing, the logic could (erroneously) be viewed as follows:

$$\text{If } H_0 \text{ then NOT } R$$
$$\frac{R}{\text{THEREFORE: NOT } H_0}$$

In full the previous example stands for: "If the null hypothesis is true, we will not observe data in the rejection region, we have observed data in the rejection region, therefor the null hypothesis is not true." This is a logically valid argument. However, it cannot be used to support the statistical inference because the first premise (if H_0 then not R) is clearly untrue. We know that if H_0 is true than we may well observe data in the rejection region, we even know that the probability of this happening is 5%. The inference underlying the hypothesis test must thus be something like the following:

$$\text{If } H_0 \text{ then probably NOT } R$$
$$\frac{R}{\text{THEREFORE: probably NOT } H_0}$$

Even if we do not include the same word (*probably*) in both premise and conclusion, we would have to include similar words. However, the inference is now logically invalid. *Modus tollens* cannot be used with probabilistic conditionals. To illustrate this, Pollard and Richardson suggested translating the previous equation into the obviously fallacious argument: "If a person is American then they are probably not a member of Congress, this person is a member of Congress, therefore this person is probably not American."

The misinterpretation of the significance level as providing a value for $p(H_0|R)$, which is essentially a probability about H_0, may thus be based on the assumption that statistical inference is based on the hypothetico-deductive method, but as can be seen the method does not work with statistical inference. It is interesting to note that since we (Pollard & Richardson) speculated that confusion about Type I errors may be based on the assumption that the previous type of argument can be used, it has actually been explicitly presented as the underlying logic of significance testing by Chow (1988, 1989), although Folger (1989) criticized the assumption of *deductive certainty* on various grounds.

CAN WE DETERMINE
THE POSTERIOR PROBABILITY
OF A TYPE I ERROR?

As the probability of having made a Type I error, given that we have rejected H_0, is the probability that we would most like to have, is there any way that we can determine this? From Bayes' theorem, we have the following relationship:

$$p(H_0|R) = p(R|H_0) \times p(H_0)/p(R)$$

where $p(R)$ stands for the overall probability of obtaining a result in the rejection region given both the truth and falsity of H_0. Unfortunately, neither $p(H_0)$ nor $p(R)$ can be calculated. For instance, in any individual situation we do not know the probability of H_0, and it cannot be calculated on a long-term frequency basis, as we do not know the appropriate base rate of null hypotheses that are tested in general. In principle, we could make an estimate of the probability by counting all tests in the literature and noting the proportion of significant results. We might be able to go from this figure to an estimate of the underlying proportion of true and false null hypotheses that generated it. However, this is clearly impossible for many reasons, not least of which is the fact that nonsignificant results tend not to be published (e.g., Greenwald, 1975).

We can, however, derive some principles from the aforementioned equation. Holding $p(R)$ constant, the lower the value of $p(H_0)$ the lower the posterior probability of a Type I error. Similarly, holding $p(H_0)$ constant, the higher the value of $p(R)$, the lower the probability of error. As Pollard and Richardson pointed out, we can thus minimize Type I errors by phrasing good alternative hypotheses (i.e., keeping $p(H_0)$ low), and running experiments with sufficient power to maximize detection of real effects (thus raising the overall value of $p(R)$).

In addition, the probability of rejection is presumably higher if H_0 is false than if H_0 is true, and thus, as $p(R)$ is based on a combination of these two probabilities, $p(R)$ will be higher than $p(R|H_0)$. It follows algebraically from this that $p(H_0|R)$ is lower than $p(H_0)$. Thus a significant result does at least tell us that the null hypothesis is less likely than it was at the beginning of the study. Furthermore, for any directional test, the probability of obtaining any data in the predicted direction is presumably greater if H_0 is false than if it is true, so any data in the predicted direction will lower the likelihood of the null hypothesis. This has particular application to replications, as replicating the direction of an effect is presumably more likely if the effect is real than if H_0 is true. Any replication of the direction of an effect, whether significant or not, will thus lower the probability of the null hypothesis being true.

This analysis shows that there are some things that we can say about the probability that we have made an error when we reject H_0. However, there are two caveats. First, although we can say in some situations that the posterior probability of H_0 is lower than the prior probability, we cannot give a value to the probability, and so the probability of having made a Type I error is always indeterminate. Second, although Pollard and Richardson argued that Type I errors may well be minimized because researchers tend to keep $p(H_0)$ low and $p(R)$ high, I feel now that there is some problem with this argument with respect to $p(H_0)$. It seems sensible to say that in the case of a really significant finding (in the nonstatistical sense of significance), the probability of H_0 would have originally been considered to be high. A higher likelihood of a Type I error is thus (perhaps unfortunately, but not really surprisingly) positively correlated with the interest value of a rejection of H_0. Although an interesting result thus may be linked to higher (prior and posterior) likelihood of a Type I error, it does not necessarily follow from this that people should be encouraged to test implausible null hypotheses.

IMPLICATIONS

Although the Cowles and Davis (1982) account of the development of the 5% criterion indicates that the choice was perhaps not so arbitrary as is sometimes thought, this is only due to it being a reasoned decision between other levels such as 10% and 1%. It is quite clear that the choice of 5% is arbitrary with respect to alternatives such as 6% or 4.78%. People have a tendency to use percentages in multiples of 5 or 10 (Baird & Noma, 1975). It seems rather harsh that, after all that time and trouble to run empirical research, we often find ourselves in a position of not being able to conclude we have observed an effect simply because we have 5, rather than say 7, digits on a hand.

I would not wish to argue that a shared criterion does not have its uses, but it can also lead to the type of disagreements that it was designed to prevent. For instance, a shared criterion means that different researchers will make the same decision about the same data—an obviously good thing. It would indeed be ridiculous if we had competing accounts of the presence or absence of an effect simply because the different researchers were using different criteria for significance. However, this can unfortunately still happen if the analyses produce p values that vary marginally either side of the 5% level. On a lower sample size, it is even possible to observe a nonsignificant result when the size of the effect is actually larger than in some other study that found a significant result. The shared criterion is thus not a universal panacea.

Furthermore, some mention should be made of the argument (e.g., Carver, 1978; Falk, 1986; Murphy, 1990) that in fact null hypothesis testing is pointless as we never test viable null hypotheses. Most null hypotheses are very unlikely, as it would be surprising if most measures did not have *some* effect. Falk (1986) suggested that significance testing may only be of use in areas such as extrasensory perception (ESP) research where H_0 (chance guessing) is considered a viable hypothesis. Indeed, many psychologists' reaction to ESP experiments do seem to suggest that people implicitly take account of possible (prior) values of $p(H_0)$ in their evaluation of significant results (McCullough, 1987). Many people are sceptical of significant ESP results who would not be at all sceptical of a more mainline finding, at equivalent levels of significance. In a sense, the fact that in most cases H_0 is not considered to be a viable hypothesis means that significance tests are treated as essentially effect size tests. The question is not whether H_0 can be rejected at infinite sample sizes, but whether the effect is strong enough to reject H_0 using typical sample sizes. There is a problem here because different studies use different sample sizes, and, in any case, if this is what is really going on this hidden agenda ought to be made explicit.

I do not wish to initiate here a *significance versus effect size* debate, as effect size measures may also have problems of interpretation (for instance, even very low effect sizes may sometimes be very meaningful; Rosenthal, 1990), and I am not actually attempting to argue against significance testing in certain areas of research. I am suggesting that significance testing could be carried out with greater flexibility, as the problem seems primarily to be that the criterion is treated so strictly as a cut-off point. Rosnow and Rosenthal (1989) wrote that

> it may not be an exaggeration to say that for many PhD students, for whom the .05 alpha has acquired almost an ontological mystique, it can mean joy, a doctoral degree, and a tenure-track position at a major university if their dissertation *p* is less than .05. However, if the *p* is greater than .05, it can mean ruin, despair, and their advisor's suddenly thinking of a new control condition that should be run. (p. 1277)

This situation, and the more general journal bias against null results (e.g., Bakan, 1966; Greenwald, 1975; Kupfersmid, 1988), is in my view undesirable. A result that is "close to" significance may well be more interesting than one that "just makes it." A more sensible alternative, as Rosnow and Rosenthal (1989) argued, involves evaluating the strength of evidence and viewing it as a continuous function of the *p* value.

These points take on even greater weight when it is considered that the significance level does not give us a probability that we are wrong if H_0 is rejected. In summary, the point is that (a) as the 5% level does not give the probability of having committed a Type I error, its status as a criterion is severely undermined, and (b) even if it did give such a probability, the 5% level is entirely arbitrary within a certain range. There is thus nothing magic about the 5% level that can, or should be allowed to, definitively discriminate between results whose significance lies above or below that level.

REFERENCES

Baird, J. C., & Noma, E. (1975). Psychophysical study of numbers. 1. Generation of numerical responses. *Psychological Research, 37*, 281–297.

Bakan, D. (1966). The test of significance in psychological research. *Psychological Bulletin, 66*, 423–437.

Birnbaum, I. (1982). Interpreting statistical significance. *Teaching Statistics, 4*, 24–26.

Carver, R. P. (1978). The case against statistical significance testing. *Harvard Educational Review, 48*, 378–399.

Chow, S. L. (1988). Significance test or effect size? *Psychological Bulletin, 103*, 105–110.

Chow, S. L. (1989). Significance tests and deduction: Reply to Folger (1989). *Psychological Bulletin, 106*, 161–165.

Cowles, M., & Davis, C. (1982). On the origins of the .05 level of statistical significance. *American Psychologist, 37*, 553–558.

Falk, R. (1986). Misconceptions of statistical significance. *Journal of Structured Learning, 9*, 83–96.

Folger, R. (1989). Significance tests and the duplicity of binary decisions. *Psychological Bulletin, 106*, 155–160.

Greenwald, A. G. (1975). Consequences of prejudice against the null hypothesis. *Psychological Bulletin, 82*, 1–20.

Hill, O. W., Jr. (1990). Rethinking of "significance" of the rejected null hypothesis. *American Psychologist, 45*, 667–668.

Kahneman, D., & Tversky, A. (1973). On the psychology of prediction. *Psychological Review, 80*, 237–251.

Kupfersmid, J. (1988). Improving what is published: A model in search of an editor. *American Psychologist, 43*, 635–642.

McCullough, M. (1987). Personal communication.

Murphy, K. R. (1990). If the null hypothesis is impossible, why test it? *American Psychologist, 45*, 403–404.

Pollard, P., & Evans, J. St. B. T. (1983). The role of representativeness in statistical inference: A critical appraisal. In J. St. B. T. Evans (Ed.), *Thinking and reasoning: Psychological approaches* (pp. 107–134). London: Routledge & Kegan Paul.

Pollard, P., & Richardson, J.T.E. (1987). On the probability of making Type I errors. *Psychological Bulletin, 102*, 159–163.

Rosenthal, R. (1990). How are we doing in soft psychology? *American Psychologist, 45*, 775–777.

Rosnow, R. L., & Rosenthal, R. (1989). Statistical procedures and the justification of knowledge in psychological science. *American Psychologist, 44*, 1276–1284.

Siegel, S. (1956). *Nonparametric statistics for the behavioral sciences.* New York: McGraw-Hill.

Siegel, S., & Castellan, N. J., Jr. (1988). *Nonparametric statistics for the behavioral sciences* (2nd ed.). New York: McGraw-Hill.

Tversky, A., & Kahneman, D. (1971). The belief in the law of small numbers. *Psychological Bulletin, 76*, 105–110.

18 Effect Size

Maurice Tatsuoka
Educational Testing Service, Princeton, NJ

It is well known that, when a null hypothesis has been rejected, it simply means that the assertion made in the null hypothesis (H_0) is unlikely to be true in the population under study. When that assertion is that the independent variables has *no effect* on the dependent variable, then the rejection of H_0 tells us only that the effect is not likely to be zero in the relevant population. It does not suggest that the effect is large or even nontrivial but simply that it is nonzero. Hence, the rejection of H_0 "cries out" for estimating the magnitude of the effect in question. This, combined with another well-known fact that the larger our sample size is, the easier it is (other things being equal) to reject a null hypothesis, makes it reasonable to give a general, conceptual definition of effect size (as Rosenthal does in chap. 20) in the following way:

$$\text{Effect size} = [\text{significance-test statistic}]/[\text{sample size}] \qquad (1)$$

It can be said we are "cutting the test statistic down to size," if the reader will pardon the pun. (Here "sample size" is to be understood in a more general way than "number of cases observed": It may be some function of the sizes of the two samples involved. This is probably why Rosenthal referred to "size of study" rather than "sample size." Examples of functions of the two sample sizes may be seen in his Equations 3 and 4.) The quantity stemming from Equation 1 may be called either a *measure* or an *estimate* of effect size, depending on whether it refers to the particular sample at hand or to the population under study.

Example. As a simple example of the previous definition of effect size, consider the following. We are interested in the extent of relationship, if any, between educational background (Graduated from College vs. High School Only) and job satisfaction. Suppose that we chose 180 individuals at random and asked each of

461

them, "Are you satisfied with your job?" The results were as shown in Table 18.1.

Carrying out the chi-square test of independence for a fourfold table, we obtain

$$\chi^2 = \frac{(180)[(82)(32) - (34)(32)]^2}{(116)(64)(114)(66)}$$

$$= 7.60$$

which, as a χ^2-variate with 1 df, is significant beyond the 1% level ($p = .006$). So it is very unlikely that educational background is unrelated to (i.e., has no effect on) job satisfaction. But just how large is the size of this effect? From Equation 1 we get

$$ES = \chi^2/N = 7.60/180 = .0422.$$

The reader may recognize that χ^2/N gives us the squared phi coefficient, ϕ^2, Thus, our effect-size measure here is

$$\phi^2 = .0422,$$

or, if ϕ itself is preferred,

$$\phi = .2055.$$

According to Cohen (1988, pp. 477–478), this effect size would be considered at best only "medium," or even rather small. We have, in shifting our focus from the significance test to effect size, cut down our "exalted" chi-square value, which was significant beyond the 1% level, to an effect-size of $\phi^2 = .0422$ (or $\phi = .2055$).

On the other hand, suppose that we had sampled only 90 individuals, and the fourfold contingency table had been as shown in Table 18.2.

TABLE 18.1
Hypothetical Contingency Table
Showing Relationship Between Educational
Background and Job Satisfaction

	Satisfied with Job?		
	No	Yes	Totals
Graduated College	34	82	116
High School Only	32	32	64
Totals	66	114	180

TABLE 18.2
Hypothetical Contingency Table
Showing Relationship Between Educational
Background and Job Satisfaction
with Frequencies Roughly Halved
from Those in Table 18.1

	Satisfied with Job?		
	No	Yes	Totals
Graduated College	17	41	58
High School Only	17	15	32
Totals	34	56	90

Our chi-square value is now

$$\chi^2 = \frac{(90)[(41)(17) - (17)(15)]^2}{(58)(32)(56)(34)}$$

$$= 4.98,$$

which is not significant at the 1% level but only (to take the next conventional level) at the 5% level. (Actually, $p = .026$.) However, the effect size is

$$\phi^2 = \chi^2/N = 4.98/90 = .0553$$

(or $\phi = .2352$), which is somewhat larger than our previous $\phi^2 = .0422$ ($\phi = .2055$).

The foregoing illustrates the trade-off between significance level and effect size, mediated by sample size. For a given (or even a somewhat lower) significance level—that is, larger p value—we get a larger effect size from a *smaller* sample size. We are, as it were, rewarded for achieving a comparable significance level from a smaller sample.

OTHER TRADITIONAL MEASURES
OF EFFECT SIZE

The measure or estimate of effect size discussed earlier is applicable only in the special case when both independent and dependent variables are dichotomous. A somewhat more general measure is the point-biserial correlation coefficient, r_{pb}, or its square, which is used when the independent variable is dichotomous but the dependent variable is continuous. As the reader may recall, this is just the ordinary product-moment correlation coefficient applied to the case when one of the variables (usually identified as the independent variable) is a *dummy variable,* taking on only two distinct values (such as $X = 0,1$—although any two values will yield the same result) to indicate to which of two treatment or classification groups each observation belongs. The formula is

$$r_{pb} = \frac{\bar{Y}_1 - \bar{Y}_0}{s_y} \frac{\sqrt{n_1 n_0}}{N} \tag{2}$$

where

$\bar{Y}_1$ is the dependent-variable mean of the group with $X = 1$,
$\bar{Y}_0$ is the dependent-variable mean of the group with $X = 0$,
n_1 is the size of the $X = 1$ group,
n_0 is the size of the $X = 0$ group,
$N = n_1 + n_0$,

and

s_y is the standard deviation of Y for the total sample.

Example. Suppose now that, in the example of the previous section, we had asked the question, "To what extent are you satisfied with your job?", instead of just "Are you satisfied or not?", and had received responses on a 10-point scale from $Y = 1$ (totally dissatisfied) to $Y = 10$ (completely satisfied). Suppose further that the distributions of the Y scores in the $X = 1$ (Graduated from College) and $X = 0$ (High School Only) groups had been as shown in Table 18.3. (Note that Table 18.3 is the result of having dichotomized the Y-scale so that individuals with $Y \leq 5$ are classified as "not satisfied" and those with $Y \geq 6$, "satisfied" with their jobs.) From this table, we get the following quantities to be substituted in Equation 2. (We carry four decimal places here—which ordinarily

TABLE 18.3
Job Satisfaction-Scores for Two Groups*

X \ Y	1	2	3	4	5	6	7	8	9	10	Total
1	0	0	4	14	16	26	26	16	10	4	116
0	1	3	6	10	12	16	14	2	0	0	64
Total	1	3	10	24	28	42	40	18	10	4	180

*College graduates (X = 1) and High School only (X = 0)

would be regarded as too many—in order to facilitate comparisons with some subsequent computational results.)

$$\bar{Y}_1 = 6.4138 \qquad \bar{Y}_0 = 5.2344$$

$$n_1 = 116 \qquad n_0 = 64$$

$$S_y = 1.7528$$

Hence

$$r_{pb} = \frac{6.4138 - 5.2344}{1.7528} \frac{\sqrt{(116)(64)}}{180}$$

$$= .3221$$

(or $r_{pb}^2 = .1037$) is our new measure of effect size. Note that these values are larger than the previous $\phi = .2055$ and $\phi^2 = .0422$, respectively. This is because, in computing r_{pb}^2 we have utilized more information about the degree of job satisfaction than the simple dichotomy, satisfied/not satisfied.

Another traditional measure of effect size is the correlation ratio, $\hat{\eta}_{y.x}^2$, where y denotes the dependent variable and x, the independent. (The distinction is important because, unlike the product moment correlation coefficient, the correlation ratio is asymmetric with respect to its subscripts—that is, $\hat{\eta}_{y.x}^2 \neq \hat{\eta}_{x.y}^2$.) This measure was developed in conjunction with the analysis of variance (ANOVA), so X may be a categorical variable representing the levels of the ANOVA factor. Its definition is

$$\hat{\eta}_{y.x}^2 = 1 - \frac{SS_w}{SS_t} \qquad (3a)$$

where SS_w and SS_t are the usual within-groups and total sums of squares of ANOVA. The correlation ratio is often characterized as a measure of "strength of curvilinear relationship," to distinguish it from the (squared) correlation coefficient, which measures the strength of the *linear* relationship between two variables. Of course, when X takes on only two values, as in the data shown in Table 18.3, there is no difference between $\hat{\eta}_{y.x}^2$ and r_{xy}^2 as the following calculations show. For computational purposes, it is more convenient to rewrite Equation 3a as

$$\hat{\eta}_{y.x}^2 = \frac{SS_b}{SS_t} \qquad (3b)$$

From Table 18.3, we obtain

$$SS_b = \frac{(744)^2}{116} + \frac{(335)^2}{64} - \frac{(1079)^2}{180} = 57.3721$$

and

$$SS_t = 7021 - \frac{(1079)^2}{180} = 552.9944,$$

whence, from Equation 3b, we get

$$\hat{\eta}_{y \cdot x}^2 = 57.3721/552.9944 = .1037,$$

in exact agreement, through four decimal places, with the value of r_{pb}^2 computed earlier.

The aforementioned agreement implies that, when there are only two groups, $\hat{\eta}_{y \cdot x}^2$ is not needed in addition to r_{pb}, which, as we know, is simply the product-moment correlation coefficient between the binary variable $X (= 0, 1)$ and the continuous variable Y. However, when there are three or more groups, it will not do to use a single ternary (or quaternary, etc.) variable X, taking on the values 0, 1, 2, 3, . . . , $K - 1$ to indicate group membership and to compute r_{xy}. This is because we would then be "forcing" a linear relationship between X and Y when such a relationship may not hold. For such cases, $\hat{\eta}_{y \cdot x}^2$ shows its distinction from r_{xy}^2. We illustrate this point by enlarging Table 18.3 to contain a third group comprising individuals who earned a graduate degree. The augmented data are shown in Table 18.4, from which we get

$$\sum_{Gr1} Y = 338, \qquad \sum_{Gr2} Y = 744, \qquad \sum_{Gr3} Y = 335$$

$$n_1 = 50, \qquad n_2 = 116, \qquad n_3 = 64$$

$$\sum_{tot} Y = 1417, \qquad \sum_{tot} Y^2 = 9493, \qquad N = 230$$

Therefore,

$$SS_b = \frac{(338)^2}{50} + \frac{(744)^2}{116} + \frac{(335)^2}{64} - \frac{(1417)^2}{230} = 80.3055$$

and

$$SS_t = 9493 - \frac{(1417)^2}{230} = 763.0478.$$

Hence, from Equation 3b

$$\eta_{y \cdot x}^2 = .1052.$$

In this context, if we were erroneously to have assigned the value $X = 2$ to members of the new group (those who have a graduate degree) and the value $X = 1$ for those who graduated from undergraduate college only, and $X = 0$ for those with only high school education in order to compute the product-moment correlation coefficient r_{xy}, we would have obtained the quantities

$$\sum X = 216 \qquad \sum Y = 1417$$

$$\sum X^2 = 316 \qquad \sum Y^2 = 9493$$

$$\sum XY = 1420$$

for substituting in the formula

$$r_{xy} = \frac{\Sigma XY - (\Sigma X)(\Sigma Y)/N}{\sqrt{\Sigma X^2 - (\Sigma X)^2/N}\sqrt{\Sigma Y^2 - (\Sigma Y)^2/N}}. \tag{4}$$

The said substitution would have resulted in

$$r_{xy} = \frac{1420 - (216)(1417)/230}{\sqrt{316 - (216)^2/230}\sqrt{9493 - (1417)^2/230}}$$

$$= \frac{89.2522}{\sqrt{113.1478}\sqrt{763.0478}} = .3038$$

and $r_{xy}^2 = .0923$, which is considerably (and misleadingly) smaller than the $\hat{\eta}_{y.x}^2 = .1052$ that we just found. This is the penalty we pay for having forced a linear relationship between X and Y when (as a plot of the group Y-means against $X = 0, 1, 2$ readily shows) a curvilinear relationship definitely exists.

In this case (i.e., when there are just three groups), a quadratic curve will provide a perfect fit to the plot of the group means on Y. Hence, if we had used X^2 in addition to X and computed the squared multiple-R, $R_{y.x,x^2}^2$, its value would have agreed with $\hat{\eta}_{y.x}^2 = .1052$. We do not carry out this calculation here, however, and instead illustrate a more general approach: *dummy-coding* the groups using one fewer binary variables than the number of groups. (Other coding methods such as *effect coding* or *mean-dependent-variable coding* could have been used just as well.)

TABLE 18.4
Job Satisfaction Score Distributions for Three Groups:
Those who did Graduate Work, Undergraduate Only, and High School Only

Y =	1	2	3	4	5	6	7	8	9	10	Total
Graduate Degree	0	0	3	5	6	7	8	11	7	3	50
Undergraduate Only	0	0	4	14	16	26	26	16	10	4	116
High School Only	1	3	6	10	12	16	14	2	0	0	64
Total	1	3	13	29	34	49	48	29	17	7	230

When there are K groups, we define K-1 binary variables $X_1, X_2, \ldots, X_{K-1}$ that take on the values 0 and 1 in accordance with the following scheme:

		X_1	X_2	X_3	X_{K-1}
Group 1	members get:	1	0	0 ...	0
Group 2	members get:	0	1	0 ...	0
Group 3	members get:	0	0	1 ...	0
.					
.					
.					
Group $(K-1)$	members get:	0	0	0 ...	1
Group K	members get:	0	0	0 ...	0

These are then used as the independent variables to do a multiple regression analysis and to compute the squared multiple-R.

Thus, for the three-group case with which we are concerned here, we use two dummy, binary variables as shown in the leftmost block of Table 18.5. To carry out the computations, we add to this pair of variables another "variable" X_0, which takes the constant value 1 for every member of the entire sample. We then construct the *raw-score* sum-of-squares-and-cross-products matrix $\mathbf{C}$, defined as follows:

$$\mathbf{C} = \begin{bmatrix} \Sigma X_0^2 & \Sigma X_0 X_1 & \Sigma X_0 X_2 & \Sigma X_0 Y \\ \Sigma X_1 X_0 & \Sigma X_1^2 & \Sigma X_1 X_2 & \Sigma X_1 Y \\ \Sigma X_2 X_0 & \Sigma X_2 X_1 & \Sigma X_2^2 & \Sigma X_2 Y \\ \Sigma Y X_0 & \Sigma Y X_1 & \Sigma Y X_2 & \Sigma Y^2 \end{bmatrix} \tag{5}$$

where all the summations are over the entire sample. From the definitions of the variables X_0, X_1, X_2, we see that the elements of the first row and first column are

$$\sum_{\text{tot}} X_0^2 = N = 230, \qquad \sum_{\text{tot}} X_0 X_1 = \sum_{\text{Gr1}} X_1 = n_1 = 50$$

$$\sum_{\text{tot}} X_0 X_2 = \sum_{\text{Gr2}} X_2 = n_2 = 116$$

$$\sum_{\text{tot}} X_0 Y = \sum_{\text{tot}} Y = 1417.$$

The (i, j)-element of the 3×3 submatrix excluding the first row and first column is

$$c_{ij} = \sum_{\text{tot}} X_i X_j \qquad (i, j = 1, 2, 3),$$

where X_3 is just a convenient label for Y. We thus see that the matrix $\mathbf{C}$, with the numerical values for its elements appropriate to this example is

$$
\mathbf{C} = \left[
\begin{array}{c|ccc}
230 & 50 & 116 & 1417 \\
\hline
50 & 50 & 0 & 338 \\
116 & 0 & 116 & 744 \\
1417 & 338 & 744 & 9493
\end{array}
\right].
$$

From this raw-score sums-of-squares-and-cross-products matrix $\mathbf{C}$, we compute the *deviation-score* sum-of-squares-and-cross-products (SSCP) matrix $\mathbf{S}$, whose (i,j)-element is given by the equation

$$
s_{ij} = c_{ij} - (\mathbf{C_0 C_0'})_{ij}/c_{00} \qquad (i,j = 1, 2, 3), \qquad (6)
$$

where $\mathbf{C_0}$ is the first column of $\mathbf{C}$ exclusive of the first element $c_{00} = 230$, and $\mathbf{C_0'}$ is the first row of $\mathbf{C}$, likewise excluding c_{00}; $(\mathbf{C_0 C_0'})_{ij}$ denotes the (i,j)-element of the 3×3 product matrix $\mathbf{C_0 C_0'}$. Equation 6 may look strange at first sight, but after getting used to it, one should see that it is merely another way of writing

$$
\Sigma x_i x_j = \Sigma X_i X_j - (\Sigma X_i)(\Sigma X_j)/N,
$$

where the lowercase xs are deviation scores from the mean. The result is

$$
\mathbf{S} = \left[
\begin{array}{cc|c}
39.1304 & -25.2174 & 29.9565 \\
-25.2174 & 57.4957 & 29.3391 \\
\hline
29.9565 & 29.3391 & 763.0478
\end{array}
\right].
$$

We now partition $\mathbf{S}$ into four submatrices as indicated by the dashed lines, and label the upperleft 2×2 portion $\mathbf{S}_{xx}$, the single element at the lowerright corner, $\mathbf{S}_{yy}$, and the remaining row and column vectors $\mathbf{S}_{yx}$ and $\mathbf{S}_{xy}$, respectively. The

TABLE 18.5
Job Satisfaction Score Distribution for Three Groups, with "Dummy-Coding" Variables X_1 and X_2 to Specify Group Membership

	X_1	X_2	Y 1	2	3	4	5	6	7	8	9	10	Total
Group 1	1	0	0	0	3	5	6	7	8	11	7	3	50
Group 2	0	1	0	0	4	14	16	26	26	16	10	4	116
Group 3	0	0	1	3	6	10	12	16	14	2	0	0	64
Total			1	3	13	29	34	49	48	29	17	7	230

squared multiple-R between Y and the two Xs may then be calculated as (see, e.g., Tatsuoka, 1988, p. 47)

$$R^2 = S_{yx} \ S_{xx}^{-1} \ S_{xy} \ S_{yy}^{-1}. \tag{7}$$

In our present example, this gives us

$$R^2 = [29.9565, \ 29.3391] \begin{bmatrix} 39.1304 & -25.2174 \\ -25.2174 & 57.4957 \end{bmatrix}^{-1} \begin{bmatrix} 29.9565 \\ 29.3391 \end{bmatrix} \left(\frac{1}{763.0478}\right)$$

$$= .1052$$

as the reader should verify. This value of R^2 is seen to agree exactly, to four decimal places, with the value of $\hat{\eta}_{y.x}^2$ calculated immediately after Table 18.4. Thus, $\hat{\eta}_{y.x}^2$ again may be said to be redundant after a squared multiple-R has been computed as shown. However, the calculation of $\hat{\eta}_{y.x}^2$ is much simpler!

The measures of effect size discussed in this and the preceding section, ϕ^2, r_{pb}^2, $\hat{\eta}_{y.x}^2$ and $R_{y.x_1x_2...}^2$ (or their respective square roots), were referred to as *traditional*, because they existed long before the notion of effect size in its present sense made its appearance. They were (and still are) more commonly known as measures of association or coefficients of determination. Nonetheless, they have every right to be called measures of effect size as well, and the ways in which they are interrelated should be appreciated.

In the next section we discuss some "newer" measures of effect size—those that were developed expressly for this purpose in the past couple of decades.

SOME RECENTLY DEVELOPED MEASURES OF EFFECT SIZE

Cohen (1969, 1977, 1988) is unquestionably one of the pioneers in popularizing the notion of effect size, although the term *effect* has been with us ever since Fisher's invention of the technique of ANOVA in the early 1920s. It is said that Fisher originally planned to carry out the analysis of variance through the multiple regression approach, but was thwarted by computational difficulties in the precomputer days. It was thus that he invented the "partitioning the sums-of-squares" approach that we now identify as ANOVA. As great a boon as this was, it did encourage the dichotomy of statistical techniques into those associated with correlation and regression analyses on the one hand and with ANOVA on the other. (Of course, recent years have seen a realliance of these two factions in the general linear model approach, which is discussed elsewhere in this volume.)

Measures of effect size were no exception in falling into one or the other of these two schools of thought. Those that were discussed in the previous section were all based on correlational methods, except for $\hat{\eta}_{y.x}^2$ (clearly an ANOVA statistic), although this, too, was seen to be replaceable by r_{pb}^2 or $R_{y.x,x^2\prime}^2$ ... if so desired. The more recently developed measures to be discussed in this section, on the other hand, are all based on ANOVA methods (including the t test for the two-group case). And, with one exception, they are very straight-forward and "elementary-looking."

The first effect-size measure, explicitly labeled as such, to appear in the statistical literature was Cohen's (1969) d, defined as

$$d = \frac{\mu_1 - \mu_2}{\sigma}, \tag{8}$$

where μ_1 and μ_2 are the means of the two *populations* under study, and σ is their common variance, as assumed in the t test. Note that d itself is a population parameter, because it is defined in terms of three population parameters. As such, it cannot, strictly speaking, be used for samples—unless we have such large samples that we are willing to assume that their respective means are, for all practical purposes, equal to the corresponding population means. (We would also have to use some sort of average of the two sample standard deviations as a surrogate for the common population standard deviation, σ.) Thus, it seems best to regard Equation 8 as a *conceptual*, as opposed to an *operational*, definition. It has the appealing, intuitive meaning as the distance, in standard-deviation units, by which the two population means are separated. When the populations are normal, d can also be converted into what Cohen called *percent nonoverlap* of the two populations; the larger the effect size, the larger the percent nonoverlap.

Next, Glass (1976) proposed what is essentially a sample analogue of Cohen's d, as follows:

$$g = \frac{\bar{Y}_E - \bar{Y}_C}{s_C}, \tag{9}$$

where $\bar{Y}_E$ and $\bar{Y}_C$ are the dependent-variable means of the experimental and control groups, respectively, and s_c is the standard deviation of Y in the control group. It is essentially rather than exactly an analogue of d because the divisor is the sample standard deviation of *one* of the groups (designated the control group) instead of a pooled estimate of the assumed common population standard deviation σ that occurs in d. According to Glass's rationale, when there are several treatment groups to be compared to a single control group, pairwise pooling would lead to a different pooled standard deviation for each control-treatment pair; hence the same $Y_E - Y_C$ value would lead to a different effect-size value. *Example.* Let us treat the first two groups listed in Table 18.4 as experimental groups, and the third (comprising those who graduated only from high school) as the control group, and compute the effect-size index g for the two experimental groups. The means of the three groups are readily calculated from the group totals and sizes shown on pages 466–467.

$$\bar{Y}_1 (= \bar{Y}_{E1}) = 6.76, \ \bar{Y}_2 (= \bar{Y}_{E2}) = 6.41, \ \bar{Y}_3 (= \bar{Y}_C) = 5.23$$

The standard deviation for Group 3 (the control group) requires our computing $\Sigma_{Gr3}\ Y^2$ anew, getting the value 1917. Hence,

$$s_c = \left[\frac{1917 - (335)^2/64}{63} \right]^{1/2}$$

$$= 1.61.$$

Therefore, the effect sizes, g_1 and g_2, for the two experimental groups are

$$g_1 = (6.76 - 5.23)/1.61 = .950$$

and

$$g_2 = (6.41 - 5.23)/1.61 = .733.$$

Whether values of g of these magnitudes should be considered large or only medium depends on the field of research and the accuracy of the measuring instrument used. Cohen (1988, pp. 20–27) recommended that for interpreting his measure d, it is best to convert it either to his percent nonoverlap measure (referred to after Equation 8) or to r_{pb} as defined in Equation 2, and gives formulas and a table for this purpose. These can be used just as well for evaluating g, because the latter is essentially a sample analogue of d. According to Cohen's table, d values of .7 and 1.0 correspond to r_{pb} values of .330 and .410, which in turn, when squared, yield proportions of variance accounted for by group membership (or by the treatment variable) of .109 and .200, respectively. In most fields of study, these values of r_{pb} (or r_{pb}^2) would be regarded as only moderate.

A third ANOVA-related effect-size measure is Hedges's (1981) modification of Glass's g, in which he replaces the s_c in the denominator by a pooled within-groups estimate of the assumed common population standard deviation σ, namely, $\hat{\sigma} = \sqrt{MS_w}$, where MS_w is the usual within-groups mean-square of ANOVA,

$$MS_w = \frac{\sum\limits_{k=1}^{K} \left[\sum\limits_{i=1}^{n_k} (Y_{ki} - \bar{Y}_k)^2 \right]}{N - K}.$$

Thus, Hedges's index of effect size is

$$g'_j = \frac{\bar{Y}_{Ej} - \bar{Y}_C}{\sqrt{MS_w}} \qquad (j = 1, 2, \ldots, K - 1) \qquad (10)$$

for the jth experimental group. Note that he gets around Glass's objection to *pairwise* pooled estimates of σ by using a *single* pooled estimate of σ based on all $K - 1$ experimental groups and the control group. Of course, this assumes that homoscedasticity holds in the population; but this assumption is inherent in the rationale of ANOVA anyway.

We illustrate the calculation of Hedges's effect-size measure with reference to the same dataset for which we calculated Glass's g_1 and g_2 in the preceding example.

We now need SS_w, from which to get MS_w. Because SS_b and SS_t have already been computed immediately following Table 18.4, we need only subtract SS_b from SS_t, getting

$$SS_w = 763.0478 - 80.3055 = 682.7423,$$

whence

$$MS_w = 682.7423/(230 - 3) = 3.0077$$

and

$$(MS_w)^{1/2} = 1.73.$$

Therefore, from Equation 10 we get

$$g'_1 = (6.76 - 5.23)/1.73 = .884$$

and

$$g'_2 = (6.41 - 5.23)/1.73 = .682.$$

These values are lower than the values of g_1 and g_2, respectively, reflecting the fact that the variabilities of Y (job-satisfaction ratings) in the two experimental groups were larger than that in the control group.

The fourth and last ANOVA-based effect-size estimate that we discuss in this section is the $\hat{\omega}^2$ developed by Hays (1963). Although it antedates Cohen's d, it somehow did not develop a following as did the latter, possibly because its definitional formula is much more complicated than that of d and its progeny—and is hence rather less intuitive. It was intended to correct (or at least decrease) the positive bias inherent in $\hat{\eta}^2_{y.x}$, and is defined as follows:

$$\hat{\omega}^2 = \frac{SS_b - (K - 1)MS_w}{SS_t + MS_w}, \tag{11}$$

where K is the number of groups involved, and SS_b, SS_t, and MS_w are the usual between-groups and total sum of squares and the within-groups mean square of a K group, one-way ANOVA.

Example. We illustrate the computation of $\hat{\omega}^2$ by using the data of Table 18.4, just as we did for Glass's g and Hedges's g'. Actually, we have already computed all the necessary quantities to substitute in Equation 11, either right before Table 18.4 or in the example for Hedges's g'. They are:

$$SS_b = 80.3055, \qquad SS_t = 763.0478, \qquad \text{and} \qquad MS_w = 3.0077.$$

Hence, with $K = 3$, we have

$$\hat{\omega}^2 = \frac{80.3055 - (2)(3.0077)}{763.0478 + 3.0077}$$

$$= .0970.$$

This is smaller than the $\hat{\eta}^2_{y.x} = .1052$ computed right before Table 18.4, as it should be, because $\hat{\omega}^2$ is intended to compensate for the upward bias of $\hat{\eta}^2_{y.x}$. Perhaps many researchers viewed the compensation to be too drastic, and hence rejected $\hat{\omega}^2$ as their effect-size measure of choice. Alternatively, it could be said that, because $\hat{\omega}^2$ is not an unbiased estimate of the population $\hat{\eta}^2_{y.x}$ anyway, why bother? (The numerator of $\hat{\omega}^2$ is an unbiased estimate of $\sigma_Y^2 - \sigma^2_{Y|X}$, and its denominator is an unbiased estimate of σ_Y^2, but the ratio of two unbiased estimates is *not* an unbiased estimate of the ratio of the two parameters.) However, there is some evidence to suggest that $\hat{\omega}^2$ is relatively insensitive to variations in sample size compared to $\hat{\eta}^2_{y.x}$. Whether this is good or bad is a moot question.

The foregoing points, in addition to the complicatedness of the definitional Equation 11, may be the reasons why Hays' $\hat{\omega}^2$ is not as popular as Glass' g and Hedges' g'.

MULTIVARIATE EXTENSIONS OF EFFECT SIZE

We have dealt only with cases in which there is but one dependent variable, Y. But there are many situations in psychological research when more than one dependent variables are involved. For instance, in the example we have been carrying throughout this chapter, we might be interested in general social adjustment in addition to job satisfaction. We now address the question of how we measure (or estimate) effect size when there are two or more dependent variables. Toward this end we build on Table 18.4 and develop a bivariate frequency distribution of Job-Satisfaction by Social-Adjustment Scores (on a four-point scale) for each of the three groups as well as the total sample, and present the results in Table 18.6.

One of the most widely used significance-test statistics in multivariate analysis of variance (MANOVA) is Wilks's likelihood-ratio criterion Λ, defined as

$$\Lambda = |\mathbf{S}_w|/|\mathbf{S}_t|, \tag{12}$$

where $\mathbf{S}_w$ is the within-groups SSCP matrix and $\mathbf{S}_t$ is the total-sample SSCP matrix and $|A|$ indicates the determinant of A.

To compute $\mathbf{S}_w$, we compute a separate SSCP matrix for each of the three groups and then add the three matrices. (This is analogous to computing the deviation-score sum of squares for each of several groups separately and adding

TABLE 18.6
Bivariate Frequency Distribution of Job Satisfaction. (Y_1) and Social Adjustment. (Y_2) Scores for Each of Three Groups and for the Total Sample

Group 1

Y_2 \ Y_1	1	2	3	4	5	6	7	8	9	10	Σ
4						1	1	5	6	2	15
3				2	5	5	7	4	1	1	25
2			2	3	1	1	0	2			9
1			1								1
Σ	0	0	3	5	6	7	8	11	7	3	50

Group 2

Y_2 \ Y_1	1	2	3	4	5	6	7	8	9	10	Σ
4					1	1	1	5	8	3	19
3			1	1	5	10	15	10	2	1	45
2			2	8	7	15	9	1			42
1			1	5	3	0	1				10
Σ	0	0	4	14	16	26	26	16	10	4	116

Group 3

Y_2 \ Y_1	1	2	3	4	5	6	7	8	9	10	Σ
4						1	2	1			4
3					4	6	11	1			22
2		1	3	5	6	9	1				25
1	1	2	3	5	2						13
Σ	1	3	6	10	12	16	14	2	0	0	64

(continued)

TABLE 18.6   (*Continued*)

Total Sample

Y_2 \ Y_1	1	2	3	4	5	6	7	8	9	10	Σ
4					1	3	4	11	14	5	38
3			1	3	14	21	33	15	3	2	92
2		1	7	16	14	25	10	3			76
1	1	2	5	10	5	0	1				24
Σ	1	3	13	29	34	49	48	29	17	7	230

the results to get SS_w in univariate ANOVA.) Thus, if the three group-SSCP matrices are denoted S_1, S_2 and S_3, then

$$S_w = S_1 + S_2 + S_3. \qquad (13)$$

(In general, if there are K groups, with individual group-SSCP matrices S_1, $S_2, \ldots, S_k$, then $S_w = S_1 + S_2 + \ldots + S_k$.)

To compute S_t, we merge the three groups into a single group and compute the SSCP matrix for this total sample, exemplified by the fourth panel of Table 18.6.

Each of the four SSCP matrices alluded to earlier is computed in exactly the same way as we computed the SSCP matrix for X_1, X_2 and Y in the example after Table 18.5, using Equations 5 and 6. (For general instructions in computing a $p \times p$ SSCP matrix using a more streamlined formula, $S = X'X - tt'/N$, where X is the $N \times p$ data matrix and t' is the p dimensional row vector of the column totals of X, see Tatsuoka (1988, pp. 16–20). We did not take this route here because it would have entailed displaying a 230×2 data matrix!

We show the details only for computing S_1 and leave it as an exercise for the reader to compute S_2, S_3, and S_t. All the necessary information is shown in the four panels of Table 18.6.

Following Equation 5, we obtain, for Group 1,

$$C_1 = \begin{bmatrix} 50 & 338 & 154 \\ \hline 338 & 2472 & 1090 \\ 154 & 1090 & 502 \end{bmatrix}$$

$$S_1 = \begin{bmatrix} 187.1200 & 48.9600 \\ 48.9600 & 27.6800 \end{bmatrix}.$$

Similarly,

$$S_2 = \begin{bmatrix} 332.1379 & 111.7931 \\ 111.7931 & 85.0603 \end{bmatrix}.$$

and

$$S_3 = \begin{bmatrix} 163.4844 & 64.0156 \\ 64.0156 & 46.4844 \end{bmatrix}.$$

Hence

$$S_W = S_1 + S_2 + S_3 = \begin{bmatrix} 682.7423 & 224.7687 \\ 224.7687 & 159.2247 \end{bmatrix}.$$

Similarly,

$$S_t = \begin{bmatrix} 763.0478 & 259.8348 \\ 259.8348 & 177.8435 \end{bmatrix}.$$

The respective determinants of these two SSCP matrices are

$$|S_w| = 58,188.39 \quad \text{and} \quad |S_t| = 68,188.97.$$

Hence, in accordance with Equation 12,

$$\Lambda = \frac{|S_w|}{|S_t|} = \frac{58,188.39}{68,188.97} = .8533$$

Recalling from Equation 3 that

$$\hat{\eta}^2_{y.x} = 1 - \frac{SS_w}{SS_t},$$

it appears that

$$1 - \Lambda = 1 - \frac{|S_w|}{|S_t|} \tag{13}$$

qualifies as a multivariate counterpart of the correlation ratio $\hat{\eta}^2_{y.x}$. In fact this is known as the multivariate correlation ratio and is often denoted by $\hat{\eta}^2_{\text{mult}}$. For our example, we have

$$\hat{\eta}^2_{\text{mult}} = 1 - \lambda = 1 - .8533 = .1467.$$

(More precisely, it should be denoted $\hat{\eta}^2_{y_1 y_2 \ldots y_p.x}$.)

However, just as the univariate $\hat{\eta}^2_{y.x}$ is positively biased, $\hat{\eta}^2_{\text{mult}}$ is also (and probably to a greater extent) biased upward. Therefore, following the lead of Hays (1963), who developed his $\hat{\omega}^2$ in order to decrease the positive bias of $\hat{\eta}^2_{y.x}$, Tatsuoka (1970) proposed a multivariate counterpart of $\hat{\omega}^2$, whose definitional formula was given in close analogy with Hays's $\hat{\omega}^2$ (see Equation 11) as

$$\hat{\omega}^2_{\text{mult}} = \frac{|S_t| - |S_w| - (K - 1)|S_w|/(N - K)}{|S_t| + |S_w|/(N - K)},$$

where K is the number of groups and N is the total sample size. By dividing numerator and denominator of the right hand expression by $|S_t|$ and recalling from Equation 12 that $|\mathbf{S_w}|/|\mathbf{S_t}| = \Lambda$, it is readily seen that an equivalent expression is

$$\hat{\omega}^2_{mult} = \frac{1 - \Lambda - (K - 1)\Lambda/(N - K)}{1 + \Lambda/(N - K)}$$

$$= \frac{(N - K) - (N - 1)\Lambda}{(N - K) + \Lambda}. \tag{14}$$

It was subsequently noted by Sachdeva (1973) that Equation 14 could be put into the simpler form

$$\hat{\omega}^2_{mult} = 1 - \frac{N\Lambda}{(N - K) + \Lambda}. \tag{14'}$$

For our example, substituting the value $\Lambda = .8533$ in Equation 14' with $N = 230$ and $K = 3$, we obtain

$$\hat{\omega}^2_{mult} = 1 - \frac{(230)(.8533)}{227 + .8533}$$

$$= .1387,$$

which is smaller than $\hat{\eta}^2_{mult} = .1467. = .1467$, as it should be, because $\hat{\omega}^2_{mult}$ was developed to decrease the positive bias of η^2_{mult}.

A subsequent Monte Carlo study by Tatsuoka (1973) dealing with the distribution of $\hat{\omega}^2_{mult}$, however, showed that this statistic itself was somewhat positively biased. He therefore heuristically derived a "corrected" $\hat{\omega}^2_{mult}$, defined as

$$\hat{\omega}^2_{mult.c} = \hat{\omega}^2_{mult} - \frac{p^2 + (K - 1)^2}{3N}(1 - \hat{\omega}^2_{mult}), \tag{15}$$

which was found to be very nearly unbiased when $p(K - 1) \le 49$ and $75 \le N \le 2000$. For the $\hat{\omega}^2_{mult}$ just computed, this correction yields

$$\hat{\omega}^2_{mult.c} = .1387 - \frac{4 + 4}{(3)(230)}(1 - \hat{\omega}^2_{mult})$$

$$= .1287.$$

CONCLUDING REMARKS

With so many different measures of effect size to choose from, the reader may well ask, "Which is the best one to use?" Obviously, there is no unique answer to this question. Different measures may be suited to different purposes. It is hoped that this chapter, by discussing the origin and nature of the various effect-size measures, has provided the readers with some basis for selecting a suitable measure for their particular purpose.

It should also be pointed out that, besides the direct use of these measures for assessing the degree to which the independent variables affect the dependent variable(s), there are several indirect, mediatory roles that they can play. Prominent among these are their use in statistical power analysis and in meta-analysis. Power analysis is, in fact, the context in which Cohen (1969, 1977) first introduced his measure, $d = (\mu_1 - \mu_2)/\sigma$, of effect size. This is a "natural" context, because power analysis deals (among other things) with such problems as determining the sample size necessary for detecting, with a desired probability, the falsity of a null hypothesis at a given significance level when the true state of nature deviates from H_0 by a specified amount—that is, when the effect size is thus-and-such.

Meta-analysis is essentially a structured, quantitative approach to reviewing the research literature on a certain topic for the purpose, in Light and Pillemer's (1984) words, of "summing up" the available evidence—or, equivalently, as Rosenthal titled his chapter (20) in this volume, "cumulating evidence." Such being the case, meta-analytic studies are focused on two things: the significance level at which the null hypothesis has been rejected in each of the studies reviewed and the effect size found in each. These two aspects are then respectively averaged in the various intricate ways that Rosenthal discusses in chapter 20.

REFERENCES

Cohen, J. (1969). *Statistical power analysis for the behavioral sciences.* New York: Academic Press.
Cohen, J. (1977). *Statistical power analysis for the behavioral sciences* (Rev. ed.). New York: Academic Press.
Cohen, J. (1988). *Statistical power analysis for the behavioral sciences* (2nd ed.). Hillsdale, NJ: Lawrence Erlbaum Associates.
Glass, G. V. (1976). Primary, secondary, and meta-analysis of research. *Educational Researcher, 5,* 3–8.
Hays, W. L. (1963). *Statistics for psychologists.* New York: Holt, Rinehart & Winston.
Hedges, L. V. (1981). Distribution theory for Glass's estimator of effect size and related estimators. *Journal of Educational Statistics, 6,* 107–128.
Light, R. J., & Pillemer, D. B. (1984). *Summing up: The science of reviewing research.* Cambridge, MA: Harvard University Press.
Sachdeva, D. (1973). Estimating strength of relationship in multivariate analysis of variance. *Educational & Psychological Measurement, 33,* 627–631.
Tatsuoka, M. M. (1970). *Discriminant analysis: The study of group differences.* Champaign, IL: Institute of Personality & Ability Testing.
Tatsuoka, M. M. (1973). *An examination of the statistical properties of a multivariate measure of strength of association.* (Final Report to U.S. Office of Education on Contract No. 0EG-5-72-0027.)
Tatsuoka, M. M. (1988). *Multivariate analysis: Techniques for educational and psychological research* (2nd ed.). New York: Macmillan.

19 The Relative Power of Parametric and Nonparametric Statistical Methods

Donald W. Zimmerman
Bruno D. Zumbo
Carleton University, Ottawa, Canada

Introductory statistics textbooks in psychology and education typically recommend that parametric tests such as t and F be replaced by nonparametric alternatives under three conditions: (a) when the assumption of normality is violated, (b) when the assumption of homogeneity of variance is violated, and (c) when the scale of measurement is an ordinal scale and not an interval scale. However, there is disagreement among authors as to how severe a violation has to be before a parametric test should be replaced. Many authors consider parametric tests to be robust and do not recommend alternatives unless one of the first two violations just mentioned is quite severe. Others believe that the bulk of data in psychology and social sciences is best analyzed using nonparametric methods. Perhaps a majority of textbook writers convey the impression that parametric tests are preferable when assumptions are fulfilled to a good approximation, because parametric tests are thought to be more powerful than their nonparametric counterparts under normal theory.

The third point mentioned—assumptions about scales of measurement—has engendered controversy among psychologists. The emphasis on scales of measurement found in textbook discussions in psychology is virtually unknown in mathematical statistics. The most prevalent point of view in mathematical statistics holds that nonparametric methods are an alternative to methods based on strong assumptions about probability distributions of random variables. Questions about the empirical relational structure and scales underlying these variables are not prominent. Accordingly, assumptions of normality and homogeneity of variance are regarded as pertinent, whereas scales of measurement are generally ignored in the comparison of parametric and nonparametric methods.

This chapter attempts to throw light on these issues by considering some

481

developments in theoretical statistics and some recent simulation studies that have been performed by ourselves and by other investigators. Also, some new simulation results that have not been published elsewhere are presented in order to illustrate some of the points in the discussion.

CLASSICAL STUDIES OF PARAMETRIC TESTS UNDER VIOLATION OF ASSUMPTIONS

Classical studies by Pearson (1931), Box (1953), Norton (1953) Boneau (1960), and others, disclosed that the t test and F test are robust under certain violations of normality (see Glass, Peckham, & Sanders, 1972, for a review). It came to be generally believed that the violations examined in these studies were representative of what could be found in practice. In these classical simulation studies, a test was most often judged to be robust if the Type I error probability remained close to the nominal significance level when the assumptions did not hold. Performance with respect to Type II error probability and the related question of the power of the test were investigated far less frequently, but studies that did examine Type II errors and power began to appear in the 1960s and 1970s. Actually, we emphasize that knowledge of both Type I and Type II errors is essential to adequately characterize robustness of statistical tests.

Most pertinent to our present concern are computer simulation studies that compared the power of parametric and nonparametric tests under violation of assumptions. Usually, the tests that have been compared in these simulation studies are the Student t test for independent groups and its nonparametric counterpart, the Wilcoxon–Mann–Whitney test. These studies are examined extensively in the sequel.

Apart from computer simulation, asymptotic relative efficiency (ARE) is frequently used as a guideline in comparing tests. Let d be the difference between a null and alternative hypothesis, and let N_a and N_b be the sample sizes employed by two tests, a and b. Then, asymptotic relative efficiency of a with respect to b is defined as

$$\lim_{N_a \to \infty} N_b/N_a,$$

where d approaches 0 in such a way that the probabilities of Type I and Type II errors remain constant.

It is well known that, under normal theory, the ARE of the Wilcoxon–Mann–Whitney test with respect to the Student t test is $3/\pi = .955$. This value is frequently presented as a guideline in introductory statistics texts that discuss nonparametric methods. Perhaps a matter of greater interest to researchers, however, are ARE values under conditions where the assumptions of normal theory are not satisfied. Hodges and Lehmann (1956), Lehmann (1975), and others derived the ARE of the Wilcoxon test and some other nonparametric tests with respect to the t test for a number of standard probability distributions, such as the lognormal, Cauchy, and Laplace distributions, and found that the ARE values frequently exceed 1. This means that the Wilcoxon test actually becomes more powerful than the t test in the asymptotic limit for these distributions (see also, Randles, 1980; Randles & Wolfe, 1979).

These findings do not reveal how the two tests compare for nonnormal distributions when sample size are relatively small—a situation that perhaps has more practical concern for researchers. As Bradley (1978) noted, researchers are not typically concerned with infinitesimally small treatment effects for infinitely large populations. For practical purposes, what is needed is knowledge of the relative efficiency of the two statistical tests for small or moderate sample sizes for various nonnormal populations. Historically, nonparametric tests have most often been recommended as a technique for dealing with small samples. If textbooks traditionally place the Student t test in the realm of "small-sample theory," then it would seem reasonable that its nonparametric counterpart be useful in the same realm.

Boneau (1960) compared the power of the t test and the Wilcoxon test applied to normal, uniform, and exponential distributions for relatively small sample sizes ($N_1 = N_2 = 5$ and $N_1 = N_2 = 6$) and found that the t test maintained a slight power advantage. Similar results have been obtained by Toothaker (1972) and Posten (1984). It should be emphasized again that computer simulation studies of comparative power are needed mainly in cases of relatively small samples from nonnormal populations. That is, they are needed when the derivation of the sampling distributions of the test statistics compared is not feasible. It is possible to derive theoretical power curves in numerous situations without need of computer simulation. Sometimes excellent approximations, such as those developed by Cohen (1988), are available. Furthermore, as mentioned previously, it is possible to derive ARE values for nonnormal distributions, as done by Hodges and Lehmann (1956), Randles (1980), and others. The need for computer simulation arises from the combination of nonnormal populations and small sample sizes, or from nonnormal populations that do not have well-known, standard probability densities. These cases, of course, have considerable practical significance in psychology, education, and the social sciences.

POWER SUPERIORITY OF NONPARAMETRIC TESTS
FOR HEAVY-TAILED DISTRIBUTIONS

A picture that is decidedly different from the one suggested by the classical robustness studies has emerged recently. Quite some time ago, in a computer simulation study, Neave and Granger (1968) showed that for a mixed-normal distribution the Wilcoxon–Mann–Whitney test is more powerful than the Student t test. More recently, in a series of simulation studies, Blair and Higgins (1980a, 1980b) and Blair, Higgins, and Smitley (1980) showed that, for quite a few nonnormal distributions, the Wilcoxon test is more powerful than the t test. Blair and Higgins (1985) also showed that, for some of the same distributions, the Wilcoxon matched-pairs signed-ranks test is more powerful than the paired-samples t test (see also Blair, 1981).

The distributions investigated by Blair and his associates included the exponential, Cauchy, Laplace, or double exponential, mixed-normal, mixed-uniform, and lognormal distributions, among others. These are examples of "heavy-tailed" distributions; that is, they are continuous probability densities defined on $(-\infty, \infty)$ in which extremely deviant values in the tails have appreciable nonzero probabilities.

As mentioned in the last section, it had been known in theoretical statistics that the ARE of the Wilcoxon test can exceed 1 for some of these distributions (Hodges & Lehmann, 1956). It is notable that Blair and Higgins found the Wilcoxon test to be more powerful in many cases for relatively small sample sizes. And, curiously, the magnitude of the Wilcoxon test's power advantage often increased with increases in sample size. Furthermore, Blair and Higgins noted that the power superiority of the t test for normal and uniform distributions was usually small, whereas, for several of the nonnormal distributions just mentioned, the Wilcoxon test often was vastly more powerful. These findings are certainly consistent with the theoretical derivations of ARE values by Hodges and Lehmann (1956), Lehmann (1975), Randles and Wolfe (1979) and Randles (1980). In fact, Blair and Higgins concluded that ARE values are a good indication of the relative power of the tests for small and moderate sample sizes.

Bradley (1977) emphasized the importance of the mixed-normal distribution, also called the contaminated-normal distribution, as a model for research data in some practical settings. The studies of Blair and Higgins disclosed marked power superiority of the Wilcoxon test over the t test for mixed-normal distributions, and the early study of Neave and Granger (1968) had already found the same thing. Further details regarding the simulation of mixed-normal distributions, as well as other heavy-tailed distributions just mentioned, are given later.

For these heavy-tailed distributions, the pattern of results was quite different from the findings of the classical robustness studies of Boneau (1960, 1962) and others. Blair and Higgins concluded that "because of the narrow ranges of populations shapes investigated in some widely cited previous studies of this type, the conclusions reached in those studies must now be deemed questionable" (1980b, 309).

These studies, taken as a whole, have extended our knowledge of the relative power of parametric and nonparametric statistical methods considerably, to various distributions not represented in the classical studies mentioned in the last section. Simulations now are available for quite a variety of nonnormal distributions and for a considerable range of sample sizes. As becomes evident, however, the meaning of these findings is still problematic as far as practical research applications are concerned. It appears that for most of the standard probability distributions investigated in these studies, the Wilcoxon test holds a power advantage over the t test. It should not be forgotten, however, that the classical studies have shown the t test to be more powerful for many kinds of nonnormal distributions, including various highly skewed, multimodal, uniform, or rectangular distributions that often appear in research practice.

Recently, Rasmussen (1985, 1986) put forward a different interpretation of the findings reported by Blair and Higgins and others. Rasmussen suggested that the power superiority of the Wilcoxon test for mixed-normal distributions is accounted for by the presence of outliers, or extremely deviant values that sometimes appear in samples. The study of outliers is prominent in the area of robust estimation (Barnett & Lewis, 1978; Hawkins, 1980; Wainer, 1982), and it is known that the t test is affected strongly by outliers in sample data.

In a simulation study, Rasmussen (1985) obtained samples from a mixed-normal distribution using a method similar to that of Blair and Higgins (1980a). Outliers were identified, using an outlier-detection statistic (Grubbs, 1969; Tietjen & Moore, 1972). Values that were found to be outliers were replaced by a z score value of 2.32, which corresponds to the .01 one-tailed probability level in a normal distribution (Tabachnick & Fidell, 1983). When samples were corrected for outliers in this way, the power advantage of the Wilcoxon test disappeared, and the Student t test became more powerful, just as found in the classical studies. On the basis of this result, Rasmussen (1985) concluded that "a researcher should check for outliers, correct them as necessary, and use a parametric test of significance" (p. 509).

According to an attractive hypothesis, the power advantage of the Wilcoxon test relative to the t test for many of the aforementioned heavy-tailed distributions is accounted for by the presence of outliers. In the remainder of this chapter further simulation data, as well as theoretical arguments, that point to this conclusion is presented. It should be emphasized that outliers tend to distort the Student t test. This has been shown in studies of robust estimation (see Hampel, Ronchetti, Rousseeuw, & Stahel, 1986; Tabachnick & Fidell, 1983). However, the ranking procedure employed in the nonparametric Wilcoxon test automatically reduces the influence of outliers, and this point is discussed in more detail in the present chapter. Consequently, the power advantage of the Wilcoxon test for heavy-tailed distributions, according to the hypothesis we are considering, is accounted for largely by a deflation in the power of the t test. In other words, there is a vast superiority of the Wilcoxon test when there is a vast deflation in the power of the t test. Evidence that this is what happens is presented in the sequel.

OUTLIER-PRONE
AND OUTLIER-RESISTANT DISTRIBUTIONS

Neyman and Scott (1971) introduced a distinction between *outlier-prone* and *outlier-resistant* probability distributions that has considerable significance for present purposes. The distinction was further elaborated by Green (1976). The basic idea states that, for certain distributions, the occurrence of a cluster of similar values accompanied by some extremely deviant values in samples is more or less probable than for other distributions.

Let $X_1, X_2 \ldots , X_N$ be an ordered random sample of size N. A probability distribution is *absolutely outlier-prone* if there exist ϵ, $\delta > 0$ and N_0, such that

$$P(X_N - X_{N-1} > \epsilon) \geq \delta,$$

for all integers $N \geq N_0$. A distribution is *absolutely outlier-resistant* if, for all $\epsilon > 0$,

$$P(X_N - X_{N-1} > \epsilon) \to 0, \text{ as } N \to \infty.$$

If the ratio X_N/X_{N-1} is considered instead of the difference $X_N - X_{N-1}$, the distributions are said to be *relatively outlier-prone* and *relatively outlier-resistant*.

These definitions imply that, in the case of outlier-prone distributions, the probability that one or more sample values will deviate to an extraordinary degree from the remaining sample values becomes greater as sample size increases. Green (1976) proved that the conditions are related to Gnedenko's (1943) law of large numbers for maximum values. On the basis of these criteria, Green (1976) classified well-known probability distributions. For present purposes, the most interesting result is the fact that the outlier-prone distributions correspond to the heavy-tailed distributions for which the Wilcoxon test is more powerful than the t test. In the case of outlier-resistant distributions, such as the normal and uniform distributions, the t test is robust and maintains a power superiority.

These results are certainly consistent with the idea that a few deviant values are involved in the power advantage of nonparametric tests for heavy-tailed distributions, as suggested by Rasmussen (1985). Another finding that points to the same conclusion was reported by Blair and Higgins (1980b). These investigators found that the power advantage of the Wilcoxon test for some of the heavy-tailed distributions became greater as sample size increased, and in this connection they pointed out that classical robustness studies that investigated small sample size are too restricted. As Rasmussen (1985) observed, this result reflects the increase in the probability that at least one outlier will occur as sample size increases.

RANK TRANSFORMATIONS

It has been suggested that nonparametric methods such as the Wilcoxon–Mann–Whitney test are more powerful than the Student t test for various heavy-tailed distributions because of the influence of outliers in samples. More specifically, extreme values in samples diminish the power of the t test, but do not influence the nonparametric Wilcoxon test, at least not nearly to the same degree. This concept can be understood more readily if we examine the nature of ranking procedures in more detail.

Ranking a set of sample values can be regarded as a transformation of the sample values. That is, it is a one-to-one function f from the set $\{X_1, X_2, \ldots, X_N\}$, the sample values, to the set $\{1, 2, \ldots, N\}$, the first N positive integers. The values assigned by the function to each sample value in its domain are the number of sample values having lesser or equal magnitude. This counting procedure is one way that a computer algorithm determines ranks.

The transformation is bounded from above by N, so it is apparent that any outliers among the original sample values are not represented by deviant values in the ranks. Otherwise expressed, the function replaces the original sample values by numbers that might otherwise be obtained by sampling from the uniform distribution on the interval $(1, N)$. Random assignment of ranks might be regarded as sampling without replacement from the discrete rectangular distribution on the N points, $1, 2, \ldots, N$. Furthermore, the *differences* between any two values in a set of ranks range between 1 and $N - 1$, whereas the differences between original sample values range between 0 and ∞. Instead of paying attention to these properties of ranks, investigators have usually emphasized the loss of information that occurs in converting continuous measures to ranks. Yet another way of expressing ranking is that it replaces the original values with values from a outlier-resistant distribution (i.e., the uniform distribution). Viewed in this way, it is clear that ranking procedures may bring about a pronounced change in the magnitude of sample values and differences between sample values, especially in the case of heavy-tailed distributions.

We now consider an important fact about nonparametric methods based on ranks that until recently has been little appreciated by researchers and applied statisticians. It has been known in mathematical statistics and recently emphasized by Conover (1980), Conover and Iman (1981), and others, that the Wilcoxon–Mann–Whitney test in standard form, that is the large sample normal approximation, is equivalent to an ordinary Student t test performed on the ranks of measures instead of the measures themselves. The relation between the two test statistics is given explicitly by the function

$$t_R = \frac{W}{\sqrt{[(N - 1)/(N - 2)] - [W^2/(N - 2)]}},$$

where W denotes the Wilcoxon statistic in standard form—that is

$$W = \frac{S - \mu_S}{\sigma_S},$$

S is the rank sum statistic, t_R denotes the t statistic calculated from the ranks of sample values instead of the sample values, and $N = N_1 + N_2$ is the combined sample size. This formula reveals that t_R is a monotonic increasing function of W; so, if both tests are performed at exactly the same significance level, either acceptance of the null hypothesis by both tests or rejection by both tests is guaranteed.

To state these results in a slightly different way, let us call two significance tests α-equivalent if, when performed on the same sample values at a significance level α, they always lead to the same statistical decision (accept or reject H_0). In that case the tests have identical power functions, but the converse is not generally true. According to this definition, the Wilcoxon–Mann–Whitney test, using the large-sample normal approximation, and the Student t test, where t_R is calculated using ranks, are α-equivalent, for all α. Even if the normal approximation is not used, the exact probabilities associated with the Wilcoxon rank-sum statistic are very close to the probabilities associated with t_R.

This means that, apart from details of computation, it makes no difference whether a researcher performs a Wilcoxon test based on rank sums, or alternatively, pays no attention to W and simply performs the usual Student t test on the ranks. The outcome is the same as far as statistical decision making is concerned. What is common to the two equivalent procedures, clearly, is the process of converting the original values to ranks, that is, the rank transformation.

A similar situation prevails with respect to some other widely known nonparametric tests based on ranks, including the Wilcoxon matched-pairs signed-ranks test and the Kruskal–Wallis test. That is, the Wilcoxon matched-pairs signed-ranks test is equivalent to a paired-samples Student t test on signed ranks instead of original signed differences. The Kruskal–Wallis test is equivalent to an ordinary F test performed on the ranks of measures in an ANOVA design instead of measures themselves, and so on. These findings have not received a great deal of attention in introductory statistics textbooks and are not widely known among researchers in psychology. They enable the role of nonparametric methods based on ranks to be viewed in a new light.

An example of the equivalence of W and t_R is given in Table 19.1, which shows power functions plotted from the results of a computer simulation. Pairs of samples of size $N_1 = N_2 = 20$ were obtained from exponential distributions that differed in central tendency in units of the standard error of the mean as shown in the left-hand column. The columns labeled t represents the results of a Student t test performed at the .01 or .05 level on the original scores. The next column in each section labeled W, plots the results of the Wilcoxon test performed at the .01

TABLE 19.1
Power Functions for Significance Tests
Applied to Samples from Exponential Distribution
(decimal points omitted)

	$\alpha = .01$			$\alpha = .05$		
SE	t	W	t_R	t	W	t_R
0	008	009	009	050	050	050
.5	015	032	032	087	122	122
1.0	056	120	120	188	309	309
1.5	147	294	294	354	553	553
2.0	290	506	506	532	747	747
2.5	464	691	691	695	872	872
3.0	642	833	833	826	947	947
3.5	786	914	914	910	977	977
4.0	880	962	962	956	991	991

or .05 level in the usual manner with rank-sums on the same sample values. Finally, the last column, labeled t_R, is the result of the Student t test performed at the .01 or .05 level on the ranks of the original sample values, instead of the sample values themselves. Of course, these ranks ranged from 1 to 40.

As is expected in the case of the exponential distribution, based on findings discussed earlier in this chapter, the Wilcoxon test turned out to be more powerful than the original Student t test. But, for present purposes, it is notable that the Student t test performed on the ranks (t_R) yielded precisely the same power function as the Wilcoxon test (See also, Zimmerman & Zumbo, 1989).

If one has examined the proofs presented by Conover and Iman (1981), for example, then it is actually pointless to refer to data like that in Table 19.1. One can be assured by mathematical proofs that for any power functions like those in the table, obtained from any distributions where there are no ties, the entries in the W and t_R columns will be the same, so computer simulation is unnecessary. However, we have included Table 19.1 because these findings are perhaps new to many readers, and some data of this sort may be helpful for emphasis. However, because of the equivalence of the two procedures, further tables of this kind in the present chapter will have a single column labeled W/t_R for brevity as a replacement of the identical W and t_R columns.

One implication of these findings that is examined in more detail later in the present chapter is that it no longer makes sense to regard the Wilcoxon test as an appropriate replacement of the t test for certain classes of data. Rather, one may now inquire whether one version of the t test (based on ranks) is an appropriate replacement of another version of the t test (based on initial scores). In other words, is ranking appropriate? If the initial data in a research study are already in the form of ranks, it is immaterial whether one performs a t test or a Wilcoxon test.

A second implication of the equivalence of W and t_R is that it is possible to view the findings about relative power for heavy-tailed distributions discussed previously from another perspective. The fact that W is more powerful than t for a heavy-tailed distribution such as the exponential distribution means essentially that, for this distribution, the t test performed on ranks is more powerful than the t test performed on the underlying values that determine the ranks. Somewhat surprisingly, this implies that discarding information by converting measures to ranks enhances the power of the t test.

Furthermore, the idea expressed by Rasmussen (1985, 1986) can be reformulated as a statement about t instead of W. An equivalent statement of Rasmussen's hypothesis is that a t test performed on ranks is more powerful than a t test performed on the original values because of the reduction of the influence of outliers by a ranking procedure. This notion implies that, in many cases, reduction of the influence of outliers is more important than loss of information, at least as far as the power of significance tests is concerned.

COMPUTER SIMULATION METHOD

In the remainder of this chapter, from time to time we mention some results of computer simulations similar to those in Table 19.1 in order to support the arguments presented. The method of these computer simulations are described briefly in this section. This method accounts for the results already presented in Table 19.1. Further details concerning simulations of this type are given in previous publications (Zimmerman, 1987; Zimmerman & Zumbo, 1989; Zumbo, 1989).

A computer program, written in Turbo BASIC (a compiler-driven version of BASIC), version 1.0, Borland, International, Inc., generated pseudorandom numbers on the interval (0, 1) and transformed these values into variates from one of the distributions described later. Significance tests of location, including the Student t test for independent groups and the Wilcoxon–Mann–Whitney test, also known as the Mann–Whitney U-test, were performed on the sample values generated by the program. The majority of the studies described in the present chapter were concerned with these particular parametric and nonparametric methods. A few other tests, including the one-sample t test, the sign test, and a one-sample version of the Wilcoxon test also were investigated.

Usually, the probabilities of both Type I and Type II errors were obtained by beginning with identical distributions and then introducing successively larger differences between population means. Sometimes entire power functions were plotted from the results of the simulations. Differences between means were usually expressed in units of the standard error of a difference between means in order to make power comparisons between tests independent of sample size and variance differences.

The entire sampling procedure and significance testing was repeated 5,000 times for each distribution or condition being examined and for each degree of difference between means. Accordingly, each entry in most tables and figures in this chapter represents the results of 5,000 significance tests. Each entry is the probability that a test statistic exceeds the critical value associated with the designated significance level. In most cases the significance level was .05, and in a few cases it was .01. Most tests were nondirectional.

The distributions examined and the methods of simulating variates were as follows.

1. *Normal distribution.* Normal deviates were generated from the transformation $X = (-2 \log_e X_1)^{1/2} (\cos 2\pi X_2)$, where X_1 and X_2 are pseudorandom numbers on the interval (0, 1). This is the exact method of Box and Muller (1958). As a check, normal deviates were also generated using the Polar Marsaglia method used in many *IMSL* subroutines (Marsaglia, 1964; Marsaglia & Bray, 1964) and the central-limit theorem method based on summing 12 uniformly distributed random numbers. All three methods were found to have essentially the same results as far as the present simulations were concerned.

2. *Uniform distribution.* This was $X = (X_1 - .5) \sqrt{12}$ so that X had a mean of 0 and a standard deviation of 1, because X_1 had a mean of .5 and a standard deviation of $1/\sqrt{12}$.

3. *Exponential distribution.* This distribution was generated using the transformation $X = -\log_e X_1 - 1$.

4. *Cauchy distribution.* This very heavy-tailed distribution does not possess finite variance. It was generated from $X = \tan[\pi(X_1 - .5)]/3$.

5. *Mixed-normal distribution* (or contaminated normal distribution). Sample values were obtained from $N(0, 1)$ with probability p and from $N(0, 25)$ with probability $1 - p$. In most of the studies described in this chapter p was .85. The normal deviates were generated using the Box–Muller method.

6. *Mixed-uniform distribution.* Sample values were selected at random on the interval $(-.5, .5)$ with probability p and on the interval $(-2.5, 2.5)$ with probability $1 - p$, where p was most often .85.

7. *Lognormal distribution.* This was generated from $X = \exp[(X_1 - 1)/.21612]$, where X_1 was a normal deviate generated using the Box–Muller method.

8. *Half-normal distribution* (or truncated normal distribution). This was generated from $Y = |X|$, where X was a normal deviate.

In addition to these standard continuous probability distributions, several discrete probability distributions, including some skewed binomial distributions, rectangular distributions on n points, bimodal distributions, and other discrete distributions having a relatively small number of possible values, were investigated.

The adequacy of the random number generator was evaluated using tests recommended by R. S. Lehman (1977) and Morgan (1984). The uniform generator met the accepted requirements of rectangularity, sequential independence, and lack of patterns in a sequence of numbers. To obtain further confidence in the method, we replicated a study by Randles and Wolfe (1979) and obtained the same results as those investigators. This data is examined later.

FURTHER EVIDENCE
THAT OUTLIERS INFLUENCE RELATIVE POWER OF
PARAMETRIC AND NONPARAMETRIC TESTS

In a previous section, we proposed that outliers in sample data play a major role in determining the relative power of parametric and nonparametric tests. Further evidence supporting this point of view is now presented. We systematically alter probability distributions in such a way that outliers become increasingly less influential, or, increasingly more influential. When this is done, one finds that the relative power of the Student t test and Wilcoxon–Mann–Whitney tests undergoes a gradual change. As outliers become increasingly more influential, the power advantage of the t test diminishes. Or looking at the matter from the reverse point of view, as outliers become increasingly less influential, the power advantage of the Wilcoxon test for heavy-tailed distributions gradually diminishes.

In a previous study (Zimmerman & Zumbo, 1990a), a standard normal distribution, as well as a uniform distribution, which are outlier-resistant distributions, according to Green's (1976) classification, were altered in a series of five steps. This was done in such a way that outliers occurred with increasingly higher probability. It was found that the initial power advantage of the t test gradually diminished in favor of the Wilcoxon test. Once the probability of outliers became appreciable, the Wilcoxon test was decidedly more powerful— just as it is for the various distributions examined earlier in this chapter.

In another procedure, in a series of five steps, exponential and Cauchy distributions were truncated at less and less extreme values so that the influence of outliers was gradually reduced. That is, the points of truncation moved closer to the central part of the distribution, so that random samples eventually came from a distribution that was very much the same in overall shape as the original one except for the most extreme values. For these distributions, the Wilcoxon test possessed the initial power advantage, but after truncation this advantage diminished in favor of the t test.

A further example of this kind of procedure is shown in Table 19.2 for an exponential distribution, for $N_1 = N_2 = 20$. This probability distribution, we have seen, is heavy-tailed, and W has a power advantage relative to t. Of course,

TABLE 19.2
Relative Power of the Student t-Test and Wilcoxon–Mann–Whitney Test
for a Truncated Exponential Distribution ($N_1 = N_2 = 20$)

SE	$k = \infty$		$k = 2.5$		$k = 2.0$		$k = 1.5$	
	t	W/t_R	t	W/t_H	t	W/t_R	t	W/t_R
0	048	049	045	049	050	050	050	048
.5	084	127	075	099	078	093	073	088
1.0	190	320	162	235	164	225	158	199
1.5	354	551	303	421	309	402	296	364
2.0	537	755	485	621	492	589	475	542
2.5	713	883	662	769	671	755	652	702
3.0	835	948	813	877	822	869	811	835
3.5	919	981	912	938	920	938	913	918
4.0	960	993	966	975	972	971	970	963

we know from the theory presented in an earlier section that t_R also possesses the same power advantage relative to t.

The four sections of the table show the initial comparison of t and W/t_R without truncation ($k = \infty$) and for three cases in which the distribution is truncated at points closer and closer to the mean. This truncation was done by eliminating sample values that were more than k standard deviations from the mean, where k was 2.5, 2.0, and 1.5. It is evident from the table that W/t_R possessed the initial power advantage, as expected, but successively more severe truncations produced a gradually decreasing power advantage of W/t_R relative to t. These results, like those already mentioned, provide some evidence that the relative power of W/t_R and t is determined largely by sample values from the tails of the distribution. The *central region* of an exponential distribution, on the other hand, behaves much like a normal or uniform distribution, as far as relative power is concerned.

A notion that is somewhat similar to the truncation just described is that of a *trimmed mean*. This concept has been prominent in the area of robust estimation, and the properties of trimmed means as measures of central tendency have been studied extensively (Barnett & Lewis, 1978; Wainer, 1982). If one has obtained a sample of N values, then a k-trimmed mean is the mean of the $N - 2k$ values remaining after removal of the highest k and lowest k values from the sample. This procedure removes outliers that otherwise would unduly influence the mean, and under some conditions it provides a more accurate estimate of a population mean. Of course, the effectiveness of the procedure depends on sample size and the probability of occurrence of outliers.

It should be emphasized that the truncation procedure described earlier in this section is applied to a population rather than a sample. That is, a truncated exponential distribution is a population distribution that resembles an exponential distribution except for removal of part of a tail. On the other hand, the trimmed-mean procedure is applied to every sample from an underlying population distribution of a standard type—that is, samples, not populations, are trimmed. One consequence of this fact for significance testing, especially when sample sizes are relatively small, is that trimming alters the Type I error probability to some degree.

For present purposes, the trimmed-sample procedure is mainly of theoretical interest. That is, it provides some further evidence for the importance of outliers in determining the relative power of parametric and nonparametric tests. Table 19.3 presents some results of a trimming procedure in significance testing based on samples ($N_1 = N_2 = 10$) from two outlier-prone distributions (exponential and mixed-uniform) and two outlier-resistant distributions (normal and uniform). In some cases (lower pair of rows in each section of the table), samples of size $N_1 = N_2 = 10$ were obtained from these distributions, and for every sample of 10 scores the highest and lowest values were eliminated. Wilcoxon tests and t tests then were performed on the remaining $N_1 = N_2 = 8$ values in each pair of samples. Under this procedure, it is quite likely that extremely deviant values in samples are discarded, if sample size is not too large relative to k.

In another procedure (upper pair of rows in each section of the table), the two significance tests were performed in the usual way on all $N_1 = N_2 = 10$ sample values without employing trimming. The table shows both Type I error probabilities (for 0 difference between means) and power (for a difference of 2.5 standard errors of the mean) for both procedures applied to the four distributions.

TABLE 19.3
Relative Probability of Rejecting H_0 for Parametric and
Nonparametric Tests (t and W/t_R) for Regular and Trimmed
Samples from Four Distributions ($N_1 = N_2 = 10$)

		Normal		Uniform	
	SE	t	W/t_R	t	W/t_R
Regular	0	051	045	052	042
	2.5	661	608	634	551
Trimmed	0	109	100	113	106
	2.5	766	734	662	609

		Exponential		Mixed-Uniform	
	SE	t	W/t_R	t	W/t_R
Regular	0	046	046	040	047
	2.5	694	776	590	775
Trimmed	0	097	102	102	106
	2.5	834	827	874	895

It is evident that the Type I error probabilities were elevated above the nominal significance level appreciably in the trimming procedure. This change was approximately of the same degree for both the Wilcoxon and the t test for all four distributions. In the case of the normal and uniform distributions, the power of the t test slightly exceeded the power of the Wilcoxon test, as is expected. Furthermore, for these outlier-resistant distributions, the power superiority of the t test remained about the same under both the regular and trimming procedures. The increase in the probability of rejecting the null hypothesis for both tests under the trimming procedure probably is related to a decrease in variance produced by trimming.

However, in the case of the exponential and mixed-uniform distributions, the result is quite different. For these outlier-prone distributions, the Wilcoxon test is markedly superior to the t test under the regular procedure, as we know. However, as a consequence of trimming, the power superiority disappears and the two significance tests become about equally powerful. These results suggest that elimination of outliers indeed diminishes the power superiority of the non-parametric method in the case of heavy-tailed distributions.

Although far from being conclusive, all the simulation results discussed in this section point in the same direction. The relative power of the t test and the Wilcoxon test depends to a large extent on extremely deviant values in samples from heavy-tailed or outlier-prone distributions. The power superiority of the Wilcoxon test relative to the t test for these heavy-tailed distributions can be reduced or eliminated by removal of outliers from samples.

BOUNDED TRANSFORMATIONS
THAT ARE NOT RANKS

For quite a few nonnormal distributions, we have seen, the Wilcoxon–Mann–Whitney test holds a power advantage over the Student t test, both in the asymptotic limit and for small and moderate sample sizes. We have explored the possibility that this power advantage is accounted for by reduction in the influence of outliers in conversion of measures to ranks. We now examine another kind of evidence that supports this hypothesis.

There are some nonparametric methods, such as the van der Waerden test, or "normal scores" test (van der Waerden, 1952), which replace ranks by other scores that are not ranks in performing a significance test (see also, Conover, 1980; Randles, 1980). In the van der Waerden test, more specifically, the N ranks of scores are replaced by N normal deviates, such that rank i is replaced by the $i/(N + 1)$ quantile of the standard normal distribution. Whereas ranks are similar to uniformly distributed scores, the numbers that replace ranks in this method are similar to normally distributed scores. It might be added, parenthetically, that the normal distribution is also an outlier-resistant distribution. These techniques are not as widely known as nonparametric methods based on ranks and are rarely treated in introductory texts in psychology. There is evidence that they have good power characteristics for many kinds of distributions. In fact, their ARE values are equal to or greater than 1, whereas for finite sample sizes, relative efficiency is sometimes greater and sometimes less than 1 depending on the distribution. Therefore, it seems that these methods are at least as powerful as the Wilcoxon–Mann–Whitney test, for a wide variety of distributions.

In this section, we employ a similar technique: We replace the ranks of the initial measures by other scores that are not ranks (not necessarily normal deviates) in order to support some of the theoretical arguments in previous sections of this chapter. We demonstrate that the power advantages of nonparametric methods based on ranks for heavy-tailed distributions are possessed by a variety of other bounded transformations that at first glance seem to entail a drastic loss of information. Our findings suggest once again that elimination of outliers by bounded transformations, of which ranking is one example, is what is crucial for the power advantage of nonparametric methods for heavy-tailed distributions.

In a previous simulation study (Zimmerman & Zumbo, 1990b), we examined the possibility that the favorable performance of the Wilcoxon–Mann–Whitney test for heavy-tailed distributions could be achieved by other bounded transformations, some rather bizarre, that are not ranks. In that study, samples of size $N_1 = N_2 = 8$ and $N_1 = N_2 = 16$ were investigated. The $N_1 + N_2$ sample values were replaced by a subset of the first $N_1 + N_2$ positive integers, or a function of that subset, instead of the usual ranks. For example, the original 16 or 32 sample values were mapped onto the set $\{1, 2, 3, 4\}$, the first four positive integers, instead of ranks, or mapped onto the squares of these integers, $\{1, 4, 9, 16\}$, and so on.

Although it appears at first glance that a great deal of information is lost in this procedure, it turned out that an ordinary Student t test performed on these numbers had excellent power characteristics. For several heavy-tailed distributions, the t test performed on the transformed values was just as powerful as the Wilcoxon test and considerably more powerful than the t test on the original values. These included the mixed-normal, exponential, and Cauchy distributions. In the case of the normal and uniform distributions, the t test performed on numbers from the sets $\{1, 2, 3, 4\}$ or $\{1, 4, 9, 16\}$ was slightly less powerful than the t test on the original values. Expressed otherwise, for both heavy-tailed and light-tailed distributions, the t test on the transformed values that are not ranks had essentially the same power characteristics as the t test on ranks.

Further evidence along these lines is presented in Table 19.4 and in Fig. 19.1. The table and the graphs compare the power of three significance testing procedures for differences in location for eight distributions. In all cases, samples of size $N_1 = N_2 = 10$ were obtained from the various distributions listed. Table 19.4 gives the Type I error probabilities for tests at the .05 significance level. In

TABLE 19.4

Type I Error Probabilities for the Student
t-test on Original Scores (t_0),
Wilcoxon–Mann–Whitney Test or Student
t-test on Ranks (W/t_R), and Student
t-Transformed Ranks (t_1) for Eight
Distributions $(N_1 = N_2 = 10)$

Distribution	Transformations		
	t_0	W/t_R	t_1
Normal	049	042	076
Uniform	049	039	073
Half-normal	050	045	076
Exponential	041	038	070
Mixed-normal	037	042	070
Mixed-uniform	041	042	077
Cauchy	020	041	080
Lognormal	020	037	070

Fig. 19.1, which gives power differences, the difference between means was fixed at 2.5 S.E.

The first procedure was the ordinary Student t test performed on the original scores (t). The second was the Wilcoxon test, or equivalently the t test on ranks (W/t_R). The third procedure was a t test performed on numbers resulting from a transformation that is not ranks (t_1). This transformation involved a mapping of the original $N_1 + N_2 = 20$ scores in the combined samples onto the integers $\{1, 2, 3, 4\}$, as described previously. Accordingly, the usual ranks 1, 2, 3, 4, and 5 were all replaced by 1; the ranks 6, 7, 8, 9 and 10 were all replaced by 2, and so on, until 16, 17, 18, 19, and 20 were all replaced by 4.

The results for t and W/t_R are as expected from the previous study cited (Zimmerman & Zumbo, 1990b). For the light-tailed distributions (normal, uniform, and half-normal), the power of the t test slightly exceeded that of W/t_R. For the remaining heavy-tailed distributions, the power of t was substantially less than that of W/t_R. Interestingly, the power of the t test performed on the transformed values that are not ranks (t_1) was quite similar in its characteristics to W/t_R. For the light-tailed distributions, the power of t slightly exceeded that of t_1, and for the heavy-tailed distributions, the power of t was substantially less than that of t_1. Apparently, a transformation of the original sample values to numbers that are not ranks but have the boundedness property of ranks yields much the same power advantage as nonparametric methods based on ranks, or a t test based on ranks, in the case of heavy-tailed distributions.

In another simulation, eight kinds of transformations that are not ranks, were applied to samples of size $N_1 = N_2 = 10$ from uniform (light-tailed) and mixed-

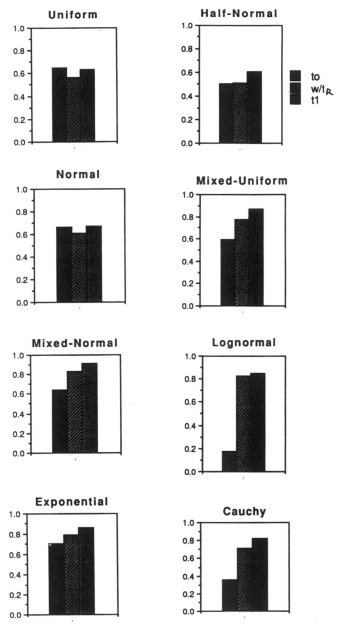

FIG. 19.1. Comparative power of the *t*-test on initial scores, ranks, and transformed scores that are not ranks.

normal (heavy-tailed) distributions. These transformations mapped the original $N_1 + N_2 = 20$ sample values onto the following sets:

1. The integers $\{1, 2, 3, 4\}$, as described earlier.

2. The square roots of the integers between 1 and 20.

3. The set $\{1, 11, 12, \ldots, 19, 20\}$. In this transformation, the first 10 ranks were all replaced by the number 1, while the remaining ranks from 11 to 20 remained unchanged.

4. The set $\{-100, -81, \ldots, 81, 100\}$. This is the set that results when the set of 20 ranks is transformed by the relation $Y_i = (X_i - 10.5)^2$, if $X > 10$ and $Y_i = -(X_i - 10.5)^2$, if $X \leq 10$, where X_i denotes a rank.

5. The set $\{1, 8, 27, 64\}$, the cubes of the first four positive integers.

6. The set $\{1, 2, \ldots, 10, 21, 22, \ldots, 30\}$. The ranks were transformed by the relation $Y_i = X_i + 10$, if $X_i > 0$, and $Y_i = X_i$, if $X_i \leq 10$. Here, the resulting scores were like ordinary ranks, except for a "gap" in the middle.

7. The set of four normal scores $\{-1.15, -.32, .32, 1.15\}$, which are normal deviates corresponding to four ranks, as in the van der Waerden test. Note here that the function from ranks to normal scores was not $1 - 1$.

8. The set consisting of random numbers on the interval $(0, 1)$ added to the original ranks. This transformation yielded a set of values such as $\{1.09, 2.85, 3.31, \ldots, 19.04, 20.56\}$, which varied from sample to sample.

Although in many instances these transformations replace the original measures by a far more restricted set of numbers, even more restricted than ranks in most cases, they all preserve the order relation in the original sample values. That is, they are all homomorphisms of order, or functions $f{:}R \rightarrow R$, such that, if $x_1 \leq x_2$ then $f(x_1) \leq f(x_2)$, for all $x_1, x_2 \in R$, even though they are not all one-to-one functions. In this connection, it should be noted that these transformations can be regarded as functions of the original sample data. Alternatively, they may be regarded as composition of two functions—the rank transformation and another transformation applied to the ranks.

The results are shown in Table 19.5 and Fig. 19.2. Table 19.5 gives Type I error probabilities for the .05 significance level. Figure 19.2 gives the power of the tests for a difference of 2.5 S.E. between means. It is evident that almost all of these bounded transformations behave in a manner quite similar to rank transformations as far as the relative power of t and W are concerned. That is, t_1, $t_2, \ldots, t_8$ have very nearly the same power characteristics as W/t_R for samples from the uniform distribution and from the mixed-normal distribution.

We see again that conversion of the original sample values to a more restricted set of numbers in which outliers are not represented has much the same effect as conversion to ranks. For the light-tailed uniform distribution the t test performed on the transformed values is slightly less powerful than the t test performed on

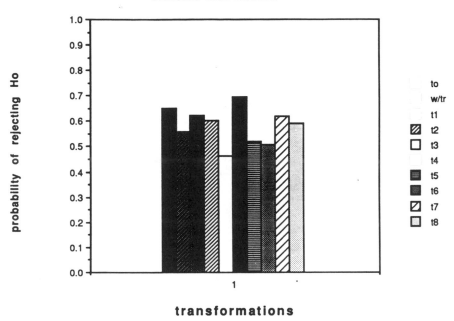

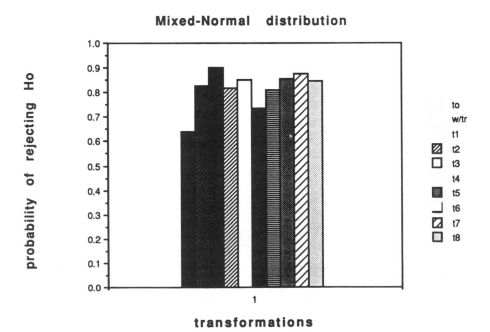

FIG. 19.2. Significance tests on transformations of sample values.

TABLE 19.5
Type I Error Probabilities for Student
t-test on Original Scores (t_0),
Wilcoxon–Mann–Whitney Test or Student
t-test on ranks (W/t_R), and Student t-test on
Eight Kinds of Transformed Ranks ($t_1, \ldots t_8$)
for Two Distributions ($N_1 = N_2 = 10$)

	Distribution	
Transformation	Normal	Uniform
t_0	049	037
W/t_R	039	042
t_1	073	070
t_2	047	043
t_3	051	056
t_4	046	051
t_5	042	043
t_6	043	044
t_7	069	067
t_8	050	048

the original values. For the heavy-tailed mixed-normal distribution, the t test performed on the transformed values is considerably more powerful than the t test performed on the original values. The effect is much the same for a variety of bounded transformations—some that are rather bizarre and quite unlike the characteristics of ranks in other respects.

TRANSFORMATIONS
THAT DO NOT PRESERVE ORDER

It is possible to introduce transformations that do not preserve the order of all scores and to perform t tests on the transformed scores in the manner described in the last section. This procedure provides further evidence that the restricted range of the transformation is more important in determining the relative power of significance tests than the information conveyed by exact numerical magnitudes of scores.

We investigate some transformations in which a random integer is added to the usual ranks. As a result of this procedure, the transformed values vary randomly from one sample to the next, and order is not invariably preserved, although magnitude of scores is to some extent preserved. In spite of the apparent loss of information under this procedure, it turns out that the power of the t test is maintained to a large extent, and the relative power of t and W follows the usual pattern described in the last section.

In a simulation study, the following transformations were investigated:

1. $Y_i = R_i + Z_i - 2$, where R_i is the rank and Z_i is a random variable. The possible values of Z were the integers $\{1, 2, 3\}$, which had equal probability. In other words, an integer was selected at random from the set $\{1, 2, 3\}$ and added to the usual rank. The mean of these integer values, 2, was subtracted, so the function incremented each rank by -1, 0, or 1.

2. $Y_i = R_i + Z'_i - 3$, where Z' assumed as its value an integer selected randomly from the set $\{1, 2, 3, 4, 5\}$. This transformation introduced a still greater degree of randomness.

3. $Y_i = R_i + Z''_i - 4$, where Z'' assumed as its value an integer selected from the set $\{1, 2, 3, 4, 5, 6, 7\}$.

Some idea of the extent to which ordinary ranks are altered by these random increments can be obtained from Table 19.6, which gives some examples of how a set of 16 ranks, resulting from samples of size $N_1 = N_2 = 8$ is altered by the random component. The table shows three examples of each of the three transformations given. (The change is extensive in the case of the third, although even in this case the order is preserved to some extent.)

Results of significance tests applied to sample values transformed in this way are shown in Table 19.7. The three transformations previously listed were applied to samples of size $N_1 = N_2 = 8$ from a mixed-normal distribution. In this distribution sampling was from $N(0, 1)$ with $p = .85$ and from $N(0, 25)$ with $p = .15$. The t test performed on the original values was compared to the t test performed on ranks (W/t_R) and to the t test performed on the values transformed

TABLE 19.6
Examples of Random Transformations ($N_1 = N_2 = 8$)

R	t_1			t_2			t_3		
1	2	1	1	0	2	−1	0	2	4
2	3	1	1	2	4	4	−1	1	4
3	3	3	4	5	5	2	3	1	5
4	4	5	5	6	5	5	4	1	6
5	6	4	6	3	4	7	3	5	3
6	6	7	5	8	6	8	3	9	4
7	7	7	8	6	6	6	5	9	9
8	7	9	7	8	10	8	10	6	8
9	9	10	9	7	10	9	10	6	12
10	9	10	11	9	9	8	13	12	9
11	10	12	12	9	11	10	11	10	14
12	12	13	12	12	11	12	9	9	15
13	14	12	12	14	12	12	13	10	16
14	14	15	15	16	12	15	12	11	15
15	14	16	14	17	16	13	17	17	18
16	15	17	17	17	16	17	17	19	13

TABLE 19.7
Power Functions for Random Transformations
for Mixed-Normal Distribution ($N_1 = N_2 = 8$)

SE	t	W/t_R	t_1	t_2	t_3
0	033	050	053	053	051
.5	071	103	105	099	097
1.0	188	251	258	247	234
1.5	365	487	486	460	425
2.0	527	679	675	651	613
2.5	652	805	802	780	741
3.0	748	872	870	849	816
3.5	821	905	905	899	870
4.0	873	928	929	921	893

by random increments $\{t_1, t_2,$ and $t_3)$. It is apparent that t_1, t_2, and t_3 were considerably more powerful than t and almost as powerful as W/t_R.

Further evidence that loss of information does not always diminish power is provided by another simulation, shown in Table 19.8. In this study, which is a replication of a study by Randles and Wolfe (1979), three one-sample significance tests were compared. The hypothesis tested was that the population mean had a specific value. The tests were (a) the ordinary one-sample Student t test, (b) a one-sample version of the Wilcoxon test (see, for example, Conover, 1980), and (c) a one-sample sign-test, or binomial test.

The one-sample Wilcoxon test, like the Wilcoxon matched-pairs signed-ranks test, involves signed-ranks of differences between sample values and the hypothesized mean. It is known that this test is equivalent to an ordinary one sample

TABLE 19.8
Comparison of the Powers of One-sample t-test, One-sample Wilcoxon
and Binomial Test for Three Distributions ($N = 15$)

	Normal			Mixed-Normal			Cauchy		
SE	t	W/t_R	SIGN	t	W/t_R	SIGN	t	W/t_R	SIGN
0	046	045	060	046	050	058	029	045	058
.5	133	108	121	143	164	178	092	179	248
1.0	235	222	219	304	378	389	191	388	518
1.5	414	390	354	495	622	635	309	584	738
2.0	607	573	506	637	798	818	404	728	870
2.5	779	748	659	735	891	927	490	818	931
3.0	894	872	783	809	935	972	558	877	963
3.5	955	944	876	867	960	990	613	913	980
4.0	984	979	937	913	975	996	654	936	989

Student t test performed on the signed-ranks (Conover, 1980) instead of the original measures.

The data in Table 19.8 reveals that, for samples of size 15, in the case of the normal distribution the one-sample t test is superior to the one-sample Wilcoxon test, which, in turn, is superior to the one-sample binomial test. However, for the mixed-normal and Cauchy distributions, this order of superiority is reversed. The Wilcoxon test is more powerful than the t test, as is expected, but the "crude" binomial test that involves substantial loss of information, turns out to be more powerful than the Wilcoxon test (see also Randles & Wolfe, 1979).

RANK TRANSFORMATIONS
AND UNEQUAL VARIANCES

We have said relatively little in this chapter about the assumption of equality of variances in normal theory. The two-sample t test and F test depend on this assumption, in addition to that of normality of the population distributions. According to many introductory statistics textbooks in psychology and education that were written in the past several decades, violation of this assumption of *homogeneity of variance,* as it is known, is another reason for using non-parametric methods, such as the Wilcoxon test and Kruskal–Wallis test, to replace the t test and F test.

We see that this point of view is doubtful in the light of present evidence and a somewhat different strategy is needed when variances are unequal. Furthermore, we see that, when assumptions of normality and homogeneity of variance are simultaneously violated—say, for example, analyzing samples from mixed-normal distributions having unequal variances, to mention an extreme case—the violations can be handled in a relatively simple way that is consistent with findings already presented in this chapter.

There is a general agreement that parametric tests such as t and F are robust under violation of homogeneity of variance, provided sample sizes are equal. But, if sample sizes are unequal, the probability of Type I and Type II errors are rather severely affected by unequal variances (Boneau, 1960; Games & Howell, 1976; Hsu, 1938; Kohr & Games, 1977; Rogan & Keselman, 1977; Scheffe, 1959). Disruption of the t test and F test under these conditions is somewhat similar to the failure that occurs in the case of heavy-tailed distributions discussed in the present chapter.

When the larger variance is associated with the larger sample size, there is a marked depression of the probability of rejecting the null hypothesis for all differences between means, including a zero difference, which gives the probability of a Type I error. And when the larger variance is associated with the smaller sample size, there is a marked elevation of the probability of rejecting the null hypothesis, including the probability of Type I error. What is not widely realized among researchers and applied statisticians, however, is that the Wilcoxon–Mann–Whitney test is affected in very much the same way by unequal variances combined with unequal sample sizes. Depression and elevation of the curves for the nonparametric test closely parallels the parametric case (Zimmerman, 1987), although it is not quite as extreme. Therefore, the nonparametric test cannot be routinely substituted for parametric methods as an answer to the problem of unequal variances.

An illustration of what can happen is given in Table 19.9. This table presents simulation data for significance tests of differences in location (t and W/t_R) for unequal sample sizes ($N_1 = 18$ and $N_2 = 6$) from mixed-normal distributions with equal variances ($\sigma_1^2 = \sigma_2^2$) and from mixed-normal distributions with unequal variances ($\sigma_1^2 = 16\,\sigma_2^2$). The latter combination of unequal variances and unequal sample sizes is the case where classical studies have revealed that the Student t test is decidedly *not* robust.

In the first method, with equal variances, both samples in each pair of samples were obtained from $N(0, 1)$ with probability .85 and from $N(0, 25)$ with proba-

TABLE 19.9
Powers of Significance Tests Performed on Samples from
Mixed-Normal Distribution with Equal/Unequal Variances
and Unequal Sample Sizes ($N_1 = 18$, $N_2 = 6$)

SE	t	W/t_R	Welch t	Welch t_R
		$\sigma_1^2 = \sigma_2^2$		
0	049	044	032	058
.5	082	105	072	122
1.0	178	271	187	294
1.5	319	491	344	499
2.0	488	701	526	665
2.5	631	829	656	763
3.0	745	900	749	809
3.5	826	933	810	838
4.0	886	954	857	861
		$\sigma_1^2 = 16\,\sigma_2^2$		
0	002	017	036	076
.5	009	046	073	140
1.0	033	133	177	315
1.5	095	311	335	540
2.0	186	527	490	736
2.5	313	722	630	863
3.0	439	856	738	934
3.5	551	931	824	965
4.0	651	969	885	981

bility .15, as described earlier in this chapter. In the second method, with unequal variances, the first sample in each pair was obtained from $N(0, 1)$ with probability .85 and from $N(0, 25)$ with probability .15, whereas the second sample in each pair was obtained from $N(0, 16)$ with probability .85 and from $N(0, 400)$ with probability .15. That is, in the first method sampling was from two identical mixed-normal distributions. In the second method, sampling was from two mixed-normal distributions in which the mixtures themselves had different variances.

The performance of the Student t test is shown in the left-hand columns of each section of Table 19.9, labeled t, and the performance of the Wilcoxon–Mann–Whitney test (or equivalently, the t test on ranks) is shown in the third column of each section, labeled W/t_R. The remaining columns in the table are explained later.

Comparing the t columns in the left-hand and right-hand sections of the table, it is evident that unequal variances combined with unequal sample sizes results in a pronounced decrease in probability of rejecting the null hypothesis. That is, there is a marked depression of the probability of Type I errors and an increase in the probability of Type II errors. However, comparing the W/t_R columns in the left-hand and right-hand sections, we observe that a similar change in these probabilities characterizes the Wilcoxon test, although it is not quite as extreme. Clearly, under the conditions represented in this table, substitution of W/t_R for t is not an answer to the problem of unequal variances. However, it is a fairly good answer to the problem of having a mixed-normal distribution instead of a normal distribution, as we already know.

Adopting for the moment the point of view that the Wilcoxon test is basically a t test on ranks (t_R), results like this become more understandable. If two sets of scores have different variances, then the two corresponding sets of ranks obtained after the scores have been ranked all together will also be likely to have different variances, although the transformation reduces the size of the difference. For example, if $X = 0, 20$ and $Y = 11, 12$, then the corresponding ranks are $R_x = 1, 4$ and $R_y = 2, 3$, and $\sigma_x = 10$, $\sigma_y = 1/2$, $\sigma_{Rx} = 3/2$, and $\sigma_{Ry} = 1/2$. Equivalence of W and t_R implies that, if the t test is sensitive to unequal variances, then the Wilcoxon test is sensitive to unequal variances of sets of ranks, and similar remarks apply to the Kruskal–Wallis test, and so on.

In theoretical statistics, there has been another line of inquiry relevant to violations of homogeneity of variance that is not widely known among psychologists and is hardly ever mentioned in elementary textbooks in statistics for psychologists. Early in this century, statisticians examined the sampling distribution of the Student t statistic for independent samples under conditions where population variances are unequal and pooling of sample variances to obtain a common estimate of the population variance is meaningless. That is, in contrast to the statistic

$$t = \frac{\bar{X}_1 - \bar{X}_2}{\sqrt{(s^2/N_1) + (s^2/N_2)}},$$

based on a pooled estimate, s^2, which is distributed as Student's t with $N_1 + N_2 - 2$ degrees of freedom, investigators examined the distribution of

$$t' = \frac{\bar{X}_1 - \bar{X}_2}{\sqrt{(s_1^2/N_1) + (s_2^2/N_2)}},$$

where s_1^2 and s_2^2 are respective estimates of the two population variances. This came to be referred to as the Behrens–Fisher problem (Behrens, 1929; Fisher, 1935).

Welch (1938, 1947), Smith (1936), Satterthwaite (1946), Cochran and Cox (1957), and others, proposed modifications of the Student t test involving approximations of the so-called Behrens–Fisher distribution. One approximation involves interpreting the t statistic with reference to a modified number of degree of freedom, given by

$$df' = \frac{[(s_1^2/N_1) + (s_2^2/N_2)]^2}{\dfrac{(s_1^2/N_1)^2}{N_1 - 1} + \dfrac{(s_2^2/N_2)^2}{N_2 - 1}},$$

Accordingly, the critical value of t' varies from one pair of samples to another under this procedure. These tests are known as the Welch–Aspin, the Welch–Satterthwaite, or the Smith–Satterthwaite approximations. The Welch–Satterthwaite version shown earlier, which is also relevant to the F test in the analysis of variance, was used to obtain the results in Table 19.9.

These ideas are not commonly presented in introductory texts, but see Winer (1971), Kirk (1982), and Howell (1987) for informative exceptions. The computational complexity of these tests has been a disadvantage in the past, but with computers this now is unimportant. These methods do effectively correct for the modifications in the probabilities of Type I and Type II errors produced by unequal variances in combination with unequal sample sizes (see also Zimmerman & Williams, 1988).

Consider now the problem of simultaneous violations of normality and homogeneity of variance. Assume also that sample sizes are unequal, so that unequal variances are truly a problem. We know from the discussion in previous sections of this chapter that replacement of t by W/t_R, or by a t test following other bounded transformations, provides a more powerful test in the case of mixed-normal, exponential, Cauchy, and other outlier-prone distributions. But these replacements fail to solve the problem of unequal variances. We have just seen that replacement of the ordinary Student t test by the Welch t test does indeed effectively counteract violations of homogeneity of variance. But the Welch t test alone fails to correct for violations of normality in the case of outlier-prone distributions. What then is to be done when assumptions of normality and homogeneity of variance are simultaneously violated? An attractive hypothesis is that both problems can be solved at once by the Welch t test performed on the ranks of measures instead of the measures themselves.

Evidence that this combination does in fact achieve the desired goal is provided by the simulation results in the remaining columns of Table 19.9. The columns labeled *Welch t* in each section of the table represent the Welch *t* test (or, more precisely, the Welch–Satterthwaite version) applied to the original measures. Furthermore, the columns labeled *Welch t_R* in each section of the table represent the Welch *t* test applied to the ranks of the measures. It is apparent that the latter significance test is superior to the other tests represented in this table for this extreme case of concurrent violations of normality and homogeneity of variance. Furthermore, just as the Wilcoxon test is equivalent to an ordinary Student *t* test performed on ranks, so also it turns out that certain nonparametric rank tests designed to overcome the Behrens–Fisher problem are equivalent to the Welch *t* test performed on ranks (Fligner & Policello, 1981).

Some further simulation data of this sort is shown in Table 19.10. In this case, the same significance tests were applied to samples of size $N_1 = 18$ and $N_2 = 6$ from two Cauchy distributions with different spread. The Cauchy distribution does not have finite variance, but it is nevertheless possible to obtain samples from two Cauchy distributions that have different degrees of variability under

TABLE 19.10
Powers of Significance Tests Performed on Samples
from Cauchy Distributions Differing in Variability
$(N_1 = 18, N_2 = 6)$

SE	t	W/t_R	Welch t	Welch t_R
			$\sigma_1^2 = \sigma_2^2$	
0	035	046	017	060
.5	053	113	038	137
1.0	099	285	100	307
1.5	166	465	180	458
2.0	243	611	264	563
2.5	316	722	344	633
3.0	388	791	413	688
3.5	451	843	477	728
4.0	505	881	528	758
			$\sigma_1^2 = 16\,\sigma_2^2$	
0	008	019	017	069
.5	012	061	033	153
1.0	027	191	085	358
1.5	057	376	170	563
2.0	101	546	242	700
2.5	160	678	316	784
3.0	216	774	385	833
3.5	274	839	447	866
4.0	326	877	498	885

some other measure of variability. The result of this procedure is essentially the same as in the case of the mixed-normal distribution: once again the Welch t test on ranks (Welch t_R) turned out to be superior. All of the results presented in Tables 19.9 and 19.10 are consistent with the idea that violations of normality and homogeneity of variance both alter the probability of rejection of the null hypothesis (both Type I and Type II errors), that conversion of measures to ranks corrects for nonnormality but not for unequal variances, that the Welch t test corrects for unequal variances, but not for nonnormality, and that the Welch t test applied to ranks (Welch t_R) effectively corrects for both violations. This is another case where a rank transformation leads to a power increase for a parametric procedure applied to heavy-tailed distributions.

There are procedures similar to the Welch t test that can be substituted for the F test in analysis of variance when samples have unequal variances (see Keselmen, Games, & Rogan, 1979; Kohr & Games, 1974; Satterthwaite, 1946). Although simulation data is not available, an attractive hypothesis suggests that these procedures applied to ranks instead of the original measures would outperform the Kruskal–Wallis test, which is equivalent to the ordinary F test performed on ranks.

From one point of view, the Student t test can be regarded as a special case of the Welch t test that applies when variances are equal. Although this is not strictly true mathematically, it is evident from Tables 19.9 and 19.10 that the Welch t test has essentially the same outcome as the Student t test when variances are equal. For this reason, one can envision a computer program that applies the Welch t test automatically to all sample data, in order to protect against possible violations of homogeneity of variance whenever they occur. If such a program were implemented, the only decision that would have to be made is whether or not to convert measures to ranks before performing the analysis.

Present evidence indicates that the relatively simple decision strategy shown in Fig. 19.3 provides significance tests with superior power characteristics for a large variety of distributions, including the heavy-tailed distributions we have examined earlier in this chapter, whether variances are equal or unequal. Furthermore, if one is willing to program a computer to perform the Welch t test routinely, irrespective of whether variances are equal or unequal, it is possible to bypass the entire lower part of the flow chart (below the broken line) and to proceed directly to the significance test. One disadvantage of this strategy, resulting from decision making about conversion to ranks, is a small power loss if conversion is made when it is not necessary.

Another possible strategy that avoids conversion to ranks is shown in Fig. 19.4. This strategy examines samples for outliers, using an outlier-identification statistic, and removes or modifies any that are identified, as may be necessary, as suggested by Rasmussen (1985, 1986). In other words, a decision is made about each sample—not as to the significance test to be used, but as to whether or not all data are to be retained. Finally, the Welch t test is applied to the sample data.

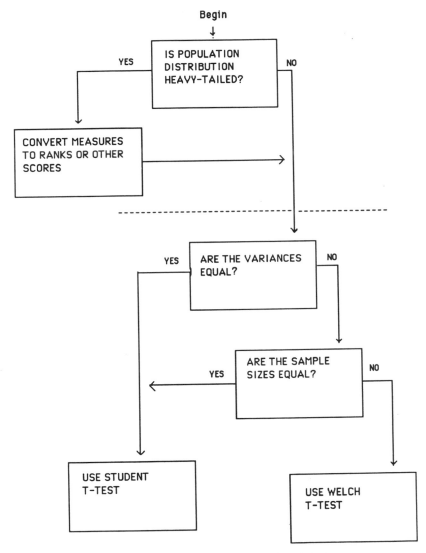

FIG. 19.3. Procedure for choice of statistical test.

This strategy avoids loss of power resulting from a rank transformation that may not be necessary, and it can be programmed in its entirety.

Finally, some very promising results are being found in the area of robust estimation and robust inference. See Hampel, Ronchetti, Rouseeuw, and Stahel (1986) for an advanced treatment or Lind and Zumbo (1990) for an introduction. Future developments in statistical computing will see further prevalence of these methods.

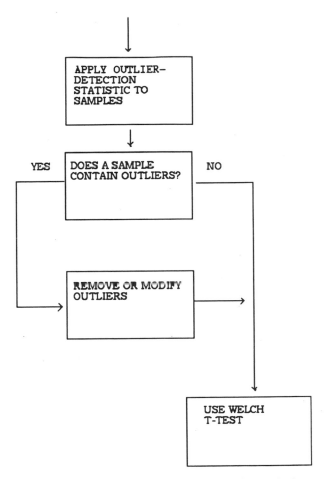

FIG. 19.4. Simplified procedure for choice of statistical test.

TRANSFORMATIONS, SCALES OF MEASUREMENT, AND APPROPRIATE STATISTICS

The general perspective developed in the present chapter has some implications for concepts of appropriate statistics that were alluded to earlier. We examine the notion that nonparametric statistical tests, such as the Wilcoxon test, are appropriate, whereas parametric tests, such as the *t* test, are inappropriate, when the scale of measurement in a research study is an ordinal scale and not an interval scale. This distinction has been routinely presented in introductory statistics textbooks in psychology for several decades. In the light of findings discussed in previous sections of the present chapter, this point of view is questionable for the following reasons:

1. The Wilcoxon–Mann–Whitney test, we have seen, is equivalent to an ordinary Student t test performed on ranks instead of the original measures. Clearly, this fact implies that, if the original data in a research study is in the form of ranks, nothing is gained by replacing the t test by the Wilcoxon test. Accordingly, the usual textbook recommendation to switch to nonparametric rank tests like the Wilcoxon test when original data are ranks is unnecessary. If the available measures are already ranks and there are no ties, it makes no difference whether one calculates a rank-sum W statistics or a t statistic. In a similar situation, it makes no difference whether one employs a Kruskal–Wallis test or an ordinary F test, and so on.

2. For numerous heavy-tailed distributions, we have seen, the power of significance tests can be increased, often dramatically, by transforming continuous random variables to ranks. This finding is usually interpreted by saying that the Wilcoxon test is more powerful than the t test for these distributions. But this finding can be just as well expressed by saying that the power of the Student t test can be increased by converting measures to ranks before performing the test. Evidence seems to be that the power of parametric tests is diminished in the case of heavy-tailed distributions because of the influence of outliers. This fact lends credence to the idea that the benefit of nonparametric methods is related to the properties of rank transformations rather than to scales of measurement. Somewhat paradoxically, one might assert that performance of the t test is diminished for outlier-prone distributions because the test is sensitive to the magnitude of differences between scores, that is, to intervals, in addition to the order of scores.

3. The power of the t test sometimes can be increased, we have seen, by converting the original measures to discrete, bounded measures that are not ranks. This means that power is increased when continuous random variables are replaced by discrete random variables having a small number of possible values. We have also seen that N ranks can be replaced by $N/4$ numbers without loss of power. In the case of heavy-tailed distributions, the replacement of the original continuous measures by these numbers sometimes results in a large gain in power. Furthermore, these transformations sometimes bring the Type I error probability closer to the nominal significance level. Textbook discussions imply that, if one has ordinal measures to begin with, it is beneficial to abandon parametric methods and employ nonparametric methods. In the case of heavy-tailed distributions, on the contrary, one begins with real-valued, continuous measures and achieves desirable ends by transforming them to integer-valued variables having purely ordinal status. This fact is somewhat difficult to reconcile with the scheme that associates interval scales with parametric tests and ordinal scales with nonparametric tests (see also, Zumbo, 1989; Zumbo & Zimmerman, 1990).

4. It is sometimes said that the statistics of means and variances are meaningful for interval measures but are not meaningful for ordinal measures. But we

have just seen in the preceding section of this chapter that unequal variances of continuous measures may be reflected in unequal variances of the ranks based on those measures. That is, sensitivity to violation of homogeneity of variance that characterizes parametric tests is generally inherited by nonparametric methods such as the Wilcoxon test and Kruskal–Wallis test that are based on rank transformations. In fact, transformation to ranks does not solve the problem of unequal variances. To solve the problem, we have seen, parametric methods based on the Behrens–Fisher distribution, which employ the Welch t test or an equivalent procedure, are required. Again, this situation is inconsistent with a simple scheme that associates nonparametric methods with ordinal scales and parametric methods with interval scales.

Let $X:\Omega \rightarrow R$ be a random variable representing an experiment in which numbers are printed on a tape by a computer. Assume that we have no knowledge of the input or the way the computer transforms the input. As in many applications of probability, the underlying sample space Ω is purely hypothetical. As long as we regard the observed output as just a set of numbers, it is possible to test statistical hypotheses without paying attention to scales of measurement, as many authors have emphasized (Binder, 1984; Gaito, 1960; Lord, 1953; and others). For example, one could test the hypothesis that the outputs of two random number generators are the same against an alternative that one generator yields larger numbers. Whether parametric or nonparametric methods are appropriate for such a test depends on characteristics of the probability distribution of the numbers. If the output 2, 4, 1, 3, 1, 2, 100 were observed, a method using ranks, or possibly an outlier-detection statistic, might be useful, and so on.

One can examine scale properties of latent variables underlying the observed values, if desired, but, nevertheless, the relative power of significance tests depends on probability distributions, not scale properties, as suggested by the previous sections of this chapter. As far as particular individuals are concerned, latent variables are considered to be nonrandom, but when sampling is involved, these latent variables are random, just like observed variables. Let $f:R \rightarrow R$ be a function that transforms values of a latent variable into observed measures, and suppose that a researcher's main interest is the latent variable. If f has an inverse, the composite function $\theta = f^{-1} \cdot X$ is itself a random variable defined on Ω, which has a mean, variance, probability distribution, and so on. Can one make decisions regarding θ on the basis of statistical hypotheses about X and statistical tests on X? Maxwell and Delaney (1985) and Davison and Sharma (1988) showed that, under certain regularity conditions, hypotheses about means of X are equivalent to hypotheses about means of latent variables functionally related to X, and that in the case of normal distributions, Type I errors, Type II errors, and power are equivalent in the two cases. In the same context, it is possible to examine the relative power of parametric and nonparametric methods both for observed variables and for latent variables.

For simplicity in the following examples, we consider one-sample tests. Suppose that X is related to an exponentially distributed latent variable θ by the function $X = 1 - e^{\theta}$, so that X is uniformly distributed. Then, a test of an hypothesis $\mu_x = \mu_{x_0}$ is equivalent to a test of the corresponding hypothesis $\mu_\theta = -\log_e(\mu_{x_0})$. If one observes sample values to be approximately uniformly distributed, but knows nothing of θ, then a parametric test will probably be more powerful and more likely to preserve the α-level. However, if the relation to the latent variable is known, and all observed values are transformed by $\theta = -\log_e(X)$, then the resulting values are exponentially distributed and a nonparametric test based on the ranks is more powerful. On the other hand, suppose that $X = \log_e(\theta)$ and that X is observed to be exponentially distributed. Then, a nonparametric test is more powerful when applied to the observed values, whereas a parametric test is more powerful when applied to the latent variable. A variety of other distributions of the forms discussed earlier in this chapter lead to similar results.

In practice, of course, one seldom knows a function relating an observed variable and a latent variable when analyzing experimental data. If all that is known is that the function is order-preserving, then, whatever X may be, the distribution of θ can be either outlier-prone or outlier-resistant. But if, in fact, the values of a latent variable are already known or can be found easily by applying a transformation, then significance tests should be performed on those values. Whether a parametric or nonparametric test is more powerful in that case depends on the probability distribution of the latent variable. However, if only observed values are available for an analysis, then choice of an appropriate significance test is dictated by the probability distribution of the observed values.

ACKNOWLEDGMENTS

This research was made possible by a Carleton University Research Grant to the first author and a Social Sciences and Humanities Research Council of Canada Doctoral Fellowship to the second author. We would like to express our gratitude to Richard H. Williams and M. M. Tatsuoka for comments on an earlier draft of this chapter.

REFERENCES

Barnett, V., & Lewis, T. (1978). *Outliers in statistical data.* New York: Wiley.
Behrens, W. U. (1929). Ein Beitrag zur Fehlerberechnung bei wenigen Beobachtungen. *Landwirtschaftlisches Jahrbuch, 68,* 807–837.

Binder, A. (1984). Restrictions on statistics imposed by method of measurement: some reality, much mythology. *Journal of Criminal Justice, 12,* 467–481.

Blair, R. C. (1981). A reaction to "Consequences of failure to meet assumptions underlying the fixed effects analysis of variance and covariance." *Review of Educational Research, 51,* 499–507.

Blair, R. C., & Higgins, J. J. (1980a). The power of t and Wilcoxon statistics: a comparison. *Evaluation Review, 4,* 645–655.

Blair, R. C., & Higgins, J. J. (1980b). A comparison of the power of Wilcoxon's rank-sum statistic to that of Student's *t* statistic under various non-normal distributions. *Journal of Educational Statistics, 5,* 309–335.

Blair, R. C., & Higgins, J. J. (1985). Comparison of the power of the paired samples *t* test to that of Wilcoxon's signed-ranks test under various population shapes. *Psychological Bulletin, 97,* 119–128.

Blair, R. C., Higgins, J. J., & Smitley, W. D. S. (1980). On the relative power of the *U* and *t* tests. *British Journal of Mathematical and Statistical Psychology, 33*(1), 114–120.

Boneau, C. A. (1960). The effects of violation of assumptions underlying the *t*-test. *Psychological Bulletin, 57,* 49–64.

Boneau, C. A. (1962). A comparison of the power of the *U* and *t* tests. *Psychological Review, 69,* 246–256.

Box, G. E. P. (1953). Non-normality and tests on variance. *Biometrika, 40,* 318–335.

Box, G. E. P., & Muller, M. (1958). A note on the generation of random normal deviates. *Annals of Mathematical Statistics, 29,* 610–611.

Bradley, J. V. (1977). A common situation conducive to bizarre distribution shapes. *American Statistician, 31,* 147–150.

Bradley, J. V. (1978). Robustness? *British Journal of Mathematical and Statistical Psychology, 31,* 144–152.

Cochran, W. G., & Cox, G. M. (1957). *Experimental designs* (2nd ed.). New York: Wiley.

Cohen, J. (1988). *Statistical power analysis for the behavioral sciences* (2nd. ed.). Hillsdale, NJ: Lawrence Erlbaum Associates.

Conover, W. J. (1980). *Practical nonparametric statistics* (2nd. ed.). New York: Wiley.

Conover, W. J., & Iman, R. L. (1981). Rank transformations as a bridge between parametric and nonparametric statistics. *The American Statistician, 35,* 124–129.

Davison, M. L., & Sharma, A. R. (1988). Parametric statistics and levels of measurement. *Psychological Bulletin, 104,* 137–144.

Fisher, R. A. (1935). *The design of experiments.* Edinburgh: Oliver & Boyd.

Fligner, M. A., & Policello, G. E. II. (1981). Robust rank procedures for the Behrens–Fisher problem. *Journal of the American Statistical Association, 76,* 162–168.

Gaito, J. (1960). Scale classification and statistics. *Psychological Review, 67,* 277–278.

Games, J., & Howell, J. F. (1976). Pairwise multiple comparison procedures with unequal n's and/or variances: A Monte Carlo study. *Journal of Educational Statistics, 1,* 113–125.

Glass, G., Peckham, P., & Sanders, J. (1972). Consequences of failure to meet assumptions underlying the fixed effects analysis of variance and covariance. *Review of Educational Research, 42,* 237–288.

Gnedenko, B. (1943). Sur la distribution limite du terme maximum d'une serie aleatoire. *Annals of Mathematics, 44,* 423–453.

Green, R. F. (1976). Outlier-prone and outlier-resistant distributions. *Journal of the American Statistical Association, 71,* 502–505.

Grubbs, F. E. (1969). Procedures for detecting outlying observations in samples. *Technometrics, 11,* 1–21.

Hampel, F. R., Ronchetti, E. M., Rousseeuw, P. J., & Stahel, W. A. (1986). *Robust statistics: The approach based on influence functions.* New York: Wiley.

Hawkins, D. M. (1980). *Identification of outliers*. London: Chapman & Hall.

Hodges, J., & Lehmann, E. (1956). The efficiency of some nonparametric competitors of the *t*-test. *Annals of Mathematical Statistics, 27*, 324–335.

Howell, D. C. (1987). *Statistical methods for psychology* (2nd ed.). Boston: Duxbury Press.

Hsu, P. L. (1938). Contributions to the theory of "student's" *t*-test as applied to the problem of two samples. *Statistical Research Memoirs, 2*, 1–24.

Keselman, H. J., Games, P. A., & Rogan, J. C. (1979). An addendum to "a comparison of modified-Tukey and Scheffe' methods of multiple comparisons for pairwise contrasts." *Journal of the American Statistical Association, 74*, 626–627.

Kirk, R. E. (1982). *Experimental design* (2nd ed.). Monterey, CA: Brooks/Cole.

Kohr, R. L., & Games, P. A. (1977). Testing complex a priori contrasts in means for independent samples. *Journal of Educational Statistics, 1*, 207–216.

Lehman, R. S. (1977). *Computer simulation and modeling: An introduction*. Hillsdale, NJ: Lawrence Erlbaum Associates.

Lehmann, E. L. (1975). *Nonparametrics: Statistical methods based on ranks*. San Francisco: Holden-Day.

Lind, J. C., & Zumbo, B. D. (1990). *The continuity principle in psychological research: An introduction to robust statistics*. In B. D. Zumbo (Chair), *Alternatives to classical statistical procedures*. Symposium conducted at the annual meetings of the Canadian Psychological Association, Ottawa, Canada. (Abstract in *Canadian Psychology, 31*, 238).

Lord, F. M. (1953). On the statistical treatment of football numbers. *American Psychologist, 8*, 750–751.

Marsaglia G. (1964). Generating a variable from the tail of the normal distribution. *Technometrics, 6*, 101–102.

Marsaglia G., & Bray, T. A. (1964). A convenient method for generating normal variables. *SIAM Review, 6*, 260–264.

Maxwell, S. E., & Delaney, H. D. (1985). Measurement and statistics: an examination of construct validity. *Psychological Bulletin, 97*, 85–93.

Morgan, B. J. T. (1984). *Elements of simulation*. London: Chapman & Hall.

Neave, H. R., & Granger, C. W. J. (1968). A Monte Carlo study comparing various two-sample tests for differences in means. *Technometrics, 10*, 509–522.

Neyman, J., & Scott, E. L. (1971). Outlier proneness of phenomena and of related distributions. In J. S. Rustagi (Ed.), *Optimizing methods in statistics* (pp. 413–430). New York: Academic Press.

Norton, D. W. (1953). Cited by E. F. Lindquist, *Design and analysis of experiments in psychology and education*. New York: Houghton-Mifflin.

Pearson, E. S. (1931). The analysis of variance in cases of non-normal variation. *Biometrika, 23*, 114–133.

Posten, H. O. (1984). Robustness of the two-sample *t*-test. In D. Rasch & M. L. Tiku (Eds.), *Robustness of statistical methods and nonparametric statistics*. Dordrecht, German Democratic Republic: D. Reidel.

Randles, R. H. (1980). Nonparametric statistical tests of hypotheses. In R. V. Hogg (Ed.), *Modern statistics: Methods and applications* (pp. 31–40). Providence, RI: American Mathematical Society.

Randles, R. H., & Wolfe, D. A. (1979). *Introduction to the theory of nonparametric statistics*. New York: Wiley.

Rasmussen, J. L. (1985). The power of Student's *t* and Wilcoxon's *W* statistics: A comparison. *Evaluation Review, 9*, 505–510.

Rasmussen, J. L. (1986). An evaluation of parametric and nonparametric tests on modified and non-modified data. *British Journal of Mathematical and Statistical Psychology, 39*, 213–220.

Rogan, J. C., & Keselman, H. J. (1977). Is the ANOVA *F*-test robust to variance heterogeneity when sample sizes are equal?: An investigation via a coefficient of variation. *American Educational Research Journal, 14*, 493–498.

Satterthwaite, F. E. (1946). An approximate distribution of estimates of variance components. *Biometrics Bulletin, 2,* 110–114.

Scheffe', H. (1959). *The analysis of variance.* New York: Wiley.

Smith, H. F. (1936). The problem of comparing the results of two experiments with unequal errors. *Journal of Scientific and Industrial Research, 9,* 211–212.

Tabachnick, B. G., & Fidell, L. S. (1983). *Using multivariate statistics.* New York: Harper & Row.

Tietjen, G. L., & Moore, R. H. (1972). Some Grubbs-type statistics for the detection of several outliers. *Technometrics, 14,* 583–597.

Toothaker, L. E. (1972). *An empirical investigation of the permutation t-test as compared to the Student's t-test and the Mann-Whitney U-test.* Madison, WI: Wisconsin Research and Development Center for Cognitive Learning.

van der Waerden, B. L. (1952). Order tests for the two sample problem and their power. *Proceedings Koninklijke Nederlandse Akademie van Wetenschappen* (A),, 55 (Indagationes Mathematical 14), 453–458.

Wainer, H. (1982). Robust statistics: A survey and some prescriptions. In G. Keren (Ed.), *Statistical and methodological issues in psychology and social sciences research* (pp. 187–214). Hillsdale, NJ: Lawrence Erlbaum Associates.

Welch, B. L. (1938). The significance of the difference between two means when the population variances are unequal. *Biometrika, 29,* 350–362.

Welch, B. L. (1947). The generalization of Student's problem when several different population variances are involved. *Biometrika, 34,* 29–35.

Winer, B. J. (1971). *Statistical principles in experimental design* (2nd ed.). New York: McGraw-Hill.

Zimmerman, D. W. (1987). Comparative power of the Student *t*-test and Mann-Whitney *U*-test for unequal sample sizes and variances. *Journal of Experimental Education, 55,* 171–174.

Zimmerman, D. W., & Williams, R. H. (1988). Power comparisons of the Student *t*-test and two approximations when variances and sample sizes are unequal. *Journal of the Indian Society of Agricultural Statistics, 41,* 206–217.

Zimmerman, D. W., & Zumbo, B. D. (1989). A note on rank transformations and comparative power of the Student *t*-test and Wilcoxon–Mann–Whitney test. *Perceptual and Motor Skills, 68,* 1139–1146.

Zimmerman, D. W., & Zumbo, B. D. (1990a). The effect of outliers on the relative power of parametric and nonparametric statistical tests. *Perceptual and Motor Skills, 71,* 339–349.

Zimmerman, D. W., & Zumbo, B. D. (1990b). The relative power of the Wilcoxon–Mann–Whitney test and Student *t*-test under simple bounded transformations. *Journal of General Psychology, 117,* 425–436.

Zumbo, B. D. (1989). *Levels of measurement and the relative power of parametric and nonparametric statistical methods: A theoretical and computer simulation study.* Unpublished master's thesis, Carleton University, Ottawa, Canada.

Zumbo, B. D., & Zimmerman, D. W. (in press). Is the selection of statistical methods governed by level of measurement? *Canadian Psychology.*

20 Cumulating Evidence

Robert Rosenthal
Harvard University

It is a common criticism of psychology and related behavioral and social sciences that they cumulate poorly. Our sciences do not seem to show the orderly progress and development shown by the natural and physical sciences. The newer work of these "harder" sciences is seen to build directly on the earlier work of these sciences. Our sciences, on the other hand, seem nearly to be starting anew with each succeeding volume of the psychological journals. Although it appears that the natural and physical sciences have problems of their own when it comes to successful cumulation (Collins, 1985; Hedges, 1987; Hively, 1989; Koshland, 1989; Pool, 1988, 1989) there is no denying that in the matter of cumulating evidence we have much to be modest about.

Poor cumulation does not seem to be primarily due to lack of replication or to failure to recognize the need for replication. Indeed, the clarion calls for further research with which we so frequently end our articles are carried wherever our scholarly journals are read. It seems, rather, that we have been better at issuing such calls than at knowing what to do with the answers. There are many areas of psychology for which we do have available the results of 2, 10, or many more studies all addressing essentially the same question. Our summaries of the results of these sets of studies, however, have not been nearly as informative as they might have been, either with respect to summarized significance levels or with respect to summarized effect sizes. Even the best reviews of research by the most sophisticated workers have rarely told us more about each study in a set of studies than the direction of the relationship between the variables investigated and whether or not a given p level was attained. This state of affairs is beginning to change.

The most general purpose of this chapter is to present the concepts and procedures that are likely to improve the process of the cumulation of evidence in psychology and its related sciences. The more specific purposes of this chapter include:

1. Defining the concept of a study's "results" more clearly than is our custom in psychology.
2. Providing a general framework for conceptualizing the quantitative summary of research domains.
3. Illustrating the quantitative procedures within this framework so they can be applied by the reader and/or understood more clearly when applied by others.
4. Discussing the concepts and procedures developed to deal with the "file drawer problem" of unretrieved research results.
5. Evaluating the practical and scientific importance of various effect sizes.
6. Considering the implications of a meta-analytic orientation for the concept of successful replication.

If we were to trace historically (and ever so briefly) the development of the movement to quantify runs of studies, we might well begin with Fisher (1938), for his thinking about the combination of the significance levels of independent studies. We would then move through Mosteller and Bush (1954) for their broadening of the Fisher perspective both in (a) introducing several new methods of combining independent probability levels to social and behavioral scientists in general and to social psychologists in particular, and (b) showing that effect sizes as well as significance levels could be usefully combined. We would end in the present day with an expanding number of investigators (including Cooper, 1979, 1984, 1989; Cooper & Rosenthal, 1980; DePaulo, Zuckerman, & Rosenthal, 1980; Eagly & Carli, 1981; Glass, 1976, 1980; Glass, McGaw, & Smith, 1981; Hall, 1980, 1984; Harris & Rosenthal, 1985; Hedges & Olkin, 1985; Hunter & Schmidt, 1990; Light & Pillemer, 1984; Light & Smith, 1971; Mullen, 1989; Mullen & Rosenthal, 1985; Pillemer & Light, 1980; Rosenthal, 1968, 1969, 1976, 1978, 1980, 1984, 1986, 1987a, 1987b, 1991; Rosenthal & DePaulo, 1979; Rosenthal & Rosnow, 1975; Rosenthal & Rubin, 1978, 1980, 1982b, 1982c, 1985; Shoham-Salomon & Rosenthal, 1987; Smith, 1980; Smith & Glass, 1977; Smith, Glass, & Miller, 1980; Walberg & Haertel, 1980; Wachter, 1988; Wachter & Straf, 1990; Zuckerman, DePaulo, & Rosenthal, 1981 and the many others cited in the references of these workers).

DEFINING RESULTS OF INDIVIDUAL STUDIES

Before we can discuss meaningfully the various procedures for comparing and combining the results of a series of studies we must be explicit about our meaning of the term *results* as it applies to a single study. We begin by stating what we do not mean when we refer to the results of a study. We do not mean the conclusion drawn by the investigator because that is often only somewhat vaguely related to the actual results. Something else we do not mean is the result of an omnibus F test with $df > 1$ in the numerator or an omnibus chi-square (χ^2) test with $df > 1$. In both those cases we are getting quantitative answers to questions that are often, perhaps usually, hopelessly imprecise. Only rarely are we really interested in knowing for any fixed-factor analysis of variance or covariance that somewhere in the thicket of df there lurk one or more meaningful answers to meaningful questions that we had not the foresight to ask of our data. Similarly there are few occasions when what we really want to know is that somewhere in a contingency table there is an obtained frequency or two that has strayed too far from the frequency expected for that cell under the null hypothesis.

What we do mean by "the results" is the answer to the question: What is the relationship between any variable X and any variable Y? The variables X and Y are chosen with only the constraint that their relationship be of interest to us. The answer to this question, however, must come in two parts: (a) the estimate of the magnitude of the relationship (the effect size) and (b) an indication of the accuracy or reliability of the estimated effect size (as in a confidence interval placed around the estimate). An alternative to the second part of the answer, one not intrinsically more useful but one more consistent with the existing practices of psychological researchers, is the test of significance of the difference between the obtained effect size and the effect size expected under the null hypothesis of no relationship between variables X and Y.

EFFECT SIZE
AND STATISTICAL SIGNIFICANCE

The argument has been made that "the results" of a study with respect to any given relationship can be expressed as an estimate of an effect size plus a test of significance, consequently we should make explicit the relationship between these two quantities. The general relationship is:

$$\text{Test of Significance} = \text{Effect Size} \times \text{Size of Study}$$

One example of this general relationship is:

$$\chi^2(1) = \phi^2 \times N \tag{1}$$

That is, χ^2 on $df = 1$ is the product of the size of the effect expressed by the product moment correlation squared multiplied by N, the number of sampling units. In this example the product moment correlation is between the independent and dependent variable after each has been dummy coded as 1, 0. Other examples illustrating the general relationship between tests of significance and effect size estimates include:

$$Z = \phi \times \sqrt{N} \tag{2}$$

$$t = [(M_1 - M_2)/S] \times \sqrt{\frac{n_1 n_2}{n_1 + n_2}} \tag{3}$$

$$F(1, -) = [(M_1 - M_2)/S]^2 \times \frac{n_1 n_2}{n_1 + n_2} \tag{4}$$

Equation 2 shows that the standard normal deviate Z (i.e., the square root of χ^2 on 1 df) is the product of the product moment correlation and $\sqrt{N}$. Equation 3 shows that t is the product of (a) the effect size $(M_1 - M_2)/S$, sometimes called d or, more accurately, g defined as the difference between the means divided by the square root of the pooled variance, and (b) an index of the size of the study taking account of unequal sample sizes (Cohen, 1977; Glass, 1980; Hedges, 1981; Rosenthal, 1984, 1991). If the sample sizes of the two groups were equal this second term would simplify to $\sqrt{n}/2$. Equation 4 shows that F with one df in the numerator is the product of the squared ingredients of the right-hand side of Equation 3. That is just as it should be, of course, given that $t^2 = F$ when $df = 1$ in the numerator.

In the interpretation of the results of any study we shall always want to compute and report some estimate of the size of the effects. Cohen (1977, 1988) has a detailed discussion of a variety of such effect size estimates, of which the most generally useful in psychological research appear to be those based on (a) product moment correlations and (b) standardized differences between the means.

The product moment correlations are widely used, easily computed from test statistics, and very general in applicability. Thus, product moment correlations can be used when both variables are continuous (Pearson r), when both variables are in ranked form (Spearman rho), when both variables are dichotomous (phi or ϕ; as in Equation 5) or when one variable is continuous and one is dichotomous (point biserial r; as in Equations 6, 7, and 8). Product moment correlations can be computed from $\chi^2(1)$, t, $F(1, -)$ very readily from the following (Cohen, 1965; Friedman, 1968):

$$\phi = \sqrt{\frac{\chi^2(1)}{N}} \tag{5}$$

$$r = \sqrt{\frac{t^2}{t^2 + df}} \tag{6}$$

$$r = \sqrt{\frac{F(1, -)}{F(1, -) + df\ \text{error}}} \tag{7}$$

One problem with the interpretation of r stems from our inclination to square r and then to misinterpret seriously the practical importance associated with any given r^2. (In other contexts, such as in comparing effect size estimates, r^2 may be quite useful.) In a later section of this chapter a method for the display and interpretation of r is presented that seems to be substantially more intuitive and informative than most of our current procedures for reporting effect sizes (Rosenthal & Rubin, 1982a).

Standardized differences between the means represent an alternative metric for reporting effect sizes. The difference between the means of two groups is divided either by the square root of the mean square for error or by the standard deviation (i.e., σ rather than S) common to the two treatment conditions. The complex issues governing the choice of the standardizing denominator, complications arising from the use of repeated measures designs, and the value of the BESD (a method for displaying the practical importance of the size of an obtained effect that is described later) have led me to lean more and more to the use of r as the effect size estimate of choice. In most cases r is very easily derived from d by a formula given by Cohen (1977):

$$r = \frac{d}{\sqrt{d^2 + 4}}.$$

(8)

Similarly, given r we can easily obtain d by

$$d = \frac{2r}{\sqrt{1 - r^2}}.$$

(9)

A FRAMEWORK
FOR META-ANALYTIC PROCEDURES

Table 20.1 provides a summary of four types of meta-analytic procedures that are applicable to the special case where just two studies are to be evaluated. It is useful to list the two-study case separately because there are some especially convenient computational procedures for this situation. The two columns of Table 20.1 show that there are two major ways to evaluate the results of research studies—in terms of their statistical significance (e.g., p levels) and in terms of their effect sizes (e.g., the difference between means divided by the common standard deviation σ or S, indices employed by Cohen (1977) and by Glass (1980), or the Pearson r). The two rows of Table 20.1 show that there are two major analytic processes applied to the set of studies to be evaluated, comparing the combining. The cell labeled A in Table 20.1 represents the procedure that evaluates whether the significance level of one study differs significantly from the significance level of the other study. The cell labeled B represents the procedure that evaluates whether the effect size (e.g., d or r) of one study differs

TABLE 20.1
Four Types of Meta-Analytic Procedures
Applicable to a Set of Two Studies

Analytic Process	Results Defined in Terms of:	
	Significance Testing	Effect Size Estimation
Comparing Studies	A	B
Combining Studies	C	D

significantly from the effect size of the other study. Cells C and D represent the procedures that are used to estimate the overall level of significance and the average size of the effect, respectively. Illustrations of these procedures are given later.

Table 20.2 provides a more general summary of six types of meta-analytic procedures that are applicable to the case where three or more studies are to be evaluated. The columns are as in Table 20.1 but the row labeled "Comparing Studies" in Table 20.1 has now been subdivided into two rows—one for the case of diffuse tests and one for the case of focused tests.

When studies are compared as to their significance levels (cell A) or their effect sizes (cell B) by diffuse tests we learn whether they differ significantly

TABLE 20.2
Six Types of Meta-Analytic Procedures
Applicable to a Set of Three or More Studies

Analytic Process	Results Defined in Terms of:	
	Significance Testing	Effect Size Estimation
Comparing Studies: Diffuse Tests	A	B
Comparing Studies: Focused Tests	C	D
Combining Studies	E	F

among themselves with respect to significance levels or effect sizes respectively, but we do not learn how they differ or whether they differ according to any systematic basis. When studies are compared as to their significance levels (cell C) or their effect sizes (cell D) by focused tests, or contrasts, we learn whether the studies differ significantly among themselves in a theoretically predictable or meaningful way. Thus, important tests of hypotheses can be made by the use of focused tests. Cells E and F of Table 20.2 are simply analogues of cells C and D of Table 20.1 representing procedures used to estimate overall level of significance and average size of the effect, respectively.

COMPARING TWO STUDIES

Even when we have been quite rigorous and sophisticated in the interpretation of the results of a single study, we are often prone to err in the interpretation of two or more studies. For example, Smith may report a significant effect of some social intervention only to have Jones publish a rebuttal demonstrating that there is no such effect. A closer look at both their results may show the following:

Smith's Study: $t(78) = 2.21$, $p < .05$, $d = .50$, $r = .24$.

Jones's Study: $t(18) = 1.06$, $p > .30$, $d = .50$, $r = .24$.

Smith's results were more significant than Jones's to be sure, but the studies were in perfect agreement as to their estimated sizes of effect defined by either d or r. A comparison of their respective significance levels reveals furthermore, that these p's are not significantly different ($p = .42$). Clearly Jones was quite wrong in claiming that he had failed to replicate Smith's results. We begin this section by considering some procedures for comparing quantitatively the results of two independent studies, that is, studies conducted with different research participants. The examples we examine in this chapter are in most cases hypothetical, constructed specifically to illustrate a wide range of situations that occur when working on meta-analytic problems in psychology and other behavioral and social sciences.

Significance Testing

Ordinarily when we compare the results of two studies we are more interested in comparing their effect sizes than their p values. However, sometimes we cannot do any better than comparing their p values, and here is how we do it (Rosenthal & Rubin, 1979a): For each of the two test statistics we obtain a reasonably exact one-tailed p level. (All of the procedures described in this chapter require that p levels be recorded as one-tailed. Thus $t(100) = 1.98$ is recorded as $p = .025$, not $p = .05$.) Then, as an illustration of being "reasonably exact," if we obtain $t(30)$

= 3.03 we give p as .0025, not as "<.05." Extended tables of the t distribution are helpful here (e.g., Federighi, 1959; Rosenthal & Rosnow, 1984, 1991). For each p, we find Z, the standard normal deviate corresponding to the p value. Both p's must be one-tailed, the corresponding Z's will have the same sign if both studies show effects in the same direction, but different signs if the results are in the opposite direction. The difference between the two Z's when divided by $\sqrt{2}$, yields a new Z that corresponds to the p value that the difference between the Z's could be so large, or larger, if the two Z's did not really differ. Recapping,

$$\frac{Z_1 - Z_2}{\sqrt{2}} = Z \tag{10}$$

Example 1.   Social intervention studies A and B yield results in opposite directions and neither is "significant." One p is .06, one-tailed, the other is .12, one-tailed but in the opposite tail. The Z's corresponding to these p's are found in a table of the normal curve to be $+1.56$ and -1.18 (note the opposite signs to indicate results in opposite directions). Then, from Equation 10 we have

$$\frac{Z_1 - Z_2}{\sqrt{2}} = \frac{(1.56) - (-1.18)}{1.41} = 1.94$$

as the Z of the difference between the two p values or their corresponding Z's. The p value associated with a Z of 1.94 is .026 one-tailed or .052 two-tailed. The two p values thus may be seen to differ significantly, suggesting that the results of the two studies are not consistent even allowing for normal sampling fluctuations.

Effect Size Estimation

When we ask whether two studies are telling the same story, what we usually mean is whether the results (in terms of the estimated effect size) are reasonably consistent with each other or whether they are significantly heterogeneous. For the purpose of the present chapter the discussion is restricted to r as the effect size indicator, but analogous procedures are available for comparing such other effect size indicators as Cohen's (1977) d, Hedges's g, or differences between proportions (Hedges, 1982; Rosenthal & Rubin, 1982b).

For each of the two studies to be compared we compute the effect size r and find for each of these r's the associated Fisher z defined as $1/2\log_e [(1 + r)/(1 - r)]$. Tables to convert our obtained r's to Fisher z's are available in most introductory textbooks of statistics. Then, when N_1 and N_2 represent the number of sampling units (e.g., subjects) in each of our two studies, the quantity

$$\frac{Z_1 - Z_2}{\sqrt{\dfrac{1}{N_1 - 3} + \dfrac{1}{N_2 - 3}}} = Z \tag{11}$$

(Snedecor & Cochran, 1967, 1980).

Example 2.   Studies A and B yield results in opposite directions with effect sizes of $r = .60$ ($N = 15$) and $r = -.20$ ($N = 100$), respectively. The Fisher z's corresponding to these r's are .69 and $-.20$, respectively (note the opposite signs of the z's to correspond to the opposite signs of the r's). Then, from the preceding equation we have

$$\frac{Z_1 - Z_2}{\sqrt{\dfrac{1}{N_1 - 3} + \dfrac{1}{N_2 - 3}}} = \frac{(.69) - (-.20)}{\sqrt{\dfrac{1}{12} + \dfrac{1}{97}}} = 2.91$$

as the Z of the difference between the two effect sizes. The p value associated with a Z of 2.91 is .002 one-tailed or .004 two-tailed. These two effect sizes, then, differ significantly.

COMBINING TWO STUDIES

Significance Testing

After comparing the results of any two independent studies it is an easy matter also to combine the p levels of the two studies. Thus, we get an overall estimate of the probability that the two p levels might have been obtained if the null hypothesis of no relationship between X and Y were true. Many methods for combining the results of two or more studies are available and have been summarized elsewhere (Rosenthal, 1978, 1980, 1984, 1991). Here it is necessary to give only the simplest and most versatile of the procedures, the method of adding Z's called the *Stouffer method* by Mosteller and Bush (1954). This method, just like the method of comparing p values, asks us first to obtain accurate p levels for each of our two studies and then to find the Z corresponding to each of these p levels. Both p's must be given in one-tailed form, and the corresponding Z's will have the same sign if both studies show effects in the same direction. They will have different signs if the results are in the opposite direction. The sum of the two Z's when divided by $\sqrt{2}$, yields a new Z. This new Z corresponds to the p value that the results of the two studies combined, or results even further out in the same tail, could have occurred if the null hypothesis of no relationship between X and Y were true. Recapping,

$$\frac{Z_1 + Z_2}{\sqrt{2}} = Z \tag{12}$$

Should we want to do so, we could weight each Z by its df, its estimated quality, or by any other desired weights assigned before inspection of the data (Mosteller & Bush, 1954; Rosenthal, 1984, 1991).

Example 3.   Studies A and B yield results in opposite directions and both are significant. One p is .05, one-tailed, the other is .0000001, one-tailed but in the opposite tail. The Z's corresponding to these p's are found in a table of normal deviates to be -1.64 and 5.20, respectively (note the opposite signs to indicate results in opposite directions). Then from the preceding equation we have

$$\frac{Z_1 + Z_2}{\sqrt{2}} = \frac{(-1.64) + (5.20)}{1.41} = 2.52$$

as the Z of the combined results of studies A and B. The p value associated with a Z of 2.52 is .006 one-tailed or .012 two-tailed. Thus, the combined p supports the result of the more significant of the two results. If these were actual results we would want to be very cautious in interpreting our combined p both because the two p's were significant in opposite directions and because the two p's were so very significantly different from each other. We would try to discover what differences between studies A and B might have led to results so significantly different.

Effect Size Estimation

When we want to combine the results of two studies, we are as interested in the combined estimate of the effect size as we are in the combined probability. Just as was the case when we compared two effect size estimates, we consider r as our effect size estimate in the combining of effect sizes. However, we note that many other estimates are possible (e.g., Cohen's d, Hedges's g, or differences between proportions).

For each of the two studies to be combined, we compute r and the associated Fisher z and have

$$\frac{z_1 + z_2}{2} = \bar{z} \tag{13}$$

as the Fisher z corresponding to our mean r. We use an r to z or z to r table to look up the r associated with our mean $\bar{z}$. Tables are handier than computing r from z, but, if necessary, this can be done with the following equation: $r = (e^{2z} - 1)/(e^{2z} + 1)$. Should we want to do so, we could weight each z by its df, its estimated quality, or by any other weights assigned before inspection of the data (Snedecor & Cochran, 1967, 1980).

Example 4.   Studies A and B yield results in opposite directions, one $r = .80$, the other $r = -.30$. The Fisher z's corresponding to these r's are 1.10 and -0.31, respectively. From the preceding equation we have

$$\frac{z_1 + z_2}{2} = \frac{(1.10) + (-0.31)}{2} = .395$$

as the mean Fisher z. From a z to r table we find a z of .395 associated with an r of .38.

COMPARING THREE OR MORE STUDIES: DIFFUSE TESTS

Although we can do quite a lot in the way of comparing and combining the results of sets of studies with just the procedures given so far, it does happen often that we have three or more studies of the same relationship that we want to compare and/or combine. The purpose of this section is to present generalizations of the procedures given in the last section so that we can compare and combine the results of any number of studies. Again, the examples are hypothetical, constructed to illustrate a wide range of situations occurring in meta-analytic work in psychology or related disciplines. Often, of course, the number of studies entering into our analyses is larger than the number required to illustrate the various meta-analytic procedures.

Significance Testing

Given three or more p levels to compare we first find the standard normal deviate, Z, corresponding to each p level. All p levels must be one-tailed, and the corresponding Z's will have the same sign if all studies show effects in the same direction, but different signs if the results are not all in the same direction. The statistical significance of the heterogeneity of the Z's can be obtained from a χ^2 computed as follows (Rosenthal & Rubin, 1979a):

$$\Sigma(Z_j - \bar{Z})^2 = \chi^2 \text{ with } K - 1 \text{ } df. \tag{14}$$

In this equation Z_j is the Z for any one study, $\bar{Z}$ is the mean of all the Z's obtained, and K is the number of studies being combined.

Example 5. Studies A, B, C, and D yield one-tailed p values of .15, .05, .01, and .001, respectively. Study C, however, shows results opposite in direction from those of studies A, B, and D. From a normal table we find the Z's corresponding to the four p levels to be 1.04, 1.64, -2.33, and 3.09. (Note the negative sign for the Z associated with the result in the opposite direction.) Then, from the preceding equation we have

$$\Sigma(Z_j - \bar{Z})^2 = [(1.04) - (0.86)]^2 + [(1.64) - (0.86)]^2 + [(-2.33) - (0.86)]^2 + [(3.09) - (0.86)]^2 = 15.79$$

as our χ^2 value which for $K - 1 = 4 - 1 = 3$ df is significant at $p = .0013$. The four p values we compared, then, are clearly significantly heterogeneous.

Effect Size Estimation

Here we want to assess the statistical heterogeneity of three or more effect size estimates. We again restrict our discussion to r as the effect size estimator, though analogous procedures are available for comparing such other effect size estimators as Cohen's (1977) d, Hedges's g, or differences between proportions (Hedges, 1982; Rosenthal, 1984, 1991; Rosenthal & Rubin, 1982b).

For each of the three or more studies to be compared we compute the effect size r, its associated Fisher z, and $N - 3$, where N is the number of sampling units on which each r is based. Then the statistical significance of the heterogeneity of the r's can be obtained from a χ^2 computed as follows (Snedecor & Cochran, 1967, 1980):

$$\Sigma(N_j - 3)(z_j - \bar{z})^2 = \chi^2 \text{ with } K - 1 \text{ } df \tag{15}$$

In this equation z_j is the Fisher z corresponding to any r, and $\bar{z}$ is the weighted mean z, that is,

$$\bar{z} = \Sigma(N_j - 3)z_j/\Sigma(N_j - 3) \tag{16}$$

Example 6. Studies A, B, C, and D yield effect sizes of $r = .70$ ($N = 30$), $r = .45$ ($N = 45$), $r = .10$ ($N = 20$) and $r = -.15$ ($N = 25$), respectively. The Fisher z's corresponding to these r's are found from tables of Fisher z to be .87, .48, .10 and $-.15$, respectively. The weighted mean z is found from the equation just above to be

$$[27(.87) + 42(.48) + 17(.10) + 22(-.15)]/[27 + 42 + 17 + 22] = 42.05/108 = .39$$

Then, from Equation 15, we have

$$\Sigma(N_j - 3)(z_j - \bar{z})^2 = 27(.87 - .39)^2 + 42(.48 - .39)^2 + 17(.10 - .39)^2 + 22(-.15 - .39)^2 = 14.41$$

as our χ^2 value which for $K - 1 = 3$ df is significant at $p = .0024$. The four effect sizes we compared, then, are clearly significantly heterogeneous.

COMPARING THREE OR MORE STUDIES: FOCUSED TESTS (CONTRASTS)

Significance Testing

Although we know how to answer the diffuse question of the significance of the differences among a collection of significance levels, we are often able to ask a more focused and more useful question (for a general discussion of contrasts see Rosenthal & Rosnow, 1985). For example, given a set of p levels for studies of teacher expectancy effects, we might want to know whether results from younger children show greater degrees of statistical significance than do results from older children (Rosenthal, 1966; Rosenthal & Jacobson, 1968; Rosenthal & Rubin, 1978). (Normally we would have greater scientific interest in focused questions relevant to effect sizes than to significance levels.)

As was the case for diffuse tests, we begin by finding the standard normal deviate, Z, corresponding to each p level. All p levels must be one-tailed, and the corresponding Z's will have the same sign if all studies show effects in the same direction, but different signs if the results are not all in the same direction. The statistical significance of the contrast testing any specific hypothesis about the set of p levels can be obtained from a Z computed as follows (Rosenthal & Rubin, 1979a):

$$\frac{\sum \lambda_j Z_j}{\sqrt{\sum \lambda_j^2}} = Z \qquad (17)$$

In this equation λ_j is the theoretically derived prediction or contrast weight for any one study, chosen such that the sum of the λ_j's will be zero, and Z_j is the Z for any one study.

Example 7. Studies A, B, C, and D yield one-tailed p values of $1/10^7$, .0001, .21, and .007, respectively, all with results in the same direction. From a normal table we find the Z's corresponding to the four p levels to be 5.20, 3.72, .81, and 2.45. Suppose that studies A, B, C, and D had involved differing amounts of peer tutor contact such that studies A, B, C, and D had involved 8, 6, 4, and 2 hours of contact per month, respectively. We might, therefore, ask whether there was a linear relationship between number of hours of contact and statistical significance of the result favoring peer tutoring. The weights of a linear contrast involving four studies are 3, 1, −1, and −3. (These are obtained from a table of orthogonal polynomials, e.g., Rosenthal & Rosnow, 1984, 1985, 1991). Therefore, from the preceding equation we have

$$\frac{\sum \lambda_j Z_j}{\sqrt{\sum \lambda_j^2}} = \frac{(3)5.20 + (1)3.72 + (-1).81 + (-3)2.45}{\sqrt{(3)^2 + (1)^2 + (-1)^2 + (-3)^2}} = \frac{11.16}{\sqrt{20}} = 2.50$$

as our Z value, which is significant at $p = .006$, one-tailed. The four p values, then, tend to grow linearly more significant as the number of hours of contact time increases.

Effect Size Estimation

Here we want to ask a more focused question of a set of effect sizes. For example, given a set of effect sizes for studies of peer tutoring, we might want to know whether these effects are increasing or decreasing linearly with the number of hours of contact per month. We again restrict our discussion to r as the effect size estimator, though analogous procedures are available for comparing other effect size estimators (Rosenthal, 1984; Rosenthal & Rubin, 1982b).

As was the case for diffuse tests, we begin by computing the effect size r, its associated Fisher z, and $N - 3$, where N is the number of sampling units on which each r is based. The statistical significance of the contrast, testing any specific hypothesis about the set of effect sizes, can be obtained from a Z computed as follows (Rosenthal & Rubin, 1982b):

$$\frac{\sum \lambda_j z_j}{\sqrt{\sum \frac{\lambda_j^2}{w_j}}} = Z \qquad (18)$$

In this equation λ_j is the contrast weight determined from some theory for any one study, chosen such that the sum of the λ_j's will be zero. The z_j is the Fisher z for any one study and w_j is the inverse of the variance of the effect size for each study. For Fisher z transformations of the effect size r, the variance is $1/(N_j - 3)$ so $w_j = N_j - 3$.

Example 8.   Studies A, B, C, and D yield effect sizes of $r = .89, .76, .23,$ and $.59$, respectively, all with $N = 12$. The Fisher z's corresponding to these r's are found from tables of Fisher z to be 1.42, 1.00, .23, and .68, respectively. Suppose that studies A, B, C, and D had involved differing amounts of peer tutor contact such that studies A, B, C, and D had involved 8, 6, 4, and 2 hours of contact per month, respectively. We might, therefore, ask whether there was a linear relationship between number of hours of contact and size of effect favoring peer tutoring. As in example 7, the appropriate weights, or λ's, are 3, 1, -1, and -3. Therefore, from the preceding equation we have

$$\frac{\sum \lambda_j z_j}{\sqrt{\sum \frac{\lambda_j^2}{w_j}}} = \frac{(3)1.42 + (1)1.00 + (-1).23 + (-3).68}{\sqrt{\frac{(3)^2}{9} + \frac{(1)^2}{9} + \frac{(-1)^2}{9} + \frac{(-3)^2}{9}}} = \frac{2.99}{\sqrt{2.222}} = 2.01$$

as our Z value which is significant at $p = .022$, one-tailed. The four effect sizes, therefore, tend to grow linearly larger as the number of hours of contact time increases. Interpretation of this relationship must be very cautious. After all, studies were not assigned at random to the four conditions of contact hours. It is generally the case that variables moderating the magnitude of effects found should not be interpreted as giving strong evidence for any causal relationship. Moderator relationships can, however, be very valuable in suggesting the possibility of causal relationships, possibilities that can then be studied experimentally or as nearly experimentally as possible.

Before leaving these focused tests it should be noted that their use is more powerful than the more common procedure of counting each effect size or significance level as a single observation (e.g., Eagly & Carli, 1981; Hall, 1980; Rosenthal & Rubin, 1978; Smith, Glass, & Miller, 1980). In that procedure we might, for example, compute a correlation between the Fisher z values and the λ's of Example 8 to test the hypothesis of greater effect size being associated with greater contact time. Although that r is substantial (.77), it does not even approach significance because of the small number of df on which the r is based. The procedures for computing contrasts given in Equations 17 and 18 employ much more of the information available and, therefore, are less likely to lead to Type II errors.

COMBINING THREE OR MORE STUDIES

Significance Testing

After comparing the results of any set of three or more studies it is an easy matter also to combine the p levels of the set of studies to get an overall estimate of the probability that the set of p levels might have been obtained if the null hypothesis of no relationship between X and Y were true. Of the various methods available and described elsewhere in detail (Rosenthal, 1978, 1980, 1984, 1991) we present here only the generalized version of the method presented earlier in our discussion of combining the results of two groups.

This method requires only that we obtain a one-tailed Z for each of our p levels. The Z's disagreeing in direction from the bulk of the findings are given negative signs. Then, the sum of the Z's divided by the square root of the number (K) of studies yields a new statistic distributed as Z. Recapping,

$$\Sigma Z_j / \sqrt{K} = Z. \tag{19}$$

Should we want to do so, we could weight each of the Z's by its df, its estimated quality or any other desired weights so long as they are assigned prior to inspection of the results (Mosteller & Bush, 1954; Rosenthal, 1978, 1984, 1991).

Example 9. Studies A, B, C, and D yield one-tailed p values of .15, .05, .01, and .001, respectively. Study C, however, shows results opposite in direction from the results of the remaining studies. The four Z's associated with these four p's, then, are 1.04, 1.64, -2.33, and 3.09. From the preceding equation we have

$$\Sigma Z_j / \sqrt{K} = \frac{(1.04) + (1.64) + (-2.33) + (3.09)}{\sqrt{4}} = 1.72$$

as our new Z value, which has an associated p value of .043 one-tailed, or .086 two-tailed. This combined p supports the results of the majority of the individual studies. However, even if these p values (.043 and .086) were more significant, we would want to be very cautious about drawing any simple overall conclusion because of the very great heterogeneity of the four p values we were combining. Example 5, which employed the same p values, showed that this heterogeneity was significant at $p = .0013$. It should be emphasized, however, that this great heterogeneity of p values could be due to heterogeneity of effect sizes, heterogeneity of sample sizes, or both. To find out about the sources of heterogeneity, we would have to look carefully at the effect sizes and sample sizes of each of the studies involved.

Effect Size Estimation

When we combine the results of three or more studies we are as interested in the combined estimate of the effect size as we are in the combined probability. We follow here our earlier procedure of considering r as our effect size estimator while recognizing that many other estimates are possible. For each of the three or more studies to be combined we compute r and the associated Fisher z and have

$$\Sigma z / K = \bar{z} \qquad (20)$$

as the Fisher $\bar{z}$ corresponding to our mean r (where K refers to the number of studies combined). We use a table of Fisher z to find the r associated with our mean z. Should we want to give greater weight to larger studies we could weight each z by its df $(N - 3)$ (Snedecor & Cochran, 1967, 1980), or by any other desired weights.

Example 10. Studies A, B, C, and D yield effect sizes of $r = .70, .45, .10,$ and $-.15$, respectively. The Fisher z values corresponding to these r's are .87, .48, .10, and $-.15$, respectively. Then, from the preceding equation we have

$$\sum z/K = \frac{(.87) + (.48) + (.10) + (-.15)}{4} = .32$$

as our mean Fisher z. From a table of Fisher z values we find a z of .32 to correspond to an r of .31. Just as in the previous example of combined p levels, however, we would want to be very cautious in our interpretation of this combined effect size. If the r's we have just averaged were based on substantial sample sizes, as was the case in Example 6, they would be significantly heterogeneous. Therefore, averaging without special thought and comment would be inappropriate.

COMPARING AND COMBINING RESULTS
THAT ARE NOT INDEPENDENT

In all the meta-analytic procedures we have discussed so far it has been assumed that the studies being compared or combined were separate, independent studies. That is, we have assumed that different subjects (or other sampling units) were found in the studies being compared or summarized. Sometimes, however, the same subjects (or other sampling units) contribute data to two or more studies or to two or more dependent variables within the same study. In such cases the results of the two or more studies or the results based on two or more dependent variables are not independent and the meta-analytic procedures we have described so far cannot be applied without adjustment.

Two common methods for summarizing the results of a single study with multiple effect sizes have been simply to compute the mean and/or median of the effect sizes. Both of these procedures are quite conservative in practice, however (Rosenthal & Rubin, 1986). More accurate and more useful procedures for comparing and combining nonindependent results have been described elsewhere by Strube (1985) for the case of significance levels and by Rosenthal and Rubin (1986) for the case of effect sizes.

THE FILE DRAWER PROBLEM

Both behavioral researchers and statisticians have long suspected that the studies published in the behavioral and social sciences are a biased sample of the studies that are actually carried out (Bakan, 1967; McNemar, 1960; Smart, 1964; Sterling, 1959). The extreme view of this problem, the *file drawer problem,* is that the journals are filled with the 5% of the studies that show Type I errors, while the file drawers back at the lab are filled with the 95% of the studies that show nonsignificant (e.g., $p > .05$) results (Rosenthal, 1979; Rosenthal & Rubin, 1988; Wachter, 1988).

In the past there was very little we could do to assess the net effect of studies tucked away in file drawers that did not make the magic .05 level (Nelson, Rosenthal, & Rosnow, 1986; Rosenthal & Gaito, 1963, 1964). Now, however, although no definitive solution to the problem is available, we can establish reasonable boundaries on the problem and estimate the degree of damage to any research conclusion that could be done by the file drawer problem. The fundamental idea in coping with the file drawer problem is simply to calculate the number of studies averaging null results that must be in the file drawers before the overall probability of a Type I error can be just brought to any desired level of significance, say $p = .05$. This number of filed studies, or the tolerance for future null results, is then evaluated for whether such a tolerance level is small enough to threaten the overall conclusion drawn by the reviewer. If the overall level of significance of the research review will be brought down to the level of *just significant* by the addition of just a few more null results, the finding is not resistant to the file drawer threat.

Computation

To find the number (X) of new, filed, or unretrieved studies averaging null results required to bring the new overall p to any desired level, say, just significant at $p = .05$ ($Z = 1.645$), one simply writes:

$$1.645 = k\bar{Z}_k/\sqrt{k + X}$$

where k is the number of studies combined and $\bar{Z}_k$ is the mean Z obtained for the k studies.

Squaring both sides and rearranging shows that

$$X = (k/2.706)[k(\bar{Z}_k)^2 - 2.706]. \tag{21}$$

An alternative formula that may be more convenient when the sum of the Z's (ΣZ) is given rather than the mean Z, is as follows:

$$X = [(\Sigma Z)^2/2.706] - k. \tag{22}$$

One method based on counting rather than adding Z's may be easier to compute and can be employed when exact p levels are not available. If X is the number of new studies required to bring the overall p to .50 (not to .05), s is the number of summarized studies significant at $p < .05$ and n is the number of summarized studies not significant at .05, then

$$X = 19s - n. \tag{23}$$

Another conservative alternative when exact p levels are not available is to set $Z = .00$ for any nonsignificant result and to set $Z = 1.645$ for any result significant at $p < .05$.

The previous equations all assume that each of the k studies is independent of all other $k - 1$ studies, at least in the sense of employing different sampling units. There are other senses of independence, however. For example, we can think of two or more studies conducted in a given laboratory as less independent than two or more studies conducted in different laboratories. Such nonindependence can be assessed by such procedures as intraclass correlations. Whether nonindependence of this type serves to increase Type I or Type II errors appears to depend in part on the relative magnitude of the Z's obtained from the studies that are "correlated" or "too similar." If the correlated Z's are, on the average, as high (or higher) as the grand mean Z corrected for nonindependence, the combined Z we compute treating all studies as independent will be too large. If the correlated Z's are, on the average, clearly low relative to the grand mean Z

corrected for nonindependence, the combined Z we compute treating all studies as independent will tend to be too small.

Illustration

In 1978, 345 experiments examining the effects of interpersonal self-fulfilling prophecies were summarized (Rosenthal & Rubin, 1978). The mean Z of these studies was 1.22, k was 345, and Z for the studies combined was 22.66 = 345 $(1.22)/(345)^{1/2}$.

How many new, filed, or unretrieved studies (X) would be required to bring this very large Z down to a barely significant level ($Z = 1.645$)? From Equation 21,

$$X = (345/2.706)[345(1.22)^2 - 2.706] = 65,123$$

One finds that 65,123 studies averaging null results ($\bar{Z} = .00$) must be crammed into file drawers before one would conclude that the overall results were due to sampling bias in the studies summarized by the reviewer. In a more recent summary of the same area of research (prepared for this chapter) the mean Z of 443 studies was 1.30, k was 443, and X was 122,778. Thus, over 120,000 unreported studies averaging a null result would have to exist somewhere before the overall results could reasonably be ascribed to sampling bias.

At the present time no firm guidelines can be given as to what constitutes an unlikely number of unretrieved and/or unpublished studies. For some areas of research 100 or even 500 unpublished and unretrieved studies may be a plausible state of affairs whereas for others even 10 or 20 seems unlikely. Probably any rough and ready guide should be based partly on k so that as more studies are known it becomes more plausible that other studies in that area may be in those file drawers. Perhaps we could regard as robust to the file drawer problem any combined results for which the tolerance level (X) reaches 5 k + 10. That seems a conservative but reasonable tolerance level; the 5 k portion suggests that it is unlikely that the file drawers have more than five times as many studies as the reviewer, and the +10 sets the minimum number of studies that could be filed away at 15 (when $k = 1$).

It appears that more and more reviewers of research literatures will be estimating average effect sizes and combined p's of the studies they summarize. It would be very helpful to readers if for each combined p they presented, reviewers also gave the tolerance for future null results associated with their overall significance level.

It is of interest to note that recent research suggests that the magnitude of the file drawer problem may be somewhat less than had been feared (Rosenthal & Rubin, 1988). Although studies published at the time of a meta-analysis are more likely to yield significant results than are studies unpublished at the time of the meta-analysis, this bias may well shrink over time because a very large proportion of the originally unpublished studies may eventually be published. In a large meta-analysis, therefore, it may be useful to conduct a subanalysis with a cut-off date for study retrieval approximately 5 years earlier than the date of the actual meta-analysis. It is likely that the file drawer problem will be lessened appreciably at least for this subanalysis (Rosenthal & Rubin, 1988).

THE EVALUATION OF EFFECT SIZES

Most of this chapter has so far been concerned with concepts and methods designed to help us improve the estimates of effect sizes and of significance levels of our cumulating evidence. In this section we try to evaluate more usefully the practical meaning of any effect size estimate and especially those that we derive from our meta-analytic procedures.

Despite the growing awareness of the importance of estimating effect sizes there is a problem in evaluating various effect size estimators from the point of view of practical usefulness (Cooper, 1981). Rosenthal and Rubin (1979b; 1982a) found that neither experienced behavioral researchers nor experienced statisticians had a good intuitive feel for the practical meaning of such common effect size estimators as r^2, omega^2, epsilon^2, and similar estimates.

The Physicians' Aspirin Study

At a special meeting held on December 18, 1987, it was decided to end prematurely, a randomized double blind experiment on the effects of aspirin on reducing heart attacks (Steering Committee of the Physicians' Health Study Research Group, 1988). This unusual termination occurred because it had become so clear that aspirin prevented heart attacks (and deaths from heart attacks), that it would be unethical to continue to give half the physician research subjects a placebo. And what was the magnitude of the experimental effect that was so dramatic as to call for the termination of this research? Was r^2 .90, or .80, or .70, or .60, so that the corresponding r's would have been .95, .89, .84, or .77? Was r^2 .50, .40, .30, or even .20, so that the corresponding r's would have been .71, .63, .55, or .45? No, none of these. Actually r^2 was .0011, with a corresponding r of .034.

Table 20.3 shows the results of the aspirin study in terms of raw counts, percentages, and as a Binomial Effect Size Display (BESD). This display is a way of showing the practical importance of any effect indexed by a correlation coefficient. The correlation is shown to be the simple difference in outcome rates between the experimental and the control groups in this standard table that always adds up to column totals of 100 and row totals of 100 (Rosenthal & Rubin, 1982a).

This type of result seen in the physicians' aspirin study is not at all unusual in

TABLE 20.3
Effects of Aspirin on Heart Attacks Among 22,071 Physicians

	Heart Attack	No Heart Attack	Total
I. *Raw Counts*			
Aspirin	104	10,933	11,037
Placebo	189	10,845	11,034
Total	293	21,778	22,071
II. *Percentages*			
Aspirin	0.94	99.06	100
Placebo	1.71	98.29	100
Total	1.33	98.67	100
III. *Binomial Effect Size Display*			
Aspirin	48.3	51.7	100
Placebo	51.7	48.3	100
Total	100	100	200

biomedical research. Some years earlier, on October 29, 1981, the National Heart, Lung, and Blood Institute discontinued its placebo-controlled study of propranolol because results were so favorable to the treatment that it would be unethical to continue withholding the life-saving drug from the control patients. Once again the effect size r was .04, and the leading digits of the r^2 were .00! As behavioral researchers we are not used to thinking of r's of .04 as reflecting effect sizes of practical importance. But when we think of an r of .04 as reflecting a 4% decrease in heart attacks, the interpretation given r in a Binomial Effect Size Display, the r does not appear to be quite so small; especially if we can count ourselves among the 4 per 100 who manage to survive (Rosenthal, 1984, 1991).

Additional Results

Table 20.4 gives three further examples of Binomial Effect Size Displays. In a recent study of 4,462 army veterans of the Vietnam War era (1965–1971), the correlation between having served in Vietnam (rather than elsewhere) and having suffered from alcohol abuse or dependence was .07 (Centers for Disease Control, 1988). The top display of Table 20.4 shows that the difference between the problem rates of 53.5 and 46.5 per 100 is equal to the correlation coefficient of .07.

The center display of Table 20.4 shows the results of a study of the effects of the drug Azidothymidine (AZT) on the survival of 282 patients suffering from acquired immunodeficiency syndrome (AIDS) or AIDS-related complex (ARC) (Barnes, 1986). This result of a correlation of .23 between survival and receiving AZT (an r^2 of .054) was so dramatic as to lead to the premature termination of the clinical trial on the ethical grounds that it would be improper to continue to give placebo to the control group patients.

TABLE 20.4
Other Examples of Binomial Effect Size Displays

I. *Vietnam Service and Alcohol Problems* ($r = .07$)

	Problem	No Problem	Total
Vietnam Veteran	53.5	46.5	100
Non-Vietnam Veteran	46.5	53.5	100
Total	100	100	200

II. *AZT in the Treatment of AIDS* ($r = .23$)

	Death	Survival	Total
AZT	38.5	61.5	100
Placebo	61.5	38.5	100
Total	100	100	200

III. *Benefits of Psychotherapy* ($r = .32$)[a]

	Less Benefit	Greater Benefit	Total
Psychotherapy	34	66	100
Control	66	34	100
Total	100	100	200

[a]The analogous r for 443 studies of interpersonal expectancy effects was .30 (Rosenthal, prepared for this chapter).

As a footnote to this display let me add the result of an informal poll of some physicians spending the year 1988–1989 at the Center for Advanced Study in the Behavioral Sciences. They were asked to tell of some medical breakthrough that was of very great practical importance. Their consensus was that the breakthrough was the effect of cyclosporine in increasing the probability that the body would not reject an organ transplant and the recipient patient would not die. A multicenter randomized experiment was published in 1983 (Canadian Multicentre Transplant Study Group, 1983). The results of this breakthrough experiment were less dramatic than the results of the AZT study. For the dependent variable of organ rejection the effect size r was .19 ($r^2 = .036$); for the dependent variable of patient survival the effect size r was .15 ($r^2 = .022$).

The bottom display of Table 20.4 shows the results of a famous meta-analysis of psychotherapy outcome studies reported by Smith and Glass (1977). An eminent critic believed that the results of their analysis sounded the "death knell" for psychotherapy because of the modest size of the effect. This modest effect size was an r of .32 accounting for "only 10% of the variance."

Examination of the bottom display of Table 20.4 shows that it is not very realistic to label as "modest indeed" an effect size equivalent to increasing a success rate from 34% to 66% (for example, reducing a death rate or a failure rate from 66% to 34%). Indeed, as we have seen, the dramatic effects of AZT were substantially smaller ($r = .23$), and the "breakthrough" effects of cyclosporine were smaller still ($r = .19$).

Telling How Well We're Doing

The Binomial Effect Size Display is a useful way to display the practical magnitude of an effect size regardless of whether the dependent variable is dichotomous or continuous (Rosenthal & Rubin, 1982a). An especially useful feature of the display is how easily we can go from the display to an r (just take the difference between the success rates of the experimental versus the control group) and how easily we can go from an effect size r to the display (just compute the treatment success rate as .50 plus one-half of r and the control success rate as .50 minus one-half of r).

One effect of the standard use of a display procedure such as the Binomial Effect Size Display to index the practical value of our research results would be to give us more useful and more realistic assessments of how well we are really doing as researchers in the psychological and related sciences. Employment of the Binomial Effect Size Display has, in fact, shown that we are doing considerably better than we may have thought we were doing. It would help keep us better apprised of how we are doing in our sciences if we routinely translated the typical answers to our research questions to effect sizes such as r (and to its equivalent displays) and compared them to other well-established findings such as those shown in Tables 20.3 and 20.4.

THE CONCEPT OF SUCCESSFUL REPLICATION

There is a long tradition in psychology of our urging one another to replicate each other's research. But, although we have been very good at calling for replications we have not been very good at deciding when a replication has been successful.

TABLE 20.5
Common Model of Successful Replication:
Dichotomous Judgment Based on Significance Testing

		First Study	
		$p > .05$*	$p < .05$
		A	B
Second Study	$p < .05$[a]	Failure to Replicate	Successful Replication
		C	D
	$p > .05$	Failure to Establish Effect	Failure to Replicate

*By convention .05, but could be any other given level, e.g., .01.
[a]In the same tail as the results of the first study.

The issue we now address is: When shall a study be deemed successfully replicated?

Successful replication is ordinarily taken to mean that a null hypothesis that has been rejected at time 1 is rejected again, and with the same direction of outcome, on the basis of a new study at time 2. The basic model of this usage can be seen in Table 20.5. The results of the first study are described dichotomously as $p < .05$ or $p > .05$ (or some other critical level, e.g., .01). Each of these two possible outcomes is further dichotomized as to the results of the second study as $p < .05$ or $p > .05$. Thus, cells A and D of Table 20.5 are examples of failure to replicate because one study was significant and the other was not. Let us examine more closely a specific example of such a "failure to replicate."

PSEUDO-FAILURES TO REPLICATE

The Saga of Smith and Jones

Smith published the results of an experiment in which a certain treatment procedure was predicted to improve performance. She reported results significant at $p < .05$ in the predicted direction. Jones published a rebuttal to Smith claiming a failure to replicate.

Table 20.6 shows the results of these two experiments in greater detail. Smith's results were more significant than Jones's, to be sure, but the studies were in perfect agreement as to their estimated sizes of effect as defined either by Cohen's d [(Mean$_1$ − Mean$_2$)/σ] or by r, the correlation between group membership and performance score. Not only did the effect sizes of the two studies agree, but even the significance levels of .03 and .30 did not differ very significantly: $(Z_{.03} - Z_{.30})/\sqrt{2} = (2.17 - 1.03)/\sqrt{2} = Z = .81, p = .42$. Table 20.6 shows very clearly that Jones was very much in error when he claimed that his study failed to replicate that of Smith. Such errors are made very frequently in most areas of psychology and the other behavioral and social sciences, a very recent example having been pointed out by Weinberger (1989). The final column of Table 20.6 shows that the combined result of both experiments is associated with a more significant t and with a smaller confidence interval (for the difference between the means and for the effect size r) than is either of the individual studies.

On the Odds Against Replicating Significant Results

A related error often found in the behavioral and social sciences is the implicit assumption that if an effect is "real," we should therefore expect it to be found significant again on replication. Nothing could be further from the truth.

TABLE 20.6
Illustrative Results of an Experiment and Its Replication

	Investigator		
	Smith	Jones	Combined
Treatment Mean	.38	.36	.376
Control Mean	.26	.24	.256
Difference	.12	.12	.120
t	2.21	1.06	2.45
df	18	18	96
Two-tail p	.03	.30	.02
Effect size d^a	.50	.50	.50
Effect size r^b	.24	.24	.24
Standard normal deviate (Z)	2.17[c]	1.03[c]	2.40
95% Confidence intervals			
Mean differences			
From	.01	−.12	.02
To	.23	.36	.22
Effect size r's			
From	.02	−.23	.04
To	.44	.62	.42

[a]Obtained from $2t\sqrt{df}$.
[b]Obtained from $\sqrt{t^2/(t^2 + df)}$.
[c]These significance levels differ at $Z = .81$, $p = .42$ (from $(Z_1 - Z_2)/\sqrt{2}$).

Suppose there is in nature a real effect with a magnitude of $d = .50$ (i.e., [Mean$_1$ − Mean$_2$]/σ = .50 σ units), or, equivalently, $r = .24$ (a difference in success rate of 62% versus 38%, as we saw earlier). Then suppose an investigator studies this effect with an N of 64 subjects or so, giving the researcher a level of statistical power of .50, a very common level of power for behavioral researchers of the last 30 years (Cohen, 1962; Sedlmeier & Gigerenzer, 1989). Even though a d of .50 or an r of .24 is a very important effect (as we saw earlier), there is only one chance in four that both the original investigator and a replicator will obtain results significant at the .05 level. If there were two replications of the original study there would be only one chance in eight that all three studies would be significant, even though we know the effect in nature is very real and very important.

If five studies investigated this phenomenon, there is only a 50:50 chance that three of more of them would find significant results. In short, given the levels of statistical power at which we normally operate, we have no right to expect the proportion of significant results that we typically do expect, even if in nature there is a very real and very important effect.

PSEUDO-SUCCESSFUL REPLICATIONS

Returning now to Table 20.5, we focus attention on cell B, the cell of "successful replication." Suppose that two investigators both rejected the null hypothesis at $p < .05$ with both results in the same direction. Suppose further, however, that in one study the effect size r was .90 whereas in the other study the effect size r was only .10, significantly smaller than the r of .90. In this case our interpretation is more complex. We have indeed had a successful replication of the rejection of the null hypothesis but we have not come even close to a successful replication of the effect size.

SUCCESSFUL REPLICATION
OF TYPE II ERROR

Cell C of Table 20.5 represents the situation in which both studies failed to reject the null hypothesis. Under those conditions investigators might conclude that there was no relationship between the variables investigated. Such a conclusion could be very much in error, the more so as the power of the two studies was low (Cohen, 1977; 1988; Rosenthal, 1986b). If power levels of the two studies (assuming medium effect sizes in the population) were very high, say .90 or .95, then two failures to obtain a significant relationship would provide evidence that the effect investigated was not likely to be a very large effect. If power calculations had been made assuming a very small effect size, two failures to reject the null while not providing strong evidence for the null would at least suggest that the size of the effect in the population was probably quite modest.

If sample sizes of the two studies failing to reject the null were small so that power to detect all but the largest effects was low, very little could be concluded from two failures to reject except that the effect sizes were unlikely to be enormous. For example, two investigators with N's of 20 and 40, respectively, find results not significant at $p < .05$. The effect sizes *phi* (i.e., r for dichotomous variables) were .29 and .20, respectively, and both p's were approximately .20. The combined p of these two results, however, is .035 $[(Z_1 + Z_2)/\sqrt{2} = Z]$, and the mean effect size in the mid-.20's is not trivial.

CONTRASTING VIEWS OF REPLICATION

The traditional, not very useful view of replication modeled in Table 20.5 has two primary characteristics: (a) It focuses on significance level as the relevant summary statistic of a study, and (b) It makes its evaluation of whether replication has been successful in a dichotomous fashion. For example, replications are successful if both or neither $p < .05$ (or .01, etc.) and they are unsuccessful if one $p < .05$ (or .01, etc.) and the other $p > .05$ (or .01, etc.). Psychologists' reliance on a dichotomous decision procedure accompanied by an untenable discontinuity of credibility in results varying in p levels has been well documented (Nelson, Rosenthal, & Rosnow, 1986; Rosenthal & Gaito, 1963, 1964).

The newer, more useful views of replication success have two primary characteristics: (a) A focus on effect size as the more important summary statistic of a study with only a relatively minor interest in the statistical significance level, and (b) An evaluation of whether replication has been successful made in a continuous fashion. For example, two studies are not said to be successful or unsuccessful replicates of each other, but rather the degree of failure to replicate is specified. Table 20.7 shows three sets of replications. Replication set A shows two results both rejecting the null but with a difference in effect sizes of .30 in units of r or .35 in units of Fisher's Z transformation of r (Cohen, 1977, 1988; Rosenthal & Rosnow, 1984; Snedecor & Cochran, 1980). That difference, in units of r or Fisher's Z is the degree of failure to replicate. The fact that both studies were able to reject the null and at exactly the same p level is simply a function of sample size. Replication set B shows two studies with different p values, one significant at $<.05$, the other not significant. However, the two effect size estimates are in excellent agreement. We would say, accordingly, that replication set B shows more successful replication than does replication set A. Replication set C shows two studies differing markedly in both level of significance and magnitude (and direction) of effect size. Replication set C, then, is a not very subtle example of a clear failure to replicate.

It should be noted that the values of Table 20.7 were chosen so that the combined probability of the two studies of sets A, B, and C would all be identical to one another; $(Z_1 + Z_2)/\sqrt{2} = Z$ of 2.77, $p = .0028$, one-tailed.

TABLE 20.7
Comparison of Three Sets of Replications

	Replication Sets					
	A		B		C	
	Study 1	Study 2	Study 1	Study 2	Study 1	Study 2
N	96	15	98	27	12	32
p (two-tail)	.05	.05	.01	.18	.000001	.33
$Z(p)$	1.96	1.96	2.58	1.34	4.89	−0.97
r	.20	.50	.26	.26	.72	−.18
$Z(r)$	.20	.55	.27	.27	.90	−.18
Cohen's $q(Z_{r_1} - Z_{r_2})$		−.35		.00		1.08

SOME METRICS OF THE SUCCESS
OF REPLICATION

Once we adopt a view of the success of replication as a function of similarity of effect sizes obtained, we can become more precise in our assessments of the success of replication.

The Replication Diagonal

Figure 20.1 shows the "replication plane" generated by crossing the results of the first study conducted (expressed in units of the effect size r) by the results of the second study conducted. All perfect replications, those in which the effect sizes are identical in the two studies, fall on a diagonal rising from the lower left corner $(-1.00, -1.00)$ to the upper right corner $(+1.00, +1.00)$. The results of replication set B from Table 20.7 are shown to fall exactly on the diagonal of perfect replication $(+.26, +.26)$. The results of replication set A are shown to fall somewhat above the line representing perfect replication. Figure 20.1 shows that although set B reflects more successful replication than set A, the latter is also located fairly close to the line and is, therefore, a fairly successful replica-

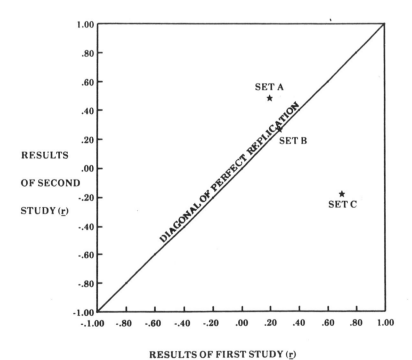

RESULTS OF FIRST STUDY ($\underline{r}$)

FIG. 20.1. The replication plane.

tion set as well. The results of replication set C, however, are shown to fall rather far from the diagonal of perfect replication. When there are more than two studies for each replication set, they can be plotted pairwise on the replication plane and different replication sets can be compared visually.

Cohen's q

An alternative to the indexing of the success of replication by the difference between obtained effect size r's is to transform the r's to Fisher's Z's before taking the difference. Fisher's Z metric is distributed nearly normally and can thus be used in setting confidence intervals and testing hypotheses about r's, whereas r's distribution is skewed and the more so as the population value of r moves further from zero. Cohen's q is especially useful for testing the significance of difference between two obtained effect size r's. This is accomplished by means of the fact that

$$q \bigg/ \sqrt{\frac{1}{N_1 - 3} + \frac{1}{N_2 - 3}}$$

is distributed as Z, the standard normal deviate, as noted earlier in this chapter. When there are more than two effect size r's to be evaluated for their variability (i.e., heterogeneity) we can simply compute the standard deviation (S) among the r's or their Fisher Z equivalents. A test of significance of heterogeneity of these Fisher Z's was described earlier in this chapter.

Meta-Analytic Metrics

As the number of replications for a given research question grows, a full assessment of the success of the replicational effort requires the application of meta-analytic procedures. An informative summary of the meta-analysis is the stem-and-leaf display of the effect sizes found in the meta-analysis (Tukey, 1977). A more compact summary of the effect sizes might be Tukey's (1977) box plot, which gives the highest and lowest obtained effect sizes along with those found at the 25th, 50th, and 75th percentiles. For single index values of the consistency of the effect sizes, one could employ (a) the range of effect sizes found between the 75th (Q_3) and 25th (Q_1) percentile, (b) some standard fraction of that range (e.g., half or three-quarters), (c) S, the standard deviation of the effect sizes, or (d) SE, the standard error of the effect sizes.

Table 20.8 illustrates a stem-and-leaf plot of the mean effect sizes (d) found in 16 categories of studies of interpersonal expectancy effects (Rosenthal & Rubin, 1978, p. 381). Tukey (1977) developed this form of display so as to preserve the raw data but display it as a frequency distribution at the same time. The top value is read as 2.0 (the stem) plus 8 (the leaf) or 2.08. The three entries beginning with the stem of 0.5, therefore, are 0.52, 0.53, and 0.56.

TABLE 20.8
Stem-and-Leaf Plot of Mean Effect Sizes (*d*) for Sixteen Categories
of Studies of Interpersonal Expectancy Effects

Stem	Leaf
2.0	8
1.9	
1.8	2
1.7	
1.6	
1.5	
1.4	
1.3	5
1.2	
1.1	
1.0	0
0.9	
0.8	9
0.7	6
0.6	
0.5	2 3 6
0.4	4
0.3	1
0.2	0 1
0.1	1 5
0.0	Average Value expected if H_0 were true
−0.0	3

Table 20.9 summarizes the central tendency, significance tests, confidence intervals, and variability information of the stem-and-leaf display. The effect sizes summarized for this research are in units of Cohen's *d* (Cohen, 1988) defined as the difference between the means of the experimental and control conditions divided by the common σ. Other indices of effect size could have been used equally well, of course.

The One-Sample Effect Size Index: π

These effect size indices are not directly applicable, however, to areas of research employing one-sample studies in which performance is compared to some theoretical value; often the level expected if performance is no better than that expected if the null hypothesis were true. In so-called Ganzfeld studies, for example, subjects are asked to guess which of four or five or six stimuli had been "transmitted" by an agent or sender (Harris & Rosenthal, 1988; Honorton, 1985; Hyman, 1985; Rosenthal, 1986a). A measure of effect size, π, has been developed for this type of one-sample situation (Rosenthal & Rubin, 1989). This index

TABLE 20.9
Statistical Summary of Sixteen Categories
of Expectancy Effect Studies

Central tendency (d)		*Variability*	
Unweighted mean	.68	Maximum	2.08
Weighted[a] mean	.70	Quartile 3 (Q_3)	0.97
Median	.52	Median (Q_2)	0.52
Proportion > 0.00	.94	Quartile 1 (Q_1)	0.20
		Minimum	−0.03
Significance tests		$Q_3 - Q_1$	0.77
Combined Stouffer Z	22.66	$\sigma:[.75(Q_3 - Q_1)]$	0.58
t test of mean d	4.42	S	0.62
Z of proportion > .00	3.50	$S/\sqrt{N}$(S.E.)	0.15
		Robustness ($\bar{x}/s$)	1.10
Confidence intervals[b]			
	From	*To*	
95%	.35	1.01	
99%	.23	1.13	
99.5%	.18	1.19	

[a]By number of studies per category; total number of studies =
345.
[b]Based on N of 16 categories.

is expressed as the proportion of correct guesses if there had been only two
choices to choose from. When there are more than two choices, π converts the
proportion of hits to the proportion of hits made if there had been only two
equally likely choices:

$$\pi = \frac{P(k - 1)}{P(k - 2) + 1}$$

where p = the raw proportion of hits and k is simply the number of alternative
choices available.

Table 20.10 shows the stem-and-leaf plot of effect sizes (π) for 28 Ganzfeld
studies and Table 20.11 shows the statistical summary of these data.

As a slightly more complex index of the stability, replicability, or clarity of the
average effect size found in the set of replicates, one could employ the mean
effect size divided either by its standard error ($S\sqrt{N}$ where N is the total number
of replicates), or simply by S. The latter index of mean effect size divided by its
standard deviation (S) is the reciprocal of the coefficient of variation or a kind of
coefficient of robustness.

The Coefficient of Robustness of Replication

Although the standard error of the mean effect size along with confidence intervals placed around the mean effect size are of great value (Rosenthal & Rubin,
1978), it will sometimes be useful to employ a robustness coefficient that does

TABLE 20.10
Stem-and-Leaf Plot of Effect Sizes (π)
for 28 "Direct Hit" Ganzfeld Studies[a]

Stem	Leaf
90	5 6
90	
80	
80	2
70	7
70	0 1 1 1 1 2
60	7 7 8 8 8 9
60	0 0 2
50	5 7
50	4 4 Average Value expected if H_0 were true
40	7
40	3 4
30	
30	
20	5
20	
10	
10	
00	
00	0

[a]Probability of a direct hit = .50 for the effect size index π.

TABLE 20.11
Statistical Summary of 28 "Direct Hit" Ganzfeld Studies

Central tendency (π)		Variability	
Unweighted mean	.62	Maximum	.96
Weighted[a] mean	.62	Quartile 3 (Q_3)	.71
Median	.68	Median (Q_2)	.68
Proportion > .50	.82	Quartile 1 (Q_1)	.54
		Minimum	.00
Significance tests		$Q_3 - Q_1$	.17
Combined Stouffer Z	6.60	$\hat{\sigma}$:[.75($Q_3 - Q_1$)]	.13
t test of mean $\pi - .50$	3.39	S	.19
Z of proportion > .50	3.40	$S/\sqrt{N}$(SE)	.04
Confidence intervals[b]		Robustness $\left(\dfrac{\pi - .50}{S}\right)$	.63
	From To		
95%	.55 .70		
99%	.52 .72		
99.5%	.51 .73		

[a]By number of trials per study: total number of trials = 835.
[b]Based on N of 28 studies.

not increase simply as a function of the increasing number of replications. Thus, if we want to compare two research areas for their robustness, adjusting for the difference in number of replications in each research area, we may prefer the robustness coefficient defined as the reciprocal of the coefficient of variation.

The utility of this coefficient is based on two ideas: First, replication success, clarity, or robustness depends on the homogeneity of the obtained effect size; and second, it also depends on the unambiguity or clarity of the directionality of the result. Thus, a set of replications grows in robustness as the variance of the effect sizes decreases and as the distance of the mean effect size from zero increases. Incidentally, the mean may be weighted, unweighted, or trimmed (Tukey, 1977). Indeed, it need not be the mean at all but any measure of location or central tendency (e.g., the median).

Table 20.12 has been prepared to give some feel for the practical meaning of several degrees of variability (S) for seven sets of five replicates each, assuming a mean effect size of zero. For our effect size indicator we have employed the Fisher Z transformation of the correlation coefficient r. When the range of the five Zr's is only from $-.02$ to $+.02$, $S = .016$; when the range is from -1.00 to $+1.00$, $S = .791$. Table 20.13 shows the replication robustness coefficients for each of the seven degrees of variability (S) for each of four levels of mean effect size (Zr): .10, .30, .50, and .70.

There are no intrinsic meanings to any particular robustness coefficients. Instead, they are intended to be used to compare different research domains for their replicational robustness in a merely heuristic way. The robustness coefficient for the data of Tables 20.8 and 20.9 was $.68/.62 = 1.10$. When employing the effect size index π we define the robustness coefficient for π as $(\pi - .50)/S$ which yields $(.62 - .50)/.19 = .63$ for the data of Tables 20.10 and 20.11.

TABLE 20.12
Seven Degrees of Variability (S) of Effect Sizes (Zr)
Around a Mean Effect Size of 0.00

Replicate	Degree of Variability						
	Set 1	Set 2	Set 3	Set 4	Set 5	Set 6	Set 7
	.02	.10	.20	.40	.60	.80	1.00
	.01	.05	.10	.20	.30	.40	.50
	.00	.00	.00	.00	.00	.00	.00
	−.01	−.05	−.10	−.20	−.30	−.40	−.50
	−.02	−.10	−.20	−.40	−.60	−.80	−1.00
S	.016	.079	.158	.316	.474	.632	.791
Range	.04	.20	.40	.80	1.20	1.60	2.00
Equal Steps of	.01	.05	.10	.20	.30	.40	.50

TABLE 20.13
Replication Robustness Coefficients for Four
Levels of Mean Effect Size (*Zr*) and Six
Degrees of Variability of Effect Size (*S*)

	Mean Effect Size (*Zr*)			
S	*.10*	*.30*	*.50*	*.70*
.016	6.25	18.75	31.25	43.75
.079	1.27	3.80	6.33	8.86
.158	0.63	1.90	3.16	4.43
.316	0.32	0.95	1.58	2.22
.474	0.21	0.63	1.05	1.48
.632	0.16	0.47	0.79	1.11
.791	0.13	0.38	0.63	0.88

WHAT SHOULD BE REPORTED?

Effect Sizes and Significance Tests

If we are to take seriously our newer view of the meaning of the success of replications, what should be reported by authors of papers seen to be replications of earlier studies? Clearly, reporting the results of tests of significance will not be sufficient. The effect size of the replication and of the original study must be reported. It is not crucial which particular effect size is employed, but the same effect size should be reported for the replication and the original study. Complete discussions of various effect sizes and when they are useful are available from Cohen (1977, 1988) and elsewhere (e.g., Rosenthal, 1984, 1991). If the original study and its replication are reported in different effect size units these can usually be translated to one another (Cohen, 1977, 1988; Rosenthal, 1984, 1991; Rosenthal & Rosnow, 1984, 1991; Rosenthal & Rubin, 1989).

Power

Especially if the results of either the original study or its replication were not significant, the statistical power at which the test of significance was made (assuming, for example, a population effect size equivalent to the effect size actually obtained) should be reported (Cohen, 1988). In addition to reporting the statistical power for each study separately, it would be valuable to report the overall probability that both studies would have yielded significant results given, for example, the effect size estimated from the results of the original and the replication study combined.

As an illustration of this procedure, consider the data of Table 20.6. Employing Cohen's power tables tells us that given an effect size of $d = .50$, Smith's power to reject at $p \leq .05$, two-tailed was .60 whereas Jones's power was .18. Table 20.14 shows that given these two levels of power there were only 11 chances in 100 that both studies would reject the null hypothesis given the effect size $d = .50$. Indeed, the odds were three times greater ($p = .33$) that neither study would reject the null hypothesis than that both would reject!

Such results are not at all unusual. It has often been documented that behavioral researchers are far fonder of making type II errors than of making type I errors (Cohen, 1962, 1988; Rosenthal & Rosnow, 1991; Rosenthal & Rubin, 1985; Sedlmeier & Gigerenzer, 1989). (It has been suggested that it is part of our Judeo-Christian-Buddhist tradition that we be deeply troubled that somewhere out there someone might be having a good time, could be getting a free ride, a significant result they do not deserve, a .05 asterisk that was actually intended for someone else.)

It is possible to index the perceived relative seriousness of Type I versus Type II errors by dividing beta (p of a Type II error) by alpha (p of a Type I error). Thus, when beta $= .20$ and alpha $= .05$, the ratio $.20/.05 = 4$ indicates that Type I errors are regarded as four times more serious than Type II errors (Cohen, 1988). Table 20.15 shows the beta/alpha ratios for three different levels of true effect size (r's $= .10, .30$, and $.50$), two levels of significance (p's $= .05$ and $.01$), and sample sizes ranging from 10 to 500. These ratios show that in the vast majority of psychological research, which tends to use modest sample sizes and is often investigating phenomena of modest magnitude (r's $= .30$ or lower), we behave as though Type I errors were from 5 to 95 times more serious than Type II errors, depending on whether we choose the .05 (5 to 20) or the .01 (40 to 95) level of significance.

TABLE 20.14
Probabilities of Various Combinations of Rejecting the Null Hypothesis
for the Two Studies of Table 20.6

Study II: Jones	Study I: Smith		
	Probability of Not Rejecting False Null (Type II Error Rate = .40)	Probability of Rejecting False Null (Power = .60)	
Probability of Rejecting False Null (Power = .18)	.07	.11	.18
Probability of Not Rejecting False Null (Type II Error Rate = .82)	.33	.49	.82
	.40	.60	1.00

TABLE 20.15

Ratios of Type II/Type I Error Rates for Various Sample
Sizes, Effect Sizes, and Significance Levels

	Effect sizes and significance levels					
	$r = .10^a$		$r = .30^b$		$r = .50^c$	
N	.05	.01	.05	.01	.05	.01
10	19	99	17	96	13	88
20	19	98	15	91	7	62
30	18	98	13	83	3	38
40	18	98	10	75	2	22
50	18	97	9	67		11
60	18	97	7	59		6
70	17	96	6	52		2
80	17	96	4	44		1
90	17	95	4	38		
100	17	94	3	31		
120	16	93	2	22		
140	16	92	1	15		
160	15	91		10		
180	15	89		6		
200	14	88		4		
300	12	80				
400	10	72				
500	8	63				

Note: Entries are to nearest integer. Missing Values
are < 1.
    [a]Equivalent to improvement in success rates of a gain
from 45% to 55%.
    [b]Equivalent to improvement in success rates of a gain
from 35% to 65%.
    [c]Equivalent to improvement in success rates of a gain
from 25% to 75%.

The Equally Likely (Non-Null) Effect Size (ELES)

A marvelous suggestion has been made by Rubin (personal communication) that
would go a long way toward helping us get over our problem with the relative
risks of Type II versus Type I errors. He suggested that whenever we conclude
that there is "no effect" we report the effect size along with that confidence
interval around the effect size that ranges from the effect size of zero to the
equally likely effect size further from zero than the one we obtained. Thus, the
ELES is the largest effect size that is equally as likely as the null value of
the effect size.

To return to Table 20.6, the "failure to replicate" by Jones provides a good example. Jones did not reject the null but obtained an effect size of $d = .50$. If Jones had been required to report that his d of .50 was just as close to a d of 1.00 as it was to a d of zero, Jones would have been less likely to draw his wrong conclusion.

ACKNOWLEDGMENTS

This chapter draws on material presented earlier in Rosenthal (1983; 1984; 1986a; 1989; 1990; 1991). Preparation was supported in part by the National Science Foundation while the author was a Fellow at the Center for Advanced Study in the Behavioral Sciences. I am grateful for financial support provided by the John D. and Catherine T. MacArthur Foundation, and by the Spencer Foundation, and for improvements suggested by Lynn Gale, Deanna Knickerbocker, Harold Luft, and Lincoln Moses. The content of this chapter is solely the responsibility of the author. I thank Frederick Mosteller for having enlarged my horizons about meta-analytic procedures over a quarter of a century ago; Jacob Cohen, a fine colleague I have never met but whose writings about power and effect size estimation have influenced me profoundly; and Donald B. Rubin, a frequent collaborator and my long-standing tutor on matters meta-analytic and otherwise quantitative. Our collaboration proceeds as follows: I ask him questions, he answers them and he then insists we publish alphabetically. What a country!

REFERENCES

Bakan, D. (1967). *On method.* San Francisco: Jossey-Bass.

Barnes, D. M. (1986). Promising results halt trial of anti-AIDS drug. *Science, 234,* 15–16.

Canadian Multicentre Transplant Study Group. (1983). A randomized clinical trial of cyclosporine in cadaveric renal transplantation. *New England Journal of Medicine, 309,* 809–815.

Centers for Disease Control Vietnam Experience Study. (1988). Health status of Vietnam veterans: 1. Psychosocial characteristics. *Journal of the American Medical Association, 259,* 2701–2707.

Cohen, J. (1962). The statistical power of abnormal-social psychological research: A review. *Journal of Abnormal and Social Psychology, 65,* 145–153.

Cohen, J. (1965). Some statistical issues in psychological research. In B. B. Wolman (Ed.), *Handbook of clinical psychology* (pp. 95–121). New York: McGraw-Hill.

Cohen, J. (1977). *Statistical power analysis for the behavioral sciences* (Rev. ed.). New York: Academic Press.

Cohen, J. (1988). *Statistical power analysis for the behavioral sciences* (2nd ed.). Hillsdale, NJ: Lawrence Erlbaum Associates.

Collins, H. M. (1985). *Changing order: Replication and induction in scientific practice.* Newbury Park, CA: Sage Publications.

Cooper, H. M. (1979). Statistically combining independent studies: A meta-analysis of sex differences in conformity research. *Journal of Personality and Social Psychology, 37,* 131–146.

Cooper, H. M. (1981). On the significance of effects and the effects of significance. *Journal of Personality and Social Psychology, 41*, 1013–1018.

Cooper, H. M. (1982). Scientific guidelines for conducting integrative research reviews. *Review of Educational Research, 52*, 291–302.

Cooper, H. M. (1984). *The integrative research review: A social science approach.* Beverly Hills, CA: Sage Publications.

Cooper, H. M. (1989). *Integrating research: A Guide to literature reviews* (2nd ed.). Newbury Park, CA: Sage Publications.

Cooper, H. M., & Rosenthal, R. (1980). Statistical versus traditional procedures for summarizing research findings. *Psychological Bulletin, 87*, 442–449.

DePaulo, B. M., Zuckerman, M., & Rosenthal, R. (1980). Detecting deception: Modality effects. In L. Wheeler (Ed.), *Review of personality and social psychology* (pp. 125–162). Beverly Hills, CA: Sage Publications.

Eagly, A. H., & Carli, L. L. (1981). Sex of researchers and sex-typed communications as determinants of sex differences in influenceability: A meta-analysis of social influence studies. *Psychological Bulletin, 90*, 1–20.

Federighi, E. T. (1959). Extended tables of the percentage points of Student's *t*-distribution. *Journal of the American Statistical Association, 54*, 683–688.

Fisher, R. A. (1938). *Statistical methods for research workers* (7th ed.). London: Oliver & Boyd.

Friedman, H. (1968). Magnitude of experimental effect and a table for its rapid estimation. *Psychological Bulletin, 70*, 245–251.

Glass, G. V (1976, April). *Primary, secondary, and meta-analysis of research.* Paper presented at the meeting of the American Educational Research Association, San Francisco.

Glass, G. V (1980). Summarizing effect sizes. In R. Rosenthal (Ed.), *New directions for methodology of social and behavioral science: Quantitative assessment of research domains* (pp. 13–31). San Francisco: Jossey-Bass.

Glass, G. V, McGaw, B., & Smith, M. L. (1981). *Meta-analysis in social research.* Beverly Hills, CA: Sage Publications.

Hall, J. A. (1980). Gender differences in nonverbal communication skills. In R. Rosenthal (Ed.), *New directions for methodology of social and behavioral science: Quantitative assessment of research domains* (pp. 63–77). San Francisco: Jossey-Bass.

Hall, J. A. (1984). *Nonverbal sex differences.* Baltimore, MD: Johns Hopkins University Press.

Harris, M. J., & Rosenthal, R. (1985). Mediation of interpersonal expectancy effects: 31 meta-analyses. *Psychological Bulletin, 97*, 363–386.

Harris, M. J., & Rosenthal, R. (1988). *Human performance research: An overview.* Background paper commissioned by the National Research Council, Washington, DC: National Academy Press.

Hedges, L. V. (1981). Distribution theory for Glass's estimator of effect size and related estimators. *Journal of Educational Statistics, 6*, 107–128.

Hedges, L. V. (1982). Estimation of effect size from a series of independent experiments. *Psychological Bulletin, 92*, 490–499.

Hedges, L. V. (1987). How hard is hard science, how soft is soft science? *American Psychologist, 42*, 443–455.

Hedges, L. V., & Olkin, I. (1985). *Statistical methods for meta-analysis.* New York: Academic Press.

Hively, W. (1989). Cold fusion confirmed. *Science Observer,* July–August, 327.

Honorton, C. (1985). Meta-analysis of psi Ganzfeld research: A response to Hyman. *Journal of Parapsychology, 49*, 51–91.

Hunter, J. E., & Schmidt, F. L. (1990). *Methods of meta-analysis: Correcting error and bias in research findings.* Newbury Park, CA: Sage Publications.

Hyman, R. (1985). The Ganzfeld psi experiment: A critical appraisal. *Journal of Parapsychology, 49*, 3–49.

Koshland, D. E., Jr. (1989). The confusion profusion. *Science, 244*, 753.

Light, R. J., & Pillemer, D. B. (1984). *Summing up: The science of reviewing research.* Cambridge, MA: Harvard University Press.

Light, R. J., & Smith, P. V. (1971). Accumulating evidence: Procedures for resolving contradictions among different research studies. *Harvard Educational Review, 41*, 429–471.

McNemar, Q. (1960). At random: Sense and nonsense. *American Psychologist, 15*, 295–300.

Mosteller, F. M., & Bush, R. R. (1954). Selected quantitative techniques. In G. Lindzey (Ed.), *Handbook of social psychology: Vol. 1. Theory and method* (pp. 289–334). Cambridge, MA: Addison-Wesley.

Mullen, B. (1989). *Advanced BASIC meta-analysis.* Hillsdale, NJ: Erlbaum.

Mullen, B., & Rosenthal, R. (1985). *BASIC meta-analysis: Procedures and programs.* Hillsdale, NJ: Lawrence Erlbaum Associates.

Nelson, N., Rosenthal, R., & Rosnow, R. L. (1986). Interpretation of significance levels and effect sizes by psychological researchers. *American Psychologist, 41*, 1299–1301.

Pillemer, D. B., & Light, R. J. (1980). Benefiting from variation in study outcomes. In R. Rosenthal (Ed.). *New directions for methodology of social and behavioral science: Quantitative assessment of research domains* (pp. 1–11). San Francisco: Jossey-Bass.

Pool, R. (1988). Similar experiments, dissimilar results. *Science, 242*, 192–193.

Pool, R. (1989). Will new evidence support cold fusion? *Science, 246*, 206.

Rosenthal, R. (1966). *Experimenter effects in behavioral research.* New York: Appleton-Century-Crofts.

Rosenthal, R. (1968). Experimenter expectancy and the reassuring nature of the null hypothesis decision procedure. *Psychological Bulletin Monograph Supplement, 70*, 30–47.

Rosenthal, R. (1969). Interpersonal expectations. In R. Rosenthal & R. L. Rosnow (Eds.), *Artifact in behavioral research* (pp. 181–277). New York: Academic Press.

Rosenthal, R. (1976). *Experimenter effects in behavioral research.* Enlarged edition. New York: Irvington.

Rosenthal, R. (1978). Combining results of independent studies. *Psychological Bulletin, 85*, 185–193.

Rosenthal, R. (1979). The "file drawer problem" and tolerance for null results. *Psychological Bulletin, 86*, 638–641.

Rosenthal, R. (Ed.). (1980). *New directions for methodology of social and behavioral science: Quantitative assessment of research domains.* San Francisco: Jossey-Bass.

Rosenthal, R. (1982). Valid interpretation of quantitative research results. In D. Brinberg & L. H. Kidder (Eds.), *Forms of validity in research* (pp. 59–75). San Francisco: Jossey-Bass.

Rosenthal, R. (1983). Assessing the statistical and social importance of the effects of psychotherapy. *Journal of Consulting and Clinical Psychology, 51*, 4–13.

Rosenthal, R. (1984). *Meta-analytic procedures for social research.* Newbury Park, CA: Sage Publications.

Rosenthal, R. (1986a). Meta-analytic procedures and the nature of replication: The Ganzfeld debate. *Journal of Parapsychology, 50*, 315–336.

Rosenthal, R. (1986b). Nonsignificant relationships as scientific evidence. *Behavioral and Brain Sciences, 9*, 479–481.

Rosenthal, R. (1987a). *Judgment studies: Design, analysis and meta-analysis.* Cambridge, England: Cambridge University Press.

Rosenthal, R. (1987b). Pygmalion effects: Existence, magnitude, and social importance. *Educational Researcher, 16*, 37–41.

Rosenthal, R. (1989, April). *Research: How are we doing?* Distinguished Lecture presented at the meeting of the Eastern Psychological Association, Boston, MA.

Rosenthal, R. (1990). Replication in behavioral research. *Journal of Social Behavior and Personality, 5,* 1–30.

Rosenthal, R. (1991). *Meta-analytic procedures for social research.* Newbury Park, CA: Sage Publications.

Rosenthal, R., & DePaulo, B. M. (1979). Sex differences in accommodation in nonverbal communication. In R. Rosenthal (Ed.), *Skill in nonverbal communication: Individual differences* (pp. 68–103). Cambridge, MA: Oelgeschlager, Gunn & Hain.

Rosenthal, R., & Gaito, J. (1963). The interpretation of levels of significance by psychological researchers. *Journal of Psychology, 55,* 33–38.

Rosenthal, R., & Gaito, J. (1964). Further evidence for the cliff effect in the interpretation of levels of significance. *Psychological Reports, 15,* 570.

Rosenthal, R., & Jacobson, L. (1968). *Pygmalion in the classroom.* New York: Holt, Rinehart, and Winston.

Rosenthal, R., & Rosnow, R. L. (1975). *The volunteer subject.* New York: Wiley-Interscience.

Rosenthal, R., & Rosnow, R. L. (1984). *Essentials of behavioral research: Methods and data analysis.* New York: McGraw-Hill.

Rosenthal, R., & Rosnow, R. L. (1985). *Contrast analysis: Focused comparisons in the analysis of variance.* New York: Cambridge University Press.

Rosenthal, R., & Rosnow, R. L. (1991). *Essentials of behavioral research: Methods and data analysis* (2nd ed.). New York: McGraw-Hill.

Rosenthal, R., & Rubin, D. B. (1978). Interpersonal expectancy effects: The first 345 studies. *The Behavioral and Brain Sciences, 3,* 377–386.

Rosenthal, R., & Rubin, D. B. (1979a). Comparing significance levels of independent studies. *Psychological Bulletin, 86,* 1165–1168.

Rosenthal, R., & Rubin, D. B. (1979b). A note on percent variance explained as a measure of the importance of effects. *Journal of Applied Social Psychology, 9,* 395–396.

Rosenthal, R., & Rubin, D. B. (1980). Summarizing 345 studies of interpersonal expectancy effects. In R. Rosenthal (Ed.), *New directions for methodology of social and behavioral science: Quantitative assessment of research domains* (pp. 79–95). San Francisco: Jossey-Bass.

Rosenthal, R., & Rubin, D. B. (1982a). A simple, general purpose display of magnitude of experimental effect. *Journal of Educational Psychology, 74,* 166–169.

Rosenthal, R., & Rubin, D. B. (1982b). Comparing effect sizes of independent studies. *Psychological Bulletin, 92,* 500–504.

Rosenthal, R., & Rubin, D. B. (1982c). Further meta-analytic procedures for assessing cognitive gender differences. *Journal of Educational Psychology, 74,* 708–712.

Rosenthal, R., & Rubin, D. B. (1985). Statistical analysis: Summarizing evidence versus establishing facts. *Psychological Bulletin, 97,* 527–529.

Rosenthal, R., & Rubin, D. B. (1986). Meta-analytic procedures for combining studies with multiple effect sizes. *Psychological Bulletin, 99,* 400–406.

Rosenthal, R., & Rubin, D. B. (1988). Comment: Assumptions and procedures in the file drawer problem. *Statistical Science, 3,* 120–125.

Rosenthal, R., & Rubin, D. B. (1989). Effect size estimation for one-sample multiple-choice-type data: Design, analysis, and meta-analysis. *Psychological Bulletin, 106,* 332–337.

Sedlmeier, P., & Gigerenzer, G. (1989). Do studies of statistical power have an effect on the power of studies? *Psychological Bulletin, 105,* 309–316.

Shoham-Salomon, V., & Rosenthal, R. (1987). Paradoxical interventions: A meta-analysis. *Journal of Consulting and Clinical Psychology, 55,* 22–28.

Smart, R. G. (1964). The importance of negative results in psychological research. *Canadian Psychologist, 5a,* 225–232.

Smith, M. L. (1980). Integrating studies of psychotherapy outcomes. In R. Rosenthal (Ed.), *New directions for methodology of social and behavioral science: Quantitative assessment of research domains* (pp. 47–61). San Francisco: Jossey-Bass.

Smith, M. L., & Glass, G. V (1977). Meta-analysis of psychotherapy outcome studies. *American Psychologist, 32,* 752–760.

Smith, M. L., Glass, G. V, & Miller, T. I. (1980). *The benefits of psychotherapy.* Baltimore: Johns Hopkins University Press.

Snedecor, G. W., & Cochran, W. G. (1967; 1980). *Statistical methods,* 6th; 7th ed.). Ames: Iowa State University Press.

Steering Committee of the Physicians Health Study Research Group. (1988). Preliminary report: Findings from the aspirin component of the ongoing physicians' health study. *The New England Journal of Medicine, 318,* 262–264.

Sterling, T. D. (1959). Publication decisions and their possible effects on inferences drawn from tests of significance—or vice versa. *Journal of the American Statistical Association, 54,* 30–34.

Strube, M. J. (1985). Combining and comparing significance levels from nonindependent hypothesis tests. *Psychological Bulletin, 97,* 334–341.

Tukey, J. W. (1977). *Exploratory data analysis.* Reading, MA: Addison-Wesley.

Wachter, K. W. (1988). Disturbed by meta-analysis? *Science, 241,* 1407–1408.

Wachter, K. W., & Straf, M. L. (Eds.). (1990). *The future of meta-analysis.* New York: Russell Sage.

Walberg, H. J., & Haertel, E. H. (Eds.). (1980). Research integration: The state of the art. *Evaluation in Education, 4*(1).

Weinberger, J. (1989). Response to Balay and Shevrin: Constructive critique or misguided attack? *American Psychologist, 44,* 1417–1419.

Zuckerman, M., DePaulo, B. M., & Rosenthal, R. (1981). Verbal and nonverbal communication of deception. In L. Berkowitz (Ed.), *Advances in Experimental Social Psychology* (Vol. 14) (pp. 1–59). New York: Academic Press.

Author Index

Subject Index